WITHDRAWN

NA
1120
E5513

Date Due

DEC 18 79			

COLLEGE OF MARIN LIBRARY
COLLEGE AVENUE
KENTFIELD, CA 94904

Printed in U.S.A.   23-521-002

ROME

The Dome of St. Peter's and the Campagna.

ROME

THE BIOGRAPHY OF HER
ARCHITECTURE FROM
BERNINI TO THORVALDSEN

BY

CHRISTIAN ELLING

WESTVIEW PRESS
BOULDER, COLORADO
MCMLXXV

ROME: THE BIOGRAPHY OF HER ARCHITECTURE
FROM BERNINI TO THORVALDSEN

Translated from the Danish from
Rom. Arkitekturens liv fra Bernini til Thorvaldsen
by Bob and Inge Gosney

Published 1975 in Copenhagen, Denmark by Gyldendalske Boghandel, Nordisk Forlag A.S.

Published 1975 in the United States of America by Westview Press, Inc.
1898 Flatiron Court
Boulder, Colorado 80301
Frederick A. Praeger, Publisher and Editorial Director

Copyright 1975 in Copenhagen, Denmark by Gyldendalske Boghandel, Nordisk Forlag A.S.

All rights reserved.
No part of this publication may be reproduced or transmitted in any form
or by any means, electronic or mechanical,
including photocopy, recording or any information storage and retrieval system
without permission in writing from the publisher.

LIBRARY OF CONGRESS CATALOGING IN PUBLICATION DATA

Elling, Christian, 1901–1974.
Rome: the biography of her architecture from Bernini to Thorvaldsen.

Translation of Rom.
Bibliography: p.
Includes index.
1. Architecture – – Rome (City) I. Title.
NA1120.E5513   720'.945'632   75-23263

ISBN 0-89158-514-1

Printed and bound in Copenhagen, Denmark

*Awarded the Amalienborg Prize on 10th June 1972
as an appreciation of a distinguished work in the humanities
written in the Danish language.*

Photographs by
Lennart af Petersens,
Vasari, and the author

FREDERIK POULSEN
in grateful memory

FOREWORD

*Tu solo vien con me;
bisogna far il resto
ed or vedrai cos'è –*

This book deals with the city of Rome and its buildings in the period between Bernini's death in 1680 and the year 1797, when Thorvaldsen came to the papal city. As the names of the two artists indicate, we are writing of Rome from the end of the High Baroque period to the beginning of the Empire style. This is but a short chapter in Roman history. Not until its end is it dramatically glorified, and there are still people who give it the label of decadence. Nevertheless that period formed an epoch in the life of the city and set the seal on Europe's culture. Regarded as a work of art, Rome in the course of these not quite 120 years took on a form which can be perceived as perfect. The appearance of the town reached its most mature beauty, the colours on the rich palette toned together, light and shade were joined in harmony. In our time, it seems to us, as if the ancient, scarred metropolis found rest after the vicissitudes of centuries, relaxed in the long holiday of peace and satiated itself with sunshine. A quiet, blissful warmth pervaded the city on the Tiber. Visitors from all over the world were refreshed by its gentle gravity. More than at any other time since the death of Antiquity, Rome now became a talisman for Europe's weary people and stirred to life its finest spirit. The Muses spoke freely and monuments flourished as in a lovely garden. In the play of life and art, that urbanity prevailed which is in itself a Latin concept and a doctrine from the South. The city which Bernini left behind him and which greeted Thorvaldsen had clad itself in the burnt-out colours of the earth itself, in smouldering ochre – and *the yellow Rome* had been born.

The beauty of the city charmed all the senses and gave its own lingering rhythm to the activity on the great papal stage. The heroic dreams of the past and of rebirth were merely waiting to unfold. The roots of

Rome reach to the depths, thunder threatens below the heights. Most often it was just a distant rumbling hidden in elegiac moods, but in the end the storm burst upon art. That Roman demonic power, once again released, blasted an architecture that had reached a state of vegetation, gave life to Neo-Antiquity with the breath of the cult of death and inspired Romaticism after the storm. Thus even the phrase "Eternal City" acquired its true pathos in the decades before Thorvaldsen.

Furthermore – was not the framework of the Rome of Pius IX and the long idyll of the artistic life beyond Ponte Molle created in that period which is to occupy us in these pages?

Our subject is classical. It must be brought up to date – so let us enter the town with open eyes.

The architectural monuments from the period 1680–1797 are exceedingly numerous. I have included all genres in my account and have put special emphasis on dealing with those types – such as monasteries, public civic buildings and town houses – which up to now have only been examined to a surprisingly small degree. My description of the subject is thus very full, perhaps the most extensive that exists. But of course at no time has it occurred to me to strive towards anything approaching a complete survey of the monuments in question. Such an attempt would prove utterly hazardous, especially in view of the fact that the specialist literature on the subject is so sparse. It has certainly never been my intention to produce a handbook, nor even a bigger work. No doubt I have committed sins of omission and fallen into error. Goethe once wrote "Rome is like the sea; the further one goes into it, the deeper it gets".

The sub-title to this work will have been noticed: "The Biography of Her Architecture". This is meant to convey that my approach is determined by an attitude differing from the usual one in similar works. I have not conceived of the history of life as completely synonymous with the history development. The existing state is for me more important than transition, the absolute more than the relative, the individual more than the collective. It is well known that architecture is a strict art which is conditioned by climate and building materials, by milieu and space, by the particular nature of the task, by the ethics, conventions and financial position of the *monied* classes. A study of these factors will always be fruitful for the writer who wishes to perform the function of the savant.

As we all know, the history of architecture – just like that of zoology and botany – can be approached by two different basic methods. One of them has as its aim the inclusion of the variety of objects in a genetically determined system, the other, the description of each object individually on the basis of its particular environment. In this book the latter principle is the predominant one. I have preferred to understand things against their own background rather than put them in a theoretical milieu, and I would far rather interpret what they stand for than state what they resemble. Instead of wearing myself and my readers out on the grindstone of types and motifs, I have stood in front of every work and according to my lights have demanded the answer to my direct question: How is your shape related to your site? Whom are you meant to serve? In which belief or in which illusion was your foundation stone laid? Have you fulfilled what was required of you? As far as possible I have relaxed the taut typological guide-lines tying the works together. In my studies in the field I have also avoided the maze of stylistics. Of course it is not possible to write about a century of architectural history without having regard for "the style" and all it stands for. It is to be hoped that I have avoided the larger patches of quagmire within the domain of "Baroque". Perhaps the art of that period can be regarded as closer to life and more substantial, once the stagnant waters of the concept have at long last retreated, and the works themselves are once more home and dry in their proper place in history.

According to the angle from which I approach Roman architecture, the work of art has a life attributed to it which is both wider and narrower than that otherwise given to buildings by the art historian. In so far as all works can be regarded as both self-aggrandizing and yet compliant parts of that composition which we call Rome, their doors are often shut to us. We take in the houses as plastic forms, as functions of the town. It has not been for me to describe the distribution of rooms and interior decoration; I have merely dissected those buildings whose features can only be understood from within. More importance is placed on the analysis of monuments as individual entities in relation to their situation. Such accounts are to a great extent based on the small but very good projections on Giambattista Nolli's map from 1748, of almost all the buildings mentioned. The greater part of this map is reproduced in the tables at the end of the book. I beg the reader to make good use of these excellent pages.

To make up for this deliberate limitation of my task, I have extended it as far as possible by reconstructing the topicality in their own time of the monuments dealt with, well knowing that such an attempt can only be carried out successfully up to a point. Consequently, I have, with greater consistency than is usual in similar works, permitted the characters of the period to be present and to give their opinions. I am persuaded that even the most laconic opinion about a new building uttered by a contemporary man in the street (not to mention architects and builders), is better evidence for me than a specialist's observation published two hundred years later. For I am a historian. As such, I have wished to illuminate genres and works by depicting – not merely sketching – the use and conception of them by living people. "The task is to provide aesthetic problems with their place in history," wrote Julius Lange in 1889 to Valdemar Vedel. It cannot be concealed that I have often wanted to feel my way into the atmosphere which surroundings give to, or receive from a monument. To be a historian is not merely a profession.

Rome's particular artistic spirit – so difficult to determine, so impossible to ignore – hangs over all edifices like a destiny. Therefore the nicest and wisest method may well be to feel one's way carefully in an effort to bring order into things. The strongest "style" in Rome – sometimes stemming other tides, sometimes releasing hidden springs – is after all the Roman style. It is with the life of this style during a century, together with the soil, history and humanity, that this book really deals.

The reader will soon discover that I have not tried to make it easy. He is spared none of the investigations that, in the author's eyes, were particularly tempting. On the other hand, I have tried to avoid making it dreary. The subject is wonderful and nothing more beautiful can fall to the lot of an art historian. It has been fermenting inside me ever since I visited Rome for the first time in 1921 and read Carl Justi's work on Winckelmann (1872) after I came home. By mentioning this work and also Henri Focillon's monograph on Piranesi (1918), I have introduced the names of my finest mentors on the subject. The Rome of the 18th century, under the banner of Antiquity, comes alive with amazing vitality in the work of these scholars. Carl Justi, the Dane, set out to study a Rome in a different key. The approaches to be found in his book – every chapter proclaims its standpoint – are made from opposing aesthetic points of view. But for him too, life in the Roman world and the atmosphere around its works of art was something enchanting.

It has always been my intention to try to obtain a personal relationship with the architecture dealt with here and, however briefly, to give expression to it. If a work of art seems to appear in character in the eyes of the beholder as well as in his mind, it becomes a part of him. The observer may feel himself in duty bound to give thanks with pen in hand, by interpreting this new acquisition frankly. In this sense, the present author has also done the work of a critic.

To write a study of Rome may be a delight, but it is also a serious undertaking, if time has been spent profitably and the mind been receptive. Whether the text be long or short, it will always represent a goodly slice of one's life, perhaps the most precious. So I must thank the people who have helped me, or who have been in my thoughts while I lived in Rome. I cannot mention all of them, but I cannot forget any of them. Madeleine and Axel Boëthius showed me great hospitality almost thirty years ago at the Swedish Institute in the Via del Boschetto and we are still in touch. Tage Bull, Ambassador at the time, and his wife, gave me precious hours of their time on the loggia of Palazzo Mattei, among priceless books. Jeanne and Andreas Basse opened up my Roman horizon to the limits of Tuscany and the mountains of the Volci beyond. Finland's Ambassador, Harry Holma, and his wife, helped me enjoy the furthest regions of the Campagna. Most of all – these Roman friends showed a stranger great kindness and strengthened his feeling of being at home in Rome. My travelling companion over many happy days was a daily source of great cheerfulness.

Those closest to me, but from whom I was separated, must also be mentioned here. A mother who handed over her savings to a nineteen year old for his first journey there. A father who never managed to get to Rome. And that dear old lady Ane Henningsen, whose treasury of memories, of books and pictures of her travels, were a boy's first introduction to Italy.

The Carlsberg Fund contributed to the publication of this book and the New Carlsberg Fund has many times paid for and financially supported my somewhat extended stays in Rome. I recognize with gratitude my great debt to J. C. and Carl Jacobsen, Danish patrons in the old Roman tradition. Finally, I wish to be remembered most heartily to the director of Krohn's Printing Works, Mr. Thorvald Jensen, who – supported by his head foreman Mr. Plougmann Larsen – guided the production with a sure and friendly hand, and I express my appreciation to Øjvind Andreasen, M.A., whose redaction of the index is signalized by his great personal skill and erudition.

In a work like the present one, it was found necessary to supplement the text with a large number of illustrations which for the most part are new. Various monuments were not known to the public, numerous buildings needed to be presented from angles other than the usual, or to be published in a more worthy manner. Of the 206 photographs reproduced, 185 were taken especially for the book. The most important and best of these, in all 119 pictures, are the work of Lennart af Petersens, who took them in 1949 on the instruction of the author. I thank this fine artist of the camera for his excellent work and for his good company in Rome.

Dr. Frederik Poulsen, the eminent archaeologist who has shown me great kindness since my early youth, also encouraged me in this work. I was at times privileged to be the companion of the greatest Danish Roman of his generation, when he visited the Palatine and saw the swifts above Monte Pincio for the last time. I feel great sorrow at not being able to hand him this book.

On 12th July, 1974, Dr. Christian Elling died after a protracted illness. Thus he did not live to see his work translated into one of the principal languages, and death forestalled his intention of writing a special preface to the English edition.

The publishers have therefore decided to reprint the preface to the first (1950) edition in extenso. For the second edition, issued in 1967, Christian Elling wrote a short supplementary preface in which he said, inter alia:

Such value as the book may possess is to be found in its entirety. The views which have determined my representation are still valid in my opinion. Although certain historical details could now be more clearly elucidated by way of recent research – in part known to me – I have nevertheless felt justified in disregarding such research without much resignation.

The book must be taken for what it is: a study at first hand made of an immense subject by a dedicated writer. To him the great Roman Era formed a part of his life history – now with a more profound perspective.

CONTENTS

The Great Motifs	1
The Capital of Christendom	33
Convents and Monasteries	159
The Common Weal	196
The Palaces	251
Squares and Streets	314
Houses in the Country	422
The Call of the Ruins	488
Bibliography and Notes	533
Index	565
Maps of Rome	587

THE GREAT MOTIFS
AN INTRODUCTION

Rome de Rome est le seul monument JOACHIM DU BELLAY
Man kann sich nur in Rom auf Rom vorbereiten GOETHE

The part of Roman architecture described in these pages is the culmination of a long history. In no other city on earth has Voltaire's century had such a glorious backcloth, nor its builders drawn on such a demanding heritage. This is deeply engraved in its art. The trivial cannot flourish on Roman soil. It can clearly be seen that all architectonic achievements, including the humble ones, have been realised in the shadow of a giant vertical yardstick. Everywhere the past makes its resurrected presence felt, and the voice of the ancients is raised in protest at the claims of youth. Napoleon aroused his soldiers in Egypt by exhorting them "Forty centuries are watching you!" In Rome too, all artistic conquests have come to pass beneath the grave gaze of eternal monuments. If we seek to understand the spirit of the eighteenth century in this city, we ourselves must feel our way into the past that brought forth that period, and accept its greatness as pure fact. If we do this, the art of the age of bewigged elegance will develop before our eyes. It leads on to the future, it fulfills itself, it follows its own nature, never concealing the vitality of its character, and only rarely in this epoch did the architectural tradition of the Romans sacrifice the elegant for cheap fashion or insensitive whim. Reserves were called on to stem the advance; the milieu demanded the fusing of plan and stylistic emphasis.

The people who lived in Rome at the time of Bernini's death considered the city a work of art, an epic and a landscape. The work of art had been created since the days of the Renaissance by ardent spirits and steady heads, by talents and geniuses all interlinked. It did not become a harmonious whole, but only a mighty fragment of "the ideal city". And there it lay now, like a torso. Rome as an epic is the work of history, a heroic tragedy. Half consciously perhaps, the city's own sons had absorbed it into their souls. Rome as a landscape – that is largely the achievement of our Lord.

In the beginning the mountains were outside Rome. They embody the horizon, they give character to the city down by the river. To the south lie the round Albano hills, green and hazy blue, surmounted by the compact cone of Monte Cavo. Raphael sketched in its silhouette as a background to his first Roman pastoral Madonna. This is pastoral downland country. From here the good wine comes in donkey panniers. This is where the Romans go on holiday. To the east, the jagged walls of the Sabine hills close the horizon. In a storm, the slopes of the mountain gleam violet and milky-white. From these savage regions Rome suffered the ever-present threat of war, and brigands watched from distant eyries. To the north in clear weather, a massif can be seen whose ridge has the lines of a couchant beast of prey. This is Mons Soracte. From Rome on a winter's day, Horace could see the white of its snow, a landmark for all in the eternal city.

Seen from the hilltop and the towns on the mountain, from Ariccia, Rocca di Papa and Palestrina, Rome lay sunk in haze. On muggy days in August one would gaze in sympathy from the high loggia of the villa down into the city veiled in fever. The traveller coming from the northern mountain chain was filled with pride, when the coachman pointed with his whip to a floating formation of grey and yellow down in the depths of the panorama, and could pick out a beautiful domed shape crowning the unknown. St. Peter's seemed a natural part of the landscape along the Tiber Valley.

The Campagna was an open stretch between the mountains and the city – grazing land and wilderness, folded, furrowed, but nevertheless flat, it went right up to the walls of Rome. In contrast to the old imperial city, Europe's capital under the Caesars, and St. Peter's throne, the Campagna must have seemed demonic. Among Rome's great motifs, it was the first and strongest. On this plain, the papal city suffered something like a Babylonian captivity; centuries' devastation of the land had imprisoned Rome behind a barrier of misery, but now the city made the sign of the cross and snarled in defiance at the no-man's land outside its gates. One's gaze was turned to the hills, sometimes in fearful anticipation, but more often in silent enjoyment of their harmonious lines. While the Roman drew auguries of storm and drought from the sight of it, his guest from afar took home a fair vision. But the Campagna was more often than not a bleak enclosure, the magic circle a strangling noose. Out there was a brooding silence. For all travellers this desert was a nightmare, pregnant with miasma, infested with brigands, not a visible human habitation for miles. Wild cattle wallowed in the swamps, and the shadows of birds of prey swooped over the short grass. Although dread was always a keynote in the interpretation of the *Campagna di Roma,* a number of variations on this theme developed in the course of the hundred years between Bernini and Thorvaldsen. With changing taste, it was seen in a different light. For Montaigne, who visited Italy 1580–1581, the wasteland was particularly forbidding because it was irrational, uncivilised: "The appearance of the country-side is displeasing (*est mal plesant*), it is covered with lumps, full of deep clefts, impossible to be licked into shape even by an army (*incapable dy recevoir nulle conduite de gents de guerre en ordonnance*) [1]. In 1650 a guide very significantly includes a story of brigands in his description of the route through the Campagna (Via Cassia) [2]: near the market town of Baccano "there was in the old days an inn frequented by brigands, and it is a local saying that this is the place where you have to keep your eyes open" – but not for the beauties of nature. Misson, the most popular guide in Italy at one time, says quite laconically that in 1688 the road between Rome and Viterbo "offers little worthy of note" [3] – and this stretch is through the most magnificent region of the Campagna. On his two-day walk (in 1715) from Civitavecchia to Porta Angelica, Holberg only had eyes for "the many snakes, so that I hardly dared to stand still, much less lie down on the ground" [4], and as a result, the Campagna made a disagreeable impression on him. He would, no doubt, have agreed heartily with a contemporary Frenchman who supposed "that Romulus must have been drunk when he got the idea of building his city in such a foul spot" [5].

Yet that fine man of letters Duclos, who made his way to Rome along the Via Cassia in 1767, even in his day refused to look at the landscape he was passing through and merely wrote down his complaints about squalid inns [6]. But following on Rousseau and his cult of back to nature, the horrors of the Campagna soon became beauty in the eye of the beholder, after Winckelmann and Gibbon had animated the empty landscape left behind by Antiquity with an enthralling melancholy. One looks back on what was once there and weeps. The idea of "the Classical soil" was conceived by Goethe. With the keen sight of a mineralogist and his alert and vital sense of perception, he felt its plasticity, and really made the landscape his own while hastening through it to Rome in October 1786. But deep in his heart was an ardent longing to read Tacitus in the original, and see the lost past in its true light [7].

In 1804, Chateaubriand wrote his international manifesto about the pathetic Campagna and said: "There is hardly a tree here, but everywhere there stand ruins of aqueducts and tombs – ruins that seem to be forests and plants, in a field of ashes of the dead and fragments of the Imperium" [8]. Madame de Stael continued in this vein in "Corinne", and for her the humble, the repellent vegetation, now speaks to the heart: "Dreaming souls, equally occupied with death as with life, find joy in observing the Roman Campagna, where the present has left no trace – this soil, which tenderly covers its dead with useless flowers, with trailing weeds lacking the strength to rise from the dust" [9]. The long rows of arches from weathered aqueducts were like skeletons in the desert (**Pl. 2**) and provided the backcloth for "the most sublime of tragedies" [10]. But from now on, they and other traces of Antiquity were not the only voices crying in the wilderness, warning that all things are transitory. Now too, the castle of the Middle Ages, defiant towers on the hillocks of the plain, called out to the traveller of sensibility. The Gothic was discovered in the Campagna. Hans Andersen studied the Romantic landscape around Rome from many aspects; he had his little improvisatore live here a while, he saw this wasteland through the eyes of a painter who selects a subject "and then chooses the barren thistle as foreground" [11]. He also sensed its macabre poetry – "in a little valley ... lay a veil of mist, we hastened through it. It was as if the elf maiden cast her cloak around me, like a clammy shroud. I closed my lips to her kiss" [12]. Dickens also shuddered and found that the Campagna, of all imaginable forms of

1. *Roman road (Via Triumphalis) on Monte Cavo.*

2. *Ruins of aqueducts in the Campagna.*

3. *Pastoral scenery near the Via Appia with the ruins of the Villa of the Quintili.*

4. *Via Aurelia Antica, view in the direction of Rome.*

5. *Bastion from the age of Paul III Farnese, situated between Porta S. Paolo and Porta S. Sebastiano.*

6. *Vicolo dello Scalone leading to the Quirinal.*

7. *Vicolo dello Scalone leading to Vicolo Scanderbeg.*

8. *Buildings along the bank of the Tiber island near the Ponte dei Quattro Capi.*

landscape around Rome, was the most suitable and expedient as graveyard for a dead city" [13].

If we are to find our way into a period in the life-history of Rome of the past, albeit the age of gallantry, we must first of all make ourselves familiar with the barren, awesome terrain which threatened Rome's very gates. The Campagna is the fate-motif in the overture –

> *Go thou to Rome, – at once the Paradise,*
> *The grave, the city, and the wilderness –*

this is Shelley's phrasing of the great theme.

It is not completely played out. The Campagna is still there; wide areas roll towards the horizon, clouds pile up over rugged uplands, poppies are flaming banners on the slopes, and the broad steppes, dried up by the gales of winter, have the colour of a lion's skin. Now and then you see those pointed huts of straw (*capanne*) which are shelters for the shepherds, and echo a greeting from Vergil. You can still, in places off the beaten track, see a peasant harvesting his fields with a sickle, as I did at the foot of Soracte. The grandiose in the character of the Campagna cannot be erased. Gravity still marks the face of the countryside, but the dread has been expelled by the work of man [14].

All the roads that led to Rome (and still do) ranked higher, to be sure, than other arterial roads in Christendom. Were they not worn by Caesar's legions, were they not paved with the hopes of millions, did they not follow the trail to the dome over Peter's grave? Various stretches of the old Roman military roads were still covered by the stone slabs from Antiquity (Pl. 1). Cultured tourists were delighted when they felt the carriage wheels jolt over this worthy paving, but few felt the need to stop and measure the slabs. Goethe's conscientious father did this in 1740 on the Via Flaminia and noted down that: "He who carefully observes the joints in the paving will be surprised, for only with difficulty can the point of a rapier be pushed into the joints, although the stones are of unequal size and shape" [15].

Encouraged in the wilderness by such traces of a cultured past, one approached Rome. The last stretches of the road were bordered by long walls in front of gardens and vineyards, and only thus was one prepared for the city's architecture. But this very *entrata* was elegant and impressive, the highway between the bare walls already possessed grandezza. Of all these lovely entrances into ancient Rome, only one is now preserved which bears witness to the noble tranquility outside the gates of the city. This is the last stretch of the Via Aurelia Antica which leads to the Porta di San Pancrazio (Pl. 4). Travellers came by this road from the papal port of Civitavecchia – and this is the route by which the sensitive traveller of the present day should always make his entrance into Rome. He follows the wall which surrounds the Villa Doria-Pamphili on his right side, while opposite, Paul V's aqueduct extends its line of arches. This aqueduct, which stretches from Lake Bracciano far to the north, to Acqua Paola on the Janiculum, is in one place carried across the road, borne by a gateway with the appearance of a triumphal arch. Then once again, garden walls with the tops of pines above them – so peaceful – and in the spring the sound of many nightingales. Finally a *casino* in ruins (Villa Benedetti), overgrown and mysterious, and a small group of humble buildings, among them an osteria with tables and chairs outside the door – and we have reached the San Pancrazio gate. Rome lies open before us.

But this can only be seen where there is a breach in Rome's walls. The ring of fortifications around Rome must be regarded as one of the city's strongest features, all the more so, because the longest stretches of wall, erected by Emperor Aurelian and made higher still by Maxentius, have a formidable appearance. In days gone by, it happened at times that particularly zealous visitors made a circular tour of the walls of Rome [16]. One admires their zeal, this was like a pilgrimage. They measured the outline of the Eternal City with weary feet – and found that their task was colossal, like everything else in Rome. Reverently they saw the lines of the scarred masonry opposing the mighty expanse of the Campagna, and at the Porta di S. Paolo they witnessed how the half-cylinders of the towers defied the pyramid of Cestius.

The fortifications of later times too, had much character. Contemporaries of Vauban or Frederick the Great might not easily have been impressed by the military efficiency of the installations, but their fortificatory style was classical. This is especially true of the bastions that were added in 1537–1542 under Paul III of the Farnese family, by a pioneer in the science of military engineering, Antonio da Sangallo the Younger.

The masonry bulwarks are just as good and severe architecturally as his Palazzo Farnese. The papal coat of arms with its lilies are set up on the corner; the crossed keys are like an enormous hinge. Everyone must feel that the heritage of St. Peter is safeguarded behind this barrier (Pl. 5).

The city on the seven hills – and a couple more – stands out in mighty relief. Down in the closely built-up quarters west of the Corso, the level is flat. But here also, the ground has bumps and hollows. This comes out in place-names like S. Andrea della Valle and S. Maria in Vallicella, but is otherwise felt only as slight dips in the roads (as in the Via dei Pettinari). The small, somewhat isolated rises often have ruins hidden beneath them, covered by layers of rubble from earlier centuries, such as Monte Cenci near Ghetto, Monte Savello which encloses the former castle of the Savelli family in the theatre of Marcellus, the Piazza di Montecitorio, from which a street slopes down towards the south, as well as Monte Giordano in Rione Ponte. A little widening of the Via di S. Stefano del Cacco, nestles a trifle isolated above the adjoining streets, raised by the deeply hidden remains of a temple [17].

But all this is only a ripple on the surface. The slopes of the true hills border ancient Rome along the river. The part of the city around Piazza di Spagna has Monte Pincio at its back; immediately behind the fashionable Piazza S. S. Apostoli rises the Quirinal, and opposite the crowded bourgeois district of Rione Campitelli, stands the Capitoline hill itself. The Aventine gives the Tiber a touch of dramatic coastline, the Palatine is an island with precipitous slopes. Trastevere lies seething as if in a bowl below the rounded uplands of Janiculum. Huddling in front of the Vatican hill is Borgo. And not for nothing has the great half-empty district towards the east the name of Monti. Compared with these august *colli*, Monte Testaccio (Potsherds' Hill) is merely a wart on Rome's deeply furrowed face.

The grand scale of the terrain has in many ways determined the artistic nature of the city and our dedication to it. Anyone who moves slowly – and so one should – over long stretches, experiences the majestic contours of Rome's physiognomy. He feels the undulations of the ground beneath his feet, all in the broadest tempo, and becomes part of a surging rhythm. Venice has its ups and downs, but the rhythm is a short one, staccato, since it is carried along only by the ever-present, humped bridges. Genoa's relief is violent, all its changes sudden; one clambers and is afraid of falling, looks down suddenly into shafts, up to dizzy roofs. But the gentle heaving of Rome is like a sea swell. If you go along the stretch Via Sistina – Via Quattro Fontane – Via De Pretis, which connects Trinita dei Monti with S. Maria Maggiore, and keep on a dead-straight course across all the hills and dales of the terrain, this is where you receive the greatest impression of the plasticity of the Roman soil.

Even short stretches of road can emphatically outline the contrasts and make us feel, within narrow limits, how the buildings are moulded to the terrain. The Via dell' Olmata nestles against the contours of the Esquiline, and when you come from its foot you see S. Maria Maggiore slowly rise over the hill with every step you take. The Quirinal's southern slope is accentuated by the level ground of the ancient Imperial squares. On a walk through Salita Del Grillo, this curving slope becomes very obvious and its finish no less; for you practically bang your head against the wall around the Forum of Augustus. The now dreary street, which laboriously runs in a south-westerly direction from the Porta Settimiana (Trastevere) and very unsuitably bears the name of Garibaldi the national hero, makes up, as it were, a segment of the slope of the Janiculum. The route is particularly impressive, because it follows exactly the inside curve of the city wall, which is delineated here by a row of old houses.

And the Via di Porta Pinciana – indeed the walk down its winding way is like a lingering glide down the hill to the teeming depths, wonderful on the wings of the downward current, but a toilsome business on the way back up again.

Because of all this, the "city on the seven hills" became the city of perspectives sans pareil. They are the viewpoints. The city takes on the appearance of a relief map from Monte Aventino, Monte Pincio, Monte Gianicolo – three vantage points which are so famous. But innumerable *veduti* also make an individual monument stand out in its full richness and gain new beauty from unexpected aspects, or merely lifts its stern profile with amazing hauteur. The dome of St. Peter's is a work of such dimensions that it inviolably predominates over all perspectives; a special setting for it was never necessary – and the fashionable peep through the key-hole in the garden gate of the Grand Master of the Knights of Malta on the Aventine does not give *il cupolone* any added greatness.

It is otherwise with the Papal Palace on Monte Cavallo, which only comes to life completely in constantly changing perspectives. Its composite, towering masses must be captured by a series of views, exactly in the same way as a large inaccessible piece of sculpture high up on a roof balustrade only becomes an entity when it is shown filmed from all sides. Viewed from the Vicolo dello Scalone, the cube of the Belvedere lies on a dizzy diagonal (Pl. 6) – and seen through the stepped passageway of that name, the city has an irresistible attraction; the promise of joyous wanderings down there puts the mind in a turmoil (Pl. 7). During the night of the 5th July, 1809, Napoleon's troops crept up these steps to seize Pius VII [18]. How many delightful and sinister flights of steps there are to be found in Rome! Vicolo delle Tre Cannelle winds up towards the Quirinal, protected it is true by the Palazzo Antonelli. The Scala Mignanelli is like an *escalier dérobé* from the Piazza di Spagna to Trinita dei Monti; the Piazza degli Zingari slopes down gently to a restful flight of smooth steps which seem just right for gypsies to doze on. Salita di S. Onofrio rushes down headlong from Janiculum. The corner house right at the top is as clear cut as a bastion.

Various churches come into view from sloping streets of steps. S. Isidoro gleams across the gorge behing the idyll of its garden, and it is a relief to arrive in the square by S. Pietro in Vincoli after having passed through the insalubrious tunnel under the Palazzo Borgia. Near the south side of S. Pietro's colonnades there is a steep stairway up to S. S. Michele e Magno; like its counterpart near the Lateran, it has the status of a sanctuary.

But truly greatly blessed is Aracoeli's lovely *cordonata* and it justifiably bears the name *la Scala del Sole*. And for the Romans, there is only one flight of steps worthy of being called merely "la Scalea" – which the rest of us calls the "Spanish Steps".

And then there is the river. Although the Tiber means far less for the life and scenery of Rome than the Thames does for London, or the Seine for Paris, it is nevertheless one of the great motifs of the Eternal City. The Tiber divides the city with its magnificent double curve, like a gigantic S. It is the horizontal plane in front of the massif of the Castel Sant' Angelo. It has met the long rollers of Ripetta harbour; the trees at the Temple of Vesta are reflected in its water. Outside the Theatre of Marcellus it is parted by an island, Isola di San Bartolomeo, sharp as the bows of a ship, the only great vessel at anchor in the river. Watermills rocked at their moorings along the bank, and clumsy ferries were dragged in its current.

The Tiber's colours are basic to Rome's palette, sometimes an oily yellow, then a milky green with the poisonous hue of absinthe. The sound of the waters cannot be banished from Rome's symphony. Many a night have I sat on a palace loggia in Trastevere and heard the incessant booming music of the Tiber, a deep tone, echoing through the sleep of the city. By day one would not have believed that its pace was so heavy. When the river becomes angry and rises – it has been known to reach as far as the Piazza di Spagna [19] – it is Rome's master. Under the arches of the bridges it always shows its latent strength, it foams triumphantly over the feet of Ponte Rotto.

In the days of Baroque and Romanticism, the Tiber was for the most part shut in by houses which ran right down to the water. Old views show [20] that the built-up area here faced the wrong way, and only in a few places (as behind the Via Giulia and along Lungara) did the palaces face the river. Thus it was bordered by fantastic architecture, miserable masonry from all ages, packed together in dirt, allied in neglect, like a lawless mob. Backdoors gave access to veritable caverns, stairs slunk up to short cuts, sewers poured out their filth, half-rotten balconies hung over the depths, side by side with privies and ragged washing. The unsavoury prison Tor' di Nona (later a theatre) projected out into the mud, as did the Collegio Clementino, whose noble façade had to be supported by tall substructures. Worst of all was the row of houses of the ghetto along the bank of the river, and this restricted quarter gasped in vain for air through its narrow breathing holes. No wonder that such condemned parts of the city, the first victims of the Tiber's attack in time of flood, was the home of every dark deed [21]. Squeezed between the houses, slipways ran down to the clayey slopes of the river bank, to discharging berths and landing stages in the mud.

The meeting point of river and built-up area has long since lost its shady melodrama. Only in one place in Rome can one still find a huddle of houses rising out of the water (although with a narrow pavement at its base), and this is on the island of S. Bartolomeo, opposite the former Jewish quarter. This tenement, with a mediaeval tower (Torre Caetani) at one corner, gives an idea of what the bank of the river looked like in the old days (Pl. 8). Since the 1880's the building of quays and their streets has cut off this frayed edge of the built-up area. It is difficult to regret this, for even the good architecture (such as the Palazzo Altoviti in Rione Ponte [22]) was flaking away and most of the houses decaying. But undeniably, the city lost a strain of wildness by this clean-up of genuine Roman *terribilita,* without acquiring any new harmonious beauty.

There is no doubt that the pride of the River Tiber is the bridges that cross it, and it is from them that the finest views can be obtained. The oldest bridges are in themselves mighty monuments. The Ponte dei Quattro Capi, the Pons Fabricius of Antiquity, built 62 B.C., bears the crown (Pl. 9). It has not changed much since then, has lost nothing of the tense grandeur of its arched back. When one walks along the narrow path and feels its backbone beneath one's feet, one is treading the same paving stones borne by arches that carried Augustus Caesar, Peter the Apostle and Michelangelo. The historical motif in these arches is without equal, and also purely artistically, the bridges of the Tiber have been a joy for all those who have loved the city since the Renaissance. The greatest Romans among the artists used them as gateways for their veduti. Raphael set the long curve of Pons Fabricius above the "Slaughter of the Innocents", and Piranesi dreamed up his *Archi Trionfali* under the influence of the Tiber's classical monuments. Nicolas-Henri Jardin followed in his footsteps [23]. A contemporary, the painter Joseph Vernet, later famous for his views of the harbours of France, became the most sensitive interpreter of the light over the Tiber and the proud outline of its bridges, all seen with the tender gaze of Rococo, enobled with exquisite tones. The River Tiber, so moody and livid, was most delicately transfigured by the brush of this Frenchman, and from him, one realises that the river had its source in the best of all worlds and its course beneath the most benevolent of heavens, for it ran sleepily through the Promised Land of art. Camille Corot later adopted Vernet's motifs, but he restored to the bridge its imperishable substance, and to the houses along the Tiber their shabby crust and stunted growth. The Ponte Molle (Pons Milvius) was especially beloved of all visitors to Rome – first as an introduction to the city of promise, and then as the point where they finally bade farewell. Innumerable artists have drawn it with care and in memory of the dawn of their Roman youth [24].

If one may compare the melody of the Tiber with a *basso ostinato,* the deep organ tones beneath the city's noise and activity, the waters of the fountains are the hundred voices, clear and silver-tongued, sonorous and soothing, dropping in slow cadence, humming, restraining, whispering. When Rome was a quiet city, a wanderer might well sense that the rhythm of the city ran free amid the stones of the houses with all these fountains playing night and day. Nowadays they are best heard after nightfall. These are the welcoming voices of Rome.

The song of the fountains frequently helps us on our way through the labyrinth. As one strolls through the quarters of the city, it is still possible to recognize their changing features by eye, by other senses too perhaps, among others a tried instinct for atmosphere, for aerial boundaries. But it happens that, even at a distance, one can hear where one is, and accordingly take one's bearings. It is a delightful feeling to trace one's way ahead through waters that speak under cover and behind corners. In which other metropolis are you kept on your course by the divining rod which leads to hidden springs? Fontana Trevi summons all in the neighbourhood with its low voice, and it often happens that the thin trickle from the dolphin's mouth, or the drooling maw of the lion in a niche at a street crossing gives a little personal warning: time to change your course. Just try late at night to take the short walk from the mouth of the Via Veneto in the Piazza Barberini to the Piazza del Quirinale, and in the stillness you will hear that the fountains are following your progress; the feeble jet from the "Bees' Fountain", a splashing fall from the Triton's shell, a murmuring behind the lattice inside the forecourt of the Palazzo

Barberini, a babbling from the "Quattro Fontane", and finally a quiet sound from the lonely column of water in the basin in the middle of the palace courtyard.

The great music of the waters is one of the splendours of Rome and for many the most precious of them all. The rich abundance of running, ice-cold drinking water, brought down from the mountains through ancient and restored aqueducts, had been utilised by the masters among the artists of the Renaissance and especially of Baroque. Of these, two masters about 1600 had, symbolically enough, the name of Fontana (Domenico and Francesco). The pulse of Rome was the rhythm of its springs, even before Bernini, that great virtuoso of the fountain, closed his eyes for the last time.

The monumental cascade in its arched gateway (*una mostra*) was the cynosure superior to all else, created to fit into the panorama of the city as background for an axis. Acqua Paola dominates the Terrace of Janiculum in the same way as an organ dominates its loft. Acqua Felice (the Fountain of Moses) in the old Piazza dei Termini was the *point-de-vue* for Via Pia. Fontanone di San Sisto (originally included in the façade of a hospital) closed the narrow prospect of the Via Giulia, and the little canopy of the Fontana del Mascherone stands at the end of a street leading from the Piazza Farnese (Pl. 14). Springs in niches gave the street intersection of Quattro Fontane its name. In St. Peter's Square all the undulating heads of water jetted from high basins. La Barcaccia gurgled in the Spanish Square, Fontana delle Tartarughe (the Fountain of the Tortoises) decorated the Piazza Mattei with its fine grouping of figures. In the middle of the Piazza Barberini the Triton blew the jet up out of his horn like a fanfare, in front of the Palazzo Farnese lilies raised their wet mouths out of the huge tubs.

And finally – with the deities of the four rivers, Bernini had transformed the Piazza Navona into a landscape, a natural theatre, a scene of bliss – as in Gioacchino Belli's own words:

Cuesta nun è una piazza, è una campaggna,
Un treàto, una fiera, un' allegria.

But in addition to the play of the large waters, secluded springs were to be found everywhere, a superfluity of small fountains – intimate and lovely. Some were full of humour, like Il Facchino (the Porter's Fountain) on the corner of the Corso and the Via Lata, where the water issues from the bunghole of his barrel. The Fontana delle Api (the Fountain of the Bees), seems as if improvised by a genius; the huge wet scallop shell was formerly fixed to a house in the Piazza Barberini, on the corner of the Via Sistina. One often sees thin trickles of water quivering above a moss-grown basin down in the yards of the common people; many an antique sarcophagus with its fluting, serves as a drinking trough for cab-horses (as in the Via Corsini). A very large granite basin from ancient times, filled to its low brim, slaked the thirst of cattle for slaughter in the Campo Vaccino. The fountains drew people from everywhere. The thirsty person put his mouth to the outlet pipe; women fetched water in vessels of wood or copper. A long stone trough, below the stables of the Quirinal at the end of the Via del Lavatore, was the meeting place for the girls of the district to do their washing, and this gave the street its name [25]. Immediately outside the Porta Cavalleggeri there was a small fountain which Pius IV had provided for the pilgrims to slake their thirst, and weary travellers from the north found a handsome fountain by Ammanati, roughly half-way between the Ponte Molle and the Porta del Popolo. People and cattle drank their first draught of Rome's assuaging waters here.

But although the city was thus provided with fountains in abundance before 1680, posterity found many problems to solve in this direction, and these we shall discuss later. The Acqua Virgo, the only one of the ancient water supplies which has functioned more or less without interruption for some 2000 years (built in 19 B.C.), lacked a worthy architectural setting for its outflow. An English traveller remarked in 1685 that this fountain, best known as the Acqua Trevi, had still not been given the embellishment it deserved [26]. In fact this was given in full measure, and the waters of Rome received their finest setting [27].

The river winds, and it divides more than it unites. The fountains play everywhere; they help you on your way but can also hold you back. An attempt was made to create orderliness in Rome by long, straight roads. Across the undulating relief, they drive tracks from town gate to monument, from square to square, from bridge to memorial. But it does not add up to anything conclusive; there are too many unknown quantities for the problem to be worked out. Nevertheless – the laws of straight lines and measured angles were written on Rome's great blackboard with a firmer hand than anywhere else in Europe, long before Bernini's last days. The network of streets down by the Campus Martius, so tangled and confusing, gradually came into being while the Rome of Antiquity lay in ruins. Footpaths twisted among decaying buildings. They made a detour round the inviolable blocks of masonry, ran along the edges of foundations, dived under a half-buried arch, perpetually seeking a short cut and forging cautiously ahead. Thus the lay-out of the city became one big fumbling attempt and was more like a delta than anything else. The streams of traffic found their own level.

The Renaissance desired geometry and a purified Latin after the period of barbarism [28]. It strove towards introducing clarity by imposing geometrical figures on this muddle. The first attempt was a triangle. This was formed in the banking quarter with its apex in front of Ponte S. Angelo; Sixtus IV began the task here in the 1470's by straightening the Via del Banco di S. Spirito (Canale di Ponte) down the middle. This was continued by Paul III who constructed the Via di Panico and Via Paola. This little *patte d'oie,* a fan of three streets through the richest and busiest district of Rome of that time, became a sort of design for the enormous triple system of streets constructed with the Via Lata of Antiquity (Via del Corso) as its backbone. To this dead-straight, north–south, middle axis were added in succession two new streets, converging on the exit from the Corso to the square in front of the Porta del Popolo. This regular lay-out, which was to be the principal feature of Rome's modern image during the Baroque period and later, was initiated by Leo X of the Medici family. He had a diagonal street constructed, the Via Ripetta, running westward and connecting the Piazza del Popolo and the river port (1517–1518). That Raphael took part in the changes in the square which were involved in this, is known for certain, but it cannot be proved whether he also had the radiation of the three streets in his mind's eye. How nice it would be to imagine that it was he, the greatest of all artists in classical Rome, who had drawn up the plans for the monumental entrance into the Eternal City [29]. In

1525, shortly after his accession to the papal throne, Clement VII (1523–1534) had the first stretch of the east diagonal road corresponding to the Via Ripetta staked out. This was the Via del Babuino, which was continued to the Piazza di Spagna in the time of Paul III. Thus he completed the great trifurcation by the addition of the Via dei Condotti (Via Trinitas) which with its continuation (Via della Fontanella di Borghese) cuts across the whole system and connects the Piazza di Spagna with the west part of the city in the direction of the Ponte S. Angelo.

At the same time as the construction of the small and the large *pattes d'oie,* during the Renaissance, a number of straight and relatively wide arterial roads were marked out. The Via Recta (dei Coronari) owes its existence to Sixtus IV who further developed the regulation of the banking quarter. The Via Alessandrina (Borgo Nuovo) is named after Alexander VI of the Borgia family (1490's). The Via Giulia and Via Lungara, corresponding roads, each on its own side of the Tiber, were sharply defined by the dominant Pope Julius II. The street first mentioned became Rome's most elegant thoroughfare, but towards 1600 it had to surrender pride of place to the Corso.

Then at the close of the 16th century, the large uninhabited parts of the city stretching to the east (the Monti district) including the hills of the Esquiline, Viminal and Caelius, were subjected to the discipline of controlled perspectives. The initiative for this urbanisation had already been taken by Pius IV (1559–1565), by laying out the Strada Pia (Via Venti Settembre) from the Quirinal to Porta Pia, a long radial road which met the city wall and originally was to have started at the Palazzo Venezia right in the very heart of the city, and at the point of origin of the Corso itself. What Pius had begun, Sixtus V continued with unerring eye and unbelievable energy. In the course of his short papacy (1585–1590), he made himself master of the wastelands of Rome by drawing lines through them. It was over three centuries before his grid was filled. With Trinita dei Monti as the points of origin, (and on paper with the intention of starting from the Piazza del Popolo) he cut an arterial road over hill and dale through to S. Maria Maggiore, an up and down stretch of roadway now called the Via Sistina and the Via Quattro Fontane. From Rome's biggest church of Our Lady, Pope Sixtus once again laid his ruler on the trackless terrain. In continuation of the Via Sistina, a new road was constructed straight to S. Croce in Gerusalemme, right out by the city wall. Another stretch of road (the Via Merulana) ran from S. Maria Maggiore towards the Lateran and a third (Via Panisperna) headed westwards straight for the centre of the city. Finally, the basilica of the Lateran, Rome's cathedral, was connected with the Colosseum by a road (Via di S. Giovanni in Laterano), which was, in fact, meant to end at the Capitol.

It can be seen that Pope Sixtus not only civilized the empty parts of Rome by turning them into a canvas for abstract linear patterns, but also served the needs of traffic and the glory of the Church at one and the same time; for he bridged the gap between scattered monuments of high esteem. Formerly, repentant sinners and pilgrims wended their way to the venerable houses of God along winding field paths, but now processions strode forward on roads which, if nothing else, had the straightness of a triumphal route. Buildings followed but slowly, and throughout the whole of the 18th century, the Via Merulana and the road to S. Croce (Via Felice) were merely passages between garden walls. The living city could still not adapt to its plan.

If one looks at a plan of Rome during the Baroque period – the best is Nolli's map from 1748 – and tries to obtain an overall impression of the strongest and most important features, we find that only very few of the sketched lines remain firmly fixed in our mind's eye. The maze of the old parts of the city is reduced by these large-scale geometrical figures, and we see that the complicated network of thoroughfares in the city results in a complete tangle. But these great figures are as if drawn by a mathematician who is not concerned with the rustling of centuries in the alleyways, but has striven towards the absolute in his concept of *Forma Urbis Romae* – whoever he may have been.

We may imagine a pendulum hanging at Rome's north gateway. It is called Via Lata, Via del Corso, and its pivot is between two symmetrical domed churches. We can move it like a radius, but its swing is limited to the west by the Tiber, to the east by Monte Pincio. Its extreme positions are clearly indicated by the Via Ripetta and the Via del Babuino respectively. As we start the pendulum off gently, and mark down the continuations of these two roads, we find that its extreme swing has stopped at two fixed points further south. On the west side this is S. Andrea della Valle and to the east S. Andrea al Quirinale. Our first attempt at this free experiment has shown its magic. It is difficult to free oneself completely from the notion that the pendulum from the Piazza del Popolo swings soundlessly back and forth over Rome like a shadow, tentatively indicating the organisation of a more permanent work of art, and at the same time measuring the progress of time over imperfection.

The other figure on the Roman blackboard is completely static, positively encaustic. I refer to the only monumental stretch of road running west–east like a heavy horizontal, namely the Via Panisperna. The eye cannot miss it on the 1748 map, for it stands out defiantly and runs systematically across the map, and thus at right angles (with Roman approximation) to the axis of the Via del Corso. The self-assertion of this impressive road in the plan is so great, that one is persuaded to ascribe to it an importance far beyond the chance fate of its survival. The Via Panisperna was obviously meant to be more than a regular traffic route, the west end of which is missing. Does it not look like a fragment of the base line of a figure traced on the ground in the shape of a pyramid? An ideal figure which was to control the whole city?

The right-hand half of the upright triangle can easily be drawn on paper. The line of the Via del Babuino when projected, crosses the Via Panisperna close to the west side of S. Lorenzo in this street. The distance from this point to the point of intersection of the Via Panisperna, with the prolongation of the Via del Corso towards the south, thus forms the base line of the east half of the large triangle. If we transfer this distance with a pair of compasses to the theoretical continuation of the west part of the Via Panisperna, we end up at the exact point where the continuation of the Via Ripetta intersects. The problem has been worked out. In short, the Via Panisperna is no less than a fragment of a stretch of road meant to join the two roads radiating from the Piazza del Popolo, so as to form an enormous closed triangle with the Corso as its middle axis. Antiquity drew the first line (Via Lata), Baroque traced the next lines but never really followed them through.

I do not know the history behind this theoretical pattern. Anyhow — everyone can satisfy himself of the beauty of this figure and — if he has a mind to do so — regard the fragmented hieroglyphic as a sign of an ever-pregnant greatness. Nobody can deny that the triangle suggested for Rome is one of the city's proudest motifs. The obelisks, most of them erected during the period of Sixtus V, are exclamation marks at the fixed points of geometry.

The art of city building in Rome during the periods of the Renaissance and Baroque, as we well know, became famous throughout Europe and was imitated all over the world. But this urbanism is not merely best on its native soil, but its very nature is different here from anywhere else. The *genius loci* has set his mark on it. Sterility is foreign to its order, the long vistas never seem endless and boring — as in later city plans, where the straight-edge prevails — because they merge into a heroic landscape; the nature of the city and its environs. The pointer directs the eye towards mountains behind a dome, the compasses measure a terrain whose rhythm cannot be subdued. The schematic plan lacks all pedantry; many obliquities in the tracing of the network of streets show the abundance of the format, and the dissonnances humanize the regularity. It should always be remembered, that the new features in Rome's plan are, after all, no more than lines in an old composition. The Corso begins at a city gateway, in a wall dating from the Imperium, follows the track of the military road of the Republic, ends at the foot of Paul III's "Gothic" tower and the Capitoline Hill of a legendary age. The Via Sistina is a Baroque processional, but it starts on a plateau dating from Antiquity, a garden terrace on the Collis Hortorum, and reaches its distant destination on the other side of S. Maria Maggiore at the Amphitheatrum Castrense by S. Croce in Gerusalemme. Even the purest mathematics flower in such fertile historic soil. Modern city complexes, whether completely homogeneous, or built at short notice, set their sights on no more than the needs of the moment, and on linear perspective.

In another respect too, Rome's great pattern may be considered as having human values. The buildings which accentuate its composition are used profitably in every-day life. If theoretical literature is to be believed, the portico at the end of a street has no other meaning than to look like something and to act as a piece of static furniture. This may be true north of the Alps and in the British Isles. But in Rome, columns have roots, and a temple's vestibule is not merely a decoration. One runs the risk of getting a false impression if one merely looks at the façade of the main elements of the prospects and only experiences them from the outside. After all, the human being is not just a passive observer of the history of style, or an extra, standing in the wings. The Roman was a consumer.

Fontana Trevi might well be a backcloth to a stage set, but it is also a small lake on whose banks one can spend a summer evening, very likely with one's back turned to Neptune. The two symmetrical domed churches in the Piazza del Popolo may be linked together in a picture taken from the city gate, but it is also permitted to seek shade in the porticos and to look out on to the square from these vantage points, even to walk past them. Which point of view is the true one? Unperturbed the Roman walked, and still walks, across the grandiose lay-out of his city, and in this way has a thorough grasp of its ideal proportions. From the day of his birth he is on intimate terms with columns and has a respect for the sun. There was hardly a single visitor of any standing who failed to go into raptures looking at the portico of the Pantheon from outside, it being elevated and "beautiful in perspective". The native preferred to see the square from deep inside the portico, for the shade was there. It can be edifying to take a different view of the famous sights in this way; the background of one becomes the gateway to another. From the outside looking in, the tourist noted the Roman as an ornamental figure leaning against a column; the city's own son watched with amazement as the foreigner dashed around out there in the sun-baked square. Thus the portico of the temple served them both, although in diametrically different ways. It must be maintained that in general Rome's inhabitants were not put to shame, since they accepted their city as it was, with natural dignity. For a change let us do as they do then, and direct our gaze from the Rotunda's porticus out towards the houses in the square, like the people of Antiquity, who walked in galleries around a forum. Let us make ourselves completely at home among the magnificent columns – one of Rome's greatest motifs (Pl. 10).

Even the colonnades of St. Peter's play their part in the beauty of everyday life. One does not denigrate the idea behind the design, by shunning the open square and wandering along the enormous avenues of columns. What is true in the abstract figure of the forecourt is not belied by closer contact with the architecture. Bernini's own age understood this very well. A mighty piece of architecture was also experienced as a part of Nature. The architect G. B. Contini (1643–1723) uses a picturesque expression for his mentor's work, and calls Piazza di San Pietro "a circular forest" (*dal foro Vaticano la cilindrica selva*) [30]. Wandering between the trunks, one sees the corridor to the Castel Sant' Angelo and the wings of the Vatican slowly turn on their axis (Pl. 11). This approach to God's temple too, has its own solemnity. One of Rome's strongest themes thus has two variations. The continuity of this façade suggests a triumphal march from the outer world. It is a gesture of universal depth. But the walk among the weighty circle of columns belongs entirely to Rome. It is its private entrance.

Anybody who cares to take the time to move observantly amid the pattern of the city's plan, must feel struck by that plastic strength residing in the houses of Rome, which stamps the architecture as art, regardless of its style. The three biggest secular buildings are the Colosseum, the Torre delle Milizie and the Palazzo Venezia, the first from Antiquity, the second from the Middle Ages, the last from the Early Renaissance (1460's). All three are prodigious through their mass. The extraordinary effect stems, to a great extent, from the size of the monuments and also from their impression as plastic entities. And this is never dependent on the yardstick. Weighty massivity is one of Rome's principal themes and varies only superficially in all epochs.

The Palazzo della Cancelleria, the masterpiece of the Early Renaissance, has finely modelled façades, but the relief of these is totally absorbed by the sturdiness of the mass. Only historians interested in the detail, regard the difference between this palace, and for example the Palazzo Altieri, which is two hundred years younger, as decisive. The person who wanders with an open mind amid the blocks of stone of these edifices finds, in actual fact, a deep-rooted relationship between the exteriors of these palaces, namely in their plastic nature. Bramante and

Raphael during the culmination of the Renaissance elicited a classical style from even the most weighty form, a skill mastered in situ by the architects of the Imperium. Just look at the enormous blocks of stone in the Via Giulia, which are the rudiments of Bramante's palace of justice (Palazzo di S. Biagio).

Those works too, which people try to catalogue as products of "maniérisme", have a thorough respect for closed plasticity, even a pronounced predilection for the bare wall (Pal. di Pio IV, Villa di Papa Giulio). And both the early, as well as the mature Baroque, deliberately made the massivity into a basic principle for all architectural forms [31]. Behind all the variations which the changing desires of the ages have called forth in the outer covering of buildings, there is always the ideal of the whole and solid house. The harmony in the townscape of Rome stems overwhelmingly from this ever-present urge towards a weighty and compact solution. Stendhal once remarked: "In Rome even the simplest shed gives the impression of a monument" [32]. This is very true. It looks big because it is formed simply and with restraint; there is an equilibrium between what is open and what is closed. It stands firmly on the ground, and its limiting surfaces are sharp, even behind the froth of the ornaments. The abstraction takes on substance in broad daylight. In Michelangelo's words: "The house is not built but indeed born" (*non murato ma veramente nato*).

Bernini said of the Tuileries in Paris that they resembled "a great little thing" (*una grande picciola cosa*) [33]. Absolutely the right words, for the palace is merely a complicated collection of petty elements arranged in order, stuck together like toys, not a unified and strong composition with the lines of mass. In Bernini's view, the cylinder, the dice, and the octagonal drum were to be reckoned perfect forms in architecture. Therefore, the greatest artist of Baroque could solemnly declare of the Pantheon, the purest monument of Antiquity: "The Rotunda has not a single fault" [34]. This grandiose judgment is a declaration of faith in the Roman heritage, of the tradition that — in the words of Anatole France — "is entirely ingenuity and beauty, beyond which there is only error and difficulty" (*hors de laquelle il n'est qu'erreur et trouble*) [35]. Antiquity's *insula* in Ostia and the hovel in Trastevere, have the same amount of

Latin in them. Weight and simple articulation, lapidary style in the proper sense of the word.

The men of the Neo-classical period could rage about those features in Baroque which could not be reconciled with the creed of architectural columns expounded by the textbooks, but the best of these people understood very well, but only in flashes, that "Antiquity" within their intellectual horizon, is a part of that unchanging concept which is called the Roman spirit, and which produces its effect by full figures and firm bodies. The Swedish arbiter of taste, Carl Augustin Ehrensvärd, in Italy in 1780–1782, was receptive to the simple and strong in the construction of Roman houses, and expressed this with his customary – somewhat affected – pithiness, in maxims such as this: "A square house is splendid; a low roof is splendid; a flat roof is splendid" [36]. The Dane Eckersberg, who was no philosopher, but saw things clearly, remarked in a letter of 1814 from Rome: "The most miserable houses have something so beautiful and elegant in form, the flat roof, the large wall surfaces and small windows" [37]. The Rome that spoke in such powerful words to Goethe was particularly the city of grandiose masses. After having mentioned the Pantheon, Michelangelo's Capitol and Bernini's colonnades in one breath, these words are uttered, a speech of dedication: "And here too the sun and the moon, like the human spirit, have something quite different to do (ein ganz anderes Geschäft) from elsewhere, here, where enormous yet shaped masses emerge before their gaze" [38].

Here we offer to the reader two plates with pictures of Roman buildings, both typical, one of them a palace, the other an ordinary dwelling house. Palazzo Rospigliosi is near the Quirinal, withdrawn behind a high garden wall (Pl. 13). It was erected at the beginning of the 17th century, was extended somewhat later, and therefore lacks homogeneity in layout, but certainly not in plasticity. It is carved out with a powerful hand. The palace proclaims its strength when seen from that corner which is faced with ashlar. It was not the intention that the façade should make any special impression, such an effect would, as it were, be beneath the building's dignity. The site itself permitted it to develop an open front, while the residence of a nobleman is often so tightly encapsulated that it usually has to produce its effect diagonally. As its proportions are generally considerable, it has little difficulty in dominating at least one street corner. The Palazzo Rospigliosi is a towering group of blocks, striking at a distance and overwhelming close at hand.

It is pointless to evaluate Roman palaces systematically on the basis of old etchings, or on new assessments of their main façades, and thus produce stylistics. Buildings live only on their own foundations; their very existence is conditioned by the space they take up. The art in them is contained in their appearance as a whole, and consequently, it is this totality which can and must be grasped. In the absolute sense, a house only exists for him who is capable of interpreting its cubic form. In the majority of cases, only God and the birds can examine the cornice, and not a single soul can perceive the façade to its full extent. Often one is content with just one section, as the plates in this book will testify. But it is possible to walk round the detached palace and bump against its corners and look at it from top to bottom. This is the way to get the measure of it; your walk around it brings it within your embrace.

The dwelling house which we show in Plate 12 is situated in the Via della Maschera d'Oro (the Street of the Golden Mask), next door to the Palazzo Lancellotti. One of the lamps by the gateway to the palace can be seen on the right of the photograph. This house has been chosen because it stands detached and always has done. A neighbouring block of buildings out towards the Via dei Coronari (in the background) has recently been removed. The building thus demonstrates its intrinsic plastic value with rare clarity. Bernini, Ehrensvärd and Eckersberg would not be ashamed of this noble cube with its low roof and the few, excellently placed openings in the wall. Innumerable buildings similar in type to this Early Baroque house, hide their cubic shape and merely show their stern lineaments where they face the street, but one realizes from these patent features, that what is behind is not a hollow shell. At a corner this becomes manifest, and after a clearing has been done it is fully revealed. Roman to the core, the house in the Street of the Golden Mask seems almost timeless, complete.

It is a significant fact that Rome's buildings have often, almost literally, developed their intensity by growth. Quite often one can see the antique column outlined in the masonry of a later façade, where it seems to

9. *Ponte dei Quattro Capi (Pons Fabricius) view from the Tiber island.*

10. *The porch of the Pantheon.*

11. *The Colonnade of the Piazza di S. Pietro with a glimpse of the Vatican.*

12. *House in Via della Maschera d'Oro.*

13. *Palazzo Rospigliosi on the Quirinal.*

14. *Fontana del Mascherone and the stables of the Palazzo Farnese in Via Giulia.*

15. *The theatre of Marcellus (Palazzo Savelli-Orsini-Caetani).*

16. *Carceri Nuove in Via Giulia.*

force its way out of the surface like a piece of sculpture out of an uncut stone. A dwelling house from Antiquity is the basis of a building from the Middle Ages. It is given Renaissance decoration, Baroque stucco, and increased in height during the Neo-classical period. Tangible continuity in architecture is a great Roman motif.

Quite a number of important memorials have acquired a genuine pathos purely through the worn traces of the stages in their slow creation, and the strata of the ages can be seen in a completed structure. The most monumental example of this may well be the Theatre of Marcellus. In the Early Middle Ages (1087), its ruins were restored and rebuilt as a palace for the Pierleone family. About three hundred years later the Savelli family moved in. In the 1520's the architect Baldassarre Peruzzi added upper storeys in Renaissance style. When the Savellis died out, the imposing structure was bought by the House of Orsini (1712), and they disposed of it a few years ago to the Caetani family, the descendents of Boniface VIII. The Roman theatre that became a palace has throughout nearly 900 years been occupied by four families of ancient lineage, the elite of Rome. No wonder that this building, with such a past, was regarded, in spite of its exceptional character and its added characteristics, as a pattern for the residence of a nobleman, particularly during the Renaissance. For it had an awesome aspect. Furthermore, its oldest part was begun by Caesar and completed by Augustus. A full, magnificent antique façade was inherent in it. Which aristocratic house in Rome – or indeed the whole world – can match it? The lowest arcades of the front of the theatre were rented out as shops (*botteghe*). They were in use until 1926, when the Piazza Montanara was done away with and the site around the monument cleared. These booths at the foot of the palace were in fact remarkable, and it is a pleasure to be able to remember them as they were. When Bramante and Raphael designed palaces in Neo-classical style (Pal. Caprini, Pal. Dell' Aquila), they borrowed the motif of the shops in the lowest storey from the Palazzo Savelli. And when Peruzzi built his Palazzo Massimo alle Colonne, the masterpiece of the culmination of the Renaissance, he was given the courage to provide the façade with a convex curve by observing the Palazzo Savelli. The remains of the Theatre of Marcellus testified to the antique origin of the bold motif [39]. Thus, this conglomeration of a building was not only able to give lessons in good style, but also develop a style itself, namely that of a developing entity. Our plate 15 shows that the building stands like a rock. It seems as if the projecting toothing, at the top to the right, has the sharpness of a cliff formation, and that the open arcades look like the caves in a mountainside. This palace on Monte Savello, a product of 2000 years of Roman history, has taken on the inviolable gravity of nature. Not built, but grown. This work is heavy with substance.

But only in such formal concepts as cubism, weight, detachment, there lies hidden a characteristic trait of the spiritual expression of Roman architecture, or – if you like – its inherent style. To Stendhal the psychologist, we owe a shrewd observation of far-reaching importance. It runs: "When you say in Italy "This building has much style", it often means that it commands respect" [40].

So it is. Roman style is severe. To the large proportions and the weightiness of the material, is joined a gravity which keeps you at arms' length. The palace is withdrawn, it ignores us. The house in the street has no intimate appeal and a fleeting glance is not enough. Even the *casini* of the villas, which might be allowed greater freedom, rarely deviate from their compact form. The decoration on the wall is only stuck on and can be scraped off easily with a measuring glance. Gravity seems to be inherent in these houses. The palace craves to show its grandezza; every façade, even of the tenement houses, wishes to show off with dignity. Nobody can enter the Roman house uninvited, only the shop is open. Thus it was before 1700; thus it remained. Rococo was introduced into a milieu which demanded respect for decorum; this style, which elsewhere was eulogised for its frivolity, learned to control itself on the banks of the Tiber. When the façade finally risks a smile, it is as if behind a fan. The ornaments of Louis XV flourish reluctantly in the streets of Rome.

We must understand that the reserved character of this architecture is not merely the result of the old building tradition in which *gravitas* prevails. It also appears as the reflection of a distinctive element in the national character of the Italian, especially the Romans. If one overlooks this, one fails to understand a great motif. Through the ages, numerous connoisseurs of Rome have emphasized the extraordinary reserve which characterizes the way of life of the population and which restrains their temperament. Even in these days, unprejudiced observers will meet with this attribute. The superficial chatter of tourists is to be ignored, so we will keep to reliable witnesses concerning the old days. John Moore, who in 1783 published a whole book on Italian national psychology, points out this very earnest solemnity [41] which Grosley rightly considered deliberately cultivated by Rome's inhabitants to prevent others forcing themselves upon them [42]. The French Dominican Labat, whose residence in Italy over a period of many years (1709–1716) made him intimate with all sorts of people, says quite laconically of the Romans: "Everything is formal with them, and everything takes its time" [43]. The astronomer Lalande also had a similar insight. His assessments of sociological conditions in the middle of the 18th century [44], enjoyed unqualified praise, even in Giuseppe Baretti's critical work in 1770 [45]. In his analysis he shows how the Romans manage to increase their *dignità* by a particularly non-committal politeness, which is disarming at several paces distance. With all shades of behaviour, from the hauteur of the aristocrat to the sullenness of the plebian taken into consideration, this permanent defence mechanism remains a recognized Roman characteristic. There is much pride in it, and the city's past has nurtured it. But there is also a natural nobility. Obstinate self-respect and at the same time respect for others. Two small details can be mentioned to illustrate this dignity in everyday life. According to a British traveller, Mr Temple, no person, high or low, would stop or turn round to stare at a stranger [46], and a compatriot of the gentleman mentioned, notes that he had never seen deformity call forth a smile [47].

This little digression also serves to interpret the houses of the Romans. The large ones dominate and call for silence, the small are closed. Inquisitiveness is not rewarded. And deformity, so rare in Rome, is ignored.

The ever latent gravity periodically became the very principle of artistic style. Bramante in 1510, Giacomo della Porta in 1600, Bernini in 1650, are all exponents of a majestic and stern manner, which is the manifestation of that same profound feeling for style which produced Paul II's semi-Gothic architecture in the 1460's, and found expression in 1485 in a treatise on architecture by the humanist Alberti (*De re aedificatoria*).

One might believe that the picturesque Baroque of Borromini and his followers was a break with the Roman tradition itself. Undeniably it introduced new forms and a changed view of many tasks, but if the matter is regarded without prejudice, it will be observed that the richly dramatic Roman Baroque at its culminating point can be conceived as a functionally conditioned gradation. "The hyperbolic and paraphrastic style" [48] was never completely fundamental to the age in question, and in Rome did not gain the upper hand in architecture as a whole. Just remember that we are only speaking of the architectural exterior. The stylistic expression mentioned, was exclusively reserved for quite definite tasks, mainly church façades. We must also go further than that to understand the situation. Without much exaggeration, it can be stated that the extreme Roman Baroque before Bernini's death could very frequently be expressed in the façade as a screen – and only as a screen, in front of a building, which, for sociological or religious reasons had a use for such. Rip this plastically modelled mask away, for it is only stuck on, and you see the true features of the building. The life-story of the so-called jesuitical façade in Rome is a masquerade, and magnificent as such, but the body of the church behind its disguise, retains its gravity. The Church of Gesù's famous façade appears in all the handbooks as a stylistic document of the first order. In actual fact, it is the principal example of a special genre, namely, the sacral showpiece, but not of a complete concept of style. Only when you supplement the façade with a picture of the church seen from behind, does the situation become clear. Then you realize that strict cubism has reached full maturity. The façade of Borromini's S. Carlino is less symptomatic of the feeling for Roman style at that time than the adjoining monastery. An undulating church façade, filled with columns, has the theatrical style of its contemporary function, but the style is not that of the age purely and simply, and certainly not of Rome. The *casa professa* of the Jesuits stands next door to the Church of Gesù, the monastery of the Theatine Order is neighbour to S. Andrea della Valle's lavish façade, the Collegio Romano flanks S. Ignazio. The three ecclesiastical dwellings mentioned have their solemn and closed characteristics; this is the style of the function, and additionally of tradition and of the city. On the other hand, as pure architecture, the façades of the churches often lack any organic connection with the buildings themselves, and are only logical from the point of view of decoration. The façade is a frontal addition which appeals to the observer in the same way as a portal or a proscenium.

If one infers a dualism from the culminating period of Roman Baroque, which is expressed by the terms "strict style" and "rich style", both effective simultaneously, one is guilty of a compromise which verges on the dishonest. A style, in its full meaning, cannot contain two violent contrasts without bursting at the seams. The facts are somewhat different. In general, the architecture of mature Baroque in Rome, is expressed now, as in the past, in the "strict" spirit which we have characterized above, but occasionally, and in special circumstances, the manner of expression is "rich".

We can perhaps most clearly demonstrate this contrast, by placing the façade of S. S. Vincenzo e Anastasio side by side with Carceri Nuove. Both monuments are roughly contemporaries from the middle of the 17th century. The front of the church, so often reproduced in pictures, constitutes a *non plus ultra* in respect of plastic fullness and turgidity; the exterior of the prison is bare, severe, almost Egyptian in its forcefulness (Pl. 16). Bindesbøll, the Danish architect of Thorvaldsen's museum, must have been delighted with this building whose forbidding aspect may have been an inspiration for Stendhal's maxim referring to Italian style, especially applicable to the Roman. This harsh prison in the Via Giulia may well have taken on a special quality based on the function of the building – the impenetrable is here something other than an artistic principle, and the bars at the windows have a greater point from the inside than is normal in façades – but nonetheless, the stamp of the architecture and its spirit, are typical for what is fundamental in Roman Baroque at the stage of its maturity. The building possesses *auctoritas* in the most true sense – and expresses it with the same coldness as does a figure in solid geometry.

The architect of the prison, Antonio del Grande, also designed the elegant façade of that wing of the Palazzo Pamphili which faces the Piazza del Collegio Romano. He was also fully capable of designing the front of a church on the lines used for S. S. Vincenzo e Anastasio. When he produced the plan for Carceri Nuove, it was completely in accordance with the prevalent style of his age and his city. A church façade with crowded columns was related to other ecclesiastical showpieces. The inviolable block in the street of palaces had family ties with the whole of Rome.

The current shortcomings in the interpretation of Roman Baroque are due to people having easier access to, and a preference for rich specialities, rather than broad, coarse generalities. Not until we fully understand the enormous number of buildings, which dominate the aspect of the city, and which embrace monasteries, institutions, houses put to all sorts of uses, and the whole of the civic architecture, will it be possible to write the true history of Roman Baroque. Then it will be realized that there is little substance to the current concept of *il Barocco Romano,* but that the architecture itself is solid in its mass.

Now that we are getting close to our real subject, which bears the name of Late Baroque, yet sometimes can be designated Rococo, it is worthwhile to stick to the point of view we have just put forward. This does not necessarily mean that we underestimate the importance of decoration for a façade. How could this be possible in a city and a period that has created the Palazzo Doria-Pamphili, a number of lavish church fronts and various finely ornamented dwelling houses? The movement of every wave in the relief, every ripple on the surface must be followed by the eye, not myopically studied. It will be remembered that decorative features do not make a style worthy of the name, for a style needs substance. We cannot award to ornament, even in the widest sense, a place among Rome's great motifs. Architecture here is only altered through slow shifts in the strict, grandiose structure. One feels that this learned playing with style resembles illusory hocus-pocus among these massifs in a tragic landscape.

In conclusion, we must visualize the colouring of Rome. If one attempts to call it to mind, it dissolves into a soft, warm, shimmering, overall shade of colour which is beyond the spectrum. The colours flourish in light and air which bring them to life in infinite variety. During the short span of a day and a night they are constantly changing. They come to life in the early morning, when everything is as fresh as on the very first day, and seem reborn as new creations. About the time when the sun reaches its zenith, they can come to fullness, but may also succumb, burnt out, dried up by the heat. At the hour of long shadows, the colour decreases in intensity, then returns to intense clarity, fades with the twilight and dies with the night, only to be resurrected in a new guise beneath the moon.

The moon silvers the faded grey, refreshes the ochre of the walls and freezes patches made by the rusty water, which seems to moisten the fronts of the houses in a slowly running stream. In the atmosphere of the sirocco, the colours sicken; they are dimmed beneath a film, as a flower is veiled with mildew, all hues are hazy with fever-heat.

Which then is the hour for Roman colour? Innumerable painters and poets have tried to make a choice; every visitor to the city has believed he has found the right one – perhaps in the light of his own state of mind. Every moment shows the wealth of beauty of our beloved. When *Roma* bathes in the dewy gleam of mother of pearl at break of day, we rejoice in the sight. Beneath the high sun, the city's complexion absorbs a warmth which glows against the darkness of the shadows, a triumph of beauty. Rome's countenance can blanch in a glimmer of flat lighting and its temperament flare up. At the flower market, or in a crowd, the colour may throw off all inhibitions, escape from the perfect harmony of the architecture and rejoice in its garishness. But at the hour when the swallows begin to circle against a lemon-yellow sky, Rome captivates everybody. The time of seduction has come; colouring swoons voluptuously like Saint Theresa herself. The colours on the palette relax into delicate tones. If the air is transparent, the lingering cadence of the scale grows as tinkling as glass, often with a tinge of pale bottle-green. When the atmosphere is filled with golden dust and the evening red bursts forth, everything is wrapped in a honey-smooth haze. It is perhaps these *soirées de Rome* which are the custodians of the city's true play of colour. Claude le Lorrain thought so and took a lifetime to prove it. You and I have also thought so – and we shall experience it again next year on Monte Pincio.

The true colours of architecture [49] reside in the nature of the building material. The most frequently used material was brick, produced in the Valle dell' Inferno. Baroque preferred unfired, sun-dried brick, which took on a soft silver-grey or dusty grey colour. Hence, there is a basic tone in Rome's colouring. The fired brick, on the other hand, assumes an orange-yellow and rust-brown colour, which is the warm and sonorous tone in the chord.

At the stage in Baroque when the bare wall started being covered with stucco, this stucco was given the colour of the brick, but in varying shades. The brown is rather the colour of a camel, or a roe-deer and can also be reminiscent of amber or fudge. New colours for the stucco developed; mainly numerous shades of ochre. A lovely egg-yellow was popular for use with country houses, such as the Villa Pia in Vaticano, Villa Medici, Villa di Papa Giulio, Villa Borghese – and also the Palazzo Barberini.

As covering walls with stucco became general, during the Late Baroque and Rococo periods, the palette grew lighter in colour. The rust-brown could melt into pale pink or a delightful orange; lemon-yellow and almond-green also appeared. The Piazza del Quirinale's three buildings each has its own colour: that of the Papal Palace is reminiscent of burnt almonds, the Palazzo della Consulta is straw-yellow (with pearl-grey shutters), the Scuderie Pontificie enjoys the deep smouldering hue which is often taken on by over-ripe tomatoes. The whole picture is completely perfect in colouring.

Rome's shading of colour is accentuated by rich use of stone. The handsome travertine is predominant. There were two sorts, one of which is inferior and very porous and ash-grey; it becomes almost white under the effect of lighting and develops black patches from oxidization, the sun and rain making it dramatic. The finer travertine is solid in consistency – and yellow. Sometimes it is saturated with pent-up warmth, sometimes unbaked looking, with the cool tinge of a toadstool. Rich in substance and colour, like a mature cheese, golden and dry like an old sherry. As one can see, the dual nature of the stone has the same harmonious effect as the brick and thus excellently supplements the latter material.

The great Roman play of colours, so engaging in its tranquil glow, has tones of an almost symbolic character, rust and dust, ash and straw. But also gold and silver – old, precious, dull gold; smooth, worn silver.

The city called eternal, has been purified by time, and this can be seen from the maturity of its colour. Its effect comes from deep down. Dignified gravity tempered with the warmth of a smile.

THE CAPITAL OF CHRISTENDOM
I

Je partis très content de l'architecture de Saint-Pierre VOLTAIRE
Je ne fus pas très frappé de la façade de Saint-Pierre STENDHAL

The first Roman church the traveller from the North caught sight of was the Basilica of St. Peter's. This was from La Storta, the last staging post on the Via Cassia before Porta del Popolo. *Guardate, guardate,* shouted the vetturino, *è la cupola di San Pietro!* With similar triumph the mountain of Vesuvius was pointed out to anyone approaching Naples.

Just as *il cupolone* towering above the city with its tones of yellow and silver was always changeless in appearance, and as an artistic concept was superior to any other view, San Pietro maintained its supremacy over all Rome's churches in spite of changing ideals. Maderno's façade was subjected to criticism in its time, but Michelangelo's dome and the mountain of a church beneath it were inviolable, possessing the eternal rights of perfection. It is an aimless task merely to defend the taste in the wonderful interior of the church which is revealed in the mighty name of Peter, and yet is so gentle and refreshing, with the drama of the Godhead filling every corner and drenched in the light from a golden age. Anybody who came from the country north of the Alps, whether he was at home in Louis XIV's cold rooms or reared behind Napoleon's military colonnades, had to forget the ABC of style and come under the spell of Rome's premier church. He had to leave with that profound joy in his mind that was given even to a doubting Thomas in the capital city of Papism.

Rome's army of churches has always been busy. They affect and pervade everything everywhere. The hundreds of voices of the bells announce the dawn, call to prayer and rest, warn in time of misfortune, rejoice at moments of festivity. When an earth tremor occurred in January 1703, all the bells started ringing spontaneously, even the little silver bell standing on Clement XI's table. The terrifying sharp knock at Rome's door could not have been answered more impressively [1]. The air vibrated with sonorous voices, supported by the roar of the cannon from Castel Sant' Angelo, when a new pope was announced from the loggia of St. Peter's by the most senior cardinal: "I bring you great joy – we have a pope . . . ." Not merely the era of every new pontificate, but also the duration of the day began with a signal from the church. Half an hour after the setting of the sun the *Ave Maria (Angelus)* announced the completion of the 24 hours. "The bell sounds, the beads are told, the girl enters the chamber with lighted lamp and says: *Felicissima notte!*" [2]. The regular progress of the church year was also marked by the bells. They all fell silent on Maundy Thursday, even the striking mechanism of the clocks, and remained so until Holy Saturday, when the ringing of St. Peter's deepest *campana* gave the signal for a tremendous, enchanting, joyful peal before the festival. Perhaps these silent days were the most stirring time for the Roman bells. Their power became more significant in the dead silence. The hours were indicated tonelessly and drily by wooden clappers which boys sounded out in the streets, an ugly melody in a low key [3].

A host of people went through the churches like a tidal wave, the great houses of God lived unceasingly, then as now, hour after hour in a changing rhythm. The poor, out-of-the-way church wakes up only now and then, but the scent, the scent of piety and incense fills the vacuum when the door is barred, and awaits the thin tinkling of the little bell ringing for mass. As we all know, the Romans do not merely celebrate the festivals, but also cultivate the daily habit of the church. In no other place on earth is it possible to vary a spiritual life so richly as here, where Peter has his grave and the Pope his throne. In Rome the possibilities of ecclesiastical experience are immense and were formerly limitless. A church can be found everywhere, whenever needed, no search is necessary as there is always an open door in sight. You enter through a leather curtain as into a living room, or you move along the nave of the church as if it were a gallery. No Roman, however poor, no pauper however miserable, is anything less than an honoured guest in these princely halls of the Church – many are more splendid than those in an emperor's palace – and he can move and have his being there with confident assurance. How great a part the Roman's right of entry here has played in his refined manners cannot be measured. He was nourished with impressions of beauty gathered from all stages of life; he enjoyed them in peace and quiet, hardly aware of the pleasure. The church interiors produced generations of aesthetics, and because of this, veneration is always alive in Rome, and works of art within the reach of every ordinary man are certain of respect. The beggar is part-owner of the golden altar, and when the crimson velvet or the tapestries are hung up in the choir for a festival, he feels with every justification that he is a participant in the rites of his church, for he is an invited guest.

The house of God is the ordinary man's constant companion on his daily round. There may be one close to his place of work and another round the corner from the osteria. Minor conventions and secret promises direct the steps to yonder chapel, or to the modest oratorium in the valley nearby. At every turn there is a *chiesuola* awaiting. The parish church itself is of immediate importance to a population which clings to its own district, but the basilica is everybody's goal. The penitent goes from station to station, and all the members of a family combine their annual excursion into the country with a visit to a popular Holy Shrine [4].

So it is true to say that the inhabitant of Rome seeks and finds his whole world involved with the wide circle of churches. Here he meets his God and himself, he honours all the saints and stands face to face with the views and fables of Christendom, with Rome's exceptional history, told by architecture and inscriptions, announced in monuments and given life in portraits. Going to church he also meets all the living; he comes across his friend, his neighbour, his enemy in another atmosphere than that of the market, yet the elements of a weekday are all there. He gets the latest news in the chapel as does the Jew in the synagogue, he catches a glimpse of the nobleman from the palace opposite, he is familiar with the archpriest's finest chasuble and on nodding terms with the usher.

In former times the Roman's familiarity with the church was even greater, his use of the interior even more intense. Members of the numerous guilds and professions [5] met together in particular churches which they either possessed, or to which they were connected in pious brotherhoods (*confraternite*). Thus the coopers owned S. Maria in Coppella (the last word means cup), cooks and cake-makers had at their disposal the little church of S. S. Vincenzo e Anastasio in Rione Regola. The carpenters gathered in S. Giuseppe near the Campo Vaccino, called after the holy Joseph, renowned beyond all other masters of the craft. Obviously fruit merchants had their centre in S. Maria dell' Orto which was surrounded by the vegetable gardens of Trastevere, and the millers in S. Bartolomeo all' Isola, the church on the island in the Tiber, for corn was ground in mills rocking on the river and driven by its waters. S. Rocco, situated close to the port of Ripetta, was the haven of the numerous seafarers (*barcaiuoli*). And it was self-evident that the elevated brotherhood of artists (now called *Insigne Accademia dei Virtuosi*) should seek shelter beneath the dome of the Pantheon. Such a charming company as the Cardinal's train-bearers had their little oratorium in Borgo Nuovo and were thus almost in the shadow of *er Cuppolonaccio* itself (as it is called with the typical mocking Roman emphasis).

All these craftsmen and other good people practised their devotions together in their chapels, perhaps now and then talked shop at these gatherings, and all according to their abilities, decorated their churches with altar paintings and holy vessels. It is said that there was quite a spicy atmosphere in these guild churches, popular with the people from the streets of small shops, and also a local tone, since the various categories of tradespeople still kept mainly to their own streets [6]. It was a happy chance that the church of the barbers, S. S. Cosma e Damiano, the temple of all Roman figaros, was, in the 18th century, situated in the immediate vicinity of the city's largest theatre (Teatro Argentina), and it is amusing too, that the architect for its restoration in 1722 was called Master Carnevale. That the honourable guild for apothecaries and doctors had established their church, S. Lorenzo in Miranda, behind the Temple of Faustina's noble and estimable porticus near the Campo Vaccino, seems obviously apt – a classical *domus medica*.

In many other ways too, the churches of Rome differed widely in use and atmosphere. Just think of the considerable number of churches to which non-Romans had special claim. Each of the great foreign nations had at its disposal special places of worship, and it is easy to understand that such buildings, protected over centuries by potentates and endowed by zealous visitors to Rome from the countries concerned, gradually came to be filled with artistic treasures in such abundance, that they developed into something more like a shrine and a national museum. The Kingdom of France had acquired no less than four churches, namely S. Luigi dei Francesi, the principal church for the French community [7], the magnificent abbey church of the French Minims, S. S. Trinità dei Monti, with S. Claudio for the Burgundians, S. Niccolo for the Lorrainers and S. Ivo for the Bretons. The Holy Roman Empire was responsible for S. Maria dell' Anima [8] (and Camposanto Teutonico near St. Peter's). The Portuguese went to S. Antonio, diagonally opposite the "Monkey Tower" (Torre della Schimia), and Spain – Spain boasted proudly of three churches. S. Giacomo degli Spagnuoli (which no longer belongs to this nation) was entered from the Piazza Navona, but quite recently it has been disfigured and lost its original main façade which looked on to Via dei Sediari (now Corso del Rinascimento). But fortunately, S. Maria di Monserrato has, right up to this very day, retained a breath of the old Spanish quarter in which it is situated (Via di Monserrato), among gloomy palaces for courtiers and prelates. When Velásquez came to Rome in 1630, his first quest after resting from the rigours of his ride was the church of S. Maria di Monserrato, where he looked at "some tombstones over painters of our nation". The next day he hurried to early mass in S. Jago in the Piazza Navona [9]. But the finest sacral monument of the Spaniards in Rome is really Bramante's Tempietto near S. Pietro in Montorio, erected at the expense of *los reyes catolicos,* Ferdinand and Isabella. England made its presence felt in a modest sort of way with S. Tommaso di Canterbury at the entrance to the Via di Monserrato, and the Scandinavian nations were only represented by the Swedish church of S. Brigida, a modest enough building, although it does in fact stand in the Piazza Farnese itself. The stately establishment maintained by the Poles has a wide frontage in the Via delle Botteghe Oscure [10]. The Greek Orthodox Church performed the special rituals of its services in S. Anastasia, and S. Basilio was used by Syrian Maronites "with cymbals and castanets" (Münter). In the port area of Ripetta, a community of Slovenes and Dalmatians rallied around S. Girolamo, most of these people being seamen and bargees. So Rome also had its Riva degli Sciavoni, but the quay in Venice probably smelt more of seaweed and cordage [11]. S. Girolamo was connected with the other seamen's church, S. Rocco for the watermen, near an institution for distressed Slovenes. Even the savages converted to Christianity could rejoice in their private church, S. Stefano "degli Indiani" or "dei Mori", these old names having been applied to Ethiopians. The black man's humble house of prayer enjoys the chance favour of being situated directly opposite the main apse of St. Peter's.

Thus, foreign nations had their own special churches in Rome, but so did the extremely varied provinces, races and civic communities of Italy itself, most of these latter being, or having been, independent states in those days, and some of their special churches were very distinguished [12]. This localized character helped to make church life very heterogenous. But the wide variation of dialects which flourished in and around these houses of prayer gave them a provincial tone which is still perceptible in the neighbourhood. The respective congregations, together with their influential patrons, found it a natural thing to put an outwardly distinctive stamp on the churches in their care. The name of the titular saint himself was a banner, the builder was often brought from outside the walls of Rome, and altar pieces were painted by masters from home. The history of art, which does not always take such situations into consideration, has, from time to time, had difficulty in working out the problem of Roman style and typology, because it has ignored this deliberate provincialism.

Thus, the national church of the Lombards, S. S. Ambrogio e Carlo, has a particularly striking silhouette, and the name itself, which refers to Ambrosius, the father of the Church, and the holy Carlo Borromeo, both bishops of Milan, gave this church a majestic *air,* (one is tempted to say *ballon*), for the shape of the dome rather detracts from its majesty. The façade was given a distinctive character, which can only be charged to the account of Lombard particularism, and of this we shall speak later. It must also be noted that the churches in Rome, supported by the fertile basin of the Po, were just where the elegant street-life of the Corso ended and where luxurious restaurants were to be found (Pl. 17).

S. Giovanni dei Fiorentini, the great temple of the Tuscans, now stands apart, outside the busy currents, but is rooted in a district in which the Florentines have preferred to live since the Middle Ages, the pulsing, vibrant street given over to banking, and its local character was stronger than many others. Close to the church which the Medici Pope Leo X made into a religious centre for all Florentines living in Rome, is the Collegio Bandinelli, erected in 1678 for children of Tuscan parents, and diagonally across from its front stands the "Florentine Consulate" (from c. 1500). A recently demolished palace on the corner of the Via del Consolato, housed the tribunal, which in former times according to special privilege, administered the law within the community of the Florentine colony [13]. The district in this corner near the Tiber still has, although partly stripped away by slum-clearance, a certain "Etrurian" severity. In the past, through the centuries, the streets near the church echoed with harsh Tuscan gutterals. Even now a few family names, famous in Florence, ring out from the palaces in the neighbourhood: Falconiere, Sacchetti; and from the square behind the choir, you see the Palazzo Salviati across the river, built in a robust style with rustic work, which – like the family itself – had its home by the Arno. Vicolo delle Palle is reminiscent of the balls in the Medici coat of arms. And inside the church, we see monuments with proud Florentine names such as Acciaiuoli, Capponi, Riccardi, while outside, on the façade of S. Giovanni – to which we shall return later – we see the signature of a Galilei.

Other Italian national churches in Rome will be summarily dealt with; some of them have an individual hallmark from the topographical point of view, or give a cue to the local dialect, or as also happens, suggest the popular humour of the district. S.S. Sudario belonging to the Piedmontese bears this out. Small and well hidden, this private chapel of the Casa Savoia is called after Veronica's sudarium which is preserved under Guarini's fantastic dome in the palace chapel of Torino. People from Lucca owned S. Croce, and the Bergamese – the compatriots of the rogue Harlequin – have settled in the Piazza Colonna, where stood S. Bartolomeo with its pertaining madhouse. Over in Trastevere, not far from the slipways of Ripa Grande, stands S. Giovanni Battista, the centre for the Genoese, most of whom were seamen. S. Spirito, the church belonging to

Naples, was rebuilt by Cosimo Fansaga, whose later Neapolitan works are far removed from the spirit in the Via Giulia [14].

Why not admit our weakness for the little Roman provincial church which no longer exists? Its name was S. Venanzio and Aracoeli towered above it: "The peaceful church enshadowed by its crown, its foot constricted by the shabby town". As it stood there – before the area around the Capitol was mercilessly cleared in recent times – it was at one and the same time the humble house of God in a Roman *paesetto* with intimate local characteristics, and a place of assembly for new arrivals from the little town of Camerino in the Umbrian Appenines. People from the Marche province, among whom were many masons, frequented S. Salvatore in Lauro, a good, domed church up near the Via dei Coronari.

This grouping of churches, at it were, according to dialects, can be juxtaposed to a far more important and obvious method of classification, namely according to the particular religious accent given to the services by the different priestly orders [15]. The Jesuit and the Trappist express themselves very differently in cult, ritual and customs (in so far as the latter opens his mouth at all). The first thing to be considered is the order of precedence with its wide distinctions. The gulf between the highborn canons and the lowest level of the mendicant friars was expressed strongly, not only in the neighbourhood in which their respective buildings were situated, but also very clearly in the architecture itself. The elegant complex composed of the rebuilt S. Maria della Pace and the square in front of it, which is on the lines of a palace courtyard befitting a dignitary of the church, was erected in the 1650's (near Pietro da Cortona) for the Augustine canons-regular (*Canonici Regolari Lateranensi di S. Salvatore*). They hold the leading position in the hierarchy of all the priestly orders, and this can be seen from their one-time residence. One is expected to approach this sumptuous temple cap in hand. What a difference between this formal *cour d'honneur* of S. Maria della Pace – as regular as the canons themselves – and the stronghold of the Capuchins near Piazza Barberini with the church unpretentiously built according to their strict rules, and the frightening comfortless walls of their monastery. Just an austere barn of a place [16]. Nothing less than an icy aura must have surrounded the principal church of the Dominicans,

17. *Via del Corso with S. Carlo. Painting by Ippolito Caffi (detail).*

18. *S. Maria in Campitelli.*

19. *S. Tommaso in Parione.*

20. *Churchyard and small square behind S. Maria in Trastevere.*

S. Maria sopra Minerva. Here, situated next to the gloomy church in the preaching friar's monastery, was that seat of judgment, the very Inquisition, and the rather oppressive Gothic seemed, in this place, to be in fertile communion with those black and white castigators, the pack of "God's watchdogs". On the other hand, a lofty profile is characteristic of the priory and church of the Knights of Malta on the Aventine. The order is both military and sovereign, a state within the state, and its isolated group of buildings also demonstrates this superior attitude.

Furthermore – are not many of the churches tinged with the colours worn by the individual orders? Formerly, the palette was more variegated, but many ecclesiastical monuments are still to be seen with their patches of black, blue, violet, white, grey, dark-brown, chocolate-brown – these are monks and nuns, in pairs or in groups, near their domicile. A cross, half crimson, half azure, sewn on the habit, can lead the way to one of the churches of the Trinitarians, a pair of white figures to the Carthusians' door. Yellow Rome is stippled from this ecclesiastical paintbox. Small vivid strokes of the brush, swiftly applied, hurried, often unsure, increase the depth in the great composition which is called *Roma sacra*. Seen from a distance it becomes an entity, when innumerable impressionistic effects tinted with all colours are unfolded as if on a fan.

There are still moments when we are lucky enough to see a bright sketch with the full impact of the past in its coloration. This can happen on the Via di S. Nicolo da Tolentino – grey, steep, shadowed – when it is suddenly illuminated by a line of lobster-red figures (*i gamberi cotti*), the German theological students making their way from the *Collegium Germanicum* down into the town. But in the old days – the time with which our book is concerned – when religious processions were the order of the day, all pious places were connected as it were, by veritable rosaries of people, monotone ranks of Grey Friars, and brown cowls with intoxicating splashes of purple and gold in their banners, crosses and monstrances, and in the vestments of the dignitaries. Thus the façades of Roman churches had a constantly changing décor as well as the permanent local tone which the colour particular to an order indicated.

We can also attack our subject from quite another direction and demonstrate a social aspect of the Roman churches in the way that they were understood in every-day life – which, in spite of everything, has always had a leaning towards the profane, even in the capital of Christendom. There were fine churches patronized by people of standing, and there were shabby ones visited only by the common herd. S. Carlo al Corso and S. Marcello (Pl. 25) were – and still are – extremely *à la mode,* due in particular to their situation in the fashionable shopping centre. S. Silvestro in Capite (Pl. 64b) also enjoyed the favour of the upper classes; it is in addition extremely well provided for, with altar silver and other elegant furniture. Several churches are particularly redolent of the aristocracy, with an aura issuing from family memorials belonging to the great nobility. This is true of Gesù e Maria, in whose interior a series of delightfully dramatic half-length portraits of the Marchesi Bolognetti and their wives seem to fill the air with conversation, almost with gossip. The atmosphere of the nave is close to that of a salon. S. Maria in Publicolis is nothing much to shout about, but the monuments of the Santacroce family echo the palace a few minutes' walk away. And in S. Francesco a Ripa, it is difficult to ignore the waft of haughtiness from the Mausoleum of the Rospigliosi's. The Dukes of Zagarolo show their bewigged heads opposite the chapel in which the Blessed Ludovica Albertoni, with the aid of Bernini, seems to be expiring with all the *abandon* of a woman of the world.

S. S. Apostoli and S. Maria in Campitelli (Pl. 18) possess, each in its own way, a splendid feeling of space. All honour to the architect, but there is no doubt that the first mentioned church gained its particular glamour from the presence of the Colonna and Odescalchi monuments (not to mention the House of Torlonia, whose name is proudly proclaimed on the façade), at least in the eyes of the Roman patriot. In the lovely interior of the latter church, memorials to the House of Altieri are given a setting which is in accord with the antiquity of this family and its high regard in the city. From the time the Altieri Pope Clement X came to the papal throne in 1670, 269 years were to pass – that is the whole space of time which occupies us in these pages, as well as another century and a half – before the next true Roman was crowned with the tiara, in this case Pius XII of the Pacelli family who was on the papal throne until 1958. In Carlo Rainaldi's very splendid church, the rattle of the keys to the Altieri tomb cannot be ignored.

As everybody knows, S. Agnese in the Piazza Navona is regarded as nothing more or less than the family memorial chapel for the Pamphilis, and hence, quite apart from any artistic merit, it is linked willy-nilly with the posthumous reputation of this family.

An extreme contrast is provided by the humble churches, the houses of prayer of the poor people in Trastevere and in other densely populated districts. We need not give examples, but we remember their smell, remember the shabby velvet, the cheap ornaments, the poor paintings. On the outskirts, although within the city walls, among the fragments of ruins and goat herds, many an ancient church led a precarious existence. It deserved to be honoured because of its remarkable past, grown up as it had on soil soaked with the blood of martyrs. It enjoyed wide-spread veneration and perhaps gave a cardinal his title. But respect was for the most part shown from a distance. Out there the miasma held sway, and it kept the faithful away; it was dangerous to go there, a real penitential pilgrimage. It is stated expressly of S. Sisto Vecchio (Pl. 38, 39a), situated in the valley near the thermae of Caracalla, that it was surrounded "by a heavy, oppressive and unhealthy atmosphere in which it is impossible to stay during the summer without risk to life" (1709) [17]. S. S. Nereo e Achilleo, opposite neighbour to S. Sisto, S. Prisca and S. Balbina on the Aventine and S. Eusebio and S. Prassede on the Esquiline, all belonged then to that family of particularly exposed, but historically famous churches – all titular in a twofold sense – since by origin they were of the so-called *tituli* (i.e. belonged to the oldest category of Christian churches in Rome), and also provided titles for cardinals. In Holberg's time they maintained their proud nobility in shadowed isolation – as did Don Ranudo di Colibrados. Only a church like S. Cesareo, by the inner reaches of the Via Appia and not far from S. Sisto, can now give us a faint idea of what could be the fate of the *pauvres honteuses* of the Roman Church in these deadly silent areas.

We can also think of Rome's churches in relation to the rhythm of the ecclesiastical year. A large number of them, the so-called stations, are functionally linked with specific festivals. As is well known, each of these has its established liturgical texts (pericopes) laid down by the *Missale Romanum,* such as the gospel, epistle and lesson. The building, the day and the scriptural passage are all mutually connected, and the custom goes back a very long time; in some cases the concordance is also determined by typographical factors valid in the days of the Early Christian Church, and taken as a whole, this cycle should be considered as a very subtle work of art [18]. Naturally, only the man schooled in ecclesiastical matters could appreciate this ingenious system properly – a sort of "unity of time and place" built into the Mass – but at that very moment the station stood out in sharp relief even for the unenlightened, the body of the church appeared in a light other than the usual. The mere fact that the believer made a pilgrimage on foot to the place of worship, that he approached it expectantly under the auspices of a holy day, gave the building a new importance. It is difficult, practically impossible, to understand completely the associations which welled up in a worshipper when the familiar front rose up before him at a select hour. But nobody will doubt in his consciousness that the existence of such a church was inextricably bound up with the day and the weather, with the bitterly cold dawn or the close summer evening, when the bronze words of the Mass were sonorously intoned.

Ash Wednesday, when the fast starts, had as its station the stern and pure church of S. Sabina on the Aventine, perhaps Rome's noblest. The walk up to where it stood on the almost desolate hill was, in itself, a serious preparation for divine service in this peristyle of the Dominicans. S. Lorenzo in Panisperna was the station church for the first Thursday in Lent. The name Panisperna cannot be clearly interpreted, but the word *panis* permits of no doubt, and we find that bread also plays an important part in the text for the day (Matth. 15, 21–28). Many worshippers throughout the ages have connected the edifice of S. Lorenzo both with this day of fasting, and with the idea of bread. That Good Friday had a particular connection with S. Croce in Gerusalemme needs no further explanation. On the other hand, the link between S. Anastasia and the second mass on Christmas Day (the first, at midnight, was celebrated in S. Maria Maggiore) can only be found by delving deeply into the past. In this case, it is the situation of the church which is decisive for its place along the line of stations. S. Anastasia stands at the foot of the Palatine, where not only the rulers of Ancient Rome, but also the Byzantine Emperors held court. The liturgical ceremony held in the church on no less a day than Christmas morning soon gave distinction to the "palace chapel", and was, at the same time, a compliment to the procurator of the Byzantine Emperor. This prelude in the early days of the Church was a hidden mystery to the crowds of believers who made their way to S. Anastasia in the dark before daybreak. But there is very little doubt that innumerable generations of Romans, in their imaginations, always saw this church looming out of the chiaroscuro of the winter dawn, crowned by the ruins of the imperial palaces. Their outlines looked menacing in the pale light – a ghostly castle from that world of paganism which crumbled beneath the Christmas star.

So many of Rome's churches are wrapped in the evergreen of legend, or reflect the glory of the haloed saints. From many places of worship there is a stairway up to heaven, made manifest to all pious souls. Why should these steps be excluded from the architecture? The *Scala Santa*, set in a chapel opposite the Lateran, but found perhaps originally in the residence of Pontius Pilate, is, after all, a tangible part of the building. The myriads of the faithful find this out to their cost, when they laboriously climb it on their knees. For them, the steps are the shrine, and Domenico Fontana's plain façade is no more than a screen, either not noticed at all, or merely accepted as a visible objective, a final obstacle. The little round church of *Scala Coeli* outside the Porta S. Sebastiano is built where the holy Bernard had a vision. On this spot he saw, in ecstacy, a ladder of fire reaching from earth to heaven. S. Maria della Scala in Trastevere gets its name and fame from a miracle-working picture of the Mother of God found on the stairs of a house.

When the chains of the Prince of Apostles are shown on August 1st, S. Pietro in Vincoli takes on its full meaning as a church. S. Pietro in Carcere, the chapel in the damp cells of the Mamertine Prison, is completely filled with the dominating shadow of Simon Peter, in the same way as a large, melancholy figure of an old man by Rembrandt emphasizes the cave of darkness around him. The chapel *Domine Quo Vadis?* near the Appian Way is just a trivial piece of Baroque, but the sacred legend contained in its husk, the scene of Christ's meeting with Peter, possesses a suggestive power which could inspire a cathedral. Paul's heroic death is signalized by three chapels (S. Paolo alle Tre Fontane), one for each of the fountains which sprang forth where the severed head of the apostle touched the ground. Catholic architecture has, apart from the tangible, an inner, invisible architecture which speaks clearly to the man in the street. This too, has its piers and flying buttresses.

There are some churches which are only comprehensible to the believing mind at one moment in time. When the new-born lambs, whose wool is to be used for the pallium of the Holy Father, are consecrated in S. Agnese fuori le Mura, the church takes on a splendour of fairy-tale beauty, which the walls of the building itself cannot produce. Every year on August 5th, jasmine, and the white, scented flowers called *maraviglie* float down from above, inside the chapel of the Borghese family near S. Maria Maggiore, in memory of that summer's day in 366 when snow covered the Esquiline Hill, and Pope St. Liberius, struck by the miracle, sketched the plan for the great new basilica (Basilica Liberiana) on the blanket of snow. A church may have passed through all the purifying fires of changing style to emerge finally in a splendid form and yet be overlooked. But the outline, drawn in the melting snow sixteen hundred years ago, will never be forgotten. It takes its place in the history of architecture among the designs by the greatest masters.

We also recall that many churches were part of the established scenery for the popular festivals in the street. No other Roman church has seen so much fun as S. Eustachio, which, until 1872, was the background for the activities of Twelfth Night (*La Befana* i.e. Epiphany); after that year they were transferred to the Piazza Navona [19]. This was, above all, a children's festival, and the little square in front of S. Eustachio and the adjacent streets, were filled with booths selling toys and pastries. A terrible cacophany of fifes, drums, rattles and horns, surrounded the church that was dedicated to the patron of hunting and decorated with stag's antlers. On this evening, the front of the church was reflected in the shining eyes of thousands of youngsters [20]. The portal of S. Antonio Abbate was linked with hoards of dumb animals. On this saint's day, an endless procession of horses, donkeys, goats and all sorts of four-footed domestic animals, as well as other small creatures, streamed past the entrance to be blessed and sprinkled with holy water. It is impossible to think of a more humane church than this chapel for Noah's Ark, its clergy being greeted by a chorus of baaing sheep and grunting pigs. The thoroughbred horses of the aristocrats and even the Pope's own team of horses were included in the cavalcade, which attracted a great many spectators to the square by S. Maria Maggiore. A café opposite was the front row of the stalls, and here sat the philosopher George Berkeley one day in 1717 and witnessed this delightful church ceremony [21]. And Goethe enjoyed "a day of jollity" seeing it [22].

The Aracoeli church took on a charming lyric splendour during the children's Christmas sermon and from the reflection of *il Santo Bambino*'s jewels; the long flight of steps up to the door of the church gave the impression of a ladder leading straight up to the crystalline heavens. And S. Biagio della Pagnotta (in the Via Giulia), the house of prayer for the Armenians – the compact front of which, with its impressive pilasters, is adapted to fit in with the enormous blocks of ashlar, which are the unfinished remains of Julius II's tribunal – assumed a gentler appearance on the saint's name day, when consecrated bread (*pagnotte*) was distributed at the portal. What could be a more amusing signpost than the little stone ship (*la navicella*) out in the road in front of S. Maria in Domnica upon Monte Celio? All children were intimate with the frightening lion's mask in the vestibule of S. Maria in Cosmedin, *la bocca della verità,* which would close immediately a perjurer, or even the smallest nipper with the whitest lie on his conscience, was rash enough to put his fist between its jaws. This moral lion's mouth gave the church its name [23]. Just imagine Struwelpeter being established in a Protestant church and made the centre of a popular cult in the porch.

At Christmas time many churches showed the most marvellous model tableaux of Christ's birth in the stable, of the Adoration of the Shepherds and the Wise Men, and particularly renowned was *il presepio* (the Christmas Crib) in S. Maria Maggiore [24]. The worshippers, who now feasted their eyes on these often brilliant scenes, created with much fantasy and a great sense of beauty, might shortly before have glimpsed the reality behind this eternal idyll of Christendom. Towards the end of Advent one could often find shepherds, who had come down from the mountains and even from as far away as Calabria, standing in front of a candlelit picture of the Virgin Mary set into the corner of a house. They would praise the Mother of God with the sound of their shawms and bagpibes. The simple, melancholy notes were as if wafted from the fields of the Holy Land. Each *pifferaro* seemed in his movements as if he were a direct descendant of those who first adored the Christ Child on earth. The musician from the Campagna had a special purpose with his hymns of praise, for he wished to ease the Virgin Mary's labour pains. If one asked such a shepherd why he frequently played outside the windows of a Roman carpenter, he would answer in the innocence of his heart: "Out of politeness to Master Saint Joseph" (*per politezza al Messer San Giuseppe*) [25]. His divine service in the street was simple and impressive, without communion table or proper vestments.

In everyday life too, Rome's *madonelle* served as small churches under the open sky and were to be found everywhere. "The place is often chosen with natural perception, it usually has something secluded and inviting about it, which lends itself to the devotions", tells a poetic observer, "at one place the Madonna has her shrine in a corner, at another in a niche" [26]. Pious conversations take place between the picture and the people in the street, also between the picture and its *lampioncello*. The former says in the words of the poet Sergio Corazzini:

> "You are my brother and I am your sister,
> See, I am fearful of standing in darkness
> Outside the gleam from your bright little flame.
> Burn and console me in my profound sorrow,
> Burn, I implore you, oh little red lantern,
> Like the pitying heart of the pure Jesus Christ."
> But the lamp sighing said: "This I cannot do."

The fairy tales of Roman churches have no beginning and no end.

The same can be said of their drama. The theatre within the walls of the churches and around their buildings knew many types of plays and excelled in every genre. Especially the pathetic style was truly incomparable; the architecture and the priesthood mastered the art to perfection. The majestic ceremonies in St. Peter's were – and are – real theatre.

Such festivals as the Pontifical Mass and the canonisation of saints are staged in a manner which is stupendous in its magnificence and impressive in its precision. Here, the inborn talent of the Italians for the spectacular is brought into full play, and you can say that the schooling of the priesthood in sculptural expression comes up to all expectations among the twisted columns and beneath the domes. Those who have been present at a canonisation and have seen the Pope on his throne accept such fine offerings as a birdcage with doves, gilded bread and a purseful of ducats for a well sung mass – or have seen a scarlet cardinal greet an archbishop in purple, and assuming the special posture which one might call "modest conceit", have witnessed the most magnificent "Haupt- und Staatsaktion" on earth. No wonder that the congregation in the church followed all the ritual scenes with the same intense participation as an audience followed the acts in an opera. The play was known from previous performances and those who now filled the leading roles were observed with keen criticism.

The interior of the basilica may have remained unchanged in structure, but not so in character. Like the scenery in an opera-house which forms the background to all the heroic episodes on a grand scale, the interior of the church seems to take on a new form depending on the spectacle, in a coloristic sense as well. Sometimes it created the atmosphere of a palatial hall (*Atrio Regio* in scenographic jargon), sometimes it completely fulfilled the strict function of the temple. For great festivals the interior's atmosphere is enhanced by the bright red of draperies and hangings, for obsequies there is a black interior, during Lent the colour changes to a soothing violet which conceals altars and chapels. The *Miserere* of Ash Wednesday and Good Friday makes the nave as dark as the grave, but gold prevails in all its splendour when the Papal Court has a day of rejoicing, and the silver trumpets raise their strident voices. The special guild of carpenters and decorators who were involved in changing the adornments of the church interiors were highly esteemed specialists. They had to move around precariously on ladders and scaffolding. The greatest master of this art was Nicola Zabaglia (died 1750), who has left us a proud record of his most elegant works. The trade of the *festarolo* was very dangerous and his brotherhood rightly chose S. Venanzio as their patron saint, for he had suffered martyrdom by being thrown from a height [27].

It is not possible to decide whether religious fervour or a sense of artistic quality was the dominant spirit in the public's idea of a *funzione* of the first rank. But it is certain that the congregation in the church was extremely receptive and attentive to the most incredible things. Mr Sharp, who at Whitsun in 1766 witnessed Clement XIII give his benediction from the balcony of St. Peter's, notes with surprise that from first to last, the tremendous number of spectators watched just as intently as did the elegant audience in the stalls of Drury Lane Theatre, when Garrick was on the stage [28].

St. Peter's reached its peak of transfiguration when solemn rites took the measure of the building and did not merely fill it with courtly pomp. Sometimes it seemed as if the church itself was superior to the religious activities, and then it became clear that this work of art overshadowed Christ's vicar on earth, and that Peter's basilica was indeed a rock. On Maundy Thursday, after the Pope had given his blessing *urbi et orbi* from the balcony of St. Peter's, it was the custom for him to excommunicate all heretics and immediately afterwards to throw down a burning torch, symbol of the stake and the fires of hell. Thousands of eyes followed the falling taper with tension and awe, and thus the crowd in the square became aware of the great height of the façade. The small figure of the Pope stood up there on his balcony [29]. Another example: On Good Friday the most venerated reliquaries in St. Peter's are shown from a balcony right at the top of one of the four piers of the dome, the Veronica pier. All eyes are lifted up, riveted on the little door up there – and the elevation of the architecture is perceived in a dizzy instant. Finally: The feast of *Corpus Domini* is signalized by a magnificent procession which moves through Bernini's colonnades and thus circles St. Peter's Square. While the Pope on the *sedia gestatoria* slowly passes through the colonnade and the monstrance with the Body of Christ, which he raises before him, emerges from behind one column after another, the forecourt of the cathedral is both encircled and emphasized. The procedure is sublime: I have seen it in action [30].

Great and noble style – but the church also made use of histrionics, realizing full well the power of the *comedie larmoyante* over the emotions, and did not disdain the thriller. Various houses of God in Rome had an aura of titillating terror. During Lent and Holy Week particularly, preachers of repentance were everywhere, creating small gloomy places of worship around them. In the Piazza Navona, fanatical clerics tried to compete with all the fun of the fair. Secular and ecclesiastical theatre, the strolling player in his booth and the preacher on his rostrum did not merely compete with one another, but also clashed with the tone of this lovely square. According to Holberg's experience, the missionary came off second best to Harlequin, – "Whereas you see people in their hundreds flocking to the entertainments, usually you see only one or two people approaching the Jesuit's rostrum" [31]. This memory may have been vivid in the great sceptic's mind when he was writing his essay, but possibly his observation should be taken with a pinch of salt.

Throughout the whole of the 18th century ostentatious penance was a great attraction, both for the people watching, and for the participants in such painful scenes. Processions traced their miserable steps from church to church, especially on Sundays in Lent, Advent and on certain days during *carnevale,* but of course, principally on Good Friday [32]. The penitents wore coats of white, red and black, and hoods with glowering eye-holes were pulled down over their faces. Some of the penitents were weighed down with a cross on their shoulders, others burdened with chains [33]. In Holberg's time one could still see processions of particularly zealous masochists who "stigmatized" themselves during the march, a form of devotion which "gives the observer a greater desire to laugh than to cry" [34]. Later in the century the flagellants preferred to practice their sport indoors. On Good Friday in 1740, the poet Thomas Grey saw half a dozen poor wretches discipline themselves in one of the chapels of St. Peter's with iron-tipped scourges, and it sickened him [35]. Pater Caravita's oratory, situated at the corner of the Corso and a street which still bears the name of this Jesuit, had built up an amazingly large congregation by specializing in severe penitential practices under convivial circumstances. Here, flagellants of both sexes carried out their pious pursuits in total darkness [36] to the great edification of an elegant audience.

When they emerged into the street, battered ladies were collected by their *cavalieri serventi* in their carriages [37].

A couple of churches were surrounded by an atmosphere of unadulterated gloom. One was the Oratorio del Cuore di Gesù (near S. Teodoro), given over to a select brotherhood called *Sacconi*, because its members wore tunics of the roughest sackcloth. They wandered out on bare feet every Friday to collect alms for the utterly helpless [38]. And even more awe-inspiring was S. Giovanni Decollato – the very name is evocative – where the famous society of Misericordia had its headquarters. When the brothers, wearing black habits and cowls with eye-holes, emerged and walked through the streets of the city, there was always an execution imminent. They presented themselves at prisons to give the last consolation to those condemned to death; they followed them to the gallows or the block and laid them in their coffins [39]. Chiesa della Morte in the Via Giulia belonged to a corporation which devoted itself to the burial of nameless corpses, murdered and drowned people, unknown victims of fires and all sorts of catastrophes [40]. In return for having managed to find a resting place in consecrated ground, the cadavers had to contribute to the decoration of the church. The sorry bones of the dead were cleaned and tastefully arranged in the burial vault, as with the Capuchins. A sacristan, who was responsible for the decoration and was an artist in his own field, expressed himself thus to a visitor: "Monsieur, this is the only place where I am happy, surrounded by my work. That's not because of the few scudi I earn every day by showing people round the chapel, not at all; but the monument that I keep in good order, which I beautify, which I cheer up (*que j'égaye*) with my talent, has become the proudest thing in my life and my greatest joy" [41]. Although sacristans succeeded in "cheering up" this earthly matter, the Romans out in Via Giulia may well have looked askance at death's Church of the Holy Virgin – an ecclesiastical theatre with the motto "Memento mori" set above the proscenium [42].

S. Angelo in Pascheria and the oratory in S. S. Trinità dei Pellegrini (a part of the great pilgrims' hospice) in which Jews were compelled to listen to the sermons, were not among the best homes of Christianity [43], and the long, menacing inscription in Latin and Hebrew which can be read above the portal of S. Gregorietto a Quattro Capi, opposite the former entrance to the ghetto, is an ugly label.

According to Montesquieu, there were no places in Rome more convenient for divine service and homicide than the churches (*à Rome, il n'y a rien de si commode que les églises pour prier dieu et pour assassiner les gens*) [44]. The author of "De L'Espris des Lois" was not suggesting that violence had particularly favourable conditions within church architecture, but he certainly felt that assailants did. And this is very true, for they enjoyed the right of sanctuary on the sacred soil. Immediately a criminal – still holding a smoking pistol, or with blood on his hands – managed to get into the vestibule of even the most wretched chapel, he was safe from arrest by the papal sbirri. In most cases, the sympathy of the population was on the side of the malefactor, and officious bodies brought enough food for his need; in fact, it was on pain of excommunication forbidden to put obstacles in the way of such supplies [45]. So the evil-doer was not only safe and sound as long as he remained within *il sacrato* – in the chapels of certain brotherhoods there was always "a couple of rooms and a kitchen at their disposal" [46] – he could also laugh derisively at the police's attempt to entice him out into the open by cunning and guile [47], and at the same time his refuge was a convenient base for new exploits. A cutthroat could carry on his trade over a wide area if he moved quickly from one church to the next. The children imitated their elders when they played cops and robbers in the street, some squares of stone being called *chiesa*, others *non chiesa*, the first being "home".

The universally popular interest in *l'amore* found fertile soil in Rome's churches. The beau monde did not go to mass until 10–11 o'clock in the morning. The ladies were usually escorted by their beaux (*cicisbei*) [48], who behaved with great decorum. At the church door they stepped forward to raise the leather curtain, then dipped a finger in the basin of holy water and offered it to the belle, who accepted it with modesty, crossed herself and tendered her thanks with a deep curtsey. After mass and the following short devotion she rose from her kneeling position, gave the breviary to her servant, picked up her fan, genuflected to the High Altar and sailed out on the heels of her cavalier, who once again offered her the holy water, raised the curtain and gave her his hand to escort her to the carriage or on a walk. But, says Baretti, to whom we owe this description, "there are also examples, especially among the young, of cavaliers whispering to one another and pointing out the lovely ladies as they come and go. The priests object strongly to this improper, quite scandalous behaviour, but even the best arguments are powerless to root out this dissolute conduct" [49]. For – as he admits – it was by arrangement that the beauties met *les petits maîtres* in the fashionable churches. Young ladies, who had very little opportunity to meet their suitors, chose very sensibly to go to late mass; this gave them time to titivate themselves and to write the love-letters which they passed to their lovers in the church – and to receive *billets-doux* in exchange.

The possibilities for flirtation were particularly opportune during late evening service (Benediction), with its short prayers and emphasis on music. Then, after the blessing, one could go straight to the opera, to the Commedia dell'Arte or to a social gathering (*conversazione*) [50], the visit to the church fitting perfectly into the day's fashionable programme. We have no need to go to the sources to realize that also young persons belonging to the lower classes used the peace of the church to ease the course of true love. The church in Rome is all-embracing. The pious and the articulate, the rogue and the lover, all are blessed in its shadows.

II

The apostolic procession of great builders, who are the backbone of the Baroque period's greatness, seemed to come to an end with the Chigi Pope Alexander VII (1655–1667). And it looked as if the succession of patrons and personalities on the papal throne who had been inspired by the Muses since the beginning of the 17th century, had for the time being its last representative in that playwright of taste, the Rospigliosi Pope Clement IX (1667–1669).

Anyhow, none of the popes in the second half of the 17th century intervened to any extent in architectural matters nor made his personal taste felt. The Altieri Pope Clement X (1670–1676) was so enfeebled with age when he took over the helm, that he could not play an active part in any building project (*attendere alle fabbriche*) [51], but had to let his favourites see to the implementation of the very limited public works in this field. That he lacked any interest in architecture is quite clear, and indicative of this is the fact that the old Pontifex never visited the mighty palace his dear family had had erected while he was on the throne. As he paid a visit every year to the Gesù church directly opposite the Palazzo Altieri, his striking lack of curiosity cannot be ascribed to failing health, but can only be interpreted as the expression of a dislike of this business of building stately edifices [52].

The austere Odescalchi Pope Innocent XI (1676–1689) lacked all feeling for architecture [53], nor could he rejoice in any artistic freedom or pleasure. The Ottoboni Pope Alexander VIII reigned for only one year and a couple of months. Innocent XII of the Pignatelli family (1691–1700) certainly built a great deal, but hardly for pleasure, for he devoted his attention predominantly to houses which were built purely for utilitarian purposes, and he acquired considerable merit thereby. He was "modern" in his attitude, in so far as he felt strongly about solving urgent problems of a practical and sociological nature in building. The passion to erect monuments (*il mal della pietra*) and create architecture for architecture's sake, which gripped an Urban VIII, an Alexander VII, was foreign to Papa Pignatelli. Without batting an eyelid, he had Rome's greatest theatre razed to the ground as a matter of moral principle, directly after it had been erected in all its magnificence.

Interest in the great evidently flagged among the rulers of the Papal States during the period 1670–1700. But it must in all fairness be remembered, that the economy of the Curia was under stress during most of this disturbed and warlike period, and the situation did not improve until the 1690's. However, church building was not at a complete standstill. Religious communities and rich aristocrats provided the resources for it. And outstanding architects, old and new, were at hand.

Lorenzo Bernini kept up his amazing creativity to the very last. Clement X seems not to have liked him, anyhow he made little use of him, but in his position as the principal architect of St. Peter's and head of papal building activities, nobody dared to interfere with him. Camillo Pamphili in 1678 entrusted the old maestro with the building of

S. Andrea al Quirinale. This serious work, whose superb interior creates a pure harmony in grey and pink marble, brings to mind the form of both the Colosseum and St. Peter's Square [54]. The great ellipse is now scaled down. Bernini himself loved this church and regarded it as his most successful work. Domenico Bernini once surprised his father regarding it with great concentration. This picture of the great artist, who, on a solitary walk, stands face to face with the creation of his declining years and finds it good, will long be remembered. When he lay bedridden from a stroke and his right arm was paralysed, he found it reasonable that this arm should be the first to die, since it had worked hard and needed rest [55]. And he was right.

Eleven years after Bernini's death, in 1691, Carlo Rainaldi also departed this life. With him died the last great figure of monumental Baroque. He had built without the passion and reckless energy of a Bernini, but his art was princely and he lived as a man of the world – "kept horses in his stables, servants in his hall, carriages in his coach house" [56] – and like a prince he departed. But it was Bernini's architecture, especially his mature, purified style, that drew Europe's attention and became a guide for the following generation of Rome's architects.

The most important among these had all been his pupils. One of them was *Mattia de Rossi* (1637–1695); he had been closest to his late master, for Bernini felt a father's love for him [57], admired his character and had great faith in his abilities. He took Mattia with him to Paris in 1665 and by his own account [58] recommended him six or seven times to the great Colbert. What better reference than this? De Rossi also became Bernini's successor as leader of *la fabbrica di S. Pietro* and thereby became primate in the hierarchy of Roman architects. He was not given great independent problems to solve, but his production is of choice quality and in no way puts to shame Bernini's assessment of his abilities.

Carlo Fontana (1638–1714) probably came to Rome as early as 1650 [59], while he was still a boy. After years of apprenticeship with various architects, such as Pietro da Cortona, he became an assistant to Bernini when the latter built his churches in Ariccia and Castel Gandolfo at the beginning of the 1660's. Every form and every line in these crystal-clear works must have imprinted themselves on Fontana. At the age of 25 he was given the final polish in Bernini's atelier and in 1666 he became *misuratore* in the building department of the Vatican, and thus set foot on the first rung of the hierarchical ladder which was to take him to the top. At Bernini's death, to what must have been his great disappointment, he had to give way to Mattia de Rossi [60]; two years after the death of the latter, he was promoted architect for St. Peter's (1697). Fontana was kept very busy by Innocent XII and had also built up a large private clientèle, from the last decade of the 17th century onwards being the uncontested leading light in Rome's architectural world.

Equipped with an extraordinary capacity for work and being a great perfectionist, he won a place for himself in every field of architecture, as we shall soon discover. Fontana was a born organizer, an outstanding technician, with an interest in history which he demonstrated in numerous publications (as did Fischer von Erlach and Lauritz de Thurah), and he seems to have possessed distinct ability as a teacher. His fame reached from Rome to beyond the Alps and as far as the Iberian Peninsula. German Late Baroque regarded him its progenitor [61].

At his peak, Carlo Fontana was the leading exponent of the Roman traditions of Baroque. He was in fact the typical intermediary, a guarantee for continuity, and also gifted in a wide academic field. This favoured official architect was however more than this. In his own quiet way Fontana became, in reality, the symbol of a style, for he was a perfectionist. He certainly cannot be called an eclectic; Bernini's purified style remained the unshakeable basis for his own art, and he made only a few concessions to Borromini's mannerisms. The secret of the power that was given to Fontana, who was no genius, is to be found in his taste rather than his caliber. It was his vocation to ease the transition from a heroic style to a cultivated one which was to be the evolutionary result – and he did it without betraying the ideals of forceful plasticity, without succumbing to the temptations of ornamentation. Thus he and his school succeeded in conveying serious Roman art through the critical period around 1700, more by judgment than by feeling, and for a long time – actually for ever – making the *Louis Quinze* style unacceptable in Rome.

As we know, Rococo in its essence is a functional art form, cultivated with grace in a cool climate. The decoration, *rocaille incarnate,* is best suited for interior use. It serves style but does not master it. Perhaps it may be expressed in this way: Fontana took the wind out of French Rococo's sails in Italy by himself applying a finely balanced rationalism, from the very start disarming the forerunners of the new trend. People of the older school lauded his respect for a glorious heritage, for he still used the Latin idiom. Architects of a younger Europe felt at ease with him, for he expressed himself articulately with a modern intonation. A personality of Carlo Fontana's stamp is predestined to be looked upon as a classicist. This he was in the same sense as Bernini was classical. But to regard him as a sort of early herald of Neo-Classicism is absurd [62]. Admittedly he renewed nothing, but he interpreted much that was old, and did it in such a clever and vital way that it retained its topicality even on classical soil. That is Carlo Fontana's achievement in Rome.

From 1673 onwards, Nicodemus Tessin the Younger was in Rome, where he was introduced to Bernini and worked in Carlo Fontana's atelier [63]. He found it logical to separate the architects in Rome at that time into two groups. To the first group belonged Bernini, Rainaldi, Fontana and Mattia de Rossi, all official architects and *cavalieri*. In the inferior category, which consisted of "mittelmässige und ordinaire, die da mehr corrumpirte *Architetti* sindt und *Muratori* genanndt werden" [64] he placed G. A. de Rossi and G. B. Contini. The inclusion of the two latter among common master masons by this promising young man, is based upon a reasoning which is as false as it is discourteous. Throughout his life, this Swedish court architect and bureaucrat never failed to put his own superior knowledge on a pedestal. *Giovanni Antonio de Rossi* (1616–1695) was an excellent artist and a cultured man. He had studied the humanities and rhetoric at the Collegio Romano, no less, but he educated himself in his own field by "private study" [65], not a bad method when a man has talent, but he was looked down upon for this reason by all the professionals, although he also had the good fortune to build up a large practice which made him economically independent. He is said to have left 80,000 scudi, a very considerable fortune. This thin, fiery little man lived in a house with good wall-hangings and felt entitled to level sharp criticism at his colleagues. As palace architect he can be considered in the first rank (after Bernini's death). His ability to utilize

21. *S. Maria in Campo Marzio.*

22. *S. Maria in Monterone.*

23. *Courtyard near S. Maria in Campo Marzio.*

24. *S. Biagio in Campitelli.*

even the most difficult sites bears witness to his fine feeling for situation and reveals imagination. Tessin could have learned a great deal from this unique character.

Giambattista Contini (1641–1723) was also a man of some distinction. He had been a pupil of Bernini and remained steadfast to him to the last, waiting by his Master's deathbed among the other beloved disciples. In taste, Contini was conservative and abominated the direction Borromini took, for he loved Antiquity. In the field, he applied a method of building which was very simple and rhythmical, and his best work never intruded on the eye, but had character. Contini was without whims, and was therefore particularly appreciated. In 1673, the very year that Tessin spoke of him *en canaille*, he was made architect to the rich Augustine order in Rome [66] as well as given a number of public tasks (as the architect for the Apostolic Court and the Fontana Trevi), but otherwise did most of his work privately, being employed by both the Altieri and the Ruspoli families [67].

This architect with the unobstrusive, practically anonymous production, must have been an interesting gentleman. He was not the sort to let himself be sat upon. As a controversialist he was very temperamental, producing brilliant paradoxical statements and inventing invective with the greatest of ease. Thanks to the biography of Contini, which his good friend Pascoli has passed on to us [68], we have a clear idea of what this touchy architect was like [69] and can practically hear his tirades against *l'ultimo moderno buon gusto*. They are worth listening to, for they summarize a generation's view of the concepts of decency and fraud in architecture, as expressed by this stubborn offshoot of Bernini. These are his words to a young hothead: "My lad, you are on the wrong track and ought to leave to the carpenters, joiners, cabinet-makers, decorators, paper-hangers and toy altars for children all these mouldings, ribs and string-courses....". He asked him if he realized that "buildings are very different from singers' platforms, from prie-dieux, sedan chairs, carriages and four-poster beds? Did he want to play *Borrominello* in the capital city of the world after having come in at 4 o'clock with three shillings' worth of plush and tassels? Such a little coxcomb, impudent know-all, popinjay, arty-crafty climber, gasbag, *disgraziatello, infarinatucolo* dot-

toricchio, ignorataccio . . . .". The master spat out the Roman pejoratives and laid the little modernist low. "No, take as an example, take as an example the façades of S. Pietro, S. Andrea della Valle, the church of Gesù, S. S. Martina e Luca, S. Maria in Via Lata, S. Susanna, and try to develop accordingly . . . .".

Among the young men who during this period received their training in Rome were two Austrians, Johann Bernhard Fischer von Erlach and Johann Lucas von Hildebrandt. The former's stay in Italy was around 1680 [70], the latter's some ten years later [71]. Neither of them thought he was "the greatest" like Tessin. Hildebrandt, a military engineer, no doubt had some lessons from the experienced technician Fontana [72], but otherwise, it looks as if both Austrian architects gained more knowledge and insight by feeling their way, rather than by sitting at a school desk and copying in the drawing office. Naturally, they also took the art of the famous masters as an example, but their own best was not brought out by this procedure. Each very different, but with equal talent, they were later to bring Viennese Baroque to its culmination in spite of Rome – and to create a universal art thereby. The most "Roman" Englishman of the age, Sir John Vanbrugh, had never been to Italy.

A fourth budding architect from north of the Alps, the Frenchman Gilles-Marie Oppenordt, completely kicked over the traces in Carlo Fontana's Rome, where he stayed in the 1690's, with a scholarship from the Académie Française into the bargain [73]. His development was very erratic; all strict and weighty styles were ignored; he copied ornaments like mad, dreamed in overgrown gardens with nymphs and mossy statues, enthused over Borromini and invented a decorative mannerism which would have driven Contini crazy if he had caught sight of it. This developed into the *Style Régence* and became a ferment in the international "rocaille" style.

Christof Marselis, working in Denmark c. 1700–1719, was a comrade of Oppenordt in Rome and shared his piquant taste. This is clearly seen from the drawings he made while in Rome [74]. La Teulière, director of the French school, stated in a report from Sept. 23rd 1698 that Antoine, who held a scholarship, had obtained valuable assistance from "a young German architect". He goes on to write: "this is a clever young man, sensible and understanding, who knew M. Oppenordt and used his room for working after the latter had left for home .... As he is both skilled in mathematics and also does architectural drawings, I have proposed to him and Antoine that they should collaborate on a project (or draw up a plan, *tirer un plan*) which they can do as soon as they have finished copying M. Oppenordt's designs" [75]. No doubt the anonymous German architect was none other than Marselis.

And so he may be looked upon as the representative of those young architects who, full of emotion, wandered around among ruins and palaces, sometimes attracted by the ideal, then enticed by the decried – witnessing Bernini's direct successors turning Rome into a great work of art. We shall follow in the footsteps of these students and visit the new churches. In August 1673, Tessin, filled with satisfaction, had sketched the most splendid of them – "it has not long been built" [76].

In 1672, after 60 years of building, the imposing domed church of *S. Carlo al Corso* was to all intents and purposes finished. Only the façade was missing, as well as a couple of flanking buildings, these being the hospice for the Lombards and the dwelling house for the priests. The annexes were built first. They became the decisive features in the appearance of the church, for they extend its front and become the backcloth to the little square given to S. Carlo, since the whole complex stands back from the building line of the west row of houses in the Corso (Pl. 17). The prototype for such a symmetrical composition, in which the plastically effective façade of the church is emphasized between subordinated side wings, and thereby stands out in greater relief, was S. Agnese in the Piazza Navona, which is framed on the one side by the Pal. Pamphili, and on the other by a building corresponding to it. S. Maria in Campitelli is flanked in a somewhat similar manner, but only the canons' residence on the right is a deliberate link with the imposing columns of the front (Pl. 18).

On the 22nd July, 1682, the foundation stone was at long last laid for S. Carlo's proper façade, and this was completed within the course of two years, being based on the design by Cardinal Luigi Omodei, the patron of the Lombard Brotherhood and also its benefactor [77]. The work of this dilettante *porporato* was harshly judged by posterity. The appeal of the massive columns of the front is certainly only slightly felt, the half-columns are lost in the wall, and the triangular pediment fails to hold the central part together because its lines are broken by rectangular projections and further weakened by a large oval opening in its panel. On its own the façade is bloated, its structure devoid of life. Compare it with Carlo Rainaldi's church Gesù e Maria, only a few years older, whose façade (1672) diagonally opposite S. Carlo, is such an excellent example of the monumental use of pilasters. But when we deliberately consider S. Carlo's façade as part of a composition which includes the flanking buildings in this long street, it gains in perspective, almost literally. Seen against the stretch of flat walls of these side buildings and the rows of windows, the cardinal's arrangement of columns seems to gain a relative strength from its subdued guardians on either side [78]. The façade of S. Maria in Campitelli stands out with greater sharpness and dominance because it is situated in a square which – in contrast to S. Carlo's – is an enclosed space and undisturbed, and it is flanked by narrower buildings, the top stories of which look down on it.

S. Galla too, situated in a dark street between the Piazza Montanara and Bocca della Verità, was supplemented on its transverse axis by simple buildings comprising a hospice for sick vagabonds and other sorts of outcasts; here they found a bed for the night and a bowl of soup. This pious institution did the Odescalchi family credit. It was started by Don Livio, and a grant in 1688 from his uncle Pope Innocent XI, expedited the work, but it was not finished until some time after the beginning of the next century by Duke Baldassare Odescalchi [79]. The architect Mattia de Rossi has tempered the façade of the church in harmony with the purpose of the whole building and it is quiet and subdued. It will be noticed that the main cornice is flush with the side wings so that the building complex is tied together, and that the volutes of the gable of the church curve out towards the flanking houses. Unfortunately, S. Galla was pulled down in 1936 when the Via del Mare was constructed. This unified, solid complex, so well balanced, was a utalitarian building of great distinction (Pl. 26b).

Usually church façades of this period, which like S. Galla used the current tripartite "Jesuit plan", are far more distinctive when decoration is reduced to a minimum and merely expressed in simple architectural terms. Then we realize that there is a great tradition inherent in them. The façade of *S. Antonio dei Portoghesi* (finished c. 1700) shows the dangers of riches easily come by; you hardly notice it because its decoration makes it ordinary. The embellishments still retain their intrinsic value – the sculpture of the figures is indeed brilliant – but the configuration itself will captivate nobody [80]. The little church of *S. Maria in Monterone* is more fortunate (rebuilt 1682 according to an inscription in the cartouche of the pediment) [81]; the features themselves are seen to advantage in the charm of their irregularity. Like a wise girl with a rather too large mouth, this front knows how to make the best of its weak points. Only a small-minded judge will see any disharmony between the wide openings in the centre section and the narrow ones at the sides, instead of enjoying these clear-cut dark holes, which are so serene in their panels, so self-confident in their function as the only door, the only true window, that they do not even cast a sidelong glance at the feeble little light at the sides. S. Maria in Monterone stands opposite an arch (*arco*) which curves over Vicolo Sinibaldi; immediately you step out into the light, the façade strikes the eye, poor, without shame, with its sharp-edged grace (Pl. 22). It is also flattered by its slim and showy partner, but this latter belongs in a different company which we shall discuss later.

S. Margherita, which stands in a little square over in Trastevere, was erected after a design by Carlo Fontana and was finished in 1680 [82]. It has a façade whose articulation is immaculate and flawless (Pl. 26a), evidently imitated from S. Maria della Scala (of Mascherino), its close neighbour, which is a hundred years older. Fontana's church deserves mention here if only for the reason that externally it keeps to a traditional plan in a manner which is very pleasing indeed. At first glance the façade seems lifeless and cold, but it is really only apparently dead, for there is life in its purely linear subtlety. That such a situation at this point in time, the year of Bernini's death, could be regarded as acceptable, also by the church's builder, the very rich Cardinal Gastaldi, is very instructive, but need surprise nobody [83]. For seen in the proper light, as it were, the significant reduction to the bare bones shows the architect's mastery of the methods of expression available to him, rather than his employment of inherited richness of form, however dextrous. The strict style in this work of Fontana's cannot be summed up as reactionary or as a product of unpleasant academic trends, but must be interpreted as a studied simplicity. S. Margherita cannot therefore detract from a work like S. Marcello, which is by the same architect and from the same period, for each of these façades individually so different has its own special importance, its own special tone. Fontana can admit to both without losing face.

An ostensibly modest plan was particularly justified in the square where S. Margherita was built. This square is small and there is another, older place of worship (S. Apollonia) directly opposite the church. Any inharmonious conflict between the two church façades had to be avoided, yet, on the other hand, it was important for Fontana to have the last word here. As the front of S. Apollonia was very restrained, with a simple arrangement of pilasters, the architect had no need to express himself forcibly. He could – and should – ensure his supremacy unobtrusively. Furthermore, Fontana's building was combined with a convent for Franciscan nuns of a very strict order [84]. The good architect is tactful on all occasions. The result was a façade of extremely reserved character.

All the same – S. Margherita shows Fontana's critical ability and refinement of taste more than the free flight of his talent. This gift is unmistakably present in *S. Croce dei Lucchesi* which was given its present appearance by a complete rebuilding 1692–1696, after drawings by Mattia de Rossi [85]. The front, which is a vertical rectangle beneath a triangular pediment holding it all together, is divided by four colossal pilasters into three sections, of which only the middle one is distinguished by a portal plus window with delicately formed copings. The sections at the side are empty, entirely passive. On the whole, the relief is rather low and static, the main cornice completely unbroken (Pl. 27).

This front elevation with its pilasters has numerous older models in Rome, but differs from these by its lean nobility. It is counterbalanced at the sides by two walls; they link half the height of the middle line of the façade with the top of the pediment. De Rossi adopted these *contrapposti* from Rainaldi's Gesù e Maria. The wing-like segments on the outside edges above the cornice are his own invention, and something of the same can be seen in his earlier work S. Francesco a Ripa. While the splendid façade of this latter church seems to flow in its articulation [86], the *prospetto* of S. Croce is frozen in its classical immobility. Late Baroque has here produced a church façade which, with its pure frontal effect and its simple rhythm, expresses the peace of the temple. Bernini's best-beloved pupil had no need to be ashamed among the Ancients.

S. Marcello al Corso was given its façade at exactly the same time as S. Carlo, that is 1682–1683 [87], but some years were to pass before the decorative figures of the saints were added. This work by Carlo Fontana can best be appreciated when its site is taken into consideration. The bare front of the old church was placed in the background of a little square which is, as it were, a niche in the Corso. It was bordered on the right by the Servites' monastery; its high and heavy façade (erected under Urban VIII) in the Corso, completely dominated the modest church which was also served by the same order.

When the church was rebuilt in 1682, the architect must have felt it right and proper to give the façade a completely distinctive character, so it would stand out in relation to its neighbour, the monastery pertaining to it, and dominate the square. In such a situation a new façade could be given a sculpturally effective style. After all – did not the whole life of the Corso, the carnival, its competitive course, the daily *trottata* – pass by S. Marcello's open forecourt? (Pl. 25).

The plan which Fontana used was old and tried. If his façade achieves such a striking effect nevertheless, it is due to the fact that its base line is concave and that he gave the free-standing column a distinguished place in its composition. There is nothing shocking about Fontana's use of this curvature in the year 1682 (compare S. Agnese), nor is it to be regarded as a special Borromini motif. Fontana's great master Bernini, had once used it in a plan for the Louvre in 1665 [88]. We may well say that S. Marcello's façade is less dominated by "a statically relaxed, purely aesthetically effective play of lines in space" than it is by architectural logic [89], for this latter never fails at any point, and a single curve cannot be regarded as excessive.

The gently curving front embraces the forecourt and stands out next to the monastery without over-emphasizing its relief. If you straighten out the façade and flatten it – an experiment in the mind which neither offends against the spirit of the work nor its letter – its traditionalism immediately becomes noticeable, and then it looks like the bottom of a box. Classicists like Milizia found Fontana's work unrestrained [90]; we find it characterized by an admirable gravity and balance. And so did the aesthetes of those days, who regarded anything resembling Borromini's work with a less favourable eye. Shortly after S. Marcello's modern façade was completed, one observer, Padre Freddi, called it *capricciosa*, but also "solid and majestic" (*soda e maëstosa*) [91]. The word "solid" is noteworthy in this connection, for the façade is just that; all elements are clear and assembled by a hand that did not shake. The changes in perspective in the curved wall are uncomplicated and no trace of any caprice can be seen (once the glaring empty frame is removed).

The brilliance of S. Marcello's façade emanates only from the curving sweep with its sparse embellishment and restrained order. And this illusion of richness which the façade possesses, has been produced by contrasting it with its monastery, a building of angles and broken lines, and this merely by planting whole columns out in the sun and making them curve in front of the hollow arc of the wall. Only two decorative elements diverge a shade from the normal – and neither of them is original, but variants. A drawing by Fontana himself, which Nic. Tessin may have been given when he was his pupil in 1688 and which is now in Stockholm [92], shows S. Marcello's façade in a form which in essentials corresponds more or less to the completed work, but in a couple of details shows interesting deviations. In the Stockholm drawing, the empty picture frame which is inserted in the broken segmental pediment is missing. It hides a window in the upper storey and in general seems to lack motivation and purpose. The large window, which in the drawing seems to be supported by the middle console of the pediment, is far more compatible with the calm totality of the façade. On the other hand, it was a fine correction by Fontana to replace the ordinary volutes, which can be seen in the drawing, in the angles between the lower part of the façade and the high pediment, by gently curved palm branches. The architect is one of those tasteful formalists who improve successfully on their own style. It is doubtful therefore whether the gaping picture frame was to Fontana's liking; perhaps it owed its origin to others, possibly to a request by the

Servites. P. Freddi says in the diary of 1693 already mentioned, that this *finestrone o quadro isolato* did not win the approval of all, but it must be remembered that a relief was to be included in it, "and when it is done, the frame will perhaps be the best of all the handsome details of the façade". The Father's pious hope, which smacks a little of bad conscience, has still not been fulfilled. S. Marcello seems to have hung out an empty mirror to reflect the vanity of the Corso.

With all due respect to S. Marcello, it must be said that none of the churches discussed here can be considered as being of extraordinary quality. The leading architects of the period however, left behind them two monuments in Rome which cannot be objected to in this way. They are by Carlo Fontana and G. A. de Rossi respectively, and demonstrate the finest qualities of these two builders. *S. Biagio in Campitelli* (also called S. Rita da Cascia) by the first-named architect, was erected as early as the first half of the 1660's (93), thus being contemporary with Borromino's S. Carlino, and with Bernini's church in the Castel Gandolfo. Hence it really belongs to an earlier stage. However we find it justifiable to include this memorial in a production that has Fontana as leading man.

S. Biagio was pulled down in 1928 [94], and later rebuilt on another site. It originally stood in a narrow street below the Capitol, immediately to the left of the steps up to Aracoeli, but it is now at the end of the Piazza Campitelli. Encapsulated in a row of houses, it had life; now it merely exists, in its detachment, like an empty conch shell. The transformation that this church has suffered has been particularly stupid, for if any sacral building was a product of its environment it was S. Biagio. Its façade could only be seen when viewed at an angle, and by far the majority of observers saw it for a moment, at the narrow entrance to the Via Giulio Romano as it faced the foot of the steps to Aracoeli [95]. One might say that the external existence of the church was fixed on a diagonal and by a momentary glance. If the architect had the legitimate wish that this work should strike the eye under such conditions – this without projecting from its building line, which was inadmissable – there was only one way open to him, and that was to follow the well-known maxim: "what is lost outwardly must be gained inwardly". The façade of the church had to be treated like a piece of sculpture which takes form by the removal of material behind a frontal plane (Pl. 24).

Fontana made the bottom storey stand firm like a heavy block in the row of houses, but he dug out a portal, windows and niches very forcefully and made these apertures so deep that the gaze was caught by them and penetrated to the depths of their shadows, thereby realizing the power of the façade. Still more deliberate is Fontana's composition of the upper storey. In spite of all the rules — keeping S. Margherita's traditional structure in mind — he bent the sides back so much, that they have a frontal effect when seen laterally. And to emphasize further the space in front of these receding surfaces, he set the massive heraldic hills (monti a monte), the Chigi family coat of arms, on the vacant corners on top of the lower storey. They catch the eye, and the gaze is instantly directed further into the depths. The confined church frees itself; we discover it. Fontana produced a masterpiece. Where S. Biagio now stands at the mercy of the winds and wide open to the sun, the meaning behind its form cannot be understood. One simply acknowledges that the strength of the modelling and the lovely colour of the stone are of imperishable nobility.

S. Maria in Campo Marzio too, is on the whole a product of its situation. A highly regarded and rich convent for Benedictine nuns owned a large area along the west side of the present Via di Campo Marzio. To the south of this area, which runs in the direction of the Via Maddalena, there stood a little church. It can be seen in Falda's prospect from 1676. The Mother Superior of this convent found it rather humble for a community of such noble sisters, and as there were abundant funds available, due partly to a miracle-working figure of the Madonna, the church was completely rebuilt in the 1680's following the plans of Giovanni Antonio de Rossi [96]. The design, a Greek cross surmounted by a dome, is ordinary, but the plastic effect of the church assumed great importance, because the simple body of the building is encapsulated in the irregular mass of the convent, and together build up to one great piece of sculpture. In Plate 21, it can be seen how the sharp cubes of the transepts and the splendid half cylinder of the tribune stand out above amorphous parts of the building.

While S. Biagio gained its authority by a process of subtraction – how solid it was could be seen when chunks were carved out of it – S. Maria in Campo Marzio became greater and better by addition; a thin body was given thick accretions. It is as if the church thrives in two spheres. At the highest level all forms are pure and the material crystalline, but in the lower half, beneath the fascia board of the apse, heaviness prevails. The enclosed balcony which curves round the choir repeats the line of the top cornice with its heavy solidity, and is of major importance when the church comes into sight. That the architect worked with the view from the Via Maddalena in mind, seems clear from the deliberate effect made by the upper part with its oval window. It breaks up the cornice, projects its wavy ridge into the upper zone, and glares like the beam from a lighthouse down into the street towards the Pantheon.

As you walk along the sides of this convent in the Campo Marzio, you may well wonder how this great uneven mass of a building is arranged inside. When passing through the noble portal from the small square to the west, you will be delighted to find an enclosed courtyard of rare beauty (Pl. 23). From the outside, we experienced a building whose character was positive, it burgeons. Here in the courtyard we feel a hollowness, a space has been carved from a mass. This secluded *cortile* is of an extremely precise form, as sharp as that of the church between its flanking buildings. The courtyard lies on the middle axis in front of the arcades of the entrance and creates a funnel-shaped space, not unlike a theatre stage. From this deep niche, side doors lead into the premises of the convent. Behind, at the exit of the funnel, a courtyard and another little church are tucked away. The Benedictine Sisters in the Campo Marzio were given a cloister garth which is without parallel in Rome. It is joyous in its close intimacy, it is elegant with conscious gravity. Even more; a breath of the fairy-tale wafts through this space. Delicate pilasters spring from the corners. In the kernel of this formless block, capitals grow like mountain crystals.

III

With the Albani Pope Clement XI, a classicist came to the papal throne. He was well read in the history of Antiquity and its literature, wrote in an elegant style, expressed himself flawlessly [97], and impressed with his eloquence. When once, as a younger prelate, he had made an academic oration before Queen Christina, she remarked: "I have heard Cicero" [98]. It was no mere chance that this crowned humanist was paternal uncle to the later Cardinal Alessandro Albani, called the Hadrian of his time, the prince of antiquarians. Pope Clement's cultivated manner was also reflected in his daily life, and his bearing was always characterized by amiability. Like Raphael he came from Urbino – and like him became a Roman in the best sense of the word, through his study of the ancient world.

Fate prevented Clement XI becoming the great patron of the art that in many ways he was so well fitted to be. His long pontificate (1700–1721) was overshadowed by political catastrophes and hampered by lack of funds. But if he did not succeed in putting his name to a single architectural masterpiece, he was nevertheless able to stamp an extremely large number of buildings, especially ecclesiastical, with the three hills of his coat of arms, these *monti* beneath a star, which are noticeable wherever one wanders in Rome. He became the great restorer, partly from his own personal urge to preserve, but also out of duty, for an earth tremor in 1703 had weakened the fabric of many churches. It has been said – with some exaggeration – in a report on the situation in Rome 1718–1721, "that there is hardly a church to be found that has not been rebuilt, improved or embellished" in the previous twenty years, so the clergy had no reason to complain about importunity on the part of profane building [99].

If Clement XI had an independent aesthetic doctrine as a builder, this may well be called classical urbanity. Such a concept was completely to Carlo Fontana's taste. The ageing *cavaliere* was certain of his new pope's favour. Clement, who was only 51 years old and full of energy, immediately set about various projects. As soon as he had been elected, even before he was crowned in St. Peter's, he sent for Fontana and the painter

Carlo Maratta, the two authorities who had been enemies for such a long time. The Holy Father commanded them to bury the hatchet and work together according to his orders. And he charged them to visit him every Sunday to be informed of his plans [100]. Thus the Albani pope initiated his period of building under the most noble auspices.

There was no shortage of architects around Carlo Fontana. He himself was active until his death in 1714, but to an increasing degree handed over less demanding tasks to his many pupils and collaborators. A couple of these belonged to his closest family, and were his son *Francesco* (1668–1708), and his brother's son *Carlo Stefano* [101]. The former's talent was not great, but all the same, he succeeded in becoming deputy to his father when he was given the directorship of the papal building administration, and in 1695 he got the job as the architect for Acqua Felice. It is quite characteristic for Francesco's level of achievement that his name is chiefly linked with the rebuilding of an antique temple (Hadrianeum), with an attempt to re-erect the column of Antonius Pius – more of this later – and with a restoration of Pius IV's casino in the Vatican garden, carried out so carefully that Francesco's part in it can hardly be distinguished from Pirro Ligorio's thin pseudo-Antique. *Carlo Stefano Fontana,* who was a priest and held a benefice at the Lateran church, practised architecture as a cultured dilettante. Other pupils of his powerful uncle – partly also his assistants – were *Romano Carapecchia,* who later worked in Malta as the architect for the Order of Knights, *Carlo Bizzaccheri* and *Sebastiano Cipriani,* also *Matteo Sassi* (1646–1723), and his nephew *Lodovico Sassi* (1678–1736).

The most important of Carlo Fontana's permanent staff however was *Alessandro Specchi* (1688–1729). In the office he was his master's right-hand man, an outstanding draughtsman and engraver, who provided plates for all his publications (earliest "Il Tempio Vaticano", 1694). Already in 1689, Specchi etched copies of stage settings for an opera libretto [102]; the main work in his graphic output is the 4th volume of the series of prospects published by Rossi "Nuovo Teatro delli Palazzi et Edificii di Roma". Specchi's handsome engravings are an invaluable source for the understanding of Baroque Rome, and have brought him a greater posthumous reputation than many an architect has managed to win with all his buildings [103]. He held the office of *architetto del Popolo Romano* or *della Camera Capitolina* (architect for the municipality of Rome) until 1728, when he retired because of advancing age and feebleness; from 1718 he had also been architect to the then Monsignore Alessandro Albani, the Pope's "nephew", and in 1721 became the *misuratore della fabbrica di San Pietro*. From 1722–1726 he is mentioned as architect to the House of Colonna. Thus Specchi had upheld Fontana's trend throughout the whole of Clement XI's reign and a good while longer.

A number of architects of the younger generation carried on the traditions of the famous *bureau*, one was *Filippo Barigioni* (1690–1753), who began his career as Specchi's assistant, when the Cappella Albani in S. Sebastiano was decorated (1706). He gave a helping hand when the cells were prepared for a conclave after the death of Papa Clement in 1721, and provided sketches for the catafalque for the following pope, Innocent XIII in 1724, on which occasion he was called *célèbre architecte* by a connoisseur [104]. *Tommaso Mattei* began to make his presence felt at approximately the same time as Barigioni. In 1701 he prepared a temporary festival theatre in the Piazza di Spagna [105], and thereby began a career as stage designer. He became a member of the S. Luca Academy in 1705. And last of all, *Antonio Valeri* in the Year of Our Lord 1736 put down his drawing pen for ever. Greatly venerated as Bernini's last surviving disciple, he had been born in Rome in 1648, and worn himself to a grey shadow in the *fabbrica* of St. Peter's. It even fell to his lot to instruct a nephew of Mansart [106]. Of course, this Fontana circle of architects is not on the whole impressive, and Clement XI's pontificate would, to tell the truth, appear rather colourless in the history of architecture, if the official staff and its assistants had not been boosted by a few figures who did not belong to the hierarchy.

One of these men, who is long forgotten, certainly did not possess any conspicuous artistic talent, but we have, by chance, inherited a couple of amusing, extremely natural close-ups of his person which deserve to be reported. They take us right back to the world of the Roman architects of those days. *Antonio Borioni* was architect to the Dominicans. He regularly went off on tours from the monastery near S. Maria sopra Minerva to the monastic houses in Latium, and carried out building work on the instructions of the General of the order. The large communities of monks and their principal monasteries usually had a particular architect whose duties could be very important. Nowadays the products of such architects are, for the most part, covered by a cloak of anonymity. Borioni also acted as antiquarian and apothecary at the Collegio Clementino [107].

We see him rolling up one day in a barouche at "Il buon Pastore", a villa with large estates, which was the summer residence of the General of the Dominican Order. It is situated in magnificent country near Gallicano, on the stretch between Zagarolo and Tivoli, and is quite well preserved [108]. We see him seated at table in the dining hall (with its fine doors of walnut), of the Very Reverend Père Cloche in the company of his principal and the latter's compatriot, the supreme head of the Celestine Order. The two Generals carry on a lively conversation in their mother-tongue; our good Borioni understands not a word of the French language, and sulks. During the night his room-mate, a French Dominican, snores so inordinately that Master Antonio fails to get a wink of sleep, and on the following day complains to him, only to receive the answer: "But you don't understand French!" Borioni may not be called an artist, but he is the only one among all the crowd of architects who has come down to posterity on a golden cloud of honest fun. And we can follow him to his door when he returns home from Anagni or Palestrina. He gets out of his carriage outside No. 31, Piazza di Spagna, a fine house near *la Scalea,* and goes through the narrow gateway, the keystone of which shows two crossed rapiers with the device: "Courteous, though armed" (*Benchè di spada armato, io son cortese*). Jacques Courtois, known for his battle paintings, had set up his coat of arms which is also befitting for artists [109].

On the other side of the Tiber lived *Giacomo Onorato Recalcati* (died 1723), another of those modest architects of the Church without diploma or knightly honours. He was in the service of the chapter of S. Maria in Trastevere, restored its campanile in 1713, and in the following years put in order the little churchyard to the north side of the basilica, opposite the Piazza di S. Egidio [110] (Pl. 20). Recalcati gave the well a fine relief by flanking the side-doors with thick piers and extending the middle part with a transverse recess. Nothing could be more unassuming, but it contributes much to the intimate charm of this secluded corner. Quite recently the soft brick tiles on the wall were pulled down and replaced by wire; clearly the value of an artist's minute attention to detail is no longer appreciated – the little square is now debased. We reproduce an older photograph to give an impression of church art in its simplest form. That the Trastevere architect could do bigger and better things we shall soon find out.

There is something fascinating about these people who are really artisans. They are tucked away in alleys and build all the small chapels, apartment houses, and coach houses, which thrive in the neighbourhood of important churches and often captivate us with their unsophisticated grace. The prospect of the city of Rome owes an honest debt of gratitude to these forgotten master masons. Only a few of them, those who broke away by doing bigger jobs, are now beginning to take on some sort of substance, but it is still not very clear. Even such a busy, able man like *Giuseppe Sardi* can still – and rightly so – be called *un maëstro misterioso* [111]. He was born c. 1680 and died in Rome some time after August 1753. He lived near S. Maria in Trastevere between 1713–1716, when he worked on this church as a mason under the watchful eye of Recalcati [112]. All his life Sardi clearly practised as a master mason; even in 1742, when he took part in an examination of the dome of St. Peter's as a surveyor. He is still called a *capomastro muratore*. This does not mean that he never built to his own design, for he is bound to have done so, but it stands to reason that independent works can only be ascribed to him with great caution and on the basis of confirmed factual argument.

While these and the older architects during the time of Clement XI were inspecting their numerous buildings at the scaffolding stage, a young man arrived on the scene who had more than a touch of genius, but for the time being he could find no wider sphere in which to express it. His name was *Filippo Juvara* (1678–1736). In 1703 or 1704 he had come from Sicily with a recommendation to Cardinal Tommaso Ruffo, a Neapolitan [113]. He soon became the pupil of Carlo Fontana, who tersely and in the best pedagogical manner, recommended that he should study the Palazzo Farnese. This did not do any harm to Don Filippo – he was in holy orders – nor was it to his detriment to attend a course at the S. Luca Academy, of which he became a member as early as 1707, after he had submitted a very mature church project [114]. The next year he was received into the exclusive society of *virtuosi* at the Pantheon. But Juvara received his best instruction by observing and drawing and measuring in that architectural world which is called Rome. He had the passion of an Oppenordt for developing detail, but also an imagination of unique daring and logical conciseness as a creator. Juvara thought and composed in the world of building like a gifted dreamer.

Up on his roof terrace at his lodgings in Vicolo dei Leutari (Street of the Lute-makers) he could see across to the cupola and towers of S. Agnese [115]. This wonderful church gave him much pleasure and later he himself built the proudest domed church in all European Baroque, La Superga near Turin. At the opposite end of the street was La Cancelleria. Here Cardinal Ottoboni provided him with a theatre to play with – and let him wave Prospero's magic wand, and this was soon to bring him fame as the greatest stage designer of the century. The dark Street of the Lute-makers certainly had bright prospects; in a house close to the lodgings where Juvara received his visions of sun-drenched, radiant architecture, Rossini a hundred years later wrote the "Barber of Seville", which still scintillates and amuses.

When King Frederick IV of Denmark was expected in Rome in 1709, Don Filippo conjured up some incredible and lovely drawings for a complete rebuilding of the Capitol and dedicated them to the monarch, no doubt in the hope of being given employment in Copenhagen. When this fell through, he turned his eyes to Paris, but here too, he was disappointed [116]. Finally in 1714 the Sicilian was called to Piedmont as court architect, and within the course of a few years made Turin the most attractive and harmonious capital of the time. The critical Holberg can testify [117].

The *Casa Savoia* had wrested the prize from Pope Albani's Rome; here, what was old and what was left of Classicism prevailed for a little longer.

Addison came to Rome in the very beginning of Clement XI's pontificate. The English Classicist quickly formed an opinion of the artistic situation. Architecture was far from flourishing, he considered. Likewise painting and sculpture, but he thought it was possible they would come to fruition during the existing pontificate, if the wars and disturbances in Italy permitted. For the Pope himself was "a Man of Learning and a Great Encourager of Art" [118]. Of Fontana, Addison knew that he was honoured as the best of Rome's architects and that he had recently written a treatise on Vespasian's amphitheatre, although it had not yet been printed [119].

The fact is that Fontana in the 1690's did work on a paper dealing with the Colosseum [120], which was published posthumously in 1725. It included a project for the erection of a large domed church inside the arena. Very likely Fontana was toying with the idea that his design might take actual shape in the jubilee year (*Anno Santo*) of 1700, and would thus in the grand manner crow the beginning of the Clementine era. But it was to be otherwise, although on paper in fact, Fontana's church was the finest work of art in Roman ecclesiastical architecture during this period. The church in the centre of the Flavian theatre was certainly thought of as a magnum opus, Roman in two senses. And we might even say that the grandiloquent idealism of the project became symbolic of the artistic wishful thinking of Clement XI, when he succeeded to St. Peter's throne, just as its ill-starred fate is indicative of the straitened circumstances of the Papal States.

But the work is also very characteristic of Fontana's leanings and ability. This basic idea was to make the ruins of the Colosseum safe for posterity by incorporating it into a cultic complex; the religious view furthers – or perhaps even determines – the urge of the antiquary to conserve. In the previous "holy year" (1675), Clement X had consecrated the site by raising a cross on the soil of the martyrs [121]. Thus formal approbation for the initiation of the project had been signalled. While the first motive for this plan was to protect, the second was purely artistic. Fontana felt very deeply about creating a synthesis of the antique and the modern, and wanted to make it clear that the particular style of an age is not at loggerheads with the patterns of Antiquity, but can, without it being an

25. S. Marcello.

26a. *S. Margherita. Engraving by Vasi (detail).*

26b. *S. Galla. Engraving by Vasi (detail).*

27. S. Croce dei Lucchesi.

28. *The Colosseum. Old photograph.*

29. *S. Teodoro seen from the Palatine. In the background the Capitol.*

30. *Model for the sacristy of St. Peter's, by Filippo Juvara.*

31. *Side portal of S. Clemente.*

32. *S. Maria in Cosmedin. Old photograph.*

imitation, continue the classical spirit in form and character. We also suspect a purely personal factor: Carlo Fontana, the architect of St. Peter's, and as such the successor to Bramante, wanted to assume the guardianship of the mighty heritage of Antiquity; it was his destiny to safeguard it. And Bernini's pupil was enthralled by this site, this enormous oval crater, which had been the source of inspiration for the form his master gave to St. Peter's Square [122].

It was Fontana's idea to enclose the Colosseum by a ring-wall. The thought may seem grotesque, a miserable fence around this mountain! But it is a sound idea if we take into account the fact that he intended to turn the whole arena into an open-air church, a sort of *basilica discoperta*. If that was so, then the architect must hold the dilapidated framework together at all costs. The multitudes of the faithful were not to infiltrate from all sides through the arcades, but were to maintain a disciplined approach, and so it was suggested that the external wall was to have only four entrances, one at each of the four extremities of the cross. Fontana also wanted the interior of the amphitheatre, which was to become the biggest church in Rome as far as volume went, to be enclosed at floor level by new colonnades all the way round the oval – veritable interior decoration, in fact. He was going to put confessionals in these "side aisles" which made up a continuous series of chapels, and in the middle of the arena he intended to build a fountain. The altar in this grandiose temple – with ruins towering above the smooth arcades and with the clouds rolling past on the airy ceiling – was to be a church, a centralized domed building flanked by towers, set at one end of the arena.

The capable engineer made all necessary estimates of weights and dimensions for this exceptional church. The cylinder was to be married to the ellipse, the outline of the dome was to be a semicircle, the lower part of the façade was to form a section of the unifying row of arcades. It was as if the regular church building sprang from the anomalous mass. Fontana certainly did his measuring and his revising, but he also borrowed; the tambour of the dome stems after all from St. Peter's, the engaged side towers originate from S. Agnese, the medallion-shaped ornaments on the spires may well come from S. Maria della Pace. The architects of later times in their turn borrowed from Fontana; the project was well known and highly esteemed by a number of his friends (e.g. Juvara), and after its publication it became the canon for church building in Europe. In Denmark, Lauritz de Thurah used it as the basis of a design for the Frederick's Church [123]. As so often happens, both before and since, architecture which has never been given form, becomes particularly inspiring. This is natural enough, as no constraint has been put on it; the originator gave of his best. Fontana's project for the church in the arena is a *tour de force*. A proud gesture in frozen immobility. In its daunting proportions it expresses what might be called "static Baroque" around the year 1700. What the inspired creators of the style had achieved has here been tamed and tempered into sober harmony; in this place doubly effective, for the building is enveloped by the rugged ruin. That Fontana felt his church could stand with such calm self-assertion within the crushing embrace of the Colosseum, is an extraordinary testimony to the passive strength in the architect and to the art of his time.

It seems a pity that Carlo Fontana failed to build his ecclesiastical magnum opus in Rome, and that Pope Albani, who orated like a Cicero, did not have the opportunity to bandy words with Antiquity on the martyrs' behalf in the Colosseum. This Pontifex with hills in his coat of arms, had to be content with his and his Architect General's greatest plan remaining on paper. Mountains were in labour, only a mouse was brought forth. The little round church of *S. Teodoro* was given an atrium hardly big enough for a cardinal's coach and four to turn round in. An inscription from 1704 informs us that this sanctuary, which by mistreatment throughout centuries had become "misshapen, half buried and almost inaccessible", now stood out in purified form [124]. Quite true, this ample cylinder was given such a clean-up that it looked really antique and reminded you of one of the beloved round temples (Pl. 29). After this job was done, Carlo Fontana with a gentle touch added a couple of slightly concave wings and a gatehouse which together formed a courtyard facing out towards the dusty road. Now the second church station for Christmas morning beneath the Palatine hill was ready to receive the faithful with dignity and yet retained its character of great age. On September 23rd, 1702, Pope Clement rejoiced at seeing the building in its complete form [125].

This was his second experience that day as a builder, for he came to S. Teodoro straight after visiting *S. Clemente*. In November 1701 the Pope had taken a look at this ancient basilica and, to his sorrow, found it in a bad state, for he loved it. Was it not an antiquity of irreplaceable value? And was it not dedicated to his namesake and patron, the martyred St. Clement I, Rome's fourth pope (d. c. 97 A.D.) [126]? He decided to restore the church's dignity as a monument, raised it in rank to the status of cardinal church and gave his nephew Annibale Albani the cardinalship. An inscription from 1705, above the main portal inside the building, as well as a treatise by Rondinini dating from 1706 [127], and dedicated to Clement XI, points out that the restoration had not ruined the church as a historic monument. According to the ideas of the time this was correct. A start was made by improving the interior, which in spite of the new picturesque decoration still continues to give such a strong impression of the Early Christian church. Not until several years later (1711–1713) was a modern façade and a campinile built under the supervision of Carlo Stefano Fontana [128]. The French Dominican, Labat, who came to Rome in 1709, mentions the building in a diary of his journey – S. Clemente was put at the disposal of his order – and says among other things, that when the great work of restoration was postponed because funds were lacking, a priest approached the Pope "at an opportune moment" and received permission to continue. On Labat's departure in 1714, it was still not finished [129]. The enterprising prelate, whose name is not revealed by Labat, was probably Carlo Stefano Fontana; he was in holy orders and is known to have taken charge of all the building work.

    S. Clemente's new façade is correct and meticulous, so pure in its cool Baroque that it in no way spoils the basilica's exterior. Moreover, it is almost out of sight, for it looks on to a closed courtyard. The most striking and best part of Fontana's modernisation is the side portal out to the Via di S. Giovanni in Laterano (Pl. 31). An older portal has here been altered by the addition of large volutes which bear a pediment. The architect has designed an ornament which has not so much the stamp of a style as that of penmanship. Fontana labelled this church in his own good hand. The portal of S. Clemente is arresting.

The papal builder progressed to other illustrious churches which needed his care. If nothing else, he saw that they were provided with an entrance fitting their dignity. Clement, the ever-pious, admitted to a private responsibility for *S. Maria in Trastevere,* for it contained the dust of a couple of old uncles of his [130]. This was the oldest of the churches in Rome dedicated to the Virgin Mary and was always certain of singular consideration, and this was one of the reasons why the Pope provided it with a new porticus in 1701–1702 [131]. Fontana had submitted various sketches, of which Clement chose the cheapest and best [132]. Of the five arcades in the vestibule, the three middle ones are emphasized by Ionic columns and bracketed trabeation. The composition is most restful; all forms have an almost classic purity. The architect here came as close to his ideal of Antiquity as he possibly could. The pediment above with its precious mosaics from the Middle Ages was respected. S. Maria in Trastevere, erected some time after 1140, is in itself a piece of Classicism in the midst of the Romanesque period. The interior of the basilica with architraves above the columns is obviously inspired by the monuments of the Early Christians [133]. Now it was once more seen that Roman soil could *nourish* a tried and tested architectural style – in the very place where, according to legend, a fountain of oil gushed forth at the hour of Christ's birth.

The vestibule of the nearby *S. Crisogono* was, in 1707, barred by an iron gate, a light lattice between columns [134]. And finally the Pope improved two such eminent antique churches as the so-called Fortuna Virilis temple (S. Maria Egiziaca) [135], and the Pantheon itself. The portico of the Rotunda was renovated, tidied up, and closed off with latticework (1719); by the earth being removed from in front of the vestibule, some of the steps were revealed [136]. There is really something very attractive about these minor and rather inadequate repairs to the great monuments of the past. Albani tidied up the front entrance and impressed on the man in the street that on the other side of the new iron gate the ground was hallowed, not only by the Christian god but also by the art of the ancients.

Pope Clement had a close personal relationship with *S. Brigida,* the only Scandinavian church in Rome. This stemmed from the days when he as Monsignore Albani enjoyed the favour of Queen Christina of Sweden and was her welcome guest at the Palazzo Riario. The Queen administered the Swedish foundation herself, including a little hospice and a chapel pertaining to it which was built near St. Bridget's house in the Piazza Farnese. After the Queen's death in 1689, Albani took over the actual administration, and the year after by being made cardinal, he also became "protector" for the whole Swedish realm [137]. When he succeeded to the papal throne he did not forget the temple of the northerners, but had the church rebuilt and provided a new façade about 1705 [138]. The master mason for St. Peter's (*il capomastro della Basilica Vaticana*) Pietro Patriarca is mentioned by one source [139] as its architect. As this man's name – in spite of its nominal definition – was so little known among the practitioners of the art, we may perhaps believe the statement. Why put it down to his account if a higher authority had the honour? We know from a drawing dated 1697 [140] how St. Bridget's looked before the rebuilding. To judge from this very amateurish sketch, Patriarca did not take any big chances. The new façade agrees very well with what can be expected of a man who was of the second rank, though trained in an atmosphere of architectural near-perfection. All the same, S. Brigida's front turned out surprisingly conservative. The two colossal solid columns bear undecorated trabeation. It looks as if Master Patriarca had studied an old-fashioned elementary textbook. The result was really not bad, and his portal has in fact the greatness of artlessness, becoming "Neo-Classical" out of pure awkwardness. That this fate, so unique in Rome, should happen to befall the memorial church for a saint from the frozen North, is quite accidental. Every enlightened Scandinavian who is fortunate enough to notice S. Brigida in the Piazza Farnese, must immediately feel at home, at the reassuring sight of this portal. G. C. Adlerbeth, Gustave III's travelling companion in Italy, has testified to its taste with the words *"snygg och anständig"* (neat and respectable) [141].

Clement XI loved columns, and that is what classicists tend to do. He took great care that Bernini's colonnades should be provided with the statues they lacked, and followed the work in his own church's forecourt with an eager eye. He was also generous to the small churches situated behind St. Peter's which languished in the shadow cast by the choir of the basilica. *S. Marta* was rebuilt in 1704, *S. Stefano* "degli Indiani", the Abyssinians' church, was re-erected in 1706, according to a design by Antonio Valeri [142], and was then given quite a powerful façade flanked by large pilasters. It still stands, but has not gained anything by the clearance of the area around it. This patching-up behind the basilica's choir was to disappear in favour of the new sacristy which Clement XI wanted to build. Through his nephew Annibale Albani, the archpriest at St. Peter's, he had Juvara draw up plans in 1715. The latter came to Rome, stayed six months, and in that time produced a number of designs which showed vivid imagination [143]. A large model was made of one of the projects and it gives an excellent impression of the building, which was to remain a castle in Spain. The *sagrestia commune* of the canons was intended and designed as a princely ballroom, and the noble canons were also to have their quarters in this group of buildings. The very grandiose style for the heterogeneous building was taken from the colonnades of St. Peter's Square. They provided the motif and the yardstick for the galleries by which the sacristy was to be connected with the basilica. The section of the model reproduced here shows Juvara's understanding of his task (Pl. 30). He thought to replace Bernini's heavy colonnades with the Pantheon's columns, and thus, to give the courtyard next to St. Peter's an Augustan air. The Pope had to be content with a whiff of this from the large wooden toy assembled for him. Once again, he had to resign himself to the fact that glorifying the Colosseum and St. Peter's was beyond his capabilities. However, Juvara's models had an admonitary effect in Rome. But they did not augur victory for mature Classicism.

The cautious Classicism of Clement XI and Fontana radiated and reached various other churches which were furbished and decorated with discretion. Prince Giambattista Pamphili had *S. Pietro in Vincoli* modernized and gave the interior, among other things, a new ceiling (1705), after a drawing by Francesco Fontana [144], but the portico of the façade from the 15th century was not molested. After the renovation of *S. S. Giovanni e Paolo,* which was carried out from 1716 onwards for Cardinal Fabrizio Paolucci by Canevari with the collaboration of Carlo

Stefano Fontana, and appraised by Innocent XIII in June 1722, only three middle intercolumniations of the entrance were left open, while the remainder were walled up [145]. There was a fine interplay introduced between the open work of the lower façade and the smooth, closed upper wall, in which three small new windows formed a triangle just above the open section of the entrance. In those days, they had such a feeling for simple yet strong effects, that even the work of a master mason was artistic. In recent years the front of this church has, at great expense and with much care, been spoiled by its titular cardinal. The Archbishop of New York preferred to see the blight of a spiritless historic reconstruction replace the bloom of an artistic and sensitive version. Since then the soul of S. S. Giovanni e Paolo has been lost. The square too, once so lovely, has withered. But Cardinal Paolucci (died 1726), in heaven, gets all the credit. His Eminence Renato Imperiali also reaps his reward in the beyond for the unobtrusive ornamentation, such as "a noble iron lattice", which he gave to *S. Giorgio in Velabro* in 1703. This church, linked with two famous works from Antiquity, the Arch of Janus and the Arch of the Moneychangers (Arco degli Argentari) has an exquisite front of Ionic columns. Clement grafted on to this well-deserving building with a gentle hand. For this reason, that true Classicist Bellicard, etched the church in 1750 with obvious pleasure at seeing the vital character of this antiquity [146].

The renovation of *S. S. Apostoli* will not be described here. When the original church threatened to collapse, the Franciscans decided in 1701 to pull it down and raise a new building after a design by Francesco Fontana. The foundation stone was laid in 1702. Francesco was in charge of the work until his death in 1708, and his father continued it until he departed this life in 1714. It was then carried on by Niccolò Michetti, among others, and was not consecrated until 1724 under Benedict XIII [147]. The church's value as a work of art, depends entirely upon its interior, which of its kind is very rich, although not particularly original. Of its façade, the vestibule erected by Julius II when he was cardinal, was retained. The elegant church thus pays no tribute to the contemporary period in its exterior. Even facing Bernini's Palazzo Chigi-Odescalchi and with the Palazzo Colonna by its side, the church conceals its modern character in Rome's most aristocratic square. The upper part of the front of S. S. Apostoli was renovated in 1827 by Valadier.

S. Maria in Monticelli is a good example of an old church whose exterior was repaired in the new sober taste. The cure has not, as is the case of much erudite treatment these days, taken the patient's breath away. Architecture has its own homeopathy. The church was transferred to the Doctrinarians, a religious order of teachers of divinity, who had a new façade built by Matteo Sassi [148]. The tri-axial front, squeezed against the Romanesque campanile, has a portal section with solid columns at both top and bottom stage, very neatly formed. The square bell-tower, which stands at the corner, had a narrow presbytery built on to its other side. The whole is a skilful game with building bricks, old and new, set upright. *S. Silvestro in Capite* has a façade made in one cast. The church stood right back from the square and in 1693 had been given a modest front with arcades at the lower stage; according to the inscription in the vestibule, it was built for the Abbess Maria Arcangela Muti [149]. Under Clement XI a front building was erected in line with the wings of the convent facing the piazza. It originally bore the arms of the Albanis [150]. The courtyard between these two façades is very attractive; here are palms and foliage between fragments of antique sculpture, and a man's head in the side wall along the Via del Gambero spouts water into a sarcophagus. The damp, sun-warmed vapour of a hothouse hangs over this ecclesiastical atrium.

One source [151], suggests that Domenico de Rossi was the originator of S. Silvestro's *prospetto*. If this is correct, the design must have been available in 1703 at the latest, because that year the architect met with an unfortunate accident on the roof of S. Pietro's colonnades while the statues were being erected [152]. After his death he was called *célèbre*. Domenico's merits were not otherwise conspicuous, but the façade of S. Silvestro is a true monument to him, for it is well suited as a screen in front of a gatehouse. The composition is unoriginal; the side ressauts with paired pilasters can also be found at the entrance to the convent of Campo Marzio (by G. A. de Rossi). But while each pilaster there is engaged with the architrave and causes it to project, the architect of

S. Silvestro has linked his pilasters together below uninterrupted architraves – a significant academic revision – and has also given the façade a low attic storey with statues standing on it. The fashionable church thus took on a more festive appearance than its slightly older model, but also became more spindly (Pl. 64b).

The hazards of respectability often threatened these Clementine churches on the borderline of Carlo Fontana's art. They are so full of respect for the traditional and are so afraid of being ostentatious that, as a result, they become the victims of self-effacement. Today we are surprised that such an enfeebled Baroque could once have caused the critics to be up in arms, shouting about irreverence. The polite style fits in best when it appears in a built-up street which can support it, and even the weakest church front develops a relative significance when seen in the company of plain unpretentious façades, like a large placard on a long wall. It is not so good when a church building with half-hearted decoration stands by itself. An isolated church was faced with dangers from the surrounding vacuum. It might just get away unscathed when a small building is placed in front. *S. Eusebio* was situated in an unpopulated area near the road, between S. Maria Maggiore and S. Croce in Gerusalemme, across the street from a grim ruin (Nymphaeum Alexandri, "Trofei di Mario"). Carlo Stefano Fontana rebuilt the church in 1711, and if a wing of a religious house had not projected at right angles on one side of it and thus given the façade some relief, its touched-up appearance would have made a very bad impression. For it takes some liberties which can only be appreciated during a leisurely *tête-à-tête*. The lower storey dissolved into nothing but arcades, and this can be seen when the gaps in between develop into a forecourt and are on the same level, but a great empty space cannot be appreciated through fragile arches. Furthermore, the middle bay in the principal storey, which is divided up by pilasters, rises neatly in a segmental arch, and the fine window is framed by large cartouches, reminiscent of the elegant touch of the builder of S. Clemente. That these decorative features in the otherwise conventional pseudo-classical style developed in the shelter of the lateral wing and can only be appreciated by close observation, is understood when we make a control test. In our days S. Eusebio is in the first place no longer solitary and is wedged in the corner of a modern square, the Piazza Vittorio Emanuele, Rome's biggest and busiest commercial centre. In the second place, the flanking wing of the religious house has been cut down to a fragment. And finally, the level of the ground has sunk so much that a steep flight of steps has been constructed up to the arcades of the entrance. The result is that this entrance seems just as unmotivated as it is trivial. S. Eusebio used to be able to give a fairly good account of itself when it dominated its own restricting enclave. Now it seems insipid.

Considering it from all angles, the same could be said of *S. Isidoro,* the church of the Irish Franciscans in the Via degli Artisti. With its monastery at the side and a long garden behind, it originally stood at the end of the street which was closed by the walls of the Villa Ludovisi. No church on the outskirts of the built-up area of Rome could rejoice in a more peaceful site. Only in one respect did it seek contact with the outside world: its façade looks down from the top of the steps of the Via dei Cappuccini [153], and seen from the bottom (now from the Via Veneto), S. Isidoro's silhouette seems to vibrate. Only up on its own level and inside the enclosed garden which is its entrance, can the façade be appreciated – and only here does it expect to be. Nothing but ornamentation can be seen. Granted, one rarely finds on a church front such an unusual motif as the cornucopia, bursting with vegetables and flowers – the sainted Isidoro was a farmer (*D. Isidoro Agricolae Dicatum* can be seen on the pediment) – but all over the façade, the plants are barbed and prickly and belong in a herbarium. It is ascribed to Bizzaccheri [154]; he showed his exuberant gifts elsewhere.

Towards the close of Clement XI's pontificate, a ferment started to develop in this Baroque Classicism. New people appeared, Fontana's circle broke up. A more lively architecture grew up in the master mason's field. Here they were not encumbered by learning, nor with any exaggerated respect for Antiquity and Bernini's "grand style". It was Borromini's name that was revered. Of course, the details of this exceptional master could be used liberally. Architects without training were able to create effects without following doctrines and by building in a down to earth fashion which gave an illusion of modernism, by merely using his decorative forms. The outward, and at times trivial effects of this brilliant builder were turned into leading motifs. This was not quite the thing to do. But the results could become superb in the hands of people of sensitivity. It is a joy to look at *S. Agata* in Trastevere. The General for the Fathers *della Dottrina Cristiana* decided to rebuild it in 1709, and in little less than a year the project got moving. It was finished in 1711 and inspected by the Pope in 1712. Giacomo Recalcati was responsible for the plan [155]. As luck would have it, the façade now stands behind a group of gnarled plane trees (Pl. 33). It has in itself the characteristics of an organic growth and seems to be surrounded by the promise of spring. The upright oval window in the pediment merges into a springy ramification of mouldings, and the angels' wings, borrowed from Borromini's paradise, here come to resemble embryo leaves, frayed like chestnut buds bursting into leaf. The ornamentation of the façade is predominantly angular, some of the panels being in the form of a rhomb, others having the dull curves of fretwork, and the pediment above the portal is very, very angled, but the best parts stand out all the more.

The handsome little presbytery which stands opposite the wall around S. Maria in Trastevere's churchyard, and which gives meaning to this secluded square (Pl. 36), can presumably also be ascribed to Recalcati. Here he uses only significant architectural motifs, all taken over from Borromini's Oratorio dei Filippini. The top with its middle section flanked by concave curves, with its "Gothic" window frame set into the arched recess, the hoop-shaped pediments surrounding wheel-like stars, all these forms are copies, but they are used in a personal way. The large has become intimate, the scattered contained and kept in place by a relief of recesses which is crisp, and opens its pores to the air and sunshine of this corner of the square. A teasing play of shadows makes the building irresistible, and it attracts us time and again when we are in Trastevere. Merely seen out of the corner of an eye this straw-yellow building in "Straw Street" sends a shiver of joy down one's back. Thank you, master builder of the poorest and most open streets of Rome.

Not long after S. Agata had been renovated, *S. Maria in Cosmedin* assumed a fresh exterior (1718). The builder was Cardinal Annibale Albani, *un homme terrible,* a fiendish politician, "hardly less hated than Satan in Hell" [156], and the archpriest at that time was G. M. Crescimbeni, the amiable man of letters and first president (*Custode*) of the Arcadian Academy [157]. Sardi is said to have been the master builder; if this is the case we may presume he followed his own plans. For though the façade was without discipline it had, on the other hand, the fire which often distinguished the art of untutored talents. Sardi's work just verges on the masterly (Pl. 32). A mediaeval front with a vestibule was to be given new form. It was no longer important to be tasteful to fit in with the old, but to give the new a strong taste of its own and see that the building made an impact in the square. The Piazza di Bocca della Verità had been licked into shape some years before. Layers of earth from centuries back had been cut away so that the church no longer looked as if it were burrowing down into the ground. In true Roman fashion, the renovation was stopped in time so that the shabby buildings for the humbler members of society could be allowed to remain standing. The square remained an irregular, enclosed space, like the market-place of a provincial town, way out in the country. But what a great provincial town! Here stood two ancient temples, concealed by masonry and disguised under the name of "S. Stefano for Carriers" and "The Church of Mary of the Egyptians". The former – also called S. Maria del Sole – is the famous round temple, the latter, the pseudo-peripteral temple which (mistakenly) is usually called "The Temple of Fortuna Virilis". And down underneath the square, the Cloaca Maxima runs its course to the Tiber.

In that year (1718), the square in front of S. Maria in Cosmedin was a part of Rome which was full of character. Antiquity was here very much in evidence, with walls intact and in reasonable proportions. It was possible for once to feel at home in temples which still had their roofs on, and whose destiny it was to function amongst the cow-stalls and haylofts in the village. The spiritual atmosphere was pungent too. S. Maria in Cosmedin, the parish church of this little Rome, had a Greek past and a Greek cognomen. S. Maria Egiziaca was the national shrine of the Armenians and attracted the people who came from the East, pale priests with enormous noses. Dull, everyday life was enclosed within a garden wall which hid the view across the Tiber. In this lively square of temples and churches, male buffaloes had rings fixed in their noses, and peasants passing through to Piazza Montanara watered the horses at the trough.

Abandoned wagons with empty shafts yawned through endless hours of midday. Only the flies on the dung showed any sign of life.

And now a new church façade was to dominate this untidy but enchanting square. It is short-sighted to assess Sardi's architecture entirely schematically, as if it were meant for an orderly street or a tidy little square. Out here, there was room to spread oneself and an opportunity to raise one's voice – one was in duty bound to let one's hair down. Had temples really any right to be so autocratic in a modern age? Sardi obviously thought not. The master builder resolutely set to work, with a sort of architectural *cavalleria rusticana* (Pl. 32). The church was hauled up out of the ground, and Sardi now made it spread out at the top with a gay border above the principal cornice of the gable. Such a doubling effect had been seen before [158], but nowhere else with such a strong inner ferment as here. Everywhere on this new front, angles and folds and mouldings spring forth. As we all know, some walls are so weak that only the plasterer can strengthen them. Similarly, it can be maintained that the squares in the outskirts which have run wild, call for a pirate rather than "Vitruvius", if one expects to satisfy the requirements of the milieu. The Piazza di Bocca della Verità was given a church front in full harmony both with the locality, and with the fountain that was erected in the square at the same time. Two Tritons writhe up from a cleft in the rocks and entwine their tails to keep their balance. A little jet of water spurts from the shell which they hold. The group, designed by Bizzaccheri, is splendid. Bernini must have stood sponsor for it. The figures are expressing their youthful high spirits to the approval of all around. Even the Danish painter Constantin Hansen, gave the fountain a place of honour in his painting of the Piazza di Bocca della Verità (1837), where it stands proudly next to "Vesta's Temple", with the dome of St. Peter's in the distant background [159]. But unfortunately he turned his back on S. Maria in Cosmedin, for its façade was, after all, of the same character as the Tritons. The square by the "Mouth of Truth" has now been cleared and levelled and the church robbed of its finery. To satisfy archaeological ethics it has all been ripped off – everything is spoilt to everybody's satisfaction. The temples were purified with a powerful lye.

I do not think that Clement XI would have been pleased. Papa Albani was a true humanist and found antiquities most beautiful when they were used. When he was at the end of his life, his nephew Annibale showed with Sardi's help – probably unintentionally – that there were hidden depths in the Romans. A more spontaneous art, full of expression, emerged among the academic columns.

IV

Innocent XIII, who was elected Pope on May 8th, 1721, reigned for only two years, nine months and twenty-nine days, so he was not given much time for building churches. This is regrettable, for this Pontifex from the ancient family of Conti in Rome (although he was born in Poli), no doubt wished to build; he delighted in pomp and circumstance, and was not without a feeling for architecture, which he put into practice in other fields. His name alone should be connected with the Spanish Steps, for this is his greatest public memorial. If death had granted him a longer respite, he might well have made his mark in the form of a new façade for Rome's cathedral itself, the Lateran Basilica. In September 1723 all that was needed was the Pope's order to go ahead with the work. The building material was already there and 150 galley slaves, able-bodied labourers, had been sent in transports from Malta [160]. In Rome, the name of the architect to whom Innocent had entrusted the vital task was surmised. In a dispatch to the French Foreign Minister of 12th October of that year, it was stated that Marchese Girolamo Theodoli had been put in charge of the church's *grand portail* (façade) [161]. This sounds credible enough. Theodoli was one of the Pope's relations – and was already at that time being commended for "his taste and experience in the art of building". In practice the Marchese had not yet shown any particular talent in this respect, no work of any size anyhow. The fact that in 1722 he had designed a barouche "of new invention", and that this magnificent creation had been presented to Cardinal Conti, the Pope's brother, may well have been useful evidence of his taste (and his flair), but could hardly be a recommendation for his employment in the biggest ecclesiastical construction in Rome [162]. At the court, Theodoli's interest in architecture had been respected, and to him had been ascribed an ability which may well be in question. Fortunately the young aristocrat was spared from coming to grips with the front of the Lateran, and the church was spared his attentions. Not until years later was he to prove that he was not entirely devoid of talent, nor lacking in artistic adroitness.

This little episode in the history of architecture – as it were acted out in the Pope's *antecamera segreta* – is really very typical of the era of Innocent XIII, which was nothing more than an intermezzo. The Pope, tempted by his ancestral pride, had a certain leaning towards nepotism, but only in minor things; a church façade, even that of the Lateran, was not a dangerous move. And building during his short pontificate was distinguished by enterprising initiatives. All the same the Conti Pope's good intentions were not in vain, leading on to the next period as they do, and giving the lead to such great works as the Scala di Spagna and Fontana di Trevi.

Three Roman churches received their external form during Innocent's reign. The most prominent of these was the important parish church of *S. Eustachio*. The Pope had been christened here, now he wanted it glorified. Out of his own pocket he bestowed 6000 scudi on the high altar, designed by Salvi [163]. Since the beginning of the century the Chapter had urged rebuilding [164], and eventually the church was given a new façade designed by *Antonio Canevari* (1681–c. 1750) who now comes on the stage. At some time before 1716 he had submitted plans for the sacristy of St. Peter's, always a good introduction [165]. He was very likely in great favour with the Conti family, and this may explain why he, in 1722–1723, surveyed Roman monumental buildings for John V, King of Portugal [166], who was an art enthusiast, and why he drew up the plans for "Arcadia's" garden which was financed by this monarch. For Innocent, who for a number of years had been Papal Nuncio in Lisbon, and as Cardinal was Protector of Portugal, had a cordial relationship with King John and his kingdom [167]. The Duke of Poli, the Pope's brother, put up the arms of Lusitania above the door of his palace, "which indicates that when the third brother, Monsignore Conti, becomes Cardinal, he will be given the Protectorate of Portugal" [168]. Behind completed architecture and the activities of a master builder there are always sources of energy hidden within the massif of society. On rare occasions, usually by pure chance, it befalls posterity to localize them. We shall see later that in the Palazzo Poli one can, figuratively speaking, strike water from the rock.

S. Eustachio's façade should not, as a matter of course, be attributed to Canevari – and he ought to be grateful for that – for it was completed by another architect, Cesare Crovara. The question of the originator is however less important, when we are faced with a work which lacks any artistic punch, as is here the case. A squat vestibule, compressed by an attic and as heavy as a packing case, forms a projecting podium under its commonplace top gable [169], and is only relieved by columns and a pediment.

It is quite another thing to look at *S. Paolino alla Regola* (Pl. 34), built by the Sicilian Franciscans close to the spot where Paul, according to "venerable" tradition, had his dwelling [170]. The church itself is built in the shape of a Greek cross with short arms, transformed by the inclusion of four corner chapels into a square building with a central dome. The lay-out of this Roman church has a closer relation to the monastic order and its members than to any local school. The architect, Giambattista Bergonzoni, was a Franciscan friar from Bologna, where he enjoyed some reputation, and where the plan mentioned was in common use [171]. S. Paolino was built at the close of the 17th century. Vasi gives 1704 as the date of its erection, whereby he presumably refers to the year when the church was completed, and he reports that G. B. Contini designed the façade [172]. If this unconfirmed information is true, the façade must have been very modest, perhaps even of an interim character, for in the 1720's a new one was built – the present one. Accounts still preserved show that in the period 1723–1729, 3000 scudi were paid out to Giuseppe Sardi *capomastro muratore* [173]. Consecration took place on September 29th, 1728. It is hardly likely that Sardi was here anything other than the entrepreneur, for Dominico Ciolli (died 1734) is expressly mentioned as the originator of the façade, and he was an academically trained builder, although little known. It seems most likely that the front of S. Paolino can be ascribed to one of Borromini's followers, who could be said to be a skilful artist with much taste. The little "buffet" in the centre window recess originates no doubt from S. Carlino; the play of alternating concavity and convexity in the architraves, together with the broken pediment, is typically Borrominesque. The composition as a whole is by no means merely a skilful patchwork, but is executed harmoniously in a smooth and fluid style. The alarming plastic rhythm of Borromini is entirely absorbed, the sharpness tempered, the relief gentle. The recesses in the panels of the lower storey give the front a certain likeness to the panelling in salons, and thus a hint of Rococo. In short, one of the "cabinet makers", whom Contini detested, carried on his little game after Contini's death (1723). It would not have been the first time that Contini was supplanted. While still alive, it had been his misfortune to see his work continued by a modernist – as in the case of *S. S. Stimmate di S. Francesco*. The building of this church, which belonged to a brotherhood, had a history full of vicissitudes that we need not go into here [174]. The foundation stone was laid by Clement XI, and Contini started the work, but he gave up, "why is not known" says Pascoli [175], and he was followed by Canevari, who is presumably the originator of the façade. Its characteristic main motif is an expressive statue of St. Francis receiving Christ's stigmata. He is borne on a cloud formed between the wings of the pediment above the portal, the lines of which have been adopted from S. Marcello. There, in the hands of Carlo Fontana, an empty picture frame was stood up against an arcade of recesses in the upper storey. In the front of the Church of S. S. Stimmate it is a saint, the ecstatic St. Francis, who is raised up and liberated in front of a crowning arched panel hollowed out like a niche. Every detail in this façade is traditional, but the composition is fresh and picturesque. And the scene lights up the narrow street of the basket-makers (Via dei Cestari). Milizia thought the work was "a very ordinary thing and full of faults" [176]. It looked alive.

In a little square close to the Tiber, stands *S. S. Trinità dei Pellegrini*, a part of the large foundation for poor pilgrims. The church itself was erected in 1614 by Paolo Maggi, who in a competition in 1611 had beaten even Maderno [177], but according to an inscription on the frieze, the façade was not built until 1723. At first glance this tall façade looks quite intricate in its articulation and full of action. But by a cool-headed analysis it can easily be sorted out. The structure behind the façade is set well back and is on one plane, as can be seen from the side section of the lower storey. Both storeys have been given a slightly concave profile, but this does not involve the whole front. At the sides and at the bottom, the outer disengaged columns of both storeys mark the limits of this vertical relief, and the background to this curving surface is emphasized in the middle by the portal and the large window above. When you have reached a clear understanding of the fundamental principle underlying this concavity, it is easy to separate the plastic additions on which the sculptural strength of the façade is based, that is the two pairs of columns with their isolated horizontals in each storey. They project in the same rhythm, they strengthen the flanks, and right at the top, aim at uniting in a complete triangle. Up here, at the apex of the gable, you can see the mechanism of the façade opened up for inspection. The apparatus reveals its construction (Pl. 35).

It is a fine work, cleverly calculated by an artist who was not beset by a demon, but in full control of spatial concepts. To some extent it is genuinely Roman, in that it is clearly based on Fontana's façade for S. Marcello and, of course, had Borromini's art in view. However, there is no similarity with the accepted, rather viscous Borrominesque works of this period (just compare this façade with its contemporary at S. Paolino), and all in all, this cool and elegant Roman façade has a foreign accent, but so far nobody has identified it [178]. I assume that the secret of the façade was buried with the architect, of whom hardly anything is known. *Francesco de Sanctis* (1693–1740) suddenly comes on the scene with this façade, and no earlier work of his is known. There is very little information about his training. If the façade was inspected by the Pope in the autumn of 1723 [179], the work must have been started the year before. So it must be a little older than de Sanctis' principal work, the Spanish Steps.

Later, when we deal with *la Scalea* we shall come to closer grips with the architect. Here, in front of S. S. Trinità, we will leave the mysterious architect for the time being, this man who has given his name to two masterpieces and still remains an unknown quantity. Was he an obscure talent, almost a genius, or merely the intermediary for a greater artist's design?

33. *S. Agata in Trastevere.*

34. *S. Paolino alla Regola.*

35. *S. S. Trinità dei Pellegrini.*

36. *Vicarage behind S. Maria in Trastevere.*

We know that the façade of S.S. Trinità dei Pellegrini was paid for by a wealthy Piedmontese, a certain Giuseppe de Rossi [180]. He was born about 1698, so he must have had the good fortune of being able to become a patron of the arts at the early age of 24. It is especially interesting that he should have come from Piedmont. Did this favoured young man seek advice in Turin before he tackled the job of building a church in Rome? If so, then he, who presumably had his ear to the ground, as well as money, must have gone to Juvara, the Piedmont oracle. The facts are, that the nearest parallels to the Pellegrino façade are two works by Juvara, one being S. Cristina in Turin (façade erected 1715–1718) [181] and a design (c. 1720) for S. Filippo in the same town [182]. The similarities they share are so great that a direct connection between Juvara's drawing office and the building in Rome is more than likely. In particular the sketch for S. Filippo – apart from the towers at the sides – comes strikingly close to S. S. Trinità's façade.

Whether the patron of the latter work obtained a design from the Turin master, or whether de Sanctis had his hidden past in the Piedmontese circle around Juvara, cannot be determined at present. But it is worth mentioning that the pilgrims' hospice was founded by S. Filippo Neri; also that the Chiesa di S. Filippo, named after the saint, was served by the Oratorians. Juvara's project for this church's façade was however not used, but the building itself was consecrated by a mass on May 26th, 1722 [183]. This makes one think that Juvara's drawings for S. Filippo – including the one which is so close to the Roman façade – became available just about the time when de Sanctis was building. This hypothesis meets the case so obviously; the seed sown in Turin was, by a freak of fate, harvested in Rome. We are not far wrong in ascribing the front of the church by the Tiber to Juvara's ideology. The smallness of the square, if nothing else, prevented the building of campaniles. The steepness of the façade may possibly indicate that the original design was put into effect in an abridged form. The Juvarian features would also have been more apparent if the linked columns had not been engaged.

As a supplement to the Juvara story, we have the information that in 1722 the master dedicated a book on Roman escutcheons (*targhe*) to Prince Giuseppe Lotario Conti, the Pope's brother [184]. The architect must have had some connection with the family, or was at least in attendance on them. His works were highly esteemed by connoisseurs in Rome, even at that time. When in 1720 Alessandro Specchi provided *S. Anna dei Palafrenieri* near the Vatican with two decorative spires, they had all the characteristics of Juvara. Don Filippo had in fact inherited a claim to the throne after his teacher Carlo Fontana. He did not manage to succeed to it in Rome. But his art approached the splendid peak to which all vigilant master builders aspired. The phase in the style was determined by him. Meanwhile, as always in the Holy City, the way to the top proved devious. And the power which Stendhal called *le patriotisme de l'antichambre* always lay in ambush.

V

A lot of things were churned up in the history of Roman church style between 1724 and 1730, and it was the new Pope who personally did the stirring. In the architecture of Baroque we find many examples of a princely builder being able to direct its development into new channels by his choice of official architects [185], but there are very few instances of the ruler's plans having such swift and direct results in building and in producing such dramatic conflicts in this field as in the years mentioned above. It is impossible to understand the sweeping changes in the style at this time without making oneself acquainted with the new Pope's extraordinary personality.

Benedict XIII was an Orsini of the Neapolitan branch (Gravina). Only in one respect did he resemble his predecessor; at heart he was just as proud of his lineage as Papa Conti, but otherwise he was by nature utterly different. While Innocent, the worldly-wise, appeared affable but reserved, Benedict was by turns obstinate, sometimes brusque, and humble to the limits of self-torture. He belonged to those people in whose character weakness and stubbornness go hand in hand. All pomp was anathema to this monk, and in his daily activities the Duke of Gravina's son liked to be in contact with the poorest of his subjects. Benedict's habits amazed the Romans. They saw this Pontifex Maximus drive out in a common carriage drawn by a pair of greys and escorted by no more than two grooms [186]. When he got the chance, he went up to the little Dominican cloister of La Madonna del Rosario on Monte Mario, sent his escort back and spent a few days on the mountain in solitude [187]. Particularly during carnival, when Rome was bubbling over down below, the Pope preferred to find peace and do penance in the simple priory which has an enthralling view and the purest air. Once in March 1727, Benedict lost his way walking in the hills. This old man, clad in a grimy white soutane without any insignia, and with a stick in his hand, was noticed by two peasants who were quarreling over their game of boccia. They called to him; he asked the way, but only got the answer: "Stop a while, you must be our umpire, and we'll tell afterwards". So Christ's Vicar settled their differences by giving a ruling on the throw, and the peasants showed him the way, but they would not go with him as they had to finish the game. The Pope arrived back tired at the monastery and told the story [188], and we are glad, for it was a story worth knowing. St. Pius X could have told a similar tale. Benedict's genuine piety brought him the reputation of a saint while he was still alive, and miracles were ascribed to him [189]. At all events, he followed his vocation as a saver of souls with fervent zeal. This totally unwordly ruler lived like a monk and ruled the state like a good bishop does his diocese. Though advanced in years he was always active and could preach for hours until the congregation was on the point of collapse. He rushed around with his team of greys to all imaginable ecclesiastical functions, was forever paying visits, heard confessions and gave the last sacrament, felt mattresses in hospitals, tasted the soup in the hospices, in fact took the priest's work to the extreme in the world's biggest parish.

Many absolute rulers – like Frederick the Great, Frederick VI, Emperor Franz Joseph – have enjoyed showing their power by pointing out where a button was missing on a uniform. Pope Benedict's blood boiled when members of monastic orders had long hair or wore wigs, for this was irregular, most un-Catholic. "Do you belong to the Greek or the Roman Church?" he asked a priest with dangling locks, angrily pulled them and boxed his ears three times. This is a story told by Valesio, who was an eye-witness to it, in his diary of May 1st, 1728. One day the Pope baptized some Jews outside the portal of St. Peter's, remaining there bareheaded for three hours in a wind so icy, that his flunkeys had not been able to stand it. Later he read mass twice, slowly and distinctly, without remembering that he had already officiated that morning, "but he always goes his own way" [190].

Narrow yet magnanimous, not of this world – this was the Pope whom a Voltaire could honour in his "Henriade":

Des Ursins de nos jours a mérité des temples ...

The Christian temples which Benedict himself looked after down here on earth, were almost uncountable. To erect churches, restore old places of worship and dedicate altars [191] was a true passion with him, so no wonder that his relationship with church building in Rome was of such a personal character. In this matter too, this tender-hearted fanatic, this meek aristocrat, always went his own peculiar way. As a result, he performed the miracle of art history – Rome's architecture now received strong and permanent influences from Benevento.

Orsini had been Archbishop in this Neapolitan city for 38 years. He rebuilt it after two earthquakes, in 1688 and in 1702, ran the whole diocese in an exemplary fashion, and for the city itself felt a love which has something very touching about it. The lonely man on the throne of St. Peter always longed to be back, and would much rather have ministered to souls in his old cathedral city than play politics with the courts of Europe. His unbounded infatuation with Benevento was no doubt detrimental to his pontificate, for it meant that he put himself in the hands of an unworthy creature from that beloved region, Cardinal Niccolò Coscia. This man, who without any difficulty at all seized the temporal power from his pious and meek master, deceived him with a vengeance, brought the state to the brink of ruin and the administration of the Curia into ill-fame. The priest of priests saw nothing – he did not want to see anything.

The Benevento tale in Rome has a more edifying side where its magic is seen on church façades. In these, as in all other religious precincts, Benedict would not tolerate any interference from Coscia. What happened was that the Pope straight away in 1724 sent for an architect and his assistants from Benevento. Without caring one little bit about the proper Roman masters, who were so highly respected, he gave the little gang from the south his total trust and a free hand with all the church building which was carried out up to 1730, with 1725, the Jubilee year, as the peak point.

Seen from a later age, the situation stands out clearly as the scene in an improvised comedy. How it appeared to contemporary spectators we shall soon see – they too, were sensible of the *coup de théâtre* in this affair. In comes a master mason from the sun-drenched province, which according to the superior Roman, was populated with monkeys on two legs. Popular humour as expressed near Pasquino had at one time dubbed the Neapolitan Innocent XII Pignatelli with the nick-name *Papa Pulcinella*. According to an ancient tradition, Benevento was the very place where this marked figure with the black nose was born [192]. That most virtuous zealot, Benedict XIII was quite innocent of the fact that he was about to take the principal part in this company of players.

The architect *Filippo Rauzzini* (Rauzzino, Ragozzini) was born at the beginning of the 1680's. He was called *napoletano,* but need not have been born in Naples itself because of that. He seems to have belonged to one of the branches of a family of building craftsmen, particularly workers in marble, who had lived and worked in the Neapolitan area since the beginning of the 17th century. One member of the family, Orazio Ragozzini, became a citizen of Benevento in 1620 [193]. The artistic altar piece, executed in stone of many different colours, rich and bizarre, is the background to Master Filippo's style. The artistic craftsman was always uppermost in him. After the earthquake in 1702, he was given work along with many other building workers who had been called in to help, in the first place as mason and *marmoraro* and then as architect. His workmanship must have impressed Archbishop Orsini, as he was called to Rome soon after the latter had become Pope. It would be very interesting indeed if we could find out what Rauzzini had produced prior to his activities in Rome. Unfortunately the heavy bombing during the last war demolished a large number of Benevento's buildings and destroyed the most important archives. An Italian scholar has recently ascribed to Rauzzini a group of buildings, taking their style as criteria, by working back from his known Roman *oeuvre* to the unknown, but this is a risky procedure. Unfortunately it also appears that the buildings concerned, except for two – a chapel interior from 1710 and a palace from 1767 – were built during Benedict's Papacy, thus at the same time as he was building in Rome [194]. So we have not got much further. Perhaps the safest starting-point is the cathedral in Benevento; its restoration is certainly earlier than 1724. Rauzzini's share in this undertaking cannot be defined, but he must have been familiar with it. And here we find in the new main gable, a motif which was later to become a characteristic of Rauzzini's style, namely a quatrefoil opening [195].

So our architect came to the Papal City with professional experiences which we have no means of assessing. It seems all the more remarkable that Benedict should have endowed him with so many outward forms of authority. Rauzzini became *cavaliere* in 1725, was made papal architect in 1726, became a member of the S. Luca Academy in 1727 and in 1728 succeeded Aless. Specchi as Rome's City architect. Nor was that all – he was inundated with commissions. Rauzzini was not content with merely producing the plans, he also took part as contractor, in partnership with two master masons, the brothers Zoppoli, and he had brought with him his own staff of craftsmen from the former scene of his activities. This imported gang of workers who were popularly called the firm of *i muratori beneventani* aroused great but scarcely complimentary attention. P. L. Ghezzi has left a somewhat caricaturized portrait of one of the Zoppoli brothers, *Mastro* Vito. He looked like a roughneck and no doubt was one. He feathered his own nest so well, evil tongues said, that he was able to buy an estate on his native soil. In the end, a downright hatred of Rauzzini and his followers grew up in Rome. People not only accused the clique of looking out for number one, but also for producing inferior work and defrauding. The two builders were nicknamed "Roof-wrecker" (*stroppiatetti*) and "Wall-mutilator" (*stroppiamuri*). So widespread was the vilification that Montesquieu in 1729 could report infamous rumours in his Olympian diary [196].

Naturally Rome's other builders were green with envy and jealousy. The Beneventani also had to share the odium which was levelled at Coscia, and which in the end was directed at their very protector, the Holy Father. We shall forthwith let Rauzzini's works – for the present only the ecclesiastical – speak for themselves. The historical facts about these building operations are available in plenty in the journals of a scandalized eye-witness [197].

Not unexpectedly, Rauzzini first worked for the Dominicans, the Pope's favourite monastic order. He decorated the chapel of S. Dominico in *S. Maria sopra Minerva* and here used that heavy, grand mannerism which is suitable for ecclesiastical furniture, but has little to do with architecture. It was far more important that the church should be given a new façade – the present one. For a long time people had viewed the blank gable with displeasure and for a festival in 1712, Antonio Borioni gave it an interim decoration "with a mass of ornaments and statues admired by the ignorant" [198]. Now the Jubilee year was the time to provide the Gothic church with a durable exterior facing the square. Rauzzini made the first measurements in May 1725, and shortly afterwards the foundations were examined, and then the whole project fell through because the architect's costing was too high (8000 scudi). The indignant Pope straightway called in Tommaso Mattei and commanded him to produce a drawing, but the project was not to cost more than 800 scudi, a ridiculous sum when the status of Saint Dominic and the dignity of the church are considered.

Mattei withdrew and died soon after in 1726. Valesio tells us that a "very conventional" drawing by "the mason and the stucco worker from Benevento" was then accepted which could be executed for 1100 scudi, and on July 17th of that year, a start was made by putting up the scaffolding. It would be wrong to trust Valesio's hearsay entirely and to believe that the façade finally approved was a work produced by the two enterprising craftsmen, or that they appropriated the profits behind Rauzzini's back. The architect, as can be seen from the rest of his work, was soon forgiven by Benedict, but it must have been awkward for him to provide plan no. 2 at such short notice and at such a low price without losing face. I consider the design accepted from the firm to be a disguised work by the master himself. Rauzzini had no reason to regret this façade, however adversely criticized it may have been. He could ask with Per Degn: "Do you want coarse sand or fine?" The Pope wanted the coarse, so he got 1100 scudi's worth and for not a soldo more. Everybody knows S. Maria sopra Minerva's façade and thinks no more of it. It is very good value for money. The admirable thing about it is that it is not eye-catching; it disdains humbug, is patently humble. Nothing but pilaster strips. Upright rectangles around Gothic circles. Rauzzini soon proved that its high quality was not solely by virtue of necessity (Pl. 37).

The same day, August 28th, 1725, that Pope Benedict inspected the new façade on the principal church of his order, he drove out to another Dominican place of worship, *S. Sisto Vecchio,* and ordered its rebuilding to be done by Rauzzini. The work was completed a couple of years later. The narrow front, facing a closed courtyard, was made strangely unecclesiastical. The middle section with its attica is higher than the projecting sides, which look like slim blocks standing on edge. Apart from the portal, part of which dates back to an earlier time, there are no columns, no pilasters, no ponderous religious emblems. The building is as light-weight as if it were made of thin layers of some exotic wood (Pl. 39a). In each of the narrow panels, so slim and elegant, there is only one ornament, the quatrefoil frame around an opening in the face of the walls; above the portal two string courses are fused together to frame an elliptical aperture. Such decoration had never been seen in Rome before. The façade disregards Antiquity and snaps its fingers at standardized authority. There is nothing assertive here. The building is purified, dry, arrogant. Looking at the side of the building (Pl. 38) this becomes very evident, and this institution belonging to the Friars proclaims an amazing worldliness. Its elegance is French, the thin framework of the pilaster strips is French, the high windows with their plain frames stem, it seems, from the mansions in the Faubourg Saint-Germain, yet taken as a whole, it bears not the slightest similarity to the Paris style of the time. And this is mainly because of the quatrefoil, the only decorative motif to be set in the wall. These everted "lips" emphasize the subtle interplay of nothing but rectangles and ethereal mouldings. A stylist of character composes like this, and the result stands out among the indigenous works with their splendid garb, like a modestly dressed cavalier who nevertheless is inordinately meticulous about the flower in his buttonhole.

S. Sisto, the church and the monastery – where S. Dominicus himself once lived, and its Romanesque campanile was familiar to him – was built in a lonely district. Pious pilgrims who saw it and vine growers on their way to the city must have regarded this collection of sophisticated buildings with scepticism. They made themselves at home, but invited nobody. It was quite a different situation when the butchers' guild rebuilt their little church *S. Maria della Quercia* in the heart of Rome, close by the Campo dei Fiori. The Pope laid the foundation stone on Sept. 21st, 1727, and Rauzzini erected the building, but this time in a very small square which amounted to merely a rectangular niche between tenement houses. The church was squashed up against the back wall, which it almost hid. The building was rare in lay-out, a Gothic quatrefoil slightly flattened at the sides. When you see the plan view of this church on Nolli's map it will remind you of a delicate organism, a fruit or a star, which is slowly trying to disengage itself from an amorphous mass. The front curve has managed to emerge. Growth has been halted at the exact moment when the swell of the wall harmonizes with the size of the square. The front of the church gradually absorbed its intimate forecourt. Our absurd modern age, more anxious to accomodate locked cars than sentient people, has removed one side wall of the little square and thus robbed this work of art of its full meaning (Pl. 40).

The architect from Benevento knew exactly what he was doing, not least when he modelled the façade. It had to be viewed at close quarters and is therefore comminuted. The horizontal members quiver as if they were pleated. Rauzzini devoted the care of a cabinet-maker to this front, but retained the good architect's respect for the boundary between structure and furniture. Indeed the church is small, *piccino piccino,* but it is not dainty and certainly not portable. The architect has happily avoided the trap that lies in wait for an artistic structure hardly bigger than a box-room let in between screens. He embellished the front with the greatest discretion. In Sicily such a small object might have looked like a fancy cake or choux pastry. Here in Rome there is no similarity to puff pastry. Among palaces and solid town houses in the Regola quarter it was necessary to resist temptation. In S. Maria della Quercia this is done by limiting the decoration to an absolute minimum and letting it gently articulate the actual structure of the building. The façade braces its body beneath the tight binding of lines in the frieze and tucks in the cornice. The large window makes the upper part of the front into a diadem, a real *coronamento,* and the scalloped Gothic flower set above the door signifies the church's hidden ground plan.

When the earthquake in Benevento toppled the archbishop's palace as if it were a house of cards, Orsini just managed to escape. He ascribed this miracle to S. Filippo Neri and forever after had a deep-rooted veneration for him. As Pope, he acknowledged his debt by building a couple of churches in honour of "Pippo bono" – an important one in his ill-starred cathedral city, an inferior one in Rome – the latter must have called for a good deal of resignation. Rauzzini was given the job here and it was executed in a great hurry. Benedict gave the order on May 26th, 1728, and during the grape harvest that same year, the building was consecrated. It was in the Via Giulia that Rome's sincere and cheerful Apostle was given the only church in the Eternal City to be named after him. People find this situation very appropriate, for the street is proud with prejudice, the most intensely Roman of all thoroughfares. But the church as architecture has certainly nothing of importance to announce. The façade is a placard advertising a saint as guest artist on the stage behind. Rome has various examples of such ecclesiastical advertisement pasted up on high, long walls between, and even under, the windows of dwelling houses [199]. *S. Filippino* however takes first prize as regards audacity. The poster is attractive and one can see that this man, in the company of saints, had a sense of humour. Chorales and organ music and monumental vacuity was called for to honour the work of Grundtvig. As his memorial, a little Italian who re-awakened the devotional life of a universal church has a plaque in relief, not unlike the pictures on the enormous banners borne in processions and planted at the shrine under the open sky. At the great mass-meetings in the Villa Mattei, a picture of S. Filippo bigger than life-size was set up [200].

Rauzzini's façade for the church in the Via Giulia was a magnificent trifle (Pl. 41). He did not enter into rivalry with the stern palaces in the neighbourhood – an innocuous adjunct, an enduring improvisation was suitable here, made in fragile stucco. A large medallion relief shows S. Filippo in ecstacy at the revelation of the Madonna and Child. The rest is merely delicate flimsiness, to be enjoyed in passing. On religious feast-days it was the general custom to hang tapestries out of windows, and

37. *S. Maria sopra Minerva.*

39b. *S. Francesco on Monte Mario.*

39a. *S. Sisto Vecchio. Frontal view.*

40. *S. Maria della Quercia.*

41. *S. Filippo Neri in Via Giulia.*

43. S. Gregorio a Ponte dei Quattro Capi.

44. *S. Maria delle Fornaci.*

these multicoloured fabrics brightened up the street and gave it a festive air. S. Filippino's *prospetto* is a similar wall-covering, but in stucco, warm as the sun and as lyrical as the message of a pious musician. Not long ago, mattocks were used to try to tear down the relief on the church (on the Plate can be seen how), but it stayed. It is to be hoped that the façade here will sing the praises of the Gospel long after the last echo has died away in Grundtvig's cavernous cathedral.

Another three churches are connected with the Beneventani. *S. S. Biagio e Cecilia* is very small and stands in the dirtiest alley that runs up the Piazza Borghese. Its owners, who formed a corporation, manufactured mattresses. A couple of dingy houses next to it were inhabited by prostitutes. The church gloried in the name *del Divino Amore*. When it had fallen into disrepair – in spite of support from owners and clientèle – Benedict lost no time in tearing down the fragile walls to build a new church under Rauzzini's direction. The foundation stone was laid in July 1729. The building stands precariously on a corner and is simple yet dignified, held together by Tuscan pilasters with cornices. It looks like a church in a gloomy and remote country parish, for there too, divine love seeks refuge behind walls which are as rough and yellow as gravel. Master Filippo seldom took a wrong turning. This unpolished contractor had a sensitive instinct for the varied nature of his subjects, and he trimmed and enlarged to the very limit, so proving himself to be an artist.

Out in the brick-fields between the Via Aurelia and Borgo there is a church, *S. Maria delle Fornaci,* which the Spanish Trinitarians had founded in 1720, as an addition to a collegium for the missionaries of the order. Below the open stairway is carved the date 1721, when work was in progress [201], but not yet completed. In March 1727, Valesio reports that the Pope had recently visited the site, "and found pleasure in the situation and the façade of the church, which he knows that the Benevento masons are in process of finishing (*fa terminare*)". S. Maria delle Fornaci is surprising in its size and splendour in this frightful part of the city, but is known by few, rarely mentioned and never depicted. When we contemplate the front, it is very obvious that it was produced in two stages, and our appreciation of it is enhanced by knowing this (Pl. 44). The lower storey has been created by a different and less powerful hand than the section above, the gable of which has splendid, bold lines. Just compare the horizontal members of the two storeys. The upper is robust and full-bodied, the lower counterpart a matter of straight lines. This is truly a façade for a district of brickmakers and labourers. The Spanish monks did not think of this, but the architect was able to boost his self-esteem by making his building shout above the rooftops of shacks and huts. Down below, people walked heavy-footed and worked in clay. The soaring façade was art for the toiling masses; it strutted like a cockerel and crowed its defiance. We are quite willing to believe that the rough-neck *Mastro* Vito and his brother had a calloused hand in the brick-workers' church of the Madonna, and the monastery doorway to the left was fashioned by a tough fist.

The Neapolitan masons also went into action on Monte Mario, whose slopes extend north of the scorching "Valle dell' Inferno". Up there stood a little parish church which Clement XI had allotted to the owners of vineyards there [202]. Even today areas of farmland are to be seen on the majestically domed range whose broad hillsides run down towards Rome. We remember Benedict XIII's love for Monte Mario; that was his personal mountain, and we have seen him walking on lonely paths among the vineyards. He had *S. Francesco,* the church for the small congregation of his retreat, completely rebuilt by Vito Zoppoli, and covered the cost by taxing the landowners in the vicinity [203]. As far as I can see, S. Francesco has remained completely unnoticed [204]. It is a pleasure to see, a Roman memorial completely in harmony with the nature of the hills, for Baroque also contains its Vergilian pastorale. The little church, so simple and so strong, is situated in the midst of a bucolic idyll; the Holy Father of the Augustan Age went on shank's pony through this landscape. The elevation of S. Francesco as seen among the trees, has a rural nobility, sinewy and sharp. Its portal is tied to the window above with bands of masonry which are clumsy, but have a fine effect when viewed from the road (Pl. 39b). At the back of the building is the priest's garden, a place of permanent tranquillity. The dome of St. Peter's down there in the lowlands looks like a distant beehive.

If you follow the road from S. Francesco for a short distance westwards, you get a glimpse of the hillside's own *cupolone* which is the pride of *Madonna del Rosario* and the Dominican monastery belonging to it, which was Benedict XIII's refuge (later a retreat for Abbé Liszt). Church and dome are older than Orsini's time [205], but he had them restored and re-consecrated at the beginning of May 1726. But the church is still unfinished, the little bell-tower has no counterpart. It is possible that the men from Benevento helped in the renovation, but it is hard to prove analytically. The real merit of the church wing does not, however, depend on the decoration, but on its basic form, that is a cube set transversely above the steps in such an abrupt way that a worshipper might almost run his head against it. Seen from a distance the entire group of buildings with the low dome fits in smoothly with the rhythm of this downland country.

After the death of Benedict XIII, Filippo Rauzzini fell victim to the purge. He was arrested on September 4th, 1731, in his house near Fontana Trevi and imprisoned for some months in Carceri Nuove, suspected of fraudulent dicharge of office. An inquiry established his innocence. He was reinstated and lived in Rome until his death in 1771. But mud sticks, and in spite of his rehabilitation, he was given no monumental problems to solve in Rome after this dramatic interlude. He seems to have worked in an advisory capacity for the Collegio Clementino [206], and probably made a living by building private houses. Perhaps one of these days we shall find out which these were.

This man was dogged by a strange fate, both in his life and in his reputation after his death. His external features too, known from a drawing by Ghezzi, have a certain silent appeal – the heavy hooked nose, the brooding eyes, the determined mouth. His life before he came to Rome has remained a closed book and probably always will; then we have five years full of information, to be followed by decline and utter silence. I had the good fortune to be able to admire Rauzzini's most outstanding works in the middle twenties. In those days he was well and truly dead, buried deep down, and had been so for gods, men and scholars for two centuries. Now, about thirty years later, all people of taste realize that Master Filippo was a genuine artist in a hazardous city.

No other master builder in Rome has had to put up with such overwhelming ignominy as Rauzzini. The unprecedentedly bitter criticism from his contemporaries is very enlightening. If we do our best to ignore the personal and political virulence directed at him, it is quite clear that he became the target for artistic prejudice, simply because he was not like the others, but an individual standing apart. Such absolute anathema must be based on one fact, namely that his architecture was conceived as being different in principle from that of all others. Public taste was offended and objected strongly. People felt sure that they did not like his mannerism. The thing that hurt most was the realization that Rauzzini had a style that ran contrary to any other, an eccentric style, a different one, his own. And he was pilloried for it. Every attempt to analyse this style must therefore be founded on the criticism made by his contemporaries. What was the basis of the complaints? Which features could not be accepted – and why?

It is reported that the day after the consecration of S. Dominico's chapel in S. Maria sopra Minerva, a notice was found fixed to the door with the following written on it: *Cappella Arabica in Chiesa Gotica* [207]. The last part of the inscription is correct, the first was close to being right – Sicilian art in the wider sense often has an acrid aftertaste of Moslem art. Both styles were extremely objectionable to Roman taste. It is clear that the spices of the men from Benevento upset stomachs from the very first. And when the old chef Benedict was dead, old scores were settled in a satirical epitaph [208]:

> *Per opera di sua mano*
> *L'ottavo sacco fu Beneventano.*

Which means that the eighth sack of Rome was his fault and was done by the Neapolitans. It was reckoned that Rome had been devastated seven times before. Orsini and his architect were the new Vandals. The scurrilous remarks quoted are just two of many. Valesio believed that the façade of the Minerva church looked as if it was going to be "nothing but a lot of curlicues" (*una vera arriciatura*), completely barbaric. The chapel of St. Dominic was said by him to be "extravagant in its forms" and "not following the good old patterns" (*senza esempio delle cose buone antiche*). This remark hits the nail on the head. Valesio could safely announce "that the city does not recognize these vulgar buildings so lacking in a sense of architecture" (*queste fabbriche ordinarie e senza architettura*), and the cultivated painter Pier Leone Ghezzi was sure of everybody's approbation when he branded Rauzzini as "a Gothic architect from Benevento who has ruined Rome with his works" [209].

In an analysis of the pejorative adjectives one finds that each of them is indicative of style: *stravagante, barbaro, gotico* refer to an art which is anti-classical. The same expressions could be used by serious arbiters of taste for Borromini and his successor Valvassori. According to de Brosses, the Palazzo Doria-Pamphili was thoroughly *gothique*. Of Borromini, Montesquieu said: *Il a mis le Gothique dans les règles* [210], and when he was in Naples in 1729 and had looked at the churches, his condemnation of them was very prompt: "No taste, a Gothic taste (*aucun goût; un goût gothique*)" [211]. In explanation he continues: "There is something bizarre in the ornamentation and nothing of the simplicity found in the works of the ancients".

However, these last assessments come from Frenchmen and rationalists, and in their mouths *gotico* just means perverted, tasteless. But when the Romans use the word "Gothic" as a pejorative it has another nuance. No observer with any culture, grown up by the Tiber and familiar with the style of his own city, would in 1725 describe a Borromini church (like S. Agata or S. Paolino) as "Gothic" with the meaning quoted above. On closer examination we realize that "the Gothic" which shocked people in Rauzzini's art is not analogous to the bizarre elements in Borromini's style. The latter's mannerism had long since settled and certainly did not cause the Romans any excitement at this time. Conceivably then, the aversion to Rauzzini's art must stem from another sort of "Gothic". In our opinion, the thing about the architect's style which caused such annoyance, was the fact that it, to some extent, could be labelled "Gothic" since it made use of a mediaeval motif – and that this amazing "Neo-Gothic" was employed in the spirit of Rococo. The common denominator for these two concepts, as surprising as they were questionable, was a powerful profanity. The quatrefoil had not been used for centuries in Rome, it now had no Church authority, was deeply suspect, no doubt even un-Catholic. And it had not the official stamp of Antiquity. Hence it was doubly barbaric. Furthermore, Rauzzini used a handful of wantonly light motifs which seemed boneless and did not conform to the fundamental laws of Classic Baroque, which still cherished a full-bodied plasticity and a logical structure. Rauzzini believed in slim pilaster strips, pilasters pierced in the middle with inset rosettes, in airy recesses, in stucco bands which seemed like strips of shoddy between panels of plywood.

Rauzzini's façades have a tendency to resemble walls from a panelled salon, like an interior turned inside out. His exteriors consist of stiles and rails framing panels, he peels off layers from the walls, he lops and clips and tacks it down. It cannot be denied that this was "building without architecture". And so the Roman thought. But in France the matter was regarded in a different light. A Parisian mansion by Robert de Cotte or L'Assurance, was choice and compact, architecture without weight, sculpture without fullness, Classicism without columns. If this finely chiselled style, which is secular in its coldness and most effective in the negative, was transferred to the front of a Roman church, its extravagance would cry out to heaven. And this is what Rauzzini experienced.

Gothic and Rococo – fragments of unadulterated Gothic, a thin veneer of French Rococo, these are the predominant elements in the art of Rauzzini. Employed by a Neapolitan they were fore-ordained to scandalize a conservative milieu, all the more so because the man was talented. It is just as much a fact that the architect was influenced by the French style of building, especially by its panelling and pilaster strip ornamentation, as it is probable that these influences were sporadic and came from works of the recent past. You will look in vain for *Louis Quinze* decoration in his art, nor is it possible to find any typical Regency motif. The master mason from Benevento had no opportunity to make a systematic study of what was French, and his knowledge of Parisian style must, in all probability, stem from a very chance selection of engraved patterns. They could bring him impulses from the spirit of a style, but not make him intimate with its details.

The Gothic quatrefoil flourished however in Rauzzini's native soil [212] – strange that he should have picked on it, but French engravings did not grow on trees. Nothing indicates that he had any contact with the *École de France* in Rome, the place where his opponents were centred. In this connection we can report a detail of personal history (missed by his biographers), which may give us a hint. In Riccoboni's famous troup of Italian players, which was invited to Paris in 1716, Scaramouche's part was played by a certain Giacomo Rauzzini. He was called "the Neapolitan" and, according to the statement of an acquaintance, had originally been an employee in the La Vicaria, tribunal of Naples. At his death in Paris in 1731 he was 45 years old, thus having been born about 1686 [213]. It is tempting to regard him as a relative of our architect. He could easily have been a brother. How intriguing if Scaramouche from the *Théâtre-Italien* – painted by Watteau himself – had at some time passed on a few French etchings to Master Filippo! Giacomo the actor was not the only one in the Rauzzini family of building workers to go on the stage. Two sons (or nephews) of the architect were opera singers; one of them, the castrato Venanzio Rauzzini, was even world-famous [214]. Winckelmann admired him: "Tomorrow I am going to Teatro Valle" he wrote on January 11th, 1764, "to see and hear the handsome Venanzio *chi fa la parte di donna*" [215].

The ending of this little French digression does not mean that we have finished plumbing the depths of Rauzzini's style, which is very intricate and not for nothing has puzzled observers in every camp. In fact, a couple of motifs could indicate that the architect also had some knowledge of Austrian architecture, in this case, the most modern. All things considered, it was quite natural for Rauzzini to look towards the imperial city, the Vienna of that time. We must make his position clear. A builder on the fringe of art wished to improve himself in order to be capable of exacting challenges, and this was the situation in the period 1710–1730. Up to 1724 he lived and worked in the Kingdom of the Two Sicilies, and we must not overlook the fact that this country had been under Austrian rule since 1707. A builder down there who wanted to make his career had one eye on the residence of the Imperial Viceroy in Naples and the other on the Viennese court. Among the Habsburg governors were representatives of those families who patronized Austria's architecture – personalities such as Field Marshal Daun, Cardinal Michael Friedrich Althan, Count Alois Thomas Raimund Harrach. In Vienna Joh. Lucas von Hildebrandt had built the Daun-Kinsky palace (1713–1716) [216] and the Harrach mansion for the above mentioned vice-regent (1727 onwards) [217]. Fischer von Erlach the Younger erected the Althan Casino in the

Ungargasse [218]. Finally, one must remember that the first paladin of the Austrian House, Eugene of Savoy, was an Italian who, during the War of the Spanish Succession, had driven the French out of the Peninsula. Now the "noble knight" had returned to Vienna covered in laurels. For a Neapolitan subject in 1720, he was almost a mystic figure, like his brother-in-arms Marlborough. Belvedere, Prince Eugene's summer residence, was visible for miles around. It was built between 1715 and 1720 by Hildebrandt, and exerted very great influence as a work of art. Here the pilasters or pilaster strips pierced in the middle (cf. Rauzzini's Spedale di S. Gallicano) and the elliptical window occur as typical features. Alternating sections of stucco and smooth surface were characteristic of the Viennese façades of the day. They could be studied in Salomon Kleiner's great illustrated work on the architecture of Vienna (1724 onwards). Belvedere was dealt with by Kleiner in a separate work [219].

In the period 1724–1730 churches were also built by people other than Rauzzini. *S. Cecilia* in Trastevere was renovated in the Jubilee year of 1725 by the titular cardinal Francesco Acquaviva, as is stated in inscriptions above the portico and above the choir. The upper part of the new façade is of a type similar to that of S. Clemente, but more squat, and with salon-like pediments over the three windows, all very elegant. The builder's name is not given in the literature on the subject. However, a festive decoration for the Piazza di Spagna, paid for by Acquaviva in 1722, was designed by Domenico Paradis, who is expressly called "the Cardinal's architect" [220]. Did this little-known man also modernize S. Cecilia? *S. Agata dei Goti* (in Via Mazzarino) with its adjacent cloister was completely rebuilt about 1729 by Francesco Ferrari. The church's trivial façade is more suitable for the atrium of the cloister than for the church itself, and glancing through the portal one is surprised to see a quiet *cortiletto* [221]. This same Ferrari also decorated the interior of S. Gregorio Magno with stucco and other ornamentation. *S. Nicola dei Prefetti* (near the Piazza di Firenze) was "concentrated into a better form" [222], included in a hospice for Dominicans and spread its clumsy pilaster front, opposite Pal. Valdina Cremona [223]. In this interior Ferrari showed his skill as a painter with an altar piece. *S. Gregorio a Quattro Capi* is a captivating work, consecrated by Pope Benedict on Sept.

26th, 1729; the architect was Filippo Barigioni. This little church, now detached, was once in a very exposed situation. On the left of the entrance is the bridge linking this bank of the river with the island in the Tiber and Trastevere. Across the road on the right was one of the gates of the ghetto, along the back of the building and its south flank was a smelly alley, and the other side was confined by the fortress-like forecourt of the Palazzo Orsini (Theatre of Marcellus). S. Gregorio's narrow front, which was often a witness of street fighting, showed the flag to the mob and to the unbelievers whom it attempted to proselytize. The façade is more of a notice board than a piece of architecture. Its lower, largest section is half taken up by a pious picture in a plaster frame which appears to hang in a bow. Above the door below this, is a flowing band with an inscription admonishing the Hebrews. From the very fine window in the top section of the façade, the priest could survey the very unruly field of his church's activities, as if from this coign of vantage he were master of all he surveyed, for Gregorietto was also his abode. If these days we look at the building from the sides which have been hidden up to now, we find that it is of a quite different caliber from that of the front. Back here it is even more eloquent as far as strong and natural architecture is concerned. Small boxes of varying dimensions are stacked up to provide the rough form of the church, and spiked firmly together; two of them (corresponding to the widening of the interior on the transverse axis) are also secured vertically by curving volutes. Barigioni was a real sculptor. In one sense his little church has considerable substances (Pl. 43) — and displays a good principle: the weak features are facing outwards, the strong hidden. We learn the same lesson from numerous buildings in Roman Baroque. Their merit cannot always be judged solely from their front.

We now turn to an ecclesiastical building which at one and the same time demonstrates a finely chiselled mask and a plain body. The building for the Servitory oratorium (*del S. S. Sacramento di S. Maria in Via*), situated near the Piazza Poli, was started in 1724, and consecrated by the Protector, Cardinal Pietro Ottoboni, in 1730 [224]. Its builder, *Domenico Gregorini,* (d. 1777), was a new figure in Roman architecture. He was born in Rome in 1700, the son of the architect Lodovico Gregorini

(d. 1723) [225], to whom we owe S. S. Leonardo e Romualdo in Lungara [226]. Domenico became a member of the "Congregazione dei Virtuosi al Pantheon" in 1722 – at a surprisingly early age. That he, hardly 25 years old, was entrusted with the building of the Servitori oratorium could indicate that he had powerful support. When we then discover that Gregorini already in 1720 had decorated a chapel in S. Lorenzo in Damaso (a part of Pal. della Cancelleria), whose titular cardinal at that time was the Ottoboni mentioned above, and that in the same year he rebuilt a small oratory (more of a chantry) for the Philippine Order at Chiesa Nuova, it is logical to point to the vicechancellor Ottoboni as his patron. Gregorini very likely worked as a scenographer for the Cardinal in the theatre of La Cancelleria during Michetti's absence from 1718 to 1723. These observations, not previously associated, might explain various things in his later career and in his style. The façade of the oratorium is moulded on to the frontal plane of the building as a particularly emphasized part of it and the rest is not elaborated at all. Considered as decorative plasticity, Gregorini's work is admirable and no doubt influenced by Juvara. The curves have just that degree of suppleness that can be tolerated in a small building and in a large piece of decorated furniture.

As a comparison we can take a somewhat later church front of similar caliber, *S. Caterina della Ruota* (Pl. 42). Here a sacral façade is combined with an adjacent building, the priest's house, and these buildings are similarly situated in an intimate square, in front of the entrance to Via Monserrato. But in the case of S. Caterina the two buildings are juxtaposed yet do not form one complete unit. The house itself is an independent item contrasting with the pilaster front, but joined to it by the principal cornice. A traditional solution effected very harmoniously in a work which is so seldom noticed, although it stands in one of Rome's most elegant districts. The unknown architect was perhaps on the staff of St. Peter's (a master mason?), the church being the responsibility of the Chapter of this basilica. The large window above the portal is wreathed by thin, reed-like mouldings which seem made of dough ("Maccheroni"). Such strips of moulding are extremely unusual in the Roman buildings of the time and should make it possible to pin down the originator.

45. *S. Claudio dei Borgognoni.*

Prospect af Porta S. Giovani i Laterano i Udkanten af Rom. 1835.

47. S. Giovanni in Laterano. In the foreground the city wall. Old photograph.

48. *Chiesa della Morte.*

49. *S. Apollinare.*

50. *Chiesa del Bambin Gesù.*

51. *S. Dorotea in Trastevere.*

52. *The back side of S. Apollinare.*

They occur around the portal window of a large dwelling house at no. 23–24 Piazza di Firenze.

When the activities of Benedict XIII as a church builder in Rome were drawing to an end, an incident took place that may well be called symbolic. The congregation of the Burgundians began in February 1728 to erect a church in the present Piazza di S. Silvestro. It is called S. Claudio and was sited in such a manner that its front could be seen from the Corso through a side street. The work was started by the Rauzzini partnership, the senior member of which no doubt drew up the plans [227]. But the Protector of the church, Cardinal de Polignac, interfered; Rauzzini was dismissed and when the foundation stone was laid on June 13th in the same year, *Antoine Dérizet* the Frenchman (1697–1768) made his bow at the ceremony as the planning architect. The Pope carried on a lively conversation with him, looked through his drawings and emphasized how desirable it was that the Virgin Mary should be given a separate altar and that the dome should not collapse [228]. Dérizet had come to Rome in 1723, with a scholarship to the French School. In Paris he had produced designs for opera scenery and now he instructed in perspective at the S. Luca Academy [229]. He was obviously a bright boy and French right to his fingertips, always responsive to the latest craze [230]. S. Claudio's façade (Pl. 45) is a textbook example of pure Parisian style, the coats of arms in the pediment correspond exactly to the cartouches which Hårleman in Sweden and Eigtved in Denmark copied from engravings showing French ornamentation. The Burgundians' suave church front would be approved without question in Dijon, but near the Corso it is extremely remarkable for Rome in a number of respects. In the first place, Rauzzini's "autochthonic Rococo" was here turned into genuine *Louis Quinze* for all to see. Furthermore, it is surprising that the latter style does not seem to have called forth any sort of criticism. The reason for this is not difficult to understand. Although contemporary French mannerism in church building marked a decline in the accepted Roman Late Baroque, there was no radical break with its formal ideals. S. Claudio's "Rocaille" did not shock anybody, was not called *gotico* and was not aggressively non-Roman, being "classical" in spirit, but Rauzzini was castigated because his modes of expression really were anti-Classical and thus felt to be barbaric. When you look at this church, it is hard not to notice the irony in the fate of the Papal builder. The monk who hated wigs, was the sponsor for Rome's only unadulterated Rococo church without realizing it. He smiled graciously at the most blatant memorial to a culture which posterity found voluptuous to its very marrow. "Style" is defined by people not there at the time.

Montesquieu, who saw S. Claudio while it was being built, characterized Benedict XIII as follows: "He only likes the exceptional on a small scale" [232]. The remark is no less apt when applied to the Pope personally as an aesthete. *L'extraordinaire dans le petit* – this sounds like a definition of the concept of "Rococo" in a wider sense. Regarded like this, the statement can also paraphrase something essential in Rauzzini's art. It was extraordinary, beyond Roman laws, at loggerheads with French rules. We must admit, all the same, that it only truly comes to life in the cramped districts of a city which taken as a whole requires massivity. The examples that Rauzzini gave to his critical contemporaries could not in any way influence the monumental church building that followed. They were more suitable for dwelling houses [233].

Juvara came to Rome in 1725 to take part in the celebrations of the holy year and in the hope of building a palace in the Vatican for the use of future conclaves. It was expected that Rome would keep him. Vleughels expressed the wish that the pupils at the French Academy should also become his disciples, "for Don Filippo is beyond dispute the most able architect in the whole of Italy" [234]. Juvara had to return with empty hands – with the formal title of Architect for St. Peter's.

VI

The new Pope, the Corsini Clement XII, who ruled during the decade 1730–1740, belonged to one of Florence's most influential families, his mother being a Strozzi. He had many of the typical qualities of the Florentine patrician; respect for spiritual values, great understanding of economics, much ambition. As Cardinal (from 1708) this very wealthy gentleman gathered around him at the Palazzo Pamphili in the Piazza Navona, a court devoted to the Muses. He entertained lavishly, spoke to all and sundry, was a good listener, and thus acquired an intimate knowledge of the Roman world. He built up a choice library, but studied little and wrote nothing. He was regarded as unbeatable at chess.

Clement XII's personal view of architecture during his Papacy was fated to be restricted. Not many years after his succession he went blind. All the same, his influence on architecture became very important, but in an indirect way. He cherished on the one hand the ambition to appear as a new Medici – the last prince of this declining family had died in 1737 – in order to satisfy his aspiration to solve monumental problems, and on the other he patently favoured the artists from his native place. After the Beneventan interlude there now followed a Tuscan period. His predecessor's parochial inclinations had, after all, been linked with a beloved diocese and had their roots in pleasant pastorality, but the patriotism of the aristocrat Corsini had been imbibed with the mother's milk. The difference in these influences was expressed in the official building activities of the two pontificates. For while there is a distinctive disharmony between Benedict XIII's personality and his architectural affinities, the most representative of Clement XII's building seem to be in full harmony with the spirit of this Florentine Pope. The blind ruler in fact succeeded in inspiring an architecture which had all the elements of a style that matched his character, and at the same time satisfied his demands.

Furthermore – and this is just as crucial as it is typical for him – Clement, a former Treasurer General, managed to increase the State's income greatly, and in consequence provided a firm economic basis for its building activities, by re-instituting the lottery in 1731 (*il Lotto di Genova*). The Italians' inborn passion for gambling was not deferred to in vain, and this financial move by the Pope brought in enormous sums. From a social and ethical point view, the lottery was no doubt just as incompatible with the Papal States as are football pools and the tote in modern society, but the State knows what is expedient and therefore claims the right to be immoral. At the first draw that took place on February 14th, 1732 at the Capitol, the Papal Treasury made a net gain of 53.588 scudi [235]. Three years later it is said that the Pope had made 900.000 scudi annually "and you can certainly do some building with an amount like that". But the figure was exaggerated [236]. Rumour also had it that the Holy Father himself won almost daily in the lottery "and so building is going along famously" [237].

The result of the unexpected increase in financial resources was that Rome's architecture boomed in the 1730's. It was reminiscent of the time of Sixtus V, for the aristocracy too, who now obtained increased liquid assets, followed the Pope's example to a very great extent [238]. But the financial weakness of the Papal States was constitutional. This fiscal coup eased the situation only temporarily, the government was stimulated to unwarranted optimism, and after the golden age of Corsini, Benedict XIV made up the accounts for that decade. The national debt had risen by 1.800.000 scudi to a total of about 60 million [239].

The credit side is the architecture, and we benefit from it. In 1736, G. B. Gaddi was able to publish an enthusiastic pamphlet "Roma nobilitata nelle sue fabbriche della Santità di N. S. Clemente XII", in which there was a survey of the Papacy's splendid achievements in building up to that date.

The builder in the Quirinal, the helpless old man, had to see through the eyes of others. Cardinal Neri Corsini, a nephew of the Pope, acted as his own private overseer. Everything seems to indicate that he filled his responsible position with discretion and loyalty. His interests were mainly aesthetic and he had moreover the advantage over other noble prelates of having spent a long time in Europe as a man of the world. Before his uncle's succession he had been the Florentine envoy to the courts of London, Paris (1710–1720) and The Hague. It was no doubt to some extent due to *il Cardinal Padrone*'s vision, that Rome's official building activities responded to impulses both from England and France.

The staff of artists was augmented by two talented Florentines; the older of these, *Alessandro Galilei* (1691–1737), was thought to be a relation of the famous scientist [240], probably without foundation. Milizia tells us that when this young man had spent seven years in England, where he had arrived in the retinue of some "foreign gentlemen" [241], presumably Britons. Strangely enough we know nothing more about this period in Galilei's life, the very time when Lord Burlington, following his first visit to Italy (1714–15), laid the foundations of Palladian Renaissance on the other side of the Channel [242]. We can imagine that Galilei was employed by an English "man of taste" and exerted his influence on the quiet at some country seat. Giacomo Leoni, who was about the same age, went to England c. 1713. After his return to Tuscany (1719), Galilei was made architect to the Grand Duke, but does not seem to have produced anything of importance. When Clement XII called him to his court in 1730, and gave him important assignments, he was an unknown quantity in Rome [243]. In a letter that Juvara wrote from Rome to the Piedmont envoy, Count D'Ormea, in 1732, he expressly states that Galilei had never produced any work (*non havendo mai fatto nessuna opera in publico*) [244]. He fumed: "Etruria rejoices and laughs". All the more surprising that the Florentine in Corsini's service did indeed provide the Papal City with an architecture of unique Roman dignity, reflecting a glimmer of light from Antiquity.

Clement XII's other compatriot, *Ferdinando Fuga* (1699–1780), of a good Florentine family, came to Rome when he was eighteen years old and obtained his education there. But he won his spurs in the Neapolitan province and in Sicily. From 1726 onwards, he directed (or took part in) the rebuilding of the Palazzo Cellamara by the Chiaia in Naples, working for Prince Antonio Giudice, Captain-General in Old Castile. We have an engraving (by Filippo Vasconi 1729) of this large establishment (which is still preserved) after its modernisation [245]. Don Antonio's brother, Cardinal Nicola Giudice, who had a big say in Roman building matters, supervised the work. We will meet this powerful personality later on. Fuga was called to Rome in 1730 [246] and was the leading official architect for the next twenty years, and he richly deserved his title. He naturally "studied Antiquity", this was obligatory. What was more important was that he had absorbed the sensitive Florentine style, a delicate, rather plain mannerist architecture which the Danes know from Frederiksberg Castle [247]. We need not call it academic or striving towards the classical; it is merely calculating, static. When Fuga met Roman Baroque and let it flow over him, his schooling in Tuscany acted as a filter. One might say that the fusion of these two stylistic tendencies came to fruition in his art. He created an architecture which is static and rational, with its formulae always clearly defined, but the very substance in which they are expressed is warm and full. Sometimes the relief is low, mostly expressed with straight lines, in one case exuberant but without vibration, and in another the plasticity is robust, the details few and heavy, the whole lacking in pictorial tension. Fuga's motive force was kept in check by a determination to make every structural feature extremely clear.

Nicola Salvi (1697–1751) was born and died in Rome, where he became a pupil of Canevari and also obtained a very general education. He wrote poetry, amongst others in the "Arcadia", was interested in philosophy, studied mathematics and dabbled in medicine [248]. The grandeur of Antiquity appealed to him, particularly through its triumphal arches, and he wanted perhaps to compete with it. When young, he only succeeded in this with decorations of momentary importance. His oldest known work is a set piece for a firework display from 1720 [249]. Another *macchina* of extraordinary dimensions was erected according to his design in the Piazza di Spagna in 1728. In the most important work of his life, the Fontana di Trevi, exact calculation and an eye for effect, created a unity which became pure poetry and immortal.

Simultaneously with the two Florentine sobersides and the light-hearted Roman, there was another important architect to appear during Clement XII's reign. He came originally from Bergamo and thus had the same background as *Arlecchino,* the hero of Italy's popular comedy. *Gabriele Valvassori* (1683–1761) endured a lonely existence in Rome until his great break-through. He was awarded a couple of minor bursarships at the S. Luca Academy at the beginning of the 1700's. For his independent field studies on Borromini, he deserves the biggest of all gold medals imaginable. He entered the service of the Pamphili family c. 1717 and remained its permanent architect after Bizzaccheri's death in 1720, retaining this position until 1739, and in this capacity produced his masterpiece, the palace in the Corso. He did, at times, work as an architect for the House of Colonna, anyhow, designed a couple of festive decorations (1728, 1729) which were set up in front of the palace by S. S. Apostoli. He was also architect for the Augustine order from 1719 to 1747, up to 1723 as assistant to Contini [250], and gave the guild of fruiterers the benefit of his art. Valvassori's extensive practice was profitable and he died a wealthy man. His demonstrative humble memorial is to be found in the strict church of the Capuchins [251].

While Galilei gave Clement a cathedral, Salvi gave him a fountain, and Fuga provided the Pope with all sorts of houses, both smooth and rough, but Valvassori worked without any Apostolic recognition. His art has approximately the same relationship to the official style as the *commedia dell'arte* had to the drama in verse – to the elevated artistic school which the Paris of the day simply called *Rome*. Master Gabriele made capital of the distinctive, bizarre dialect spoken everywhere by workers in stucco, and by masons; his father was a carpenter. That this unashamed response, echoing from the small market-squares, could steal an important scene in Clementine Rome, is clear evidence of the healthiness of architecture even at this point in time – and of the profundity of Valvassori's originality. He continued to speak his own tongue.

OMNIUM URBIS ET ORBIS ECCLESIARUM MATER ET CAPUT – that is the title of the Lateran Basilica. A correspondingly pompous façade would have been fitting, but was missing. There had been no lack of tentative efforts to build one. After his accession, Clement XII had the opportunity to leaf through large portfolios of older projects (by Borromini and Theodoli among others). And he could lay his hands on a not inconsiderable capital to pay for the work. The Pamphili Pope Innocent X left the sum of 60.000 scudi [252]. Innocent XIII on his deathbed had assigned 10.000 [253]. These sums were far from adequate. When, in the end, Clement had the pleasure of giving *S. Giovanni in Laterano* the desired front, it was due mainly to the fact that he had means. In August 1733 he donated to the building fund the sum of 100.000 scudi, proceeds from the lottery, and promised a further 10.000 scudi from every draw [254]. It must be admitted that the Pope turned this filthy lucre to good account, and Rome's cathedral received the proudest front that the 18th century could provide.

It was in October 1731 that Clement called together a special "congregation" in preparation for building. Towards the end of November this exalted selection committee had resolved to reject all the old projects and hold a big competition [255]. A committee of judges was appointed which consisted of two architects (Valeri and Dérizet), two sculptors (Maini and Rusconi), two painters (P. L. Ghezzi and Pannini), together with the president (Seb. Conca) of the S. Luca Academy, and its secretary (Nic. Ricciolini); the architects, the two real specialist members, were only outstanding in an academic sense. Over a score of projects were submitted by Italy's best architects, but nothing from Juvara, although the Pope seems to have taken council with the great architect when he came to Rome [256]. Galilei presented his model to Clement on July 4th, 1732 [257]. Some time later the Pope called in Gregorini, no doubt in connection with the façade, the archipresbyter of the Lateran, Cardinal Ottoboni, being his protector, but nothing came of it [258]. In the course of the summer, the designs sent in were assembled in one of the galleries of the Quirinal [259]. The committee of judges gave Galilei's work its recommendation with four votes, Vanvitelli got three and Sassi one only. Naturally the competition aroused feeling and rumours flourished. Vleughels reported later that "after the fashion of this country" the architect had been chosen beforehand, that four of the judges had "been bought", one of them being a Frenchman (thus Dérizet) [260].

The "congregation" repudiated the specialists' choice without ceremony and supported Vanvitelli wholeheartedly, but in the middle of July 1732, Clement decided on the project by his compatriot Galilei. The Florentine's work was also the cheapest to put into practice, so it was said, the estimate being 300.000 scudi [261]. Repercussions from the great *imbroglio* were felt for a long time. Milizia burst out indignantly: *Che concorso fu mai quello!* ("Has anybody ever seen the equal of this competition!") [262]. Its outcome was, all the same, a fortunate one; none of the other designs known [263] can measure up to Galilei's.

The triumphant architect returned to Rome in August and wasted no time in starting the excavations for the foundations. In September, 230 men were at work, later 300 came from Aquila, for there was a shortage of workmen in Rome [264]. Galilei received 4000 scudi as his fee and the promise of a reward [265]. The arms of the Pope were put up on the façade in October 1733 amid a fanfare of trumpets [266]; at the end of 1735 the statues were in place on the roof balustrade, and the floor of the vestibule was laid in 1737. The total expenditure was 489.000 scudi.

Any architect who wished to solve this demanding problem with wisdom and spirit would have to reckon with three essentials facts. The first and most important was the view from the church, which in those days extended beyond the city wall across the Campagna to the mountains (Pl. 46). The façade was to stand face to face with Monte Cavo. This demanded strong lines, simple divisions and a striking effect from the distance. Then, because of its status, the church was bound to be compared with St. Peter's and must be considered as the decisive reply of the age to Maderno's front. Last of all, the Holy Father's diocesan church had to be centred around a loggia from which he could bless the world on Ascension Day and on the morning of Pentecost. Galilei squared the account fully. In the first place, he saw his façade as set within the great space, and therefore built on a grand scale. He realized that the building, which rose like Rome's own countenance above a wasteland, had to have firm lineaments, and for this reason he left the architraves over the columns and pilasters unbroken. He saw that the front gained greater power in relief if arches were carved out of the flat surface, so he had the upper storey – the one seen from furthest away and the one seeing furthest, divided up by arcades. He understood that a church which was called the "head of the world" had to bear its crown high above its subjects for all to see, so he set a towering balustrade upon its brow and bestowed on its figures a special stature (Pl. 47).

By thus fashioning his work on the large-scale site itself, instead of working it out in the drawing office, Galilei acted like an artist of genius, for in this way he found the proper solution to St. Peter's. He did not "improve" on it, he simply took no notice of it. One basilica raised its voice to the east, the other to the west. Maderno and Bernini involved their church with the city, so that it turned its back on the nearest hill. But Galilei made his cathedral's façade hail the whole of Latin territory. He had no quarrel with S. Pietro as architecture and kept its loggia in mind. Christ's Vicar steps forward on a balcony set between windows in the front of St. Peter's. Galilei opened up half his building in his honour and made the whole upper storey into a portico. The arch in the middle, which emphasizes the standing figure of the Pope, is more finely articulated than the rest of the storey, but still remains one loggia among many. So wide is the gallery's span up there, that the Pope could bless *urbi et orbi* – it seems –while making a slow promenade, even turning the corners if necessary. How lovely this serene, this deserted belvedere which breathes in the winds from the plains through its yellow arcades!

The people of those days who witnessed the event must have been absolutely arrested by this grand work. A poet described in 1738 how mightily impressed one was by the façade on the road into Rome [267]. Richard called it majestic [268], even de Brosses recognized, albeit reluctantly, its good points [269]. But during the following period, Galilei's masterly work had to pay the penalty for its originality in harmonizing earth with heaven; one could not close one's eyes to the sublime in its outline. The followers of Neo-Classicism looked at it in close-up, examined details and found much to criticize. Aspersions were cast by arithmeticians like Lalande, who found fault with the proportions while standing on the steps [270], and were publicized by Volkmann's guide (1770), the one most used in Goethe's time (in front of me now lies Nicolai Abildgaard's copy). People learned that the enlarged details were declamatory and the taste impure. "The façade is and remains far too theatrical", decided Münter in 1786 [271].

Certainly it is problematic. The situation is, in fact, that what was classical in Galilei's work, had come too soon to count as a model and that its Neo-Classical elements were incorporated in a mighty Roman idiom rooted in Baroque. In the analysis of its style we must first recognize this rhetoric [272], a strong character's proud answer to the Campagna. Did he seek and find help in Rome to determine its form? If we wish to follow Galilei, as he reconnoitered the terrain to have his resolve substantiated by the art of others, we must avoid all that is commonplace and only visit those places which can provide an inspiration on an elevated plane. First of all, it would be a good idea to follow him to an area where architecture is deliberately set against a background of disorganized nature. This is done with great effect in the Campo Vaccino. In Galilei's day this was a furrowed field, which, seen from the back of the Capitol, ended in an impressive church front. When in 1615 Carlo Lambardi built the façade for S. Maria Nova (S. Francesca Romana), it was his definite intention to make it watch over the deep, overgrown space of the Forum Romanum, and this can be seen from its structure. He used only one massive arrangement of pilasters bearing a triangular pediment and set this upright rectangle on a very high plinth. Whatever else Galilei had in mind, he could, with advantage, have considered S. Maria Nova which is also adapted to a demanding situation and should be seen from a distance. Perhaps he remembered Lambardi's bold work, if only in outline, when he developed the middle elevation of S. Giovanni.

Nor is there any doubt that the Florentine Galilei learnt from his great compatriot Michelangelo, who became a Roman – you realize that from the Capitol. Here you see the "giant order" and you find in the porticos of the palaces there, supports that have the same function and effect as those in the façade of the Lateran church. This Capitol aimed at Caesarian stature and was Rome's other "head". Only the wisest humanists have seen straight away that the Lateran front should be compared with kindred works. When Taine got over the first shock, he too, had to capitulate, and compared Galilei's façade to *quelque arc de triomphe érigé pour recevoir dignement le César spirituel* [273]. The ever-superior Carl Justi, Winckelmann's eulogistic biographer, called this spectacular building the last important architectural work in Rome (1868) [274].

But they were voices crying in the wilderness. Hardly had Baroque been accepted than those concerned with the history of style went in pursuit of the poor church, which had no wish but to be left alone. If previously its ethics had been challenged, now the architect was being criticized for plugging Neo-Classicism before its time. While people frantically hunted down his borrowings, Galilei was now being called one of the Palladians. He had, after all, lived in England. But this description of him is just as erroneous as the prejudice was unfair. A "temple pediment", four supports beneath a triangular fronton, was not necessarily imported to Rome from Venice or the British Isles [275], and the so-called "Palladio motif" in the middle section of the loggia, already used by Bramante in the Vatican [276], need not stem from the loggia in Vicenza, for the Lateran church has no connection with it [277]. Galilei's composition is classical (i.e. exemplary) by its great and simple form; its "style" proclaims *Maiestas Domini;* it is a ceremony expressed in imperative phrases. Is this not enough? By comparing the Lateran's pilaster front with English counterparts in the Burlington artistic circle, it becomes obvious that the Roman masterpiece has the individual character which was lacking in British Classicism in 1720, namely originality as well as textural authenticity, and natural harmony between expression and task. As a "Classical architect" on Baroque soil, Galilei has only a slight kinship with James Gibbs, who was Fontana's pupil in Rome about 1708 [278]. Definite signs of Galilei's English training are only apparent in details inside. The strikingly pure "Neo-Classicism" in the decoration of the vestibule of the basilica (e.g. the cassettes in the barrel vaulting) should probably only be interpreted as evidence that the architect – like Leoni and "the gentleman plasterer" Bagutti, who was brought in by Gibbs after 1709 [279] – had the opportunity to pursue the study of Classical ornamentation and possibly put it into practice at the home of a British Lord. Galilei very likely knew Leoni's English Palladio edition from 1715, but as an architect in Rome he suffered no ill-effects from it.

The *Corsini chapel,* which Galilei added to the Lateran church 1732–1735, was to be a mausoleum for Clement XII and his family [280]. The work was, to some extent, restricted by the Pope insisting that it should be built on the pattern of the Cappella Sistina in S. Maria Maggiore [281]. We will not go into details about the fine interior, the structure of which is based on Domenico Fontana's work of the 1580's and thus continues the tradition of Florentine Renaissance. It is not without reason that the style of the chapel has been called "Neo-Cinquecento" [282]. Its Classicism is backward-looking, fossilized in Tuscan neatness. Corsini thought he had provided a building in the noble style of the ancients, if somewhat polished up. He established the Capitoline Museum at this time – he wished to be buried in an antique porphery urn, which he transferred from the Pantheon to his new chapel [283]. It was thought to have been used as a sarcophagus for Agrippina, Nero's mother [284]. This article, which was to contain the mortal remains of a pope by way of a change, was eulogized by Vasari [285] and thus sacrosanct for a new Medici. The chapel put Galilei in an exposed position.

When he was assigned the job of providing *S. Giovanni dei Fiorentini* with its long-awaited façade, he, like Uriah, was set at the forefront of the battle. He now had to compose a large front in a place where it could not breathe, and had to use a conventional plan which must produce a tripartite building with a raised middle section. It is said that as Galilei was far too busy with the Lateran, the Pope gave this task to Fuga [286]. If this is true, it is easier to understand why Galilei failed to come up to expectations when the work was forced upon him all the same. Towards the close of September 1732, he was on the site to measure up [287]; a few months later Clement approved his drawings [288]. The façade is lifeless, without inspiration. The design could well have been made by a man who was working under pressure, and only wanted to rid himself of the problem as quickly as possible without getting into trouble. He made no personal mistakes, did not put a lot of himself into it, and was satisfied with a sober disposition of his columns and with keeping the architraves smooth. This sincere talent, which was sublime when given freedom to move, produced tasteful ornaments when the "student" in him was called forth, but threw in the towel when he was forced to build *alla romana* in the proper sense of that architectural school. It bored him stiff to build the screen in front of S. Giovanni in the Via Giulia. It bores us too.

Perhaps Fuga's artistic temperament was less unstable than Galilei's. The two churches he erected while his colleague's works were in process of being built are different, but equally good and both personal, very much in accord with the rest of his work. And in them the Roman local tone has absorbed the Tuscan idiom. *S. Maria dell' Orazione e Morte* in the Via Giulia, an entirely new building, was designed by Fuga. According to Valesio "he put his hand to the plough" on December 25th, 1732. The foundation stone was not laid until June 1st, 1733, and the building was consecrated in October 1737 [289]. The little church, which was owned by a pious brotherhood, is built on a plan elliptical in depth and was given a bold front, but it was only partly visible from the approach road (Pl. 48). This façade gives clear indications of Fuga's mature meditative psyche. It is obvious that he used Rainaldi's S. Maria in Campitelli (Pl. 18) as model [290], but he omitted the outer layer of disengaged columns which made that façade so vital. It completely changes its character, and the motifs on the second level now become predominant. Most important of these are the connected detached columns. In the Campitelli church, they increased the depth of the relief by retreating. In Chiesa della Morte, they appear as the strongest links in the building and its only full members. It was rather rash of Fuga to misuse these detached columns right out in the open, for they lack all function and are merely forms within small boxes. But it was a bright idea to make this façade in a narrow street a strong element in a negative way. Fuga may have remembered Michelangelo's vestibule to the Laurenziana library in Florence, where such incapsulated pairs of columns constitute a principal theme. The "church of the dead" has a great deal of substance and much gravity. The framework is solid and the rounded shafts rise in solitary quietude through the shadows. We know of no sepulchral monument of the time which is so inviolable.

In September 1731, a start was made on the foundation for *Chiesa del Bambin Gesù,* which was part of an educational establishment for poor girls. It stands in the Via Urbana opposite S. Pudenziana. The drawings were by Carlo Buratti, who was in charge of the work until he died. Since, at this time, the building had risen to a height of 20 palmi, both its type and the plan of the façade must have been decided upon, and thus did not permit Fuga, Buratti's successor, to make any essential changes [291]. Nevertheless, the finished church, consecrated on September 9th, 1736, was given an accent which made it Fuga's own (Pl. 50). The façade is a narrow rectangle between giant pilasters which are an integral part of the body of the building. Such an arrangement had often been seen before (e.g. S. Maria dell' Umiltà and S. Egidio), but not with such a violent contrast between the solidity of the building and the church gable. This was Fuga's handiwork. The ornamental foliage of the capitals intertwines over the re-entrant angles, the zig-zag cornice above, anticipates the *fortissimo* in the heavy, broken pediment. It can be seen from our plate that the effect is almost that of jagged lightning. Fuga let the whole bare cube of the building burn out its pent-up energy through this portal [292].

And now a plunge down from these heights to the masters of the small squares and their churches. A group from the 1730's continued the brisk, cheerful style which second-class architects itched to express. *Carlo de Dominicis* was one of these, having in 1716 taken an examination for entry to the third class of the S. Luca Academy [293]. After 1733, he worked in Rauzzini's drawing office as *giovane di studio* [294]. *S. S. Celso e Giuliano* in Banchi Vecchi was built from the foundations to his design in 1735. Its plan is a transverse oval. The only fresh feature of the façade is its rich plant motifs. The oak and the laurel, the palm and the lily, are profuse in foliage, but in vain. The architecture itself is without fertility. De Dominicis also built *S. Bartolomeo degli Bergamaschi* in the Piazza Colonna (1738), a little Borromini play on the theme of Bernini's S. Andrea al Quirinale, but of course he replaced the latter's entrance of detached columns with an ordinary framework, which is not without artistic virtues. The curved gable includes the whole façade and seems to put it in parenthesis from above. *S. S. Vincenzio e Anastasio alla Regola,* a funny little church with a dome, mellow and compact, which the guild of pastrycooks built beside the Tiber (it was pulled down shortly before 1888), was perhaps the work of de Dominicis [295]. For the saddlemakers, he erected *S. Eligio,* by the Piazza della Gensola, in Trastevere in 1744; this has also disappeared [296]. In 1738 an unknown architect amused himself by giving the oratorium *S. Simone Profeta,* in the Piazza Lancellotti, a transverse oval light in a Rococo cartouche and by providing the window above it with a curved balcony rail [297]. This coquettish place of worship is now in ruins.

In Clement XII's time three religious institutions erected their churches between flanking buildings (hospice and cloister). Two of them can be dealt with quickly, namely *S. Giuseppe alla Lungara,* built between 1730 and 1734 by Ludovico Rusconi Sassi [298], and the church of the Poles, *S. Stanislao* in the Via delle Botteghe Oscure. The first, cowers between its supporters, as well it may, for it has no face. The Polish façade assembles the whole into a noble unity of airy elegance. *S. Maria Maddalena in Campo Marzio* is, on the other hand, quite unique, and so much has been said about it that it requires comment (Pl. 56). It belonged to, and was built for, the Community of *Ministri degl' Infermi,* who were pledged to comfort the dying all over Rome, and who were never to desert the victims of plague during epidemics [299]. The church, the first design for which was provided by Carlo Fontana, was then entrusted to G. A. de Rossi and completed in 1698 by Carlo

Quadri, but had no façade until 1735, when the scaffolding was put up in February [300]. Who designed it is not known. Vasi states that perhaps the drawings for it were found among Mastro Carlo's papers after his death [301], but in guides from the end of the 18th century, Sardi is said to be the originator [302]. However, it is not so much the architect who intrigues us as the plasterer. Bereft of its stucco ornaments, the façade is a feeble imitation of the Borromini style; the master's name makes no difference. If the work stimulates the observer, and it has teased many, and has even been called the prototype of the provocative Rococo, the reason is predominantly to be found in the nodular, spiny and twisted organisms which are applied above and below the statue niches, and which stress both the portal and the panel above it. The "rocailles" are rather abominable and also foreign to the Roman emotional make-up. I assume that the plasterer got the idea from engravings of German decorative art. Fasolo rightly spoke of "northern pedantry" [303]. But the ornaments which are decorative in Munich, look a little hysterical in Rome, and seem tinny. We have the assessment of two Teutons of the attractions of S. Maddalena (the institution also looked after loose women). Joh. Caspar Goethe "estimated the beautiful façade highly" in 1740 [304]; Norbert von Grund forty years later called it "an intolerable monstrosity" [305]. The Imperial Councillor from Frankfurt knew a thing or two; the painter cultivated Greek ideals. Carlo Quadri, the year of whose death is not known, probably belonged to a known and numerous family of workers in stucco, one of whose members worked in Denmark at the time of Frederick IV. The warped façade for the church of the ministering angels can only in a qualified sense be taken as contributing anything to genuine Roman architecture [306], and did not belong in Corsini's Rome.

The domed church of *S. S. Nome di Maria* near Trajan's Forum, built by Dérizet 1736–1738, has not improved Rome's appearance either. A model of it could have been useful for instruction in the academy where the architect was a teacher; it is so faultlessly drawn and formed, but there is such a lack of character in its French regimentation of Roman motifs. "The bribed judge" in the Lateran competition was a true professor. The extremes the German and the French produced do not really count. The Corsini era of only ten years weighs heavy in the scale of the history of Roman churches, the Lateran and Fuga's work being the deciding factors.

VII

Benedict XIV was the greatest pope of the eighteenth century. Prospero Lambertini, this robust Bolognese, had a bright, warm personality which brings him very close to us as a human being. What was in his generous heart he had to get off his chest. Very few occupants of the Papal throne had been so plain-spoken. He was a quick-witted scholar – this becomes the ruler in the Vatican. His character was magnanimous and energetic – this befits Peter's heir. Other popes have resembled him in such virtues. But Benedict's greatest personal attribute was his profound sense of humour. Whether he expressed himself in his blunt, sometimes extravagant terms, or sparkled with raillery, it conveyed a message from a free and noble mind. The contrast between the high rank of this hot-headed gentleman and his outspoken utterances was for ever shocking people, but rarely failed to captivate. His frankness certainly withheld nothing. Papa Lambertini was irresistible and was loved by all those in Europe who had any opinion to express.

As a builder, Pope Benedict recognized his full responsibility towards Rome and took a pride in beautifying the city. But the economy of the Papal States was so bad, when he succeeded Clement XII in 1740, that public building seemed doomed to stagnate. Thinking of his predecessor's papacy, Benedict himself said: "Ten years of merry-making and entertaining (*allegria e conversazioni*) have ruined this country; but if God wills, then it will get on its feet again, but this will need time and patience" [307]. Neither of these boons was to be granted him. At the beginning of his reign the national debt, as already mentioned, was very considerable, and although the finances improved, he always felt himself seriously hampered by lack of funds.

Nevertheless, Papa Lambertini succeeded in carrying out such impressive architectural works, that his pontificate – with the Jubilee year of 1750 as its focal point – stands out in splendour in the history of architecture. This balanced ruler with his strong personality put the finishing touches to that work of art called Roman Baroque. Under his auspices, the division of the city into 14 *rioni* made an exemplary improvement [308] and the whole area of the city was mapped out with unique precision and attention to detail by Giambattista Nolli (1748). Parallel with this, the engraver Giuseppe Vasi, produced an almost exhaustive graphical picture of the triumphant papal city in the *Delle Magnificenze di Roma antica e moderna* ("The Splendours of Ancient and Modern Rome") a volume illustrated with 250 plates and published in 1744 and the following years [309]. Benedict XIV stands out as the last great *Restaurator Urbis,* and his good, steady hand has the right to sign the prospect of the city *perfecit opus.*

All the same, his taste for architecture was not very developed. It seems more limited than his respect for its reputation. Once one of his predecessors had erected a church and stamped it with his armorial bearings, the papal builder had nothing more to say, and so posterity believes that he was content with his work. But in the case of Benedict, there was a dialogue between official "approval" and personal evaluation, and he was not afraid of it being heard beyond his nearest surroundings. It has reached our ears too. So we can enjoy the unique experience of seeing a great builder tear his own works apart. While from the portal, Benedict's name is accompanied by a fanfare of trumpets, we hear His Holiness rage in the council-chamber about the trash he had been hard put to to pay for. This sums up the whole man. A pope must not pretend to be wiser than a famous and experienced architect, and the latter can claim just as much respect as his principal, whose aristocratic coat of arms on the gable is a due receipt. The architect is the sovereign lord of the drawing board and his employer must preserve an apparent solidarity with him. But it did not occur to Lambertini within his own four walls to make a secret of his feelings. When the splendid rebuilding of S. Maria Maggiore was completed, he remarked: "We have no reason to glorify ourselves by this work; one might almost believe that We have turned ourselves into a theatre impresario, for the church looks like a ballroom scene" [310]. And after S. Croce in Gerusalemme had been totally renovated, the Pope passed sentence in no mean fashion: "Now that the work has been brought to an end at enormous expense, We are rather dissatisfied at having destroyed this venerable monument by such modern muck (*porcaria moderna*), as the saying goes" [311].

When we rejoice in Lambertini's Rome during Voltaire's gay and sceptical century, being stimulated by the sight of the Church of the Holy Cross's excesses, and become light of heart in the greatest of all spiritual ballrooms, because its art holds us in its spell, we also have the pleasure of hearing the laughter of the good Pope Benedict, and we are thereby reminded that this joyous art must be taken seriously, but not too seriously.

Horace Walpole, who said of himself that he was neither servile to a prince nor humble to a priest, erected a monument in his park with a long inscription in honour of Benedict XIV, the best of all Rome's popes. Lambertini was sent a copy of Walpole's *éloge* and commented on it to a friend in the following words: "We feel like one of the statues on the top of St. Peter's which seen from a distance down there in the square makes a nice show, but in close-up proves to be wearing a horrible mask (*orribili mascheroni*)" [312]. It is quite likely that the Pope was as wrong in his self-criticism as he was in his judgment of architecture. The Maecenas in his swaying litter was too close to it all.

In contrast to his predecessor Clement XII, Benedict was no friend of artistic nepotism and in fact detested it. *Fuga* held his powerful position until he went to Naples in 1750, and he apparently had no rival for the Pope's favour. It was not Lambertini's inclination to involve himself in the details of the building administration. "We have enough to do with the activities of being Pope", he expressed himself on one occasion, when an attempt was made to persuade him to interfere with the affairs of a subordinate [313]. However, it must be admitted that even a pope with a profound personal involvement in architectural matters would have found it difficult to direct the course of style towards fertile soil at this very time, for in the middle of the century it started to taper off and slow down to a trickle and threatened to seep into unproductive sand. In the field of architecture Christ's Vicar cannot perform miracles. The number of independent and talented architects was reduced and then increased only slowly again, keeping pace with the decline in monumental building activities towards the end of Benedict's papacy in 1758.

Barigioni, Salvi and *Sardi* died shortly after 1750. Two masters of the old school, namely *Valvassori* and *Rauzzini,* survived Benedict XIV, and worked on well into the following period (dying 1761 and 1770 respectively), but of their later activity little is so far known. They served mainly ecclesiastical foundations and private employers, even persons of the third estate. They were no match for the new age and were swallowed up in Rome's great unknown.

Among the younger people, the architects of Fuga's generation, *Luigi Vanvitelli* emerged as one of the first rank (1700–1773). He was born in Naples, the son of the distinguished Dutch landscape painter Gaspare van Witel [314], and was still an infant when he arrived in Rome. When he came to the years of discretion, he followed in his father's footsteps and so became very familiar with the architecture of the Papal City as seen with a painter's eye, and this, in its own way and its own time, was no mean training. He could not have been a pupil of Juvara in Rome, as has been stated, but trained himself as an architect eclectically, although at one stage he is known to have given the ageing Antonio Valeri a hand in the *fabbrica* of St. Peter's [315]. As a cultured artist and by his participation in the Lateran competition he had made a certain name for himself in artistic circles before he won any fame as an architect. In 1736, Vleughels wrote in a letter to Paris: "There is now only one good architect in Rome, and he is also a painter. He found architecture easier to practise and therefore has given up painting, for in truth he was not as proficient at it as he is in his present profession" [316]. This artist, whose name is not given, can hardly be anybody else but Vanvitelli. It is known that he had helped Barigioni in 1732 during the interior restoration of two churches in Urbino, but no independent work of any importance is known from his younger years. In 1747 he succeeded in supplanting Valvassori as the Augustines' architect. He was in full career!

Gregorini, the third prominent architect of Fuga's generation, had won his spurs already in Benedict XIII's day by designing the graceful oratorium for the Servites. Now, under the next Benedict, he played a greater part on the mighty Roman stage, and as architect for S. Croce completed his life's one and only monumental task. He had made preparations for this leading role while waiting in the wings during the decade of Clement XIII's reign, in fact quite literally, for his activity had apparently continued to be confined to the theatre. The project for the reconstruction of the opera house Teatro Tordinona (1734) is his [317]. *Pietro Passalacqua* (died 1748) also produced theatrical architecture in two senses of the word. In 1710 he won first prize at the S. Luca Academy [318] and is expressly stated to have been a pupil of Gregorini as well as his assistant (*primo giovane di studio*), and to have helped him in the erection of S. Croce as well as the Teatro Tordinona. Passalacqua undertook a rebuilding of Palazzo Sforza-Cesarini and this, no doubt, has some connection with the fact that in 1731 the head of the ducal family had built the Teatro Argentina, Rome's leading theatre, situated directly opposite the palace mentioned above. Passalacqua may have been helping Theodoli, the architect for this playhouse [319].

However that may be, various things seem to indicate that Passalacqua, little noticed by history as he appears to be, spent his early days under the rigging loft, and like Gregorini was brought up among columns on canvas. Like Juvara, he was born in Messina and was only a few years his junior. He presumably knew his fellow-townsman, the leading man in scenic design, and this can be proved in a roundabout way. Juvara went to Lisbon in 1719 at the invitation of King John V of Portugal. He stayed in Rome in the spring of 1721 on his way back to Turin [320]. We know for a fact that Passalacqua had made some models of St. Peter's and the Vatican for John V at the time that Canevari made the surveys previously mentioned for this monarch [321]. Canevari delivered his drawings to the Portuguese ambassador in March 1723, after having worked on them "for more than a year"; at a rough estimate this takes us back to the beginning of 1722, or perhaps the end of the 1721. Passalacqua's wooden models, which were large and very detailed, must have taken much longer to make. It would not be too far-fetched to suppose that Juvara, while in Rome, acted as the intermediary for King John's order and got into personal contact with the two architects, one of whom was his compatriot in the strictest sense of the word.

Alas, we know so little about all these long-gone relationships and can only grope our way in the dark and plot our path from one sporadic light to another. Can the strange and unusual name of Passalacqua perhaps cast some light upon the man? An actress cum singer went under the name of Passalacqua; she belonged to Imer's troup in Venice about 1735, being the faithless mistress of Goldoni. She was given the directorship of the theatre in Mantova in 1749, and died in impoverished circumstances c. 1760 [322]. Her real name was Lisabetta d'Afflisio and she was a daughter of an actor. She was, no doubt, related to the Neapolitan adventurer Giuseppe D'Afflisio (D'Affligio), who went on to become director of the Hofburg theatre in Vienna and who died as a galley slave in 1787 [323].

As we can see – the very name of the Sicilian architect spotlights the world of the theatre. As was the case with Rauzzini.

Carlo Posi (1708–1776) was one of the lesser lights, although he was architect for St. Peter's. Like Marchese Theodoli he found his clientèle among the beau monde, was connected with the Colonna family, and employed occasionally by fashionable convents. Of all his colleagues *Cavaliere* Posi was perhaps the only one who was a member of the salon and in this way had more chance of coming into contact with Parisian Rococo. Justi called him a copy-cat [324]. His gravestone can be seen in S. Alessio; his cenotaph, complete with portrait, was erected in S. Caterina da Siena (which he had rebuilt) at the expense of his heir and pupil, Giuseppe Palazzi. We must not forget to mention *Tommaso de Marchis*, who has left a couple of elegant works, but is otherwise little known [325].

Benedict XIV's Secretary of State, Cardinal Silvio Valenti, who held office from 1740 until he had a stroke in 1754 [326], was a shrewd judge of art. He built up a considerable collection of paintings – some prominent works from it were sold to the Danish King [327] – and as a private builder displayed distinctly modern ideas, meaning French and Classical, and included chinoiserie in the interior decoration of his villas [328]. Valenti's collaboration with the Pope was exemplary, and one might expect the Head of the Church to have let himself be influenced by his trusted premier in building matters as well. This can only be proved in one single case – and will be dealt with later – characteristically enough, it concerns a little secular building of the intimate type.

As our introduction to church architecture during the reign of Benedict XIV, we present *S. Cecilia's portal façade* dating from his second year in office. Fuga was the architect, the builder a paladin of the first order. Cardinal Troiano Acquaviva loved display more than any other dignitary in Rome at this time. As ambassador for Spain and Naples, and the Protector of these Royal Houses, his words carried weight and his domicile was correspondingly impressive. He had a princely income; the archdiocese of Monreale in Sicily alone is said to have brought him 600.000 livres a year. De Brosses summed him up in January 1740: "He has noble, somewhat stoutish features and his face reflects his spirit; he is powerful, respected, esteemed, regarded as a worthy man and chases after anything in skirts (*grand débrideur de filles*)" [329]. Casanova served for a short time in 1744 as secretary to this corpulent courtier and prelate [330], whose extensive interests also included well-built houses. Fuga's talents had previously been appreciated by him, and after Juvara's death on January 31st, 1736 in Madrid, he suggested to the Spanish court that Fuga should be chosen as successor, but in vain, fortunately for Rome.

When he was elevated to Cardinal in 1732, Acquaviva was given the benefice of S. Cecilia, thus becoming the successor to his paternal uncle, Cardinal Francesco. The nephew now carried on the work of his uncle, and did so in far greater style. S. Cecilia stands withdrawn behind a deep forecourt (atrium), and in consequence the church's outer façade is on the portal which faces a smallish square surrounded by heterogeneous buildings. Out here, Cardinal Troiano put his uncle's unimpressive work in the shade. The new portal is said to have been started at the beginning of August 1741 [331].

Fuga decided to give the façade of the building itself a discreet articulation in low relief, and he used the recess as motif with great skill. It is admirable the way the window frames of the upper storey merge with the pilaster strips and thus form a continuous framework. It will also be seen that the cornice has an extremely flat moulding and that the four triglyph consoles beneath the frieze of the middle section are very indecisive. The architect has deliberately played down the façade in order to make it a fitting background for the portal. An observer might, at first sight, regard the building as an elegant mansion – Acquaviva's sonorous name is set almost unobtrusively below the cornice – did not the prominence of the portal make such an illusion impossible. Those heavy Doric disengaged columns with their very angular architrave and broken middle pediment, announce that this is the hallway to the house of an absolute ruler. But to God's house? The symbolism of the church is weak and insignificant, a cherub's head above the keystone of the archivolt, a couple of martyrs' crowns above the side doors, that is all. The Cardinal's heavy coat of arms which fills the segmental pediment, and the fleshy figures of angels at the side of it, dominate this church portal in a particularly worldly fashion. We have seen this sort of thing innumerable times before in Rome, but hardly so blatantly as here (Pl. 55).

Considered stylistically, Fuga's new façade for the revered church of Saint Cecilia is altogether a strange piece of work. A summarized analysis of it would run like this: 1) The front is in good civic taste, for behind its walls are residences for clerics, but no altar; 2) The portal is more secular than ecclesiastical, for although the way through it leads to a great shrine, it is not itself the temple door; 3) The columns' plasticity is out of the ordinary in that it expresses the Cardinal's own contours. No Roman architect was better able to articulate so emphatically and tersely as Fuga. Here, in front of S. Cecilia, his idiom is most audibly called forth. His voice is suddenly raised.

The echoes resound across the dusty square. Even a house from the Middle Ages, black with age, which faces the portal, shrinks at Fuga's stentorian voice, and is dazzled by the saffron yellow of Cardinal Troiano's building.

The renovation of S. Maria Maggiore came first on Benedict XIV's list. Fuga's design from 1735 was all ready, and a building fund was started in 1740. The old vestibule to the south threatened to collapse, so there was no time to waste. The foundation stone for the new façade was laid on March 4th, 1741, and everything was finished at the beginning of the 1750's [332]. The interior restoration does not concern us here, only Fuga's alteration of the front (Pl. 53). The problem here was to pin a portico with a benedictory loggia between two palatial corner blocks, the east one of which had been built in 1605 by Paul V, the other having been added in 1721, for the sake of balance [333]. Fuga's solution has been praised to the skies. It is certainly ingenious, but not really arresting,

53. *S. Maria Maggiore. Painting by Pannini.*

55. *S. Cecilia in Trastevere. Front building.*

56. *S. Maria Maddalena.*

57. S. S. Annunziata in Borgo S. Spirito.

58. *S. S. Quaranta Martiri e S. Pasquale Baylon.*

59. *S. Alessio sul Aventino.*

60. *Il Priorato di Malta.*

and in quality is inferior to his façade for S. Cecilia. Circumstances forced him to build a light structure between two blocks which are divided up into small sections, to assemble a simple framework, erect a dais which is also a portal for the largest church in Rome dedicated to the Virgin Mary. But it is difficult to build a work which is of a provisional character, yet has to endure *per saecula saeculorum*. Lalande was not entirely wrong when he compared Fuga's portico with a sort of birdcage [334]. Galilei had been successful in giving that forceful exterior of the Lateran façade an extraordinary energy as architecture. Fuga's façade for S. Maria Maggiore is no more than a permanent decoration. With cool significance he gave the edifice the benefit of all his mathematical skill; he wisely alternated between triangular pediments and segmental arches, "he turned the thing into a pyramid" (as they said in those days), and did in fact create an outstanding spectacle. But there is no depth of spirit breathing through these arches. Only the Papal Court, not Christ's Vicar, could make an impression here. The question is – where else in those days could you find a church portico with the courage and ability to outdo the backdrop to the final act of an opera?

S. Croce in Gerusalemme was renovated throughout 1741–1744, leaving only the campanile as it was. Considering that this venerable memorial had been Benedict XIV's titular church when he was cardinal and was therefore assured of particular respect, it is easy to sympathize with Lambertini's indignation at the final result of its modernization. Although today we would by no means call it "muck", our criticism can only be unfavourable. It is obvious that Gregorini, who with Passalacqua directed the operations, was consciously competing with Galilei's façade to the Lateran. But apart from that, methods quite different from those of Galilei were used by Gregorini to create his effects. Compared with that of the Florentine, his composition is melodramatic. This is very evident in the middle section, with its strongly chiselled structure set off against plain flanking walls. This recipe for a church front, simple in principle, was time-honoured in Baroque (remembering S. Maria in Campitelli, S. Carlo and S. Galla) – the church's own *prospetto* bulges between two lean monastery wings. It is true that Gregorini trimmed his work with a unique sense for effect, for he too, practised the mannerism of simplification. Seen from a distance it is a church of great attraction, but only when looked at aslant. This can only to a certain degree be considered a virtue, especially for a basilica expecting all sorts of processions, for although S. Croce is seen to its best advantage in this way (viewed from S. Giovanni in Laterano), a symmetrical façade should never forfeit its right to be looked at fair and square. But this S. Croce does and yet is one of the finest churches of its class in the whole of the Christian world. The façade can therefore be identified with painted stage scenery, for ever frozen into a perspective seen from sideways on, but is wrong from any other angle. If we look at S. Croce from the front, head-on, its grossness is revealed.

In the Lateran Church's façade the details were scaled in size for an edifice which had greatness in every respect; in S. Croce their dimensions are greater than the building can sustain. The Servites' oratorium possessed a stature which did not strain Gregorini's talent. S. Croce did. The archivolt above the main portal, in type borrowed from the benedictory loggia of S. Giovanni, has acquired a couple of clumsy protuberances which straddle the base of the tall oval window (a Juvara motif), and make the supports beneath them ridiculous. The distracting way the figures on the balustrade are grouped is also of a doubtful nature. The convexity of the façade unquestionably has an underlying motivation; it is distended by a vestibule having a transverse ellipse as its ground plan, forming a new head for the church. Inside this *atrio* the cupola, its "calotte", is borne by a ring of detached columns. Richard was far from edified by the vestibule to the Holy Cross Church, which is more like "stage scenery than the entrance to a house of prayer" [335]. Classicists of the first water were of course disgusted with this rotunda. In order to stimulate the soul to reverence "*müssen* die Säulen wie die vor dem Pantheon seyn", snapped Münter [336]. Jagemann decreed that even the finest colonnades were neither noble nor splendid if they were not more or less like those of the Pantheon [337]. For his part, Richard was quite right in his characterization of Gregorini's rotunda, which could be said to have been conceived in the world of the theatre. Similar *atria* can be found in Juvara's scenery for Ottoboni's theatre [338], which Gregorini presumably knew, as well as the work of all the Baroque scenographers who followed the trend of Galli-Bibiena. This last important Baroque church in Rome had an affinity with "The Temple of Fortune" or "The Palace of King Cyrus" in opera seria. It must have cost Benedict XIV some 100.000 scudi to be the impresario for S. Croce [339].

Not the theatrical as such, but the theatrical appearance, was a warning of decadence, and was particularly striking when bombast detracted from a church. Benedict XIV was no enemy of play-acting and theatrical illusion, but of turgidity. In 1745, it was not the done thing in Rome to build an important church façade without the same emphasis that is played out among the columns of a proscenium. But from S. Croce came merely a hollow echo. At the last curtain call after a *rappresentazione sacra* in the grand style, Gregorini had to admit to a work which showed the weakness of the times, as well as his own.

If we take a survey of Roman church building during Lambertini's papacy, starting with S. Maria Maggiore, we soon see that the retrogression in originality is expressed in three different ways. Some churches attempt to keep the picturesque, plastic manner alive as long as possible by calling on the reserves. Such buildings are roughly in the same situation as human beings who burn out all their passions in a short Indian summer – their carriage, their expression seem to regain a painful youth. Features sometimes take on a crystal-clear, translucent beauty, just like the opalescent light before a storm. Other works of art wearily abandon the style they have inherited, an apathetic resignation makes them formless. They are mostly written off by posterity. Finally there are those of a third category which attempt to save themselves by penance and fasting; they try to turn over a new leaf and pull themselves together, sometimes shrinking with fear. This sort of artistic individual is usually called a forerunner. We shall deal briefly with a few examples, the best in each of these three groups.

A church in Trastevere with the long-winded title of *S. S. Quaranta Martiri e S. Pasquale Baylon* demonstrates Baroque in its death-throes, but as yet fully conscious. The façade is bold and clearly articulated. No pilasters are used, merely linked pilaster strips, which might be regarded as imported from French Rococo had they not already been used by

Carlo Fontana – the lovely little church of S. Maria ad Nives in the Via del Colosseo shows his talent for this to great advantage [340]. The exterior of the church is subdued, and the ornamentation of the portal and the flanking doors is to some extent emasculated. However, the angles in the double pediment are still drastic, and the cornice, which reaches out around the sharp corners of the monastery, soars up in a trenchant arch. S. S. Quaranta Martiri was built 1744–1745. Terribilini refers to it in his diary of May 23rd of the latter year and says that during the excavations ancient coins had been found on the site [341]. The monastery had been built in 1736. The Spanish discalced Franciscans who owned the church are said to have employed the local architect Giuseppe Sardi [342]. If this is the case and if the plans are his, the contractor from Trastevere produced something excellent in the end. But it is worth noting that he had a son of the same name in the profession [343]. Plate 58 shows S. S. Quaranta Martiri with a sharp-edged shadow falling across it. We chose the hour of this deep shadow for our photograph to give the church of the forty martyrs a little of the drama that it surrendered when it lost its neighbour, a rustic fountain called "la Fontana Secca". In former times the church created its own little forecourt at the entrance to the long Strada di S. Francesco a Ripa, and the diagonal line of the monastery to the right shows the direction this street takes. The church retreated decorously behind this sharp corner, using it as a buffer.

The little oratorium of *S. S. Annunziata* was set opposite the Hospice of the Holy Spirit's new wing in Borgo S. Spirito in 1745 (Pl. 57). The architect, probably Passalacqua, overreached himself here. His house of prayer dedicated to the Annunciation is boastful and bursting with "sacral appeal". It projects slightly in the middle, yawns above the minuscule portal, indolently parades its flanks, which are profaned by pretzels over the doors, and by drawing-room windows; sticks a cross up in the air on top of a sort of épergne, sets the dove of the Holy Spirit within a burst of rays. Right at the top it retires into a balcony, which, in its delight and emotional curves, looks as if it is expecting a visitor from on high. The "Baroque" of this stage manager had certainly not breathed its last. Faced by this work, so splendid in its way, one is disinclined to take motifs of a serious architectural nature into account (Juvara has been sedulously plundered); the whole set-up is theatrical, as catching as a rick fire, completely unprincipled but enchanting.

> *"Cheeks have blushed a flaming crimson,*
> *Eyes are lowered to veil the reason."*

The oratory vaunting itself in the street of the hospices was called "la Nunziatella" by everybody, in such an intimate and caressing way, that it was as if one were speaking of an actress or an extravagant courtesan – "la Faustina", "la Diamantina"...

While the first of these two churches was vital and the other was vivacious, the façade of the contemporary *S.S. Trinità degli Spagnuoli* in the Via dei Condotti lacked any life at all, in spite of the fact that it has both concave sweep, several columns and also figures of manacled slaves above the door. The founder, belonging to the Trinitarian order, was Mgr. Diego Rubio, Archbishop of Lima and Viceroy of Peru. The architect brought in was the Portuguese Manoel Rodriguez dos Santos, but Sardi was in charge of the work on the site, as the entrepreneur. Building started in 1741, and the church was consecrated in 1750 [344]. When we analyse the front we find that in spite of its richness of detail it is very unsophisticated in its relief and only half alive. It was a marvellous situation, a clever man could have dominated the lower part of the Via dei Condotti as seen from the Corso by giving his building here an appropriate character. Now the lukewarm recess of the church is merely a break in the building line of houses, just something a little different, never even hinting at the beauty of the elliptical interior. Its colourful frescoes were produced by Guglielmi and the Madrileno Antonio Gonzales Velázquez (1749–1750), and Goya, no doubt viewed them with interest during his visit to Rome in 1770–71 [345].

S. Giovanni Calibita on the island in the Tiber was rebuilt in 1741, by Romano Carapecchia; its interior was decorated "from head to foot" [346]. As far as the façade is concerned, this church too, must be considered as one of the "tired" ones. The best that can be said of its exterior is that the campanile of the corner is very effective as the finish to the adjoining hospital wing which runs along the river – and it counteracts, if rather awkwardly, the Torre Caetani. The two towers look at one another with disdain from each side of the exit of the Ponte Quattro Capi. We, on the other hand, see them as in a picturesque harmony.

Among the churches from Lambertini's time which underwent a cure for purification, *S. Apollinare* is the finest work of art. And well it might be. Fuga, to whom the building is due, was the architect of this period who found it easiest to purify his style, for it was healthy in all its tissues and had good bone-structure. He had no need of any "process of regeneration" with regard to absolute values of form; to build in a more simple style than before was all that was required. S. Apollinare (1741–1748) has original ideas in its plan (vestibule resembling a transept, deep quadrilateral chancel). But there is none in the façade (Pl. 49). Fuga's more recent critics have declared that it has no life and "is weighed down by memories of the past" [347]. But what if the architect had no intention of creating a vigorous front? Or tried to forget the memories of the past? No one can deny that S. Apollinare has a physiognomy whose traits are traditional; it is equally clear that features like the hollowed-out panels between the top gable and the vertical flanking sections in no way enliven the front. Let us assume that Fuga intended it to be in a low key. He succeeded in this by divesting an ideal of all the passions which, with increasing violence, had played havoc for a century and a half, even since A. da Sangallo invented this type of façade for the church of S. Spirito in Sassia.

S. Apollinare is like the final fair-copy of a paraphrase of the themes on the most famous Roman church façades. The portal and the large window above it are reminiscent of la Madonna dei Monte (by G. della Porta). The whole, so cooly interpretative, has a temperature corresponding to the successive stages of the Renaissance. But Fuga's version is not just a weary echo; he cultivates the original and the essential with an ingenuity which is deliberate. He has the stamina of a surgeon. How confidently he uses his knife can best be seen at the back of S. Apollinare, this side which is so rarely appreciated (Pl. 52). It might be audacious to insist that "Jesuit Baroque" has never at any time been expressed with greater authority than in this edifice which is empty and plain, pregnant in cut, perfect in balance. All talk of "academism" is just as unwarrented here as it was with Carlo Fontana's S. Margherita. It is merely that the stamina is greater because the way back was longer.

S. Dorotea in Trastevere, right next to Porta Settimiana, also has a façade which is traditional but made firm and new by rationalization (Pl. 51). The architect, Giambattista Nolli, the most experienced surveyor in the Rome of the 18th century, originator of the classic map of the city (1748), had in 1751 [348], made his church façade into a function of the curve of the street, as perfectly and naturally as if he was using a well-tried form for the first time; it was also the last. The much-boosted "Borromini motif" is reborn in the authoritative spirit which Fuga admired in Bernini (cf. "Triclinio Leoniano") – this impressive pilaster arrangement which the French of the time would have called *mâle*.

We must take great care when the style of a couple of churches from Lambertini's days is to be classified. The first was encumbered with the hidden pretentions of its monastic order. The other's architect was an intellectual and an amateur, and therefore a prey to every fashion.

The learned Spanish hermits of the order of St. Jerome had monasteries like palaces. "Our Lady of Guadelupe" in Estramadura was fabulously rich and, after Santiago de Compostella, Spain's most popular place of pilgrimage. This enormous group of buildings could easily accommodate Philip II and his very large retinue for 20 days without incommoding the 26 friars [349]. The very name (*Nuestra Senora de Guadelupe*) was Hernan Cortes' battle-cry when he conquered the New World [350]. Charles V spent the last two years of his life in San Geronimo de San Yuste; "el Real Monasterio de San Lorenzo del Escorial" was an Hieronymite monastery and a royal palace all in one, the biggest building in the world for a monastic order. Philip II died there. San Jeronimo in Belem near Lisbon, is a Portuguese Pantheon. As well as monarchs, Vasco da Gama and Camoens rest in the care of the Eremites. Privilege entails responsibility also in Rome, so when the friars of this order's Lombard congregation completely rebuilt their church *S. Alessio* on the Aventine in the Holy Year of 1750, it was given a very elegant appearance. Cardinal Angelo Maria Querini, Prefect for the Vatican and Benedict XIV's rather troublesome friend, was in charge of the building activities. He had donated a fine library to Brescia, his cathedral city (1747), as *titolare* of S. Marco in Rome he supplied this church with splendid interior decoration [351]. This Venetian patrician, who had extravagant tastes and knew Voltaire personally, employed the architect Tommaso de Marchis to be in charge of the Eremites' building [352]. A description of it after its completion was the work of the abbot of the monastery (1752).

In front of the new, very secular façade, with its vibrant and fasciated pilasters (cf. Pal. Costa) an atrium was laid out, which at the sides was enclosed by a monastery wing and a decorative barrier wall respectively (Pl. 59). The frontage to this palace yard was a two-storied building. The top storey has a balcony in the middle set between Ionic columns; the portal beneath is flanked by recesses with tabernacle-work in an extraordinary pure, but fragile "Classical" style. The architect had obviously studied the Late Renaissance ("Mannerist Architecture") and among other things, remembered the middle loggia (ascribed to Michelangelo) in the Villa di Papa Giulio [353]. By a remarkable freak of fate the Hieronymites' *coenobium,* which gives the impression of being a refined ecclesiastical country seat, was to be the home of a king of Spain. When Carlos IV was driven from the throne by Napoleon and took refuge in Rome, he acquired the monastery of S. Alessio, which had been dissolved three years previously by the French, and lived here for a short period as a royal hermit in the truest Habsburg fashion.

S. S. Marcellino e Pietro, on the corner between the Via Merulana and the Via Labicana, also tried to simplify its style by assuming archaic guise. It was erected 1751–1752 following a design by Girolamo Theodoli [354]. The dome in particular shows that the Marchese felt which way the wind was blowing. On the outside it is built up of concentric rings of bead moulding. This squat monster had nothing to do with Baroque, nor – in spite of what people may say – with Borromini [355]. Theodoli aimed at the ideal; he copied the stepping at the base of the Pantheon's low dome but went no further, content to stop in the run-up to his jump. His peculiar product looked like a cross between a pear and a Dutch cheese. In a way, this zealous dilettante deserves recognition for having failed so splendidly in a sphere in which others have since been successful by merely copying. The linked pilasters of the church's front are terribly hard and flat, this was considered moral. Only the four shafts of red granite standing guard at the entrance and bearing the arms of Lambertini have complete dignity. They really do stem from Antiquity.

None of these works, which each in its own way wished to succeed by looking backwards, pointed the way forward, neither towards a greater art nor a living "Neo-Classicism". S. Apollinare bordered on the "Classical" only by being negative, like a metal memorial tablet. The plan could not be reduced any more without ending up as calligraphy. S. Dorotea is swallowed up by the street which nurtures it. S. S. Marcellino e Pietro started the rebirth of the dome in innocent ignorance, and S. Alessio resigned as a house of veneration in order to find favour as an ecclesiastical mansion. Only two big places of worship in Benedict XIV's later years aspired to approach the sublime beyond the Baroque. How revealing that both these works leaned on ruins for support, and one of them also by exploiting Michelangelo.

As mentioned earlier, Fontana had worked on some projects for a mighty religious complex in the Colosseum at the end of the 17th century. Fifty years later this idea became something of a reality, although in a much reduced form. The Jubilee Year of 1750 provided the occasion for erecting a circle of separate altars and a chapel (S. Maria della Pietà) with living accommodation for a hermit, who took it upon himself to keep an eye on the site during any pause in his meditations. It was consecrated by Benedict XIV in 1756 before an enormous audience [356]. Now pilgrims and other devout people could follow their Via Dolorosa by doing the round in the large oval arena. It was unfortunate that the "Stations", the stone altars, had such a likeness to articles of furniture; they were built as plain as wardrobes at the back (Pl. 28). To Madame Du Boccage, who viewed them through her lorgnette in 1757, they looked like sentry boxes [357]. Having entered the arena thinking only of lions, this change of ideas was most unwelcome.

The authoress, on the other hand, declared herself greatly edified by the sight of the interior of *S. Maria degli Angeli,* a part of Diocletian's thermae, and thereby made herself the mouthpiece for the enlightened of the time. "Love of Antiquity, which has captured my imagination," she wrote, "has captivated me to such an extent that I prefer this great temple to the magnificent St. Peter's, the interior of which seems to me to be far too decorative" [358]. Pope Benedict was of the same opinion and expressed it with polemic vigour: "Fuga, at great expense, has turned a great basilica (S. Maria Maggiore) into a barn, the Carthusians, with few resources, have turned a barn into a magnificent basilica" [359]. As far as the latter is concerned this may be true, as the church is majestic in size. However, its greatest merits were there before Vanvitelli set his hand to the rebuilding. Antiquity and Michelangelo had created the spatial entity. Vanvitelli's renovation, which took place in 1749, resulted in a different orientation, for he built a new chancel in one of the long sides, and the vaulted transept which now goes across the building, creates an overwhelming effect. He gave strength to the interior by walling up niches and hanging a series of enormous paintings, all of the same height, in imitation of St. Peter's. This veritable gallery of altar pieces included masterpieces by Domenichino, Maratta, Subleyras and Battoni [360]. The interplay between these low-key, but colourful surfaces and the eight mighty antique columns (supplemented by four new ones) is impressive. It was a proud form of spatial interior decoration called forth by the ideas of imperial architecture in the 1750's; it was true Classicism before Neo-Classicism reduced the concept to stucco. In Vanvitelli's low apse, which stands a little above the level of the transept, the two paintings on each side wall are set in frames with cresting and cartouches in French Rococo at the top, and at the end walls of the main body of the church are altar pieces painted *à trompe l'oeil*. But these concessions to the taste of the time mean no breach of faith with the sublimity of the temple. The statue of St. Bruno, the founder of the Carthusian order, which Houdon executed in 1766 [361] and which stands at the exit from the circular vestibule, is completely enigmatic, cold, white and silent [362]. Linking this figure, which stands out like purified nature, ascetic and subtle, with the group of cypresses of the Carthusian monastery, is an architectural work to which the best men of the time ascribed pathos. It was beyond the apprehension of a Winckelmann, truer than Piranesi's visions. Here the architect did not express a style but a Roman art-form.

VIII

Then it was the turn of a Venetian to occupy the papal throne and to try to do it satisfactorily. Clement XIII Rezzonico, who ruled from 1758 to 1769, belonged to a family of the minor aristocracy from Como which had moved to Venice at the beginning of the 17th century. The father of the future pope, a rich banker, did not pay his entrance fee for inclusion in the golden book of patricians until 1687 [363]. Palazzo Rezzonico by the Grand Canal, begun by Longhena and completed about 1750 by Massari, conveys a clear impression of the splendid conditions in which the family lived [364]. All his life, Clement had a gentle yet exceptional air of Venetian *morbidezza* about him. This man, as fat as he was soft-hearted, had the amateur's sensitive instinct for art; beautiful things were a part of his life and were perhaps the only luxury to which this otherwise meek servant of the Church had any inclination. But it was sculpture particularly that appealed to him. When he was Pope he increased the Vatican collections by several famous pieces, one of which was the "Meleager" statue bought in 1770 for 6000 scudi from the Palazzo Pichini [365], and he really felt little regret that no important Roman building ever bore his coat of arms. One gets a hint of Clement XIII as a connoisseur of art when he is seen in two situations – as a private individual in his gallery and as Christ's Vicar. In 1740, de Brosses was admitted to the Palazzo Altemps (north of the Piazza Navona) where the then Cardinal Rezzonico lived, to view some fine antiquities. The master of the house received him affably. Great was our president's surprise when he noticed a relief showing a bacchanalia in which goats and satyrs were on more than friendly terms. It made the otherwise broad-minded de Brosses gasp, and he aired his feelings in a letter to friends at home: "Oh dear, Monsignor Cardinal, to tell the truth, it is a trifle heady in Your Eminence's antichamber!" [366]. Twenty years later this truly pious Pope had metal fig leaves affixed to the statues in the Vatican, and the thanks he got for it were these words by Winckelmann: "Never has there been a more asinine administration in Rome than the present one" [367]. This did not prevent him accepting the post of Keeper of National Antiquities (*Commisario delle Antichità*) three years later (1763) from

149

the same Clement. There were conflicting sides to the character of this easily led Pontifex from the lagoons. When on Maundy Thursday he read aloud from the loggia of St. Peter's the Papal Bull *In Coena Domini* with its condemnation of heretics, he wept bitterly [368]. During the eleven years of his compassionate rule 4000 people were murdered in Rome [369].

The Eternal City now settled down in the afterglow of sensibility. More strongly than ever before did it attract the intellectual and fashionable élite of Europe [370], and so became the noblest sanctuary for culture in the whole world. There was plenty to be sad about. No architecture of importance was created; they only made museums, and that is a bad omen for any civilization wishing to remain alive. At the same time as building was at a standstill, printing presses worked on happily and spewed out treatises on archaelogy. There were far more ladders down into the depths of ruins than scaffolding up against new walls. The smaller the number of new houses, the larger the number of engravings of ruins, the fewer the buildings on the ground, the more works on paper. And the outcome was that Rome was acknowledged as being entirely immortal.

We shall, in an epilogue, examine further this sad state of affairs which emerges clearly during the papacy of the well-meaning Clement XIII and develops even more fatefully in the time of his more immediate successors. For the present it is enough to remember the most important cause of this decadence: the sentimental cult of Antiquity. Pompeii, the city of ruins, which became more and more popular after 1748, was considered to be even more ideal than Rome. Here was nothing but ruins. This did not do the city of the popes any good at all. Architects developed an unhealthy urge to go underground or to dangle below weathered cornices. And the critics got into the unfortunate habit of looking askance at houses still standing in their entirety, and at this most recent heritage which had solid assets but preached no dogma. This Latin had no philological roots in the past.

A spirit of lethargy had in fact developed in Rome's architecture. The symptoms had been present even before 1760. It could be thought that after centuries of inspired work a great need had been met. However,

Rome is forever growing. The unfortunate thing was that the best brains of the time now grew so immensely zealous with regard to the architecture, that with their enthusiasm they paralysed its reduced energy with phrases about the immortal and with interpretations of the past. No wonder that church building declined so completely. The tumble-down temple overshadowed the serviceable church and sapped the confidence of its builder. In 1756, one year after Winckelmann's arrival in Rome and while Benedict XIV was still in office, a mediocre sculptor like Johannes Wiedewelt felt entitled to associate S. Maria Maggiore and S. Croce with "little sugar houses for cake decoration" [371]. He had cultivated a taste. And so had C. A. Ehrensvärd ("Antiquity had taste and we have sought taste"). And yet no doubt, truth dawned on the Swedish Classicist when in 1780, with a sigh of resignation, he made the following remark about the attitude of his age to Antiquity: "Why people are supposed to have had more taste then than they have now nobody knows, and why we must still admire that which we neither intend to, nor can imitate, I have no idea either" [372].

The truth was perhaps that a debilitated art lost itself in daydreams. Impotence begot ideals, moral hypocrisy and a carping spirit – *les vieillards aiment à donner de bons préceptes, pour se consoler de n'être plus en état de mauvais exemples* ...

In the discussion of the building activities of this papacy, these interim remarks are meant to excuse our inability to mention the name of more than one important architect as representing the epoch. One must remember that Rezzonico's period was lived under a tremendous pressure of Church politics, that is the European propaganda against the Jesuits. But also from the narrower angle of politics in art, it will be seen that *Urbs Roma* was faced by a situation of a very paradoxical nature. The official guardian of Roman Antiquity was a German with a poorly developed sense for architecture – Winckelmann. The best architect in Rome was a Venetian who never built a proper house – Piranesi. Deep down in their hearts these two oracles despised one another. The archaeologist and the lithographic artist had pride of place in the drawing office, they were both men of genius. How could any poor earthbound builder be expected to withstand the pressure from these giants?

Giambattista Piranesi (1720–1778) had conquered Rome with his engravings some time before Clement XIII came to the throne [373]. The gloomy *Carceri* series introduced his epic of Rome's magnificence in light and shade, the tragic city of the ancients and the fair metropolis of the moderns. With his *Vedute di Roma* he demonstrated that the papal capital of the Baroque period was also the capital of the world. And with the four large folios entitled *Antichità Romane* (1757) [374] he produced such a monumental record that it made the living city wilt in comparison. Piranesi, Rome's passionate lover, breathed so much pathos into the ruins that he must have frightened himself with all the spirits he conjured up. And like a gravedigger he dug away the foundations from under his own ideal: Rome as an organic and plastic entity. It fell to the lot of this neurasthenic poet to tear down where he wished to build up, to sow the seeds of doubt where he wished to substantiate. If any man in Rome can be called a schismatic, then that man is Piranesi. Neo-Classicism rests fair and square on his shoulders [375]. He taught the age and the world, that dead architecture is of more consequence than living, because it is more beautiful. Only Rome could foster such a fatal illusion – and an artist of Piranesi's daemonic character. A Roman from the Venetian scene . . .

Papa Rezzonico could not possibly increase the fame of his fellow townsman, but his official importance he could. The stormy artist was made a knight in 1767, but he preferred the burin to the sword. In 1760 another Venetian, Giacomo Casanova, had also been given the Order of the Golden Spur, the motto of which was *Praemium Virtuti et Pietati* [376]. The Pope should have provided work for the man who proudly called himself *architetto veneziano* in his publications. Clement was only too willing, for he had a weakness for all Venetians, as Goldoni also found out in Rome [377], and had a personal liking for Piranesi, sharing his mania for Antiquity.

But here too, the Pope had to realize his incapacity. There was no task great enough for an artist who had modelled the whole of Ancient Rome, had investigated and perceived its richness and made it his own. Piranesi could not, in the very nature of things, carry out a small and simple task. He was commissioned to design a high altar for the Lateran Basilica, but it was never carried out [378]. It was Piranesi who presented the Pope with works, buildings in atlas folio. *Delle Magnificenzi ed Architettura dei Romani* (1761) and *Antichità d'Albano e di Castel Gandolfo* (1764) are both dedicated to Clement XIII. When the members of the Conclave were to assemble after the Pope's death in 1769, Piranesi was obviously in charge of the preparations for their quarters in the Vatican. The greatest cicerone of Imperial and Papal Rome showed a young German painter around this temporary structure of boarding set beneath Michelangelo's "Last Judgment" [379].

While Clement XIII was on the papal throne, only one church of any standing was given form, and a poor one at that. We refer here to S. Lucia del Gonfalone, which was renovated 1761–1765 for a fraternity, according to a design by Marco David [380]. The front is quite stereotyped, a product of superannuated ideas. Few notice it, nobody remembers it. One small church had the good fortune to be decorated during Clement's reign on the initiative of his brother's son Giambattista Rezzonico, Grand Prior of the Knights of Malta. This was the order's church on the Aventine. And it had the good fortune to get into Piranesi's hands. No work could be more typical of the stage reached in the 1760's than *S. Maria del Priorato*. In the first place the church has such a picturesque situation that it seems designed for the special edification of sensitive souls (Pl. 60). The church stands on the outermost point of the Aventine hill and can, by some stretch of the imagination, be taken for a baronial castle; it is surrounded by the sighing of palms of an unusually proud stature. Also, as we know, the renovation of the church was left to a sorcerer whose greatest wish it was to give it an antiquated appearance. Piranesi the poet almost succeeded.

His compatriot Algarotti once said that everywhere else ruins become ruins by themselves, except in Venice, where they were constructed (*par tout ailleurs les ruines se font d'elles mêmes, à Venise on les bâtit*) [381]. This bon mot about Venetian architecture may well be applied to Piranesi's only achievement as an architect in Rome. He did not, of course, erect an artificial ruin, but he did something even more suspect – he fabricated a building which according to all temporal laws should by this time have looked like a genuine ruin. He had begun by building castles in the air in the smouldering atmosphere of Venice, now at last, the time had come when he was to use stone and mortar on the very hill where Hercules stole the oxen from Cacus. The front became nothing but a confused suspension of Antique and Egyptian ornaments looking as if they were nailed to the wall. In the white interior of the church, Piranesi showed himself to be an architectural artist by using lighting effects in the chancel, which isolate it with the cold illumination of a stage. Behind the coup de théâtre we see Palladio's magic [382]. It took Il Redentore in Venice to show the Aventine church, meant for a decaying Order of Knights, what Roman pathos really was.

> *For God's sake, let us sit upon the ground*
> *And tell sad stories of the deaths of kings.*
> SHAKESPEARE, RICHARD II

IX

The last chapter in the history of the decline and fall of Roman church building began around 1770. No Gibbon felt pain at watching this decay. A great tradition, without equal in the world, went to its grave amid the scornful laughter of all who witnessed it, the artists especially. Their sorrow was only felt for those places of worship which had been standing in ruins for thousands of years. The square in front of S. Maria del Priorato was like a churchyard in which one bade farewell in elegiac style to the living, struggling Rome of true believers, then to go forth purified towards lofty aims with that bold gait which can, at times, be a characteristic of mourners still in rude health.

Beyond these crossroads we need not identify popes with their new churches, for none of them have any claim to our attention. Clement XIV Ganganelli (1769–1774), one of the most pure figures of the Holy See, sank under the burden of responsibility which the abolition of the Society of Jesus had laid upon him. His most favourite place of worship was perhaps the woods around the Castel Gandolfo where he, the son of a doctor, delighted to botanize. And his successor Pius VI Braschi (1775–1799), who wished to cut the figure of a Renaissance prince, gained nothing but invective for his additions to Michelangelo's St. Peter's; this, after all, could only be regarded as a commendable resolution and a dignified task. No great architect was in despair because he had nothing to do. Piranesi wandered around in Rome like a soothsayer whose prophesies had come true. He now welcomed adulation, sometimes playing the part of a *père noble,* at others snarling like a wounded lion. It was in 1771 that Mrs Millar said of him that when he was in a good temper he was extremely helpful, informative and amiable to strangers; in England he would be called "a humorist", hence unreliable and fickle. To get on with him you needed to be acquainted with his oddities [383].

Three years later Bergeret, that connoisseur of art, visited this important person, looked at his beloved collections and noted quite drily: "He sells his antiques to the highest bidder" [384]. Roland de la Platière, whose visit to Piranesi took place in 1778 [385], had even less of an opinion of him: he imparts to objects a stronger emphasis than Nature herself, his burin is not always trustworthy, his aim has been to reveal Antiquity without the help of a spade (sacrilege!), he employed a pen with that heaviness and ignorance peculiar to him, said many fatuous things and amassed a great fortune. His conclusion was: "Shoemaker stick to your last!" So that was all the prophet got for his trouble. But nobody saw any reason to deplore the terrible taste in interior decoration which this fine talent made universally fashionable by his decorative engravings. And hardly anybody failed to appreciate the decorations by which Piranesi and his imitators put Antiquity to shame indoors. Clérisseau with the help of the paintbrush turned Père Le Sueur's cell in the Trinità dei Monti monastery into a completely different cella, such as would be found in a ruined temple with a leaky roof. The learned mathematician's pate was exposed to the winds of heaven, but no divine eye watched from above. This delusion could well be reminiscent of "Happy Cottage, T. & M. Plornish" in "Little Dorrit". Piranesi himself is supposed to have made sketches for such foolery in the Villa Malta, for M. de Reteuil, the Knights Templars' ambassador [386].

Is it surprising that the ecclesiastical enthusiasts for Antiquity, whose initial introduction to ruins was in the first instance a flight amid storm and stress from the empty church, should so soon feel at home among them? P. Le Sueur had the illusion brought indoors for his constant delectation. While the familiar, faithful Roman churches seemed slowly to become overgrown with mould, the presentient world from the heathen past was gradually vulgarized into an archaeological promenade for the clergy as well:

> *Les prêtres fortunes foulent d'un pied tranquille*
> *Les tombeaux des Cantons et la cendre d'Emile*

In which buildings then could one erect new altars for the gods of the Papal State and Christianity? Those of Antiquity were now beautiful ruins; behind the mutilated walls scholarship had supplanted the choir. It was hardly possible to erect new houses of prayer, for though they might be in one piece they were neither beautiful nor mysterious. And mysterious they had to be. When Harsdorff was in Rome (1762–1763), where he struggled with the problem of "the noble church", he asked in despair: "Where among all Rome's modern churches can one find anything that can be considered a pattern and which can satisfy the dictates of true art? Where is the mystery?" [387].

It is possible to evaluate Rome's relationship with the visible church in the period 1770–1790 by taking the measure of two buildings, the Colosseum and St. Peter's, those monuments in whose shadow an active past has chosen to try its strength since Bernini's death. It will be remembered that after 1750, Benedict XIV had consecrated the Colosseum for religious usage and intended it to be the biggest church in Rome.

It appeared however that the past of the shaken and hard-tried ruin as a playground for unsavoury elements could not be exorcised from the soil, no matter how many crosses were put up, and that the hermit did not really prove equal to the task, for soon the arena, drenched in the blood of martyrs, became once more *le rendez-vous des filles de mauvaise vie*. Then at the beginning of 1770, big divine services with confessions and the distribution of indulgences were held within the oval. But it was still nothing but a circus. Scandalous incidents took place [388], and as they gradually died down, the ecclesiastical props arranged in a circle merely became a frame for burlesques and sentimental tableaux (Pl. 28).

To the first type belonged the weekly sermons of the Capuchins. A monk expiated on the catechism to the assembled gang of half-civilized beggars and guttersnipes who like monkeys expressed their feelings with grimaces [389]. Sensitive individuals were edified by this, for no tourist could resist a ragamuffin lost in prayer by the light of the moon or torches, nor could he forget the *salade à la ruine* which he enjoyed in the hermit's little vegetable garden [390]. The hermit's hut itself, built in conjunction with a chapel, was just as charming as "Pensieroso" and the other Gothic summer-houses in the romantic gardens of the age [391]. When Goethe in 1787 mentions the pious man's "Kirchelchen" [392] and his friend Moritz in the same year speaks of the hermit's "artiges Stübchen" [393] we realize from the caressing diminutives alone that the disposition spoke to the heart. Goethe revelled in the idyll in the Colosseum. But William Beckford (1780) was seized by a violent urge to pulverize the whole of this circle of saintly nests and chapels, and visualized with amusement how the fat clerics would make a lion's mouth water [394]. The Englishman was exclusive. He wanted the place to himself. The Colosseum could provide those of an elegiac inclination with everything they wanted. Here was Antiquity in unrivalled magnificent decay, here was a febrile plant growth, here was a gruesome past, here were bells calling to prayer and childlike piety, here bandits could lurk in every cave. The moon did its duty and the curious brought their own torches.

Canon Meyer from Hamburg had good reason to note that there was no more fertile place for artists in Rome than this amphitheatre and its vaulted, half-collapsed passages, out of whose ruins grew luxuriant shrubs. By day there was a feeling of exultation, by night of horror [395]. Frederik Münter, later Bishop of Sealand, was just as delighted with the theme, "the uncertain light and the hard shadows gave an aura of infinity" [396]. For a couple of generations after 1780, painters found a rich "repertoire" within the walls of the arena. The Danes J. P. Lund and Eckersberg show in their studies of the Colosseum that the Baroque additions were of particular interest. A drawing by Hubert Robert was reproduced in an aquatint by J. B. Mornet and given this cumbersome title: "While the hermit of the Colosseum prostrates himself in prayer two young girls are robbing him of the flowers decorating his painting of the Madonna" [397]. This is the vignette, delicate and sweet, which concludes the long chapter of the Church's struggle with the greatest memorial to Antiquity.

Thus Benedict XIV's church under the open sky was overtaken by a curious fate. In Clement XI's day the place might have been tamed. Now it was too late. By daylight, the hunting ground of the ejected whores became the reserve for models and a religious centre for lacrymose *beaux-esprits*. In the darkness, Nature returned with all its magic. Here was the end of a true *Via Crucis*. The arena was under the spell of its mighty past, and the church was overwhelmed by the ruins. Had not the mass itself been transformed into an overgrown hollow like Lake Nemi's volcanic crater?

The last great ecclesiastical work of our period suffered a sad fate. *The Sacristy of St. Peter's,* erected 1776–1780, according to a design by Marchionni, Villa Albani's architect [398], was dwarfed by the proximity of the basilica. It was meant to be an annex on the lines of a treasury and to serve as a palace for the high and mighty canons. Marchionni did right to flatten the dome and reduce his building by graduation, giving it a certain amount of individuality by siting it at the end of the two galleries which connect it with the basilica itself. His artistic skill lies in this well-calculated distribution of mass, not in the details of the façade. The reward for his insight was an unprecedented scathing criticism. The Classicists, who had lost all feeling for architectural tact and sense of situation, and who cried out for an indivisible monument with a temple façade, dismembered Marchionni's work with their criticism. Palmstedt, who watched the sacristy being constructed (1779–1780), calls it a monstrosity and a catalogue of all offences against taste [399]. His immediate successors among cultured travellers described it as a sugar-loaf and a doll's house, a mess and a pustular boil [400]. Civilized Romans scorned Pius for this *coglioneria* by the cathedral of St. Peter's.

In our day we do not regard the sacristy as a piece of architecture which stands or falls on its own merits. We see this straw-coloured creation as a piece of controlled nature which enfolds us on our walk at the foot af the basilica. We saw the top from the Campagna. Now at close quarters we realize – and this feeling gives us great happiness – that the church cares nothing for our snap judgments.

CONVENTS AND MONASTERIES

> *C'est une belle chose que Rome pour tout oublier,*
> *pour mépriser tout, et pour mourir*
> CHATEAUBRIAND TO Mme RECAMIER, 1819

I

There is a strange, inaccessible town looking across the roofs of Rome, an airy city of balconies and belvederes. Down in the streets is another special world. The houses are widely distributed, included among others, but as an entity this collection of remarkable buildings is just as exclusive as the lofty district of roof loggias. By this we mean the community of religious houses, "a different Rome", withdrawn from the world.

It has been estimated that in 1709, the Papal capital had approximately 148,000 inhabitants. Of these 3556 were monks and 1814 nuns, in all 5370 cenobites [1]. That is to say, the ratio of the inhabitants of religious houses to the total population of Rome was 1:28. The mathematician Lalande arrived at a similar statistical result in 1765 [2]. In other words, every twenty-eighth person who lived in the Rome of the 18th century belonged to a monastery or a convent. This is a considerable percentage. In absolute terms 5–6000 people were in those days quite a number to accomodate [3]. Around the middle of the century they monopolized about 140 religious foundations, some of which of course were on a large scale. The figures quoted are exact. According to the index of Nolli's very accurate map from 1748, there were then 135 religious houses, of which 128 were connected to churches. This figure is in close agreement with the information in the index to Venuti's exhaustive description of Rome from 1766, which gives 145 such institutions in all, 102 for monks and 43 for nuns. The term religious house, is here to be taken in the wider sense, for it also covered community houses for members of congregations (e. g. Jesuits) and various academies (places of education under strict monastic discipline), but not the residences for communities of "secular" clerics, such as the Penitents or the canons who served large churches.

Those cenobites of the segregated Rome who did go out – many nuns never or very rarely did – were very much a part of the street scene. And their houses, which only very few other people ever entered, were an extraordinary distinctive feature in the city as a whole. They were so imposing on their sites that they have essentially determined the face of Rome – and still do to some extent. For that, if for no other reason, the cloisters deserve careful study.

However, Rome's numerous religious houses have for so long remained a closed book as far as the history of art is concerned. Workers in this field usually come up against a brick wall. Our knowledge of the finer points of the architecture of these buildings is thus of necessity very limited, particularly in respect of Late Baroque, and this is a great pity, since Roman monastic architecture from various points of view is of considerable interest. Perhaps it only rarely presents particular merits individually, although the best masters of Baroque were there for the asking. But in general the important community houses were examples of a special aesthetic form.

For the very reason that the genre of the monastery is so unambigious, its secrets should be penetrated. These austere buildings are likely to work out their own special problem with the greatest possible economy of architectural effects. The portal of the church is high and the door wide, appealing with pride to the beholder's feeling for beauty, and inviting him in to the solemn ceremonies. The palace is at liberty to raise its voice in the street, announcing the power of its owner. But the monastery is under strict discipline on all occasions. It is enclosed on principle, by nature subdued, since its only vocation is to conceal nameless people in a communal dwelling. And so the situation is that the cellular houses of the cenobites, which according to the general opinion among Protestants of our day are mere relics from a dark past, in reality express the purest functionalism and in the final analysis may be considered in essence and character the most up to date buildings which the Baroque period has bequeathed to us. Such buildings have no direct appeal. Architectural criticism of earlier days completely neglected the Spartan barracks for monks and nuns, and, to tell the truth, these provided little pabulum for a more detailed analysis of style. However, our modern age ought to be able to appreciate such basic expression in any building of a social nature, and in consequence pay respect to Baroque's biggest monuments to collective living.

We shall discuss the influence of traditional monastery architecture on the development of Rome's apartment houses in a later chapter. For the present, while examining this sector, prominence will be given to the most important of its type, characteristic features of the special idiom of the cloisters will be noted and the effect of religious houses in the prospect of the city will be dealt with briefly.

Like the church buildings the monasteries and convents differ widely within the strict limits of their purpose. Some of them are so age-old, despoiled by nondescript additions, that no architectural style at all can be ascribed to them. They seem more related to organic formations, such as cliffs honeycombed with caves, or giant oaks, rotting and misshapen with age. It is impossible to look upon such worm-eaten religious houses without feeling perturbed. Their mere exteriors have nourished phantasies about *Les Secrets de Rome* [4], which Romanticism engendered in rivalry with *Les Mystères de Paris*. This group of venerable and decayed monasteries provides a gloomy background to rational building activities after 1600.

Rome's monasteries from the period of Late Baroque vary both from the religious and the social point of view. The greatly divergent character of the various monastic orders was apparent in the buildings. The aristocratic Theatines' requirements in respect of external merit and internal comfort were vastly different from the ordinary, friendly simplicity of the Capuchins. Listen to what a friar said of the Theatines in 1709: "In spite of its strict poverty the order has larger and more magnificent monasteries than any other in Italy" [5]. Granted, our informant was a Dominican and fairly critical in his opinions of his colleagues in other communities, but anybody can see that the house of the Theatines of S. Andrea della Valle has a façade which in its proportions is as simple as it is exquisite, and it commands much respect. On the other hand, the Capuchins "who are poor in another way" built systematically in the most humble manner. In the past, their monastery in the Piazza Barberini showed this clearly. Now it has been severely reduced, but in the 1760's this large complex housed about 300 monks within its bare walls [6]. But it was not repellant. These brown-hooded friars, for the most part sons of the people, surrounded their gaunt house with an air of joviality. Benedict XIV, always astute, had doubts about most of the orders, and only the Capuchins received unconditional praise from him, and that is why in 1743 he ordained that the Papal Court Chaplain (*Predicatore Apostolico*) should in the future always be a Capuchin [7], and this has since been the case. Even such a rancorous anti-cleric writer as Gorani had to admit that these mendicant friars enjoyed universal affection – but in his opinion unjustly, for they were thieves, the lot of them. "As a result," he remarks, "their monasteries look like those caves in which brigands gather to strip travellers to the buff" [8]. The fatuous demagogue saw only what he wanted to see, Pope Benedict, respected by Voltaire, knew what he was about. Of course an opinion like Gorani's gradually won a hearing, and in the century of liberalism it was particularly the Capuchins' decorated grave cellars that Lutheran tourists seized upon, making the whole establishment into a sort of ecclesiastical mortuary. This has been dealt with by various writers.

Nowadays we need only state without any bias, that the Capuchins quite obviously lived in great poverty and that their domestic requirements were extremely modest. Their monasteries may not have been surrounded by the halo of all the virtues, but they diffused the light of poverty, although they smelt terribly. According to Münter the Capuchin monastery in Tivoli was unique in that it did not stink [9]. And the popular revivalist preachers, who went forth from their Roman centre, left a trail of cheerful and earthy stories on the way to their dismal domicile. It is worth noting that a collection of anecdotes entitled "Capuchin Recreations" (1738) [10], which was by no means meant to increase the reputation of the brown-cowled friars, actually improved their image, for the tall stories are either entirely harmless, or salted with a humour not always possessed by missionaries. There were more ha'pence than kicks. Had the Capuchins occasioned no other popular legends than this cycle of picaresque tales, they would have been enough to show what rough and ready members of the Franciscan family they were. And although the Capuchins were selected scapegoats for the Church's castigators on the wrong side of the Alps, they also helped to give a more pleasant but equally false impression of monastic life by providing Northern painters in Thorvaldsen's day and later artists with countless droll and pathetic subjects. These words may serve to help you reflect before condemning a shabby monastery wall.

A monastic order with even stricter rules – the Carthusians, had completely different requirements in the way of buildings. What was called severity in the Piazza Barberini was merely a bad joke in *la Certosa* and vice versa, in more ways than one. The Carthusian was always a loner, the Capuchin a mixer. The former was lord of all he surveyed in his own little dwelling within the framework of the institution, and was more or less a hermit within the community. This had been so since the first beginnings of the order. The division of the houses into cells had already been laid down by statute in 1134. Since the days of St. Bruno the Carthusians' rules have never been modified on any essential point, and the order is the only one that has never been reformed [11]. Its monasteries had to be on a grand scale and to some extent became imposing, since the rows of cells required a lot of space. But every single room had a minimum of size and comfort. If we look into the pantry of the Carthusians, we find here a parallel to their studied asceticism in the buildings they erected, for the White Friars were exemplary in their frugal food regulations. They ate only fish, plus various cereal and egg dishes, but never touched meat and only one sort of game-bird was permitted them, namely teal. These birds live on fish [12]. The Carthusians' very special blocks of cells are no more likely to appear in the codex of architecture than teal would on a menu. Nobody can deny that a sustained and enforced diet of both specialities would demand considerable resignation.

We need not point out that the Carthusian's lonely meal, supplied through a hatch in the door, was at no time brightened up by the product, which for many is the best claim the order has to recognition in the outside world, namely the liqueur called Chartreuse (*Elixir végétal de la Grande Chartreuse*). Monks of other orders have also produced such distillations of high quality, for example *Padri dell' acquavita* made by the Jesuates [13] (not to be confused with the Jesuits, the Fathers of the Society of Jesus), while in our days the Trappists produce a eucalyptus liqueur which is well thought of by many. But the Carthusians' decoction of wild herbs is particularly in character with this order. Its nature was at one and the same time contemplative and rustic; you might say that this mixture exudes a mature aroma [14]. The order's houses may well have been forbidding, but were also ennobled by a chilling discipline which is close to aestheticism. It is significant that in the Roman monastery near S. Maria degli Angeli, the corridors through the arcades of the courtyard are not embellished with colourful paintings, but the walls are covered with fine engravings and maps [15], an exclusively black and white decoration. Francisco Miranda, later the liberator of Venezuela, who visited the monastery in 1786, remarked on this feature [16].

The contrast between the world of the Brown Friars and that of the White is also significant when we realize that the buildings of the two orders were used as background for widely divergent figures in literature. Hans Andersen made his little improvisator grow up in the care of a fine Capuchin and become a spiritual foster-son of the monastery in the Piazza Barberini and a choirboy in its church. This all sounds very idyllic; decadent Romanticism exulted in sepulchres, the somewhat skeletal interior of a church was even felt to be "charming" – and thus this pious genre picture introduced its figures: Bødtcher's cowled monks, Pater Joseph, the monk with his toothache . . .

But the Carthusians' houses attracted the passionate characters, rebels and negators – Miranda, a dictator in embryo, belonged to this type. The Swedish statesman Gustav Adolf Reuterholm, the "equal of tyrants", had himself depicted (in an engraving by Francesco Piranesi) sitting in the great courtyard of the Roman Certosa in the moonlight and beneath tall sighing cypresses [17]. And Stendhal was on to a good thing when he chose the title *La Chartreuse de Parme* for his new novel, for although this imaginary monastery plays a minor role, its very name aroused tense anticipation and provided the hero in the book with a noble exit. The monastery may be remembered as a mausoleum for Fabrice del Dongo and is a frame for his energetic character. For Stendhal *La Chartreuse* was just an idea synonymous with a grand institution. As a young man in Grenoble he had lived close to the mother house and centre of this order and it had made a great impression on him. Stendhal may have expressed contempt for two of the order's most famous monasteries in Italy. To him *la Certosa* in Pavia was nothing but a "sugar-loaf" [18], the buildings in Florence "a satire" and its eighteen "fakirs" ought to be thrown into gaol, and the whole institution turned into Tuscany's major prison [19]. Nevertheless by giving his novel a Carthusian label this stubborn atheist improved the chances of his book. Its redeeming feature in Rome was that the name of that Titan, Michelangelo, was connected with the monastery [20].

Finally Taine, whose insight was extraordinary, brought out very strongly the Capuchin-Carthusian antithesis by basing it on the Roman buildings themselves. The cloisters of the Brown Friars are full of bad portraits, and here a strange gaiety is prevalent among the bones and the edifying posters – "we need to breathe a different air" – and he hurries to S. Maria degli Angeli to relax in the courtyard: "I believe that there are few things on earth so great yet so plain; the utter simplicity, so rare in Rome's architecture, makes a unique and unforgettable impression" [21].

A special category of cenobites, namely the priests regular (*clerici regulares*) were more likely to live in community houses which in type resembled a canon's residence (*canonica*). Nobody could confuse a formal "professed house" for Jesuits with the sealed-up wing in which Franciscan sisters of strict observance spent their lives.

But there was a hierarchy that cut across that of the order's own. Some convents enjoyed a certain fame merely because of the rank of their members, since only ladies of the aristocracy were accepted. The rigorous laws of the order were to some extent cross-bred with the rules of court-like etiquette. The opposite extreme is represented by convents used as houses of correction for female sinners in more ways than one. So Roman convents can range between two such vastly different types of building as the aristocratic pension and the actual prison. Whether the Lord God, who divides the sheep from the goats, will in due course readjust these conditions, is a moot point. Anyhow – from the point of view of architectural history we children of dust have plenty of types to operate with between the palace and the prison.

We shall first deal briefly with a few selected examples of both fashionable, and humble, almost wretched convents. We must at once point out that the rank of those living the cloistered life was in many cases in inverse ratio to their lodging. The most elevated convent in Rome, the *Tor' de' Specchi* in the Piazza Campitelli was, and still is, established in the most squalid of all buildings. The more high-born the nobility the less likely to worry about outward appearances, so they say. Gloria superba twines best on broken columns. As far as neglect is concerned, Tor' de' Specchi came up to all probable expectations. This irregular group of sad-looking buildings stems from the Middle Ages [22] and looks like it to an almost exaggerated degree. The few barred windows are like deep caves in a cliff face, set haphazardly, and the whole complex stands like a walled-up sepulchre, though not a whited one, even more suspicious-looking now when the creation of the boulevard Via del Teatro di Marcello has given an unimpeded view to one side of the building; in spite of the sunlight, the masonry seems frozen. But inside the convent things were brighter, orange trees appeared in the courtyards, and in the nuns' cells one could find flowers, birds and complicated toys as evidence that innocent pleasures were encouraged – as we learn from an English lady at a later date [23]. Dickens would smile if he knew, and think of Mr Pecksniff's daughters.

The convent of Tor' de' Specchi was founded here in 1433 by S. Francesca Romana (died 1440), and it has remained here ever since, a somewhat unique instance in Rome [24]. The nuns, who are called Oblates (i. e. those who have given themselves to God) and who make neither vows nor are subject to sequestration, are – as Vasi says [25] – "exclusively virgins of Rome's highest aristocracy who observe chastity, poverty and obedience". When a pope of the Rococo period paid them and their *Presidente* (for this was what the abbess was called) a formal visit, the little alley was blocked by richly gilded coaches of the aristocracy [26].

The convent of the Benedictine nuns of *S. Lucia in Selci* on the Esquiline, also housed "the happy few" in a building of the most lugubrious appearance. It still exists – for the moment anyhow, for this district is due for clearance – and is a grim lesson to all visitors from the North, even the most hard-boiled, as they pass by [27]. The architecture would have been just the thing for Sir Walter Scott when describing some hair-raising deed or other. The convent wings of *S. Cecilia in Trastevere,* particularly the building to the left in the forecourt (Pl. 62) are also very forbidding; behing these gratings sat little countesses, their minds in secret turmoil. Maria Clementina, the titular queen of Great Britain, retired here to this place in the 1720's, because living with her husband, the Old Pretender, had become unbearable [28].

A young maiden of the nobility, who had taken the veil, ended up here, and one day when the family was visiting burst out in her distress: "I am a despairing nun and my soul is damned, for I am unable to forgive my father." This admission was made as late as the 1840's; a small boy never forgot his aunt's words and included them in his memoirs, published in 1944 [29]. The spirit of the Middle Ages enveloping these very aristocratic houses of correction was even more oppressive in Benedict XIV's time, although the gloom of asceticism could now and then be pierced by a glimpse of the fashionable way of life which still held good in that epoch. Our informant, mentioned above, who because he had lived so long was able to give evidence of the tragedy, so remote in time, that he had witnessed in the aristocratic convent, also remembered that his aunt Olimpia in another select and strict religious house (S. Lorenzo in Panisperna) always had to speak through two close-meshed screens in the *parlatorio,* and these were furthermore set 70 cm (28″) apart in the wall, the outer screen being provided with sharp projecting points, and during Advent and Lent the poor wretch was moreover hidden behind a curtain [30]. The screen was obligatory in the parlour of all convents, and, as far as is known, still exists in places. In a vigorous apologia for the situation in Rome, published by Baretti in 1770, who particularly polemizes against the distorted view tourists had of convent life, he says straight out: "The screen is generally double and very close-meshed. Only in Venice can a hand be passed through the iron bars, but the Venetian screens have ruined the nuns' reputation in this city" [31]. With good cause, Père Labat describes the screen as a *machine* which was invented "to strengthen the sex's frail virtue or to counter it" [32].

But of course, parallel with communities of aristocratic nuns in decaying buildings there were also "noble foundations", whose buildings were in the main up to date and which made as much show a possible, encouraging elegant sociability. This was true of the convent of the Benedictine nuns in *Campo Marzio* and above all of the Dominican nuns' palatial edifice by *S. S. Dominico e Sisto*. The fashionable church with its ostentatious horseshoe-shaped stairway was like a *corps de logis;* to one side stood the large building for the ladies, and in front, a splendid courtyard behind a fine portal invited entrance. Lalande found the stairway handsome but out of place, its shape being more suitable for a park. On the basis of his French ideas about *bienséance* in architecture he may well be right [33]. This ecclesiastical edifice standing there on the corner of Largo Magnanapoli and Via Panisperna – a quiet, well-kept street – with the majestic garden wall of the Villa Aldobrandini and the Casino as neighbours, is a proud sight, if a feudal one. It is possibly the only one of its type in Rome which by its outline reminds us of a princely German abbey. Nowadays, when Magnanapoli has been widened and the square crowned with lovely palms, the former residence for pious women (now the Collegium Angelicum) has become even more impressive than before in the configuration of the city.

The convent accepted only maidens of noble birth and exclusively those brides of Christ who brought with them rich dowries, "so it is no wonder that it is the richest convent in Rome" [34]. On December 5th 1726, a troup of tightrope walkers were invited to entertain "certain nuns of S. Domenico's order who are nearly all princesses (*principesse*)"; presumably these were the sisters in this very convent. The acrobats "performed inside the building, where the ladies had had a little stage erected at their own expense, while Princess Borghese took it upon herself to pay the tumblers". It caused a general scandal, for not only were these strolling players let in, but for some considerable time carpenters and other artisans had moved freely about the sanctuary in order to put up the stage [35]. But after all, it is nice to think that the nuns' cheeks glowed red with pleasure merely at seeing the players' white faces.

Another convent for Dominican nuns, situated opposite the one just mentioned and flanked by *S. Caterina da Siena,* had similar social pretensions. When Innocent XIII paid it a visit in 1721, he was accompanied as a matter of course by the "Princesses of the Blood", that is by his relations, Princess Acquasparta (the Pope's sister) and the Princesses Cesarini and Ruspoli [36]. They felt perfectly at home in the company they found inside the walls. In 1706, the exiled Queen of Poland had persuaded those nuns with some life still left in them to play-act; they fared better than the sisters of the convent in the Campo Marzio a year later, for the abbess of this convent fell from grace [37]. The convent of S. Caterina possessed an antiquity of the first rank within its precincts, that is the Torre delle Milizie. The religious house clung to its base just as Mary Magdalene did to the foot of the cross on Golgatha. The good ladies used this unique tower for relaxation and amusement, and who would begrudge them this small pleasure? On the occasion of the election of Clement XII in 1730 they let off fireworks from the top of the tower [38], and at other times they used its platform as a watch-tower. It was certainly Rome's highest belvedere (present height is about 51 metres). The ladies may have forsaken the world, but at least they made sure of a splendid bird's eye view of the earth-bound creatures below. For this reason the steps of the tower were made more negotiable in 1728, following a design by Clemente Orlandi; the prioress, Maria Costanza Bolognetti, had asked advice of another noble, the architect Marchese Theodoli [39].

Sequestration was very strict in this nunnery, and in the middle of the 19th century it was the rule that the convent could only be entered by male persons five times a year. The regulation must have been at least as strict a hundred years earlier. From this it is obvious that only very few eye-witnesses, apart from the highest ranking clergy, could report their impressions of this closed community. One such privileged, naturally a diplomat, was Baron Schlözer, who has left some notes about his visit in 1866. I assume they can also cast some light on the atmosphere inside the building as it was around 1750; it is doubtful if such circles moved with the times.

Cardinal Hohenlohe read mass in one of the private chapels for all the twenty-five nuns dressed in their white habits, "all fine elderly ladies, most of whom took the veil 15–20 years ago, and since then have never left their convent [40]. After mass", continues Herr von Schlözer, "the whole company went into a large hall, where we took chocolate with them and spoke to every one of them. In spite of their secluded life they were all extremely direct, talked a great deal, told stories, laughed and repeatedly assured me that they felt not the slightest desire to come into contact again with the outside world ... They giggled immoderately every time I told them how little taste and understanding I had for such a religious life (fine example of Prussian tact) and always received in reply: *C'è la vocazione!"* [41]. A worthy retort.

The Augustine nuns in the *convent of S. Marta* were no fools either and according to Père Helyot they belonged to the very highest stratum of society [42]. They had only taken simple vows, but never went out. This sacrifice was alleviated by the fact that the nuns to a certain extent kept open house. "They received visitors in salons without the restriction of gratings," says D'Orbessan in 1750, "and did the honours at their assemblies with the same easy manner as would a hostess in one of Rome's most splendid houses" [43]. Rome's governor took care that uninvited intruders, including monks, did not gain access to the reception rooms of such foundations. The Commissioner of Police (*il bargello*) and his minions (*sbirri*) had to be on their toes to catch any miscreants. "But there are certain convents full of princesses and ladies of high rank where the *bargello* dares not show himself, for he would be the victim of nasty and unpleasant incidents if he molested a man of the church in these precincts" [44]. This little detail, handed down by a Dominican, confirms in no uncertain terms how well the sisterhoods of the nobility were protected. It may also demonstrate how the chastity of these virgins was respected. In 1704 a disreputable Frenchman tried to abduct a nun from the convent of S. Marta, but without success, and it is to be hoped that such a shameful plot was not repeated. The rascal, 16 years old, was put to the torture, confessed and was executed [45].

Another elegant congregation of nuns was the Oblates' *dei Sette Dolori*, approved by Clement X in 1671. The founder was Donna Virginia Farnese, the Duchess of Latera. The "Convent of the Seven Sorrows" accepted only noble ladies who because of ill health could not find refuge elsewhere [46]. The convent thus functioned as a sort of upper-class nursing home. The sisters in attendance were probably of common stock. The appearance of the church and convent compares well with the Oblates' circumstances, for the façade, a masterpiece by Borromini [47], is based on a great sovereign gesture, the concave movement. On the other hand the façade is interrupted, sedate in its development, its subtlety suppressed, all hardened into a mask, yet imposing. The handmaidens of Madonna's Seven Sorrows have hidden Borromini's crumbling face behind a wall and the sequestration is still so inexorable that not even the church can be entered [48]. When on rare occasions the ladies left their pious pension to go for a drive in a closed carriage, they pulled a black hood over the white wimple to be on the safe side [49].

Among the monasteries there were hardly any that could be said to belong to a fashionable category, this being the prerogative of the weaker sex. There were of course communities of monks in which concessions were made for the upholding of dignity. This was particularly so in the case of the monastery which was the order's headquarter and contained the General's residence. Visiting prelates could expect to be received and housed with dignity. But entertainment on a grand scale was non-existent, and one can search in vain for places, such as chapter houses, audience chambers and refectories, which could compare with the luxurious interiors found in German and Austrian abbeys from the beginning of the 18th century.

It is significant that in 1756 when the Dominicans had a meeting of the chapter in the Minerva monastery to elect a new General, the first time in the order's history that this event took place with the Holy Father presiding, it had to be held in the library (*Casanatense*). The Friars Preachers did not have a chapter house of a suitable size at their disposal [50]. We have a description of the General's residence at the time of Antonin Cloche (1686–1720). When this prelate's extraordinary power is considered, he being a figure of European stature and comparable to a sovereign, his official quarters could only be described as extremely modest. In conformity with the common practice in large Roman houses two official apartments were included, one for summer, one for winter use. The first, which was the most spacious (*le grand appartement*) and faced the General's garden, consisted of three rooms: an anteroom with three windows, the conference room of the Inquisition and a study. Mediocre pictures on the walls, a few writing desks and leather-covered chairs, otherwise nothing. The only private room the General had was his bedroom which contained an iron-framed bed without hangings [51]. The Jesuit General's summer residence in the noviciate on Monte Cavallo was (1716) during Tamburini's rule even more chilly. No monumental stairways or extravagant vestibules gave access to this prelate whose power made a world tremble. A Provincial Immediate in Bavaria could play at making his monastery look like Versailles, nor did cardinals practise economy in building matters, but the heads of the important monastic orders were very conscious of the impression they made with their grim style.

In the new kitchen of the Augustines there was a spit turned by a water-wheel. The apparatus was constructed by the famous engineer Zabaglia [52]. I can never walk past the building in the Via della Scrofa without smiling at the thought of the learned brothers' *tournebroche,* and being reminded of both Anatole France's philanthropist and Daudet's *Trois Messes Basses*. I beg the reader's indulgence for this digression.

It is now time to visit the humblest of Rome's cloisters. Near *S. Apollonia* in Trastevere stood a convent for sisters of the Franciscan Trinitarians, which was overwhelming in its inexorable severity. According to its rules these fervent women scourged themselves every Monday, Wednesday and Friday; they fasted to excess and like other sisters "who did penance" were clad in grey [53]. Their poverty was so great, so it is stated in a diary from the 1650's, that they died from hunger [54]. The Inquisition knew what it was doing when it deported a girl to the convent of S. Apollonia. This happened in 1789 to Serafina Feliciani, the wife of the adventurer Cagliostro. He was sentenced to spend the rest of his life in prison and died there in 1795. She, who was not guilty of any other crime except that she had followed him through life, was incarcerated with the penitents and forgotten. The year of her death is not known [55].

In the Suburra quarter there was a nunnery behind whose walls a human word was rarely spoken and about which people only talked in whispers. Situated as it was in the middle of a rough and busy district, the convent all the same managed to hide itself away from all contact. Facing the College of the Neophytes and across the road from the Madonna dei Monti a little alleyway slunk into the darkness. A real cul-de-sac, it came to an end at the entrance to an institution whose door was barred and whose inhabitants lived in sackcloth and ashes. To make contact with them the intrepid visitor had to bang on a barrel set high above the door. A muffled voice answered from inside the building. If one's errand was approved, the barrel turned round and revealed a key. With it the door could be opened and a cramped chamber be entered. In one of the walls, which bore frightening inscriptions, was an aperture with a double lattice. Behind this was a metal plate, pierced by holes like the rose of a watering can. Through this the visitor could converse with the abbess who was furthermore draped in heavy linen from head to foot, even her face being hidden [56].

The sisters were called "The Living Entombed" (*le sepolte vive*). They were "Poor Clares", nuns of the strictest observance, looked upon as female Capuchins, their convent church being also called Chiesa della S. S. Concezione like that of the hooded friars, but they usually went under the name of *Farnesiani*, because the order was instituted by Donna Francesca Farnese in 1631. The convent was built under the protection of Cardinal Francesco Barberini (died 1679) [57]. It no longer stands, having been pulled down in the 1880's, a sacrifice to the Via Cavour. But the entrance to the cul-de-sac can still be found and the built-up area in its immediate neighbourhood (Via Madonna dei Monti) is very old, in places mediaeval. A house in Late Gothic style seen in an engraving by Vasi [58] is still standing. The place has more or less the same atmosphere that it had in the hey-day of the entombed virgins.

Benoit-Joseph Labre loved to walk along these mouldering walls in those days. He was a pious vagabond for whom the conditions of the Trappists had proved to be too stringent, so he chose to make his way all over Europe as a penitent, a Wandering Jew on all roads leading to shrines. In the end he capitulated to Rome (after 1774). At night he often slept behind one of the chapels in the Colosseum, where tourists took him to be part of the picturesque scenery, not knowing that a hundred years later he would be canonized. One day he fell on the steps of Madonna dei Monti and died shortly after (April 16th, 1783) in 2, Via dei Serpenti. His legend quickly spread and is still alive in the district [59].

This ragged and scruffy character is remembered here because he hovers like a ghost around the graves of the Farnesians and in the street of the gypsies nearby. This man, a bird of passage, could never meet the women in their cage, for the two circles of asceticism were forever closed. The pilgrim carried the house of his order with him on his back, and cast down his burden on the threshold of Rome's most lonely dwelling.

A few particularly unpleasant establishments thrived under the auspices of compassion and morals, but it was not good to tarry there, for the admonition of Christ was paired with the discipline of correction. Such institutions were sometimes called "asylums" (in our ears a jarring word), sometimes convents. The alumni consisted partly of fallen women, partly of wives who were unhappily married. The former were raised up, the latter supported. Grosley wrote, obviously with mixed feelings, that he had never heard of any similar refuges for men who were unhappily married [60]. The methods applied in such "homes" were of course inhumane, and recruitment of members was done with brutal high-handedness and sometimes on a hypocritical voluntary basis. We find that a harlot was taken by the scruff of the neck and dragged off to the home of virtue [61], and we also hear that destitute and unkempt individuals begged to be allowed to eat the black bread of humiliation. I ask the reader to look at the following street scene from about 1715, showing a little group of penitents like liberty horses in training: "There were seven in all. The girl leading them carried a large cross of purple-painted wood; they all had bare feet and were dressed in long purple kirtles with ropes around their waists and wore a sort of shoulder cape ("Domino"). Their heads were shaven and covered only by a thin mauve veil which did not prevent people from seeing that they were barely 18–20 years old and very pretty...". The group stops, a cleric on duty delivers a homily and ends: "Have ye not voluntarily accepted confinement? Are ye kept there by force?" Whereupon the uplifted women knelt down on the ground and declared with ardour that they wished to die in their haven of safety. The plate was then passed round the crowd of greatly affected bystanders [62].

Rome's architecture for all these broken-hearted people still stands – as monuments to two well-known orders whose names are not included

61. *The Convent of the Servites near S. Marcello in the Corso.*

63b. *Monastery in Via S. Giovanni in Laterano.*

63a. *The Dominican Monastery of S. Maria sopra Minerva.*

64a. The Turchine Convent on the Esquiline. Engraving by Giuseppe Vasi.

64b. S. Silvestro in Capite with the Franciscan Convent; on the left the Convent of S. Maria Maddalena (delle Convertite). Engraving by Giuseppe Vasi.

65. *The Monastery of S. S. Giovanni e Paolo.*

66. *Monastery in Via del Lavatore.*

67. *Corner of courtyard of the Convent of S. Margherita in Trastevere.*

69a. *Corner of courtyard of the Minerva Convent.*

69b. *Corner of the Ursuline Convent in Via Vittoria.*

71a. Convent wings of S.S. Pietro e Marcellino in Via Lubicana.

71b. The Passionist Convent on Monte Cavo.

72. *The Monastery of S. Bonaventura on the Palatine.*

in the Church's Calendar, the masochists and the sadists. *S. Giacomo delle Convertite,* between Lungara and the Tiber, offered peace (or was it hell?) on earth to profligate women "who desired to be freed from the chains of sin, and contritely devote themselves to the service of God" [63]. When their lot, not necessarily voluntary, is considered, these poor girls may be said to have jumped out of the frying-pan into the fire. They were now chastised by harsh nuns "who themselves were a good testimony to rehabilitation". No wonder these overseers "always kept their countenance hidden behind a veil", and that this same grim convent was practically the only one to resist Napoleon's abolition of the cloisters in 1810 with all its might, and had to be taken by storm [64]. This unique heroism of the converted Amazons was due not so much to support from above as to a determined wish to keep their charges inside. The chronicler of this episode, Louis Madelin, has apparently overlooked the character of the convent of S. Giacomo which can explain – but not excuse – the "unfortunate excesses" of the brutal and licentious soldiery on this very occasion.

A Frenchman of letters in Voltaire's time said of the English that they were only superior to his nation in that they had excellent horses and fine dogs as well as freedom from wolves and monks. Guidi, who is our informant, had to concede that the defamation of those who lived the cloistered life was now in fashion. After having stayed for some time in Rome (1773) and seen the situation at first-hand, he counselled moderation all the same. It was impossible to overlook a great many shortcomings. But – "one should look at the land these people cultivate and compare it with the fields of the landowners, should observe the help that monks give to their neighbours, should remember the many hands to which they give work". In his retort he also points out that when monks and nuns are criticized for all sorts of abuses, this word in itself indicates that religious orders as such are of value, since it is impossible to abuse *une chose essentiellement mauvaise* [65].

This compatriot of Candide went into the matter with his eyes open and showed discernment. And when Napoleon gave the deathblow to the religious orders in Rome by driving monks and nuns out of their cloisters, it soon became clear how much these people, now so maligned, had meant in day to day life by fulfilling the obligations that the State had shrugged off. The children lost their teachers, the poor went in vain to the cloister gate to obtain bread, the homeless lost their refuge, the lonely their rare visitors. "What profiteth it the tyrant if he gaineth the whole world yet driveth out the Holy Benedict from Subiaco, Francis from Assisi and Dominic from the Aventine?" [66].

II

After this sociological introduction we are now going to examine the religious houses as architecture. We pointed out earlier that these buildings, often so extensive, could, merely by their cubic solidity give character to, or indeed dominate whole streets. This is still true in many cases, although the monastic buildings concerned have been adapted to secular use and thereby reduced to a seedy state, shamelessly besmirched by neon signs and placards. However, the mass of the building has retained its power. Many people have been greatly impressed by a certain harmony in a Roman street without realizing that this harmony depended upon the long, solid wall of a monastery. We do not actually see it, we merely feel it.

The Via *delle Vergini* and the Via *dell' Umiltà* get their names from two very large cloistral buildings. This part of the city, near the Corso, has undergone changes, but the two enormous cubes of the cloisters still dominate the surroundings. Where these two streets intersect at a right angle, the pietistic barracks control everything; your gaze is drawn upwards and your eyes follow the monotonous rows of windows. The Vergini convent for Augustine nuns as well as its church are said to have been built by Mattia de Rossi [67]. The Umiltà cloister was given its accent by Carlo Fontana who included a narrow church front in the large façade, thereby making it seem even bigger [68]. A narrow street, Vicolo del Monticello, follows the side wall of the convent closely, like a gorge between the severe yellow walls.

The Dominican building by S. Maria sopra Minerva is a large irregular block, in Italian *un' isola,* with steep walls on all sides and with changing profiles. It is exciting to wander around the outside of the old stronghold of the Friars Preachers and see how its appearance alters when viewed from the surrounding squares and streets; the whole quarter is under its sway. Only in one place can a wanderer reach its centre by following a public road, and that is along a little side road, the Via Beato Angelico, which makes straight for the chancel of La Minerva and turns into an intimate little square between the church, the older part of the monastery (Pl. 63a) and a row of plain dwelling houses standing on Dominican land. This passage was originally called "Vicolo dietro la Minerva". The Danish composer Rudolf Bay, who lived there 1841–1842, called it irreverently "Minerva's backside" and described its character in the following terms: "no wider than Peder Madsen's Gang, no longer than Trompetergangen and closed at the end like Pistolstræde" [69]. The Copenhagen flavour is easily recognized in this; the lane is warm and friendly. It can be recommended to tourists from the North who wish to gain their first impression of the might of a Roman monastery from close at hand, for the building makes no concessions to the idyllic site. A wing of the monastery behind the alley is topped by a lofty belvedere. It was a part of the General's residence [70]. His view reached to all the corners of the world.

Quite different is the effect of the Augustines' compact monastery in the Via della Scrofa; this now busy street is well supported by a very plain and solid stretch of wall. You might think it was the side elevation of a palace. Its frigid uniformity relaxes however in a little humorous aside, the relief of a sow (*scrofa*), transferred from the former building, where it was part of a little wall fountain. An alley along the south side of the Servites' monastery in the Corso gives the pedestrian a peaceful refuge where he can recover his equilibrium. In this secluded spot he can enjoy the sight of a fine rhythmic play produced by the staggered parts of buildings which are topped by a belvedere overlooking the Piazza S. S. Apostoli.

And then again – the stretch of the Via della Lungaretta (in Trastevere) which runs along past the cloisters of S. Margherita and S. Rufina, is indeed dominated by these dark buildings which break up the lively melody of the street. It is not necessary to give any other examples, only to remind the reader that the wall enclosing a monastery garden in former times often controlled the appearance of a street which might otherwise have looked disorganised, particularly of course on the outskirts of a built-up area [71]. The Via del Quirinale lost its character when the wall in front of the Jesuit noviciate of S. Andrea was sacrificed, and now instead there is the emptiness of a public park, visited by few and giving pleasure to even fewer. Because they have such good outer walls, buildings belonging to religious orders are particularly suitable for the formation of public squares. Examples are the Dominicans' little square in the Via del Seminario and the square at the entrance to the Campo Marzio convent. The Piazza di S. Silvestro (Pl. 64b) was once a peaceful haven between large religious houses, and the square over on the Tiber island, between S. Bartolomeo and the hospice, in our time still had a mighty monastery wing on each side. The one to the south has now gone; the square is incomplete [72]. It can be argued that the Piazza del Popolo might have been more of an entity before Napoleon's architect turned it into a park-like square and rounded it off at the sides. Seen from the city gate, the long garden walls and the monastic lodging houses held the whole site together, and in those days the view was concentrated on the two domed churches and the entrances to the three main streets.

Roman monastic architecture of the Late Baroque period carries on the traditions of the normal and also monumental building which was started within this genre at the beginning of the 17th century by masters such as Domenico Fontana and Maderno [73]. Borromini, who was a specialist in the building of religious houses, further advanced the development of the genre by a series of profoundly original experiments [74]. However, the rule governing all planning and shaping of the religious houses, in effect since the Middle Ages and with its roots in Antiquity [75], is founded on one basic type: the long many-storied house with corridors, whether such a building stands on its own, is attached to a church, or is a wing of a complex surrounding an inner courtyard (*chiostro*). The function of this building is to house a plurality of people in one-roomed flats; employing an expression used nowadays, it can be called a "block of flats". But it differs in principle from modern "blocks of flats" by the inhabitants not only having uniform flats (with a common room for catering, work and recreation), but that they themselves wear uniforms and live under domestic discipline. As a result, the form of this type of building tends to approach that of an asylum, prison and barracks. On the surface this only means that the architecture expresses a stricter civic character, the utilitarian emerges undecorated. In addition there is the particular circumstance that the community life of the inhabitants and its discipline are devoted to a voluntarily chosen ideal. The occupants of the little flats are taking part in a form of worship merely by being such occupants. To be in lodgings is a sort of cult. Where numerous people lodge, the building is the expression of a great collective cultic activity, at the same time as quite simply being the roof over the heads of many people.

The religious house will thus be tempted to announce its religious mission externally. This can only be done by giving the building one or more motifs taken from the church. They take the sting out of the monastery's otherwise harsh appearance without repudiating its clearly practical purpose. It is interesting to see how the sacral emphasis throughout the whole of the Baroque period tries to keep pace with the patently functional in monastic architecture – and to notice the victory of the "civic". The further the 18th century progresses, the more secular becomes the style of the monastery. But the development proceeds without vital conflicts, slowly, always within the limits of synthesis.

The struggle between what is basic and what is borrowed develops of course where the ecclesiastical character needs to make itself known, namely in the façade of the monastery, given that there is a recognizable façade, or where the monastery is important in the prospect of a city (e. g. when seen on a diagonal). The symbolic sacred elements used in this instance are gables containing clocks or bells, attic gables and the large arched window. The first (*l'orologio*) is the sure sign of a religious institution [76] and has continued to be so especially in rural monasteries and religious houses which have no independent church building. Everywhere, where the often fragile little belfry sticks up in the air, it is easy to make the diagnosis: here cenobites live or visit, however secular the building may look [77]. The main example is Borromini's clocktower on the Philippine monastery and a similar one on the Capuchins' which has now been taken down.

The attic storey, which raises the height of the frontispiece, does not intend to hide its meaning either; it is in itself a church gable on a small scale. The motif cannot possibly be mistaken in a town where the civic architecture does not include the gabled attic. The decorated church gable appeared on only very few Roman monastery façades. It makes its greatest impression on the *religious house of the Servites* in the Corso (Pl. 61); this has been made especially imposing because it stands in Rome's main street and is the General's residence. The building was erected by Urban VIII Barberini (1623–1644), Casoni being the architect [78]. No ecclesiastical building could be more authoratitive; its sculpture is strong, a church and a residence carved out according to a formula which is inviolable. The façade is a masterly piece of composition, based on the figure III – can anything artistically superior be seen in the Corso? And yet this monastery in the maelstrom of the city is disregarded and seldom discussed. The group of windows beneath the gable, an angular variation on the "Palladio motif", is repeated in the *piano nobile,* and the three separate windows below this are echoed in the next storey but one towards the top, where the circular opening and two small arched windows break through the thick wall. All the frames are heavy, almost crude. One could say that the building follows the life-style of the coarse cowls; here hard bread is the daily bread, here the dogma of infallibility is forged, here concise commands dominate.

The house of the Servites is older than our period, but in this prospect of the city it is not to be missed as a bastion of the cloistered city in Rome. The church gable also occurred on the *Capuchin priory* (facing the Via S. Basilio), erected by the same Casoni [79], and in a few other places where there was a view from the top storey. The *Minerva priory*'s two façades, set at a right angle in the little square by S. Ignazio, which we mentioned earlier, have attic gables resembling the large central gable of the church belonging to the Dominicans [80]. Such raised middle sections were not very popular after Urban VIII's time, the motif had meaning only on a façade which had to be self-contained and independent. Normally, the front of a monastery is paired with a church façade, the latter being the more important. Such was not the case with the part of the Dominican priory we have just discussed, and although the Servites' stood next to S. Marcello, this had in the 1620's such an undistinguished exterior, and was at the same time set so far back from the building line of the street, that the priory had to act as the herald for the whole pious establishment. We see also that two such outstanding buildings as *the headquarters of the Jesuits and of the Theatines,* both symmetrical and with a strong frontal effect, are bereft of all religious accentuation because they are overshadowed by two of the richest church façades in Rome.

On the other hand, the large arched window soon became popular everywhere. And no wonder, for this fulfilled two important conditions for leading a monastic life; it was "ecclesiastical" in character and practical in use. The false gable was mostly pomp and symbolism. Roomy refectories, wide corridors and stairs in large complexes meant for habitation, had to have light. The isolated large window is therefore properly included among the many small windows set in rows. We shall later come across several examples of its use [81]. It is the true trade-mark of the monastery; in the large ones it is one of a number of motifs, – every traveller will remember the huge arched windows in *the monastic mansion of the Minims* at Trinità dei Monti – in the small and humble monastery this high opening is often the only way it can assert itself. Now and then such a window needs its own rectangular attic above the main cornice, as in the Minerva priory, for it is a cheap substitute for both the ecclesiastical attribute and the belvedere [82].

Let us sum up the situation. The Roman architect who has to build a monastery in the period we are dealing with, has at his disposal the special elements we have just mentioned and can apply them according to the given circumstances. But the fact is that they are of secondary importance to him; as an artist he is also tied down by the uncompromising regulations which the monastery as a type is subjected to from the bottom upwards. We must try and understand what the consequences were as far as the exteriors of the monasteries were concerned. A façade of several storeys and many windows can be divided up rhythmically both horizontally and vertically. Let us look at the horizontal. The typical storey of a monastery contains a number of room-units of equal size (cells). As these are situated along the outer wall of the building, the windows appear to follow the regular plan of "1–1–1–..." (cf. Pl. 64 a–b). Nowadays, we would not find such a row of equidistant windows particularly strange. But in the Rome of Baroque it was far from predominant. It is in absolute contrast to two other widely used plans for horizontal division, namely 1) the ancient "civic" plan which has the formula "2–2–2–...", and 2) the rhythm distinctive of palaces, which although symmetrical is also elastic, since it depends upon the alternation of wide and narrow spaces between the windows [83].

That the monastery only in very rare cases uses one of these other schemes – the Servites' distinguished looking house is one of the exceptions which is influenced by "type 2" – emphasizes more than any other feature that this kind of building is entirely functional in its expression. The monotonous rhythm of windows at regular intervals showed clearly that behind them was a series of rooms, and that they were all the same size. The two other formulae for façades are suited to other circumstances. The "2–2" scheme has come up from the ground floor and is based on a regular alternation down there between shop and door (with steps). The variation in the grouping of windows in a palace is indicative that the rooms behind can differ in dimensions and that the façades do not give a damn about the interior of the building. We can throw light on the specific nature of the monastery's plan in an indirect way by answering the following questions: Are there any ecclesiastical community houses (buildings not used as monasteries or convents) that use the "2–2" scheme? If so, which and why? Yes, such buildings do exist and the characteristic thing about them is that they resemble monasteries in all ways except one: their storeys are not made up of cells but divided into rooms and accommodation of varying sizes. This applies to colleges (for example "the hundred poor priests" by S. S. Michele e Magno near St. Peter's Square) and particularly to the large building (now demolished) opposite S. Maria Maggiore which was used as a dwelling for the Penitents of the basilica, who are not cenobites [84]. That the latter building made use of the *taberna* scheme (2–2) was due to the fact that the ground floor was to some extent broken up by lock-up shops being included (cf. Coll. dei Propaganda Fide). Such a practice – the establishment of private shops – was certainly unthinkable for convents with strict sequestration [85].

We have thus established that the 1–1 rhythm in the division of a storey's windows is, and must be, indicative of a cloistered building; it is determined by the structure itself. How it came to be transferred to civic architecture and in the course of the 18th century gained further ground, we shall explain below.

It is however possible for the architect to lend variety to the series of cell windows without breaking with the principle of sequence. In the first place he can make openings of a different shape from the usual, or he can merely alter the frames. Such variations do not occur just at random but are grouped together and form either a particular section in the pattern of the building [86] or change with each storey. The latter alternative is also common in other genres, the former is not. Moreover, one row of cell windows can be made distinct from others by the addition of screens, shutters, blinds, lattices, balconies, each type in its own row (Pl. 64a). But the arched window can be set anywhere, the circular window too, meandering all over the place, but used mostly as the light for a staircase.

In the upward development of the façade, storey above storey, we find corresponding specific characteristics. The storeys can vary in height, depending on the requirements of the interior, but the monastery is reticent to emphasize the important storey on the outside and does not follow the traditions of the palace. Just as the row of windows is "democratic" – there is equality and brotherhood between the windows – so the piano nobile does not pull rank but distains any ostentation. A tendency can therefore be seen towards omitting the string-course; the straight-edge is certainly always used, but its lines are effaced (Pl. 64a–b, 67, 71b) [87]. If we sketch a typical monastery façade from memory, we are reminded at first of windows marshalled in endless rows, then we are aware of these rectangles without bodily form, nothing but holes in serried ranks. The façade is not built up, it is divided up. The entresol is usually involved with the palace's piano nobile, but in the monastery the mezzanine only serves its own purpose, and can be put anywhere, often at the very top of the building; the Minerva priory had three mezzanines one above the other on top of the three normal storeys [88]. Some monasteries divided the top storey into simple arcades, these being a belvedere for the monks where they could study during the hot season [89]. Last but not least we take note of the fact that the monastery wall does not care to attract the eye to its middle section – if the wall is on a line with a church front, the attraction is directed towards the latter, and if the façade is on its own there is no focal point. What it expresses is profound all the same. The claustral front is an aesthetic phenomenon as unique as the monastic life. Late Baroque made capital of the extraordinary. It shaped each block on the basis of a total sum of uniform cubes and treated the external surfaces geometrically. The immaculate monastery of this period in this way assumes an organic similarity to the functional architecture of our own time as represented by the plain block of flats with small units, and the standard office block. And there is also a relationship in other ways with the sophisticated puritanism of the 1920's style. A play on sobriety, an unexpected dissonance, a stimulating syncopation, a porthole bulging like a soap-bubble – all these balconies and awnings . . .

The architect of the monastery acquired the difficult art of producing a good job while under constraint. This is particularly evident when it was a matter of renovating an old building and changing bare walls into architecture. Just three windows grouped together was an ornament – and the token of asceticism (Pl. 62). But poverty brings its own reward. Such an external but specific detail as a window-shade, a merciless screen from below, a merciful one from above, gave the architect an aid, the one most readily at hand – the shadow. Was its help taken into consideration as it is by us? Many a house of penance is redeemed by the abstract when shapes of intense blackness glide slowly over its surface (Pl. 63b). And when the deep shadow of a neighbouring wing cuts across the battered wall with its triangle, the building is as if touched by a secret benediction (Pl. 63a). Just look and see how the heavy, black flame from the cone-shaped canopy above the Madonna (Pl. 69b) scorches the façade of one of the most reserved convents in Rome.

III

Kind reader, join me in a walk that will take us to a number of cloisters, starting with buildings that stand within the city itself. We shall discuss them in more or less chronological order and let each in its own way, very briefly contribute to our understanding of the nature of this type. Pride of place goes to the beautiful convent which Donna Camilla Orsini, widow of Prince Marc' Antonio Borghese, erected on the Esquiline for a community of nuns called *Turchine* or *Celeste* because their habits were of a brilliant sky-blue [90]. The foundation was approved by the Pope in 1670 when Donna Camilla made a deed of gift of 80,000 scudi, one half of which was to be a building fund and the rest invested for upkeep. For once we have some details connected with the building of a convent [91]. The administrators of the Borghese estate undertook to find a site which besides being close to S. Maria Maggiore would also be in peaceful surroundings with a wholesome atmosphere, and not be overlooked by other buildings in the neighbourhood. A suitable piece of ground was acquired in the present Via dei Quattro Cantoni. Building started in 1670 and the convent was ready for use in April 1676. The architect was G. B. Contini [92]. Although the convent was principally for ladies of blue blood, Donna Camilla wished to do away with all luxury. The foundress, as pious as she was generous, had plenty to worry about – for one thing a further sum of 25,000 scudi was needed when the architect departed from his original plan and "the Devil will always try to hinder those works which serve his destruction and glorify God". An obstinate neighbour aimed too high with his new house and might have been able to take a sly look at the nuns' sanctuary, but his evil designs were foiled. The powers that be were invoked by the princess, and the foolhardy fellow had to wall up his prying windows. In 1685, having taken the name of "Sister Maria Vittoria", Donna Camilla died in her convent surrounded by the aura of sanctity.

An engraving by Vasi (Pl. 64a) shows the convent of the Celestines. The church pertaining to it has a façade of the desired simplicity; it is extremely chaste, but in the convent itself the various apertures are so sensitively diversified that the front becomes alive. Thus the circular windows are extremely effective; they seem to float upwards against the rhythmic stream. The shutters on the first floor, which open outwards from the bottom, make the windows look as if they are yawning, while the little balconies at the top project with impunity, being nearest to the sun and the sky and heaven too. I wonder if people in the street in those days appreciated the architect's calculated use of simple elements. The composition must subconsciously have given pleasure – good artists, who are the interpreters of their age, usually get the approval they expect. The nuns themselves were probably not aware of it, for they saw the building more from the inside and in any case, their gaze was for ever fixed on higher things.

The large convent for Augustine nuns by *S. Marta,* opposite the Collegio Romano, took form about the same time as that of the Celestines under the supervision of Carlo Fontana. It was an extremely fashionable institution [93], almost palatial, with tall, regularly distributed windows. The building is still extant and is well suited to its present secular use as the *Questura;* large yellow cubes, solid like Egyptian mastabas. A similar purified style is to be found in those parts of the Minerva priory which were erected while Père Cloche was its General [94], as well as later in the century. Antonio Borioni, the architect of the order, must have had a hand in it, for we know that he enlarged the magnificent library, built to Castelli's design, to house the books donated by Cardinal Casanate [95]. A part of the priory is shown in Pl. 69a. The arched windows have a slower vertical tempo than the rows of ordinary lights. There is an inherent peace in this arrangement, so bare and noble, with its light-coloured walls and wide corridors, which are paved with stone and lime-washed [96]. The echoes from the tribunal of the Inquisition fill this built-up hollow square and the spirit of domination decides between black and white.

Now to Trastevere – to the convent by *S. Margherita,* probably built by the architect for this church, C. Fontana, about 1680. This building, now secularized, famed for its discipline, exemplifies the claustral building methods which reduce all aesthetic expression to a minimum without losing the artistic basis. We see the now so neglected building from its courtyard (Pl. 67); simple balconies have been added, windows made larger; flowerpots and washing, small children and a broken-down fountain are the signs of life of people who are supposed to be free. Remove these traces and you are left with a house showing remorseless discipline. Piers like boxes set up on end, dull moulding, stark arches. A building erected by numbers, made for discipline. Here, if anywhere, is where you can see the spirit of oppression in its most concentrated form. But we only see the patched-up shell. The nuns' confined daily round of self-denial and strict regimentation may have lent the building a beauty, brutal and mute, echoing the cloistered life. Messages from the past cannot be expected behind these walls – all the same, one cry of distress has reached us. One day in the spring of 1722 a Portuguese nobleman, Don Francisco Lopez, was caught climbing down from a nun's window by rope ladder. He was thrown into prison, but pardoned by the intercession of his master, Cardinal Pereira, and sent back to his native land [97]. I imagine that this rope ladder will help the untutored layman to understand the architecture of the S. Margherita convent and consider it a redeeming feature.

A Latin inscription in the vestibule of *S. Silvestro in Capite* states that the adjacent convent for Franciscan nuns (the so-called *Urbaniste*) had a new and more spacious building added to it in 1722 [98]. This is seen on the right in Pl. 64b. The façade of the church is now on a lower level than the flanking houses, of which the narrow one on the left on the corner of the Via del Gambero, having retained its projecting cavetto moulding at the top, is still in existence, while the main part of the building on the right, has been rebuilt and is now a post-office. The top windows of this wing were framed by the string course which edged the façade, an artifice that is frequently used and always has an elegant effect. Compare it with the back of the forbidding priory in the Corso, where it stood next to *S. Maria Maddalena delle Convertite,* which has now been pulled down. With its barrier wall and by its sullen exterior it displays the recalcitrant character of the prison inmates.

No. 38, Via del Lavatore is an ecclesiastical building of high rank. Reliable information about it has not yet been found, so our assessment of it is advanced with due reservations. As far as we can judge it has some connection with the church of S. S. Vincenzo e Anastasio a Trevi which stands in the immediate vicinity. If that is the case, the building was no doubt erected for "the Minorites", a community of priests regular (also called *Caracciolini*), who served this church [99]. The stately façade, which we photographed from the Vicolo Scavolino (Pl. 66), has exactly the character befitting a community house for clerics of high standing. In its exterior it is closer to a patrician's house than a monastery. The architect is most likely to be found in Borromini's circle; the herma pilasters of the middle window are particularly significant of this. A very personal touch is the formation of the pediment above the portal, the volutes of which curl towards the oval cartouche in an interplay of curves. A very similar composition occurs over a door in the presbytery of S. S. Quirico e Giulitta and is attributed to Valvassori (1750) [100]. The plain window frames of the Minorites' building with their double flat mouldings, each of a different depth, also occur here. One might with reason regard it as a work by the architect of the Palazzo Pamphili-Doria, as long as the true dating of the building does not contradict this. There is a certain disharmony in the façade, caused by unequal conflict between the ponderously bizarre and the personally discreet domestic style, so well represented both by Valvassori's palace from the 1730's and by his presbytery, which are some 15–20 years younger. The dating of the building we are discussing here may possibly explain this conflict, and its somewhat ambiguous purpose may also have something to do with it. All things considered, Valvassori's great name is not likely to have been taken in vain in the Via del Lavatore. The front unquestionably demonstrates a strong individuality, an obstinate character. If only as an ecclesiastical memorial it forces the observer to query it.

Our friends, "the Minorites" had the tall broad building put up, and together with *S. Lorenzo in Lucina* it makes the square in front of the church look very regular. Venuti says (1766) that the monastery was renovated *modernamente* [101], and in fact the whole square was. The property of the good fathers looks like a solid block of flats [102], with high ceilings, many balconies and large windows. The community of nursing sisters (*Ministri degl' Infermi*) who owned *S. Maria Maddalena in Campo Marzio*, gradually managed to build up a whole square block for their purpose, partly under the supervision of Bizzaccheri [103]. A new wing was being built in 1738, and we know this from Valesio's note about an accident on the side [104]. The most interesting part of the complex is the narrow section on each side of the church façade (Pl. 56); small arched windows have been included in these very limited spaces. Behind *S. Maria di Montesanto* in the Piazza del Popolo is a Carmelite convent, built from the base up, by Theodoli. When a topographer assures us "that it is a fine embellishment to the Corso" [105], referring in fact to its northern, poorest part, he is quite right. The high walls of the convent provide a support for the entrance to this important roadway, and a fine portal with a segmental pediment, which is almost Classical, is a worthy greeting to a traveller entering the city's network of streets.

The Redemptorists (*Congregazione del S. S. Redentore*) formed one of the few communities founded in the 18th century. It was instituted by Alfonso de' Liguori (died 1787) at Amalfi in 1732 and specialized in missionary work among country people. Its Roman house was linked with S. Maria in Monterone and probably dates from the middle of the century (Pl. 22). The founder of this order, *Doctor zelantissimus*, was also a musician and in 1760 composed a duet between Jesus and the soul [106]. Without intending to trade on this information, one could say all the same that the priory of this new order (on the corner of Via dei Redentoristi) sings treble to the church's alto and intones in gayest Baroque. The cornices and other members have been moulded into supple, undulating forms by a virtuoso, and here indeed is a confection of roulades. The expression is aptly reminiscent of the pastrycook's craft. The popular revivalist preachers out in distant fields used both sweet and sour effects, particularly in the Neapolitan area [107]; tassels and scourges were equally effective on the missionary scene. In this façade the Redemptorists did not disdain the charm of entertainment.

It is refreshing to come to the *Ursuline Convent* in the Via Vittoria. It was founded by Duchess Laura of Modena, opened in 1688, increased as time went on and reached its present size by the extensive building activity between 1745 and some time in the 1760's [108]. Excavation of the foundations for a new wing in 1763 revealed remains of ancient buildings. The architect was Mauro Fontana, a grandson of the great Carlo [109]. The convent was famous for being a high-class establishment for young ladies, and the Roman nobility had their little girls educated here [110]. The cenobitic character of the buildings is toned down, noticeably refined; no other house of this kind in Rome is so delicate in relief. Its appearance is temperate and as clear as a cloudless day in September. And there is a soupçon of something French in its atmosphere (Pl. 69b). When Countess D'Albany ran away from her unhappy husband, Prince Charles Edward Stuart, and sought refuge in Rome (1780), she locked herself up in the convent of the Ursulines and remained there until the next year [111]. The building now houses the Roman Conservatory of Music (S. Cecilia).

A couple of quite late monasteries, each connected to a church, are offset by a similar ecclesiastical building on the other side of the church. This creates symmetry. One of these foundations came into being through the Spanish Trinitarians in the Via Condotti with *S. S. Trinità degli Spagnuoli* as centrepiece. On the left in the street stands the monastery, thus in the quietest place; on the right on the corner to the Corso a hospice and a lodging house, which we shall discuss later. The two buildings were erected by Sardi [112] in 1741 and 1734 respectively. Equally well balanced, but better planned, is the pair of buildings which the congregation of "pious workers" (*Pii Operai*) added to *S. Giuseppe alla Lungara* in the 1760's; this church stands near the Tiber. The little-known architect Giovanni Francesco Fiori gave these houses a bold elevation and a somewhat fussy decoration which is particularly trivial on the Palazzetto's central axis [113]. Small scale architecture began to run to seed about this time and the large architectural works developed growing pains, becoming stiff and nodular.

The Augustinians' priory was a new building which was erected from 1747 onwards under the aegis of Gioia and Vasquez, the Generals of the time, following plans by Vanvitelli [114]. Its qualities are indeed outstanding. The plan is harmonious, the colonnaded cloisters dignified, the stairs and corridors decorated with discreet opulence [115]. This imposing design suffers all the same from one essential weakness – it makes concessions to the secular style of the palace. The main façade in the Via dei Portoghese is divided into three sections, all of the same width. The middle one stands out like a buttress; such modelling is in itself quite exceptional for monastic buildings. And the two lower storeys are ashlared as if they were meant to be the foundation; this feature too, indicates a close kinship to the aristocratic mansion. When you have finally turned the corner of the interminably long side of this building in the Via della Scrofa, which continues the directional lines of the front, you discover to your horror that the monastery looks boring. And this is an entirely new experience on our peregrination. Ordinary priories have no visible rear, only outer walls, but the rear of the Augustinian priory looks like the back of a castle. The alignment with aristocratic style has not intruded until now, and by the priory's attempting to ingratiate itself with the secular, it becomes hopelessly degraded. It rates as third class merely because it has high-class aspirations to splendour. Vanvitelli's error is the result of the crisis facing architecture. The instinct for what is fit and proper had gone by the board. Or to put it another way, the ideals of Neo-Classisism were beginning to take over. When in the end they gained the upper hand, during the decade of revolution, the great days of monastic architecture were over in Rome. Napoleon's men tore down the buildings of the Olivetians by *S. Francesca Romana*. The monastic barracks which were put in their place when papal rule was restored were erected in a cold and declamatory style [116]. Of course it is a vocation to be a monk, but it is no profession.

The monasteries out in the dismal district between the city and the walls were extremely isolated. Many of them had an ancient core and resembled citadels, towering massifs, hard, rough-hewn, such as the buildings by *S. Balbina* on the Aventine with the square creeper-covered tower and *S. Pietro in Vincoli*'s monastery and its grove of cypresses (Pl. 182), and more than any other, the fortress called *S. S. Quattro Coronati*. Faced with such armour-plated monastic houses, Baroque was impotent, and it can be seen in the courtyard of the latter monastery how the additional walls and the inset windows are of less durable substance and different calibre. The new country abbeys in Rome which are erected after Bernini's time were, like the old ones, compelled to be highly concentrated. They were outlined against the scenery and the sky, seemingly free but in fact confined. The monastery surrounded by streets became isolated merely by the manifestation of its outer walls, the rustic cloister withdrew into itself; its very form was that of the intransigent individual, caring little for the artistry of a façade. So the citadel and the villa had to be the basic architectural types on which the monastery out here modelled itself. Its situation, the style of the order and its economic potential determined the character of the mixture.

Up on the Palatine stands a group of buildings which contains both these types. *The monastery of S. Bonaventura* was founded c. 1675 for Franciscans of stricter observance (the reform of S. Pietro d'Alcantara) [117]. The first little group of monks selected this secluded spot as particularly well suited to the contemplative way of life, for the top of the hill was profoundly peaceful. A prospect by Falda from 1676 shows the original building, the outline of which remains almost unchanged (Pl. 72). The monastery and the church were approached along a footpath up the slope opposite S. Gregorio. The monastery of S. Bonaventura is the perfect example of a poor and exposed monastic dwelling which began its life among thorn-bushes and ended in an idyllic garden. From this towering "skyscraper", with rough loggias hewn out at the top, the brothers kept a look-out; from their poor church they went down to preach among the crowds and to travel Italy's white highways.

One of the most respected friars from the Palatine was Leonardo da Porta Maurizio (died 1751), who enjoyed the widest confidence as a spiritual adviser and who advanced the cult of the Via Crucis with great fervour. He is said to have instituted no less than 572 ways of the cross and to have founded the most famous of them all, the *via crucis* in the Colosseum [118]. Even today the monastery of S. Bonaventura has its own little stations of the cross which is full of poetry. It follows the path shaded by acacias that runs along the wall in front of the Villa Mills and leads to the church. An old inscription conveys the Cardinal-Vicar's instruction that no games of any kind can take place in this consecrated yard; it reminds desecrators of the pictures of the Agony that they will be prosecuted, and refers to letter of Jan. 18th, 1731 concerning indulgences. The present shabby stucco reliefs hardly deserve to be spared [119], but the place inspires respect with its piety and shade. The entrance to the monastery is through a little door with a porch roof over it and a rusty bell-pull at the side. A skull and crossbones carved on a stone plaque bids welcome. A fit setting for Frater Leonardo.

Moritz, Goethe's friend, walked into the garden and was vexed with the monks who sat there "in dull, brooding silence", and complained about "the ugly habits" hanging there to dry after being washed [120]. Here lived the ridiculous foes of Antiquity, next-door neighbours to Emperor Tiberius. After all, Moritz was a mythologist and an expert of classical hangings [121]. We prefer to remember Fra Pietro, the gentle Kückler, bending over a vegetable bed or sitting up in his cell with the shade over his old eyes and the Roman landscape at his feet. The little community of S. Bonaventura had one fine thing in common with lesser mortals – the lofty palm, cherished as much by the friars as by the tourists. Madame de Stael [122], Hans Andersen [123], Reumont [124] all mention it with delight. The sough of the wind in the fan of palm-leaves seemed far more glorious than all the tail-feathers of ostrich and peacock around the Apostolic See.

In the little square by *S. S. Giovanni e Paolo* it is not the church in fact, but the outworks of a monastery which dominate. Behind a long flight of steps stands the most powerful part of the building, a cube as in a fresco of Fra Angelico (and Mary's visit to the temple could be re-enacted on the steps). Even a Romanesque campanile of high quality is impoverished by this block, whose front has the imprint of a master: just two big details, the arched window and the door, keep one another tensely balanced. The principle of the composition is Gothic [125]; its power in simple architecture was appreciated in the Baroque period. As the principle is employed here, it gave the monastery's projecting front a striking authority, all the more effective because the church has only a weak façade. The monastery, with its rambling rear, was handed over by Clement XI to a newly founded (1705) community of missionaries (*Padri della Missione*), who kept it until 1773 [126]. The building was possibly renovated to some extent after the transfer mentioned. Canevari is stated to be its architect [127], but in its bare bones the prominent part is older than his time (Pl. 65).
and a rusty bell-pull at the side. A skull and crossbones carved on a stone plaque bids welcome. A fit setting for Frater Leonardo.

like a fortress, and looks particularly menacing facing the uphill Via Porta Pinciana. The wings which form a square are hidden, and only inside the forecourt of the church can a stretch of monastery wall, with its watchful arched window, be detected. A supramundane silence must have prevailed in the Fathers' garden when all around was nothing but empty, aristocratic parks. Thomas Grey – the author of "Elegy in a Country Churchyard" – had been intoxicated by the moonlight and the scent of orange blossom on the lonely path by S. Isodoro [128]. Münter too was spell-bound here, but by the songs of Ossian and Fingal, "those famous heroes", which he listened to in Pater James MacCormack's cell (1786) [129]. The learned classicist from the North (like his compatriot Zoega) found it easy to pour out his Gothic soul when the moon played its deceptive tricks and isolation was relaxed a little. Then the monastery became more human.

The so-called *Philippines,* a community of high-born nuns (Oblates), could not put up with anything less than a country-house belonging to the aristocracy, so they obtained the Villa Sforza on the Esquiline and renovated it in 1740 [130]. The core of the casino, a square block with a central belvedere, can be seen in Falda's bird's eye view of Rome from 1676 [131]. It was presumably after its sale to the order, that the building was lengthened to form a rectangle, and it looks as if the windows were given new frames on that occasion (Pl. 68). The nuns then had the transverse wings erected. These differ from the older structure by having ashlar courses in the lower storey. The extreme right wing of the convent is a very engaging piece of architecture, a true country-house. The Philippines enjoyed the sunshine on the same hillside by S. Maria Maggiore that the good Donna Camilla had chosen for her foundation, but this stands a bit further down; the Oblates, who moved here at a later date, got the better of the bargain. *The Teresians* also moved out into the country. They left the wretched Via delle Botteghe Oscure in 1750 and transferred to *S. S. Pietro e Marcellino* [132], a definite improvement, although the new site was low-lying and the air unhealthy. Older buildings here dating from the time of the Basilians, were in the course of time extended along the Via Labicana. As this long wall behind trees now stands (Pl. 71a), it shows clearly how a contemporary religious house can assert itself with dignity near a lonely country road. The great nunnery spread itself as if it were a little suburb on its own. Isolated "skyscrapers" usually look so forlorn on the outskirts of a town – religious houses did not, for, gregarious by nature, they were held together by a church and did not rely on a network of streets. Another example of a long cloister by a country road within the city walls is seen by *S. Eusebio*. The great estate is superbly planned [133].

We now say farewell to the Roman world of religious houses from the top of Monte Cavo. *The Passionists,* a more recent community (founded 1720), erected a hospice on the highest peak of the Albani hills in 1758. The founder, St. Paul of the Cross (died 1775), preached repentance. His flock built up a cult around the Passion – and no other place near Rome was better suited to direct the thoughts of the friars towards the Hill of Golgatha than Monte Cavo's summit, which stands at an elevated distance, swept by the winds, with a magnificent view over the Campagna as far as Soracte and the Mediterranean (Pl. 71b). Down there stands the papal city, looking like a rubbish tip, full of rusty bits and pieces.

The present monastery of the Passionists was erected in the 1780's by Cardinal Stuart [134]. The buildings are strictly cubist. The connection between the prince of the church mentioned and the most remote monastery belonging to Rome is an ironic master-stroke of history. The Cardinal Duke of York, Bishop of Frascati and Dean of the Holy College, was the last of his ill-fated family. After the death of Bonnie Prince Charlie in 1788, he called himself Henry I of Scotland, Henry IX of England and France. Just a breath of hot air – lacking the power of the wind around Monte Cavo. This old dotard now took a chilly pleasure in seeing bare monastery walls encroach upon the foundations of the temple of *Jupiter Latialis*. One might believe one is looking at a fortress – even more dominating than Edinburgh.

Heinse made an assault on Monte Cavo in 1782 along the triumphal route of the Latins (Pl. 1) to hail the humbled Jupiter – the Passionists were perched there like vultures [135].

THE COMMON WEAL

Al gatto del Papa si dice Monsignore

I

The first public building in Rome that any traveller would make an acquaintance with was a papal customs house. A building of that kind was to be found in several places; two were built by the river harbours, a third – the largest – was right inside the city. There were also guards at the main gates. Innocent XII Pignatelli organized the customs and excise for the express purpose of obtaining funds for the enlargement of a large charitable institution for underprivileged children. The two customs houses which he established were meant to give visitors to Rome as favourable a first impression of the city as possible. Had the irritable sea-captains and the exhausted travellers known of the good intention of the Pope, in which he partly succeeded, they might perhaps have delivered up a small prayer of thanks as well as the tribute money.

Along the bank of the Tiber opposite the ridge of the Aventine is a district which still retains much of its Baroque character. It is worth a visit from those who do not merely seek the picturesque but who also wish to savour the spirit of daily life as it was in the Rome of a bygone age. By this stretch of the river, with clayey slopes running down to the yellow oily water, lay the city's harbour for ships coming up the Tiber from the Mediterranean. This harbour, called the *Ripa Grande,* was a simple berth without wharfs. The bales of goods which were to be inspected by customs and put into storage were hauled up a ramp to a customs house overhanging the river. It was sited in line with a street which, at right angles to the bank, leads up to S. Maria dell' Orto. The terrain here along the harbour and out as far as the Porta Portese, squeezed in between bastions from Urban VIII's time, in 1680 formed a large rectangle of walled-in gardens backed by a road running parallel to the river. This area on the southern outskirts of Trastevere was at that time meant as a building site for the combined workhouse and orphanage which was given the name of Ospizio Apostolico di San Michele (Pl. 75).

The old customs house (*Dogana Vecchia*), which resembled a dockside inn suffering from dry rot in a river painting by van Goyen [1], had to be pulled down to make room for the future monumental building. So the Pope decided to build a new customs house with a storehouse right next to Porta Portese and to include it in the corner bastion facing the Tiber. Here the building was not in the way, and had a clear view along the river bank in front of the hospice which had by now been started. It is necessary to be acquainted with these circumstances to be able to understand the shape of the building [2]. The new customs house, erected at the beginning of the 1690's by Mattia de Rossi [3] and completed by Carlo Fontana, was built on a very irregular plan so as to fit into the angles of the bastion. As was proper for a building which was to further the fiscal interests of the State, its exterior was given a somewhat stern appearance, but "the function" did not entirely undermine the artistic expression. The projecting portico, keeping a benign eye on the whole of the harbour was ashlared according to military precept and topped with a superstructure decorated with sculpture [4]. We recognize the style from Christian VI's customs house in Copenhagen. It was probably Fontana who added the arcade; under its arches the customs officers and the traders could take shelter (Pl. 85).

La Dogana di Ripa Grande no longer exists – more's the pity. It dominated this busy quarter by the harbour and city gate. And the corner-stone is missing in the magnificent Baroque complex which we shall discuss later.

La Dogana di Terra, where duty was levied on goods arriving overland, is situated in the Piazza di Pietra and was given its modern appearance when Hadrian's temple was converted. The work, completed in 1695, was supervised by Francesco Fontana and he may well have provided the plan as well. In Specchi's engraving from 1696 it is expressly stated that "the architecture" is by Cavaliere Francesco [5]. Nevertheless a not very closely defined, but presumably decisive influence on the project has been ascribed to Carlo Fontana [6]. The conjecture is obvious.

All the same, why should the not very prominent son be named as the originator, if the design comes from his famous father? Whoever it was that did the work, it shows great talent and much credit to the designer. It is also typical of the refined taste which at that time was expressed in additions to antique buildings, particularly in Fontana's circle.

The architect realized at once that the portico of the Hadrianeum with its tall Corinthian columns could best come into its own by being included in a modern façade and by being used in a building that was alive. The colonnade was like a buttress which was self-contained and waiting for the rest of the building to catch up. Fontana drew the natural conclusion without hesitation. He added a section at each end of the colonnade, made these parts (each of two bays) recede and enclosed them with pilasters, the capitals of which were made from an example by Borromini (Oratorio dei Filippini). This shows the architect's genuine taste; any close competition between the old and the new, which would inevitably occur if he made the capitals for his pilasters imitate the antique, was to be avoided. So a capital was deliberately chosen which was unobtrusive. The central projection of the portico was further strengthened by an attica, which was going to be decorated with statues.

The appearance of the customs house after it had been rebuilt showed that the temple had been respected, although the intercolumniations obviously had to be filled in, and *Roma moderna* was enriched by a palace which was in the spirit of the mature Bernini. The Palazzo Chigi-Odescalchi (1665) could be glimpsed in the background, and here again, the contrast between a wide central section with large columns and subordinate end sections is the principal motif. But the substance of Fontana's work is Antiquity's own.

It is our belief that the customs house in the Piazza di Pietra was the most majestic building of its kind in Europe at that time. And where is its like today? The Romans were presumably proud of it, and one might well believe that even worshippers of Antiquity who came to Rome for the first time and were immediately faced with his magnificent peristyle must have felt edified. But this was not the case with the French adherents to Rococo, for they were too schooled in pedantry. When dear de Brosses came face to face with Fontana's masterly show-piece in 1738, he was extremely indignant about "those filthy swine who have filled in the spaces between the columns with an ugly patchwork just to make a hang-out for scoundrels" [7]. How can a nation with any sense of greatness and nobility in art commit *une action si basse?* The president's anger was aggravated by the humiliation which he like many other tourists suffered; he had a book confiscated, Misson's guide into the bargain, which was on the blacklist of the Inquisition [8]. Duclos escaped a similar fate in 1767, for he knew all about it in advance and had omitted to bring the criminal manual with him [9].

Thus from its very inception *la Dogana di Terra* witnessed innumerable squabbles between travellers and customs officials. Every day the columns looked down on indignant people who had their entry into the Eternal City spoiled – and afterwards got their own back by condemning the taste of the building. A sensible man got off lightly by admiring the façade "which is well designed". That was in 1773 [10]; otherwise all true believers among the Neo-classicists in Goethe's time were disgusted at the defiling of this temple. Not until the Romantic period was the merit of the work appreciated. It was found intriguing, a fitting example of "the miraculous city, where the old has grown together with the new in such a way that both form an indivisible whole – the only one of its kind the world has to show" (Chr. Molbech) [11]. It was the great spirit of Baroque which made the relics of Antiquity unfold and break out from the lifelessness of the ruins.

This central customs house at once gave the traveller the strong impression that he was visiting a capital without parallel. The building showed a Janus head and proved that the rock of Rome had deep fault lines. Here the gap caused by the passage of time had closed. Elsewhere the seams were visible which resulted from the strange stratification of the Roman community.

As the Papal State was constituted it was inevitable that its official architecture at one and the same time had the same general tone, yet a tendency towards disharmony. By far the majority of public buildings in Rome were religious houses. The rest belonged to the Church. The concept of the common weal had a different meaning here from in the other capitals of Europe, and necessarily so, for Rome resembled none of them, neither in spirit nor structure. Just as the Pope's tiara is made up of three rings, Rome was a capital in three realms. It vindicated its title of *caput mundi,* was the seat of government for the universal Catholic Church whose boundaries reached to the ends of the earth and cut across the frontiers of all monarchies. Then again Rome was the seat of government of an Italian state which was secular in its mechanism, if not in its motive force. Finally Rome was itself, the heir to the Imperial City, a municipality raised up on the dais of history.

In each of these guises Rome had to have public buildings. Some were common to all three forms of government, others were not. The administration by the Curia of a spiritual state within the world at large needed government offices and courts; the Church-State also had use for such, but needed all sorts of other buildings for civic welfare. And finally the City of Rome had to have a say in the architecture. This it did in the *Capitolium,* a resounding name and a Michelangelo masterpiece, the proudest town hall in Christendom, visible from everywhere and in influence on municipal architecture throughout the whole of Europe.

A state organization *in spiritualibus* is particular in its attitude towards architecture. The more superior the administrators, the more ethereal their relationships become. Right at the top where Christ's Vicar beholds God's handiwork and pronounces infallible judgment, there are no housing problems. The papal throne and the dais of the Prince of Apostles are pieces of furniture without substance. And as the autocratic ruler over his secular State, the Pope as the final authority only needed a cabinet. The palace which houses it is the centre of government. It was the same in the France of Louis XV. But Versailles has its *Cour des Ministres* in front of the king's palace. The Vatican did not know what the concept of ministry was, in the normal meaning of the word, and so had no ministerial building. The College of Cardinals neither has been, nor is today, comparable with a Cabinet of Ministers; it is more like a House of Lords, but without constitutional rights. It acted as an advisory senate and, at the accession of a new pope, as an electoral body. As such, their Eminences have no need of offices.

Those members highest in the administration, who aided Pontifex Maximus in the execution of his duties, were the so-called congregations,

73. *Castel S. Angelo. – Painting by Gaspare Vanvitelli. (Detail).*

74. *Piazza del Quirinale (Monte Cavallo)*.

75. *Ripa Grande and Ospizio di S. Michele. Engraving from the age of Pius VI.*

76. *Piazza del Quirinale with Palazzo della Consulta and (on the right) the Papal Stables. Painting by Pan*

of which many, among them the most renowned, are still maintained. They can be compared with the specialist councils, which under the name of Colleges handled the affairs of the Ministries in Denmark between 1660 and 1848. The majority of these *Congregazioni,* each of which was made up of cardinals and other high prelates with a prefect at their head and who made up the core of *la Curia Romana,* in those days held their meetings in the Vatican or in the palace to which their ruler summoned them. At times they assembled in the house of the prefect. Such central bodies – some of which (e. g. Congregazione Consistoriale and the Congregazione dei Sacramenti) are invested with universal authority, while others (such as the Congr. Ceremoniale and Congr. della Reverenda Fabbrica di S. Pietro) have only a very narrow sphere of influence – had to do their work wherever they could, but performed an influential and secret function. There was no inscription above any portal announcing that the government was carried on from here. The inner cabinet (as we would call it nowadays) neither desired nor needed to advertise itself. Even today the State Secretariat, the Papal Ministry for Foreign Affairs, is housed on one of the Vatican's most inaccessible top floors [12]. Only a couple of the congregations had always had special buildings at their command, namely the College of the Inquisition (*Suprema Sacra Congregazione del Sant' Officio*) and the College of Missionaries (*Sacra Congregazione di Propaganda Fide*), since their activities required a considerable amount of space indoors, but even in such huge hives, a council only needed a cell for its meetings.

Another category of papal administrative bodies, the so-called *Uffizi,* in spite of being hierarchically of lower rank than the congregations, had a more extensive power and influenced the life of the community to a greater degree. The Chancellery (*la Cancelleria Apostolica*) was the best situated, being housed in the palace of that name, the masterpiece from the early Renaissance. The Vice-Chancellor of the Holy Roman Church had his residence here, and holders of this office – people like Cardinal Pietro Ottoboni and the Cardinal Duke of York – were particularly demanding and claimed much of the palace space. The largest hall, a room of enormous dimensions, was however reserved for the officials of the Chancellery when they assembled to prepare the Papal

Bulls. The interior had to inspire confidence, hence Clement XI in 1718 had its walls decorated with Franceschini's cartoons for the mosaics in the dome of St. Peter's, and beneath these a series of paintings of buildings which this pope had erected or restored [13]. While Archinto, the Cardinal Secretary of State, had the Cancelleria at his disposal, he gave his librarian Winckelmann an enviable bachelor apartment on the third floor of the palace. The proud young scholar mentions in a letter that his sitting-room facing the square had a balcony [14]. We know from Vasi's engraving [15] that only a single window on this floor was provided with one. So Winckelmann's window was on the middle axis of the façade, right above the portal. No member of the Cardinal's household (*famiglia*) could have been better placed nor have had a more magnificent view. If he looked straight ahead, he could look right into the Square of the Poultry Keepers (Piazza Pollarola). Many public buildings gave accommodation to laymen. In the Neapolitan Embassy (Palazzo Farnese) a few steps away from the Chancellery, the engraver Giuseppe Vasi had found a refuge – although on the first floor facing the courtyard; he was after all the Duke of Cerisano's *guardaroba*. The palace swarmed to such an extent with hangers-on that it was nicknamed *il Ghetto di Farnese* [16]. Even the official buildings that were most wrapped around with red tape suffered no loss of status because of the noise of the lodgers upstairs, or the sight of nappies blowing in the wind. We should not disregard this very human, truly Roman characteristic before we venture further among the façades of officialdom. The back premises could be fitted in with the front premises without the piano nobile losing its dignity.

At the beginning of the 1730's a building was erected for two important State bodies, the Secretariat for Apostolic Briefs and the so-called *Consulta,* which had various juridical and administrative powers, revised death sentences, supervised provincial governors and kept an eye on the sanitary authorities. This College corresponded roughly to a "Ministry of the Interior". By virtue of its situation in the Piazza del Quirinale, opposite the papal residence, and because of its artistic form, the Palazzo della Consulta became the most representative building of the Roman civil administration. Its elegance was also due to the fact that the two prefects of these offices, both cardinals, were domiciled within the walls of the palace, one being the renowned bibliophile Domenico Passionei, who was Secretary for Apostolic Briefs from 1738. The building was moreover erected as barracks for the Papal Horse Guards. These colourful warriors provided the architect with a stimulus for his chivalresque style.

Fuga, to whom the task was consigned, had to solve a complex problem. He was to give the Piazza del Quirinale a new enclosing wall to balance up with the palace and the recently finished Papal Stables. He had to adapt, yet not lose his grip. The bulk of the Quirinal Palace could not possibly be outdone, but the authority of the Consulta and the splendour of the cuirassiers had to be proclaimed. The new building was one of inherent contrasts; its purpose was divided between the civil and the military, and each of these bodies was again subdivided: two "offices", two guards. We shall in the first instance see how Fuga came to terms with the façade. He divided it horizontally into two storeys; the upper was the haunt of the cardinals; the cavalry jingled at the bottom. The distinction between the ostensibly equal authorities in the "piano nobile" and the two rival guards on the ground floor was cleverly managed by dividing the front into three sections with the help of a centre ressaut containing the main portal; this established the high rank of the palace. The martial elements could come on parade through the gateways on either side. The completed building was lower than the Quirinal Palace and to some extent subordinate to it (Pl. 76).

But nobody would take the Palazzo della Consulta for being the wing of a princely *cour d'honneur;* the architecture is too expressive for that. The disciplined plan of the façade is translated into a relief on several planes and with closely drawn lines. Fuga, austere at other times, in this instance realized that the building could only retain its individuality by being in the light when the palace is in the dark, and by forming a contrast to the weighty colossus opposite. In the same way that Fuga faced up to the way the wind was blowing from the Quirinal, he also built in a more modern idiom. It was as if he here received a certain impulse to demonstrate the strength of subdivision when confronted by a massive building with unbroken surfaces. It is moreover quite possible that Cardinal Corsini, a nephew of the Pope, who was acquainted with the courts of Europe, had a strong hand in it. Although the Consulta as a State institution could not be compared with the Reichskanzlei in Vienna, with Whitehall in London or with the red ministerial building in Copenhagen, the Palazzo most elegantly represented the Curia in Rome. Both the architect and the Cardinal may well have had in mind the Chancellery wing in the Hofburg, J. B. Fischer von Erlach's creation, with its severe pilasters and the mezzanine below the top cornice, as found originally in Rome [17].

The Consulta has indeed a milder tone than the Austrian palace, which is so imperial and arrogant. Apart from one feature – the segmental pediments of the windows in the piano nobile – the composition shows no French influence, but is Roman with a touch of a north-westerly breeze. The palace has a certain similarity with the architecture in Turin without being directly influenced by Juvara. The luxuriousness of the relief is both a trifle bombastic and rather lifeless. And the delicate straw-yellow colour looks faded against the full-blooded hue of the stables.

The old palace which stood on the site was pulled down in 1732, and the foundation stone for the new one laid on October 9th of the same year. In August 1733 the completion of the roof trusses was celebrated. The Pope treated each of the 160 workmen to 1 lb of macaroni and provided 10 barrels of wine as well as bread, cheese and sausage. By 1735 Clement XII's coat of arms had been set up in the middle of the roof balustrade, but it was not until 1739 that the main portal was given its allegorical figures (by Maini) [18]. The painting reproduced in Plate 76 dates from as early as 1733, so Pannini, who is the artist, must have used Fuga's drawings. De Brosses saw the palace when it was brand-new and found the architecture "extremely tasteful" [19], although he was otherwise very critical of contemporary architecture in Rome. When he in this case showed his approbation, it is clear that it was the elegance in the work more than anything which struck a chord in his French heart.

Pannini's view of Monte Cavallo is seen roughly from the position where a steep street (Salita della Dataria) runs past the Papal Palace down towards the Trevi district (Pl. 74). This road gives the impression of being a dignified backstairs to the residence, and there is an unmistakeable scent of chancellery, dust and sand issuing from the papal office buildings with *la Dataria Apostolica* in their midst. The two most important facts about the building are that it dates from the time of Urban VIII and that the authority housed in it could grant dispensations. Otherwise the building is completely negative, but on the other hand the governmental palace built a hundred years later in the Piazza del Quirinale has something to boast about [20].

The finance department of the Papal State, the focal point of which was the Apostolic Chamber, had put its stamp on three excellent works of architecture – all older than our period, but we cannot possibly overlook them. *Banco di S. Spirito* (founded 1605) seems to have been named after the Holy Ghost. Very creditable indeed, but it benefited the establishment's credit far more that its real namesake and guarantor was the Hospital of the Holy Spirit whose riches were immense. Rome's most important bank enjoys the honour of having called forth a work by Borromini, but this is not generally recognized. The building is still extant and stands in the Piazza dell' Orologio, near Monte Giordano, but has lost its original character by being renovated at the end of the last century. It is mentioned in the literature under the name of Palazzo Spada. However, there is no doubt that Borromini designed the building as a bank. A property had originally been rented in the old banking quarter in front of Ponte S. Angelo, but these premises in the Casa Sterbini proved to be inadequate. Mgr. Virgilio Spada, *commendatore* for the S. Spirito Hospital therefore had a new building started in 1661, but after Spada's death at the end of 1662 the officials of the bank, who did not want to leave the time-honoured financial centre, were successful in halting the construction. Virgilio Spada's heir, Marchese Orazio Spada, was forced to take over the half-finished bank building [21]. According to old engravings [22] this was very different from the usual types of palaces in Rome, and naturally so, for Borromini was a true architect. What is surprising is that art historians have, without a murmur, been able to accept the building as a private house, albeit Alexander VII's name was there to be read in large letters on the attica of the façade [23]. Properly evaluated, Borromini's work is an interesting attempt to compose a special style dictated by the task; the bureaucratic style. He has for once designed a façade which is not "baroque" and almost dull.

In 1667 the Bank of the Holy Spirit was transferred to a palace, which could be said to be the oldest example in Rome of a monumental utilitarian building with a purely secular purpose – that is the "Mint", *la Zecca Vecchia*, built during the reign of the Medici Pope Clement VII (1523–1534), following a design by A. da Sangallo [24]. This is where the Banco di S. Spirito still is, the place where cardinals and princes raised their loans when they were going to build palaces and repay debts, in the building, erected *con bellissima grazia* (as Vasari said), where once the pope's ducats were struck.

The hunt for ready cash led the Roman to the pawnbroker. The loan bank *Monte di Pietà* – again a money box with a holy name – was established under the protection of a saint, Carlo Borromeo, and in 1604 took over a palace owned by the Santacroce family. The building was restored by Maderno [25] and was extended a number of times, so that in the end it embraced a very large rugged block. A wing towards the Piazza S. S. Trinità was added from 1735 onwards by Sebastiano Cipriani, aided by Salvi, who became the former's successor as architect in 1740 [26]. The establishment does in fact seem like a mountain, and during walks in the district one is constantly aware of its bare walls rising steeply above the crowded dwelling houses, shutting out the views and making churches seem small (Pl. 77). Of all municipal buildings in Rome the Monte di Pietà is the most impressive, being completely homogeneous, the later additions too having the rugged style of a massif. Its authority is not bruited abroad by distinctive marks but expresses itself in Spartan form by its hugeness. The best of Late Baroque's public buildings with a mundane objective all learned a lesson from the "Mountain of Compassion". They achieved true greatness by not pretending to be more than they really were (Pl. 85).

On the very fringe of the history of architecture there are some public buildings which were of major importance in the daily life of the people and which were regarded by the man in the street with far greater attention than all the beautiful palaces. We refer here to the provision depots.

Providing the city with corn and oil, the most important foodstuffs, was the monopoly of the State and was administered (not without some abuse) through the prefecture *dell' Annona* [27]. Rome has, as we all know, an incomparable ability to give the simple but important things of life proportional house-room; a store becomes a monument, or is one; for if necessary the ancient ruins open their gates. Octavia's portico lent the public fish-market (*la Pescheria*) its arches [28]. The large corn stores (*Granari*) had since Gregory XIII's time been accommodated in Diocletian's thermae and were thus neighbours of the Carthusians. Fontana undertook an extention in 1705. After a fire in 1763 the restored granary was given a new portal of rare nobility [29], which showed respect for both the magnificent ruin and the poor man's daily bread.

The paternal care of the government was also extended to the Romans' stimulants. A public building, which really did serve the common weal, was the papal tobacco factory. Its product did not however envelop the Apostolic See with sweet-smelling incense; no miracle is known to have taken place under State monopoly. A number of popes in the Quirinal had a real appreciation of "the great God Nick O'Teen" as well. This was true of the hedonist Innocent XIII, who according to Kreyssler [30] liked a pipe of tobacco and, self-indulgent to the extreme, "spent much time on the night-stool"; the last named pose seems fitting, for Conti always did things in style, but it is difficult to imagine this particular pope with a pipe in one hand and the keys in the other. It is more surprising that Benedict XIII was also enamoured of tobacco, and he is said to have lifted the ban which his predecessors had imposed upon snuff-takers in St. Peter's; the reason may have been that he considered the contrast between the basilica and a snuff-box out of proportion [31]. Besides, tobacco in suitable doses was regarded as an anti-aphrodisiac and therefore appreciated by many priests. This was not necessarily the reason for Benedict XIV's devotion to the delicious weed, and he was flattered by the name "Papa Tabaccone". When a prelate, to whom he offered a pinch, sanctimoniously refused it, saying that he was spared this vice, he was met with the apostolic answer: "It is not a vice and if it were, you would surely have it too" [32]. And we see Lambertini at the Pearly Gates with his snuff-box. Pietro Bracci placed it in its usual place beneath the apostolic thumb when he carved the figure of the Pope for the sepulchral monument in St. Peter's; Benedict is giving his blessing with the other hand. It is not known whether Clement XIV Ganganelli was a devotee of tobacco – he had so few trustworthy friends and deserved at least one – but he had plenty of opportunity. He received considerable consignments from the King of Spain, the finest snuff manufactured in the factory in Seville (completed 1757, later the place where Carmen worked), and the Bishop of Havana presented him in 1774 with "a crate made of Indian wood containing 24 porcelain jars filled with tobacco" from his fortunate See [33].

The manufacture of tobacco in Rome was farmed out until Benedict XIV made the State take over the business and set up a factory in the present Via Garibaldi. The building, large but quite plain, stood opposite S. Maria dei Sette Dolori, next door to the Assunta sanctuary (Pl. 70) and can be seen in an engraving by Vasi [34]. Like the mills on the slopes of Gianicolo it obtained its water power from Acqua Paola above the Arcadians' garden.

Papa Tabaccone's factory was followed by the grandiose concern which Pio Nono built in the middle of Trastevere. It still pleases the smoking public with its inscription, in which the curial Latin consecrates pipe tobacco and snuff:

PIUS IX P. M.
OFFICINAM NICOTIANIS FOLIIS
EXSTRUXIT
ANNO MDCCCLXII

II

The Roman legal machinery creaked horribly and was very complicated, numerous courts putting obstacles in the way of one another. Tribunals had ill-defined powers and their jurisdiction fluid boundaries, so the poor subject had to run from pillar to post, in a literal sense too, for the courts were scattered all over the city. It mattered less that the courts of the Roman Church with universal competence in spiritual affairs were also widely distributed, for these high authorities were not exactly popular or sought after, nor was there any danger of their premises being confused, even less overlooked. Who was ignorant of the Inquisition's headquarters? The ecclesiastical Court of Appeal with the harsh sounding name *Sacra Romana Rota* held its sittings in the Vatican itself. Or, when the Pope was in residence at the Quirinal, in the Chancellery, and *la Penitenzieria* with the Grand Penitentiary as president, the special court in "matters of conscience" [35], called those in question to the Palazzo dei Penitenzieri, a cadaverous building in the Piazza Scossacavalli, which has recently been pulled down.

Minor courts flourished like weeds. It was imperative to fuse together most of these courts whose activities were wholly or predominantly local, and which often interfered in the daily life of the population. This was done to some extent during the time of Innocent XII. To this end he bought the Palazzo Ludovisi on Montecitorio, which Bernini had started building in 1650 but never completed. Carlo Fontana was ordered to finish the work and convert it into a palace of Justice. His first plans were so high-flown that they could not be put into practice [36]. The idea was to have the building surround a large courtyard, closed to the north on the tapering site of a semicircular building. In the autumn of 1694 a very abridged design was approved and three years later the work was finished. Two narrow wings at the back and an exedra of decorative barrier walls with niches now enclosed the cortile. The façades facing inwards were divided up by arcades, some of them bricked up. The central ressaut in Bernini's main front was increased in height by the addition of an attica and an *orologio,* thereby giving the *Curia Innocenziana* its proper official character; the minor courts could now safely proliferate to their hearts' content in unison and in cold premises. "All the procurators and such people who plague the human race under the name of servants of the law, and who like doctors are a sinister aftermath of original sin, have their offices or haunts in one and the same place ... here all cases are heard and all documents kept, so that without leaving the palace one can ruin oneself and one's neighbour without undue effort" [37]. This characterization of the Law Courts, made roughly twenty years after completion, is from an Inquisitor with a sense of humour.

The Palazzo di Montecitorio played the difficult role of a dispenser of justice in a city with a background of harsh Roman Law and of a mediator in a society where, according to Winckelmann, "nobody commands and nobody obeys". But the building itself stood firm, based on Bernini's authority. The papal regime, ever paternal and wordly-wise, later used the balcony above Fontana's columned portal as the stage for drawing the beloved lottery, which took place to the sound of music and much rejoicing. On C. F. Hansen's courthouse in Copenhagen are the words: "A country must be built upon law"; its stern portico emphasizes this. Rome's *curia* proclaimed a different maxim from the balcony: "The public weal is furthered by lottery". The inhabitants sometimes looked at the stronghold of Justice through rose-coloured spectacles and were not always confronted with the harsh truth as they passed by. In a building opposite the palace the stamped paper introduced by Benedict XIV was on sale. In the lawyer Goldoni's time there was much coming and going by attorneys and officers of justice in black robes with small white collars (we are reminded of the inevitable notary in old plays, e. g. Don Curzio in "The Marriage of Figaro"), and lo! when the lots were drawn from the silver urn, it was "a boy in a large black hat" from the White Friars orphanage who brought the glad news. This is recorded by Hans Andersen in his diary of January 23rd 1841.

The Governor of Rome was a very powerful personage; he belonged to the prelature, surrounded himself with a guard of honour of Halbardiers and was invariably created cardinal after his retirement. He presided over his own tribunal which embraced both civil and criminal courts, and was the city's chief of police with a large corps of sbirri under his command (in 1758 this was in the region of 1000 men), legitimate brigands under the direct command of a *bargello*. To this could be added several hundred spies. An English observer, Charles Hervey, regarded them (1761) as second to none [38]; a Frenchman of the same period gave the whole Roman police force a splendid testimonial: "They solve everything without being seen or heard" [39]. Every legal authority used paid snoopers, even the Cardinal Vicar (i. e. the Pope's representative as Bishop of Rome) could not, at the diocesan authority, keep his eye on the priesthood without plenty of assistance from a "secret service"

[40]. The Governor had his offices and law-courts in the Palazzo Nardini, a handsome building from the Early Renaissance period, until Benedict XIV transferred them to the Palazzo Madama which was taken over from the Grand Duke of Tuscany [41]. Rome's Governor was thus given a truly magnificent residence. When the original governor's palace was vacated, the street in which it was situated was re-christened Via del Governo Vecchio, a resounding name. It was in the middle of the last century that *il Governatorato* was transferred to Pal. di Montecitorio. One was received here by the latest Roman prefect of police of the Papal State, Monsignore Randi [42]. Vilh. Bergsøe has described an audience with this talented numismatist (the poet calls him Renzi), "a tall, thin man in magenta silk stockings" [43].

Rome's ancient prisons were appalling. This was especially true of *il Carceri Capitolino* hidden in the vaults of the Tabularium beneath the Palazzo Senatorio and reserved for the felons condemned by the municipal tribunal [44]. Throughout the day the convicts clung to the bars of the large windows shouting piteously to the people outside: "Give a bajacco to the poor prisoners!" (*Date un bajacco ai poveri carcerati!*) [45] and pushed rods with bags on the end out through the bars bawling *Mosiu! Milord!* [46]. Still worse were the underground dungeons in the Castel Sant'Angelo, which the curious nowadays only enter with a shudder of horror. The very fact that it is necessary to bend so low to get through the doors of the cells is enough to send a shiver down your spine. Here the darkness of the grave prevails, the cells put you in mind of wells and indeed some of them were once used to hold grain. The towering citadel weighs upon the prisoners, grinding them down. The cells for political prisoners were slightly better and higher up, facing on to a small courtyard which is neither devoid of humanity nor art. The galley slaves, many of them en route to the naval base of Civitavecchia, were quartered in a wing at the foot of the fortress, in the damp shadow between Sant'Angelo's outer defences and the drum of the citadel itself [47]. You cannot pass by this place – with Clement XII's chapel for those condemned to death – without remembering the exercise yard for the prisoners in "Fidelio", and the echo of Tosca's scream seems to hang over the castle's dizzy battlements. Languishing in the depths from Dec. 27th

1789–April 7th 1791 was someone who can vie with the most dramatic figures of grand opera. This was Giuseppe Balsamo, called Count Cagliostro [48].

However, the atmosphere surrounding this papal Bastille was not as horrific as was that enveloping the prisons of the Inquisition, nor was the fog of secrecy so impenetrable. These were situated in the palace where the ecclesiastical court had its official premises, and still has, in a deep square immediately west of the colonnades of St. Peter's. The building has, in recent times, been given a completely characterless façade, but old photographs show that by its gloomy exterior alone it could instil fearful forebodings; small spy-holes scattered across a menacing, towering wall [49]. The palace was not old as Rome understood it and in fact took shape in 1569 [50], but gradually became rather neglected in appearance. But nobody was encouraged to inspect it at close quarters. Its solidity left nothing to be desired, even if the plaster did fall off the walls.

Officially the General of the Dominicans was the "first counsellor" in the College of the Inquisition and the strongest man after the cardinals of this court [51]. Only by closer contact with this powerful prelate could one hope for an entry into this sealed building. On June 10th, 1709 the Dominican General Cloche drove out to the Palazzo del Sacro Uffizio and took his compatriot Père Labat, a young friar of the order, with him in his carriage. The third member of the party was the General's secretary, Frater Baptiste, known in the history of art as the flower painter Jean-Baptiste Monnoyer [52]. We can well believe that the drive of these gentlemen from the Minerva monastery to the repelling tribunal was interlaced with amusing conversation, for the General possessed a sarcastic wit that spared no one – he compared Cardinal Orsini, later Pope Benedict XIII, with a hunting horn "harsh, twisted and empty" [53] – nor was Père Labat backward in this respect. But if this latter, encouraged by his General's *bonhomie,* imagined that at the end of the trip he could subject the Inquisition's prison to a close scrutiny with his protector as guide, he was to be disappointed. He had to be satisfied with a view of the barred windows from the outside, and by his estimate they measured 4×3 feet, and sloping screens cut off all contact with the outside world, allowing the prisoners only a glimpse of a narrow strip of sky. To judge from the distance between these windows, the cells must have been about 10 feet wide. Labat was told that they were quite airy and light, "more than sufficient for that sort of people". The good Dominican felt very uncomfortable "in this holy place" and only wanted to get away, to the great amusement of his guide [54].

If a visitor with such good connections as Labat did not have his curiosity satisfied, it is not surprising that John Howard went there in vain. This man of humanitarian sentiment, a pioneer in the history of criminal law, examined Italy's gaols in 1778 and has described them in his classic work on the prisons of Europe. Doors otherwise closed were opened to this fearless man in most places, even in Russia, but when he tried to make his way into the building belonging to the Roman Inquisition he came up against a dead end. In his "State of Prisons" he writes that the rooms in this silent and melancholy house were always forbidden him, although he managed to spend nearly two hours in the courtyard before his presence there began to arouse suspicion [55].

So we have to make do without any really authentic detailed description of the most notorious prisons in Rome and in the world for that matter, since only a few people ever came out and even fewer were at all anxious to draw attention to themselves by talking about it. We have however an account by one person who succeeded in escaping from the house of the Inquisition. He was in holy orders and named Giuseppe Pignata, being secretary to Prince Gabrielli. One morning he was arrested on his way from the palace (the present Pal. Gabrielli-Taverna on Montegiordano) down to the Via del Governo Vecchio and was taken to the Palazzo del Sacro Uffizio. This probably took place in 1690. Pignata's later escape (1963) was no doubt just as great an achievement as Casanova's from the leads of the Doge's palace in 1756, but our priest is certainly far from being as brilliant a raconteur as the Venetian. Various things seems to indicate that his account, which was published in 1725 in a rare and little noticed book [56], may well be veracious, so perhaps we can trust some particulars, such as the height of his cell which was 17 feet, measured with a broomstick. He does leave us with the impression that the regulations in the prison were not inhuman, and this adds credence to Pignata's information. He and his cell-mate had at their disposal three tables ("two to study at, the third to eat at"), as well as a couple of armchairs, and of course a bed. Our hero was even somewhat put out that he was refused a harpsichord [57]. The terrifying thing about this building was its silence.

The great papal State prison for common criminals, called *Tor' di Nona* after a mediaeval tower, was situated on the Tiber in the Via dell' Orso, not far from the Ponte S. Angelo. In a little square in front of this bridge, public executions took place. This prison, which was a gloomy collection of buildings, some of which were very old, had its outer walls washed by the waters of the river. A stink of corruption filled its vaults and when the Tiber rose the poor wretches incarcerated here found themselves in what amounted to a sewer [58]. During his time as judge advocate at the Rota court, Innocent X Pamphili became familiar with the Tor' di Nona, which was always filled to overflowing like a nest of vipers, and was deeply moved by the plight of the prisoners [59]. Shortly after he became pope (1644) he had the foundation stone laid for a new and properly run prison in the Via Giulia, called *Carceri Nuove* from that time onwards. It was completed at the beginning of the pontificate of his successor, Alexander XVII Chigi (1655), and is still in good condition, but has now been turned into a museum of criminology [60].

When you consider that this gaol was planned at the time of Charles I, its modernity is amazing. You find broad staircases with low risers, airy corridors, plenty of room, good organization. The prisoners were no longer treated like wild animals, but as men created in the image of God, who had misbehaved and were in need of discipline. The actual word clemency appears in the inscription over the gateway [61]. In the same way as the principles of humane punishment were laid down by an Italian, Cesare Beccaria, whose epoch-making work "Crime and Punishment" came out in 1764, so it is a credit to the Rome of the popes that it built a prison which may be considered the oldest humane one in Europe. It is worth noting, as Howard did, that the sanatorium with its 17 beds was spacious and thoroughly clean. This can be compared with the ghastly prisons in Siberia which were built and used two hundred years later to the eternal shame of Czarist Russia [62]. The old tradition of monastic architecture benefited this main Roman prison of the Baroque period, for the gaolbirds were now incarcerated in rooms that were bare, clean and whitewashed like a monk's cell. In the Carceri Nuove it was still the custom to put several prisoners in the same cell, where they had to remain both day and night, a practice which easily lead to permanent overcrowding [63]. But a commendable segregation into various categories was put into effect; boys, priests, prisoners with skin diseases and Jews were accommodated separately. Although the isolation of the latter was in no way dictated by humanitarian considerations, it must have made things easier for the barely tolerated Hebrews. As in Sant'Angelo, the cell door was lower than the height of a man, which had no other purpose than to teach the prisoners humility. In our eyes a repelling detail, yet a penitent in a church had to submit to far more severe penance than merely bend his head.

Carceri Nuove was not only an admirable institution for its time but it was also superb architecture (Pl. 16). Antonio Del Grande, who was the architect, experimented with very large and very simple details and swore by each of them. The smooth window frames and the plain string course above the ground floor look like stone planks. The "Egyptian" ashlar portal with the side posts converging towards the top is as solid as the rock of ages. The entrance to the burial chamber of a papal sepulchral monument was similar, and it later became the central motif in Thorvaldsen's mausoleum. The tablet bearing the inscription above the gateway to the prison is a sharp-edged block with tooth-like projections at its base. But the windows are large and let plenty of light into the interior. The front is finished right at the top by a cavetto cut on generous lines, which is reminiscent of church façades in Rome from the Middle Ages (Aracoeli; S. Maria in Trastevere; S. Maria sopra Minerva) and goes right back to a temple in the days of Pharaoh.

Two new prisons were built in the 18th century, both on modern lines. Rome's streets swarmed with little ragamuffins who were a complete pest to inoffensive people. Clement XI decided to put the worst of them all together in a special *Youth detention centre* which was erected in 1703 as an annex to the Ospizio di S. Michele, following a design by Carlo Fontana. His praiseworthy intention was not so much to render these small needy bandits harmless, as to rehabilitate them. They were divided up into classes according to age and conduct and were to work as a community, though isolated at night in individual cells. There was no previous architecture to provide for such a system. Fortana sought the solution along the lines where it was most obvious, namely in the galleys. He planned a large hall two storeys high, and across this workshop, called *la galera,* long benches were set up to which the miscreants were chained, just like slaves in the floating prisons. Spiral staircases in the corners of the hall led up to the galleries on the long sides, onto which the cell doors opened [64]. The exterior of the prison, facing on to a back street, is a pure geometrical pattern of barred windows, small squares closely grouped between large rectangles. This specialization in penal reform was continued during the time of Clement XII by the building of a *Women's House of Correction* designed by Fuga and paid for by the lottery. It was set out along the same lines as the prison for young offenders, but this theoretically ideal system was not to remain so in practice [65]. This prison too, was linked to the S. Michele hospice, and the extensive façade takes up one side of the square opposite Porta Portese (Pl. 79). By this, the tall building obstructed the view from the monastery by S. Francesco a Ripa; the prison disturbed the peace of the cloister, and this annoyed Cardinal Spinola, the protector of the pious institution, so much that he became quite ill from indignation [66]. Fuga's work is certainly well worth looking at. Carceri Nuove is clearly something of a pattern for its severe style, but the building's structure is both delicate and dry. The unobtrusive pilaster strips finished at the top with slightly raised panels, form a framework with the very fine returned cornice. In its style the façade is reminiscent of the Palazzina of the Quirinal, but it is, as it were, fined down. In fact, we can but agree that the compulsory nature of this task has in no way made the architecture bleak, still less dispirited. It is very extraordinary that Fuga was able to avoid anything forced; the polite spirit of his age is expressed in this way. Carceri Nuove was a serious building, the women's prison is a reserved one.

That this civic idea of a prison as an architectural concept had become established can be seen from the institution for young offenders which was erected as late as 1826. It is an annex to the Carceri Nuove in the Via Giulia (Pl. 80) and keeps to Fontana's ideas. Ennobled utilitarian art, Baroque functionalism, with a studied subtlety in the staggering of the horizontal features and the contrast in the size of the windows, the pure monastic style. A modern architect would appreciate the building. But the rest of the monumental prisons of the time in Europe were quite different. Radical and often hysterical Neo-classicism thought it necessary to give the prison a propagandist exterior meant to scare people out of their wits. Think of Newgate Prison in London (1770–1782 by George Dance the Younger) and of the women's prison in Würzburg (1809) whose overpowering rusticated masonry can only be penetrated by force and gives an impression of terrible weight. C. F. Hansen's county gaol in Slutterigade in Copenhagen is of this same type. The prison vaulting found in operas (and Piranesi's Carceri series) have inspired such façades; Antiquity dressed them in grim ashlar. As we all know, the Italians of Schiller's time were very conversant with real robbers and with vainglorious make-believe. But it was not in their nature to transform a building for captive outlaws into an inferno in stone. People out in the street realized that the building was a house of cells, dependable, and simply a rehabilitation centre – like the monastery. That was all they knew and cared about. They admired fantasies about torture-chambers on the stage. Those tourists who thirsted for sensation could go to the Castel Sant' Angelo.

III

The learned republic in Rome had two strongholds, the original university, *L'Archiginnasio della Sapienza,* called *Lo Studio* for short, and the Jesuits' own academy, *Collegio Romano.* Theology ("The fear of the Lord is the beginning of wisdom", in the words of the Psalmist, as is stated above the portal) as well as the classical languages, the study of antiquity and jurisprudence, medicine and mathematics were taught at the former, and Cardinal Valenti endowed two chairs in chemistry and physics. The Jesuits' college concentrated on the scholastic disciplines and the humanities but did not include the natural sciences. There was also a third *alma mater,* the *Collegium de Propaganda Fide,* Urban VIII's magnificent foundation. This was an international university for missionaries and consequently gave pride of place to instruction in all the languages of the world. All three institutions were housed in awe-inspiring buildings. It was believed in those days that it was not right for temples of learning to look like factories but divine enlightenment should be striven for from the architectural point of view as well. External extravagance is just as unpleasant as internal poverty, and this also goes for buildings containing lecture halls. Rome's authorities and those who held the purse strings, understood that elegant style need not be at the expense of practical aims. What is best in art should not be stuck on the walls but be inherent in the building. There is much to indicate that good architecture does more to improve the rising generation than the finest thought processes exchanged across the professor's lectern; the activity of a builder is fully as reliable, and his work is longer lasting. La Sapienza carried on its activities in Giacomo della Porta's austere palace which contained Borromini's church (S. Ivo), while the Jesuits' academy took up the enormous block in the Piazza del Collegio Romano [67]. Bernini and Borromini had built the Missionary Institute in the Piazza di Spagna, thereby creating an unsurpassed pattern for pedagogic architecture on a large scale.

Around these seats of learning were arrayed numerous colleges, some of which housed and prepared students at the universities, while others served special purposes. A number of them were reserved for young scholars from particular provinces. In fact most of the smaller colleges were nothing but seminaries. We shall only deal with those whose buildings are characteristic of our period either wholly or in part. It is very thrilling to roam round the city hunting out the lodgings of students from long ago. Try the Via Giulia and look at No. 81, close to S. Giovanni dei Fiorentini. In this prim, yellow dwelling house the *Collegio Bandinelli* was established in 1678 for twelve alumni from Tuscany. They spoke the dialect of the district. The lower storey follows the recipe, shop – door – window – door – shop, a fine composition, common to innumerable *case* of the artisans and small shopkeepers. At street level there was the bustle of everyday life, above it the pupils struggled with grammar and the

77. Monte di Pietà and S. Salvatore in Campo.

79. Women's prison at the Ospizio di S. Michele.

80. *Prison in Via Giulia.*

tribulations of piety. Or find your way to the steep, crooked alley which leads up past the right side of Palazzo del Grillo's front. In the corner stands the *Collegio degli Ibernesi,* a building from the period around 1650, originally the home of seven scholars from Ireland. When they had finished their studies they were sent home to their emerald isle by the Jesuits to be missionaries. Their Roman building is stuffy, shut in, a good habitat for parchment books (Pl. 86b). When the heat got on the Irish students' nerves, they marched off to the college's vineyard at Castel Gandolfo and enjoyed a landscape studded with chestnut trees, which after the rain took on the warm splendour of the emerald.

Collegio Cerasoli for students from Bergamo stood on the corner of the Piazza Colonna and the street leading into the Piazza di Pietra. The building was modernized at the same time as the church of S. Bartolomeo (S. Maria della Pietà) by Carlo de Dominicis. The English seminary in the Via Monserrato has a fine square too and is full of atmosphere. *Collegio Inglese,* linked with S. Tommaso di Canterbury, was rebuilt in the 1680's under the patronage of Thomas Philip Howard, who belonged to the arch-Catholic family of the Duke of Norfolk. He was driven out of heretic England in 1674, received the cardinal's hat in 1675 and lived in Rome from then on. Bishop Burnet, who visited his countryman in 1685, commends his kind heart and finds that the dignity of the purple had in no way spoilt his simple monastic habits [68]. This may all sound very attractive, but this prince of the church belonging to Great Britain's foremost family (its head is the hereditary Earl Marshal of England), retained all the same a certain taste for pomp and circumstance. This was probably why the still more humble Innocent XI lent him the papal villa itself in Castel Gandolfo for his summer residence [69]. Cardinal Howard saw to it that the best architect of the time, Carlo Fontana, took charge of the rebuilding of the college [70]. In the courtyard you can see a wing with restrained recesses and a clock-tower, which resembles a crown with hoops.

The Englishmen's college in its tranquil street, perhaps Rome's most serene, was the scene of an unexpected event in 1773, when Cardinal Corsini brought Ricci, General of the suppressed Jesuit order, to safety behind its walls, where he enjoyed an honourable captivity until the gates of Castel Sant' Angelo closed behind him. After this episode the college was for some time teasingly called "Rome's Tower" [71]. Coloured people were also to be found among the huge crowd of students. The young scholars from Syria and the Lebanon had their centre in the *Collegio dei Maroniti,* the remains of which – now reduced to garages – are hidden away in a passage behind the Via del Tritone. It is an out-of-the-way place with ochre walls, with some balance between line and form, a moment of quiet amid the noise, far removed from the delights of Sharon.

The Greeks had their college at S. Anastasio in the Via del Babuino, and after it was enlarged and completely rebuilt in 1769 [72] it was reckoned to be the most elegant of the national student hostels in Rome. *Collegio Greco* however was not given any new style and resembles a variant of the Neophytes' college (Rione Monti) from Urban VIII's time. Like other contemporary palaces in the days of dawning Classicism, it is ennobled by borrowing from cool Early Baroque. Only in the Rococo window of the mezzanine is there any light relief, otherwise the building is as ponderous as an armoured tank (Pl. 87). Although many constituents were borrowed from Della Porta and his circle, something was missing. The secular innocence is obviously in the process of being lost, and whereas the ecclesiastical buildings had formerly shown no sign of uncertainty, the present architecture deliberately built for ethical purposes is clearly produced under difficulties. The result was the invention of an official clerical setting that is abominable. With the increasing want of faith the buildings lose their humility. They now look like institutions, which is bad. In our plate it will be noticed that the Greek college overlooks a low, peculiar building quite lacking in "style" but not in personality. It is an old studio for sculptors [73], a piece of architecture full of character. The papal mosaic factory situated south of St. Peter's was of the same type. The building expresses its use, tersely, clearly, correctly; this is a workshop that needs light. The Collegio Greco drones on in a rusty voice. The *Collegium Germanicum* (c. 1748, by Fuga) near S. Apollinare may well have a forceful exterior, and is still without affectation, but becoming standardized, not merely formal, in character.

In comparison let us look at two scholastic institutions reserved for the education of young gentlemen. These buildings stem from a more mature age and have all the signs of elegant naturalness. *Il Nobile Pontificio Collegio Clementino* took pride of place [74]. It was founded in 1595 by Clement VIII Aldobrandini and accepted only the children of the nobility, including those from abroad. Two Counts Ulfeldt, great-grandchildren of Christian IV of Denmark, were educated here among young noblemen from Europe's most famous families. This completely aristocratic institution put special emphasis on training its pupils in chivalrous activities, dancing and music, riding and the practice of arms, as well as play-acting. Their minds were also taken care of, for they were taught Latin and courtesy. Instruction was in the hands of the Somaschi fathers, wordly-wise and mature teachers who brought a breath of humanity into this *Gymnasium Illustre* [75], beneficial to people who are favoured by fortune. Popes and cardinals pampered this educational establishment of international fame, many of them (like Benedict XIV) had themselves been alumni. The Collegio Clementino was instituted in 1600 in a palace near the Piazza Nicosia and remained here until it was demolished in 1936. The academy was given its final form by being extended and rebuilt in the 1680's and the beginning of the following decade under the supervision of Carlo Fontana. Since the complex was completed in stages, it could not boast of a proper plan. The buildings were assembled around a more or less square courtyard, and there was no regularity whatever in the lay-out. But the wing right at the back which rose directly above the muddy waters of the Tiber was extremely impressive in its plasticity. Fontana here created a brilliant piece of architecture by force of external circumstances. This heavy mass, striped horizontally by the pattern of windows, extends between two slim cylinders set on the diagonal axis. The one to the east projects as if it were a stair-well at the gable end of a functionalist block of flats; the sophisticated cubism in the architecture of our time has not surpassed this style in utilitarian buildings (cf. Pl. 85) and only rarely has its instinct for balance. Such a work has sixteen noble ancestors.

Collegio Nazareno vied with the Clementine foundation for precedence – as does Eton with Harrow – and in the 18th century the first mentioned boarding school was for a time particularly fashionable [76]. It had a zoological and mineralogical collection and the pupils gained a sound knowledge of these subjects, something incredible in Rome [77]. The poet Parini was a member of the teaching staff from 1754 to 1762 and could here find material for his satirical poem "Il Giorno" (1763 onwards) on the dangerous habits of the nobility, of which Pietro Verri, the man of letters, bore the marks on his body when he was a pupil (1744–1745), having been beaten-up by some vicious fellows from Abruzzi [78]. From an architectural point of view, Nazareno is less harmonious than Clementino. The college occupied an older building provided by the titular Archbishop of Nazareth (1630). This palace, the dominant feature of which is its belvedere [79], is built along the line of the wide curve of a street behind the Via del Tritone to which it was extended after 1700, and it oppresses its surroundings with its weight. Its outer appearance is more or less unchanged since the days of Clement XI. Schoolboys from all walks of life now fill the building where once only little noblemen romped in lilac tunics. There are indications of the alterations made to the main building at the beginning of the 18th century within the courtyard where ochre-yellow panels are set in the dark walls. The straight lines of windows are not very different from the cell windows in a prison designed by Fontana. At the back of the cortile is a wall fountain built to set off an antique statue. The inscription on the plinth gives the name of the figure and the patron: *Caius Iulius Caesar / Dict. Perp. / Alexandri / Cardinalis Albani / Donum / Anno MDCCXXI.*

The Cardinal in his capacity as antiquarian in 1721 thus set up an excellent example for the alumni to consider during break: dictator for life. On a handsome corner house out in the Via del Nazareno can be seen another inscription which is an injunction against defiling the square in front of the college and refers to a decree of June 18th, 1720. Read in conjunction, the two inscriptions inform us that at the time Caesar's statue was raised in the courtyard the college had been modernized – and that by now the Cardinal, nephew of the Pope, cast his shadow as far as the corner of this street. The so-called *Seminario Romano* was the lyceum of the Jesuits. Up to a hundred young nobles were educated here (on their way to the Collegio Romano) in languages and the fine arts as well as in riding, fencing and dancing. The alumni's theatre was established at the beginning of Innocent XIII's papacy, and its auditorium had marble columns and a ceiling decorated by Pannini [80]. Among the churchmen educated here were the later popes Innocent XII and Clement XI. While this seat of learning had to be content with an oldish palace (in the Via del Seminario), the school for priests, whose pupils were brought up to do special duties in St. Peter's, obtained a new building close by. *Seminario di S. Pietro,* said to have been erected in 1729 [81], was given an eccentric façade; ten papal crowns were inserted in the semicircular recesses above the windows of the piano nobile, as well as the private tiara in the Corsini coat of arms. This was almost too much of a good thing, and the front became no more apostolic because of it. Was the unknown architect chosen by the cathedral chapter merely a gauche person, or an eccentric? The recess motif mentioned is an archaism. Rauzzini is known to have been employed by the Vatican at this time [82], but the seminary does not resemble the other works by this capricious master, so it is out of the question to put forward any argument that he was the originator of this strange building.

Primary education was in a poor state in papal Rome. The most fortunate infants were sent to a dame school where they learnt to sit still, rattle off prayers and knit. Far into the 19th century discipline was remorseless [83]. Thousands of children learnt nothing at all, for it was far more enjoyable to romp in the streets than be dragged off to filthy little infant schools to be thumped by half-educated ignoramuses – all clergy of course. In convents, girls from wealthy homes got a basic knowledge of life in general. But there was a spot of light in this pedagogical gloom, and that is the work of the Scolopi as teachers. The congregation of *della Scuole Pie* – hence the name of the fathers (in Austria the name *Piaristen* is used) – was established in Rome in 1617 with the aim of giving free tuition, particularly to poor children. After having led a precarious life in a couple of rooms behind the sacristy of S. Dorotea and later in a number of other places, the school was transferred by the founder of the order, S. Giuseppe Calasanzio, to the Palazzo Torres (Lancellotti) on the south side of the Piazza Navona, and was at the same time entrusted with the church of S. Pantaleo. The order still has its headquarters here (31 Piazza dei Massimi). But it had grown at such a rate, and requests for admission to its schools had grown so overwhelming that in the 1740's it was able to set up a large purpose-built academy. The Scolopi obtained Pal. Cenci (opposite S. Nicola de' Cesarini), had it partly demolished and erected on the site *una sontuosa fabbricca,* to which they transferred their establishment in 1747. The architect was Tommaso de Marchis [84]. Under the name of Collegio Calasanzio the institution became very famous. The pupils were not only given biblical instruction but also courses in Latin, Logic and Theology, and were taught by enlightened and humane teachers. Before the Revolution the college was regarded as perhaps the best boarding school in Rome [85].

Only Sorø Academy in Denmark (founded 1740) can bear comparison with Collegio Calasanzio, but then this was an aristocratic foundation. Holberg, its founder, was made a baron in 1747; Giuseppe Calasanzio was made a saint the following year [86].

Leaving the seats of learning and preparing to visit the many buildings that cater for the sick and helpless, we need to pause a moment for a breath of fresh air. Let us go to the *Botanical Gardens* up on Gianicolo. Here was a wide view of the distant horizon, green trees everywhere, and the sound of the waters of Acqua Paola playing over the neat flower beds. The park was laid out under Alexander VII Chigi and can be seen immediately behind the fountain in Falda's prospect map of 1676. Clement XI had G. B. Contini erect a house in which the lecturer in Botany at the Sapienza University had his lecture hall. Shortly after 1770 the Jesuit Minassi was given the chair. This pleased Linnaeus, and he noted in 1774: "The Pope, who previously proscribed Linnaeus' writings in his territories, is nominating a new professor to read his system *publice* in Rome" [87]. Denmark's Martin Vahl, pupil of the king of flowers at Hammarby, visited Rome in 1785 and must have walked in the park on the hill, but he avoided his colleague, Professor Martelli, like the plague [88]. A couple of years later Goethe wended his way to this garden and gained much profit from it. His tour of it encouraged him to continue his studies of the life of plants. *Il giardino de' semplici* no longer exists on this site; its casino has been replaced by a new building, but the place still remains a garden and retains its scent (Pl. 188).

Up there night sometimes conjures up the silhouette of a renowned figure. He could be seen in many parks during the day and mixed with those who practised the sciences, though not with the naturalists. The terrace above the grove of the Arcadians underwent a pagan transformation when the fountain and the trees on the hill were completely alone in the limitless depth of a summer night. It could happen at times that two men appeared on a path running up the slope. They crossed the empty space in front of the pool, took off their clothes and let themselves down into the water of the basin beneath the great arches of the fountain. Winckelmann was given a swimming lesson [89]. The greatest of Roman scholars cooled his Greek brow in dignity and in silence.

IV

"I wish I could describe the misery in which the Roman poor languish," wrote Bonstetten, "but I feel that it is impossible; it knows no bounds." He once saw a man lying in the middle of the Corso amid the swarming beau monde and hurrying equipages. He had fainted from hunger. The traffic split up round the motionless heap of rags [90]. A sight like this was common in Rome. Stifled cries of misery echoed from the alleys and passages. The Romans were not heartless, and normal charity was particularly common among the moneyed classes. Aristocrats vied with pious confraternities in meriting the praises of God and man by establishing homes for the poor [91], and a host of poor people were handed their daily bread at the doors of a great number of convents and monasteries. Neither the Church nor the papal government turned a deaf ear to the gospel's message "Love thy neighbour". But in face of the poverty which thrived like an endemic disease in the marrow of Roman society, even such an extensive welfare system was powerless, and it was beyond all capability to redress the situation completely. The masses living close to subsistence level, and often below it, were ravaged by disease. The idea of hygiene was unknown in daily life, the climate dangerous; malaria predominated in the Campagna and fever was always present in low-lying and crowded districts. People were born in ordure, breathed in stench, drank the poisonous waters of the Tiber, stumbled over carrion in the streets.

A view of Rome from above in the 18th century can be interpreted in many ways. Sometimes the churches stand out in relief and we see only the "Holy City" below a forest of domes and towers. Or the cubes of the palaces rise out of the mosaic of the map and conjure up a city of happiness and pride. Perhaps we would do best and be more honest if – for a change – we regarded the Rome of the past as an enormous slum sprinkled with a few large buildings, not much to look at, but clean within and a blessing to many.

All big cities had an infinite army of poor, but Rome's was increased every year by pilgrims from all over Europe. Hordes poured into a city which was already boiling over with a starving and bigoted proletariat. The great complex *l'Ospizio della S. S. Trinità dei Pellegrini* (founded 1650) was prepared to receive these thousands, lodge them and feed them for three days. The capacity of the institutions was put to the test in the "Holy Year". Just one evening in 1675, 5–6000 pilgrims were admitted, given a proper meal at tables covered with white cloths and decorated with flowers, and laden with all sorts of meat dishes [92]. From Christmas Day 1724 until January 25th 1725 the hospice welcomed over 10,000 guests [93]. In the whole of the year 1750 about 195,000 were accommodated, who were served 466,000 free meals. The figures for 1775 were respectively 13,000 and 333,000 [94]. On their arrival the lodgers were washed and examined by doctors [95]. Their beds were impeccably clean and the food must have been beyond reproach, for an English nobleman, who visited the hospice in 1779 on a day of fasting, has listed the tasty menu: good rice soup, fish salad, peaches and vin du pays in large jugs [96].

The Hospice of the Holy Trinity and other Roman hostels from both "the great" as well as "the gallant" century are extremely simple externally. But they did not demean their inhabitants by putting on a show of excessive poverty. Plastered walls, well distributed openings in them, strong corners – these are also the components of the side wings of palaces and monasteries. To judge from the exterior, the Monte di Pietà might just as well be housing small ragamuffins as bags of sequins. This sober, vague style, derived from Domenico Fontana's school about 1600, has an all-embracing discretion which above all benefited the public buildings erected to help the underprivileged. Here again one appreciates the delicate Roman sense of tact. No occupants of an institution are degraded here by having their wretchedness or sins proclaimed from above the portal. In London above the entrance to the mental asylum of "Bethlehem" (Bedlam) (founded 1675) were hair-raising figures of "Lunacy" and "Melancholy" – Great Cibber's brazen brainless brothers (Pope) – so that nobody should confuse the madhouse with the houses of sane mortals. The gateway to the women's prison in Amsterdam (built 1645) was distinguished by a relief showing a symbolic female figure with a scourge in her hand and a beggar woman grabbed by the scruff of her neck [97]; the madhouse here was so purpose-built that the afflicted had only a view of an inner courtyard with the statue of a madman in the middle [98]. In Rome's hostel for "fallen women" these words could be read: *Neglectis Rejectisque Ab Omnibus,* which might be rendered "the sanctuary for all neglected and rejected". This is the voice of Rome.

The Holy Trinity Hospice stands in the centre of a district crowded with large buildings that serve the common weal. It begins at the Monte di Pietà and ends at the Tiber. If you turn off from the Via dei Giubbonari, which is always a-buzz with its small shops, the street of these institutions appears through a huge arch (Arco del Monte) connecting the pawnbroking establishment and its annex (originally Pal. Barberini). From this restricted viewpoint you are only aware of the Trinità hospice as a large flanking wall, nor does it stand out in the Piazza dei Pellegrini as an isolated piece of architecture. The church of S. S. Trinità is an elegant screen for the wings hidden behind. It is only down by the Ponte Sisto that these blocks become manifest and show their strength. Here also was *l'Ospizio dei Mendicanti,* erected in 1587 by Domenico Fontana. The building is still standing, but cut back by the Tiber quay, and can be considered as the pattern for the "Roman institutional style" which was in use through the whole of our period. The institution at Ponte Sisto was decorated in a way which, it must be admitted, could only be accepted in Rome. The part of the building nearest the river gives a *point-de-vue* of the Via Giulia, and the Borghese Pope Paul V, realizing the requirements of the prospect, had a fountain set into the wall where the front of the building faces this elegant street (1613) [99]. Via Giulia had acquired a splendid background, and the poorhouse wealth all at the same time. To the people outside in the sun, the cascade was refreshing as they drank of the water in the shell; "a very pleasurable sight" wrote Olof Celsius the Elder in 1698 [100]. We should keep this exemplary composition in mind when we now turn to the monumental architecture for social purposes in the Papal State after 1680. Instead of insisting on isolating institutions for the destitute and ignoring them, they are displayed here as works of art with as much right as any other in the city. The liberal mind was profound enough to make silent monuments of the benevolent buildings.

L'Ospizio Apostolico di S. Michele, the biggest welfare institution in Rome and one of the most important in Europe at the time, had quite an interesting history. A Neapolitan named Lionardo Caruso, who had been in the service of several popes, established an orphanage for boys about half-way along the Corso, near S. Silvestro in Capite, during the reign of Gregory XIII (1572–1585). Since this honest butler went under the name of *il letterato,* due no doubt to his literary pursuits, the name was transferred to his poor little charges. At the funeral of the French ambassador in Rome in 1687 the procession was headed by "the little grey children usually called *letterati*" [101]. There was already then quite a crowd of them, and their home in the Corso was becoming too cramped. During the pontificate of Innocent XI, an orphanage for girls was also founded. The Lateran Palace, which had long been unoccupied and was in a poor state, opened its gates to the little girls. In itself this was an excellent idea, but in practice it was a dubious solution, for the Lateran is the coldest building in Rome and made for very grown-up people. That Bernini was given the job of preparing the accommodation was also a fine idea [102], but of no benefit to the children. But Tommaso Odescalchi, who was related to Innocent XI, founded in the middle of the 1680's an orphanage by the Ripa Grande with a chapel dedicated to S. Michele, and the austere Pope was even persuaded to inspect it (1685)[103]. And so the foundation was laid for an institution which was purpose-built architecturally and large enough to absorb older refuges. And this did happen. Mattia de Rossi began the work and it was continued after his death in 1695 by Carlo Fontana [104]. It was the apple of Innocent XII's eye and he managed to see its main features completed before he died. The stage they were at then can be seen in an engraving by Specchi from 1699 [105].

The home for children gradually took in other occupants – cripples and old, destitute people, asocial individuals, ne'er-do-wells, and finally also criminals were transferred to S. Michele, which thus began to take on the rather doubtful character of a mixture of workhouse, orphanage, prison and all-purpose welfare home. As a result the institution grew at a great rate, buildings were added at both sides as long as there was room and in the end, during the papacy of Pius VI, that is when one hundred years had passed, the huge building had become as long as a month of Sundays and stretched almost as far as the Vatican does between the Belvedere and the Sistine Chapel. An engraving showed its triumphal progress [106] (Pl. 75).

If ever a building was destined to become a bleak barracks, it was the beggars' Versailles in Rome, for its dimensions, its purpose and its piecemeal growth were all a terrible strain. All the same – S. Michele became true architecture and remains so. Its monotony was relieved by the raised roof section of the original building (the "long belvedere" or "workshop floor") being repeated in rhythmic alternation on the extensions. The seemingly endless walls along the Tiber are plain and dead, but up in the roof zone the complex comes alive. One might say that the building is an entity in so far as it is a series of houses in mutual dependence, and this is very Roman. La Salpetrière (finished 1669) in Paris, on the other hand, has the logic of an isolated mathematical problem, and that is French Classicism. Inside the main courtyard of S. Michele, one can appreciate Fontana's very moderate style with plain arcades and windows set into right-angled recesses, everything very unostentatious. The courtyard might have felt oppressive, were you not aware that the architecture breathes by the expansion of the middle bay of arches. The storeys above the cornice soaring upwards as if of lighter substance, the wings projecting and directing the movement forward. A fountain is the centrepiece in the inmates' courtyard (Pl. 78), not a monument to infamy.

What an extraordinary community this interminable palace of poverty housed. Boys started their lives here, old men finished theirs. For those who had reason to fear, the very name of S. Michele constituted a threat. But the worn-out and weary must have praised the name of Innocent XII, who called them "his nephews (nepoti)" and preferred to have all the Roman poor under one roof [107]. There was something colourful about the workhouse, for Clement XI set up a tapestry weaving workshop supervised by a French craftsman with the assistance of journeymen from *Les Gobelins* [108]. But the industry was never really a success (although the principal became a canon [109]); by 1729 there were only fifteen workers, according to Montesquieu [110]. The young men were also taught various trades, for it was realized that regular occupation is the best cure for the socially maladjusted. During his visit in 1778, Howard had nothing but praise for what he considered a most excellent institution.

It could also be regarded as an asset to the townscape of Rome. The Ospizio di S. Michele provides the Tiber with a monumental wall to balance the steep slopes of the Aventine on the other side, and nowhere else has the river a calmer flow than along this stretch. The area between the hospice and the harbour, which lay in front of it, was strengthened by a proper quayside, the only one in Rome at the time, and planted with trees from the very beginning. Lalande rightly points out that the Papal City missed a great deal of beauty it might otherwise have had by not having the embankment promenades, which gave Pisa, Florence and especially Paris so much character [111]. So the Frenchman rejoiced in "the extremely pleasant walk" along S. Michele, beneath the foliage of the trees and with decent architecture on one side, thinking no doubt of the Quai des Galeries du Louvre. By building on such a wide frontal plan on behalf of the underdog, Rome developed its first modernized perspective. In Paris, the Place de la Concorde was created (1748 onwards by Gabriel) around a royal equestrian statue. The buildings in this all-embracing panorama across the Seine are nothing but a decoration – pure aestheticism. The Adelphi complex by the Thames Embankment in London (1768 onwards by the Adam brothers) was nothing but speculative building disguised as archaeological fantasy. British cant, French *gloire* – the Romans had integrity on their side.

Numerous orphanages for children and young people who either had no parents or else lived in very bad conditions were built near S. Michele. The girls only escaped from the so-called "homes" when there was another door opened to them – either marriage (if they had a dowry) or the convent. *Il Conservatorio della Divina Providenza* at Ripetta was instituted in 1674 in an even older building, which is still extant and well preserved in its gloomy exterior. An oratory designed by Theodoli and consecrated in 1728 was a small measure of light relief for the girls in purple [112]. Rather more attractive, seen from the outside, was the *Conservatorio delle Zoccolette*. A pious prelate, the privy almoner for Innocent XII, founded an orphanage for up to 200 beggar girls near the Bocca della Verità. There they had a roof over their heads, lived on charity and home industries, were clad in unbleached linen and wore clogs, hence their name in the vernacular [113]. Just imagine them in procession through the streets of Rome: "They wore gloves and a white veil which covered their faces. At the head walked one of the girls carrying a cross. Behind her followed the others two by two, very modestly and without saying a word, such as is not common in their sex. Their teachers in dignified black marched at the flanks to keep order, and the principal brought up the rear with the oldest pupils, one at either side of her" [114]. We can conjure up the clattering crocodile in front of their new home (after 1715) in a wing of the S. Sisto Hospice. Its façade has a certain warmth, for two shades of ochre have absorbed the sun (Pl. 86a).

The onomatopoeic word *zoccolette* must have surrounded the orphanage with a very particular atmosphere, most likely based on kindly feelings towards them; a certain coquettishness may also have been in the air concerning the well-behaved column of clog-shod girls – Labat alludes to reckless pedestrians who were only prevented from taking a closer look at them by the prospect of the galleys. However that may be, it is certain that the word *scalette,* which also contains a dry and sharp clip-clop in it, by no means called forth pleasant associations, for the "home", whose official name was *S. Croce della Penitenza* but was called *delle Scalette* in the vernacular, was a fearsome institution. Young women fled here to avoid the temptations of life; they made no vows and their escape from the world was the result of despair. The double flight of steps which has given the institution its name, stands out in the endless Via della Lungara, and you cannot avoid seeing it or remembering it [115] (Pl. 85).

In Trastevere itself there were two "homes" whose buildings date from the 18th century, and here the wind seems tempered to the shorn lamb. The *Conservatorio di S. Pasquale Baylon* is on the corner of the Via dei Genovesi, behind S. Cecilia, and makes a good corner house, clear and honest, plain and therefore right. It is reproduced as a good example of a public building on a small scale for ordinary people (Pl. 82a) [116]. *Conservatorio dell' Assunta* had, like many other institutions, changed its address a number of times and at every move it rose higher, appropriately enough for a refuge with the Ascension as its title. During the papacy of Clement IX it began down at the bottom of Trastevere by the triangular frying-pan that is called Piazza S. Egidio. In Innocent XI's time it made its way up the steep Salita di S. Onofrio to settle down right at the top of the Via Garibaldi, opposite S. Maria dei Sette Dolori. The building has an identity of its own and we reproduce it in Pl. 70. As shown here it looks like an engraving by Vasi [117]. This whole section of the street has remained largely unchanged since then and is a delightful, out-of-the-way corner of the city amid sloping gardens. I do not know whether it was erected as a new building for the "home", but it must have taken shape with this in view, for on a tablet in the anteroom can be read: *Sub Auspiciis / Benedicti XIV P. Max. / Anno Dom. 1744.* The façade would display a completely bourgeois character if the small cross-barred lights did not interrupt the rhythm of the windows. This lean building at the end of the built-up area on Janiculum clearly had a purpose quite different from that of housing suburbans (as it does now); something "authoritative" manifests itself, particularly in the changing rhythm of the rows of windows. It is admirable how gently, how delicately the note has been struck. Disillusioned women sheltered inside, and their shield against the world has the graceful pattern of Rococo. The trees on the hillside produced a play of light and shade as well as a little cool air; now and then came a faint whiff from the Pope's tobacco factory next door. Today the small stunted palms in front of the building are no more presentable than if they were the cuttings from the dead spinsters' flower pots.

We have spoken above of the modern orphanage, which "the Sisters of the little Christ-child" had erected in the 1730's, when we dealt with the church of the order (Il Bambin Gesù), for the latter is architecturally a part of the huge asylum building. And we come finally to a reformatory erected by Pius VI in 1790. Its sonorous Latin *Domus Mendicantium Pupillarum a Tempio Pacis* was fully justified by the building's style and position. The ashlar portal in the Via del Colosseo roars at the small beggars whose lot it was to pass through it. We have now reached the age of pedagogical Classicism. And the institution was indeed partly built into the "Temple of Peace" (Constantine's basilica). Not even Dickens could imagine a children's home of such a grotesque nightmare quality as the complex which was pushed into the back of the vaulted ruin. There the street is dark and gloomy, the antique structure is blockaded by this implacable barracks, and in the front, facing the Forum, the basilica opened its three tremendous jaws. In between was monumental chaos. Romantic engravings show us luxuriant plants twining like snakes beneath weathered arches from ancient times; since Piranesi, the works of the ancients had developed megalomania. We can suddenly understand *Templum Pacis* as the puny, skinny youngsters saw it. Frederikke Brun is an excellent cicerone: "The building with its courtyards and gardens takes up a fairly large area. Everywhere are traces of Antiquity, as in the sculptures set in the walls. We climbed up many large flights of steps to get to the back of three huge vaulted arches; between the landings there extended large cultivated areas with terraces for vegetables..." [118]. This cannot have been the province of the pupils. They were trained downstairs in plain rooms while the tourists were delighting in the panoramas from the roof. During his stay in Rome in 1844, Dickens naturally looked over the institution by the Temple of Peace, but a passing remark in his Roman diary may well be applied to the establishment: "The false truth and the true are fused into a monstrous union" [119].

The hospital system could pride itself on a glorious past. *L'Arcispedale di S. Spirito* had been world-famous for nearly 1000 years and served as the archetype for so many hospitals in the rest of Europe. The Helligaandshus at Amagertorv in Copenhagen is an off-shoot; King Christian I had admired the parent institution in Rome in 1474. The care of the sick in the centre of Christendom benefited also from the incomparable, ever-present generosity on the part of the popes and the wealthy. Imposing buildings were put up for the great mass of the sick in the Baroque period which were at the same time impressive architecture. Two important hospitals date from the 17th century, namely *l'Arcispedale del S. S. Salvatore* near the Lateran, and the Consolazione Hospital in the valley behind the Tarpian Rock. The former, intended for those suffering from fever, stands on a corner, and its main wing (1636 by Giacomo Mola) [120] forms a quiet side wall for the great space of the Lateran square. The north wing was built in 1655 by G. A. Rossi. A hospital was in principle a long, unpartitioned room (*una corsía*), a long wing being the basic type. The Consolazione Hospital, the narrow passage added to the church of the same name, which can be seen from Falda's prospect of 1676, is of this type. This infirmary, which was renovated at the close of the 1680's [121], was meant especially for people with injuries and wounds. When it is realized that in 1785 alone, 560 people were murdered within the Rome city boundaries [122] and that anything up to 20,000 persons are estimated to have been killed during the rule of Pius VI (1775–1799) [123], there must have been quite a number of admissions of patients with gunshot and knife wounds.

It is obvious that the Roman hospitals of those days left very much to be desired, but the standard was higher than that in the other capitals of the time north of the Alps. Italian hospital wards benefited from century-old experiences, knowledge tested and tried in monasteries and convents, whose large communal rooms and many corridors, paved with stone and whitewashed, provided the pattern for hospitals and charitable institutions. Nor should it be forgotten that all those who cared for the sick carried out their tasks as a religious vocation; deep devotion is always a fine qualification for nurses and doctors, even if at times treatment was more edifying than curative. The various statements about conditions in Roman hospitals which we have from strangers to the city are surprisingly favourable. Weinlig noted in 1768 that every patient in the city enjoyed the privilege of having his own bed, while the Hôtel de Dieu, the biggest hospital in Paris, packed 6–8 poor wretches into one bedstead, where they lay like sardines. He also praised the regular ventilation, finding the hygiene beyond all his expectations [124]. Frederik Münter, who visited the Consolazione Hospital in 1786, gives it a certificate of cleanliness, all the windows being open and the air in the wards impeccable [125]. And the very critical Howard was in the main satisfied with the departments he inspected in 1778. The humanitarian principle of many streets outside hospitals being obstructed by chains to prevent the noisy traffic of carriages was a striking feature. We have not yet progressed to this in our civilization, but motor cars do after all provide an excellent source of clinical subjects.

If we intend to visit all the hospitals built or anyhow thoroughly renovated in the 18th century, this being no mean undertaking in a short space of time, we must start on Aesculapius' own island, Isola di S. Bartolomeo, in the Tiber. Nearly all Roman undertakings have a heroic overture and so have the hospitals – elsewhere the story starts with an isolated lazar-house, but here it is begun with a god and a temple. This narrow wedge in the river has medical traditions going back more than two thousand years [126]. According to the myth, passed on to us by Livy, Aesculapius himself came in the form of a snake to this island in the Tiber, brought there by ship from his Greek home. The Romans built a temple to the god and shaped the *Isola della Salute* like a vessel with a sharp bow, making it a sanctuary for medicine. Christianity consecrated a church here to the Apostle Bartholomew, who ended up by being flayed alive, and thus gave a surgical tone from on high. Since the Middle Ages the cramped island between the bridges of Antiquity had become a common breeding-ground for churches, clinics and religious houses. The ghetto glowered at it from one side, Trastevere snarled at it from the other, while a great silence, that of sickness and death, reigned over this strip of clay in the middle of the moody Tiber.

Soon after 1580, a newly created order of nursing monks, called the *Bonfratelli* or *Fatebene-Fratelli,* moved to the island and built a hospital which can be seen in Tempesta's city plan from 1595. The establishment gradually encroached upon the confusion of buildings there, sent out its tentacles between the sailors' hovels and mixed its odours with those of the mud. A narrow cross street (Vicolo della Moletta) twisted and turned down to the water-mills anchored in the river in the direction of the Piazza Molara over in Trastevere and the ill-famed pot-house of La Barchetta, "a grimy, smoky, ramshackle building projecting halfway into the Tiber . . ., over the entrance the dry laurel leaves rustle in the evening breeze" [127]. The island of healing certainly needed cleaning up, and a beginning was made by clearing the slums around the hospital. This took place during the period of Clement XI and on this occasion it was given its present front; its height was increased in 1742 and has been reverently preserved [128]. Its rhythm has subtleties in its simplicity. The part on the left concentrates its three windows around the portal (with a medallion above the bend in the cornice) and towards the ashlared corner; the part to the right is subordinated to the adjacent church of S. Giovanni Calibita, and one can see that its low campanile close to the Ponte dei Quattro Capi corresponds in height to the top storey, the two outer windows of which, on this side, are emphasized by linked pilaster strips. Pull and counter-pull are in balance (Pl. 82b).

Only once a year was the silence of the island of healing broken, and that was on St. Bartholomew's Day (August 25th) when the people of the river headed for the church. The spacious square was filled with boatmen, sailmakers and longshoremen from the Ripa Grande, and the tanners too, turned up in honour of their patron who had been skinned. They drank wine in the osteria by the Caetani tower and ate watermelons, whose juicy blood-red slices resembled segments of the saint. The Fatebene monks exhibited anatomical wax models, and a confraternity in purple sackcloth (*Sacconi Rossi*) was not to be outdone. They arranged *rappresentazioni sacre* with a superabundance of thigh-bones in the form of crosses. By the column in the middle of the square was set up a list of sinners who had refused the Lord's mystical table at Easter. The whole island sailed through a mist of piety and of steam from the cookshops, while along the bank of the river ran the streams from the latrines.

When the day of rejoicing had come to an end, the Tiber island withdrew once again into the world of hospitals, like a snake into its hole.

81. *Central part of the S. Gallicano Hospital.*

83. *The S. Gallicano Hospital.*

84. *Collegio Calasanzio.*

The whole of Isola di S. Bartolomeo is today as it was originally, although the square has been cut about and the new hospital bestrides the north part of the island like a colossus. The south is filled with the neglected monastery wings and gardens of the Franciscans – all is quiet here. The bridges of Antiquity form narrow sluices for through traffic, so the island retains its independence and its flavour of *Vecchia Roma*. Neither Belli, who sang the praises of *er tabellone,* nor the artist Pinelli, who once found his good name included on that outrageous notice [129] would today fail to find a place to order a drink in the corner beneath the Gothic tower; the neighbouring monastic building with the shops has stood for over three hundred years. Hans Andersen might have met the two arch-Romans here: "When it got dark we went to an osteria on an island in the Tiber. It was a veritable cookshop with its boiled lobsters, fried fish and vegetables. A lamp burnt in front of the Madonna on the wall, various kinds of people sat eating at the tables; outside some children were singing sweetly . . ." (Diary October 22nd, 1833). An inscription on the parapet at the end of Ponte dei Quattro Capi states that Innocent XI restored the bridge in 1679 "with stronger sides and as a more permanent memorial". Nothing more than a bit of masonry. As you rest your hand on its worn travertine and look across the square by the hospital you get a moving impression of Roman continuity from this island with the shape of a ship. *Fluctuat nec mergitur.*

The holy year of 1725 gave rise to the foundation of two special hospitals which served the most ostracized of all the sick – patients suffering from venereal disease, and lunatics. Could the jubilee year and Pope Benedict XIII have bequeathed finer memorials? The Pope decided personally that the *Ospedale di S. Gallicano* was to be erected for those suffering from venereal disease in particular. He had a trust-fund at his disposal whose statute he arbitrarily changed for the furtherance of the purpose mentioned, and he laid the foundation stone in March 1725. He inspected the still unfinished building in October that year, and the chapel and institution was consecrated on October 5th, 1726 [130]. And, most remarkable of all, he must have sanctioned the style of the building, which was quite amazing. Never before had there been a charity hospital, particularly one for the diseases of vice, which looked so full of optimism.

For that is what Rauzzini's building in the middle of poverty-stricken Trastevere did. It must have been done deliberately, but there seems to be no reason other than a desire to give the place dignity. The inscription quoted above also indicates some form of rehabilitation.

The building plan is simple – two wings flush with one another, one for women and the other for men, are linked together by a tall chapel, as gay as the pavilion that unifies the long wings of an orangery. This architecture is so warm (Pl. 83) that one's thoughts fly easily to the palatial hothouses of a Baroque garden. It is quite unreasonable to call it bizarre [131], and to point the finger of scorn at its light-heartedness is really naughty. The façade is bright and clear because it reflects an entirely rational construction. The wings are divided horizontally by a narrow balcony with iron railings. The motif looks picturesque, but its motivation is surprisingly modern, for this external passage-way is built primarily to enable the nurses to open and close the windows without disturbing the sick. A great deal of ventilation was needed in these wards, so the building was left open to the air as much as possible and was as light and as dry as a conservatory. The ground floor is divided up by pilaster strips, and circular recesses are set in the walling between. They have now been bricked up, but should not by mistake be taken for mere ornament, for from Vasi's engraving [132] we discover that these circles were originally the moulding around apertures in the wall which were only filled with fine latticework.

I assume that the Gallicano hospital, designed by a much advertised "Rococo architect", is the first one in Europe to have the healthy atmosphere and purified beauty of a sanatorium. Its exterior would not jar in any new town – with the exception of the chapel (Pl. 81). As far as that is concerned the architect took time off, for now he was building for the Church. The portal is on the exact axis of Vicolo di Mazzamurelli, the name in Roman dialect meaning poltergeist and thought to be the only capricious phenomenon in the district. The chapel's façade, visible at the end of this narrow street, is a calculated siting. It is not in the centre of the hospital building – the wings are of unequal length – but has been shifted over to form the focal point of a prospect in depth. The pavilion closes the view along the street with its curves and angles, enhancing the large entrance and the niche above it, as if it were a benediction loggia looking upon an afflicted people. On a medal which Benedict ordered to be struck on the completion of the hospital are his words: "Our heart has grown fuller" (*Cor nostrum dilatum est*). In keeping with this, Rauzzini made the portal high and the building exceedingly cheerful.

The first hospital in Denmark specifically for skin and venereal diseases, that of Rudolph Bergh, was erected in 1886 and could easily be confused with a prison tarted-up for a special occasion.

The building of the *Ospedale de' Pazzarelli*, the mental hospital at Lungara, was, as already mentioned, decided on in the Anno Santo of 1725, but was not started until February 1727 [133]. It is possible that Rauzzini was the architect. Up till then the madhouse had been squeezed in behind S. Bartolomeo degli Bergamaschi in the Piazza Colonna [134]; now it came out into the fresh air and strangely enough had room to enjoy it. The site adjoined the S. Spirito hospital and spread across the gentle slope right down to the Tiber. Nolli's plan and Vasi's prospect (V, Pl. 87) show that the building turned its back on the street and was open to the river through two big courtyards separated by a transverse wing. There was of course a barrier wall, but the buildings higher up the slope on this side were completely broken up into arcades with an unobstructed view across the Tiber and to the whole district around S. Giovanni dei Fiorentini on the opposite bank. What was the point of arcades in front of every storey if they were not accessible to at least the quietest of the institution's inmates? The question is pertinent, for everywhere else in the world, the lunatic asylum was in those days the most hermetically sealed of all buildings, and barred cellars and punishment cells the usual home of the mentally deranged. Can we really believe that the institution in Rome permitted people with clouded minds to vegetate in these wide loggias facing east, facing the morning light, the garden below, the living city itself? There can be no other answer than a hesitant affirmative. Once again we stand amazed at Roman maturity [135].

And of course that reminds us that it was a fool who first recognized Francis of Assisi as the Chosen One. He spread his cloak in the dust at the young man's feet. Giotto painted the scene and has here presented what was probably the first serious picture of a mental case in the history of painting [136]. An intelligent observer once said that St. Francis, the most Italian of all saints and the most saintly of all Italians, "shared the love the demented had for the paradox, the disguise of truth" [137]; and he loved the poor in spirit, the silent comrades of animals and flowers. We have a suspicion that Francis of Assisi's own people, so elegant in their way of thinking, so inspired by the constant cultivation of the hidden depths of the heart and of faith in their profound nature, hide the gentle tact of an artistic race towards the completely irrational in the human soul. Tasso, driven by his persecution complex, was treated with respectful care by his guard in Ferrara's madhouse. Did not Arcangelo Corelli express a soulfully shaded sympathetic insight in his famous variations on *la Follia,* and thus give the theme and name of the dance an explanation? The tragedy of madness was depicted compassionately by the numerous Italian composers – from Vivaldi and Antonio Pollarolo to Guglielmi and Piccini – who in the 18th century set *Orlando furioso* to music, and by the mastery of Paisiello in his *Nina pazza per amore.* For to these musicians it was not only the inmate of a madhouse, rattling his chain and ringing his fool's bell, who was mentally sick. The monk in his hair shirt, the hermit crawling like an animal, the penitent nun behind her double set of bars all lived as if they were raving mad; they were respected for their resistance to human frailty. Among the large community of saints it is perhaps the possessed who stretch out their hands to the sane and lead in the dance, the dance of the blessed before the altar of miracles. Such strange ideas can be interwoven with our picture of the Roman lunatic asylum with its galleries raised above the throng.

A spring had its source at the foot of the building. Giovanni Maria Lancisi (died 1720), personal physician to three popes and a famous professor of medicine – Goldini's father was his pupil [138] – proved the healing power of the waters, and his patient Clement XI therefore provided the spring with a handsome surround (debased 1830). It is very noticeable in a veduta by Eckersberg from 1815. *Acqua Lancisiana* still exists and was once an ornament to the sad institution above it. It was also called the Fonte della Barchetta [139], because the ferries from the Via Giulia came alongside at this spot. The passengers who climbed up to Lungara by a ramp on the slope along the walls of the mental hospital could take a sip as they went past and give thanks for their mental faculties. When I last went down the modern concrete steps to Dr. Lancisi's medicinal spring they were slippery with excrement. People who seemed sane, were bathing in the river.

L'Archispedale di S. Spirito in Sassia formed a complete little town in the bend of the Tiber opposite the Ponte district. The southernmost of the four *Borghi* towards St. Peter's was – and is – its main street, the Porta di S. Spirito its triumphal arch. The principal of this extremely well endowed foundation has his commanding palace next door to the church of the Holy Spirit. All the buildings in this community carried their own device, a cross with double arms. Sixtus IV's hospital (1471–1482), very considerable in extent and as architecture [140], was increased in length by Benedict XIV with an extra *corsia* towards Castel Sant'Angelo. This added structure did not permit Fuga to express himself independently as an artist except in its compact portal, but Guglielmi painted fine pictures on the ceiling of the gallery for the sick. However, although the exterior of the hospital buildings had to accept the inevitable, the situation outside provided a compensation. The street's very extended, stern perspective demanded an enlivening accent. This was supplied without delay. The oratory of S. S. Annunziata was moved to a position opposite the new wing, providing Fuga's work with a striking contrast (cf. p. 142). Once again an example of the over all view, of the finely balanced development of a district in sombre guise – like a gleaming weight, moved along a steelyard till it finds its point of rest.

Pope Benedict was satisfied with his hospital, which had cost him 100.000 scudi. When his personal physician died, he thought jokingly of reserving a bed in this expensive wing "so as to be carried to it in case of illness and thus save both the choice and the expense of a new medical man" [141].

It was without any ulterior motive that the part of the complex on the other side of Porta di S. Spirito was improved by the Lambertini pope, for it was here in Lungara that the buildings of the foundling hospital were located. This institution, established in 1198 and perhaps the oldest in Europe, and the maternity hospital, had to provide space for a very large population. There were about forty wet-nurses, up to a couple of thousand orphans (who were either left on the doorstep or handed over) and about five hundred young mothers who were kept inside the walls of the hospital until they married or became nuns [142]. What an awful hustle and bustle! To this must be added a large number of nursing sisters with their own nunnery. The rebuilt Benedictine edifice (erected 1749) no longer exists, nor does the addition to the wing in Borgo S. Spirito, but old photographs tell us enough to be able to judge its character [143]. An inscription stated that this barracks for women was erected "for the greater comfort" of the inmates [144]. As far as room inside the building was concerned, the girls had no cause for complaint, for the dimensions were better suited to Guardsmen. The size of the windows indicates barrack-rooms big enough to hold a whole company, and the doors could be sally-ports in a fire-station. The Holy Father thought big on behalf of his exposed flock. No – the intimate touch was out of place here – if nothing else could suppress it, the neighbour of the orphanage certainly did so very forcibly.

Antonio da Sangallo's half-finished city gate bearing the name of the Holy Spirit, and the adjoining bastions which confine the Via della Lungara between their steeply sloping walls, no doubt controlled the architecture of the home for mothers. The whole of this space is crowded with solid geometrical forms, with obtuse and acute angles. Open a pair of dividers, lay them with the hinge at the city gate. Then the line of the road along the river is one leg and Salita di S. Onofrio, which runs up towards Gianicolo, is the other. On closer investigation we notice that the doors of the foundation have an acutely angled shape as well as spiked side posts very reminiscent of a fortification. It is quite possible that Fuga tried his hand at being a military engineer when he designed the sparse details for the beleaguered mothers' wing. Architecture was the art of building cities. Today this powerful city panorama is spoiled by the carriageways of Lungotevere.

This leading hospital provided death with a big yearly harvest. Statistics from 1833 show a mortality rate of about 25 % in the children's ward [145], before that it was probably even higher. In London, where the first orphanage was built in 1742, the mortality rate for "children on the parish" under five years was not less than 80–90 % at this later time [146]. The burial ground up to then had been between the hospital and the Tiber. It was crammed with bodies, and the river frequently flooded over them. It was high time to give the dead some peace and, what was more important, to provide a better atmosphere for those still alive. Papa Lambertini created order with his usual bluntness.

Immediately outside the Porta di S. Spirito a path wound its way under the cover of the bastions to the churchyard of the hospital. This was in the foundation's vineyard on Gianicolo – where Propaganda Fide's new college now stands – and a more beautiful place could not have been chosen. Seen from here the whole of Rome seems to lie prostrate at the foot of this lovely hill. The churchyard was designed as architecture, and Fuga was responsible for that [147]. *Campo Santo* with its flat gravestones set in rows was surrounded by a high wall with blind arcading and finished behind a niche on the vertical axis by a chapel built on an elliptical plan and crowned with a shallow dome. Gravity and Doric forms.

V

As we all know, Peter did not carry a sword in vain. It is a pity to say farewell to official buildings in Rome without having feasted our eyes on the military establishments. The security of the community under the white and yellow banner was minimal, but its symbols were outstanding. Was Castel Sant'Angelo not the most warlike citadel in the world? It looked like it and much can be built on faith. Whether the Roman fortress was weak or strong, it had solid foundations. At the time of Marlborough, Prince Eugen and Frederick the Great, it was still the archetype of a defiant building. The Archangel hovered above the tower and a swarm of winged figures kept guard along the bridge to the gateway, but Castel Sant' Angelo was never just a hollow shell. Antiquity had given it body, history a stentorian voice which drowned all cannon. It stood over there, heavy and fierce, the stronghold sans pareil in Christendom (Pl. 73).

Apart from this almost mystical asset the pope had very few military buildings at his disposal in Rome. There was no need for them to be big, for his army was small. The armed land forces of the Papal State amounted to 50,000 men around 1700, but in the course of the following century they were constantly reduced. In the 1760's there were only about 1500 men under arms in Rome [148] and twenty years later the Pope's entire land-based force numbered 2500 men with a garrison of 600 in the capital [149]. The navy had five galleys at Civitavecchia. Just prior to the French occupation in 1798 the weight of artillery in Castel Sant'Angelo was reduced to thirty cannon first used in the days of the Borgias [150]. A Hanoverian officer who went there noted in 1783 that the defence works were poorly provided with guns and the arsenal badly equipped, but to make up for it the colours were decorated with pictures of saints "which in an emergency will presumably be more effective here than mortars" [151]. According to Gorani, formerly a full lieutenant in the Imperial army who took part in the battle of Hochkirch, huge pyramids of cannon-balls were found everywhere, but they were of a different calibre from the guns [152]. Ballistics as a science was perhaps infected by the art of heraldry.

The only section of the army deserving of modern architecture was naturally the most decorative, the flower of the army. The pope had two corps of personal Guards, the Horse Guards, "the light cavalry" (*chevaux-légers, cavalleggeri*) and the Swiss Guard, both under the command of the court chamberlin (*il Maggiordomo*). The former was composed of men of noble birth and in Clement XI's time consisted of 100 men, who stood guard in the ruler's antechamber and escorted him at important ceremonies. The corps wore scarlet uniform and was technically two companies of lancers. It now goes under the name of *Guardia Nobile* and was reorganized in 1801. The Swiss Guard, formed in 1506 by Julius II – these incomparable "knaves of clubs" (Hans Andersen's phrase) – from the original cantons on the Lake of Lucerne, also served in those days as a trusted palace guard. The so-called *Lancie spezzate*, young noblemen dressed in black *à l'antique* and armed with both pistol and sword, was a semi-civilian household guard or – if you like – a sort of military corps of gentlemen in waiting (*con cappa e spada*). Benedict XIII, always so humble, dissolved this elegant club of palace warriors, but by 1730 it had regained its position in the privy antechamber. To the household troops must also be added the corps of cuirassiers, formed by Innocent X. Its strength was from 50–100 men in blue uniforms. Pius VII turned them into dragoons.

The rank and file of the army was made up of a few regiments of foot, among them a contingent from papal Avignon. The garrison of the Castel consisted mainly of sturdy craftsmen who in papal uniform served the saluting battery and ignited rockets. A Corsican company, highwaymen pure and simple, acted as military police and these gendarmes were the effective fighting strength of the Papal State. Bonaparte's compatriots were fighters [153].

While the papal army was not distinguished by its offensive character, its common sense left nothing to be desired. Experience had taught the Roman, always a simple soul, that come rain or sun all resistance is futile and the only sensible thing to do is to lay down your arms at once and surrender unconditionally. A soldier on sentry duty rushes straight into the guardroom when a shower beats the retreat or the sun launches its fiery darts [154]. Even the most responsible front-line position could fire a papal man-at-arms to deeds of heroism when faced with such odds. This Clement XIV found out when in 1774 he went in procession through his capital after having chased out the Jesuits. Immediately a *temporale* burst, the escort of Horse Guards turned one by one into side streets, dismounted and sought shelter in doorways, so that the Pope had to march into the Piazza della Minerva unescorted [155]. He might have died of pneumonia and so set his army a glorious example in the hour of victory [156]. That soldiers could at times be seen parading with umbrellas is an unconfirmed report, but a footman sent shopping without an umbrella considered himself a martyr [157].

One sort of military activity was particularly trying for the Roman infantryman and was therefore heartily detested by him, and that was to stand on guard in front of the opera house during performances [158]. Montesquieu overheard one day in 1729 the bitter complaints which an armed *sentinella* confided to his servant: "He had to stay where he was whether it was hot or cold, had only time to eat three small loaves and drink a *fiasco* of wine a day. He had caught his death, he insisted, from parking carriages" [159]. The situation, indeed the words, are echoed in Leporello's first scene in "Don Giovanni": *Nott' e giorno faticar ...*

One can quite see that such an obstinate civilian as the typical Roman followed the rule: "Be Prepared" ("Immer bereit sein ..."). While carrying out his military exercises with lack of precision and enthusiasm he could also show the public the greatest courtesy, this latter being especially praiseworthy when it came to breaking up a mob. Several eyewitnesses have described their impressions of troops being drilled. One of them saw (1710) the Horse Guards parade; it was all very colourful, but the officer had the greatest difficulty in getting the men to carry out the movements on command [160]. Another observer relates (in the 1760's) how a young officer got carried away while issuing his commands. One of the troops began to feel it was all a waste of time, he stepped forward and asked: *Ma quando finisce 'sta storia?* (Tell me, how long is all this lark going to last?") "Hang on a bit longer lad," answered the officer, "it won't be long now" [161].

The cavalry had the greatest respect for the heavy chargers they entrusted themselves to and endeavoured to keep them in a permanently phlegmatic condition so that they should not precipitately endanger the riders' lives and disgrace the Holy See [162]. For, as the old Italian adage had it: "A galloping horse is an open grave". A cuirassier on a bolting horse is never a pleasant sight and at Corpus Christi it is positively indecent. It was the invariable custom at cavalcades for the pope to ride a mule that was past its best, so that he at least could get the business over with in style [163]. But the armed forces had to be self-sacrificing and could not very well saddle up on donkeys. When the Guards were on parade, the heavily accoutred men felt they were done for; they appraised the terrain in fear and trembling, and the spirit of the corps might then find expression in the shouts of *Guardatevi! Guardatevi!* ("Look out! Be careful! Watch it!"). The soldiers' fear of the animals they thought they could not control was only exceeded by their love of their neighbour [164]. Such warnings were the battle-cries of the

View from the Gianicolo towards the Scalette Conservatory and the Regina Coeli Convent (on the left). In the background the Carceri Nuove. Old photograph.

96a. San Carlo ai Catinari, balcony. (Foto ex Vaticis.)

96b. The Irish College in Via degli Ibernesi.

87. *The Greek College in Via del Babuino.*

88. *The back part of the Palazzo della Consulta.*

army. The pope's light cavalry preferred no doubt to turn up when it was all over, thereby confirming the peace-loving policy of the Church.

All the Holy Father's military bands played splendidly and noisily. The men received decent pay and were well dressed, their uniforms resplendent with so much braid, and cut on such generous lines that one of them "would be enough to dress three Prussian heroes" belonging to Old Fritz. There was one officer to every ten men. God's watchful eye could be sensed up in the clouds above the legions of the Roman church, and the pope's blessing finger a little closer at hand. "The Shadow of an army obeys the shadow of a leader" [165], and a prelate in skirts inspected the ranks.

With the exception of the garrison at the citadel, as far as can be ascertained, only the personal Guards of the pope were housed in barracks. The light cavalry was next-door to the Inquisition's palace in the Borgo, just inside the city gate, named after the corps (Porta Cavalleggeri). The building, a bare monstrosity, dated from Pius IV's time. The cuirassiers were quartered in equally plain barracks in the Piazza dei Termini, which in those days was the parade ground [166]. The horses' long tails flipped up the dust in front of the home of the Carthusians. As the special palace guard, the Swiss were always quartered in the Residence itself, at the Vatican, in the same place as now, behind Bernini's colonnade and the corridor to the citadel. The little church of S. Martino was part of the territory of the Swiss, and a semi-cylindrical fortified tower dominates their courtyard. At the Quirinal too the papal mercenaries were assembled around an old-fashioned fortification, the bastion-like tower which juts up on the way to the Via della Dataria.

As a result of the Quirinal taking over the function of the Vatican as the principal residence, the guards had to be concentrated on Monte Cavallo and accommodated in large buildings. We have already discovered that the Palazzo della Consulta was erected as a combined barracks and administration building, and have analysed its front, the smiling face of the Ministry of the Interior. But this is a mask. The body of the building expresses its true nature and proclaims it most articulately at the rear. It has concise lines, suitable for squadrons of *chevaux-légers* and the cuirassiers. This palace, the headquarters of the Guards, had to adapt itself to the site allotted to it and did so by taking on the form of a trapezium with the short side at the back towards the slope of the Quirinal hill. Seen from here (Pl. 88) it looks completely different from Monte Cavallo's level. The extended façade was counterbalanced by its height at the back, a block imposing in its mass, splendidly articulated and finished at the top in a forceful manner by the strong main cornice between the mezzanines. These contained barrack-rooms for the troops; the loose-boxes were behind the high barred windows. The gateway, forceful without being bombastic, opened on to a broad riding ground between the two converging stable wings and then into the courtyard which Fuga adroitly laid out on a rectangular plan within the acute-angled shape of the complex. There were passages right through the building from the middle of the yard's long sides which formed an internal link with the large flights of steps behind the main gateway facing the palace square. Easy communication was thus paired with an excellent ground plan, the four entrances being set symmetrically in the form of a cross. This planning was not purely for aesthetic reasons; the purpose is obvious: the horsemen on their large (and cumbersome) horses had to be able to turn in a hurry in every direction.

Detachments of foot were on guard at many places in the city, including the Piazza di Pietra opposite the Customs house, at Monte di Pietà to guard the bank, in the Piazza Giudea to keep the Jews under control, in the Campo dei Fiori, Rome's busiest market, and several other places. The main guardroom was in the Quirinal square and consisted of a brick-built arcade which Fuga at the beginning of the 1730's erected around the handsome sweep of the papal stables opposite the Palazzo della Consulta [167]. From a strategic point of view, the guard on the ghetto side of the Ponte dei Quattro Capi was particularly important as they had to cover the bridgehead against possible attack from Trastevere, which was always in a state of turmoil. The ordinary guard posts were large cages (of wooden timbers), designed for hasty retreat. In them the soldiers stood like wild animals behind bars hissing at the people outside. It is very typical that when the inhabitants of Trastevere during riots in 1736 streamed across the Ponte dei Quattro Capi and attacked the guardhouse, the squad withdrew to S. Gregorietto and counter-attacked from there. The church was the safest cover and nobody would dare to make an assault on it [168].

Napoleon's era left behind projects for the only really martial barracks in Rome. The Consulta building's rear elevation is merely grave and stiff and offers no challenge to civilians. Its discipline is just a slight variation of the utilitarian buildings of the time. As part of the grand redevelopment of the Piazza del Popolo by the new Augustus, a barracks for gendarmes (Carabinieri) was planned, having the main guard and octroi at the adjacent city gate [169]. It was erected 1822–1824 according to Valadier's design, but for Pius VII, who in this case did not disdain the Napoleonic left-overs. The building, faced in strident rustication, shouts "Empire" to the true Martian Field below, but receives no answer in return. The soldiers appeared on occasions in the arcaded front with their threecornered hats and black side-whiskers, but this was hardly enough of an Imperial style to restore the spirit of a Caesar to the entrance to the Holy City. Here began and ended the Rome of the artists. Stendhal mentions that he entered the city through the Porta del Popolo in November 1825 and showed his passport to the gendarmes in the brand-new guardhouse. The former Imperial lieutenant of dragoons found the entrance *plein de petitesse*. He sent his servant to look for lodgings, gave the French propylaeia a cursory glance before throwing himself into a carriage to get to the Colosseum. During his first walks he found unqualified pleasure in noticing that "the noisy footsteps of a brigadier-general" were nowhere to be heard. A Minister of State would walk home like any other citizen, and "at his gate meet three or four chickens who undisturbed peck the ground for something to eat. Nobody seems to be in a hurry here" [170].

The road linking these two genre pictures – from the fortified city gate to Cardinal Consalvi's home in the street of government offices (Via della Dataria) – runs through official Rome, where nobody commands and nobody obeys, through the idyllic village of the artists, and heads straight on to the biggest ruin. To the end of the time of Pius IX this route was paramount for all visitors. The popes' building activities for the common weal, however good or up-to-date, were regarded merely as deserted enclaves or considered antagonistically as the nesting boxes of clericalism, if anybody noticed them at all. At the Porta del Popolo you came up against a barrier, in Pio Nono's time, particularly when you wanted to get out. No other public architecture was so vilified as the guardhouse, for it stood for a régime which was as corrupt as it was philistine. "We were just about to leave by the Porta del Popolo when we were suddenly stopped by an enormous papal policeman, who, in spite of his martial appearance, in the politest possible way advised us against going outside the walls. "Why?" was the general outcry, which almost simultaneously rang out from us all. "Because the road to Viterbo is not safe," answered the policeman. "But we only propose to go to Ponte Molle," objected one of the older artists.

"The road to Ponte Molle is not safe either," replied the gendarme in the same imperturbable manner . . .".

THE PALACES

> *Un bâtiment, pour être beau, doit commencer à l'être dans la rue*
> DE BROSSES

I

The home of the aristocrat in Rome is on a large scale corresponding to the style of his life and the honour of his name. The head of an ancient and powerful family is full of pride, perhaps even puffed up with arrogance at being a Roman noble [1]. Many of the Roman clans profess to be descended from the patricians of Antiquity. Prince Massimo counts Fabius Maximus Cunctator among his ancestors (and has the motto *cunctando restituit rem*). The Santacroce family derives its origin from Valerius Publicola. The Muti family from Mucius Scaevola, and the Pamphilis even put the legendary king Numa Pompilius, whose beloved was a naiad, at the head of their genealogical table. The Crescenzi family too, insist that they are continuing a direct line from the days of Antiquity, like the house of Frangipani, who claim to carry on the ancient Roman *gens Anicia*. Mere belief in such a majestic family tree made the owners of noble names into a unique phenomenon among other lesser mortals. Even famous first names from the heathen past could increase the family name's resonance – Marcus Antonius (Borghese), Julius Caesar (Rospigliosi), Hasdrubal (Mattei), Hannibal (Albani), not to mention Trojanus (Acquaviva). You bow to the Duke of Devonshire, although his name may only be John, but every Julius Caesar is at a special advantage if he lives in a palace.

Illustrious above all others were the feudal families whose origins are lost in the Early Middle Ages, such as Conti, Savelli, Caetani, Colonna, Orsini, the five most noble names. Throughout the centuries they had lived and fought as ruling clans, had defied one another and stood up to the pope. The house of Savelli, among whose legendary forefathers was that Aventinus who defended the hill in Rome which was later called after him against Aeneas, died out in the male line in 1712, and the Contis became extinct in 1808 after a period of regeneration during the papacy of the family's Pope Innocent XIII (1721–1724), but by then this house, perhaps Rome's most ancient, had presented the Eternal City with twelve popes and more than sixty cardinals. The Colonna family, who maintain their supremacy in Roman aristocracy equally with the Orsinis, to this very day has only been able to produce one Pontifex Maximus, but in this case quality made up for quantity, for it was Martin V, who in 1420 brought back the power to St. Peter's throne in Rome after exile in Avignon. The fourth pope of the Orsini line (Benedict XIII) became the greatest builder of Roman Rococo.

The heads of these and other ancient aristocratic clans substantiated their claims to prestige with their large estates. A couple of noble families possessed actual sovereign rights, namely the House of Ludovici-Boncompagni, who ruled the principate of Piombino (and a part of Elba), and the Carpegnas, whose little hereditary state was situated near Urbino.

The nepotic families of the popes vied with Rome's ancient nobility by reason of their enormous wealth, which fell to them because of their progenitor's power and dominion. They bear such sonorous names as Albani, Aldobrandini and Altieri, Barberini, Boncompagni and Borghese, Chigi and Corsini, Odescalchi and Ottoboni, Pamphili and Rospigliosi. Every one of these magnates – with the title of Prince (*principe*), Duke (*duca*), Marquis (*marchese*), Count (*conte*) – felt that he stood close to the throne. He considered himself a minor monarch, and with reason, when he surveyed his many small towns, his boundless estates, his country mansions and villas, his churches, chapels and charitable institutions. Many a picturesque market-town in Latium still bears the stamp of the country seat of a Roman prince, his coat of arms set over the town gate; the palace dominates the square, the fountain bears his name [2].

The Roman scene itself made the aristocrat of ancient lineage stand out in brilliant relief, inscriptions praised his ancestors in loud tones. No Borghese can attend mass in St. Peter's without seeing his own name in letters two feet high above the portal of the basilica. The members of the great houses time and again recognized their coats of arms on public buildings as they drove through Rome. Hardly a noble family could be found which did not count cardinals among its members. Each of these *porporati* held the rank of crown prince among the potentates of the rest of the world, nursed secret expectations of the papal tiara and corresponding aspirations in everyday life. Various cardinals were only too pleased to fill the official role of Protector for one of Europe's crowns. Honorary posts could invest their holders with extraordinary importance. Since the papacy of Sixtus V, the heads of the Colonna and the Corsini families had functioned as papal crown princes (*principi assistenti al soglio*), but as a result of hereditary enmity between the two houses, these dignitaries alternated in the practice of their duties, the most important task of which consisted, and still consists, in making a fine show around the papal throne. The head of the House of Colonna in Rome was the hereditary Constable for the Kingdom of the Two Sicilies. After the Savellis died out, every Prince Chigi at birth inherited the title of Marshal of the Conclave, the electoral assembly of the cardinals. It was also illustrious to be able to call oneself the Standard Bearer of the Holy Roman Church, the Commander of the S. Spirito Hospital or Senator of Rome. The aristocracy had a rich and melodious keyboard to play on.

Descendant of an Augustan senator or of a mediaeval tyrant, related to Christ's Vicar on earth, Protector of an empire, and in addition millionaire – is it any wonder that such Roman patricians were exacting in their demands regarding their houses? They made sure they were carried out and continued to do so during the period which is our subject.

According to his means, every aristocrat desired all the circumstance of a real court to function within his walls. Expressed in architectural terms this means that the palace had to express "an inner perspective". In order to inspire respect, the noble insisted upon distance separating the gateway from the inner sanctum. He who pays a visit or is granted an audience, has to walk a long way through apartments before he is ready to be received. As a result, an unbroken series of rooms, an imposing suite in the piano nobile, is absolutely necessary, the longer the better. This requirement alone, dictated by ceremony, makes a lot of work for the architect.

All witnesses from those days emphasize the tremendous machinery which was set in motion at official receptions in the houses of the higher aristocracy [3]. The owner lived his daily life modestly in a couple of rooms, but when he flung open the doors, the guests had to obey the rules of precedence according to the rank and lineage of their host, approach with increasing deference and show him all due reverence. We know the ceremonial from audiences at Court.

The carriage drove into the *porte-cochère*, the doorkeeper banged his staff on the flagstones, the chasseurs and footmen lined the shallow steps in the huge dark hall. Cardinals, Ambassadors and Princesses were escorted up by servants carrying torches (*torce*), the less favoured made their own way upstairs [4]. In the first *anticamera* there was a swarm of lackeys, in the second anteroom the ordinary liveried servants were superseded by grooms of the chamber; gradually as you gained ground through the high-ceilinged, half-empty reception rooms, the status of the personnel increased noticeably as almoners and chaplains, pages and secretaries took over from one another. From apartment to apartment the dignity of the guest is proclaimed; he makes his way amid a salvo of titles, a fusillade of *Eccellenza,* and if a foreigner, he finds his name gradually deformed beyond recognition. The great Montesquieu once entered the vestibule in the house of a Roman prince with his illustrious name intact, to have it changed in no time at all to Montedieu, then to Montieu, again to Mordieu, finally to be denuded of all rank and introduced as plain "Monsieur Forbu" [5]. At the end of the journey stands the major-domo (called *decano*) with the chamberlain of the house, who is himself of noble birth, and he performs the presentation to the lord of the palace and his consort from the door of the apartment or inside the presence-chamber itself. D'Orbessan reports that the masters of ceremonies were dressed in black uniforms with short capes "very like *les pères* in our plays", and they extended a white-gloved hand to the ladies whom they introduced. He also tells us (1750) that a list bearing the names of the guests was on view on a table in the first antechamber.

The cardinals and Rome's princes had legal right to hold court. Above the throne hung a portrait of the ruling pope, of another monarch to whom this prince owed homage, or perhaps of the family's most famous son. When the nobleman stepped up on the dais, he was resplendent in all his glory. This privilege of erecting a *baldacchino* was also given as

89. *Via Giulia with the Arco dei Farnesi. Beneath this the Palazzo Falconieri.*

91b. Depot behind the Palazzo Altieri.

91a. Garden wall of the Palazzo Borghese in Via dell' Arancio.

92. *Via della Pilotta between the Palazzo Colonna (on the left) and its garden wall.*

a special favour to four Roman families with the rank of margrave, namely the houses of Costaguti, Patrizi, Sacchetti and Theodoli.

"Respect yourself, if you wish others to respect you" – this famous maxim which Cardinal Mazarin instilled into Louis XIV held good in Rome's palaces. Applied to the building it runs: "Show my greatness in a spacious and well-arranged manner."

However, it was not only etiquette that required a lot of space to make a suitable display; the special way the Romans entertained also demanded a lot of room. The aristocratic Roman was to some extent inhospitable, in so far as he was reluctant to invite anybody to his table [6]. The exclusive dinner-party or buffet supper, which was a Parisian social institution, very rarely took place here; a very noticeable exception was Cardinal de Bernis' ever ready laid table. Nor did the French salon way of life, where the convention is a group (*cercle*) of people surrounding the armchair of a wise and charming lady, become very popular in the Papal City. A few derivatives were noted towards the close of the 18th century [7]. Social gatherings such as these, of an intimate character, need only a few pleasant rooms of moderate size. The French deliberately cultivated the exclusive interior.

But when the Roman noble finally did invite people to his home he kept open house. The guests came in large numbers to be seen, to bask in admiration and converse with guarded frankness. Such gatherings were therefore called *conversazioni*. Music might be provided and card-playing take place. Refreshments were limited to refreshing drinks and chocolate, biscuits and various iced collations. While French entertainment is stationary, the participants sitting either at a table or in a group in front of the fireplace, Roman assemblies are peripatetic and the guests are constantly on the move. "One can choose whether to sit down, walk about or converse with whoever one wishes," says Abbé Richard, "great freedom paired with politeness is the rule" [8]. Another distinguished traveller emphasizes "that there is no general conversation, coteries are formed (*on se cantonne*), small companies within the large one". People come and go [9], from party to party as well.

There was of course a tendency to crowd together in the salon where the hostess and the dignitaries were [10], yet the Roman *conversazione* was indeed dependent on having many large reception rooms available. Not only the continuous movement of numerous people – at a reception given by Cardinal de Bernis there were up to 3000 guests present [11] – but the radius of action of the individual dignitaries also demanded room for movement in the palace. For although the gathering may be informal, the respect for status is by no means neglected. A cardinal in *cappa magna* has a wide train many feet long. Just imagine ten princes of the Church circulating; everybody gives way to them and salutes them, the tails of the exalted peacocks sweep slowly across the marble floors. A single one of these guests in purple could, with a few measured steps, play havoc with a Danish count's salon [12].

This traditional institution of red tape and ceremony was only possible with a large staff of servants. The greater the number of liveried servants hovering in the antechambers and the more footmen escorting the coach, the more impressed the spectator was by the owner's position. "The magnificence of the great consists mainly in having grandiose palaces, many pages, lackeys, horses and carriages," explains Lalande [13]. But there was plenty to do for the many hands in the princely residence and its annexes, and frequent repairs gave the workmen on the staff regular occupation. The daily meals for the family, taken in withdrawn solitude, required the least effort, and it was not at all unusual for the food to be brought in from an outside caterer. The contrast between outward show and a poor way of living astounded all foreigners. While a crowd of lackeys "spent most of the day in the anteroom playing cards or stretched out on the benches", the prince went to his frugal meal and sat down on a creaking chair with leather upholstery dating from the time of his grandfather. Grosley tells us that he visited a sick cardinal who occupied one of the largest and most splendid palaces in Rome; the place he lived in was a smoke-filled, badly lit room on the mezzanine floor only 8 feet by 6. Horace Walpole, in Rome in 1740, asserted that the most powerful princes expended merely eighteen pence on their daily food and that some increased the expenditure to five paoli or half-a-crown. Cardinal Albani was considered extravagant because he spent ten paoli on his lunch and evening meal. Members of the papal aristocratic families were so haughty and so miserly that they had no contact with anybody in the daily round, but shuffled around in an enormous palace with two miserable candles and a couple of monsignori whom they were forced to keep alive so as not to be completely alone [14]. The luxury-loving son of Sir Robert Walpole was shocked by these conditions. But Holberg looked upon this simple way of life with a more friendly eye and made a mental note of a number of things: "In the palaces and the houses of the nobility it is not unusual," he noted in the first letter of his autobiography, "that the left-overs from lunch are kept for supper."

We must point out that the relationship between master and servant was exceedingly patriarchal. Wages were low, tips being the most important income, but the jobs were much sought after, because the servants, who were mostly married and frequently also had other jobs in the city, enjoyed various material benefits including a claim on provisions, as well as being in a safe environment under the protection of their employer. Faithful old retainers and their widows received free accommodation. So a little community grew up round every palace, and its members, even remote ones, did not consider themselves merely domestics in the home of a rich man, but also his dependents connected with the family, often through several generations. This excellent relationship is well expressed by the very word *la famiglia,* which is used of the domestic staff in the widest sense [15]. Indeed, it frequently happened that domestics and their children took the honoured family name, and this practice has contributed much towards keeping a splendid nobility alive. The world-famous singer Caterina Gabrielli was the daughter of a chef employed by the prince of this name and thus brought honour to it far beyond boundaries of the Papal State.

It is easy to see why an individual's responsibility for such an unusual number of people had architectural consequences. In most cases the noblemen made the necessary room in side wings, or reserved a certain part of the palace for his *familiares.* This part was then given a suitable modest exterior, and a glance at the façade looking towards a side street would soon tell you that this was the part which housed the staff, because it was revealed by the low storeys and the plain frames of the windows [16]. But when the employer neither could nor would accommodate a whole "colony" under his roof, it was necessary to build a special complex. From this developed a special category of buildings called *il palazzo di famiglia;* palace indeed, for the house is often of surprising dimensions. The type is altogether remarkable (and has been ignored by research). The buildings concerned, outwardly have certain grand-scale features, which are dictated by the neighbourhood, but are in reality nothing but small flats. In this respect, the type lies somewhere between the charitable institution and the ordinary apartment house.

If a systematic study is made of Nolli's very detailed plan of Rome from 1748, five *palazzi di famiglia* are found to be included, naturally only the largest and the most striking. Of these the annex of the Colonnas, which was built abutting on to a mediaeval tower in the present Via 4 Novembre, has been completely renovated [17], but it is still possible to admire the size of the building. The servants' quarters of the Barberini palace in Quattro Fontane have also been completely rebuilt. The *Grand-Commun* of the Chigis [18] was on the corner of the Corso and the north side of the Via di Pietra. The large and picturesque annex of the Palazzo Santacroce, which we shall later discuss in another connection, still exists. The Borgheses' palace for their underlings is far and away the genre's proudest representative from the Baroque Period, an impressive cube facing the side elevation of the residence and equally as long. It has a magnificent corner facing down towards the Via della Scrofa [19]. At the sight of this stern barracks, which, in dimensions, far exceeds the Chancellery in Copenhagen, one gets a very good idea of the size of the richest patrician's household.

Prince Lancellotti's *abitazione per la famiglia* behind the Via dei Coronari probably dates from the first half of the 18th century (Pl. 90). Like that of the Borgheses it is situated parallel to one of the side elevations of the main palace and thus forms one side of a small private square. The building, which has been completely overlooked and is now in disrepair, is attractive in a discreet style entirely in harmony with its purpose. It looks to us like a respectable property with flats for the less well off. The general impression is that of light and cordiality; the façade is neither stamped with the presumptuous emblems of the prince, nor degraded by any skimpiness in its features. The only allowance made to the palace opposite is an indication of symmetry in the distribution of the bottom storey.

There really is something fascinating about these beehives, formerly buzzing with activity and gay with colourful liveries. The buildings are so natural and seem so at home in this arrogant territory, in spite of the formal garb they are made to wear. A little world of its own, ruled paternally and charitably by a petty autocrat. They strove and suffered, sang and complained in one great fellowship behind such walls as these – with the family's dominating portal opposite. The servants were able to make some extra money by renting out rooms to tourists who, for a small outlay, obtained both pleasant lodgings with well-disciplined servants and an important sounding address. In 1777 the elegant French civil servant Roland de la Platière established himself in a couple of rooms overlooking the street in the domestic wing of the Duke of Bracciano's palace. His host, a coachman, tucked himself away in a garret [20].

Many servants, and also an enormous number of horses and carriages were needed. For transport alone many animals were required, for the heavy vehicles could not be dragged up Rome's hills or to the villas in the Albani mountains by less than four horses, and six were customary for a ceremonial drive. But the large amount of horseflesh was also determined by the aristocrat's position in life. Whenever foreign visitors such as ambassadors made an entry into Rome, the nobility turned up with an enormous show of splendid coaches – as with servants, the greater the numbers, the more important the person. When in 1731 Cardinal Grimaldi returned to Rome from his nunciature in Vienna, his procession numbered 80 carriages, not counting Cardinal Corsini's and his own [21]. The Duke of Choiseul, the French envoy, made his *entrate della campagna* with more than 110 vehicles in 1754 [22].

Furthermore, the concept "Corso", that daily drive in the main street also called *la trottata* [23], indicated an extremely large number of carriages and horses. It is believed that on festival days during the carnival, there were over 1000 carriages driving slowly up and down the Corso. This number of vehicles would – at a modest calculation – require about 4000 horses.

One witness concluded that the less well-off cardinal could make do with but 12 carriage horses. The head groom of the wealthy Cardinal Grimani, Imperial Ambassador in Rome, wrote full of pride to his brother in 1703: "I am in full charge of over 30 horses and more than 15 people and do not have to account for anything" [24]. But Prince Borghese usually had 100 horses in his stables, with 83 coaches and other vehicles in his coach-houses [25]. Prince Rospigliosi, whose stud was particularly renowned for, among other things, its dappled biscuit-coloured bays (immortalized by Guido Reni in the "Aurora" fresco in the Casino Rospigliosi), had a couple of hundred horses in his stables [26].

Although people in the Papal City did not indulge in the luxury of bloodstock to quite such an extent as did those in Naples, the magnificent teams of horses must have been an impressive feature of Rome's streets and provided a splendid decor for the townscape, especially when the heavy steeds (mostly Spanish breeds [27]) jingled past on ceremonial occasions with their luxurious harness and shook the tassels on their head trappings. These *fiocchi* on the equipages of cardinals and princes indicated their rank. The governor of Rome was also entitled to use them [28]. The first mentioned personages of rank furthermore enjoyed the privilege of being allowed to send a footman with an umbrella in front of the team, so that at the sight of this awe-inspiring *ombrella* (still however rolled up) all other vehicles should give way [29]. The people in the street could admire a Prince Gabrielli's best racehorse when it came first in the annual *corso de' barberi* in Rome's main street. They could identify an ambassador's new team of black-headed horses or blue roans, could ridicule the mean old archbishop's magenta rattle-trap and applaud the coachman who, like a virtuoso, negotiated a corner at some speed with his six in hand [30].

Where were all these horses and carriages accommodated? Generally in the subsidiary courtyards of the palace, if there were any. For example, the stable yard for the Palazzo Altieri was in the second and largest *cortile,* which had none of the characteristics of what the French call a *basse-cour.* Prince Colonna's main stable was on the ground floor of the palace's side wing, directly beneath the banqueting hall, that famous gallery; but the wing mentioned, which now faces an elegant and very busy street (Via 4 Novembre), originally stood along the narrow Vicolo de' Colonnesi. The Roman gentlemen who lived on the grandest scale had to accommodate most of their horses in stables specially built for the purpose – in some cases these were counterparts to the *palazzi di famiglia*. In regard to situation, that of the Borghese could be counted as the most splendid; it closed the family's square at the Tiber end, and was not pulled down until fairly recently [31]. The Rospigliosi's famous stables were situated on the right side of the palace's large courtyard along the present Via 24 Maggio. An engraving by Vasi [32] shows that this courtyard was used as an exercise yard, and this was also the case with the Piazza Borghese. The very rambling *Stalle Barberini* sprawled at the foot of the palace, the entrance to it being at the east corner of the Piazza Barberini, and we know that Thorvaldsen established his atelier in a part of this large building [33]. The Palazzo Farnese's stables and domestic wings from the 16th century were connected with the main building by a fine arch (Pl. 89). They dominate a whole stretch of the Via Giulia in the same way as the Villa Farnesina's palace-like stables – possibly designed by Raphael – formerly dominated Lungara on the other side of the Tiber. The stables of the Quirinal took on such a monumental character and became so intimately connected with the palace, that the buildings will be discussed below when dealing with the papal residence.

It is only a short generation ago that Rome smelt of horses. Although is was mainly the cabbies' nags that exuded this odour, it hung all the same over the whole of the city as the last whiff of the atmosphere of old papal Rome. Anyone wishing nowadays to make contact with the milieu of feudal coaches at close quarters would not find it by following his nose. Or his ears. It is of course still possible to hear the crisp clip-clop on the stone paving, but the melody is thin. The resounding clatter of hoof-beats that filled the city for centuries and was the *continuo* amid its clamour, has vanished for ever with the stink of dung and of horses' sweat.

By seeking humble places and concentrating on the backs of palaces, the patient wanderer may yet come upon traces of the Age of Elegance and its mode of conveyance. Most promising is a little crooked lane behind the Palazzo Altieri that runs in the direction of S. Stefano del Cacco. Here stands a one-storeyed building jutting out from the palace and facing north. This was once a stable – or perhaps a remise – belonging to the noble house [34]. As it stands here, overpowered by the towering walls of the palace, this plain building could tell us a lot about the people who lived in the front of the house and at the back; the contrast between the sunlit façade and the rear premises in constant shadow. But it is also worth noting that this low annex took up so much space in the very heart of Rome. When one walks along the crooked path on the reverse side of the Palazzo Altieri it is right into a deserted city and a community long since dead (Pl. 91b).

Having asserted this, it becomes evident that a Roman palace was formidable by virtue of the status of the family and the conduct of life behind its walls. However, the nobleman's house was also built on a grand scale as a veritable monument to the owner. Matching the internal character, established according to the activities of the traditional way of life, were the external features which conveyed the idea of a memorial pure and simple. Even when the building was half empty, used only rarely, or completely deserted and boarded up, as a work of art it clearly proclaimed the importance of the owner by its own superiority. The architecture classified him, making his means and his taste obvious to everybody.

It is part of the aristocrat's nature to "cut a figure" (*far figura*). In Italy, palace architecture in particular gained great benefit from this distinguished occupation. An English observer wrote in 1685 that there was nobody less afraid of spending money on building palaces than the Italians, and none that did so little to preserve them [35]. This was very natural, even with the plaster peeling the memorial serves its purpose, a ruined palace is still a shell around an indisputable reputation. All patina is noble, perfect neatness is unmistakably bourgeois.

The Italian *far figura* in architecture is an almost demonic drive, with a streak of Quixoticism too, perhaps. The French did not appreciate this Roman *trait*. And the English frowned both on the lack of comfort and all the neglected sills. "What in France is called cutting a fine figure consists of having a well-laden table," reflected President de Brosses, "a rich man who wants to make an impression employs many chefs." Not so with the Italians: "One shows off by expending large sums on the erection of a large building, which serves as an adornment for the nation and is at the same time imperishable evidence for posterity of the builder's name, rank and taste." And he finished up with this delightful and instructive assertion, so truly Gallic and as polished as an epigram: "A beautiful fluted column is well worth a good fat fowl" (*une belle colonne canellée vaut bien une bonne gélinotte*) [36]. Nugent expresses the same sentiment when he remarks that the Italians prefer to spend their money on buildings and gardens (as well as equipages) rather than using it for "luxurious tables and strong liquors", and in fact the nobility had made building "their favourite amusement" [37].

Stendhal expressed his ideas of this situation – as a characteristic of the Italian and perhaps especially the Roman psyche – with his usual insight and pithiness. At one point he states: "Having a fine house in the city makes for a greater reputation than having millions in your wallet. If the house is of outstanding beauty it will soon be called by the name of the owner. People say: The law court is in such and such a street, in the *Casa Clerici*." A proud façade ennobles a man. And he describes some gentlemen "who have the good fortune to be building; they are filled with passion like generals launching an attack" [38]. And he joined them on the scaffolding.

If an attempt is made – as we intend – to survey and assess the Roman palace architecture of a certain period, it is wise to take three important factors into consideration. The first is that the builders threw themselves into the work with great passion; they were personally involved as people of rank, possibly too, as men with a feeling for beauty, and connoisseurs. By and large we may assume that the aristocrat is not just a somewhat indifferent client for a piece of architecture, but a demanding principal and the unsparing critic of the architect, a "general" on active service, if you like. This idea by no means denigrates the architect's personal achievement; it merely serves to put the two contracting parties on an equal level, and up to now this is what the history of architecture has largely neglected to do.

In the second place it must be borne in mind that "cutting a figure" by building, can be done in various ways. A brand-new count, who perhaps has recently moved to Rome, wants a "figure" different from the descendant of a family whose mediaeval tower already stands on the building site (Pl. 106). The aristocrats bent on building palaces formed a clan which outwardly showed a united front, but each one went his own way. The individual members were inclined to have reasons for their building activities which were determined by inherent tradition, respect for the family, special milieu, personal prejudice, perhaps wild aspirations and ancient blurred symbols. They kept an eye on their neighbours, wanted to outdo them or merely be different, and not to be looked down upon at any price. They remembered a great-grandfather's abortive projects and now desired to learn from them, to alter them and in the end to achieve their aims.

The palace is after all a dwelling; its builder is a human being, a person for whom the historical view of long-gone ages and dead heroes is just as indispensable for guidance as keeping an eye on rival houses. The activity of the builder is interwoven in a network of associations. Only in exceptional cases are we now able to sort out some parts of this, but its existence is a fact. To ignore the matter is the easiest thing, but this sort of attitude is hardly favourable evidence of the scholar's judgment.

Thirdly and lastly, the building site of the palace, its position in the perspective of the city, is always important and often decisive for the architecture. Roman topography has many traps for the unwary; every new work must look out for itself if it is going to hold its own. The terrain often makes serious demands and so do older buildings in the neighbourhood. There is no other city in the world which puts the architect to the test as much as Rome does. He must not neglect to take all aspects into consideration, and is a prey to the existing company and the spirit of the place. And the architect, who is to build a domicile on the grandest scale, is perhaps particularly at risk, for he has in fact to serve two extremely demanding masters, the overwhelming heritage from the past and modernity itself.

A historian, who arranges a number of palaces in order of precedence without having regard to the special external and internal conditions pertinent to each single work, is counting his chickens before they are hatched. His brilliant evaluation according to all the rules of typology is, seen in the proper light, only a construction on paper having little to do with the real situation. An interest in transition has often hampered a true insight into the real state of affairs.

In the following survey of Rome's palaces in the hundred years after 1680, we shall not only review them in chronological order, but also inspect each façade, assuming that, like the building behind, it is a work *sui generis*. We would rather seek out the particular in every problem, than search for distinctions as far as history of style is concerned. To us it is preferable to understand a building's individuality and, as far as possible, assess the style of each palace rather than give it a number in a series.

The most Roman thing to do would be to fall in with the impassioned generals who joined battle on the scaffolding of the palaces.

J'ai monté moi-même aux échelles...

II

Across the road from S. Andrea delle Fratte stands a palace. It is not very large by Roman standards. But it has great dignity of style. The architect and first owner of the building was also a figure with strong contours and of immense artistic consequence. This palace was Bernini's home. "Popes, princes and whole nations knelt to him here in homage," runs an inscription on the façade (Pl. 93).

Anyone who intends to study Roman Baroque palaces might well make a beginning by regarding the heavy corner house in Capo le Case with due deference. It shows the matured building traditions of a century. The palace represents the common denominator of the strict Roman style in which Giacomo della Porta is the first important name. Bernini's house is the criterion of the fully developed form. Like any other classic solution, it is expressed very simply. All superfluous decoration is banished, only the bare structure emerges. The only ornament on the façade is a discreet wave scroll moulding in the fascia under the piano nobile. This very antique motif is the mark of the building's classicism. Everything is straightforward, tested and weighed in the balance

– and not found wanting. The relief of the façade decreases in strength upwards towards the coping above the windows, but it is only a slight *diminuendo;* the unity of the building cannot be disputed. It is an elegant building in the full sense of the word, so reserved in style that it seems almost self-effacing, yet it controls an outstanding corner in the new Rome of the Baroque period. But there is a tinge of arrogance in this reserve. It would be a temptation to regard this as deliberate, especially when you look at the building opposite, for there, facing Bernini's dignified house, stands that part of the Propaganda Fide palace which Borromini designed. The works by the two great architectural rivals present a dramatic antithesis. With Bernini, controlled tradition is predominant, Roman Baroque at a Classical stage; with Borromini the new, vigorous and eminently individual art of form prevails, which brought about a revolution in Baroque as an international style.

When old Bernini died in his sober house on November 28th, 1680, the struggle between the principles in Roman palace architecture was already raging. They clash with unique acrimony at the corner beneath the windows of the genius.

We have already pointed out that the plain cube was never abandoned as being the ideal form for a palace, not even in the last phase of Baroque. The solid, practically burnished mass, maintained its position throughout the whole of the 18th century and continued to be the archetype for the smaller palace. The following are good examples. *Palazzo Cini* is situated at the end of the deep and narrow Piazza di Pietra (Pl. 94). Its style is completely traditional, the stern character retained. A striking detail is the large belvedere which dominates the square but has not been designed for the centre of the palace's façade. Above the portal is carved "Joseph Cini", the name of a banker who was ennobled in 1818 and bought the palace about that time. It was in this solid, genuinely Roman building that Stendhal was a frequent visitor, when he was consul in Civitavecchia, having made friends with Count Filippo and flirted with Donna Sandre in the green salon [39]. It is pleasant to imagine this virile palace as the setting for the great French Roman, perhaps because it corresponds so aptly to his own definition of Italian "style". Although Casa Cini presumably dates from the period around 1700 [40], it is just as cold in its exterior as the Palazzo Caetani (1564, by Ammanati) in the Via delle Botteghe Oscure, which Stendhal also visited at the end of his stay in Rome.

Another example of belated austere Baroque is the *Palazzo Clementi* which, like the Casa Cini, stands at the end of a narrow square, the Piazza di Campitelli. But we notice here that the belvedere has been incorporated as a raised section in the middle of the building. The cube has been given a new silhouette, but its surfaces are as smooth as ever (Pl. 95).

At the time these two palaces were completed, a break with the severe style in palace architecture had long since been made. This was due to a small group of architects of Bernini's school – and especially the talented Giovanni Antonio de Rossi. Any attempt to record Rome's palaces in the period 1670 to 1700 as a regular development in style would be forced – the warning against easy systematization, which we spoke of before, is particularly applicable to the first part of our period, the early phase of "Late Baroque". But of course a generation of aristocratic architecture has its own special trends. The most noticeable showed an inclination to altering the squareness of the building. The smoothly modelled block was, as always, the ideal pattern and an abstract cube was still inherent in the body of the building, but it was brought out with less sharpness than before and the Absolute lost its emphasis. The sharp corners are now smoothed off and the façades modelled in relief. The *Palazzo D'Aste* (Bonaparte) on the corner of the Corso and the Piazza Venezia, probably built before 1665 by G. A. de Rossi, was the real pioneer. Not for nothing did J.-F. Blondel design to discuss this façade in detail in his "Cours d'Architecture" (III, 1772). This French arbiter of taste praised the sober elegance of the narrow front at the expense of older Roman palaces, whose monotony and undecorated surfaces must have been an affront to his eye. The basic plan now becomes more flexible, windows are placed closer together, and if the palace is composed of several units around a courtyard, the architect makes great use of contrast between high and low. The influence from French palace architecture appears sporadically. The shape of detail is inspired by Borromini, and his signature can be detected more frequently than present opinion will concede. But local tradition is strong; its latency is present like a sort of living academism throughout the whole century and has a delaying action; it breaks out from time to time and acts effectually as a steadying influence on the architecture.

In the *Palazzo Muti* (Bussi) at the end of the Piazza d'Aracoeli, which is now entirely changed, G. A. de Rossi broke away from the time-honoured rectangular and used the difficult site for a building with a regular pentagonal ground plan. His solution to the problem is neat, and he has taken the existing conditions into account with a fine feeling for the possibilities. One of the two entrances to the central courtyard is set in the chamfered corner of the bastion-like edifice, the other is immediately opposite, thus in the middle of the figure's base line, the longest of the façades. The position of the portals and the whole arrangement of the building has been adapted to the little church of S. Venanzio. De Rossi has located his building in such a way that the line through the gateways is at right angles to the façade of the church.

Anyone entering Palazzo Muti through the gateway at the corner of the pentagon (Pl. 96) would soon catch sight of S. Venanzio across the courtyard. The church seemed like an annex to Marchese Muti's residence. When the little church was recently demolished this calculated effect was lost. De Rossi practised his art in vain, and the palace has now unfortunately only an uninterrupted view of the Victor Emmanuel monument across a boulevard. All the individual features of the palace are terse, even the portal at the flattened corner has a frame with simple moulding enclosed by ashlar pilaster strips, but at the top it has a handsomely carved cartouche which contains the device of the Muti family, two crossed clubs or sceptres. The family's other emblem, a charred hand, refers to the reputed founder of the family, Mucius Scaevola [41].

The *Palazzo Altieri* is a magnificent monument, with its main front facing the Gesù square. It is one of Rome's very biggest noble residences, covering a tremendous area in the centre of the city. The princely family of the Altieri culminated in Cardinal Emilio, who became pope in 1670, assuming the name of Clement X. Since he was the last Altieri in the male line, he adopted a relation, Paluzzi degli Albertoni, and bestowed upon him his name and coat of arms. This man, Cardinal Paluzzi-Altieri (died 1698), was the real builder of the palace, and Don Gaspare (married to his cousin Laura Altieri) completed it. Its erection was spread over quite a number of years, the oldest part near the Gesù dating from the 1650's (it can be seen in a prospect by Lieven Cruyl from 1665) and started by the Pope's brother. After 1670 a large extension was built out towards the Piazza Venezia. The work was done with *furia*, 1672–1673, "both by day and by night" [42]. The growth of the palace surprised even the Romans. Pasquino quoted a couplet by Martial about Nero's Golden House:

> *Roma domus fiet. Veios migrate,*
> *Quirites,*
> *Si non et Veios occupet ista domus*

– and this satire suggests that when the Altieris had filled Rome and driven its citizens out to Veii, the papal family's megalomaniac building activity might well spread its tentacles right out there as well.

Deseine the topographer, a cultured bookseller, described the Palazzo Altieri in 1713 and pointed out that "this grandiose and double palace, standing on its own and able to house a king and his whole court, is remarkable in the distribution of its windows and receives light from all four points of the compass" [43]. The expression "double" indicates the most important problem in the situation. This was to extend a self-sufficient building, the older one, by building a new one which was longer on its transverse axis and flush with the original façade. Should an attempt be made to unite the two parts into a harmonious whole or should they be juxtaposed? Subordinate or coordinate? These two principles, held by two rival architects, were at odds in the planning. We know that Antonio de Rossi was employed as architect and was in charge of operations up to his death. The Altieris must nevertheless have had recourse to Carlo Fontana as well, for a project of his which differs greatly from the design that was finally accepted is in existence. Fontana's idea was to include the earlier palace in a completely evenly proportioned complex around a transverse courtyard with the main portal set in the middle of the new façade, thus reducing the entrance from the Piazza del Gesù to a side gateway. The solution is doctrinaire yet radical, dignified on paper and doomed to remain there [44].

We shall now compare Fontana's project with an anonymous design which N. Tessin the Younger copied in Rome; it has never yet been discussed (Pl. 98b) [45]. Here an entirely different course has been pursued, and that is addition: a new palace is planned as an external prolongation of the older one. The colonnaded courtyard of the latter is clearly meant to be the main palace yard, while the new and larger one is subordinate and has only been lightly sketched in. The courtyards are however not merely juxtaposed but are also connected by two separate areas; the first leading from the palace yard is the *cortile minore,* then follows a portico which is narrower, together forming a funnel-shaped passageway, all beautifully conceived and designed. We see that the bent line of the Strada Papale has not been straightened (as in Fontana's project), and this results in an interruption in the straight line of the façade.

Who is responsible for this design? We know in the first place that Tessin, while he was in Rome in 1673, was a pupil of Fontana; he worked in his office, industriously copying his drawings, and that he put a lot of effort into transcribing a treatise Fontana had written on the new-style palace architecture. We find too, that the young Swede followed the building of the Palazzo Altieri, in full swing at that time, with great interest. It would be logical to assume that his drawing is a copy of a design by Fontana. If that is the case, it is presumably of a later date than his project that was never used, and shows Cavaliere Carlo going back to building habits of an earlier period. One feature in the plan (the gradually diminishing passageway between the courtyards) is reminiscent of de Rossi's *chiostro* in the convent in the Campo Marzio. But it is hardly likely that Tessin, Fontana's admiring disciple, should attempt to copy designs by an architect, whom he himself reckoned among "the corrupt" and (1687) contemptuously calls "a person by the name of Antonio Rossi, who has built nearly the whole of the palace".

De Rossi won, in so far as he pushed through the composition based on addition. But Fontana left his traces in the final project, which had been drawn up by his older opponent, and according to which the palace was built. They greatly enhanced the layout – the symmetrical projections and varying heights of elevation in the lesser courtyard, which contribute such a powerful rhythm to its interior, are without doubt taken from Fontana's unadopted plan (Pl. 100).

Master Carlo's German biographer, Coudenhove-Erthal, has in his here oft-quoted monograph, denigrated de Rossi to the advantage of his hero, and he considers that the Palazzo Altieri is a conglomeration, lacking "eine baugedankliche Verbindung" between the two parts of the palace. He calls the later of them "eine Verlegenheitsschöpfung", and would prefer to see the united front elevation constructed with the main portal in the middle. We cannot agree with this excellent scholar's criticism of de Rossi's work as we now see it, nor regret that Fontana's uniform arrangement was not put into practice. Coudenhove-Erthal may not have studied the existing surroundings of the palace. A glance at Nolli's map from 1748 shows that only the original part of Palazzo Altieri faces an open space, that is the square in front of Il Gesù, while the rest – by far the greater part of the total front elevation – is restricted by the narrow street (the present Via del Plebiscito) which runs along the side of the Gesù church.

It must have seemed quite logical to distribute the front in such a way that one part which seemed to be detached should project out towards the square by its middle ressaut and the other, subordinate and facing the dark street, should be less accentuated. If Fontana had had his way, the palace in its completeness could not have been viewed from the front. This splendid harmony was only justified on paper. It was no less obvious to take advantage of the site in planning the complex, and distinguish between the main building (with its deep courtyard matching the depth of the square) and the side building (with its transverse courtyard).

When this writer says of de Rossi that he worked to a given formula and was then forced to compromise with the "building space", while his rival "considers this space as the primary object" and then makes the building express this idea, he has not really reasoned it out. It is the other way round. De Rossi adapted himself to the demands of the site as a part of the city as a whole. But in contrast to Fontana, he did not forget the long, restricted façade. He avoided pointless divisions in its relief, merely let it continue as a decorated wall, and he appreciated that since it could only be seen in its entirety at an acute angle from the Piazza del Gesù it had to be given a striking silhouette (disregarded by Coudenhove-Erthal). This was done by erecting a two-storeyed belvedere on the roof, sited so cleverly that it both accentuates the independence of each of the two buildings and yet links them together visually (Pl. 98a) [46]. De Rossi was a first-class architect. He not only built for Rome, but identified with Rome. His contemporaries endorsed his views.

Because of the exceptional integration in the Palazzo Altieri, the details, although skilfully accomplished, are of less importance. The back wall of the palace yard has at the top a terrace motif which is a stroke of genius; the cortile, otherwise so austere, is softened by this unexpected interruption. The curving pediments over the windows, visible above the balustrade, seem to change, to become fuller when seen in conjunction with the high-up, fenced-in gallery. In the regular triangular tympana further down, are set the Altieri stars, here looking more like the spokes in the wheels of a celestial chariot (Pl. 99). A detailed description of the palace can be read in Fokker (op. cit. pp. 195–199), and here – as well as the number of windows etc. – the word Baroque occurs some twenty times, although with variations of "the Early", "the High", "the Late" phases of this period, all simultaneously making their mark on the building. It sounds as if a delicate difference in style could be quoted like the size of shoes. The palace is extremely homogeneous. Naturally the back is presented differently from the front, facing the flamboyant entrance to the Jesuits' church. The horses in the stable yard need no pilasters and the entrance from a side street should not be a triumphal arch. De Rossi's masterful *isola* is on a great enough scale to benefit from more than one kind of climate; its very appearance is alive. Towards the north, the complex even tapers off to a low point and this is certainly not Baroque.

Until fifty years ago, a very remarkable palace stood at the south end of the Corso. It had a particularly conspicuous situation, in that its front faced the present Piazza Venezia. Here the horse-race during the carnival ended at the Judges' platform in front of the façade (Pl. 101a). From nowhere else could the race be watched to better advantage than from the balcony of the palace, which Count Giovanni Antonio Bighazzini had built here in 1680 from a design by Carlo Fontana [47].

93. *The Palazzo Bernini in Via della Mercede.*

94. *The Palazzo Cini in Piazza di Pietra.*

95. *The Palazzo Clementi in Piazza Campitelli.*

96. *The Palazzo Muti.*

97. *The Palazzo Cimarra.*

98a. *The Palazzo Altieri (after Vasi).*

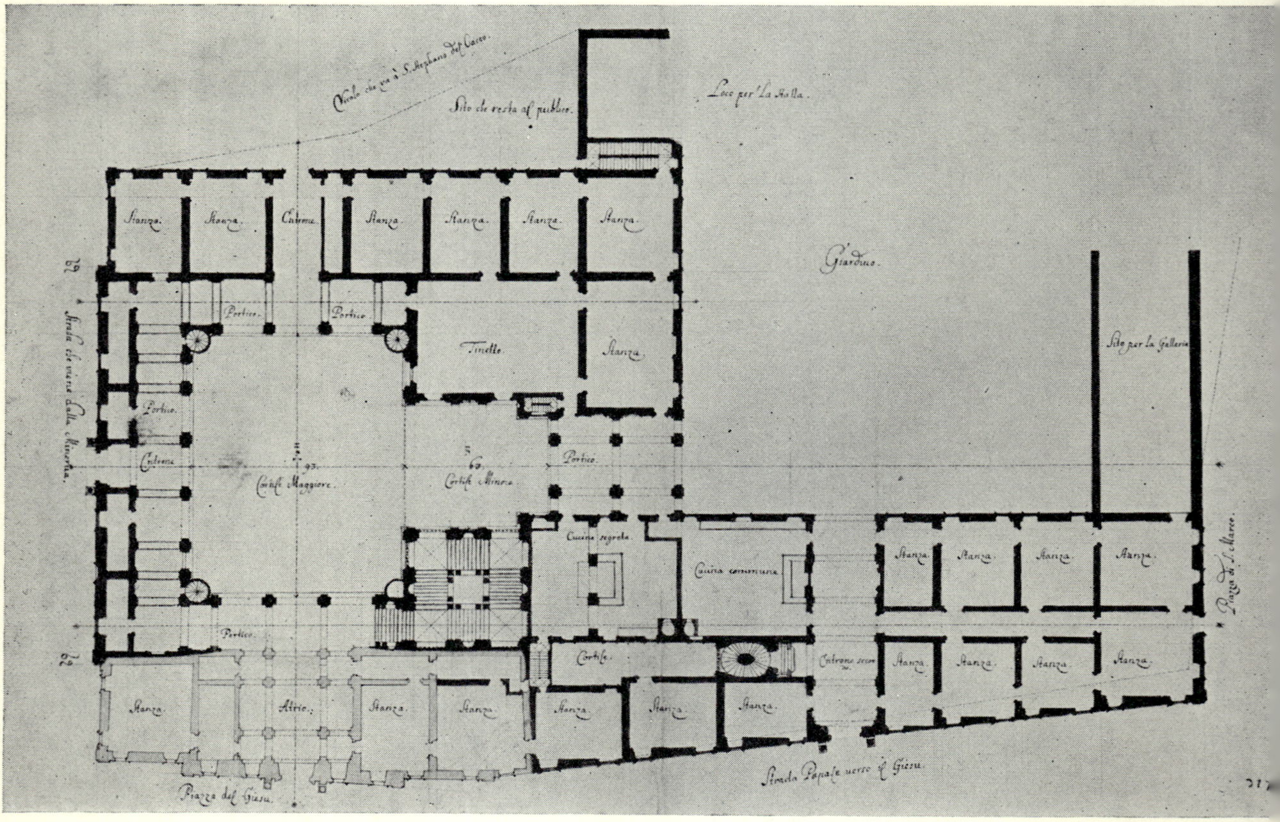

98b. *The Palazzo Altieri. Copy by Nic. Tessin of a project which was never carried out.*

99. *The Palazzo Altieri. The first courtyard.*

100. *The Palazzo Altieri. The second courtyard.*

101a. *The Palazzo Bighazzini in Piazza di S. Marco. Detail of engraving by Vasi.*

102. *Corner of courtyard of the Palazzo Gabrielli (Orsini-Taverna).*

103. *Glimpse of the Palazzo Grimaldi.*

104. *The Palazzo Gambirasi near S. Maria della Pace.*

105. *The Palazzo Gentili in Via in Arcione.*

107. *The Palazzo Pichini in Piazza Farnese.*

108. *The Palazzo Pamphili-Doria.*

At first glance, one is surprised by the conservatism of the façade of the *Palazzo Bighazzini*. We seem to have taken a big step backward since the Palazzo Altieri. The front has no central projection, in fact there are no salient details. The end sections do not protrude, although the intention seems to be there, with narrow sections enclosed by pilaster strips in rusticated work, as it were "crypto-ressauts". The motif is characteristic for the period just before 1600, the time of Giacomo della Porta. It seems difficult to believe that the important works of Bernini and Borromini had occurred in the meanwhile. We also notice (seen best from a frontal close-up of the palace) that the architect tried to bring a little movement into the monotony of the rows of windows by changing the spaces between them, wide in the middle, narrow at the sides. But this rhythm too, was out of date in 1680; della Porta's Palazzo Chigi in the Piazza Colonna brings this to mind [48]. The signs of the new age are to be found in the tripartite portal with free-standing columns and in the more richly moulded cornices dividing the storeys.

We may well ask why Fontana worked here in such a conspicuously conventional manner. Classification according to the history of style can give us no acceptable answer. We may find a clue if we take the trouble to look at the square as it was then. The Palazzo Bighazzini made up one side wall of a rectangular space and had a domineering building as its opposite neighbour. The two closest analogies are the Piazza Colonna and the Piazza Borghese. In both these places we find a palace facing the main building in the square; opposite Pal. Chigi stands Pal. Del Bufalo, opposite Pal. Borghese its *Grand-Commun*. The two, so to speak, subordinate palace buildings therefore correspond in character to the Palazzo Bighazzini in its relationship to the Palazzo Venezia. It is indeed strange and extraordinary that the two "secondary" palaces have their façades divided up in a similar way to that of the Palazzo Bighazzini – Pal. Del Bufalo even has the same number of windows – and both have the "crypto-buttresses" which are not at all common in Rome. This similarity is not likely to have been by chance. We believe that Fontana (or his employer) consciously chose what one might call a "situation style", not caring that this was about a hundred years out of date. Tradition has always been strong in Rome; what is a century there? The new palace opposite Paul II's harsh fortress would rather be subordinate yet strong, be number two with old-fashioned honesty, than bedizen itself with modern finery and experience the fate of the parvenu – to have a finger pointed at it.

In the social respect, the palace of the Bighazzinis came into the limelight with its later owners. While the Counts Bolognetti were the occupants, Maria Pizzelli Cuccovilla held her salon here, and was visited by Alfieri, Goethe and Herder [49]. In Thorvaldsen's time and also later, the aristocratic banking family Torlonia held open house in Fontana's discreet building for fashionable Europe. Stendhal has given a brilliant but malicious description of a soirée given by Don Giovanni Torlonia, Duke of Bracciano, who did not merely show off his art treasures with pride, but also, on occasion, mentioned their price [50]. Thorvaldsen was able to contemplate in silence one of Canova's principal works, "Hercules and Lichas", in a room specially set aside for it – and at one of the balls in the palace, he perceived with his sensitive eye, perhaps for the first time, the most beautiful female profile of all. His rapture is felt in his bust of the Marchesa Florenzi, the lady who was introduced in 1821 under Torlonia's very roof to King Ludwig of Bavaria, later to become her lover [51]. Did not Paganini scintillate with his diableries in competition with the glittering ceilings and Torlonia's shining ducats? The ponderous "second-rate" palace in this way occupied the front row at Vanity Fair; the real horses in the race were pulled up to a halt at the finishing post below the balcony. When the palace was demolished (1902) and replaced by an assurance company's building – ugly and boastful, like most such palaces of commerce – the great spectacle was transferred to the balcony of the Palazzo Venezia opposite.

This was where *il Duce* trod the boards.

It was ten years or so after the Palazzo Bighazzini was finished, that a large new palace was erected in the Corso. This was the *Palazzo Mancini,* also called the Palazzo Salviati. It has been neglected by modern textbooks and is not even mentioned in the most complete of them [52]. That is a pity. But perhaps understandable. For the palace is outrageously anomalous. All the more reason to understand it, and particularly necessary because it was certainly not overlooked in the 18th century (Pl. 101b).

That the façade of the Palazzo Mancini was nearly complete was stated in November 1689 [53]. Its architect Carlo Rainaldi died in 1691. He is of course one of the most distinguished masters of Roman High Baroque. His works prove him to be an outstanding sculptor who used the motif of the free standing column like a virtuoso. His diverting, somewhat theatrical art is best represented in S. Maria in Campitelli's façade and interior and the front of S. Andrea della Valle. The latter work is particularly extravagant in relief, with closely set, full and half columns, the round shafts of which make the decoration merge into the surface. Let us now look at the Palazzo Mancini. What a difference and what a surprise! The composition is still concentrated, the large, plain walls of classic Baroque are here completely enshrouded. But the many details have not the character of luxuriant vegetation forcing its way out through the wall from within; it is taut and full of vitality. The character of this palace façade is of a more pointed, severe and crystalline type. Just look at the wall itself. Its network of joints seems rough and grooved. If you could run your hand over the surface you would graze or perhaps even scratch yourself on all these ridges. If given the chance to make the same experiment with S. Andrea della Valle, you would feel the surface move under your hand and the cylinders of all the columns would caress it with their smooth and lissom curves. The difference is not merely objectively determined by the contrast between the sacred and profane styles, but lies deeper. If you look at the horizontal band of balusters which ties the Mancini façade together below the piano nobile, you see that it is a very emphatic motif, as hard as metal. Such balustrades beneath the windows are foreign to mature Roman Baroque (but they appear in the High Renaissance of Bramante and Raphael) and so are the balconies with the strongly projecting consoles in the form of volutes. The cold, dry forms seem to stem from a different clime; the work is calculated, rationalistic with strongly emphasized rhythm. We perceive a foreign "Classicism" in the Corso, which can only originate from France. However, not a single element is purely French and French alone, nor is there one detail that does not echo the Roman past, but in its entirety, it is extraordinary for the Rome of Late Baroque. This is no doubt why the textbooks regard the Palazzo Mancini as a suspect phenomenon and maintain a conspiracy of silence.

What is the explanation? The influence of the owner might be the reason. He may have wanted to give his house distinction, an individual note, and after all, the one who pays the piper calls the tune. In this case he was not a Roman, but a Frenchman (although of Italian lineage). He was the son of Cardinal Mazarin's sister and his name was Philippe-Julien Mancini, Duke of Nevers, married to a French lady. In conformity with his origins and his combination of names, he divided his life between Paris and Rome. A man who knew him well states that the Duke moved as nimbly between the two cities "as other people cross from one pavement to another" [54]. He rises one morning in his Parisian mansion, orders his carriage and says to the Duchess: "Prepare yourself Madame, we are leaving." She enquires in a conversational tone: "For where, Monsieur?" "Rome," says her consort nonchalantly. Or it might be the other way round.

The Duke of Nevers, who was an ornament to the court of Louis XIV – *bel esprit,* "incomparable poet both in French and Italian", but moody (inconstant) – apparently wished his palace in Rome to appear bilingual as well. And so it does. When the Duke's carriage stopped outside the portal in the Corso, Mazarin's nephew soon realized that he was in Rome from the exterior of his dwelling; it was not hard to acclimatize himself, for the building spoke with an accent – a Frenchified Italian.

It was not only coincidence that the Hôtel Mancini (in 1725) was taken over by the French state in Louis XV's time and turned into an academy of art for holders of scholarships to Rome awarded by the Louvre. It functioned as the *École de France* until this moved to the Villa Medici in 1803. Here Bouchardon and Pigalle, Hubert Robert and Fragonard and many other French artists of repute lived during their stay in Rome. Saly and Jardin stepped out of this house into the Eternal City. The directors of the academy were in their element behind the indifferent walls of the Nevers' palace and praised the elegant style. Piranesi had his *bottega* opposite the palace for a time, and many a young Frenchman crossed the street and felt more Roman in his atelier. Parisian visitors of the older generation breathed a sigh of relief when they caught sight of this thoroughly logical façade. All those barred windows in the other palaces gave this Roman street a prison-like character, thought Duclos, but the Palais de France was soothing, its façade was *la plus noble* [55]. The men from the Saint-Honoré understood it.

What a candid analysis of the Palazzo Mancini has disclosed, is confirmed by the assessment of a Frenchman. Lalande clearly states what the art historians should have discovered long ago: "The decorative style of the façade is half French, half Italian. The massivity is Italian but the embellishment is in French taste. The whole is neither beautiful nor ugly, which is true of most cross-breeds." To sum up: "There is a combination of lean and heavy, a hint of taste and little understanding" (*il y a des maigreurs et les lourdeurs, un peu de goût et peu de science*) [56]. We shall let this evaluation stand on its own merits – it was given by a pedantic astronomer – but the analysis of the style carries weight. Whether Rainaldi compromised with the demands made of him or purely and simply followed directives from Paris cannot be decided.

The *Palazzo Cimarra* is also a rich man's dwelling which the specialist literature has disregarded. This is quite extraordinary for it is full of majesty. Unfortunately it is not typical in any way, merely extremely personal (Pl. 97). It must have been built in the last decade of the 17th century, probably before 1695 [57]. The ground plan seems strange; the palace is sited in such a way that it forms an acute angle, which is very unusual for Rome and at odds with all the rules of regularity. The way in which this massive building appears before us, it could be the re-entrant to an unfinished square. This impression is to some extent the key to understanding the otherwise enigmatic building. In Falda's bird's-eye view from 1676 you cannot see the Palazzo Cimarra, but you can see its site, a right-angled corner enclosed by garden walls. This little square is composed in harmony with the church of S. Lorenzo in Panisperna, which stands on a slightly higher level opposite. As the front of the church is at an angle to the line of the road, a re-entrant had to be made on the other side for S. Lorenzo to have a proper forecourt. The garden walls indicated this shape, the design for a projecting court. Palazzo

Cimarra takes up its own half of this, hence its angular plan. In our plate, you see in the foreground a couple of spheres which are part of the church's higher standing flight of steps. The church watches its neighbour *de haut en bas*. But the palace refuses to be put upon; it towers to keep up with its companion. Seen in isolation, it is out of the ordinary and deformed, seen in its milieu, it appears well-considered yet more like a piece of civic architecture than just a private dwelling. It is also in keeping that the abruptly sheared corners of the blocks are supported by giant pilasters and that the unknown architect has increased the height of the building with an enclosed belvedere, set exactly opposite the front elevation of S. Lorenzo. The rusticated window frames have their counterparts in the Palazzo Patrizi-Nari-Montoro (in Via di Montoro). The architect may well have been one of those whom Tessin considered "corrupt". The family of Count Cimarra was not very important and a hundred years later were said to be in reduced circumstances [58]. Their intractable house (now a barracks) up on the ridge of the Viminal is certainly worth looking at and it stimulates the imagination – one feels it could be an aspiration to grandeur.

The *Palazzo Del Grillo* too, is to a great extent dependent on a given situation and on older buildings nearby, especially a tower, the magnificent Gothic Torre Del Grillo. It has on each side of it a palace building, the east (and larger one) connected to the tower by an arch (Arco Del Grillo), while the building out towards Trajan's Forum and the Casa dei Cavalieri di Rodi abut on to the flank of the tower (Pl. 106). Deseine says (c. 1713) briefly and to the point, that "The Marchese Del Grillo's palace consists of *deux* corps de logis joints par une arcade" [59]. The main building took on its present appearance in the 1690's following a plan by Carlo Rainaldi, who designed pleasing window pediments. In the inner courtyard, which is on a higher level, there is a portal resembling a sumptuous altar piece with profuse details (Pl. 178). This may have been added by Bernardino, the son of the original builder Cosimo Del Grillo. The former was perhaps the legendary wag "Marchese Del Grillo", about whom a number of fantastic stories were told. Strangely enough, one of the figures on the portal is Mercury. High ranking aristocrats did not usually boast of being connected with trading;

does the explanation lie in the fact that in 1743 Marchese Bernardino became *Custode a Deputato della Porta Portese,* this being the entrance to the harbour of Ripa Grande? The statue of Pallas Athene needs no explanation in the courtyard of a person of *esprit* [60]. The building on the other side of the tower is also of a later date than the main palace. It has two terraced storeys on different levels, and the flowers on the top terrace compete with the ornamentation above the doubled windows. The real distinction of the Del Grillo residence lies in the picturesque grouping, a piece of Roman nature in stone. There are vantage points from various levels in the complex, and this outpost from the Baroque period on the edge of the Imperial fora, takes over the terrain of the ancient ruins as if it were the Marchese's glacis. And the palace keeps its romantic back garden in reserve. We shall visit it later.

In the first couple of decades after 1700, the period of Clement XI, very few Roman palaces deserving of study were built, but some of them will be described. The exiled Queen Casimira of Poland, John Sobieski's widow, who had settled in the *Palazzo Zuccari* (Torres) by Trinità dei Monti, had an arch built in 1702 (demolished in 1799) from here to the newly established convent in the Via Sistina. She could in this way – like the Del Grillos – make her surroundings exclusive. The Via Sistina itself was described as *sotto l'arco della Regina* and Winckelmann among others, used it as his address [61]. It was far more important however that the queen, in 1711, gave her palace – which juts out like an inert bastion between the exits of the Via Sistina and the Via Gregoriana – a loggia supported by columns, facing the church square. It has the effect of a monumental theatre box looking towards the slope that a decade later was to turn into "The Spanish Steps", Rome's immortal stage-setting. Casimira's architect was Filippo Juvara. This was at the same time that he was preparing Cardinal Ottoboni's theatre in the Cancelleria and designing scenery for the Polish Queen's intimate opera house in the Palazzo Zuccari [62]. It would be quite true to say that with the help of the columns, Juvara gave the palace by Trinità dei Monti a very theatrical façade, the only one in Baroque Rome. The building's situation was an invitation to the architect to give the narrow front an elegant loggia – and the opera house behind, gave him the idea of turning it into a *tempietto,* a set piece from a heroic scene. Perhaps this served as the foyer for visitors; from the step of the coach, they were swept straight into the ideal world of make-believe. However that may be, as a central element in a palace façade, the motif is unique in Rome; the nearest analogy as far as form goes, is the semicylindrical portico in front of S. Maria della Pace.

As far as present knowledge goes, the "half temple" of the Palazzo Zuccari, so compact and gentle in its lines, was the only work which Juvara was ever to build under the Roman sun. But it certainly commanded the most favourable view. About 1708 he designed a palace for a member of the Florentine family of Panciatichi [63], probably the old Cardinal Bandino (died 1718), the Patriarch of Jerusalem [64], but it was not built. Neither could Cardinal Ruffo, Clement XI's *Maëstro di Camera* (up to 1706), the Sicilian magnate to whom Juvara was recommended when he arrived in Rome from Messina, offer his brilliant compatriot a building site. The Cardinal's palace was no doubt complete when Juvara arrived. It was by G. B. Contini [65] and stood in the Piazza S. S. Apostoli. To judge from engravings, the *Palazzo Ruffo* belonged to a large category of mansions, which did not differ very much externally from large bourgeois houses. They avoided all emphasis on feudal privilege but were no less noble art for all that. The high-born aristocrat from Messina was ensconced behind plain walls. He was in select company; his neighbour to the left was Duke Odescalchi (Pal. Chigi), living opposite was the Constable of Naples (Pal. Colonna), in the palace at the short north side of the square (Pal. Muti) lived the Pretender James Stuart (later also his son "Bonnie Prince Charlie") and in the palace on the south side of the Piazza S. S. Apostoli (Pal. Bonelli), resided Prince Ruspoli (who had the young Handel perform his *Oratorio la Resurezzione* here in 1708) [66]. Tommaso Ruffo did not need to feel like a poor relation; his house possessed the dignity of simplicity, and a painted coat of arms as bright as an official seal, surrounded by the many tassels of a cardinal's hat, was the only decoration.

The Palazzo Gambirasi, by C. Fontana [67], is another elegant house which shows off as little as possible. And it is still there. Over the door is carved a lobster, i. e. "armes parlantes" (this crustacean is called *gam-*

bero in Italian). The lobster is not particularly heraldic and is more common as an inn sign (compare Via del Gambero, called after an osteria), and the claw as an emblem may have a certain plebeian connotation. Facetiousness aside, it is clear that the palace here does not set out to gratify the eye, and that the owner conceals his magnificence. But of course, it maintains the feudal right of its social type to rise above the masses. We have often emphasized it as a merit that the Roman palace is adapted to its situation. This means that the building is composed according to the circumstances of the site, but it reserves the right to go on better. The Palazzo Cambirasi stands in a street which leads to S. Maria della Pace. Its forecourt is a compact work of art, a finely balanced correlation with the church's façade, which curves outwards in a semicircular portico (Pl. 104). The only compromise the Palazzo Gambirasi makes with the uniform building in the church square is by having its string courses flush with the horizontals in their façades; apart from that, it overwhelms the view. As our picture shows, the palace holds sway over the street partly by its cliff-like mass, partly by the chamfered corner with its balcony. For the true appearance of the building is on the diagonal; seen aslant it dominates completely, and so the corner is paramount. The front *en face* is not the palace's proper countenance, and it comes to life only in three-quarter profile.

Fontana's work is awkward frontally [68], but in its setting it has class. For the inhabitants of the district in those days, the palace had extra merit because the Gambirasi family lived there and was rich. Even now, when the building has been stripped of its aristocratic prerogatives and stands there merely as a piece of architecture, it still has the character of a mansion.

In the Via in Arcione, that ever cheerful street dotted with provision shops, which runs its crooked course to Fontana di Trevi, there is a palace now suffering from present conditions. It has been cut back by *il traforo* running under the Quirinal gardens, is shaken by the ceaseless roar of the traffic in the tunnel, and a silly car-park has been made in front of it. When it faced the church of S. Nicola in Arcione, the *Palazzo Gentili* was less visible, but the façade had its effect in this narrow space. In contrast to the Palazzo Gambirasi, it is not the mass of the building but the surface relief that counts here. To the conventional eye there is more "style", here meaning decoration, which can be more easily defined, but as a monument, the palace has been overlooked in the history of architecture. The portal with the hermae (columns tapering towards the base) set edge on, and the returned cornices, are in the Borromini manner (cf. Collegio di Propaganda Fide); the windows of the top storey, which are knit together by a band of moulding, points to the Pal. Pamphili-Doria by Valvassori. The palace is said to have been built in 1720 by Mgr. Antonio Gentili, a prelate of the Curia, later (1731) cardinal and datary [69] (Pl. 105). He had S. Nicola opposite modernized (1738, by Theodoli), and was thus safely home and dry with a reassuring prospect into the bargain. The palace's architect is unknown, but it is logical to think of Valvassori, to whom we have above ascribed the monastery of S. S. Vincenzo e Anastasio in the same street. Later in the century the Palazzo Gentili was acquired by the last Marchese Boccapaduli, whose wife vied with Signora Cuccovilla in collecting celebrities. Donna Margherita held her literary *conversazioni* in the large salon where Count Alessandro Verri was to be found every evening. The Marchesa with the awkward name, stood in the same relationship to this poet as Madame Récamier did to Chateaubriand [70]. Verri's principal work *Le Notti romane* was inspired by antique ruins, also presumably by his hostess and by the palace, in an intriguing street that sidles down into nocturnal Rome.

Palazzo Negroni in the Piazza Nicosia was extensively rebuilt by Bizzaccheri [71]; a corner with elegant window frames can be seen in Vasi's engraving of the Collegio Clementino and indicates that details gave the building its strength. Something of the same is true of the *Palazzo Grimaldi* (Lazzaroni) opposite S. Croce dei Lucchesi, in so far as the rhythm of the closely paired windows, a throbbing double beat, is the melody of the façade. Later we shall examine this motif more closely, for it does not often occur in aristocratic architecture. Here it has a fine effect, especially when the long front gradually comes into view through the narrow passage, and the lines of the double lights increase (Pl. 103). The palace has not been dated and might well come from the 1700's. As far as I can see, it received its original name from the Genoese Niccolo

Grimaldi, a former governor, who became cardinal in 1706 and lived for some time subsequent to that [72].

In the 1720's a large palace was erected on one of the Corso's best sites, opposite S. Marcello and its little forecourt. It was an enviable situation for a builder and for a house with aspirations. Interestingly enough, it was not a representative of the old patrician families who exploited the advantageous possibilities of the site, but a newly created noble, the Marchese de Carolis. The director of the French Academy called him a fortune-hunter (*homme de fortune*) [73]. J. G. Keyssler put on the debit side the rumour that his father had been a pig-dealer [74]. The Marchese himself was a banker and built up such a fabulous fortune, that in the opinion of the Romans he could not possibly have acquired it even by crooked methods of speculation – hadn't he found a treasure under an old hovel in the Regola quarter? Or dug up a Roman army's military chest of 8 millions buried in one of his fields? [75]. Whatever the truth may be, this ambitious financier and his brothers (one of whom was a prelate) had the means for making a grand show in the main thoroughfare. *Palazzo De Carolis* tried to knock the other residences in the Corso into a cocked hat (Pl. 119).

The building of the palace, which lasted from 1722–1727, is said to have cost the exorbitant sum of 300,000 scudi, furniture and fittings included. The Marchese chose the papal architect Alessandro Specchi to design it for him. He was also experienced in the building of more elegant private houses. The *Palazzo Verospi* (further north in the Corso) had been thoroughly rebuilt by him in 1705, and when the foundations were dug in that year, a treasure of 60,000 scudi was found, buried since the Sacco di Roma in 1527 – so such things do happen after all [76]. Specchi had also extended the *Palazzo Albani* by the Quattro Fontane. Now he was at last to stand on his own two feet. He took advantage of course of all the benefits the site offered. The façade of the Palazzo De Carolis, which takes up all the available space, is symmetrically constructed, so that the central portal section is on the middle axis of the square, but not quite on the church's, which is a little out of line. Specchi's façade is somewhat lacking in energy, but we cannot entirely blame the architect. That the relief is weak, although the space in front of the building would seem to lend itself both to movement and an original plasticity we must acknowledge as a stylistic trait in the façade. In the façade of the Palazzo Mancini across the road, which was built 35 years earlier, the vigour of High Baroque still prevails, but here, in the Palazzo De Carolis, economy of decoration is evidence of new ideas in architecture.

We are now in the first dawnings of Rococo; the lighter features in the façade are an indication, but not the composition or the details. The very long stretch of wall with a total of 19 windows has been carefully divided into three sections by slim clustered pilasters, and all the details are traditional. The immediate forerunners of the portal, with four columns and a balcony, are already to be found in the Corso: the Palazzo Sciarra-Colonna, where free-standing columns appear for the first time in Rome (1640), and the Palazzo Mancini. A similar tripartite type of portal, but with only two detached columns, was used by Carlo Fontana in the Palazzo Bighazzini. Specchi has borrowed the pointed gables from the Palazzo D'Aste. Here too, a couple of other characteristic details appear, namely the auriform shell included in the tympanum and the folded leaf capitals of the pilasters. The plinths of the portal columns of the Palazzo Massimo di Rignano, designed by the same Fontana, have similar folded leaves twining around them. Thus you can see a direct transition from the school of G. A. de Rossi through Fontana to Specchi. The most modern and the only French element in the façade of the Palazzo De Carolis, is the small head of a woman peeping out over the doorway; it is an *espagnolette* from the Régence period in Paris. The somewhat plain front originally had a couple of small irregularities, a jest and a blemish. Below the window to the extreme left on the ground floor, nearest to the corner by S. Maria in Via Lata, was included the splendid little wall fountain called *Il Facchino* [77], the figure of a man carrying a barrel, from the bunghole of which a thin stream flows. It would appear that even a banker's sources could dry up. Furthermore – when in 1729 the man who built the palace was granted the licence for the papal postal service in succession to Marchese Del Bufalo, he – says a witness – "ruined the second window from the portal" to make an entrance to his office; it was on March 2nd of this year that the first letters were handed in [78]. A genuinely Roman situation – pomp and circumstance with foot-notes, one burlesque and one practical.

Inside the palace it was clear that the new, fashionable interior decoration at any rate had gained a footing in Rome. There were many rooms hung with tapestries and no end of imported drawing-room furniture in the latest, or the next to latest, Parisian fashion. "Everything that strikes the eye is new" says a contemporary witness, and this is very significant information; it was an upstart who so quickly made the Romans – otherwise so conservative in their housing – toe the French line. Characteristically enough it was in the following years that the Palazzo De Carolis was to experience its greatest splendour under the banner of the Bourbon lilies. When the builder died in debt and childless, the Director of the *Académie de France* suggested to his government that it buy the palace and convert it into a residence for the ambassador. "It has," he wrote, "the finest situation in Rome, in the Corso, and in front of it is a beautiful square with a new and splendid church" [79]. The fastidious Frenchman certainly knew how to appreciate the good things. The sale did not take place. But soon afterwards the palace was rented by the Abbé De Canillac, a French judge (Uditore di Rota) in the Supreme Court of the papal city since 1735. This extremely cultured man, who at one time had been France's ambassador to the Holy See, set great store by the home of the parvenu. He lived in great style, surrounded by artists (P. L. Ghezzi drew him in 1744 and brought out his *buonnissimo gusto*), and was a sedulous collector. A connoisseur like de Brosses, who visited Canillac in 1739, lauded the palace and the abbé's cuisine [80]. The fashionable life in the Palazzo De Carolis and Monsignore Canillac's artistic activities were however resented by the otherwise liberally minded Benedict XIV. "It would be better if all the money he squanders on tapestries, engravings, music and refreshments were used to benefit S. S. Trinità dei Monti," he wrote in 1745 to a friend [81]. The church referred to was the responsibility of France.

From 1752 onwards, the palace went through a more acceptable phase spiritually, because the Jesuits took it over and extended it to the rear [82]. But this was only a transitional period, a pause for refreshment, as it were. For in 1769, Cardinal de Bernis, Louis XV's newly appointed ambassador, moved into Specchi's building. It would be no exaggeration to say that from this point onwards and right up to the revolution, the palace was the unqualified social centre of the papal city, indeed one of the leading houses of the civilized world. People called it "The French Hotel", and the square between its portal and S. Marcello was given the honorific title of "The Pivot of Europe" [83]. The Marchese de Carolis would have jumped for joy, even in his grave, if he could have known the international fame his expensive property had acquired. Now it is a bank and full of money-bags.

Opposite the Palazzo Farnese – a vulnerable position to be opposite neighbours – stands the *Palazzo Pichini,* which assumed its present form at the same time as the Palazzo De Carolis and which is also Specchi's work (Pl. 107). Once again we find the faint-hearted treatment of the façade's relief, which is very low, but we also see something new, the modelling of the front wall on several planes. On the one hand, the steep façade is divided vertically into five sections – a middle section and two end sections (ressauts) on the same plane, and in between two retracted sections. Then again, the window recesses form one composition. Such a systematic division is foreign to Rome, a modern phenomenon with French influence. The Palazzo Pichini's front is close to the true, meaning French, Rococo, although there is not a single genuine rocaille ornament present (the shell at the top is *Style Régence*).

The palace is basically Roman underneath the thin covering of the façade. If we observe the middle axis, we find a portal with detached columns plus balcony, above this the most important window, also with columns and curved "wings" to the pediment, and above that a simpler window. A very compressed, almost squashed section which is far too narrow altogether. I think I understand why there was such a compression. Specchi made preliminary studies of Bernini's design for the Palazzo Chigi-Odescalchi. Here we have a similar construction of the portal section, but in this case there is a reason for the narrowness: it has to fill a narrow space between pilasters [84]. Form and type, elevation and outline betray a direct relationship between the two palaces, and this reveals that Specchi worked from a famous pattern which he has completely changed by removing the close row of pilasters and using instead a composition with alternating projecting sections. The experiment failed. The proportions are poor, the whole thing seems forced, but it does tell us one important thing: Bernini's conventional design for a palace façade was used as a basis for French experiments. Such surprising jumps from tradition to modernism, such breaks in the continuous development, are characteristic of Roman Late Baroque. We must move warily not to stumble or fall in the snares of typology, must feel our way from work to work. Every single one of the palaces has its own countenance and its own mystery.

Palace architecture in the 1720's was terminated by the building which one of the most doubtful members of the Holy College erected in the Via del Tritone, that is, the statesman Giulio Alberoni – "witty, spirited, inconstant, contemptible, without morals, without consideration, without principles", that Prince of the Church, in whose cynical eyes a cardinal was "a Harlequin dressed in red" [85] and who later, while he was the Papal Legate in Ravenna, conceived of the fine plan to conquer the Republic of San Marino. In his Roman palace, finished in 1729 (now disfigured beyond all recognition) [86] Pannini had decorated the walls with paintings in a triumphant and imperial style.

III

Now in the 1730's came the glorious building period made possible by the shower of gold from Clement XII's lottery. Three aristocratic families of the very first rank – the Houses of Colonna, Pamphili and Corsini – gave their palaces a new exterior and thereby added three distinguished features to the Roman scene. The buildings concerned differ greatly. And last but not least, the papal residence on the Quirinal was greatly improved. Its wing-span was extended and the surroundings made more palatial.

The *Palazzo Doria-Pamphili* in the Corso is Rome's most extraordinary palace from the 18th century. It has long mystified students of architecture. Up to about twenty years ago, it was believed that the magnificent façade had been erected in 1690 [87], but in fact, it is nearly half a century younger, a discovery that has upset the interpretation of its style quite a lot. But it is not really difficult to date it correctly, for two such famous and excellent writers as Baron Karl Ludwig von Pöllnitz and President de Brosses have given us eye-witness accounts of the construction of the palace in their Roman memoirs. But as we all know, art historians have a tendency to read only the works of colleagues and to forget that the erection of these large palaces and similar buildings has been observed by people in the street as well, people with eyes in their heads and notebooks at the ready, people who had the great advantage over the historians in that they lived at a time contemporary with the work and were intimate with its style and spirit.

Due to a couple of such wide-awake persons, we are fortunately able to feel that we were almost present during the most magnificent building activity which took place in the Corso in the 18th century (Pl. 108).

Baron Pöllnitz writes that the Palazzo Pamphili in the Corso would become the finest palace in Rome externally "once the great façade which is being built at the moment is finished" [88]. The pertinent "letter" in Pöllnitz's journal is headed "Rome, December 5th, 1730". Could this be an invention similar to Stendhal's references to dates in his books on his Italian travels? It may be so. But his factual knowledge is proved further on in the text. Pöllnitz reports en passant, that the builder of the palace had lost his brother the cardinal "a short time ago" and had inherited from him the tidy sum of 400,000 scudi in hard cash (as we can see, Prince Pamphili did not belong to those aristocrats for whom it was necessary to gamble in a lottery to get hold of ready money). However, it is a fact that Cardinal Benedetto Pamphili died on March 22nd, 1730. So we have reason to put our trust in Pöllnitz and can take for granted that the façade of the Palazzo Pamphili was started before December 1730. This is in conformity with a report that Prince Camillo Pamphili in February 1731, began the demolition of an old house next door to S. Maria in Via Lata, to make room for extensions to the palace along the Corso [89].

In the course of the following years, the mighty front rose higher and higher. One day in 1739, President de Brosses visited the French Academy of Art in the Palazzo Mancini on the other side of the Corso. He looked out of one of the windows in the director's apartment, took in all the details of the neighbouring building and gave a snap estimate of the Pamphili's new house: "Work is at present proceeding on the Pamphili Palace, and a new style is being tried out in which lilies and cocks' combs are used as ornaments." He continues in a shocked tone: "This is considered wonderful, but in my opinion it is not only close to Gothic but is even more barbaric. A shameful sight among so many buildings of elegant and simple taste. Rome, which these days cannot boast of a painter, has obviously no superfluity of good architects either" [90].

The architect, who is not mentioned by name, and at whom the criticism of our French connoisseur is levelled, was Gabriele Valvassori. He is no unknown quantity. For a long time he was just a name connected to one work very incorrectly dated. We have gradually obtained considerable information about him, and he begins to take on substance. This important work in the Corso confirms that he was an artist.

In 1730 the Palazzo Pamphili consisted of an extensive complex of buildings both old and new. The main building proper (erected 1661–1663 by Antonio del Grande) faced on to the Piazza del Collegio Romana. The oldest part of the complex, which may date back to the beginning of the 16th century, had a very diversified front in the Corso and was to some extent only a barrier wall. Behind this was a courtyard with arcades. This part of the palace was not worthy of a Prince Pamphili and made a bad display in Rome's main street, having the Palazzo Mancini as an opposite neighbour and the Palazzo De Carolis on the left hand side. At the very time that the latter palace was finished, Valvassori's patron commissioned him to give the Palazzo Pamphili a dignified countenance which would make a suitable impression in the architectural ensemble already there. The new wing was to take up the full width of the site as far as S. Maria in Via Lata. In order to understand the building that was erected here, we must realize that the architect had to fulfil two conditions when solving his problem, an outer and an inner. The external condition was laid down by the situation itself. The building stands in a relatively narrow street and so the façade had to make its effect by strong sculptural details to be able to assert itself, and this was all the more necessary because the Palazzo Mancini opposite had a dominating relief. A pronounced diagonal perspective was not important for the Palazzo De Carolis, for it could be viewed frontally from the Piazza di S. Marcello where it stood, not to mention the fact that Specchi deliberately played it down. The Palazzo Pamphili's vehement façade can therefore be regarded as the product of the pressure of circumstances. The internal conditions for the elaboration of the façade was dictated by the use made of the wing. This large building was created primarily to house a gallery, a long banqueting hall in the piano nobile which could contain the family's large collection of paintings, and which was suitable as the background for ceremonial entertainment. There can be no doubt that Camillo Pamphili wished to create an interior which could be the immediate rival of the famous gallery in the Palazzo Colonna. An art gallery must have plenty of light and, if possible, light from high up. If it faces a narrow street, it needs big windows. This is what Valvassori's façade has, and the windows have been supplemented by further lights beneath the high-sweeping cornice. And then again – the façade of the lower storey does not cover an actual dwelling, but is to some extent the screen for the inner arcade. The usual Roman Baroque palace is tightly sealed at the base, on guard against the surrounding world. But not so here. The Palazzo Pamphili offers a row of very large, close-set windows. They give the effect of light and air, and are full of gaiety; and the very exterior seems to promise a sunny courtyard with palm-trees.

Thus we find that the special features which were important for the façade of the Palazzo Pamphili were the logical fulfilment of particular structural conditions. But of course the way the architect gives architectural form to this demonstrates his style, his art and his originality.

The style – opinions have differed considerably about this. As long as it was believed that the palace was built around 1690, it seemed obvious to call it High Baroque in its highest degree. Now that we know that the building comes from the 1730's there is some wild talk of Rococo in a special Italian manner. Let us invoke the judgment of a specialist. As we mentioned a while ago, de Brosses thought that the architect here had introduced "a new style"; he does not like it, and not for a moment does it occur to the celebrated and cultured Frenchman that it could

109. *The Palazzo Corsini, view from the garden.*

110. The Palazzo Chigi (Odescalchi) in Piazza S. S. Apostoli. In the background the Palazzo Muti, Palazzo Colonna on the right. Engraving by Piranesi.

111. *The Palazzo Colonna with Chinea decoration. After an engraving.*

112. *The papal stables on Monte Cavallo (Piazza del Quirinale).*

113. *The Palazzina of the Quirinal.*

114. *The Palazzo Boncompagni in Via del Babuino.*

115. *The Palazzo Boncompagni. Portal.*

116. *The Palazzo Testa-Piccolomini.*

possibly have anything to do with *style Louis Quinze,* meaning the true Rococo. Nor has it, for that matter. When on the other hand, de Brosses states that the style is close to Gothic, he is in a way correct from his own personal point of view. He would have used a similar expression for extravagant works by an Oppenordt, a Meissonier, who are the exponents of French ornamentation derived from Borromini's world of decorative form. And he would have designated Borromini himself "a Gothic", a barbarian, a corrupter of good taste.

Palazzo Pamphili's style cannot be called "new"; Valvassori is a successor to Borromini in so far as he makes use of the master's characteristic details, and of these, the most striking is his borrowing of the high-swept window pediments from the Collegio di Propaganda Fide. Many other architects still drew on Borromini's rich treasury of form; Valvassori was by no means the last Borrominian, nor was he a reactionary. The thing that is extraordinary about his Pamphili façade is the fact that he had courage to use the great master's style to solve quite a monumental, secular problem and that he had the talent to turn it to good account, to advance along the path indicated. Valvassori's façade is a brilliant creation, it is vibrant but with nothing vague about it – we notice how firmly the horizontal is made to stand out in the perspective, an interwoven band of balconies, bulging above the portals without breaking the supple continuity and running out across the low terrace wing where it ends in a knot. The upper, flatter braiding follows the rounded corner and right at the top, the windows in the cornice form a chain with large, flat links. The vertical division is done mainly by the rhythmic distribution of windows in groups. Seen very much foreshortened – and this is the usual angle of sight – the detached columns of the windows give the impression of smooth, bold hatching, while the pediments are assembled into long, vigorously undulating, ornamental friezes. The transition from high relief through a lower, to almost fretted forms, which seem stuck to the surface, is masterly. The large window frames in the bottom storey have also been created by a strong, sure hand and set with a delicate feeling for their distinctive form, so unlike architecture, for while the frames in the top cornice merge into a taut band which seems to hold them in place, the heavy window frames at the bottom seem to hang on heavy spikes with ornamented heads. The rest of the windows in the façade – the proper ones – have supported pediments.

All this amazing wealth of sculpture is sprinkled with a number of very charming decorative details – hardly one too many, hardly one out of place. As an instrumentalist, Valvassori is the perfect virtuoso; he is determined to work with full-bodied tones and has every right to. De Brosses, being a Frenchman of Rameau's generation, prefers a more translucent effect; he spoke scornfully of "lilies" and "cocks' combs" meaning unconventional figures in the ornamentation. His comparisons are very much to the point; there are indeed lilies everywhere in the façade, for this flower is the device of the Pamphilis (also the dove with the olive branch); a Robert de Cotte or a Gabriel would never dream of turning the Bourbon lilies into capitals; for that they had too much good taste and too little sense of humour. Nor is there any doubt that the cartouches in the top window frames really do look like cocks' combs. Valvassori must have considered them (if he ever thought of the likeness) just as acceptable as the Barberini bees or angels' wings. The Frenchman had no understanding of the finer subtleties of the Roman orchestra.

It is not likely to have dawned upon de Brosses that the façade of the Palazzo Pamphili was the Italian answer to the Palazzo Mancini, his beloved *Académie de France,* across the road. And it must have been so. Carlo Rainaldi's façade, 40 years older as it was, must to Valvassori have seemed to be his destiny: his own building was to stand face to face with it for a very long time to come. Both buildings are about the same length. The Pamphili palace could not consider being the subordinate. There had to be an architectural dialogue between equals – and the Roman would prefer to have the last word. We should make the situation quite clear: the head of one of Rome's first families kept a wary eye on the King of France's palace which stood there bursting with arrogance, but his architect calculated it openly. The façade of the Palazzo Mancini is strong in relief, self-assertive, with sharp shadows. The Palazzo Pamphili had to be the same. But how was it possible to make it strong, if the architect used the unaccentuated language of a Specchi? Just imagine a façade like that of the Palazzo Pichini in this place and in this conflicting situation! The Palazzo Pamphili would then look like nothing more than an annex to King Louis' Academy. An architect who worked in the cautious academic manner of Carlo Fontana would fall down here, so now the only way to find a good solution to this difficult building task was to use Borromini's sculptural High Baroque freely. There is a profound inner significance in it being used here for the last time in a monumental palace. Valvassori's façade is far from being a strangely delayed and isolated phenomenon in Rome; on the contrary, it is very topical, and considering the milieu, it is a logical conclusion. Nor can this work be said to be due to Parisian contemporary style. It is autochthonic.

If we compare these two opposed façades in the Corso, we find that in composition too, Valvassori plays up to the Palazzo Mancini. Both fronts are covered with ashlar, the joints of which are strongly emphasized, this being an unusual feature in those days. The two horizontals of the window balusters are also common to both, which is worth noticing as the motif was decisive for the Palazzo Mancini but is otherwise found only rarely in Rome. The vertical division of the façades is also in principle the same in both buildings. These common features confirm that Valvassori has certainly taken the building opposite into consideration. But the individual details are certainly different, and this is where Valvassori finally gains the upper hand. He not only articulates differently but also more strongly. Contrasting with the hard and angular is the soft and full; straight lines are broken and bent, right angles rounded off. Camillo Pamphili and his architect were victorious in the Corso. Everybody looks at this palace and either enjoys it or hates it. The Palazzo Mancini is merely noticed in passing.

Don Camillo died in 1747. His successor in the palace, Prince Girolamo Pamphili, left no sons when he died in 1760, and the greater part of the family's possessions then passed to the Doria family [91]. A traveller noted in 1777 that the new owner, who was Genoese, was unacquainted with the Roman patrician's delight in showing off his works of art, and only reluctantly permitted access to the palace [92]. But ten years earlier, Lalande had been able to get in, and on this occasion the rather bigoted Prince Doria permitted him to be shown, not the paintings, but a magnificent ciborium designed by Juvara. It is said to have cost the preposterous sum of 130,000 scudi (693,000 livres) and had been commissioned by Camillo Pamphili [93]. This valuable object found its proper niche in the palace which is also a piece of decorative Baroque in the de luxe class. It would be an idle exercise to try to imagine the interior decoration Juvara could have created for this sum.

The Colonnas had lived in the Piazza S. S. Apostoli since time immemorial. It was obvious that the palace had noble ancestors. It was a particularly discordant complex; old and new tried in vain to unite around a broad forecourt which lay behind a barrier wall with gateways out to the square. This is how the *Palazzo Colonna* appears in two prospects by Bart. Poli, dated 1730 and 1731 [94]. A *cour d'honneur* was a rarity in the city, here – on the doorstep of the premier noble in Rome – it would be unique as an entrance. If only from the point of view of a stage-setting it should have been one. An explanation is required here: the Casa Colonna of all the palaces in Rome had, outside the building, an advantage over all the others, since it was here that for a few hours on a certain day every year, it became the solid background to a flashing scene. Many aristocratic façades were decorated on special occasions. When a prelate became cardinal, his home was extravagantly embellished (*la facciata*) with ornaments of stucco and painted canvas [95] but most houses were illuminated from time to time only. But the Palazzo Colonna was the only one to give a gala benefit performance every year. At the feast of Peter and Paul (29th June) the so-called *Chinea* festival was concluded by an incredible firework display in front of the Palazzo Colonna, one also having taken place the previous evening. As hereditary Constable of Naples, the head of the Colonna family had the job of presenting the Holy Father with a symbolic feudal tribute from the King of the Two Sicilies. This tribute, which consisted of gold ducats in a silver vase or in an embroidered purse, was carried into St. Peter's by a white ambler (la chinea, or l'acchinea, cf. Fr. haquenée) which knelt prettily in front of the throne. The Danish architect Niels Eigtved has described the ceremony in a letter from 1733 [96].

This regularly recurring firework display, which was introduced again in 1722 after having lapsed for some time, was the palace's great distinction and attracted an enormous audience. The Romans are great lovers of fireworks. To think that this was just a round of catherine wheels and rockets would be a mistake. The art of pyrotechnics aimed higher than that. A complete architectural structure was to go up in flames and every year proper architects used all their brilliant inventiveness to conjure up yet another *machine;* Elysium and Hell, temple and arbour, the Ancient Egyptians, the yellow sons of China, all the world provided motifs for the one day structures, beneath Prince Colonna's windows. It would indeed have been strange had the competition from the fiery, spluttering sham architecture made no impression on the palace and we can well believe it did. I am convinced that the renovation of the Colonna palace cannot be properly evaluated without taking the *Chinea* festival into account. The blazing fantasies greatly affected the building behind. There is no doubt that the front wall of the Palazzo Colonna had a theatrical character unique among the houses of the Roman nobility. The situation is really without equal. For 363 days of the year this elegant residence was extremely insignificant, if not to say bare. The remaining two days, most of its exterior was concealed by extravagant decorations. In the end the building itself ran amuck, tricked out, as it was, in a permanent fancy-dress.

The matter had another more positive side to it. The owner of the house could not tolerate living in a building whose main role was to be a backcloth. It should also perform the role of a royal box as well as being an integral part of the performance. If Prince Colonna could not readily enjoy the costly spectacle from his own forecourt (the Apostoli Square) there was something nonsensical about it all. And this he was not able to do before 1730, because the main building of the palace stood too far back, almost covered by the barrier wall. The north transverse wing parallel to the church of S. S. Apostoli may have projected into the square, but it was so antiquated that it was no use at all. The only place where the building could successfully assert itself was at the south corner. This was the side where the most modern part of the building, the gallery wing, stood, and it formed an angle with the main building, with its front facing what is now the Via 4 Novembre. The building was erected between 1663 and 1688 by Antonio del Grande and the magnificent banqueting hall at the top was completed by Girolama Fontana some time after 1700 [97]. But please note that this gallery wing was not very long and did not reach right into the piazza, and this was where the work was started.

On September 26th, 1731 Valesio noted in his journal: "They have commenced building to extend the gallery as far as the Piazza S. S. Apostoli." This meant that a lower terrace wing was added which finished off with a tall pavilion on the very corner. The engraving showing the decorations for the Chinea festival in front of the Palazzo Colonna in July 1732 that we reproduce here, shows that the pavilion was then completed (Pl. 111). It shows how it must have served as a large-scale theatre box for the owner. Rome is full of belvederes set up on the roofs, but a loggia on a street corner is something peculiar to the Palazzo Colonna – a raison d'être. We see from the engraving that the plain barrier wall was still standing at this time. But its days were numbered, for the building programme included further alterations. The wall was to be replaced by a terraced front building and the end section of the old north wing was to be rebuilt symmetrically with the corner pavilion. This took place in the course of the following years, and in an engraving of the Chinea festival from 1733, the portal can already by seen to the right of this building. Quarters for the servants (*per la famiglia*) were provided in its mezzanine storey [98].

The Palazzo Colonna now at last possessed a contemporary exterior, rich and striking – but architecturally it was not typical of its age nor was it artistically of great merit. The responsibility is the designer's. Aless. Specchi, architect to the Colonna family for many years and the originator of numerous set pieces for fireworks, had to stop practising in 1728 because of advancing senility. Don Fabrizio Colonna did not chose his successor from among the most notable in the profession. *Niccolo Michetti,* a pupil of C. Fontana, must have been something of a hothead. He dropped out of his studies in Rome (1718) and went to Russia with two masons. There he worked for a number of years to his detriment [99]. A couple of years after his return (1723) he became a member of the Luca Academy, after which he probably earned his living mainly by being a stage designer. His stay with the Muscovites had schooled him in heroics. He also produced sets for Cardinal Ottoboni's theatre (1729) [100] and had presumably done this before he left, for the "Italian sculptor, who was in Ottoboni's service and who served the Czar in Moscow" mentioned in a letter from February 1st 1724 from Poerson [101], can be none other than Michetti. He reported on his activities to this cardinal immediately he arrived home.

As noticed, he was described as a sculptor. The decoration of the Palazzo Colonna is also merely extrinsic and rather presumptuous. The window frames merge with one another, but to no avail. In Rome it was not the custom to prop up a façade with the help of ornamentation, like a general being kept on his feet by encrusted gold braid. When some ten years later, around 1750, the north part of the palace was extended by the addition of a new wing along the Via della Pilotta, the opposite extreme was adopted and this time the building came under the influence of the blandest French style. The middle part has a low apse (*un' ovato*) as seen in Rococo mansions in Paris. The motif is used in one Roman casino (Villa Vaini), but apparently not in any other palace. This part of the building activities was the brain-child of Cardinal Girolama Colonna, brother of Don Fabrizio and major-domo to Benedict XIV [102], a cultivated man of the world who could have been influenced by French ideas at court where Valenti was the arbiter of taste. The architect, Paolo Posi, was also a shrewd fellow. What the front of the Palazzo Colonna did not achieve, meaning original dignity, the back made up for. It was adapted to the intimate character of the street (Pl. 92). The façade is without emphasis, merely a wall opposite the garden wall and only the slight bulge betrays the latent strength of the mansion and forms a happy balance with the flat-arched bridges leading to the Giardino Colonna. One of Rome's greatest palaces became human and charming on the reverse side, turned towards the secret garden.

Up behind this, on Monte Cavallo, important things had happened in the meanwhile. The *Quirinal* had, since the 1690's, been the popes' customary town residence [103]. This had not been accompanied by much significant change in the architecture, but some new buildings were added to meet the requirements of the enormous papal household. Innocent XIII especially, was full of ambitious schemes and Clement

XII carried on with his plans and invented some of his own. It is to the credit of the latter pope that he turned Monte Cavallo into a real palace square and into an artistic entity. This soaring prospect reaching up to the sun, resembling no other princely courtyard in the world, is absolutely individual. In Goethe's apt words: "so unregelmässig als grandios und lieblich" ("Ital. Reise" 3rd Nov. 1786). Across the square from the Quirinal's mighty corner, through which the diagonal of the complex is drawn [104], the papal stables were erected. The building for the pope's horses and mules was indeed elegant and resembled a villa's casino, open in front around a gently rising flight of steps in the form of a horse-shoe. Along this curved entrance the apostolic steeds closest to the throne – 86 in all – could waltz up to the piano nobile. Apart from the horses in "the best room" there were another 42 on the high-ceilinged *rez-de-chaussée*. Flats for the coachmen and other stable servants were provided in the mezzanine. A festive piece of architecture, this broad niche-like building in orange – an ideal background for the rearing stallions of the Dioscuri and for the stern palace itself (Pl. 76). The pope could now look on to a perpetually moving scene, very like the staircase scenes in the "open-air theatres" winding their way behind the villas high up in the Albani hills.

And funnily enough – this stately home for the ecclesiastical stud was built in the style of St. Peter's; the giant pilasters, the attica and its windows, are all borrowed from the basilica's façades [105]. The architect must be sought among those most familiar with S. Pietro's *fabbrica,* but, strange as it must seem, his name cannot be given with any certainty. The work, which took place 1723–1724, was discontinued at the death of Innocent XIII and remained static during his successor's reign. It has been ascribed to Alessandro Specchi. G. B. Gaddi, who in 1736 published an account of the buildings erected by Clement XII, expressly states that the architect for the stables was Michelangelo Specchi [106]. Once again we must query why a well-informed contemporary source should mention this obscure architect if the famous one with the same surname had the honour. Stylistically the building would certainly fit in very well with Alessandro's other work, but as we know so little about Michelangelo's, we are really no further. Did the stables in any case acquire their present frontal style in the first building period? All we do know is that Aless. Specchi disappeared from the scene in 1728, and when building is resumed in 1730, we see to our surprise that another old man, Antonio Valeri, is in control [107]. Can we really believe that this man, "Bernini's very last pupil", pulled off the one coup of his life, with one foot in the grave, by supporting this equinine palace with St. Peter's pilasters – and got away with it? One thing is certain: when Fuga at some time during 1730 replaced Valeri, he took over a job which was more or less completed. Only the device on the mezzanine and an arcade which was built round the corner towards the castle hill and served as a *corps-de-garde* can be ascribed to him [108]. This guardhouse was later removed. The rounded corner of the stables stands out now in its great simplicity and strength (Pl. 112), a fine contrast to the brutal prow of the Quirinal. When one is drawn up from the town towards the palace by way of the powerful sweep, it is the curve of the stables which controls one's steps and opens the gate to the magnificent view.

A dead straight view is mostly patterned on the residences of autocrats. We find one at the Quirinal too, but in this case it is a street along the side of the palace, the Strada Pia. And it is characteristic for Rome, where the unusual in the art of the long perspective is so often triumphant. Think of Michelangelo's gateway at the street.

During the period of Alexander VII and Innocent XII the pertinent part of the palace was lengthened by stages; Papa Conti extended the wing even further; Clement XII then added an appendix on *la Manica Lunga* and finished it off with a palazzina, designed as a dwelling for one of the dignitaries of the Curia (the secretary for secret messages in code). The building dates from 1732 and was planned by Fuga, and here again, it was his fate to have to complete the work of others [109]. The façade is of low relief, almost delicate, and choicely proportioned. The ashlar pilasters are as dull as slabs of chocolate (Pl. 113). All the same, the front is self-assertive in the company of the other extentions; the interminable wing on one side is only effective as a vertical plane, nothing but wall. *Il Palazzo della Famiglia Pontificia* was not merely the largest Roman building of its kind, but thanks to Fuga's pavilion, it also became the city's most distinguished. The best way to judge how deep-seated is the elegant simplicity would be to compare the Palazzina with the uninteresting square block which Clement XIII built for his courtiers in 1766 along the Salita del Quirinale – not to mention Pius IX's "barracks" for the same purpose (from 1864) situated on the other side further down the sloping street. Here, a century later, self-effacement has turned into an arid desert waste of bureaucracy.

It was on the Monte Cavallo that Fuga also built the monumental Consulta palace, which has already been discussed as a public building. In doing so he gave the palace square in the early 1730's an up-to-date character, what might be called a touch of Louix XV in the wider sense, without for a moment neglecting Roman vitality and colour.

Soon after Fuga's work at the Quirinal had been completed he was invited to build a palace for Don Bartolomeo and the Cardinal-Protector, the sons of Pope Corsini's brother. Artistically he had a freer hand in this private task, but only as far as the external circumstances allowed. The *Palazzo Corsini* must be evaluated with many reservations, which are often overlooked by those purely interested in style. We find in the first place that the chosen site in Lungara was unconventional. According to Roman ideas it was not only remote, being outside the gate (Settimiana), but its situation close to Trastevere was considered rather undignified. de Brosses said in 1739 that as long as Clement was alive people would make an effort to seek out his relations, but as soon as the pope died (and this happened the year after) Prince Corsini would either have to look for another domicile or get used to his own company [110]. On one side the terrain was bounded and restricted by a narrow suburban street, but at the back it rose attractively up the slope of Gianicolo. This means that the palace had to accommodate itself to the conditions of a villa, with the result that its real front faced the garden, from where, dead against the usual conventions for a town palace, the best view of it was obtained. The façade we pass in the road must be regarded as secondary, almost a rear elevation. When it is criticized as being "cold" [111], the fact is ignored that an inviting warmth would have been out of place here. The long façade is not easily taken in by people using the road; it is not meant to arouse attention or to vie with the monasteries and hospitals in this down-town Rome (Pl. 85).

Thus the architect obtained his directives for the building's dualism from outside pressures. Towards Lungara a finely chiselled face is shown; its central part is only slightly emphasized with ashlar pilaster strips and an almost imperceptible projection. We recognize this reserved style from the Quirinal's palazzina. A plan by Fuga confirms that the original idea was to stress the central section more, partly by making it taller and partly by facing it with a subdued rusticated masonry in which all the windows were set in a round-arched recess [112]. A true Florentine feature, acknowledging the home of both pope and architect, and reminding us of Fernando Ruggieri's design c. 1730 for the rebuilding of Palazzo Pitti [113]. However, the position on the bank of the Tiber was a success, the Tuscan experiment was nipped in the bud.

As we regard the Palazzo Corsini from the garden (Pl. 109) it opens up completely and without reservations. We now realize another reason for its structure. Fuga's work is in fact a conversion. The Palazzo Riario had stood here from the days of High Renaissance; it was Queen Christina's Roman castle [114]. At the ends of the main building along the street there were two transverse wings, the longer one at the south end, together forming a quadrangle. The area north of this was an equestrian exercise ground. This space enabled Fuga to almost double the size of the existing building by incorporating the south wing and building a new transverse wing at the other end to balance it. He also created a central building which absorbed the old short north wing. This balancing trick is calculated to a nicety, but the attention that had to be paid to the existing walls put the symmetry somewhat out of kilter in the execution. Fuga was successful in masking the irregularities by setting porticos between the unevenly broad and tall wings.

The garden façade was then given plenty of plasticity of a bold nature. The specific motifs obviously gave wings to the artist's fantasy; we are aware of his pleasure in modelling on a grand scale, adding a cube and then knocking holes in it to create deep shadows, carving out large courtyards and erecting arches for the sun to shine through. The broad strokes of this architectural design made Fuga truly Roman. The block of the central part, which stands out and is broken up by enormous windows, corresponds to an atrium resounding like the nave of a church and to a stairway of rare monumental size.

Work on the Palazzo Corsini was started on August 6th, 1736 according to Bagnari's diary [115]; in 1739, de Brosses could observe the paintings inside. But a number of years passed before the interior decoration was finally completed. Grosley reports that he saw (1758) a fresco painter at work "in a palace in Lungara"; this must have been Corsini's. That the young artist was a talented violinist there is no doubt, for "from the scaffolding he played 5–6 *impromptus* for us with the verve and ease of a Neopolitan" [116]. This French traveller was of the opinion that the distribution of rooms here – under Parisian influence – was far better than in older Roman palaces. "What the interior decoration loses in splendour it gains in comfort" – it was the maxim of Rococo. The Palazzo Corsini's special attraction was its library, probably the largest private library in Rome, containing about 70,000 volumes distributed in six large rooms. There was no competing with the graphical collection which Giovanni Bottari, the renowned Florentine connoisseur, had assembled for the Corsinis. No sooner had Winckelmann arrived in Rome than he hastened out here to pore over the engravings in this treasure-house [117].

Not only the palace itself, but also its surroundings have been wonderfully preserved. The quiet lanes around the garden look much as they did at the time when Bottari, Foggini, Paciaudi and other members of the circle of Tuscan scholars wandered around and discussed antiquities. In Via dei Riari, one can still admire the garden wall (cf. Pl. 183b), an obstacle which Joseph Bonaparte overcame on December 28th 1797. During the bloody tumult in front of the palace where he lived as French Ambassador, he ventured out of the gate to pacify the mob, but had to beat a hasty retreat round the corner and up over the wall to his own back-door [118]. The street on the other side, the Via Corsini, is quiet and empty. People with a feeling for atmosphere sense here the special aura which often hangs over small streets sheltered by a very grand mansion. They vegetate in silent awe – and are frequented (like the renowned little alley behind Park Lane) "merely by gaudy footmen, by butlers – lonely and reticent men distrustful of all other butlers – and by wicked little grooms". A splendid magnolia stands in the middle of the carriageway.

Having now surveyed the most important palace buildings from the 1730's we then make our way along from work to work, down in time and through the town. By looking at *Palazzo Testa-Piccolomini,* a building by an unknown master, we probe in the first instance, the ordinary local style which characterizes these strongly individual works of first rank. It occupies the acute angle between the Via della Dataria and the Via dei Lucchesi and is very elegant in plan (Nolli No. 257). The elevation is no less admirable (Pl. 116). The body of the palace – irregular in shape between the two streets, with its footing adapted to the sloping street – looks at first sight like a planed-off block, one among many, in the great sculptured design called Baroque Rome. We sense that the building is a component part, not an individual on its own, the way it fits in so perfectly with the rest. Its art learned in Fontana's school is very fine. It is on the basis of works like these, which seem spontaneously generated, that the aristocratic architecture of the following period must be evaluated. This is the norm which Rococo prettified and on which Neo-Classicism waged war.

In the Via del Babuino, about midway along the right hand side from the Piazza di Spagna, stands a palace which attracts attention with its vital façade. It has 13 bays and the seven middle ones project in a low ressaut. This section is emphasized in another way too, for the bottom storey's masonry is pointed horizontally and the windows have copings of various rich types, while the windows in the side sections merely have plain framework (Pl. 114). Thus the side sections of the façade have a spare and airy effect in contrast to the relief of the ressaut – only down at the ground floor do they become both heavy and, as it were, anchored. The windows here are covered with lattice-work and the two side portals are surrounded by rock-faced rustication derived from the savagely "natural" cliff-like shapes which Bernini used on the Palazzo di Montecitorio. In the segmental pediment of one portal, a winged dragon is struggling to emerge from a shattered boulder, as if it were petrified in a grotto (Pl. 115). Above the corresponding side portal, a pair of scaly dolphins glide forth from a rocky crevice.

The four-winged palace is not remarkable in plan. The main gateway leads into an arcade along the rear of the front building and provides access to the stairs in the north side wing. If only for the sake of the curious portals one would like to be able to date the palace and find out the builder's as well as the architect's name. A collection of letters from that time which has been overlooked by art-historians will provide the answer to two of our questions [119].

Don Gregorio Boncompagni, Duke of Sora (died 1707), had made a brilliant match when he married Donna Ippolita Ludovisi, Princess of Piombino. As daughter of Niccolò Ludovisi, the son of Gregory XV's brother, she was heiress to the Ludovisi family fortune, while her mother, Constanza Pamphili, was a niece of Innocent X. In order to unite the estates of the Boncompagni and Ludovisi families, Don Gregorio arranged the marriage between his oldest daughter Eleonora and her maternal uncle, Antonio Ludovisi. As the latter died in 1731 and Donna Ippolita passed away two years later, Princess Eleonora was left a widow with an enormous inheritance. She preferred to stay in her little duchy of Sora, part of the Kingdom of Naples, by the river Liri. But in her later years, this very pious lady developed the urge to build a palace in Rome. You could not say that she lacked a residence in the papal city, for she owned the lovely Villa Ludovisi outside the Porta Pinciana; all the same, she felt she could indulge herself by acquiring an up-to-date dower-house as well. In one of her numerous letters to her son Gaetano, she mentions the building project, if only in passing. The young man had asked for some money. Donna Eleonora refused his request in the kindest way in a letter from January 28th, 1738 and mentions among other reasons the *capriccio* that had taken hold of her. The expression "caprice" for the building of a palace of some considerable size is rather amusing and very indicative of the nonchalance of these aristocrats. The princess, in other ways so meek, adds a modest reflection: "The building will give me but little pleasure since I am old, but I shall at least be able to die in a house of my own." This house is the palace at 51, Via del Babuino, which faces the Via di Gesù e Maria.

Armed with this information, we are now able to interpret the strange portals of the *Palazzo Boncompagni-Ludovisi*. The winged dragon can be accepted without comment, for it is the heraldic beast of the Boncompagni family. But the Bernini rock-work, whose appearance on a 1738 façade is rather unexpected, can now be allotted to its proper file. The Palazzo di Montecitorio's erection was started under the supervision of Bernini, and was the town residence for Prince Niccolò Ludovisi, Donna Eleonora's maternal grandfather. So, in a way, the out-dated motif has been placed on the building in the Via del Babuino as a sort of family symbol, to commemorate the family's period of glory under Pope Gregory XV Ludovisi and in memory of the huge palace, which in 1692 had passed out of the family's possession.

Donna Eleonora's architect is not mentioned in the correspondance. It may well have been Gregorini as the following indicates. As mentioned above, he had previously worked for Cardinal Pietro Ottoboni. We now take notice of the fact that Eleonora Boncompagni and the Ottobonis were related twice over, since the princess's sister Giulia was married to Don Marco Ottoboni, whose daughter (and heiress) married Donna Eleonora's own son Pietro in 1730. Marco Ottoboni, who had incidentally bought his duchy, Fiano, from Niccolò Ludovisi's estate, was the paternal uncle of the cardinal, at that time the most important member of the family. Another pointer is that Gregorini in 1748 had completed Prince Ludovisi Boncompagni's sepulchral monument in Isola del Liri and in the same year converted the Villa Ludovisi in Rome. He was apparently in high favour with the noble family. The palace front in the Via del Babuino is in complete agreement with Gregorini's gentle, theatrical style, but any direct basis for comparison is lacking, for his known and still preserved *œuvre* includes only church architecture.

An epitaph to Donna Eleonora, *matrona spectatissima,* who died on January 9th, 1745, can be seen on the left of the entrance in S. Maria del Popolo. Her children Gaetano, Pietro and Maria Francesca put up this memorial whose crowning pediment is Borrominesque. The very beautifully modelled dragon that we know from the Via del Babuino not far from here stands out on the plinth. The "Baboon" figure, after which the street is called, can be seen in the palace courtyard.

The palace that Bernini had erected in the 1660's for Cardinal Flavio Chigi the Elder, was taken over by Innocent XI's nephew, Don Livio

Odescalchi, in 1694, the year after the cardinal's death. His sister's son Baldassare Odescalchi, Duke of Bracchiano, who was his heir, extended it and had it converted by N. Salvi in 1745. The Palazzo Odescalchi's great merit in its original form was based mainly on the effective contrast between a central section, held together by giant pilasters, and two shorter flanking sections with horizontal jointing, thus severe verticals are opposed to delicate horizontals. The conversion which doubled the length of the façade, destroyed this contrasting motif by the width of the ressaut being increased from seven to fifteen bays. The portal was duplicated at this time, whereby a dominant centre line disappeared, and the increased number of large pilasters caused the rhythm to dissolve into monotony. Opinions of a later date has censured Salvi and his age because of this drastic conversion. Gurlitt found it "to the detriment of the palace" [120], Riegl went so far as suggesting that the palace now lacked harmony (Einheitlichkeit) since it was too wide in ratio to the height, looked like a side elevation and was no longer distinguished-looking. "The Romans are slipping down from their superior level; this form of art can no longer claim to be in the lead" [121]. Similar complaints are echoed by Fokker when he insists that the long line of pilasters is "dreary" and the remodelling regrettable [122].

Nobody can deny that the loss of an authentic and outstanding work by Bernini is a pity. But it does not follow that its successor has no right to exist. The critics overlook the fact that there were other things Salvi had to take into consideration besides a reverent attitude towards Bernini. As often happens, they can only see their object in the light of a topical artistic evaluation and disregard the past. The Palazzo Odescalchi was built to fit in with a very busy square which had changed in many ways since 1665. Salvi had taste and sense enough to entertain respect both for the location and his employer. In Bernini's golden age the Piazza di S.S. Apostoli was an incomplete space, a narrow corridor with gaps here and there. The Palazzo Colonna stood on the same side as the church with an untidy outline and looked more like suburban architecture. When the Palazzo Chigi was built opposite, it could quite happily retain a large garden on its north side and stand there in lonely majesty, for this was the boundary between town and country.

In 1745 the situation was completely different. The church of S. S. Apostoli had in the meanwhile been rebuilt from its foundations and was now – though as yet lacking an up-to-date façade – a church which attracted a very select clientèle. Also, only about 15 years previously, the Palazzo Colonna had been pulled together and cleaned up. Now it was Salvi's task to utilize the facilities of the other long wall of the square, in short, to turn it into architecture. He also made drawings, unfortunately never used, for a new façade for S. S. Apostoli [123], which stood directly opposite the Palazzo Odescalchi, and this shows that it was his dream to create an entity here. When therefore, Riegl scornfully compares the new front of the palace to a side elevation, he has some justification, but in a very different sense, for Salvi's work should really be construed as a long side wall of a final solution. When however the same scholar finds the length too great in ratio to the height, he is making a mistake, for the façade should not only be appreciated as a building's exterior, but also as the inside walls of this square, and from this standpoint, the proportions leave nothing to be desired. Riegl's conclusion that the palace is not sufficiently dignified must therefore be discounted. Just look at Piranesi's engraving (Pl. 110)! Duke Odescalchi has by Salvi's artistic sense subjugated the rest of the Piazza di S. S. Apostoli, and has surpassed even the Casa Colonna which had been master here for seven hundred years. The discord in Michetti's pavilions and terrace was muted by the neighbour on the opposite side of the road, much to the benefit of the square.

Another observation must be advanced. After the popes had chosen the Quirinal as a permanent residence, the Piazza di S. S. Apostoli took on a function it had not had when Bernini built Palazzo Chigi. It became an enduring stage at the pope's splendid procession, when, after his accession, he drove through Rome to the Lateran to claim his episcopal church (*il Possesso*). The first stretch of the route was, according to custom, as follows: from Monte Cavallo across Magnanapoli through the crooked Via delle Tre Cannelle and then along the flank of the Palazzo Bonelli (Ruspoli) – and when the cavalcade arrived in front of this palace it had (as Venuti says) *un nobilissimo prospetto* of the Piazza di S. S. Apostoli. This was in fact the procession's first proper, proud view into the papal city. And it was precisely the left side of the square containing the Palazzo Odescalchi which was displayed to view. At the corner of the Palazzo Colonna, the procession turned sharp left past S. Romualdo and arrived in the Piazza Venezia. After the Via 4 Novembre was constructed, the above topographical details were basically changed, but it is easy to follow the pope's route on Nolli's map.

Now perhaps my readers have realized that Salvi's façade was, in those days, felt to be particularly distinguished-looking because of its length and that the "dreary" row of pilasters was rich seen in diagonal perspective (which it usually is, not only by popes on mules). Assessed on the basis of these facts, the Palazzo Odescalchi is not only absolved from criticism, but can claim full restitution as a work of art of its time. Even when we think of the style without taking the surroundings into consideration. The regular rhythm of the giant pilasters was in no way a half-hearted mechanical process which was merely the outcome of the architect's lack of inspiration, but a reflection of a deliberate artistic trend. Call it "Academism" if you like. We prefer to accept the use of this motif as an influence from French architecture. It was given sanction by Mansart in his classic squares (Place des Victoires, Place Vendôme). We are thinking only of the plan, not the execution in detail. Salvi could take heart from the example of classical Paris for the extension and rhythm of the palace wall in his own Roman square.

It would be a good idea to pursue our subject by following the papal triumphal route. We left the procession in front of the Palazzo Venezia. From there it crossed the entrance to the Corso and moved into the present Via del Plebiscito (formerly Strada del Gesù). To the right, opposite the Palazzo di S. Marco's dark un-classical walls, stands an aristocratic house of ample size waiting to be appreciated. It was erected at the beginning of the 1740's by Prince Camillo Pamphili as a supplement to the family's existing palace complex [124]. One is struck primarily by the enormous demand for living space. Before analysing the new building it is important to take its use into account. Don Camillo himself, or his family, had no need of it, for his normal residence was in the wing facing the Piazza del Collegio Romano, while the part on the Corso was used mainly for banquets etc. The building in the Strada del Gesù was

117. *The Palazzo Petroni (Bolognetti) in Piazza del Gesù, seen from a salon in the Palazzo Altieri.*

118. *The Palazzo Mastrozzi.*

119. *The Palazzo Mellini in Piazza di S. Marcello. On the left Via del Corso with the Palazzo De Carolis.*

120. *The Palazzo del Cinque on Montecitorio.*

121. *The Palazzo Santacroce in Piazza Benedetto Cairoli.*

123. *The Palazzo Rondinini in Via del Corso.*

124. *The Palazzo Braschi.*

erected partly for relations and dependents of the Pamphili family and partly as a high-class apartment house; Cardinal Ferroni lived here in the 1760's. Or more precisely: it was an eligible residence but not the residence of a noble family. Fokker queries whether there were originally shops on the ground floor [125]; these are clearly seen in an engraving by Vasi (II, 1752, Pl. 39). These shops follow the rhythm 1–2–2 (2–2) 2–2–1, a decidedly "middle-class" beat. When we also notice that the building surrounds two courtyards next to each other, therefore having two portals, and that the façade stands face to face with the Venezia palace, which it cannot possible challenge frontally, it will then come as no surprise that the Pamphili annex has its emphasis at the sides and is an ambiguous composition altogether. The façade is divided vertically into three sections (6–9–6), the outer ones of which are covered by jointed ashlar, but this distribution fails to unite the extensive front, five storeys high (including a mezzanine). The portals with their balconies are pulling in opposite directions, the shops break up the façade, the middle window in the ground floor is bricked up and a relief in stucco takes the place of an opening. The façade is split up because there is no impulse to cohere. The diffuse is calculated and the mixture natural. Like the sylph maidens – two merge into one, and one turns into three. Why should we expect this *palazzo di tutti* [126] to parade with the banner in front? The only attempt to indicate a symmetrical axis appears in the top storey where there is a balcony to the three middle windows, belatedly and of course without effect. This Palazzo Pamphili thus provides further evidence of the importance of internal and external factors for a Roman work, as in the case of the Palazzo Altieri, whose façade in this same street is similarly conditioned. If such analyses are of no interest, we can at least enjoy the elegance of the details – curving balconies, rounded latticework like flower baskets, consoles with rigid precision of form (Pl. 122) or, if we feel so inclined, indignantly condemn the building because it does not look like a real palace. The architect was Paolo Ameli, who was in the service of the Pamphilis from 1739 to 1758 [127]. He succeeded Valvassori, but did not follow his artistic form.

Palazza Petroni (Cenci-Bolognetti) in the Gesù square was rebuilt by Fuga in the 1740's – more definite information is lacking [128] – and was given a new façade of the "giant order" (Pl. 117). This is merely a screen covering an irregular building complex. Both Count Petroni and his architect had obvious reasons for giving the façade this ceremonial character, for its opposite neighbour was the Palazzo Altieri, and the building was situated in an exposed position at the place where the triumphal procession to the Capitol suddenly changed course. When in 1769, Clement XIV led his cavalcade diagonally across the Piazza del Gesù, one of the Captains of Horse, Don Emilio Altieri, saluted his wife who was standing on the balcony of the family palace. The papal Master of the Horse, Don Alessandri Petroni, who also rode in the procession, was then able to pay his respects to his own house in a similar fashion [129]. It made a fine impression on this great day. It is almost impossible to overestimate the importance that ceremonial had for the rationale of a prominent building. Characteristically enough, Palazzo Petroni's long and much lower façade in the Via d' Aracoeli was not elaborated, as it was seen only from the side. The giant pilasters which Fuga erected should be assessed rather as contrivances to make a smaller building more presentable, than as a stylistic feature with certain curious trends. The façade's most personal – and finest – members are the fluted posts at the portal; there is craftsmanship in them. Otherwise the work is merely one part of a greater whole in this locality and does not set out to demonstrate any special characteristics.

One appreciates this dignified aloofness when examining several palaces from the period immediately following. They diverge from the lines of their surroundings, break away too, from the tectonic solidity which – even in a screen – was a sign of good architecture, and try to become individuals through decoration. The architects were men of the second rank. Large mansions of this type can be a lot of fun and captivating for a limited time; their often attractive ornaments spring forth at the edges of all the windows – but they are not able to hide the weak form and ambiguous proportions. We will list the most important monuments in the group.

The *Palazzo Mellini* near S. Marcello in the Corso was completely renovated by Cardinal Mario Mellini shortly after 1747. It was this year that he was raised to the purple [130]. The architect was Tommaso de

Marchis. He added pilasters to the rounded corner of the building, overdid the pediments of the windows in the piano nobile with cartouches, and bent the corners of the top window frames as if they were made of cardboard (Pl. 119). A similar treatment of details is seen in the *Palazzo Santacroce* which was extended and renovated somewhat later, presumably for Prince Antonio Santacroce [131], married (1761) to the fêted Donna Giuliana, Cardinal de Bernis' dear friend. If the soft pink colour of the walls is really the original, then the architect has harmonized it prettily with the frivolous decoration (Pl. 121). The palace infects the whole district with its pointed humour; only the corner possesses the pomposity suitable to the home of people who claim to be the descendants of ancient heroes. To judge from appearances it is difficult to believe that this sophistical palace is the haunt of ghosts. The story goes that two statues of cardinals, both Santacroces, come down from their pedestals at night and drag their clattering marble trains behind them through the long galleries [132]. One of these unfortunates must have been Cardinal Prospero who, in the 16th century, introduced Rome to the pleasures of tobacco [133]. Anyway, it seems very likely that a house belonging to the distinguished Santacroce should be honoured by apparitions, the most unmistakable of all feudal attributes. The first of the line to reach princely rank (in Clement XI's time) had committed a murder [134]. The *Palazzo Del Cinque* on Montecitorio is built on a very grand scale but not even the rhythmic staggering in the rows of windows helps to control its bulk. It is really a town house with delusions of grandeur, ready to take on the Palace of Justice itself. We like the building for its insolence and its superb fullness of body (Pl. 120). The *Palazzo Mastrozzi* (Graziosi) at the entrance to the Via di Monserrato also belongs to this category of patrician houses, where it is a successful example of its kind. Venuti called it (1766) "a little palace with very charming and unusual architecture" [135]. Grace not only emanates from the jewel-like decoration of the windows, but also resides in the fragile form of the house itself. There is verve in this building which seems designed by an unrestrained hand (Pl. 118). By a lucky chance, we are able to get some impression of the atmosphere that surrounded the Casa Mastrozzi as it was experienced by a small boy who lived on the second floor [136]. Everyday life in the family of Count Brigante Colonna was on a modest scale, but formal, lived out in a restricted little world. *Il contino* went to school in the nearby Vicolo delle Grotte; he ran across the square (Piazza della Ruota, Pl. 42) to visit the room behind S. Girolamo della Carità, where his beloved S. Filippo Neri had lived, and his nurse told devout stories about S. Leonardo da Porto Maurizio who had once preached in this neighbourhood [137]. But Giulio was not aware that Juvara had designed a chapel in S. Girolamo dedicated to this saint, nor that Cagliostro had gone to ground like a hunted animal close to his home [138], for he was only a little Roman boy who lived in the finest house within this narrow environment.

In spite of the Louis Quinze ornaments here and there, we hesitate to give the name of Rococo to these and other noble houses. The cool mood, which is the spirit of genuine French Rococo, is noticeable only in very few Roman palaces. The best of these is the *Palazzo Rondinini* (Sanseverino) in the upper part of the Corso. As far as we know it was restored throughout in the 1760's for Marchese Giuseppe Rondinini. The front as an entity was devitalized in the cleaning-up process, the Parisian is evident only in the double portal (Pl. 123). We can ascribe a "Pre-Classical" tendency to the detached columns under the balcony; the arches of the gateway are crowned by cartouches and shells in the late, natural *Style Rocaille*. A similar framework appears in the portal of the *Palazzo Pediconi* in Montegiardano (and in Vanvitelli's chancel in S. Maria degli Angeli). In the 1790's there was a hotel called "The Golden Eagle" under the roof of this palace [139].

It was about this time that the last great palace of the century was erected in Rome. In 1790, Pius VI bought the Palazzo Orsini-Santobono on the south side of Piazza Navona, and had this as well as the adjacent houses razed to the ground in order to build a residence for his relations – Luigi Braschi-Onesti, Duke of Nemi, and Cardinal Romualdo Braschi. The gentlemen moved into the palace in 1793, but the interior was far from complete, when the duke in 1798, after the Pope's imprisonment, had to flee from Rome. The architect was Cosimo Morelli from Imola [140]. The very extensive palace, built on a trapezoid ground plan with the short side facing the Piazza di S. Pantaleo, bulked very large, and this was its greatest asset. The building barges into the city scene with a force, which might be yet another expression of this family's ruthless determination to exploit every situation (Pl. 124). In Rome, the newly created Duke was hated for his greed and brutality [141]. The palace too, is hard as stone. Its "Classicism" is nothing but reaction; Morelli rejected the humanity of Mature Baroque and went back to designs used at the close of the 16th century (cf. e. g. Palazzo Alessandrino-Bonelli, 1585), to the time when the aristocrats' mansions were influenced by their owners' chilly arrogance. The lower storey (with mezzanine) of jointed ashlar and the columned portal, may well have been planned with the Palazzo Borghese in mind. The architecture is sterile throughout. This is the first time the exterior of a Roman palace makes a brazen proclamation of the fact that its builder is a millionaire; the highly polished "Renaissance" of the main staircase is later repeated in bank buildings (and in some national museums).

One spring day in 1803, Frederikke Brun wandered through the bare and unfinished rooms of the Palazzo Braschi, with Zoëga as her guide [142]. At the top there is a room whose wall decoration in Egyptian style would have interested Bindesbøll. All the same, he was the more able man. His museum in Copenhagen built to house Thorvaldsen's works, designed while he was under the spell of the great sculptor, is perhaps the only building outside Italy in whose corridors and vaulted chambers even the owners of Roman palaces could move around with confidence.

SQUARES AND STREETS

On y fait plus, on n'y fait nulle chose LAFONTAINE

I

The built-up area of Rome had, by the end of the eighteenth century, been so thoroughly constructed that only a little remodelling here and there was necessary. The orderly layout of streets from the Renaissance period and the large three-pronged fork running from the Piazza del Popolo had long since settled into the mosaic of the plan and become as ordinary as the thoroughfares that were a result of a natural development. Yet the underpopulated areas between the Sistine main roads were to remain something of a backwater for a long time to come. It must be regarded as beneficial for Rome as a work of art, that this contrast between the slowly growing, teeming city and empty districts with their carelessly drawn axes was still allowed to exist. The Campus Martius could not be subjected to a process of redevelopment, as was later to be successfully done with common land in other towns. There is a peaceful rhythm of the streets in the time-honoured districts; all thoroughfares proceed at a leisurely pace and make allowances for the construction of intimate little squares, odd corners, dead ends. The Via del Governo Vecchio too, although the most important stretch of the popes' triumphal route from the Vatican to the Lateran, serpentines its way with indifference and disintegrates into a series of short prospects. Even the monumental squares in the city – the narrow bowl of the Piazza Navona (Pl. 125), and the Campidoglio Square lying like a plateau above the roofs of the city – are self-contained.

Individualism is deeply inherent in Rome's nature in contrast to Paris, which tries out every experiment on a geometrical basis and aspires to uniformity. Even in ancient times Rome's monumental sites, temples and imperial squares had a pronounced tendency to isolate themselves from the rest of the city [1]. And when the straight lines, which the Renaissance boldly tried to transfer to the centre of the city from a Vitruvian ideal metropolis, were lost in the mediaeval maze, history itself acted in the interest of "Romanity". Devastation by barbarians and the long years of decadence which followed had been a clearance in the true sense of the word, not so much because it cleaned up, but because it left behind scattered remains. These constituted an ever-present active resistance and helped Rome to be true to its own self; they encouraged division into smaller areas. So we find that owing to both its antique origin and its later destiny, it was never Rome's fate to fall victim to a schematic town planning system. The city of the popes is *paesistica*. This expression, which we owe to Marcello Piacentini [2], could be taken to mean that Rome has always tended towards small divisions, that it has a hankering for village systems.

The marvellous thing about it is that this particularism can be identified with the overall good, a feeling which must be the most stirring in the world.

Architecture can take the credit for this, so good is the art of building on the banks of the Tiber. High quality is the common factor; every patch in the city's restless pattern contains a work of mature plasticity, moulded fearlessly to its environment. Roman urban architecture is controlled by harmonious anomaly [3].

In the period following Bernini's death there was no lack of attempts to develop along strict lines and make great changes. In every epoch we find architects whose dreams of an immense building site fire them to improve taste. But all attempts by the state to prune with a large knife came to nothing. Powerful forces resisted, especially lack of funds and habitual inertia. It was in some way as if the city itself quietly suppressed every radical design that might impair the tranquillity of its streets. Rome was mature and wise; it was relaxed, secure in its wealth of humanity and its dominion over souls.

The most far-reaching of Late Baroque's never realized town planning schemes was a project by Carlo Fontana for a complete rearrangement of the Borgo district and a huge extension of Bernini's St. Peter's Square. The drawings were published by Fontana in his "Templum Vaticanum" (1694) [4]. Significantly enough, this particularly enlightened suggestion aimed at clearing up a part of the city which was completely subordinated to St. Peter's and the popes' residence and on which ceremonial made extraordinary demands. And it was no less instructive that Fontana exploited Maestro Bernini's square to the full. He wanted to raze *la spina* between the two *Borghi* and create a wide street prospect, which in later years has been put into practice far less artistically [5].

The vividness of Fontana's idealistic project for the recasting of a whole section of the city is realized when we compare it with a couple of earlier, very typical alterations to the city prospect. These were local in form and as always, they were based upon those narrowly confined mansions which were in need of air – a better drive up to the door, a wider view and thus greater possibility of being seen from a distance. The church, the monastery, the palace, all create their own urbanism; what they needed could be compared with a clearing being cut in a primeval forest. The straight stretch of road which bears the names Via della Mercede – Via di Capo le Case and runs towards S. Giuseppe [6] was systematized in Paul V's time and radiated from S. Maria Maddalena's convent *delle Convertite*, situated between the Corso and the Piazza delle Monache di S. Silvestro (as it is called on Falda's map); the walls of two convents formed the square and controlled the lines of traffic. In front of the Chiesa Nuova, the Oratorians, with the approval of Urban VIII, had the road running past it widened into a square, and erected there large uniform *casamenti* (destroyed when the new Corso was put through) [7]. And in 1675 the same religious order laid out the homogeneous Via di Chiesa Nuova, still extant, along the east flank of their church. It was at about the same time that the Piazza della Cancelleria took on its present form after a number of old houses had been pulled down. The church of S. Lorenzo in Damaso and the Vice-Chancellor's palace, under one and the same roof, had thereby put a suitable distance between themselves and the alleyways of the *canaille* by this side of the princely building being detached. When the Corso Vittorio Emanuele was carried through, it laid this side completely bare, and this operation weakened it considerably. In 1690 plans were put forward to pull down a group of houses in the real Corso near S. Maria Maddalena and the old *Letterati* orphanage, in order to create a square with a fountain [8],

125. *Piazza Navona seen from the air. At the bottom the Palazzo Braschi.*

127. *Porto di Ripetta. Old photograph.*

128. *Niche at the top of Salita di S. Sebastianello.*

but the densely packed street staved off all attacks and avoided being equipped with a large niche in competition with the Piazza Colonna.

As we now begin the process of examining the large Roman squares of our period – where the architectural status can best be evaluated – we must from the onset remember an important concept for composition. Effected with talent, it puts a new construction on the predominantly utilitarian planning of modelling on the grand scale. This concept, created by Baroque, is frequently discussed in the topographical literature of the 18th century, in a phraseology which is particularly lucid. It states that some buildings *formano teatro alla piazza,* i. e. give the square the character of a theatre. The phrase is used for example of Pietro da Cortona's square in front of S. Maria della Pace and of the square in front of S. Ignazio. The word *teatro* is also used for the niches that accentuate the central parts of a terraced garden [9], and it was a common everyday term for the first wide landing (with its steps like an amphitheatre) in the Scala di Spagna. In Holberg's time *theatrum* meant the stage itself.

When the Italians of the seventeenth century described architecture by referring to a playhouse, they naturally thought of the stage scenery. It has a backcloth to which the wings are adapted and on which the perspective is focussed. Something of the same is true of those squares which are described by the expression used above; their *fond* is a monumental building, very often a church. In other words they are the stage. However, every theatre has two opposing aspects; one view is from the auditorium towards the proscenium, the stage itself, the other from the stage to the auditorium, the stalls and the balcony. Both in the playhouse and in the mise en scène of the square, the former aspect is the most important, but the "front of the house" also has a claim, for it is the reason for the theatre's existence. We will find that both views were of significance when new squares were laid out in eighteenth-century Rome.

It was no mere coincidence that the public theatre with its scenic arrangement started its period of greatness in 1670 with the Teatro Tordinona [10] as the first one, nor that Carlo Fontana, the father of Late Baroque, was epoch-making within the field of theatre architecture, even internationally, as the type of plan laid down by him still has universal validity. The relationship between the decorative square and the view of the stage was not merely an academic exercise in the drawing office. Nor can the matter be dismissed with the argument that the squares we are dealing with were "theatrical" in the same broad sense as is all Baroque. Here we are concerned with concrete matters, with the direct influence of stage architecture on urbanism. The Romans were used to seeing large scale temporary theatres of all kinds in their squares. They were erected on festive occasions, and the man in the street had no difficulty at all in readjusting from illusory spectacles lasting only a day, to a permanent stage built of solid stone designed to last for generations.

The way Cardinal Ottoboni celebrated Innocent XIII's accession was by erecting a magnificent concert theatre in front of *La Cancelleria,* and the square now seemed to have come into its own [11]. The Piazza di Spagna itself was, on a number of occasions, enhanced by a temporary scenic spectacle before La Scalea became a permanent stage as, for example, when Prince Vaini built a temporary operatic stage (1727) outside his Palazzo Mignanelli [12]. Even after the Spanish Steps were built they had, on occasions, to compete with great events, as in August 1727 when people admired "a magnificent theatre with more than 100 musicians" in the square [13], and when Nicola Salvi two years later conjured up a decoration so enormous that it entirely hid the steps [14]. We may well ask where the piazza's real theatre lay. In the same way it is also amusing to see how nonchalantly the owners of palaces had wooden balconies fixed on to the most beautiful façades when a "show" took place beneath their windows. The balcony which Queen Christina built on the corner of the Corso in 1660, from where the finish of the horse-race could easily be followed, was in fact called *un palchetto* [15]. The stage itself was the Piazza Venezia. When Prince Ruspoli during the carnival of the jubilee year of 1775 built a platform in front of his palace at Largo Goldoni, he destroyed, without compunction, wall paintings on the inside of the wall, not to mention the external one; this extravagance did however bring him a satirical verse from Pasquino:

> *Per fare una loggia guastare un palazzo!*
> *Samara architetto! Oh, principe pazzo* [16]

Which in translation sounds something like this:

> To desecrate a palace in building a private box,
> The architect's a fathead, the princeling a dull ox.

The Roman squares experienced one benefit and gala performance after the other, performed in changing settings. Of these, just a few have never lost their place in the repertoire and can still be found. They are the shining lights of the present chapter.

Michelangelo had made the Capitol the first square in the world with a stage décor. Handbooks from the Augustan Age spoke proudly of *il bel teatro di Campidoglio* [17]. But this elevated stage could not really be an inspiration for later structures, because the situation was unique from the point of view of terrain as well as others. The stage is set on a hill and gradually soars into view as the steps are ascended one by one; "The rising palace" is a tremendously dramatic experience. Strictly speaking, it is the steps that provide the drama for ordinary people. They could only become part of the scenery by taking an active role and enter the stage. However, the Capitol as theatrical applied art suffered from one serious drawback: the pope's procession and the carriages of the nobility could not drive up the steps, so in 1692 these were supplemented by a most unheroic roadway on the right hand side, designed by the municipal architect Filippo Tettoni [18]. A trophy was set up at the start of the ramp, its motif being three jars (*pile* or *pignatte*), an allusion to Pope Innocent XII Pignatelli's name and coat of arms. The detour to the back of the scenery was therefore given the name of Via delle Tre Pile.

A keen and clever scenographer would surely have been disappointed with the approach to the Capitol. It was lopsided and thoughtlessly reduced by the Jacob's ladder of the Aracoeli. In sketches from 1709 Juvara showed how the site could have been made the finest drama in the world, had the space up there been filled with tempestuous architecture – a couple more churches in symmetry, flights of steps, fast-moving lines [19]. This improvisation on Rome's most splendid theme was – believe it or not – composed in honour of Frederick IV of Denmark, who intended to visit Rome but was prevented by the plague.

At the time the Via delle Tre Pile was driven up to the Senator's Capitol, Carlo Fontana was trying to turn Montecitorio into a forum [20]. The Roman *curia*, which he himself had constructed in the heart of the city, was in need of a proper parliamentary square. The project was stupendous and without doubt an attempt to compete with Antiquity. This task encouraged the learned architect to express himself in Latin. He wanted to place a building with a semicircular ground plan opposite the front of the Court of Justice. A street was to run through this concavity continuing the middle line across the square to the portal, and a triumphal column, which might be a brother to that of Marcus Aurelius in the Piazza Colonna just around the corner, set up on this line. Strangely enough, this antique column of which Fontana had dreamt, was discovered at Montecitorio itself in 1703. It will appear later in our account. The motif of the large hemicycle, though derived from the ground plan of the palace, might be interpreted as a concave, somewhat blown-up imitation of the tribuna's semicircle to the north. But Fontana must also have wanted to construct a copy of a monumental square from Antiquity with the help of his curved building. For very good reasons he did not know the shape which the Imperial fora originally had, but he would have seen the niche-like buildings found in the thermae and studied the bold reconstructions made by antiquarians. An engraving by Donati (1695) of "Agrippina's Thermae" shows an exedra enclosing the square in front of the main building [21]. As seen from the ground plan, it was Fontana's intention to include shops in the residential complex in the parliament square which were to alternate with matching street doors in the rhythm a–bb, this being the accepted scheme then. His design for the square has in actual fact an amazing similarity to the *Mercato di Traiano,* which was excavated more than two hundred years after his death. As a classicist, Fontana was remarkably good at guesswork.

An antique forum in Baroque guise – and a stage into the bargain. The concave building forms the auditorium with circle and gallery in the back wall; the central street enjoys the frontal view usually reserved for people in the front row of the circle. We take note of the fact that on the ground plan the corners of the hemicycle have been cut off, so that the perspective includes the whole palace in its full extent. Where the amputation has taken place, porticos have been added which could give the impression of being theatre boxes set obliquely to the stage. And seen from the Palazzo di Montecitorio – a theatrical castle-like building – the actors up in their salons or emerging from the entrance could take in all the hollow space at a glance. For it was Fontana's great achievement to have established the "horseshoe" plan as the one best suited for a theatre auditorium [22]. It was not possible to use it here, for the optical perception of the palace on the middle axis was far more important than the view from "boxes" at the curving sides. This circumstance resulted in the architect simplifying his ideas and returning to the semicircular figure of the antique theatre. His love of Antiquity served him well, but he was also a modernist. It is a great pity that Fontana's sublime solution was not carried out, for it was fully Roman. But the streets put up a resistance and the houses here were not to be moved.

It was easier on the bank of the Tiber. A few years after the Montecitorio project had fallen through, Rome was given a *teatro* of the first rank in the *Porto di Ripetta*. There was here a rutted stretch of bank with discharging berths for the craft that brought wine, oil and coal from Umbria and Sabina. A filthy dockland in the middle of a shocking district, the haunt of thieves and harlots [23]. Ripa Grande had recently been tidied up. Its example would have to be followed, and also the harbour area to the north was in need of tighter customs control. Very likely the whole idea of building might have come to nothing had the earthquake of 1703 not forced it through. This vigorous intervention caused part of the Colosseum to collapse, and in this way a large stock of building material was at once at hand for next to nothing. And it was good stuff. So they started building and with great urgency. Clement XI was able to appraise the completed construction in August 1704 [24]. It can be seen in Plate 127.

Deseine described the Ripetta harbour as built *en forme d'un théatre spacieux* [25]. The monument which was to catch the eye in this setting was S. Girolamo degli Schiavoni. Alessandro Specchi, Fontana's right-hand man and municipal architect for Rome, now showed what he could do as producer and scenic artist, schooled as he was in the opera house among other things [26]. In front of the church, on its middle axis, he projected a semicircular podium which is the central figure of the layout. Seen from out in the river it looked like the base of the church façade and it also acted as a belvedere with a panorama across the river taking in the green meadows on the other bank (Prati di Castello). Nothing is more satisfying than watching other people work. The observation platform by the harbour could expect a swarm of sightseers, so the idlers were invited to rest on comfortable circular stone seats. Apart from that, the decoration was very sparse indeed, the most original being two columns shaped like milestones on which the water-level of the Tiber during its most severe flooding was recorded [27]. For once the columns with ship's beaks were omitted. These *columnae rostratae* were otherwise so often found in the maritime architecture at that time (as on the Arsenal Island in Copenhagen). But for convenience and comfort, a little fountain was set up, the water of course spurting from the three Albani *monti* (they also braved the winds on S. Girolamo's gable).

We recognize without difficulty that this platform was the basic element in the whole composition. Following the curve of this "apse", concentric flights of steps were built to enclose it. This upset some people, for the normal thing would have been to set rows of steps parallel to the quay and the bank of the river. Here the semicircular block seems to have been, as it were, plunged into the water, displacing it in the middle to create waves at the sides, combers along the straight line of the steps with a supple motion, a lingering, shallow, constantly falling ripple. A rhythmic meeting of earth and water. This was more or less our impression of the Porto di Ripetta as a work of art. But was it at that time? We have Clement XI's own verdict on first seeing it. A courtier present has passed it on to us: "His Holiness was not particularly satisfied, partly because of the small amount of water given forth by the fountain, partly because from the podium it was not possible to enjoy the spectacle (*come per non godersi dalla cima il prospetto del teatro*), a great drawback, which the architect blamed on Mgr. Giudice, the Pope's majordomo and comptroller of this building activity [28].

This is an extremely instructive assessment. The edifice lacks a vital architectural spark, it lacks an urgent pressure that could be released in a vertical jet, like a gusher. The Pope sees the whole "spectacle" as an apparatus, and he finds it inefficient. The whole thing is too low and too short. Confined between the two fascinating perspectives, you do not stand in the middle of things and see the movement of the architecture beneath your feet. On the face of it our impression coincides with that of those days, and we have the words of the best possible witness that the structure was considered mechanical. Statements of such fundamental importance are rare. We are grateful to Papa Clement for his comment on a theatrically aesthetic basic law used in Roman secular architecture. Ripetta was an approach to something great which external features restrained. With all its weaknesses, Specchi's creation was nevertheless charming and no other period could have produced such a basically good design and yet seen its faults so clearly.

The scenes of daily life must have been gay on this fair quay, which made a pretence of being a harbour. Old southern ports of call tend to have an atmosphere of easy optimism, and neither seamen nor vessels seem to be in any hurry to set sail. Every pile of bales resemble a *nature-morte;* the ships might have been designed for the seven seas of an opera. Just think of the lovely dock basin in Marseilles, a rectangle of water between tall, vivid buildings, or the sleepy arcaded street along the waterfront in Leghorn, hardly changed since the days of Antony Adverse, and also Ligurian fishing villages with hefty iron rings set in marble slabs, and lateen sails flapping in a lazy breeze. Views of Vernet harbours in the Mediterranean, dominated by fortresses, inhabited by lounging Levantines, combine with intense visual sensations of one's own – and from a youth long past emerges the picture, shimmering in the haze, of the Molo in Naples, where the lazzaroni assumed sculptural poses and recited endless heroic poems for the compatriots of Thorvaldsen. I remember best of all a sweaty crowd clinging to the quay like lizards, and tall wheels of a gig slowly creaking forward between freight and people. The Italian harbour of Baroque times was an everlasting promenade, frequently the final destination set at the end of a city's corso, with its scenery peopled by actors who on their rope ladders performed tricks as amusing as Punchinello's on his trapeze. No maritime scene was as refined however as the Ripetta by the Tiber.

People of leisure nestle in the embrace of its lines. And what a background for tender elegies, farewell scenes, deserted lovers. *Le jeu de l'amour et du hazard* has given us various sketches of such episodes by the Roman quay, and it would be a pity not to include them in the picture. The French language master, living at 31, Piazza di Spagna, has closed his door to his daughter's suitor. Casanova, who is sorry for Barbaruccia, one day meets her unhappy lover and goes for a walk with him past Ripetta. "When I noticed that he was gazing upon the waters of the Tiber with distracted eyes, I feared an act of desperation, and in order to calm him I said that I would ask for news of his beloved ..." [29]. Just the outline of two figures on the surging steps. Forty-five years later, in April 1788, Goethe went down to the same harbour to say farewell to "the lovely girl from Milan" who had made him so happy up in Castel Gandolfo. When he left her lodging and came out on to the street, his coachman had gone and a small boy had been sent to fetch him. So he was granted another moment. "She looked out of the window on the mezzanine floor of a splendid house where she was staying. It wasn't very high up and it seemed as if I could touch her hand." They talked for a moment. Engravings (and the old photograph reproduced here) confirm that only one of the two large houses at Ripetta had a mezzanine. This was directly above the ground floor. Maddalena Reggi showed herself that day in one of those low windows above the shops. And from here she looked out every day: "For a long time now I have seen ships come and go, unload and load; it is very entertaining, and I often wonder where they all come from and where they all go" [30].

As will be remembered, the building of Porto di Ripetta was started after the collapse of masonry in the Colosseum. The ruin provided the material for modern architecture. And then for the second time in the year of the earth tremors the very soil of Rome brought forth new features for the city. In September 1703, when excavating the garden of the Missionary Fathers (Via della Missione), an ancient pedestal and a granite column of very large dimensions were unearthed. Reliefs and inscriptions on the plinth proved that the column was erected in honour of Emperor Antoninus Pius [31]. Clement XI was delighted with his antiquity found in the middle of Rome and wished to have the monument set up in front of the Court of Justice at Montecitorio, this being close to the place where it was discovered. Carlo Fontana and his son Francesco were able to overcome all the technical difficulties involved in raising such enormous pieces. While this took place other suggestions were advanced for the siting of the column. One of these was the idea of incorporating it in the new work around the Fontana di Trevi, which had also been damaged during the earthquake.

It would be interesting to know more about this project. In my opinion it is indeed possible to obtain authentic information about it by comparing a couple of documents not read in mutual context before. The sculptor Pietro Bracci, who was later responsible for the important part of the sculpture for the Fontana di Trevi, left behind not only his own drawings but also a sketch, which his biographer [32] refers to as Clement XI's project, without however producing definite proofs and without being in a position to determine the originator. The pertinent drawing is produced here (Pl. 130c), but unfortunately only from an engraving. By a lucky chance a bright Frenchman interested in art, M. de Blainville, who was in Rome during the business of the column, obtained information on the spot and has passed it on in an account of his travels, published 1737 [33]. This seems to have been overlooked by the history of architecture. De Blainville reports that one day when visiting Carlo Fontana he saw his design for a *Piazza Clementina* which the Pope had wanted executed near the Fontana di Trevi. The French traveller's description is exhaustive and concise. It runs like this: "As the Albani device is three hills, three such made of white marble have been erected with a statue of the holy Clement on top. The *place* is to be oval, surrounded by splendid palaces *d'une égale symmetrie*. From the three hills set in a large basin there are to run three streams, because there is an abundant provision of water, the best drinking water, to feed them, and as the saying goes in Rome: he who has once drunk of this water will come to drink it again."

While we, in passing, take note of such an early assertion of the magic powers of Fontana di Trevi, we must admit to an almost exact accordance between de Blainville's description and the drawing mentioned. This must then be a reproduction of Carlo Fontana's project from 1703 or the year after. As the plan is missing we can only assess the work with reservation. His siting of a Piazza Clementina betrays the breadth of vision of the architect who wanted to improve Bernini's St. Peter's Square.

After all, Trevi is at the foot of the Quirinal and it was clearly Fontana's idea to provide the papal residence with something like a lower forecourt with connection to the Via della Dataria. We must remember that Monte Cavallo still had no monumental buildings on it. De Blainville said that the Clementine square was oval. The shape of the basin might also indicate this same figure. But it seems unlikely that the whole periphery was ever intended to be completely rebuilt, for in that case such a rich and relatively modern piece of architecture as S. S. Vincenzo e Anastasio would have to be pulled down. There can be little doubt that one long side of the square, presumably the one which now contains the Palazzo Poli, was to curve in the form of a large niche. If de Blainville's words can be trusted, then the opposite long side would have been correspondingly concave, resulting in the intended oval. The two niches facing each other need not have been connected in their entirety. On the transverse axis, where streets emerge and where the church in question stands, gaps could be left in the formation and in this way serious sacrifices could have been avoided. The large hemicycle as a motif for a square, we know from the plan intended for the Montecitorio, and Pietro da Cortona had used it in a project for adjusting the west side of the Piazza Colonna, where it was also to be the background for a fountain [34]. In the execution, however, little similarity can be found between the two architects' plans [35]. The ellipse was particularly dear to Fontana because of the Colosseum and Bernini's St. Peter's Square.

The construction of the Piazza Clementina was never to be done. But the antique column which Fontana intended to set up at the Acqua Vergine was an indication of the destiny of the Fontana di Trevi.

II

The previous history of the Spanish Steps is long and involved, and it is necessary to delve into it before we ascend this wonderful creation to look across Rome. Many factors, both topographical and individual, political and economic, were contributory to the making of *la Scalinata di Piazza di Spagna*. And they agree only with difficulty. Historians have spent much time trying to elucidate the matter. A comprehensive monograph by Pio Pecchiai provides plenty of local material and summarizes in a scholarly fashion the results of earlier research [36]. Here we shall put forward a new interpretation, based to some extent on sources which have been overlooked or not fully interpreted.

The first motivation for the creation of La Scalea was concern about the traffic. The fashionable church of S. S. Trinità dei Monti had an inadequate access from the streets from where the congregation in their carriages mainly came, namely the Piazza di Spagna and the Corso. The piazza at the foot of the hill on which Holy Trinity Church stands was in the Baroque period a fashionable meeting place and the centre of the foreign quarter. Here were the best inns, here the most expensive carriages halted. Between the square and the high level of the church there was a gently rising slope planted with trees here and there (Pl. 126). Only people on foot could use it; coaches from the city had to make a long detour up through the Via Gregoriana or Via Sistina to get to Monte Pincio which lay past Trinità dei Monti. The inevitable procession of vehicles which took place in the Via del Babuino or in the Corso itself, going from there through the Via dei Condotti to the Piazza di Spagna, could not get from the latter by any direct route to the road which runs along the verge of the sloping gardens.

It had been a long-standing wish to adapt the slope and include it as a monumental element in the network of Roman streets. Since the Renaissance period it had been known that a large structure of steps and terraces leading up to the *collis hortorum* had once existed here [37]. Plans to renew the ancient tradition hung fire until another motivation made them more immediate – a mixed motivation, composed of political and aesthetic reasons. The Trinità church was entrusted to the French order of Minims and was under the official protection of the diplomatic representative of the French government in Rome. The church's titular cardinal was a Frenchman. The Gauls also had the undisputed right to dispense justice not only in the church precincts on the ridge of the hill, but also on the slope, indeed in the whole of the northern part of the Piazza di Spagna. As the southern part of it was under the authority of Spanish police, which was imposed by His Catholic Majesty's hirelings and supervised by the ambassador in the Palazzo di Spagna opposite the unprotected hillside, it can come as no surprise to anybody that the locality became a battlefield for ambitious spirits. The papal government watched with covetous eyes and looked anxiously to its shaky prestige.

The French had the best cards for they kept a tight hand on their rights over the area. And they played their hand well. The steps, which the whole world calls Spanish, were erected on French initiative. Or rather initiatives. First we shall unravel them one by one and then plait them together.

In Louis XIV's time there lived in Rome a gentleman from Le Mans by name of Etienne Gueffier; he had come here in 1626 as a secretary to the legation and in his later years he became their *Chargé d'affaires*. As such he superintended the French institutions, especially the national church S. Luigi dei Francesi with its hospice and S. S. Trinità dei Monti and its monastery. Gueffier lived in the Piazza di Spagna and the slope was always before his eyes. His old legs knew the steep paths well and in the end he conceived of a plan to defray the expenses for a flight of steps; this would glorify the French church and serve as a memorial to himself. He drew up a will on January 1st 1655 in which, among other things, he provided that after his death 20,000 scudi should accrue to the Minims and be used for a *cordonata*. Gueffier left nothing to chance and stipulated that the steps should be built "according to the model (i. e. design) appended to the will, or a more suitable plan to be produced by the same architect who made the project in question". The name of this architect was Orazio Torriani [38].

This was a handsome endowment, and the will was of course contested by the inevitable nephew who felt cheated by his rich uncle. Etienne Gueffier could however depart this life on July 30th 1660, half an hour before midnight, more or less certain that sometime in the future he had secured a dignified approach for the French church on Trinity Hill. The subsequent court case between the monastery and the nephew (actually the son of the old diplomat's niece) ended in a compromise which reduced the sum for the steps to 10,000 scudi, still a good basis to work on. Further developments in the affair are characteristic of the fate of good intentions in this world of ours; the only solid thing about Gueffier's dispositions was the capital sum itself. His express wish that a design by

Torriani should be used, sank into oblivion, and the drawing is not known. But the money multiplied in the hands of the Minims and this was very necessary, since the basic capital was far from sufficient to cover the expenses of such an exacting architectural work.

Having now discussed the Gueffier episode, we shall concentrate on the next stage in the affair. This is linked with the name of Mazarin. The Cardinal-Minister wrote to his agent Benedetti in Rome in 1660 ordering him to have the best architects submit designs for a *scalinata,* the cost of which was estimated not to exceed 80,000 scudi. Mazarin, who knew about Gueffier's will, was not of course acting in his own interest, and being something of a miser was not going to delve into his own purse either, nor was he, by this gesture, "preparing an asylum for himself in Rome" [39], but he did it on Louis XIV's behalf, wishing to provide the Great Power of France in the papal city with "la gloire". Who were the architects that the cardinal's intermediary approached? Rumour has it that Benedetti chose "four young men" and set them to work [40]. A strange way to proceed when such an enormous sum was to be devoted to the glory of the Sun King. It is known that François Dorbay presented a design, and this pupil of Levau may have been one of the young architects mentioned [41]. We also know of an anonymous drawing bearing Mazarin's coat of arms, and perhaps its originator was another one of them. So this was a pretty lean harvest for the cardinal's talent scouts in Rome. However, there does exist a project which can with certainty be ascribed to the initiative of the French statesman, but this is so impressive that it is not likely to be the work of a beginner in this field. The design, which is in the library of the Vatican (Coll. Chigiana) and has been reproduced by Hempel [42], bears Mazarin's coat of arms and at the bottom right the legend *dell' Abbate Benedetti*. Hempel has correctly interpreted this as meaning that the design was submitted by Benedetti, not conceived by him, but omits to give the name of the artist responsible for the plan. Pecchiai shows less caution and suggests that Benedetti may have drafted it with Dorbay's assistance [43]. A very gratuitous deduction, but in its conclusion obviously incorrect.

This is where it is important to take a closer look at Benedetti. Abbot Elpidio Benedetti, of good Roman stock, had been Mazarin's secretary before he became his diplomatic agent in Rome, specializing in artistic matters. He was later to work for Lionne and Colbert in the same way. We must, for good reasons, point out (and this has not been done in previous arguments about the early history of *la Scalinata*), that this extremely cultured man was a genuine admirer and a close friend of Bernini [44]. In 1645 and the following years, he had, on Mazarin's behalf, tried to persuade Bernini, the great Roman, to enter the service of the court of Versailles, but without success. In 1664, when the rebuilding of the Louvre was on the agenda, he recommended Bernini to Colbert with such fervour that the undertaking was accomplished this time [45]. Benedetti can truly take the greater part of the credit that Bernini was given the opportunity of creating his magnificent architectural projects in Paris.

It must not be overlooked that our abbot had himself taken a hand in building in Rome. He had a very remarkable villa erected outside the Porta S. Pancrazio called *Il Vascello*, because it was a fanciful rendition of ship motifs and full of whimsy. It was also full of French ornamentation, and the arms of the Bourbons as well as Henri IV's, Louis XIII's and Louis XIV's busts were included in the façade. This architectural abortion probably came into the world on the express instructions of Benedetti. "Il Vascello", destroyed during the French attack on Rome in 1849, is a monument to a lover of art, whose face was turned to Paris but whose heart was in Rome [46].

The Villa Benedetta received a notable visitor in 1687, namely Nicodemus Tessin the Younger. His diary of his stay in Rome has been published, but only in extracts [47]. In the original there is a description, not publicized until now, of a work of art in the villa which interested Tessin tremendously. In translation his account runs as follows: "The Villa Benedetta, belonging to an abbot who has been secretary to His Eminence Cardinal Mazarin, contains divers curiosities among which is the model which *Cavaliere* Bernini made for the slope of Monte della Trinità. This is a fine composition designed for the ascent of carriages. A is the steps to the Trinità dei Monti church, B is the pedestal for an equestrian statue of the King of France who desires to bear the expense of the whole structure so that his statue can be erected, but this the pope has been loathe find in Juvara's *œuvre* certain general bases for the truth of Maffei's statement; the architect often introduced the subject of the picturesque *cordonata* in such a diverting way that the Spanish Steps are immediately brought to mind [56]. But of course one cannot put forward a convincing argument on the basis of stylistic similarities of a general nature. We must seek our reasons historically, and to do this it is necessary to undertake an excursion to the Tiburtine hills. It has never been done before with this purpose in mind, so we set off happily to investigate.

Up there, near Poli, stands a villa called Catena. To a Dane it might seem that the history of its building beats that of any other Italian villa, for the cost of the erection was in fact defrayed by stout Jutlanders in the time of Christian IV. The builder, Torquato II Conti (died 1638), was one of Wallenstein's generals and as such General Officer Commanding in Jutland 1627–1629 during the Thirty Years War. An inscription on the villa's wall establishes that the general had built his country residence out of the rich booty he had obtained from the defeated Danes after the battle of Aalborg on October 18th 1627 (*Copia Ad Alborgum De Victis Gothis, Norvegis, Danis ... Die XVIII Octobris Anno MDCXXVII ..... Pecunia Ex Captivis In Ea Expeditione Commutatio ... Vinetum Fecit Suum*).

When Innocent XIII became pope in 1721 the Villa Catena was owned by his brother, Prince Giuseppe Lotario Conti, Duke of Poli, a descendant of the famous member of the Imperial war council. Papa Conti did not have a *villeggiatura* during the first year of his pontificate, but in March 1722 it was learnt that he proposed to stay in the Villa Catena during the summer [57]. It was about this time that his brother began to make preparations for this, i.e. modernizing and decorating the country seat, for we hear in April that he was *continuing* his building operations. They had no doubt been started in 1721. The Pope's visit did not after all take place in the spring of 1722, so building was continuing through the month of June [58]. In December of the same year the Duke was in residence [59], but it was not until April 1723 that it was finished [60]. Innocent visited his family villa on April 26th and spent a week there [61].

An on the spot investigation enables us to understand this most extraordinary building. In front of the highly situated casino, which is rather like a fortress [62], terraces have been constructed in combination with ramps and flights of steps. These surround a nymphaeum at the bottom. An inscription above the basin dedicates the large structure to the Pope. We quote it word for word:

>INNOCENTII XIII PONT. OPT. MAX.
>FAELICI FAUSTOQVE ADVENTUI
>JOSEF LOTTARIUS DE COMITIBUS
>D (AT), D (ONAT), D (EDICAT)
>DIE XXVI APRILIS MDCCXXIII.

It may in addition be noted that the stepped front of the Villa Catena in its important features is obviously derived from Bernini's project for the Spanish Steps. One is immediately struck by the nymphaeum and the two convex ramps which enclose the composition on the outside and were intended as an approach. The structure is now in disrepair but the original is verified in its details by a contemporary painting [63]. It was an inspired work; no Italian country mansion except Caprarola did in those days have an entrance from below on such a magnificent scale. Assuming the correctness of our observations, it could be demonstrated that the Duke of Poli and Innocent XIII used Bernini's long-neglected project immediately *before* the design of the Spanish Steps was decided upon. The question now is, which architect provided the version used at Poli? For there is no doubt that it is an adaptation. On this hypothesis we venture to suggest that Juvara was the man. This is supported by an important circumstance which has already been mentioned: it was in 1722 that Juvara dedicated a publication on aristocratic escutcheons to the Duke, which clearly indicates that the latter was a client of his. We must also remember that Juvara had worked for the King of Portugal, who was very close to the Pope. There is indeed some reason to suppose that Juvara's design for the steps in 1719 was roughed out as a variation of Bernini's project, which the monk from the Trinità monastery must have been familiar with.

However that may be, we have some justification for keeping an eye on these possibilities in our continued search for the real author of the

Spanish Steps, this man who remains an enigma. Brilliant works are usually created by brilliant people, but nothing obliges them to leave proof of it behind. Bernini has also at times concealed his authorship.

Back in Rome, in the Curia, the affair now entered its decisive phase. This is in obvious continuation of the building of Villa Catena. The fact of the case in Innocent XIII's first years was that two architects led the field. Neither of them were particularly outstanding, but both had powerful influences working for them. The war of the steps was fundamentally a struggle between political bodies, not between artistic principles. On one side was the papal administration, supported by Rome's building commission (*il Tribunale delle Strade*) – this was the local, arch-Roman authority. On the other stood the French Ambassador as the protector of the monastery and its terrain, as well as being the executor for Gueffier's will – he was the spokesman for the French desire for glory. The former power supported Alessandro Specchi, the architect for *la fabbrica di S. Pietro* and municipal architect, an experienced man who had long ago shown his competence by his solution to a similar problem, the flights of steps at Porto di Ripetta. The French candidate was the official architect attached to the Trinità monastery, Francesco de Sanctis. He had no reputation but technically had first claim for erecting the French monastery's *cordonata* [64].

Pecchiai states that de Sanctis carried the day because Innocent at the beginning of his pontificate set out to please France, whose representative was able to intimidate him [65]. But the problem is not as simple as all that. In fact there is a way of delving further into the matter. We can follow the pope's craftiness through overhearing snatches of his conversation with various authorities, thanks to sources of which Pecchiai had no knowledge. A flood of light has been shed on this very dramatic building affair, particularly during its last and decisive phase. We can follow it week by week, right up to the climax.

A prelude took place in April 1722. According to Poerson the pope had by then suggested to the General of the Minims that the French fathers should now set about things without delay [66]. This explicit wish was expressed at the very time Prince Conti was building his pontifical steps at the Villa Catena, and it gives food for thought. In August 1723 the

French Ambassador, Abbé de Tencin, approached the Holy Father. During an audience the discussion came around to Palazzo Poli and Fontana di Trevi. This was an opportune moment and Tencin himself has related how he made use of it: "I said to the Pope that I had hopes that the steps might be the first public work to be undertaken during his reign." Innocent caught hold of his hands and said: "Would you like to know what has so far prevented the work being carried out? It is the fact that former popes have not had confidence in the French ambassadors here. As for me, I have confidence in you. You and I, we two shall build the steps, we understand one another. I will choose a plan with you as well as an architect. Until that time, you in conference with the General of the Minims, who is a Frenchman and my friend, should embark on ordering the necessary building materials." This was indeed an impressive conversation. Following on this Tencin asked Louiv XV for further instructions, and makes it a cardinal point that the matter should be kept clear of interference by the Pope's ministers [67]. On September 21st *le Bienaimé* requested a detailed plan, accompanied by one or more "models". The one the Pope preferred was to carry his mark. And, wrote King Louis, "I will then mark the one I have decided on" [68]. The stage was set for dignified decisions at top level.

But down at the level where things were to be decided, all those involved were at variance with each other. A diplomatic despatch of September 28th to the French Foreign Minister lifts a corner of the veil covering this lively affair. Some days previously a special "congregation" had been assembled by the Pope to adjudicate the disputed plans. Participants in the meeting were several cardinals, the Duke of Poli and other relations of the Pope (worth noting), a number of prelates and Roman patricians (also rather strange), together with the General from Trinità dei Monti. The meeting voted unanimously to reject Specchi's project on the grounds that it was in bad taste and also because it was too expensive. All the same – in spite of the fact that Tencin and others were strongly opposed to the Roman architect, "they" (i. e. the Pope) decided to implement it. According to our informant this shocking decision was brought about by Monsignore Giudice, the papal maggiordomo, called *le protecteur de ce méchant ouvrier* meaning the valiant Specchi [69].

129. *The Spanish Steps. The "theatre".*

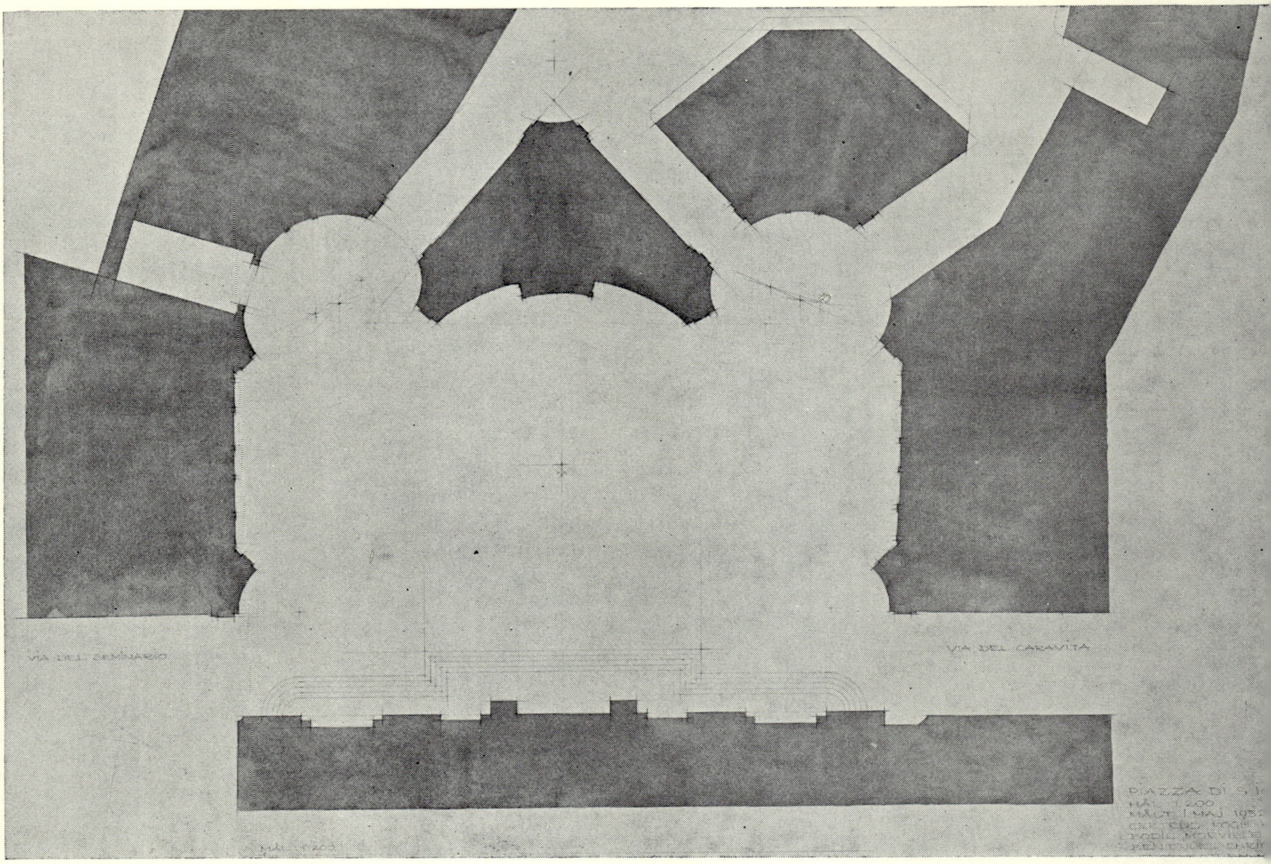

130a. *Plan of Piazza di S. Ignazio. Survey 1953.*

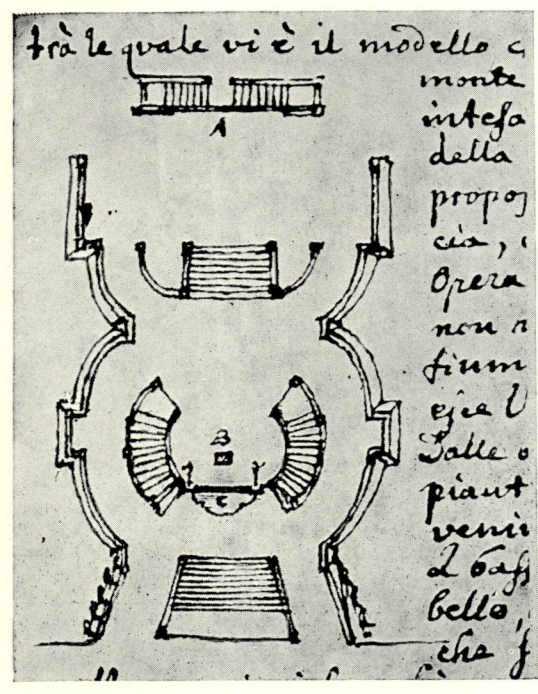

130b. *Copy by N. Tessin the Younger of Bernini's sketch for the Spanish Steps.*

130c. *Drawing for the Fontana di Trevi by Carlo Fontana.*

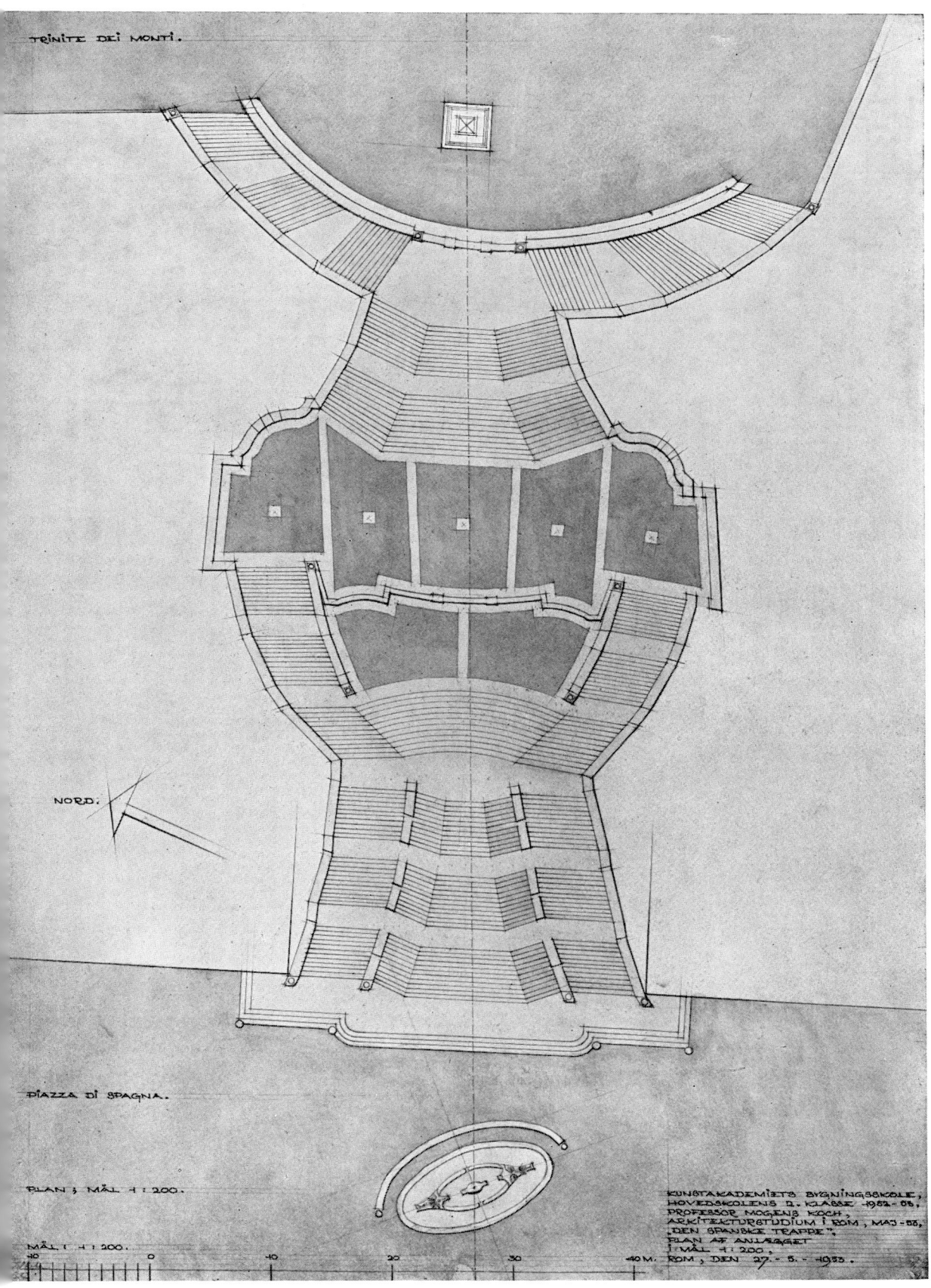

131. *Plan for the Spanish Steps. Survey 1953.*

132. *The Spanish Steps.*

The instigator of this daring intrigue was a difficult man to deal with. Giudice was rich, came from a powerful family and was experienced in artistic matters. He it was who had supervised the construction of Specchi's Porto di Ripetta. Once when Cardinal de Polignac had a look at his collections and stopped to admire a Raphael, Giudice made a point of having it placed in the Cardinal's carriage the moment His Eminence was leaving [70]. Obliging circumstances!

Despite all this – the major-domo lost this time, much to his exasperation. During the following two weeks all the cards in his hand gradually had to be relinquished. On October 12th two reports were sent from the French headquarters to Versailles. In one, from Tencin to Louis XV, it was stated that the Pope's final decision was expected at any moment. In the meanwhile he desired that foundations be laid, since they could be used in any case, but this Tencin had turned down. It could safely have been done, for at this point Innocent presumably knew the result [71]. In the other letter of the same date (from the consul de la Chausse to the Foreign minister in Paris) it states in so many words that the Pope had finally decided on de Sanctis' design and desired him to take on the work. We also learn that Marchese Theodoli had offered to assist the architect mentioned with his good advice. This aristocratic builder was always busy-bodying. In this instance he was acting in the interest of the Pope, his own relative [72].

How this sudden change in the affair came to pass is explained in the despatch which Tencin sent to his king on October 15th, if read properly. The abbot reported the outcome, of which he had been informed during an audience with Papa Conti, in the following words: "The matter of the steps has been decided in a way that will be most pleasing to Your Majesty, since all will depend on Your Majesty's orders and no papal minister shall have anything to do with the work ..." There had been many intrigues (the ambassador is shocked) even in the choice of the design; *il Maggiordomo* and *il Presidente delle Strade* had a candidate in common. "But I," says Tencin "have thwarted their machinations." And then comes a passage of great importance, quoted word for word (the italics are my own). *"I have had* a *new* plan drawn up by the Minims' architect in which *I* made use of all the best suggestions (*les meilleurs observations*) which have previously been put forward and which were most to the Pope's taste. This project has enjoyed the approbation of His Holiness" [73].

We cannot deny that Tencin's self-satisfied account is very instructive. It gives us to understand that with de Sanctis, Tencin obviously called the tune. The architect's plan which had been approved is, without mincing matters, defined as an eclectic work. Tencin knew of the earlier plans as also did de Sanctis. The information that Tencin and his tool accommodated themselves to "the Pope's taste" is particularly significant. This establishes that Conti had made up his mind. Did he perhaps have a plan taken from an existing prototype? It is emphasized that every allowance had been made for the Pope's "taste" in de Sanctis' final version – with a guided pen.

Let us imagine the scene – an interior in the Quirinal with two figures. The two cunning old diplomats are sitting there bluffing each other, covertly, simulating frankness, flattering and tempting. They are agreed on one thing: to keep the Curia out of it. Who won this game of poker played for the most celebrated monument of Roman Baroque? The penultimate hand went to the ambassador, the French side, French money; the French choice of architect for the work was sneaked from under the Roman noses. This outcome, the Bourbons' triumph, was reported amid fanfares to Louis XV. But the last hand was won by the shrewd Roman pontifex because the steps were built according to a design adapted to his personal wishes. It was *his* favourite ideas which form the nucleus of the project, whatever the name of the architect may have been. Tencin boasted of having cooked the Pope's goose by flattering his taste. Innocent laughed up his sleeve, for his taste was the trump card.

Abbé de Tencin then quickly despatched the plans to Versailles. The accompanying letter is delightful. He commended the Pope's determination, imagining that it was of benefit to himself. And he quoted the following statement by Innocent: "Of course nobody has yet succeeded in putting a ring through my nose, as happens to oxen in Italy which are to be led; nevertheless I am reproached for letting Abbé de Tencin make me do what he wants." Just remember, this is Tencin himself making this reference, bragging to Louis XV. Did it not really dawn on him that Pope's words were full of malicious irony? It is perfectly correct to say that Innocent eluded the nose-ring his court wanted to lead him by – so he could graze in peace. But Tencin without noticing put a ring through his own nose. And the ambassador had no sensation of this adornment.

Subsequent events are quickly told. When Louis XV examined the three drawings submitted by de Sanctis and saw the Pope's mark on the best and most thorough of them (A) he, as a true chevalier, put his sign of approval at the side of the Holy Father's. The drawing is now in the archives of the French Foreign Ministry [74]. This authorization took place at the beginning of November 1723 [75]. Before the end of the month the foundation stone had been laid and the work commenced. "If people continue with the same zeal," wrote Poerson to D'Antin on December 7th, "there are good reasons for believing that the Pope, who is very desirous of seeing the building finished, will have this pleasure within a short time" [76]. But Innocent was to be disappointed, for he died before this. In 1725 the French fathers, who were now short of money, stopped the half-finished work [77]; all the same an inscription on the steps gives that year as the date when the work was completed – for this was *Anno Santo*.

La Scalinata was not fully completed until 1726. But the rejoicings were short-lived. In September 1728 a part of the retaining wall for the top terrace collapsed and the whole edifice threatened to cave in [78]. The fathers brought a case against de Sanctis, but otherwise let things take their course. *Un mauvais ouvrage,* grumbled Montesquieu in 1729 [79]; "carelessly done," declared de Brosses ten years later. It was not until 1731 that the work of restoration was started, the French authorities having consulted Valvassori and Fuga [80]. In one place there was not only talk simply of a restoration but also of a totally new structure, and this was the terrace wall at the end of Via di S. Sebastianello. Pecchiai has strangely enough overlooked the fact that this section of the structure, with its monumental niche on the visual axis of the Via della Croce, can clearly be ascribed to a very famous architect. Cardinal de Polignac, Tencin's successor as French Ambassador, had obtained from Rauzzini a statement with a rough estimate. In this document, dated March 3rd 1731 [81], the architect introduces himself as *Architetto di detto luogo* (i. e. the Minims' church and monastery). This official information can be interpreted in no other way than that Rauzzini had become the successor of the compromised de Sanctis as the duly appointed architect for the establishment (and the steps). The information about this – not fully used by Rauzzini's latest biographer – is interesting. It comes as a surprise that Pecchiai [82] can refer to "il Rauzino" as a person of whom "no architectural work of any repute has been preserved"; he clearly refuses to recognize "Filippo Cavaliere Rauzino" (which is the signature on the document) unless he is called "Raguzzini". It seems quite obvious that Roman "Rococo"'s greatest artist did indeed leave his imprint on its proudest work – if only in the wings. The niche portal (Pl. 128) need not be ashamed of his name, or of being seen. It is meant and designed to be viewed from a distance, situated as it is right at the top of a long ascending prospect. This is why the triglyph capitals are so drastically enlarged and the broken pediment so enormous. Its visual effect carries a long way, right down to the Corso. It is strange that Rauzzini's side niche became the only part of La Scalea's entire architecture which can be observed in its full impressiveness from Rome's main thoroughfare – and is frequently overlooked, as is the architect's name.

As shown by the above information, the implemented project for the Spanish Steps was a collective effort. De Sanctis was its executor and supervised on the site. The general outlines and the inspired features were borrowed from others. We cannot give chapter and verse for the different contributions, for we do not know how comprehensive and how tangible the borrowings were. A great deal would be gained if we knew of an authentic draft by Specchi, for his share in it might well have been full of character. We know that Loret attributed a drawing of the steps to Specchi, but with doubtful justification. In its execution it resembles so exactly a design which is ascribed by the same historian to Cipriani – so much so that one and the same architect must have drawn them both. It is difficult to understand why Specchi has a greater claim than Cipriani (or a third, unknown architect) [83]. There are some grounds for conjecturing with Hempel that the elegant wave-like motion in the rows of steps of la Scalinata might have been influenced by the originator of the Ripetta harbour [84].

There can be no question that the structure at the Villa Catena had an influence. Here, Innocent discovered a composition, designed in honour of his family and himself, which could be taken as a last dress rehearsal for la Scalinata. We have already put forward arguments that Juvara might have provided a plan for the Villa Catena. Furthermore, the circumstance that the approved drawing for Scala di Spagna has turned out to be a collective product, strengthens the probability of a sketch by Juvara being among its components. The circumstances might have been that the principal idea inherent in the design which Juvara is supposed to have sketched in 1719 was used in two instances, suitably adapted: 1) for the structure at the Villa Catena (1721–1723): 2) in la Scalinata in the Piazza di Spagna (1723ff.). In the latter case this could have been the leaven which helped this dough of suggestions, already kneaded together but still heavy, to rise and prove. For one thing is certain: the project actually used differs from all the others by its supreme rhythm, its swelling lines. Not merely the motifs but an *imponderabile* of artistic sense sets it apart. One can well believe that the swift strokes of a Juvara brought the idea of a Bernini into full play in a free and fitting manner.

Specchi could easily have brought the steps up to the level where the scene becomes all-embracing and the work comes into its own. Its individuality lies at the very heart of it – *above* the stepped frontal approach, *below* the upper landing, which is a traditional motif (used in Specchi's Ripetta, in front of S. S. Domenico e Sisto, as well as in numerous terraced gardens). But what about de Sanctis? We are very unwilling to push him to one side. As a stage manager he had shown talent. Is his sympathetic insight due to the fact that he was schooled by Juvara earlier on? We have pointed out before that his only known work previous to the Spanish Steps, the façade for S. S. Trinità dei Pellegrini (1723), probably was an adaptation of the great Sicilian's drawings. It is tempting to surmise that on yet another occasion de Sanctis was chosen to put into practice the designs of the absent Juvara. Perhaps at the Villa Catena – before doing so at the Piazza di Spagna? We dare go no further in our search, but now turn to the Steps as they rise before us.

The scale drawing (Pl. 131), made by some young Danish architects, gives the outline. The figure is crooked and lopsided and bulges like a baluster. Plates 129 and 132 show the shape of the figure from two important angles. We shall not give any detailed description, but let the illustrations speak for themselves. There are so many other pictures to supplement them, which are frequently reproduced in the literature. The best is Piranesi's engraving.

We see from the plan that the vital composition is built up on the rhythm 1:2. The scheme can be set out as follows: one middle flight – *pause* (landing, called *teatro,* with rows of steps as in an amphitheatre) – two lateral flights – *pause* (wide landing, called *piazzone*) – one middle flight – *pause* (*caesura* at the terrace wall) – two lateral flights – extended *final pause* on the top landing. This alternating effect again produces the basic number three – no doubt an allusion to the fact that the structure leads up to the church of the Holy Trinity. In an anonymous explanation of an unknown project, the author expressly mentions that the figure three has this meaning in the composition of la Scalinata [85]. It is repeated again and again; the lowest frontal flight is divided by it both horizontally and vertically; in the concavity of the "theatre" the division comes to the fore, the upper pair of lateral flights is divided into three sections like the lower, the corresponding flights of the theatre being included, and the last full flight has three facets. But although the key to the figure 3 is carefully forged and of some size, it is concealed from the observer. To his eyes and beneath his feet it spreads out in a delightful free play.

One is gradually raised by all these steps to a world bathed in light. It feels like a procession to a banquet behind a balustrade by Tiepolo. One is conveyed down by curving ramps, finding one's feet on a level plane, washed onwards by the surge of steps, once again to find repose as one walks across a disciplined level – until finally, by an increased rhythm, one is borne forward and down into the Piazza di Spagna. The architecture of the Steps has absorbed us, the system expands and then contracts, we feel the strong calm beating of its pulse and we are enveloped in something mighty and vibrant and warm. I cannot imagine that a person of artistic disposition could possibly walk up these amazing steps for the first time without feeling influenced by them and know a feeling of being set free. Hardly anybody is ever likely to be unaffected by their spell.

This structure is called simply *la Scalea* by the local population. For them they are the true Roman Steps, not the "Spanish". And this is the case. La Scalinata della Trinità dei Monti has no equal, not even outside Rome. Other cities have majestic stepped structures which have a rich scenic effect in the townscape, but none of these, as far as I can see, are comparable with la Scalea. The endless steps up to the cathedral in Gerona is a magnificent motif, but the Spanish church stifles the life of the street. Some people have suggested Bom Jesus do Monte on the hill outside Braga, the Rome of Portugal, but without justification; the steps up to this church are a decorative pilgrim's way, like many others built during the Rococo period, but it is certainly not urban art and does not in the slightest resemble la Scalea [86]. Nor has the handsome cordonata between the houses in front of S. Giovanni in Modica (Sicily) any real relationship to the Spanish Steps, either in their shape or usage. Many other examples which are supposed to be analogous must be rejected.

The reason for this can be explained. The great originality of the Roman structure springs from its complex and unusual function. The most frequently emphasized elements in it are really the least characteristic. Certainly the Steps are constructed as a *point-de-vue* for the Via dei Condotti and its continuation further back, but the effect is most noticeable on a map, and the theme as such is elementary in the Rome of Baroque. The effect of the Steps belongs to the Piazza di Spagna, and only there can it be seen in its entirety. Then again it is true that it serves as a dais for its church, but S. S. Trinità is not vigorous enough to absorb the Steps. It is altogether strange how lightly the religious side is emphasized. Tencin's attempt to embellish the site with statues of saints carved by French artists was stopped (perhaps because both the sculptors and models were his countrymen [87]), and there is not a single religious symbol to strike the eye; only the names of various dignitaries are apparent. Strange as it may seem – no incense hovers over the Minims' precious steps, erected as they were by the efforts of three popes, beneath the zealous gaze of various cardinals and with the approval of *le Roi Très-Chrétien*. The public quite calmly took over the Steps in a true Roman fashion. Among the driving forces responsible for the work and which made it a *macchina* without parallel, traffic was the strongest. And note well, traffic of a very special kind.

Traffic here was mostly a matter of marking time. The passers-by were in no hurry. Progress over the hill to and from the city was in those days so limited that in the end it was decided to omit the outer ramps for the carriages. The essential function of the Steps was to connect Rome's most popular promenades: a lower one among the cafés and shops in the Piazza di Spagna, an upper one in the peaceful gardens, along the walls of the monastery and the Villa Medici. The Steps carried loungers from one level to the other, and were therefore made both slow and easy. One could say that la Scalea was constructed mainly as a Corso for pedestrians, a rising promenade with places for repose. The task was unique, the solution should match this – and it does – demonstratively. The elevated plateau in the middle took on the atmosphere from the two planes they connected – the fashionable world mounted the Steps in a leisurely way to mingle with the rustic idyll above; it was marking time with ceremony and grace. The Steps with all their meanderings were in themselves a public pleasure-garden in stone, both formal and sensuous. One rambled at leisure, sat down on the yellow steps, saw and was seen, circulated, posed and dozed. Each step was at one and the same time a bench and a plinth.

This great work of art has a life which has nothing to do with style – the long history of daily life which knows no cry for beauty but accepts being part of it. More than two centuries' traffic by countless pairs of shoes is a silent process which leaves as little trace in the annals of the past as do waves any permanent ripple in the sand. So if we hear no word from dead passers-by it does not mean they were unobservant when they climbed the Steps. They were conscious of them, however vaguely. We find little to impress us on the beaten track of our daily round. Now and again a detail emerges, in the flash of a moment. We are aware of some of the features that have always worked as stimuli and which made the passers-by appreciate the Steps if only for a moment. Two important factors, close at hand, are cubes and spheres. The lower flights of the Steps are divided, as we saw, into three parallel flights, separated by horizontal travertine blocks. Each of these corresponds to the height of five normal steps and viewed collectively, they seem to be stairs reserved for giants, who with long strides aim to leave the rabble behind. As seen by the climber, these boxes beat the rhythm of the relentlessly rising scale. The pauses make them less awe-inspiring and they steady down to a slower beat. There is also the possibility of sitting on the blocks; when going down it is almost impossible not to do so; seen from above, the sun-warmed surfaces invite you to accept them as a cadence of restful seats. The sphere, on the other hand, is a halt sign. There are four of them where the Steps debouch into the Piazza di Spagna. These splendid round stones are borne by pedestals which in their shape seem to be fashioned from metal, and they carry the devices in relief of Louis XV's lily and the eagle of Innocent XIII Conti. On the lowest section of la Scalea even middle-aged gentlemen may be seized with a desire to slide down the ramp and glide out with great aplomb. The four spheres prevent such unseemly progress; they accentuate the exit and entrance with equal dignity. One's hand caresses the smooth stone with delight.

Two identical houses in the Piazza di Spagna provide a frame for the beginning of the Steps, and they were erected by the Minims when older properties had to be rebuilt, without doubt according to designs by de Sanctis; they are contemporary with la Scalinata. You hear people complain that these *palazzetti* confine the approach to the structure and hide its further upward ramifications. An unfair criticism – the houses are meant to narrow the middle flight, they act as a sluice forcing the current upwards and at the same time provide a setting of great benefit to the prospect. The façades themselves have a restrained decoration, very distinguished-looking indeed. As a pair they are excellent corner-stones, as individuals their features are patrician. From the monks' standpoint, these buildings were purposeful, even necessary, for they brought in considerable rents. Large cellars to hold wine and oil had been made under them – some went right under the Steps – and very up-to-date apartments were fitted out upstairs. The owners without a doubt intended them to be used as rented accommodation for visitors of substance. The gamble paid off, for they were eagerly sought after by the upper ten. Princes and noblemen took up their stance at the foot of the Steps and kept an eye on the world from the windows of these fine houses. The Romans soon grasped the meaning of the Steps which were a palliative for their needs. On August 1st 1726 Polignac wrote: "When the great heat is here everybody prefers to spend the nights out of doors, and this place has become more popular than any other because of its beauty and the good air" [88]. At the same time of the year in 1734 – tells Valesio – people danced in the moonlight on *il piazzone* to the music of an orchestra which the Spanish Ambassador, Cardinal Francesco Aquaviva, sent over from his palace. *Il teatro* became a stage and the Steps a nocturnal camping site. During the daytime they were swept by the ladies' full skirted gowns. The swaying of Canterbury bells across the stage and on to the top. "I am convinced that if the ancient Romans could see these steps they would blush for their descendants' architectural style," a cavalier stated in 1730 [89]. But Baron von Pöllnitz was a Saxon. What he meant here was "Gothic taste".

The Jubilee year of 1725 was celebrated in the middle of a decade when artistic excess effervesced in Rome. Never before or since did architecture express itself so ebulliently and graciously as when the heaviness was toned down on the façades of a couple of well-endowed churches and at the meeting places of an appreciative public. Hardly had the Spanish Steps been opened before the Piazza di S. Ignazio took shape. In its spirit the *escalier d'honneur* of the Minims corresponds to the Jesuits' forecourt. And the circumstances leading up to it are also very similar. Like the French fathers of Trinità dei Monti, the fathers of the Society of Jesus wanted to take over an area through the influence of their own architecture, to give their church a proud approach, and they also intended to profit from building houses to let here. It seems amusing to think that the most elegant square in Rome was established by the most militant religious community.

At the beginning of the 1720's the Jesuits wanted to take over the little church of S. Macuto which stood across the road from their great church bearing the name of Ignatius Loyola. There was strategy behind this. A quick look at the map will show the situation clearly: S. Macuto bridges the Jesuits' two large establishments in this district, namely Seminario Romano behind this little church, and the Collegio Romano next to S. Ignazio. Benedict XIII allowed the Society of Jesus to take over S. Macuto, but on certain conditions. They had to undertake the pulling down of the wretched houses opposite S. Ignazio and provide a proper prospect instead. The purchase of the site necessary for this was costly – in the course of a week the good fathers were forced to expend 32,000 scudi [90] – so their intention was of course to obtain the best possible investment. Regard for the decorative was combined with the desire for a fully effective utilization of the site. And this was very limited. So this fairy-tale square took shape in the midst of rugged reality.

On August 14th 1727 Valesio entered in his journal: "Today the Jesuits began to dig the foundations for the *fabbrica* with a tiny square (*con pochissima piazza*) ... and they are employing the Beneventan architect (i. e. Rauzzini) and his design" [91]. In 1729 his *casini nuovi* are included in the census returns, so they must have been occupied by then.

At first sight, the Piazza di S. Ignazio appears to be a perfect synthesis of space and sculpture. Cubes with concave façades are arranged in a symmetrical composition (Pl. 133). If you enter this square at an angle, its transverse siting, which at the back is closed by two prismatic blocks forming a pattern of projections, can be seen as a grouping of skilfully adapted bodies, a play of concavities (Pl. 134). All according to how you feel – you may enjoy the scene in all innocence, like entering a picturesque work of art – or you may appreciate its similarity to a Baroque stage and rejoice at meeting it again, in this case under an open sky. As far as form goes, there is not much difference between the buildings here and the solidity of the clipped hedges in a private garden theatre [92].

Vilh. Wanscher has described the site through a painter's eyes: "The square must be seen in strong summer sunlight, when strange shadows made by the cornices are cast down across the façades' curved surfaces" [93]. And it is almost too inviting to animate the stage with scenes from Goldoni's *Le donne curiose* or make it the setting for an *opera buffa* by Pergolesi or Galuppi. The introductory scene in the "Barber" would find a perfect setting among Rauzzini's spirited houses – Rosina's balcony is all prepared, Figaro could easily appear from round one corner singing, and escape like a cat round another. After the serenade the musicians disperse by the streets in the background: "And so adieu then, good gentlemen ...". Indeed even the tones of the square are lyrical and beautifully varied, changing in shades from orange to pale pink.

It would not be irrelevant to introduce these comedies in the Piazza di S. Ignazio, but it would perhaps be better to extract its basic outline and see it all in its naked beauty. The figure on the drawing-board (Pl. 130a) is very expert and very beautiful, calculated with geometrical skill. It shows clearly that curves made by the walls of the buildings indicate three ellipses; the front of the triangular block is a broad and central ellipse, the two smaller ones are seen at the sides. These last two are not quite symmetrical – contrary to what old, incorrect surveys show [94] – the ovoid concavity to the left is forced by external conditions to be irregular, and it is this little irregularity that confirms that the architect had no intention of forcing his abstract pattern through. It was enough for him to have based it on very precise spacial conceptions, and to have constructed an edifice whose *raison d'être* is only seen piecemeal by the observer – so that the total impression becomes one of caprice.

Synthesizing, the aesthete may characterize Rauzzini's work as an elegant *objet d'art* and consider it polished by its "Rococo". And we could leave it that. But the historian cannot avoid asking: Why is the complex at S. Ignazio the only one of its kind in Rome which makes use of detached prismatic bodies? Why is this sophisticated game being practised here of all places? Should we consider it merely as a reckless individual performance in which the artist let himself go? A certain knowledge of local conditions for building may possibly increase our understanding (in no way reducing our admiration for the artist). It is clear that the originality of the complex is based in principle on a diffused background. If we could imagine this area enclosed by its solid side walls and an uninterrupted wing at one end, cut short by the streets, the square would be considered "normal" (cf. Piazza Lancellotti), and all possibilities for an ingenious system of forms and concavities would be excluded. But the important thing is that the square neither could, nor should, be closed by one building as *fond* – partly because a network of streets at the back had to be respected, partly because such a plan would waste space. The architect was forced to take these factors into account. Speculation in building cuts down space, regard for traffic carves it out. The awkward external circumstances inspired – as often happens – the artistic sense of the architect and made him give of his best. Rauzzini sharpened his instruments, trimmed his blocks so that carriages would be able to drive and turn in *la pochissima piazza* and the streets around.

An added gain was the extremely attractive form both these *"casini nuovi"* took on. This was appreciated by the prosperous tenants and produced an ample income for the Jesuits. Valesio has reported that sarcastic remarks were not lacking from people who had watched the site being excavated and were surprised at the bold experiment. It is an amusing situation: a group of Romans, always ready with their criticism, stand and gaze in bewilderment at the jigsaw puzzle of blocks, at the foundations to Rome's most frequented square. Will all the pieces ever fit together? Neo-Classicism was not content with merely being perplexed with the Piazza di S. Ignazio but regarded the virtuoso's performance as buffoonery. Milizia called them "ridiculous houses looking like chests of drawers". The derogatory term may have given the name to the Via dei Burrò (bureau) which connects the square with the Via di Pietra [95]. You could say that Rauzzini's houses do in some way resemble chests of drawers in "angular Rococo" – in the same way that candlesticks in the French Empire Style resemble antique columns. But it was much worse for a building to resemble a piece of furniture meant for storing nether-garments, than to look like a broken-off piece of temple. For a couple of generations the Jesuits' houses were disregarded and only thought of as antiquated and old playthings. Even Fokker [96] can say patronizingly that the plan "certainly affords amusement to the spectator". The answer to this Victorian utterance is: "We are not amused!" Serious thought was bestowed on it before it took benign shape. It is the obvious outcome.

III

Two Roman poets are now going to lead us to the extravaganza called *Fontana di Trevi*. Once upon a time a citizen from one of Rome's back streets came home from Paris and his friend bombarded him with questions about the strange city up there in the north. Perhaps the testing time came when he was asked: "Say, does the mist of Trevi's water reach as far as there?" (*L'acqua de Trevi, dì, fuma là puro?*) This is a line in a sonnet by Gioacchino Belli. On cool days a haze hangs over the reflecting waters of the fountain and Old Romans look upon it as one of the seven wonders of the world [97]. The fountain certainly seems to be one of them when we stand inside the magic circle of Belli and Rome – as we do now. We receive a poetic impression which makes us think of the fountain as a landscape within a town, a part of nature generating its own climate.

Another poet – also an interpreter of Rome in its own dialect – has left us a shrewd assessment of the fountain's style. This is Pascarella, who one day sat with Carducci on the steps in front of the basin, revelling in the sight, and then remarked: "This may be a work from the eighteenth century, but it looks like the seventeenth" [98]. Pascarella was not appraising the capitals. He meant that the architecture of the fountain and the whole great spectacle was Classical, like one of Racine's plays. And so it is. For it is when you imagine a far-away prospect behind the Trevi fountain in the narrow square – a horizon of Roman hills, a view of heroic columns – that you comprehend the spirit in which it was created. But the fountain's tangible, indeed immediate history, is just as limited as the space which it dominates.

Acqua Virgo rises in the high ground of the Campagna between Tivoli and Palestrina. It runs straight from Antiquity to Rome. At one point in the seventeenth century, as the poet reminded us, the conduit's gushing outflow was included in a fantasy by Bernini. Before 1635 the Virgin's Spring discharged its waters through three outlets in the Piazza di S. Maria in Trivio [99] and it was this year that the fountain was moved to its present position. Urban VIII directed Bernini, who in 1629 had become supervisor for the Acqua Vergine in succession to his father [100], to put forward suggestions for a more lavish design for the fountain with the use of marble from Cecilia Metella's sepulchral monument on the Appian Way. We do not know the artist's plan, but his sketch for one of the details may reflect the idea behind the project. The drawing referred to shows a Neptune figure standing on rocks above a cascade. The god of the sea was to be the lord of the fountain.

But in Bernini's mind the hills of the Campagna were to provide the basin for the waters and their slopes its background. The sound of the miraculous spring was to be echoed in grottoes, its streams were to play among rocks. Thus Bernini was the instigator of the fountain's greatest motifs – and stones from a monument of Antiquity were ready at hand. What he dreamed of creating, later took shape in a different landscape, in the Piazza Navona. Bernini's plan for Trevi was abandoned because of shortage of funds, but hopes of resurrection were kept alive, awaiting only an impulse to become fact. For a long time the fountain retained its simple form. We know it as it was, from a drawing by Lieven Cruyl (1665) [101]. The water is gushing out into a semicircular basin in front of the back wall of the Palazzo Conti. Women are doing their washing in a long brick-built trough at the side.

Then in 1703 there came an unexpected call to action. This was the discovery of the Antoninus Pius column which gave birth to the above mentioned project by Carlo Fontana (p. 320). The design, to some extent, continued the Bernini tradition in that the basis of the scheme, here too, was a sort of artificial cliff landscape. But the motif of the column, which was new, required the fountain to be disengaged from the wall behind it and to be transferred to the middle of the square, as its monument. This imaginative plan had to be given up as it was considered to be on too large a scale and out of keeping with the existing circumstances. These were in fact decisive. The Acqua Vergine poured forth its waters at the base of a wall and it was linked with a certain building, this being the Palazzo Poli. This situation was and remained a factor of constant importance; the spring demanded a specific type of fountain, the wall fountain. It also follows that the owner of the palace would want a say in the architecture which was to adorn his house and be its façade. The moment the call went forth from the master of the Palazzo Poli and he allowed scaffolding to be erected in front of his house, the fountain would have to change its appearance. The aqueduct was the State's, the wall was the Duke's.

The palace's demand for a new design came in 1721 when Innocent

XIII became pope, for it was his family home in Rome and was now owned by his brother Prince Giuseppe Lotario Conti, Duke of Poli, whom we remember from the Villa Catena. The Pope's family feeling is now the decisive factor; he, more than any others, had reasons for wanting to put Clement XI's plan for Trevi into practice, for in this way he would be serving not only the community, but would enhance the glory of his own kith and kin. As early as August 1721 we find him occupied with such thoughts. Poerson wrote: "Since the fountain with Rome's best drinking water is situated at the very Palazzo Conti where the Pope was born (this was incorrect), His Holiness has decided to pull down some wretched houses in the vicinity and to lay out a square and a terrace in combination with the Palazzo Conti" [102]. A few days later we find that the plan with the columns has been discarded, since it would cost 10,000 scudi, and the Treasury was complaining [103]. But the Duke of Poli started having alterations made to his palace, and the idea of enlarging the fountain was not given up and was still being discussed in August 1723 [104]. And then Innocent died on March 7th 1724. Soon afterwards a notice was affixed to the Contis' not yet finished palace containing the following words: "Here contributions are gratefully received to help complete this great building" [105]. The Conti episode had by no means been in vain, for behind the low basin of the Fontana di Trevi there now rose a monumental building, which was not just a simple wall. This front was divided (no doubt with a view to the coming architecture for the fountain) into three sections, two side pavilions and a lower middle section, which for the time being was left unfinished. This disposition ensured that all future designs would be dependent on the wall.

Benedict XIII had a project with sculptured figures drawn up by Benaglia, but the Pope's death put a stop to it and the figures were rejected by his successor [106]. Now at last, the hour of completion for the Fountain of the Virgin was at hand. Clement XII, who was able to ensure an abundant flow of money into his coffers, also cherished the ambition of giving the Acqua Vergine a splendid outlet, and as a lover of Antiquity, he had his eye on the illustrious column. From 1730 to 1732 he encouraged various artists to produce designs for the fountain.

We know of several suggestions by Vanvitelli, one of them (dated 1730) intended the column to be erected in front of a niche in the lower middle section of the façade. The fountain itself was to play a more subordinate role, although it was to spray a couple of sea gods lying at the foot of the column [107]. In another, and presumably later, project by the same artist [108], the column had been omitted and replaced by the statue of "Roma" at the back of the niche; two similar curving stairways lead up to the middle section of the façade. Both of Vanvitelli's designs are uninspired; there was no effervescence in them and the basic ideas were without force. Bouchardon and Lambert-Sigismond Adam, two scholarship-holders from the French Academy, also tried their luck [109].

All the Trevi projects, a total of 16, were publicly exhibited in the Quirinal in 1732 and submitted to the Pope for his verdict. Clement vacillated. First he gave the palms of victory to Vanvitelli, then changed his mind, and in the end the work was given to Salvi. This was a wise decision. Vanvitelli was compensated by his employment as architect for a hospital in Ancona (1733–1738), and this was much better suited to his sober talent. The Fontana di Trevi deserved to be staged by Salvi, an artist of abundant merit. The work was quickly started, but there were difficulties, especially from the hydrotechnical point of view, and several interruptions took place. By 1736, the large inscription could be set up and the Pope's coat of arms placed above the attica. The situation as it was in 1739 can be seen in an engraving in Campiglia's supplement to Falda-Specchi's "Nuovo Teatro". A copy of this work (in the Biblioteca Corsini) bears the following legend in Cardinal Neri Corsini's own hand: "Clement XII left this fountain as shown here, with 40,000 scudi for its completion" [110]. De Brosses saw the work the same year, describes it carefully and considers that it will become one of Rome's most beautiful fountains, yet he was more attracted to Bouchardon's model, *d'une noblesse singulière,* which he had studied in the St. Luke Academy [111]. In 1742 the enclosure around the large basin and the steps down to it were completed, and on a hot August day in 1743 the water flowed for the first time. In 1745 Benedict XIV was able to have an inscription set in the architrave of the middle section establishing that he had brought the task to completion. He overstated things a little, for the last and most difficult part still remained to be done. Just like the builder in a folk tale, Salvi became a victim of his mighty creation, the more his work progressed, the greater was the deterioration in him. Those who envied him persecuted him with hatred, but he held on to his precarious position defiantly, although he received attractive offers both from Turin (after Juvara's death) and from Naples (where the palace in Caserta awaited him). Through his daily struggle with lime and water and ashlar, he developed arthritis; he was crippled by it and died in 1751 [112]. His task was inherited by the architect Giuseppe Pannini, who countermanded some of his measures, for he divided the wide cascade that Salvi had intended, into three smaller streams. Some time after 1754 Hubert Robert made a lovely red chalk drawing of the Fontana di Trevi as it looked behind boarding covered by sailcloth. By now the Romans had long been waiting for something great and wonderful in the little square, so when would the curtain be going up? Not until May 20th 1762 could Clement XIII view the Fontana di Trevi in the form it has today.

We will now also analyse Salvi's composition. The façade is divided into three parts, but not in the same way as Vanvitelli intended, where the middle section was receding and lower, like a decoration between two pavilions. It was now united by the central part being emphasized like a heavy ressaut with columns set beneath a very high attica. The side sections were given pilasters. This is the front of a castle – you might call it a *château d'eau.* At long last the Palazzo Poli had acquired an immaculate façade and the square its closed back wall. A vacuum had been filled; now the waters could be dammed up and the space be pervaded by the sound of the rushing streams. A god in action was now required, a central figure commanding the cascades to pour forth and dramatizing the scenery with his presence. Now that the wall behind the fountain had become a monument and columns had given it a powerful relief, it was time for the god to appear. In heroic architecture the mystical must come forth; the languishing figures of the Virgin's Fountain had no place here. It was the Lord of the Seas, Neptune or Oceanus, standing in his conch shell chariot, drawn by snorting horses, who held his triumphal entry here – with his own triumphal arch (Pl. 136). The broad ressaut is divided by three arcades and thus forms a *mostra,* so characteristic of

133. *Piazza di S. Ignazio.*

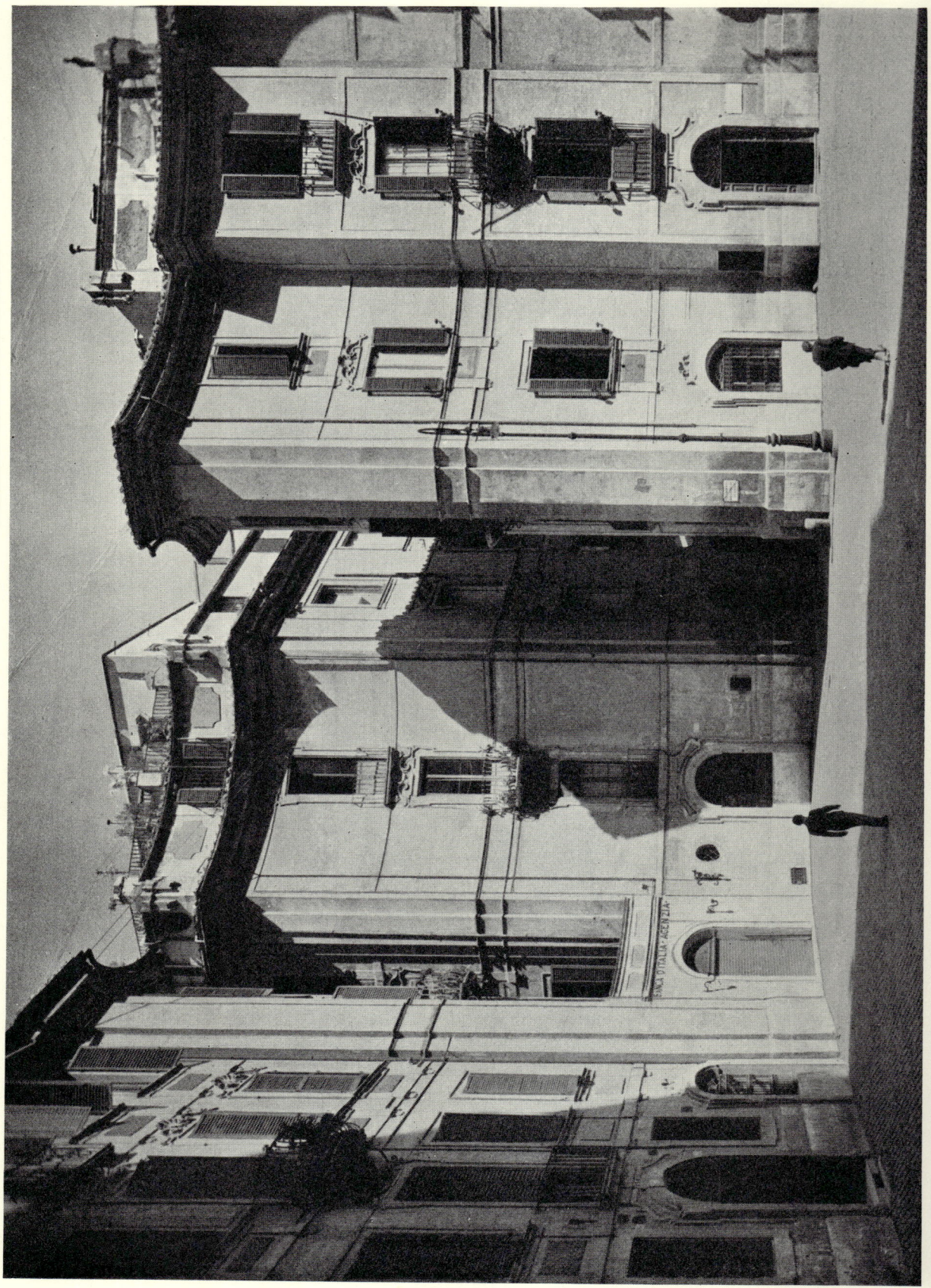

135a. *The corner of the Corso and Via Condotti with the Palazzo Ruspoli (on the right) and "Goldoni's House".*

135b. *The fountain in Piazza della Rotonda.*

136. *Fontana di Trevi.*

137. *Fontana di Trevi.*

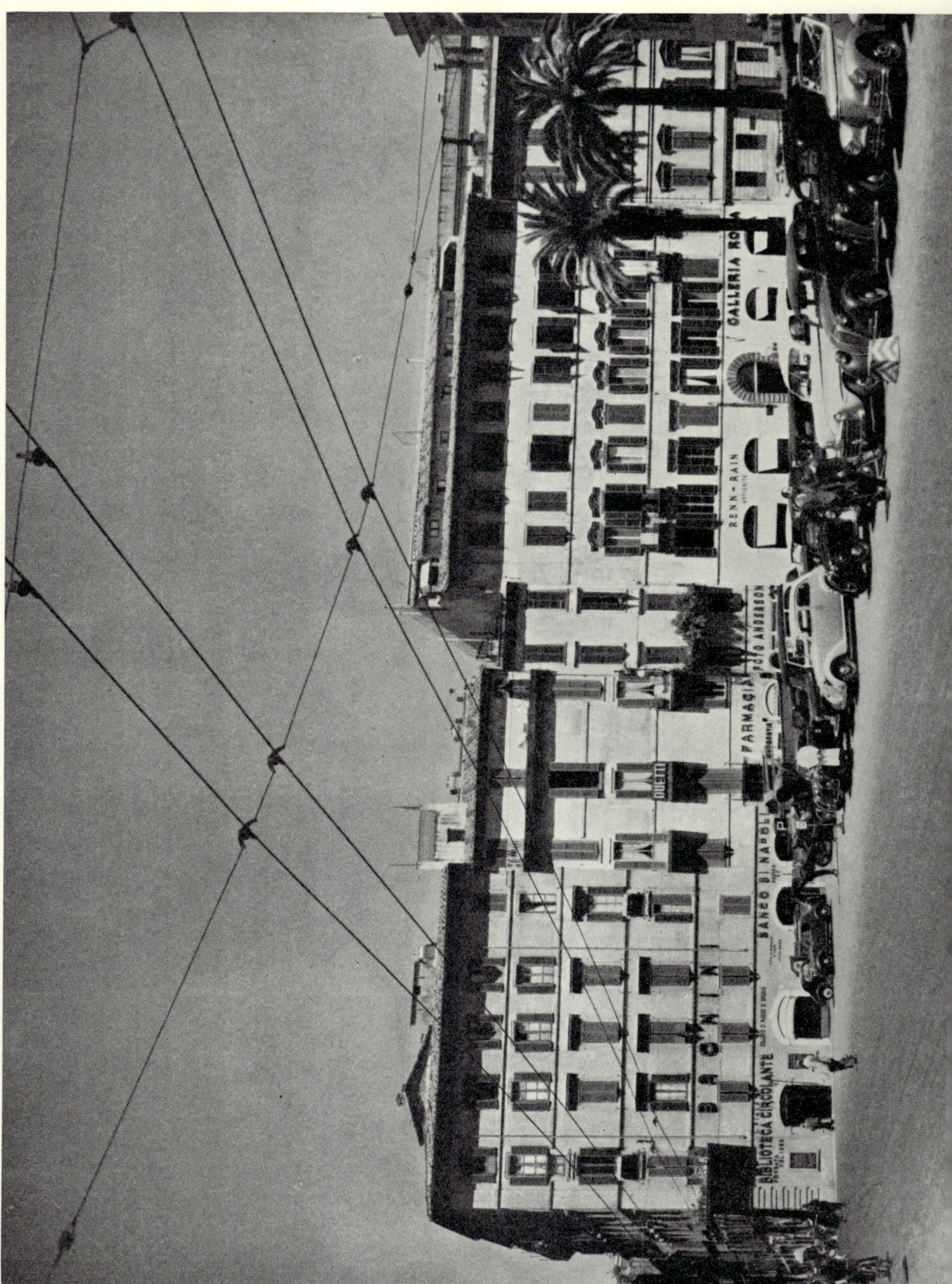

139. *Piazza di Montecitorio.*

140. *The Maltese Square on the Aventine.*

earlier large-scale fountains, and it might in fact be likened to a triumphal arch. Salvi however, was not content with the outline of a classical type but chose a definite pattern: the Arch of Constantine, feature for feature.

The idea is magnificent – the Emperor of the Seas and the Waters, with the rush of waves at his feet and storming winds above his head, steps out from Antiquity's most turbulent, most restless *Arco di Trionfo*. The Baroque of Late Antiquity is fused with the Classicism of Baroque – as a critic of style might phrase it. He might also feel inclined to ask why Salvi chose this very ideal. We know that he, an artist schooled in literature, cultivated "the Antique" with particular zeal. Very well – he was not the only one – all the same, it is probable that his temperament was more receptive to a direct influence from the famous memorials of the past than was that of others of his calling. It is worth noting that while he was struggling with his projects for the Fontana di Trevi, the Arch of Constantine was being restored from top to bottom (1732). This might have provided fruitful impulses for his studies and called the great, maltreated handiwork to mind. And who improved its sculpture? None other than Pietro Bracci – participator in the competition of 1732, the sculptor who was later to execute the figures of Neptune and the seahorses for his own fountain [113].

Pascarella was right. Fontana di Trevi does look like a decoration from *le grand siècle*. Bernini himself might have created Oceanus. The arch rising above the sea-god's head and the temple-like niche has the same outline as the entrance to the Vatican, Bernini's *Scala Regia*. His pupil, Nic. Tessin the Younger, had also used the motif of the Constantine Arch at Stockholm Castle, on the façade facing south, from whence the triumph was proclaimed. Trevi's portal is regal.

And so the great fountain became part of Rome and everyday life. The people made free with the scenery and, as is always the case in Rome, they accepted the sublime surroundings as something perfectly natural. The basin was a lake which cooled you down on hot summer nights, and the water was good to drink. The mountain scenery surrounding this Roman *lago* held many secrets; things grow and stir among the stones, algae and strange plants cling to the porous travertine, which seems to have brought them into existence (Pl. 137). Tassels and fringes, as from a cardinal's hat, weave around copper coins.

When the fountain's author died, one of his friends, the musician and poet Benedetto Micheli, wrote a sonnet to the waterscape – "this creation by the unappreciated maestro Nicola Salvi" – and published it "in happy memory – dear God – of my dearly beloved friend and benefactor". The poem, in Roman dialect, begins with the lines:

> My soul, what joy to smoke a pipe's tobacco
> And look upon the beauty of this fountain!

Through the smoke from the tobacco, as it mingles with the water's own *fuma,* we see how the Fontana di Trevi has become one with the Roman people [114]. Early in the morning Alfieri used to visit the square and sit on a step or an outcrop of stone, eating bread and cheese, meditating [115]. How many people have bidden the day farewell here, listening to the darkened waters? One January night in 1834, as Hans Andersen was going home from the theatre, "the streets were empty and the cascade of Trevi falling with all its noise" [116]. The echo of this sound is buried deep in the memory of all visitors to Rome, the voice of *le torrent séculaire* [117]. From the time of Micheli up to this very day, Salvi's great work has symbolized the gateway to the joy of everyday life. Here the hours of the day and night are dreamed and danced away.

The musically inclined are completely entranced. Not all arbiters of taste felt so liberated. Far too many were overburdened by clichés. One of the first witnesses among the swarm of visitors, Madame du Boccage, was at once overcome by enthusiasm when in 1757 she unexpectedly came upon Fontana di Trevi: "I was driving past, nobody had mentioned it to me, my amazement almost launched me headfirst out of my carriage. I stopped to admire the most beautiful staging of sea deities" [118]. But the people who were under the spell of Classicism found much to object to about Neptune and his castle. Lalande felt that the cliff structure should have dominated the building more, in the same way as the ravine in Tivoli dominated the Sybil's Temple – which was asking a lot [119]. Guidi, in 1773, was one of the first to complain that the square in front of the fountain was too small [120]; time and again people who know no better have called for a "clearance", the one certain result of which would mean ruination for the monument, for the restricted space is the basis for the dynamic strength of the fountain. "Sturm und Drang" found its spokesman in Heinse when he considers the sea god and the Tritons superfluous among the rugged rocks; the figures interfere with his conception of awesome Nature, "the whole is a scandal for Rome" [121]. In Ramdohr's eyes, Neptune looked like a dancing master, lacking in simplicity [122]. Kotzebue disputed the apparently widely held view that the springing of water from a palace was ridiculous: "I find this objection baseless. Wherever Oceanus stands, water will spring forth" [123]. The Rationalist made concessions – but only just. In Thorvaldsen's time the work was regarded as a *rodomontade* [124].

Other fountains were built in Rome at the time when people wore three-cornered hats. Only one of these minor fountains should however be mentioned in the same breath as Acqua Vergine. This is the excellent piece of sculpture in the Piazza di Bocca della Verità (Pl. 32), designed by Bizzaccheri, and executed about 1715 by Francesco Moratti [125] and mentioned earlier in this book. Onorio Lunghi's fountain (1575) in the Piazza della Rotonda was completely rebuilt in 1711. The upper part of an obelisk, which had formerly stood in front of S. Macuto, was set in the middle of the quatrefoil basin (Pl. 135b). The sculptures, the usual water-spewing dolphins, as well as various masks, devices and cliffs, were added by Barigioni. It is recorded on an engraving of his design for this structure [126] that the initiative for the alteration came from *il Presidente delle Strade,* who happened to be a cousin of the Secretary of State, Cardinal Paolucci. Through him, Clement XI was stimulated to take an interest in the matter – "the Pope is now occupied with it and it takes his mind off other things" [127]. The fountain is a clever piece of craftsmanship, excellent in its proportions. It is instrumental in making the square in front of the Pantheon, this elephant-grey colossus, so attractive.

Once when Queen Christina, during a ceremonial drive through the city, saw all the fountains spring and believed that it was being done in her honour, she modestly requested that they should be turned off. She received the answer: *Madame, ces cascades vont ainsi jour et nuit.*

Joseph II, the affable Holy Roman Emperor, was also once chiden in a similar fashion by the Romans.

IV

About 1730, at the time when Scala di Spagna and Piazza di S. Ignazio had just been finished and the Fontana di Trevi began to take shape, the Roman civic architecture of the 18th century had reached its climax. No later work in this field came anywhere near the qualities of these structures. But the following period, up to the occupation, was signalized by another kind of building activity which has enriched Rome with features it can never lose. The first that comes to mind is the readjustment of *Piazza di Montecitorio,* which became a substitute, albeit of inferior design, for the "Forum" planned by Fontana. Clement XII ordained in 1732 that the cramped square in front of the Court of Justice should be enlarged and that the street running towards the building made so broad that the façade of the palace could be perceived at the widest possible angle, when viewed from the front. There was no longer any question of repeating the niche motif, but the idea was to create a harmonious rectangular forecourt on the transverse axis. An inscription on the Palazzo Di Cellere, which became part of the new structure, states that the work took place in 1733 and that its purpose was the creation of a view towards "the Roman Forum", this being done by demolishing tumble-down houses in a humble street (Pl. 139).

The Piazza di Montecitorio, which has remained largely unchanged since the time of the Corsini pope, is unjustly relegated to the shadows as a work of art and is rarely mentioned in the specialist literature, presumably because there is a lack of bravado in its style, merely a civilizing influence. The Law Courts of Papal Rome however form an entity which is dignified; the façades have firm lines of great simplicity. This simple style, which is Rome's contribution to modern metropolitan architecture in the form of blocks of flats, goes back to Fontana's artistry, as we already know it from the project for the "Piazza Clementina". But of course the buildings on Montecitorio are taller; they respond to the huge dimensions of Fontana's own *Curia*. The architect is not known.

Perhaps the shallow rustication, which covers the middle section of Palazzo Di Cellere and resembles weather-boarding, may help to track him down. Such a form of decoration, quite foreign to Carlo Fontana, was adopted by Fuga. We find this characteristic *à refends* jointing as a principal motif in the courtyard of Palazzo della Consulta, built at the same time as the houses in the Piazza di Montecitorio. I see nothing to prevent the assumption that Clement XII employed his favourite architect to design the homogeneous architecture in this square about this time. When Benedict XIV had the plinth to the Antoninus Pius column (discovered in 1703) set up as the focal point in the renovated square, it was Fuga who was in charge [128].

Papa Corsini had wanted to decorate the square in front of the Lateran Basilica's new façade with an "Egyptian" obelisk. This, a rather poor piece of sculpture, had been presented to him by Donna Ippolita Boncompagni (whose palace we remember). It was situated at her famous Villa on Pincio and originated from Sallust's gardens [129]. The obelisk arrived safely at the Lateran, but after the Pope's death in 1740 it was still lying on the ground and remained there for some considerable time [130]. A couple of minor improvements to the city were carried out without any trouble by Clement; for example the Piazza Pollarola was given a better form [131] and the Corso was widened in 1736 by the Palazzo Sciarra, mostly to benefit the carnival traffic [132]. The Piazza di Pietra, the customs house square, was paved in the 1730's and given a handsome east wall by the large property, still extant, which the Bergamaschi community erected behind their church and institution in the Piazza Colonna [133]. In 1734 a little harbour was built north of Ripetta, *Porto di Legno,* with slipways and enclosed yards specially meant for the import of timber [134]. In the following decade too, a number of localized clearances took place in the general aspect of the city; these were more concerned with daily life and its movements. We note that in 1742, the Piazza Sforza-Cesarini was squared up (*riquadrare*) [135], as was the Piazza del Monte di Pietà (1747), where the erection of the bank's new wing caused older buildings to be pulled down [136].

An item of civic art with a breath of vision was eventually carried through by Lambertini. He completed what Clement left undone in front of S. Giovanni in Laterano. By now he not only had a great creation behind him, but in front of him lay another compelling attraction – S. Croce in Gerusalemme, whose façade was on the line of sight and about to be rebuilt in the lofty style of the Lateran. Soon after his accession, Benedict conceived the noble plan of connecting the two basilicas by a wide avenue, half road, half square [137]. And he put it into practice. Vineyards were destroyed, depressions in the ground filled in, a level surface was laid down over the rough Campagna within the city walls and trees were planted in rows. The façades of the sister churches, so splendid and so isolated, could reflect one another through a lattice formed by the crowns of the white mulberry trees.

A look at Nolli's map from 1748 shows that Benedict XIV's magnificent promenade, when measured from its start with posts and chains, to where it ends outside the Amphiteatrum Castrense, has exactly the same length as is the distance from the east end of *la spina,* between the Borgo Vecchio and Borgo Nuovo, to the ellipse of the colonnades in front of St. Peter's. This is not merely by chance; an intention is clearly there, and we admire its ambition, recognizing at the same time that Baroque in this consummate composition had changed its direction. For although a unified architectural prospect has been realized, it has a list – S. Croce does not meet S. Giovanni face to face, but sideways on, in a diagonal perspective. Such a liberty in a directional view could be tolerated because a horizon higher than the peaks of the church gables and even St. Peter's dome, indeed beyond the doctrines of architecture in those days, extended above the wide scene – and this was the Albani hills and infinity itself. The view was not so much the straight line through a landscape, as an approach road to something of a greater nature, where even the tallest monuments are mere set pieces. Conceived in this way, we here see Baroque as a style heading towards its dissolution. The Lateran's *stradone* and the Colosseum as a roofless church – Papa Lambertini's most grandiose experiments – are both poignant witnesses to the fact that the most powerful urban art in the world was soon to fall under Nature's sway.

Up on the Aventine stands a little square which certainly has something of the atmosphere of a park. Don Giambattista Rezzonico, the son of Clement XIII's brother and Grand Prior of the Knights of Malta in Rome, had laid it out in 1765 in conjunction with the erection of an entrance in front of the priory's villa. It is stated in an inscription that the work was done "to increase the majesty of the site". This had already been granted the square by the terrain, which stood high and remote, and which was almost equal to the grandeur that history has ascribed to this sovereign and military order of knights. Piranesi, who was once again entrusted by his patron to set the scene, created here a truly pictorial effect by closing the equilateral square at the back by two walls at right angles to each other; nothing could have been simpler. But he also embellished them in a way which is stimulating, perhaps too stimulating. From his treasury, filled with goods from antique graves, he selected particularly memorable articles, made them heavier, played down the big, enlarged the small and then set them up on the wall as a warning to all (Pl. 140). In one place you find a fluted stele dwarfing the obelisks, in another, a tablet bearing the Maltese cross surrounded by a very heavy garland enclosed in a stylized sistrum; the mystic past of the hill is suggested by pipes of Pan. The individual forms in this disposition are sometimes full-bodied, sometimes extremely pointed. When classical trappings are transferred from the lithograph to natural surroundings they become completely unreal. One discovers how wrong it is – not merely in proportions – and that a perfect illusion can only be created when seen through a medium far more "Roman" than is the atmosphere on the Aventine hill. The splendid cypresses are very much in the spirit of Piranesi and allow his artistic creation to seem like a Garden of Remembrance. Romantic gardens also mellowed with age; when art is allied with nature it can, in the end, make an architect's dreams come true.

Within the walls of Rome the time soon came when the only artistic innovations worthy of mention were produced by the engrafting of borrowed monuments. Now it was Antiquity itself which gradually came to power. It became easier to erect obelisks than good stout houses. The period of Baroque was ushered in with obelisks during the time of Sixtus V, but they were certainly supplemented by much contemporary architecture around them. If, in the following two centuries, the choice lay between the erection of a new building and the ancient stone needle, it was after all the latter that lost. But in the era up to the French Revolution and French supremacy, building activities were allowed to decline and Egyptian pillars permitted to advertise the splendours of the past, not always in the best of taste. Triumphant Classicism crowed over this rhetoric – with some justification, as their "Romanity" at least was genuine. Did not these monuments rise up from the soil of the Imperium, from Rome's very own ground? The spirit of history surrounding the obelisk could not be exported; in the cities beyond the Alps such columns had to be reproduced, bought or stolen. However skilfully it was handled with circles or octagonals of houses produced around its shaft, it still remained nothing but a piece of academic furniture. It is all right to move obelisks from place to place in Rome; Roman soil would always be clinging to them. When in 1802 Canova was working in Paris on the model for Napoleon's bust, the First Consul liked to discuss Rome with the sculptor and used every opportunity to emphasize the advantages of his own capital. "Here in Paris we make every effort to provide people with shade, we plant our boulevards with trees," said Bonaparte. "We haven't got room for things like that," retorted Canova, "we plant obelisks" [138].

When Pius VI became pope (1775) there was a small selection of antique obelisks waiting to be set up. In a witty pamphlet entitled *Supplica dei quattro obelischi* the arch-Roman Cancellieri put forward their case. And from his writing-desk in Leipzig the famous philologist Joh. Fr. Christ hinted that the Ludovisi obelisk was waiting for another Sixtus [139]. Pius, always inclined to the grand gesture – the empty one as well – was just the man to put the tall memorials in their proper places. He began with an obelisk that had once stood in front of the Augusteum and which not long before had been dug up behind S. Rocco [140], and he had it erected, which was quite natural, outside his own windows on Monte Cavallo. It was not to stand in lonely majesty, for it was placed among the statues of the two horse tamers (Pl. 74, 76), whose pedestals on this occasion were swivelled round and set at an angle to each other. In May 1786, Fr. Münter saw these colossi being manipulated and was not satisfied with the way they were arranged under the supervision of Giuseppe Antinori [141]. Andr. Chr. Gierlew felt the same way, finding it "peculiar" to squeeze such a unique monument as an obelisk in between the figures of unruly horses [142]. The idea was indeed bold and certainly original. Pius VII later (1818) added the splendid granite basin from Campo Vaccino. By then all sorts of relics had been collected in the palace yard, the medley of this decoration is a true *Quodlibet*, wholly in harmony with Monte Cavallo's enchanting, preposterous beauty. Even the inscriptions on the plinths of the Dioscuri (*Opus Phidiae, Opus Praxitelis*) are lies; everything is out of this world. Of the Roman spirit which produces this Goethe states: "Hier brachte der Zufall nichts hervor, er zerstörte nur" [143]. Pius could not leave things alone and everything had to be on a big scale.

The Ludovisi obelisk had long been lying about in the square, left in front of the Lateran palace. Its turn had come at last. Cardinal de Tencin had at one time tried to get hold of it on Louis XV's behalf in order to erect it in front of S. S. Trinità dei Monti, above the Spanish Steps, the apple of his eye; still, the Cardinal was too late off the mark [144]. Perhaps Pius VI got wind of this old idea; it is however certain, that in 1787–1789 he caused the Ludovisi obelisk to be erected in this place under the supervision of Antinori [145]. It was not a particularly good solution, for if the site is too small and not the right one, the obelisk is defeated from the start. This one overshadows the delicate architecture of the Steps and stands out immoderately. To make an impression from down in the Piazza di Spagna, the stumpy thing had to be erected on an inordinately tall plinth which on closer inspection, did not increase its charms. The Romans were amused. One disguise during the carnival in 1789 included headgear shaped like a huge white pedestal, on the top of which balanced a little obelisk painted red [146]. Seen through the narrow Via Sistina however, this much criticized monument has an admirable effect; it is characteristic of the artistic phase of that time that it looks best from the side, having a rather blurred space – the concept of a view round the corner – as background. It is at its most impressive when it stands out there at the end of its narrow street against a sunset or the night sky. The Romantics thought so too; Fioroni turned the Trinità obelisk into a portent in his evocative nocturne from 1830 (in Thorvaldsen's Museum). Goethe saw the foundations laid (February 1787), and his perruquier found a fragment of an antique vase in the rubble, but had to relinquish it to the poet [147].

The third obelisk on the pope's list, the "gnomon" of Augustus' enormous sundial in the Campus Martius that Pliny mentioned, was found once more in 1748 behind S. Lorenzo in Lucina and raised by Zabaglia, but as it was broken and expensive to repair, it was left lying in the courtyard of the Palazzo Conti at Largo dell' Impresa. Here it was viewed with admiration and pity by Bergeret in 1773, by Münter in 1785, by Goethe in September 1787 [148]. It was not until 1792 that Pius succeeded in having this imposing article erected in the *Piazza di Montecitorio* (Pl. 139), very close to the gnomon's original site, and in exactly the place where Carlo Fontana had wanted a column. The person in Rome on whose mind this Renaissance of the obelisk weighed heaviest, was the Dane, Georg Zoëga. The enigmatic memorials had long attracted him, and as early as 1786 on an excursion with Münter, he was able to demonstrate that the Ludovisi obelisk was not an Egyptian original but only a Roman copy [149]. A few years later, Pius VI gave him the task of preparing a comprehensive monograph in honour of the pontificate. He reluctantly agreed to take it on, for it was likely to become an enormous concern with him in charge. By 1792 he could begin printing the mighty tome *De origine et usu obeliscorum* (Rome 1797, i. e. 1800) in which he piled up a pyramid of facts [150]. Zoëga nearly killed himself by this intense labour, "I regard the book as my cenotaph" he wrote in 1796 [151]. It was to become the cornerstone of his reputation.

Not long after Zoëga had put the finishing touches to the magnum opus about Pius VI's exclamation mark, Thorvaldsen arrived in Rome (March 8th, 1797). It is a well-known fact that the archaeologist acted as his stern mentor in the first difficult years. It might well be that one of the obelisks that Zoëga had glorified with his quill stood as a landmark for the brilliant young sculptor – just by pointing to two sculptures – Monte Cavallo's horse tamers (Pl. 74). Some people were of the belief that the pair represented two examples of Alexander the Great taming

Bucephalus [152]. Anybody in their right mind could see that the colossi were heroes. In the 1790's, the decade of the Convention and the Consulate, there was a tremendous enthusiasm for all heroic figures, for patriots and the destroyers of tyrants. "The genre of the strong and the violent" (A. W. Schlegel's expression) burst into sudden, if short-lived flower in the Rome that had fostered Brutus and possessed the real Martian Fields. Artists had the opportunity to study the magnificent antique models in the Holy Father's palace yard, and made good use of it. Through her Corinna, Madame de Staël interpreted these statues to the whole world; according to her they not only glorified human physical strength but also spiritual nobility [153]. Curbing a wildly rearing steed with one hand falls to the lot of only a chosen few (like Bonaparte in his march across the Alps). It was Goethe's experience that neither the eye nor the spirit was quite able to grasp the magnitude of the Dioscuri [154]. Canova too, as a young man went into ecstasies when faced with *i cavalli del Quirinale* [155]. Their passion was later to find a graceless echo in his group "Hercules and Lichas" (1796) which is nothing but a tour de force. So was Thorvaldsen's "Jason" (1803). The artist admitted many years later that he had "wanted to show off" in this work, i. e. vie with Antiquity and Canova [156]. In anticipation, he had in 1799 made a smaller model of "Pollux" on the Monte Cavallo, when Zoëga helped him by obtaining access to a window in the Palazzo della Consulta [157]. There is no doubt that Jason belongs to the great family of horse tamers, anyhow by elective affinity (Apollo Belvedere is a more distant relation) – and Fernow was right to describe it as "made in the true antique heroic character" [158].

The 1790's was more or less the last time an obelisk played any part in the conception of artistic works of passion. Valadier had in 1793 designed the complete renovation for the Piazza del Popolo using the obelisk from the Circus Maximus as a dramatic accent. His project was logical enough and held together well; he intended to retain the square's original trapezoid form and to enclose it with nothing but peristyles according to the precepts of Vitruvius' fifth book, chapter one [159]. "The Empire" desired a Caesarean Forum long before Napoleon. But Valadier's project, the last mature work of Roman urbanism, was put aside.

During the clerical and bourgeois reaction, when giant stones from Egypt had lost their glamour, a creation of debased beauty was carried out (1816 ff.). The new Piazza del Popolo, following the lines of two opposed hemicycles, was only "Classical" on paper, not in its execution, for Romanticism – ironically enough from France [160] – was the solvent for its composition. This new square became as much the beginning of the Pincio Gardens, which were laid out at this time, as the entrance to Rome. This very antithesis betrays the weakness of the plan. The view to and the view from the belvedere up on Monte Pincio competed deliberately with the two domed churches down in the square; the elevated promenade imposed a vista at right angles to the principal axis from the gate to the city. While Baroque had only imagined Piazza del Popolo as an architectural prospect in depth, Romanticism made it a transverse panorama as well. Once again the landscape, in this case a park, had proved its power over pure architecture, this time – and finally – at the very door to the capital of the world.

Up on Monte Pincio the fourth obelisk was eventually erected (1823), the last one to have figured on Cancellieri's agenda, and which lay in the side courtyard of the Palazzo Barberini [161]. It became an ornament in the "Winter Garden" where the fashionable carriages circled round the elegant restaurant (Casino Valadier, 1817) [162]. The Piazza del Popolo's own obelisk had four recumbent lions added to it in the 1820's. The jets of water issuing from their jaws refreshed the stray bystanders – artists and beggars – who in the summer months sought rest in the dusty, somewhat pompous square. "When the obelisk's shadow like a huge pointer touched Monte Pincio, we gathered once again by its noble hieroglyphs to listen to the chatter of the fountain" – and to Bergsøe's tales.

V

"I remember that in Rome everything proceeds at a dead pace; carriages and pedestrians all move like tortoises". This was Pietro Verri's impression of the rhythm of the Eternal City as he remembered it from school days 1744–1745 [163]. Ten years later Winckelmann expressed a similar experience, although this was acquired in a position of greater responsibility: "In Rome everything must be undertaken with a certain phlegm, otherwise you will be taken for a Frenchman". Following this come those fine words which have the emotional sound of a confession: "It seems to me that the seat of learning for the whole world is in Rome, like others I have been purified and tested" [164]. Goethe was a witness to this statement, "it corresponds to my way of thinking" [165].

Anybody merely wishing to form a comprehensive and lasting picture of the papal city's appearance under normal everyday conditions would do well to follow in the footsteps of these true connoisseurs, and wander around at his leisure. What we are describing in the following pages is meant to be something like a sketch for a mosaic frieze, assembled from the small impressions aroused by a long stroll through ordinary Roman streets. We enter a modern city which retains the features of ancient times, but we try to recognize reality in historic tones (Levertin's words) and fill up the gaps as best we can by borrowing from the maps, pictures and texts of the 18th century. As everybody will realize, it is only possible to know a city when you have got into the routine of a regular life. Once this stage has been reached, your daily life runs as if on rails and the streets are noticed in strips with the addition of a few unexpected sights [166]. This experiment must be tried out in the Rome of the Age of Reason. Before we distinguish between the types of houses and give histories of style, we shall be content to take in the walls enclosing the streets, as if we were simply somebody out for a walk – these walls between church and palace and monument, these long emotive stretches of wall which are the city itself. And as we walk along without analysing, it is, for the moment, enough to look at the walls of the square and the streets as they appear to us at eye level. The storeys above the shops exist only in our consciousness as neutral vertical planes, for we are just lazing around. The city becomes a series of strips, somewhat unclear, often flickering with a few arresting details – long lanes which unroll before our half-seeing eye. They leave us an impression of stretches of arterial roads, of cuts made in the massif of structures; they remind us once again of the walls surrounding the squares and remain in our minds as abstract lack-lustre prisms.

And so as we wend our way through Rome, we often feel that the moving stream in the network of streets becomes dammed up, forming a backwater, a little square or a group of squares in which movement stagnates. For hesitation is perhaps the most characteristic feature in Rome's streets and in their use. The rhythm changes constantly to a *ritardando*. The square pertaining to a palace always cries "Stop!" by its regular plan and its dominating building; such a square by its very nature forces the passer-by to take his bearings and then start off in a new direction – the Piazza Lancellotti and Piazza Borghese come to mind, the latter being used as late as the 1880's for the prince's equestrian exercise ground [167]. The square in front of a church is also imperious, challenging every passer-by to turn and face it, demanding his attention, in a way even his reverence. What the square performs as a theatre we have already discussed. The little squares, which have developed unplanned, behave quite differently. They slow people down, reduce the speed a little, then send you on refreshed along your chosen path. Where these squares are all grouped together, as often happens, it can create the effect of being caught in an eel-trap.

There are many examples and we shall mention just a few which are particularly typical. Piazza di Pasquino is the widening of the east end of the Via del Governo Vecchio funnelling into the Piazza Navona, whose basin is the great reservoir of the district (Pl. 125). The Piazza di S. Egidio is also funnel-shaped, the narrow outlet pointing towards Trastevere's main artery, the long Via della Lungaretta; and at the wide end four streets spurt out, three of them heading for the Tiber. Whichever way you cross the square, its very shape provokes expectancy; you may either be guided from one of the many fairways through smooth waters to one definite inlet or vice versa – the inertia of the square helps you to make a leisurely choice of direction. The Piazza di Scanderbeg is a small pot that has gone off the boil in the maelstrom of back streets behind S. S. Vincenzo e Anastasio; Piazza Margana is a resting-place in its own little area, the alleyways lead into it in such a gentle manner – the modest palace has authority among the humble houses, the mediaeval tower makes compact this *paesetto* not far from the Capitol and the tranquility is that of the Sabine Hills [168]. The Piazza in Piscinula is a noisy little hillside square as it distributes the crossroads that go up into Trastevere, overlooked by S. Benedetto's dilapidated campanile. Piazza della Pigna is intimate and reverent, a closet well hidden inside a fine house; I am astounded each time I come across it – like the prince who once in a remote part of his palace suddenly came face to face with one of his own children of whose existence he was not aware.

In many places a street wall falls back, a small section intended by a force which we now cannot always grasp. Teatro Argentina, whose façade is from 1845, is joined on to a projecting Baroque building. It marks the corner of the original complex and seems to have no point at all, since the block opposite has been removed. But originally, when the theatre was confined by the narrow street, its front was pushed back to allow the carriages going to the opera house to turn. The building mentioned forms the flanking corner of the little forecourt, and is moreover the only part of the famous theatre which remains as it was in Farinelli's days. Piazza del Drago in Trastevere (Pl. 158) used to be called "della Crocetta" because it abutted on to a very straight crossroad. But the call of an alley and an inn nearby was stronger than that of the cross. One wall of the square retires a few paces and so the ideal figure is denied.

This elasticity in the body of the city always comes as a surprise. If we take as an example the maze of streets and small squares, and mixtures of both, in the triangle between La Cancelleria, S. Andrea della Valle and Campo dei Fiori, it is apparently a muddle. But when the plan is analysed, it becomes clear that the five streets and three squares make up a very supple configuration with distinct objectives: the Piazza Pollarola points towards the Cancelleria and its square, from its wider end facing east, it forks in two small streets to Piazza del Paradiso (Pl. 141) which again speeds narrow streets on their way, towards the north, to the portal of the Palazzo Massimo alle Colonne, to the east, to the side façade of S. Andrea, southwards, to Campo dei Fiori through the funnel of the Piazza del Biscione. From here, another passage runs into two remarkable courts (Piazza di Grottapinta and Piazza dei Satiri) set within the *cavea* of Pompey's theatre. Seen on the map, this section of the city is an ingenious mosaic of triangles, quadrilaterals and segments of circles. Experienced on the spot, all the figures even out and fuse into a continuous kaleidoscopic series. The Piazza delle Coppelle suffers similar lateral tension, but no turmoil results. The pedestrian is delayed on his way, but not held back. All movement in Rome is cautious and takes its time, and detours are often short cuts.

When wandering in the naturally developed parts of the city, one sometimes feels as if it were a movement through defiles in a low plateau which have been worn away by erosion. The streets have, it feels, the organic structure of a canyon and they follow a course seemingly full of obstacles. The endlessly slow process of its development has apparently left behind a strange impulse which has lead generations of people to move along in a cautious rhythm. The reader will perhaps find this description of its nature put too strongly and not in keeping with the benevolent intimacy of the Roman street. There are other old towns that are cut up into a confusion of aimless alleys, of withdrawn squares and unexpected retreats, but they do not in any way encourage the observer to comparisons with geological phenomena. However, one must remember that it is not only the solid geometry of the streets, but also the substance of the structures themselves which determines the character. And in Rome, the architecture which has been shaped on the basis of time and space, possesses a fuller textural effect than we find anywhere else in the world. All honour to Baroque for having modelled Rome into a plastic mass of balanced consistency. The material, which makes thorough use of stone and mortar and stucco, is satisfying in all respects, tough when it is soft, hard when it solidifies, easy to smooth, impossible to break. It never flakes like flint, its edges never scratch like broken glass. If fabric of this material were to be crushed, the process would be covered by the French term *écraser,* not by the verb *briser.* Out of this perfect matter, streets can easily be moulded; their walls give way and then stand fast. It is significant that while the French word "*carré*" describes the concept on the drawing board (a four-sided figure), the Italians perceive a detached block of houses as an island and use the word for it (*isola,* Latin *insula*); their conception is clearly intelligible, for their islands are cliff-like and are hence sculptural.

So now as we walk through the solidified mass of Rome we discover repeatedly that in the homogeneous structure from which the streets are carved, consideration has been shown at the very place where the most hazardous incisions have been made. Right-angled corners on the houses have been strengthened by ashlar since the time of the Renaissance, provided the owner felt inclined to spend the money. Rusticated masonry distinguishes a corner, and a crossroad is given emphasis. This motif remained paramount in the Rome of Late Baroque; modern civic architecture rejected its merits, yet the houses with ashlar corners were thought of as being patrician, continuing the ancestral style. We show a classic example (Pl. 148); here lived Rafael Mengs 1758–1764 (and Casanova, while a guest of the court painter, happened to meet Winckelmann here in a state of inebriation) [169]. The corner certainly stands firm and the blocks of stones are rooted in the ground, but the rustication appears all the same as an addition which is only a support when seen close up. The situation is different when two streets after a long stretch intersect at an acute angle – here the pointed corner is in a particularly exposed position, for it protects more than just a house; it is the end of a "peninsula", a deep incision. Rome has many thoroughfares which produce such a spit. As good examples we can quote Via Monserrato>Via del Pellegrino, Via dell' Orso>Via di Monte Brianzo, Via in Arcione>Via delle Scuderie, Via Sistina>Via Gregoriana, formerly also Via dei Falegnami, which outside S. Carlo ai Catinari formed an acute angle with the Via della Pescheria. Facing such a forked road which penetrates deep into the heart of the city, one gets a strong impression of both the amplitude of the mass and the power of the sculpture. And this is particularly apparent because of the solidity of the building standing on a corner (*la testata*). It is not merely a dovetailing but an integral part of Rome's massivity. Exposed houses such as these guarantee the city's textural unity.

In the numerous instances where short streets form a sharp angle by converging, Baroque tends to reduce the angle, as at other house corners, by chamfering or recessing. Plates 142 and 143 demonstrate a typical case. Two streets run from the Via Capo di Ferro, to the left, Vicolo delle Grotte, which bores its way up to the Via dei Giubbonari, to the right Vicolo della Madonnella, which is a blind alley. The corner is flattened, a commonplace survival in all Rome, and the roof follows the angle. These two narrow streets can indeed be taken as representatives of the great majority of ordinary streets in Rome. The *cul-de-sac* disintegrates; Vicolo delle Grotte (called in one place Vicolo delle Cripte) curves beautifully, as if carved out. Greyish yellow and shabby, complete and dignified, a crevice leading to other passages and caves. We might mention the fact that it was in this alleyway that Cagliostro found his wife, a child of the bottomless pit of Rome. These streets that curve, express a strong organic existence; they adapt themselves to their locality. Just look at Via dei Polacchi, whose distended concavity is magnificent (Pl. 144), or the row of houses in the Piazza del Paradiso opposite S. Andrea della Valle and the back wall of the Piazza del Febo. The three streets (della Vetrina, delle Vacche, della Volpe) which run out towards the north-west side of the Piazza Navona from the Via dei Coronari, have taken their curve from the lines of the ancient racecourse.

A touchstone for the sculptural character of the Roman street is its frequent connection with great monuments. We speak here only of "chance" connections, not of official staging. It is a constant pleasure to witness the assurance with which civic architecture does obeisance without being cowed. Via dei Pianellari is a quiet corridor around the transept and apse of S. Agostino; an alley imitates the shape of Tor' de' Specchi's tribuna. The tiny space of the Piazza di S. Stefano del Cacco prepares the wanderer for the towering mass of Palazzo Altieri. Nothing can surpass the way S. Tommaso in Parione is combined with a large neighbouring house (Pl. 19); at one side a re-entrant is formed to allow the church free play, thereby creating a diminutive square, and the obtuse angle is softened down by a round belvedere. We have no need to emphasize that all the disguising and renovation of antique ruins that took place in the Baroque period was often of a very artistic quality; nameless master masons possessed the sensitivity which is a gift rarely bestowed upon learned restorers. Let me remind you of the house next to *le Colonnacce,* so superb in its polish [170], and the delicate building to the left of the Antonius temple in the Forum; both can be seen in Vasi and Piranesi.

We can also test the elasticity of the roadways by measuring their greatest resistances. These were masonry arches erected across the roads, heavy and oppressive, narrowing the streets. Such constrictions may have

141. *Piazza del Paradiso.*

142. *Vicolo delle Grotte and corner of house facing Vicolo della Madonnella.*

143. *Vicolo della Madonnella. The photograph is a continuation of the one opposite.*

144. *Via dei Polacchi seen towards Via delle Botteghe Oscure.*

145. *Via dei Cappellari with the birthplace of Metastasio.*

146. *Section of housewall in Via delle Carrozze.*

7. *Section of Via della Purificazione. The house with the three bays was the habitation of Alexander Trippel.*

148. *The corner of Via Bocca di Leone and Via Vittoria – Rafael Mengs' house.*

given the impression that the city was resisting and that the streets only reluctantly opened up. All the same – they were more, and something other than *caesurae*. They provided a frame for the views and threw the destination ahead into relief. The people of those days may not have been aware, in the same way as we are, of the artistic effect. Yet we suspect that they intuitively sensed these arches as beats in the everyday rhythm of the streets. Besides the previously mentioned *cavalcavie* from palaces, we can mention the Arco di Parma at the exit from the Piazza Lancellotti to the Via Tordinona (and the opera house of the same name), Arco di S. Marco with a view towards Palazzo di Venezia, Arco di Grottapinta, the shallow channel into Piazzetta del Biscione, all now disappeared [171], together with Arco dei Cappellari (Pl. 145), Arco della Pace (Pl. 164), Arco dei Tolomei in Trastevere and the arch of the Cenci by the ghetto. Add to these the five entrances to the Jewish quarter which were menacing openings to streets in a completely different city, and do not forget the gateways in the fortified corridor from Castel Sant' Angelo to the Vatican – the reek of people and smoke oozed out through them from Borgo Pio's side streets into the prelates' highway (Pl. 149).

Obstructions – and slowly moving streams along worn beds. The ever indissoluble dualism of function and structure [172] was completely inherent in the city of Rome, a slow mechanism, weighed down by traditions, silted up by social inertia, but constantly in motion – a structure as if of malleable clay. The shapes rose above solid earth. The foundations of the city might undulate under the old districts, but the houses lining the streets were all on the same plane. Thoroughfares – apart from the Corso – had no narrow platforms to be used as pavements, nor any gutters. The house and the pedestrian were always on an equal footing [173]. So here we follow in his footsteps – in this instance not into a void veiled by the abstract, but down on the more mundane level of the well-worn threshold. Dwellings will be observed from the outside to try to understand what life represents here.

The lowest zone of the street wall, which harboured men at work and was in intimate contact with all on foot, was slit by openings, particularly doors, gateways and shops. They took many forms, but all the same, the ordinary street prospect was far from lacking in harmony. Certain basic types could be found in most places; among entrances to houses it was the narrow door with the fluted side posts of peperino and the grilled semicircular light, accentuated by a keystone (Pl. 48, 147). This handsome feature, which originated in the 17th century, is repeated so often in the many *portoncini* with curved and broken pediments, and during the 18th century, architects used it in all manner of rich variations, according to the prevalent taste [174]. Pl. 146 shows the combination of an old-fashioned entrance and a modern one in the Via delle Carrozze, where people of humble means lived and hired out cabs to the affluent tourists.

Another important factor, indeed the guiding spirit in all busy streets, was *la bottega,* both workshop and trading place. They were all very alike and had not varied in type since the time of the Imperial City of Ancient Rome, remaining the same throughout the Middle Ages and the Renaissance [175]. We have seen a truly Classical *taberna* at Ostia, and the shops during the Baroque period did not deviate much from this, either in form or function. A large square opening was the connection between house and street, the masonry counter with its large stone slab on top [176] reduced the gap, allowing free passage on one side. Door, counter and "window" were all created by the half-wall which gave the opening on the front of the house a special configuration. The bartering was done in the street. As a protection against sun and rain, strutted awnings were set above each booth; where there were several of these, it gave an impression of a row of porches, like a survival of the covered walks (mignani, Latin maeniana, in Venice liagò) so popular in earlier times [177]. The authorities had systematically tried to root out these excrescences, but with little success (Pl. 17) [178]. At the end of the day the shops were barred with wooden shutters, like the stalls in a covered market – "put out the lights and bar the door".

The outside of this time-honoured type of shop was improved upon in the 18th century, when the angular outline at the top was curved like a flat basket-handle and was given a shouldered architrave and keystone, like street doors – but in principle it was not really altered. As far as I have been able to ascertain in my quest around Rome, you can no longer find a genuine *bottega* here. I reproduce two examples, one primitive and one Baroque, which with others have survived unscathed in the little remote town of San Gregorio, somewhere between Poli and Tivoli (Pl. 151a-b), and it shows us what an ordinary Roman shop looked like. And its linear motif, this big mouth, is still a predominant feature in the old Roman street, although now it has been veiled by modern display windows. Even today it is not all that difficult to see in our mind's eye Goldoni's and Goethe's *botteguccie* while we gaze at the windows and make purchases.

This continuity in the city scene is to some extent a miracle. There was a calm, imperturbable rhythm along the close-set streets, no shop claimed any special attention by its position in the wall. To this austere aestheticism in general, corresponded an untrammelled individualism in the way the goods offered for sale were arranged. Many witnesses have laid stress on the extraordinary feeling for beauty which enabled the traders to brighten their caves. The grocers in particular were outstanding in this respect. In 1834 Hans Andersen gave a description of the shop of his opposite neighbour in Capo le Case, and his little improviser conveys his admiration for it: "Amid beautiful garlands of laurel hung the white cheeses made from buffalo milk which could pass for big ostrich eggs; the candles, wrapped in gold paper, resembled organ pipes, and the sausages had been stood on end to represent columns supporting a Parmesan cheese which gleamed as if it were yellow amber" [179]. In Madame du Boccage's opinion, the flowers were exhibited here in a far better way than in Paris; they were laid like a mosaic in a variety of colours. We are reminded of the "Flower Festival in Genzano" [180].

The Romans do not seem to have gone in for shop signs with the same passion that the cities further north displayed; there was too much discipline and too little Gothic in Rome's atmosphere. But of course there were many, usually very ordinary, professional signs such as the barber's brass basin, the glover's red fist, the tobacconist's grim-looking Turk's head with a pipe in its mouth. It was on inn signs that the imagination was given full play and many of them still recur in the curious street names. Quite a few found their subject among animals – the ostrich (Vicolo dello Struzzo), the peacock (Via del Pavone), the lion (Via del

375

Leoncino), the monkey (Vicolo della Scimia), the bear (Via dell' Orso), the turkey (Vicolo del Gallinaccio); the inns with the two last-mentioned names are still standing. Also "Three Robbers" (Via dei Tre Ladroni). A multiple in the sign made a good impression – "The Five Hams", "The Seven Kings" and "The Nymphs"; the "Two Columns" doubled the single column in Prince Colonna's arms. "A Woman with a Rosary in her Hands" advertised the inn situated in a religious establishment, and as "The Quill and Octopus" stood in the Parione district, we imagine the lawyers' clerks and the public scribe from the nearest street corner to have been among the customers. This host of expressive signs has long ago been dispersed. Only on old pictures do we see some of them, such as The Black Cat that jumped out above the arcade in the very old Osteria del Gatto Nero (Vicolo del Cardello, demolished before 1870) [181].

It could not have been easy to entice people into a bar with fabled beasts hanging over the door, here in this city where the Borgheses' and the Boncompagnis' dragons, the Contis' chequered eagles and the Pamphilis' doves with olive branches in their beaks swarmed everywhere [182]. Dismembered sculptures and busts found all around were such a powerful spectacle that painters of sign boards were no match for them. We remember here the enormous foot (Il Piè di Marmo) in the street of that name, the column drum with the scar from the Paladin Roland's sword (Vicolo della Spada d'Orlando) and the split head of a man (Via della Testa Spaccata).

What an atmosphere "The Five Moons" (Via delle Cinque Lune) conjure up; the sickle moons are emblazoned on the Piccolomini escutcheon; or "The Golden Mask" on the wall in a dismal alley (Via della Maschera D'Oro); they could indeed make a tavern swing. But few Roman signs have called forth such derisive laughter as were provoked by some Parisian inn-signs – *le chat qui pêche, le veau qui tette* ...

The most usual of all Roman signboards was both the oldest and the one that has remained longest in existence, namely the green bough (*frasca*) of laurel or olive which heralds a tavern. In the rural outskirts of the city, the little banner of vine leaves may still tempt you to enter. It is the most ordinary sign in the mountain villages; quite recently at

Castel Gandolfo it was this that waved enticingly outside a house. There is another characteristic and poetic street fitting that is regularly to be found in the old Roman Streets and that is *la Madonnella,* the religious picture set on a wall or placed on a corner. This may be either a painting in a frame or a relief in stucco, a proper little *edicola* with three-dimensional figures. Anyhow – a place of worship in the open. Once there was a very large number of these popular shrines. By the time of Pius IX there were no less than 2739, but now the amount has been reduced to just over 500; of these about 80 are to be found in Trastevere and about 50 in Rione Monti, two of the most plebeian districts [183].

The pious pictures, like the fountains, were a guide through the city and might also arrest the wanderer's attention enough to make him stop for a moment. During Advent they attracted the fife-players in much the same way as a flower in bloom lures the bees. Mme Vigée-Lebrun, who had arrived in Rome at the beginning of December 1789 and lodged in the dark Vicolo Mancini (where the French Academy stood), was kept awake by the bagpipes droning until dawn [184]. One grows heartily sick of this nocturnal music, wrote a German painter a little earlier [185]. These pastoral scenes were, on the other hand, much beloved by the tourists, and Pinelli's prints bear this out. On feast-days, frequently very local ones, an altar was erected in front of the blessed picture and it was decorated with flowers; ice-cream would be served and a little band from the street struck up a tune [186]. On summer nights much merriment took place; the young people of the district celebrated their *Madonnella* with songs, fireworks and dancing [187]. All according to her capabilities she performed miracles for the congregation and gave them consolation in time of need. One July day after the new revolutionary calendar had been introduced in 1798, Princess Colonna wrote to a friend that a figure of a Madonna in the neighbourhood had opened its eyes. "I would like to see anybody who is not wide-eyed in times like these," noted her correspondent dryly in his diary [188].

Late Baroque and Rococo rendered it particularly easy to instil into the street shrines that sweet cheerfulness which made simple people rejoice to the heavens. It is rather charming to see angels soar up into the clouds on a house which exudes poverty. We reproduce a particularly graceful one (on the corner of the Via della Dataria and Via S. Vincenzo), which is shown in Vasi [189]; it lends a golden touch of the voluptuous chapels to the crossing (Pl. 150b). The coquetry in many of these reliefs is brought out by canopies which provide a shelter of scallops and tassels. The Virgin Mary is placed under a parasol. Especially fine of its type is an *edicola* on the Palazzo Castellani, where two upright angels proffer the Madonna dell' Archetto's miracle-working picture with a zest and fervour that may well have a moving effect on the passer-by here at the exit from the Via del Lavatore at the very moment the Fontana di Trevi comes into view [190].

All in all the most vivid appointments in the street scene must have been the cheapest – washing hanging on the line. Around 1710 we find de Blainville serious in his condemnation of this widespread form of decoration, finding it irreconcilable with good taste. Underclothes and napkins dishonoured the greatness of the city [191]. A generation later Mrs Piozzi from London was shocked that princes, whose income was equivalent to that of the Duke of Bedford, hung wet rags to dry out of the palace windows [192]. She could just manage to ignore the common people's nappies. But these scandalized people from abroad made a great mistake. Festoons of underwear, frayed and ragged, were not merely evidence of cleanliness. They also made a pure, aesthetic impression and livened up Rome. It was as if the whole city was waving scarves in the air. A fine Rococo interior with its panels has never looked ordinary and lived in, as museums would have us believe; behind the walls it is nothing but a skeleton. Not until curtains, portieres and bric-a-brac had been included, did it take on the spirit of the age. Nor does the street exist as history without the additions that the moment presents. Should we believe that what is without style is beyond style? The lines from house to house, with the capacious Baroque underpants and handkerchiefs the size of towels, must have been invaluable in Fontana's and Galilei's Rome. We remember how beautifully lines of pennants form a bridge from the Madonna in her halo on one street corner to the stars of a Prince Altieri on the other. A little study in this very subject can be seen in Plate 150a; the house is the clear-cut block, the pure essence of architecture; the madonnella represents the seal of the Church, as put up by her pious servants in the street. The washing fluttered across the shadow – we could call it civilisation's own little paean to the lowest strata of society, in the same way as a ritornelle or a satirical song might be. This festive decoration – timeless, pitiful and moving – still turns many a street into an interior where piety makes merry (Pl. 152).

At night it was really dark in Rome. Street lamps were first introduced during the French administration, but could not be tolerated. The ordinary street lighting came mainly from the little lamps placed by the images and the rays of light falling from the open-fronted shops. The Roman was an individualist and the night belonged to himself. When he walked through the darkness his lantern was used with discretion for his own peace of mind and so as not to interfere with the dark deeds of others. Pedestrians were loud in their demand that carriage lamps should have their blind side turned outwards – if the flickering cone of light was likely to reveal their activities, the shout went out: *Volti la lanterna!* The intense darkness possessed a latent dramatic poetry. In a place where the gleam of a little candle was the normal lighting, the lighted torch held aloft engendered a melancholy festival. Celebrations and fireworks were loved by the Roman for the very reason that he cultivated the darkness with such a passion – the night was illuminated by lightning flashes, the clashing of extremes of contrast. The tepid half-light did not suit his temperament. When Rome slept beneath its dark sky, those keeping late hours would be found at the tavern table and by the images of saints, the only hollows of light. In contrast to the daytime city, it increased in size and became changed, an entirely new entity [193].

VI

And now to the everyday life [194]. There was a certain number of markets that dealt with the capital's supplies of food, and it was here that the greatest activity took place. *Il Presidente della Grascia* and his employees checked up on both the bipeds and the quadrupeds. The cattle market was held every Friday in the Campo Vaccino; in the months following Easter the lambs were brought in; in the winter it was the pigs that occupied the pens situated between S. Maria Liberatrice and Orti Farnesiani. Here the butchers and small provision dealers (*pizzicaroli*) did their buying. The office of the market authorities stood by the Phocas column; the animals drank out of the large basin at the fountain (from 1593) close by the Temple of Castor and Pollux; it now adorns the Monte Cavallo. No other meat market could be as Classical as this. The horse markets were situated at the Piazza Farnese and Campo dei Fiori; in the latter, donkeys too, were offered for sale and grain was sold here. The poultry dealers filled the Piazza Pollarola with their fowls. *La Pescheria* took place in the Portico of Octavia. All these were indeed priceless trading centres; from booths by S. Carlo al Corso, grilled fish was offered for sale, much to the discomfort of the fashionable congregation. Wine carts from *i Castelli Romani* steered their unsteady course towards the Piazza Madama; we can see one of them in Vasi's engraving.

The largest food market with provisions of all sorts, as well as fruit and vegetables, was in the Piazza della Rotonda, in front of the Pantheon's peristyle. It was assembled in a shed forming three wings of booths [195]. An inscription on a house right opposite the temple states that Pius VII had this undignified "belly" removed to provide a better view of M. Agrippa's building. The adjacent Piazza Crescenzi was an extention of the Pantheon market; along the east side of S. Eustachio was a row of properly built shops. The Piazzetta di Macel de' Corvi, behind the Palazzo Venezia, was a Rotonda market in miniature – and there were, of course, similar small market squares where food was sold in all the outer districts.

Piazza Navona, the most Roman square of all, carried on the traditions from Domitian's stadium and was the gayest playground in the city. At the Wednesday market, *roba* of every conceivable kind were sold; it was a real medley. At the street stalls, brought into order by Maderno and Valadier, the general public bought both food and clothing and cheap luxury articles; a girl would find a bodice and a string of coral, a man buckled shoes and cheese, the children their amulets. Stout materials, useful articles, second-hand goods.

All the fun of the fair was here. Strolling players set up their stages and Harlequin vaulted across them; Punchinêllo horrified and amused with his dirty brutish face; tight-rope walkers swayed on the thin line; puppet players raised their braying voices and the air echoed with the thumping of cudgels on the puppets' heads; charlatans screamed the virtues of their love-potions and "magic pills" and their ointments to cure the bites of mad dogs; tricksters would prophesy lucky numbers in the lottery for a couple of *bajocchi;* pilgrims offered water from the River Jordan for sale; barber-surgeons and tooth-pullers boasted of their skills. A poor wretch who had sold Mortadella sausage made from horsemeat was shackled in an iron collar; a confidence trickster had to ride *il cavaletto,* egged on by the hangman's whip.

The Piazza Montanara was the gathering-place for the farm workers; these dark-tanned people who looked like Indians, came from the Campagna and the mountains, sometimes all the way from *la Ciociaria,* to buy implements or to find work in the Roman vineyards. A small market was held every Saturday in the Piazza alli Monti for the simple inhabitants of the district, and it was very similar to a market day in a provincial town. Even today it is quite easy to people the square by the Madonna dei Monti with life as it was once, for as far as rhythm and atmosphere goes, it cannot have been very different from the present way of life in this small market-town. When I last visited it, a local saint was being celebrated with the help of a brass band, which sauntered slowly through all the streets of the neighbourhood; one of the buglers was always falling behind to have a chat at some shop or another. In a little square, in the shelter of Palazzo Massimo alle Colonne, stands a column which is now quite overlooked. Nowadays, few people visit this out-of-the-way corner that the ancient column has given so much dignity, although it is not rooted in its original place. The curled acanthus of the capital has almost been eaten away by time, like the decoration on the palace wall. But in the past, things happened here, the small space echoed wiht the hoof-beats of the post-horses, for Piazza della Posta Vecchia was one of the coaching stages. Only a few steps – and the traveller was in the Piazza Navona. The little Piazza Padella behind Carceri Nuove, which has now disappeared, was a kind of police-station yard, where masses of gendarmes could always be found.

The various guilds and corporations of traders were, to a great extent, still closely bound up with their own special street and the surrounding ones. However, by the middle of the century or thereabouts, these ties were beginning to loosen. Merely by a handful of street names we can imagine life as it was in the mediaeval districts around the Campo dei Fiori; we hear the din of battle and see the flourish of short capes in these streets. Their inhabitants made crossbows (Via dei Balestrari), jerkins and doublets (Via dei Giubbonari – *vesti la giubba*), locks and keys (Via dei Chiavari), trunks of leather for the many travellers staying at the inns in the district (Via dei Baullari), hats (Via dei Cappellari), guitars and lutes (Via dei Leutari). Some of this knightly equipment may not have been in fashion during the Rococo period, but stringed instruments (mandoline and colascione) were always in demand, and right into this century the clever locksmiths still had their workshops in the Via dei Chiavari. Tailors and glovers kept to the Banchi Nuovi. If an impression of an old street of these craftsmen is required, you must visit Via dei Cappellari (and pull your cap down over your face as you walk along). It is depressing, dark as the bottom of a well and very smelly. You look into caves from whose depth the glow of a lamp calls forth sweaty faces in the semi-darkness, revealing bent and emaciated figures as in Krøyer's painting of the hatters' workshop. Here you fathom the bitter reality behind street names such as Via delle Botteghe Oscure and Via delle Grotte, although no ancient vaulting strung its low arcades along this particular alley. At the place where it becomes almost squashed by a masonry arch, Metastasio, the prince of heroic opera, was born. He knew from his childhood both "The houses of the damned" and the prison vaults (Pl. 145).

There was the loud noise of the coppersmiths in the Via dei Calderai behind the Piazza Navona that was difficult to drown. In the Via dei Falegnami near the Piazza Mattei, swished the planes of the carpenters; the quieter work of the basket-makers took place in the Via dei Cestari near the Minerva square. The more superior goldsmiths were, by a further edict of 1680, restricted to the Via del Pellegrino, also called "degli Orefici". In Specchi's engraving of Cancelleria we see that the ground floor of this grandiose palace has been entirely given up to shops selling these expensive articles. As evidence of Carlo Rainaldi's extravagant way of life, Pascoli mentions that he was in the habit "of buying the most expensive jewellery available *al Pellegrino*" [196]. Vasi mentions in 1754 that the goldsmiths and silversmiths lived here, although some had now moved to other streets; all the same, the majority were still to be found in the traditional street [197]. Lalande confirms this a few years later, for in the street of the jewellers one got a stronger impression of Rome's wealth and trade than in even the Corso [198]. Today too, nobody goes in vain to the Via del Pellegrino if he is looking for a piece of jewellery for his beloved, for there are eight goldsmith shops here. We may just add that the city assayer lived in the side-street Vicolo del Bollo, that the goldbeaters worked in the rather dismal Vicolo del Fico at Montegiordano and that the second-hand dealers hawked their wares in the same neighbourhood.

The booksellers' district was centred on the Piazza di Pasquino. The damaged statue, which has given its name to both the square and the concept "pasquinade", stood at the sharp corner of the Palazzo Orsini (now by its successor Palazzo Braschi) and thumbed its nose at the bookmakers' little angular square. A painting by Sinibaldo Scorza (from 1627) depicts in detail the large bookshop in the most elegant building [199]. The adjacent part of the Via del Governo Vecchio, which was literally called Strada de' Librari, was also full of bookshops, publishers and printing works. The respected firm of Pagliarini, whose printing house, among many other things, printed several volumes of Vasi's "Magnificenze di Roma" had as its address "a Pasquino". The books were of a high quality typographically, although they could not measure up to the standard of Bodini's editions in Parma. Nicola Pagliarini later moved his concern round the corner into Via dei Leutari, to the Palazzo Mignanelli (street no. 32–36), where Rossini later composed "The Barber of Seville" [200]. The scandalmongering aria was created in a building which had once been filled with religious writings, for in 1773 Pagliarini bought the Jesuits' library in their Casa professa, after the society had been suppressed [201]. There were also large bookshops in the Via di Parione (Pl. 19).

The books have now left their own district by Pasquino, and this is a pity, for the quarter has a very special intimacy, the friendly warmth that comes from booksellers' crates and old engravings displayed on the façades. The smell of printers' ink and musty paper is sadly missed. It may be a consolation that one small door is left open to one of the houses in the Strada de' Librari, which had its heyday in Voltaire's young days. François Deseine's establishment, very patriotically named after St. Louis, must have been an exclusive Parisian community in Rome [202]. The bookseller knew his papal city, as his cicerone bears out, and he entertained his customers with outspoken commentaries. Like the shop in the Quai Voltaire in Paris (no. 9) where Anatole France's father and later Honoré Champion sold books, Deseine's premises were *une librairie à chaises* [203] – those splendid straw-seated chairs that can bear learned people and piles of printed matter with equal grace. At Deseine's, it was like a club of literati and artists, who discussed and read the newspapers ("Nouvelles"). One day M. de Blainville asked the philosophical bookseller if he knew Bayle's Lexicon (which had been on the Index of banned books since 1700). "Do I know it?" he answered, "I have sold several copies here in Rome and even members of the Holy College hurried to buy it." When de Blainville expressed his surprise, Deseine said that Père Cloche, the Dominican General, patronized him, and that was sufficient answer [204]. The anecdote is amusing, considering that Holberg a few years later (in the winter of 1715–16) only managed to get a quick glance at the heretical work, when, by mistake, he was supplied with the wrong book at the Minerva Library, whose chief patron, of all people, was Cloche [205]. Should Holberg perhaps have tried to look under the counter in St. Louis' bookshop ...? Deseine himself died in 1715.

The Piazza di Pasquino is useful as a starting-point for further excursions to districts which show the influence of particular occupations. The west part of Via del Governo Vecchio formed the main axis through the quarter frequented by members of the legal professions who bustled about the governor's palace and the law courts [206]. This street came to an end at Montegiordano and the Piazza dell' Orologio in front of Borromini's clock tower. According to tradition, the famous meeting between the boy Pietro Trapassi, the later Metastasio, and the lawyer Gian Vincenzo Gravina took place here. The budding poet charmed the man who was to become his influential patron with his improvisations, and this enabled him to leave the unsavoury hatters' lane [207]. Attorneys, notaries and officers of justice had their offices in the small streets which do not look much different now from what they did in Montesquieu's time, as far as the exterior goes, but now they have a very bad reputation. Vicolo della Campanella, Vicolo del Corallo, Via della Vetrina, Via Panico on the other hand are shabby-genteel; here the pettifogging lawyers felt as contented as maggots in a cheese. No client can feel safe in the Vicolo del Micio, the name of which may be translated as something like "Mangy Tomcat Alley" – it looks like it too; in most doorways you see petty practitioners ready to pounce. It is strange to think that distinguished barristers at the ecclesiastical courts and eminent jurists of the Vatican – precisely the members of the not very numerous Roman bourgeoisie – can once have lived and worked in this down-at-heel part of the city. And yet several archbishops and more than one pope have made their way up with the help of the goose quill. Francisco Miranda lodged in 1785 in the Strada Papale (del Governo Vecchio) near l'Orologio in the very rooms that Papa Lambertini had occupied while he was still only a young legal official at the Curia [208]. Eugenio Pacelli, later Pope Pius XII, son of a consistory advocate, was born not far from here, in the Palazzo Pediconi by the clock tower, and he spent his youth in the Palazzo Rossini, 19 Via della Vetrina, whose mighty belvedere surveys the whole district. Even in Gioacchino Belli's days it was occupied by more than a hundred solicitors [209].

We promised more than one excursion from Piazza di Pasquino. The second one is also through streets where paper and typography is the main business. Many engravers and graphic publishers set up their presses in the vicinity of the Piazza Navona. The addresses printed below the engravings are the signposts. The publishing house of the de Rossi family was known all over Europe as being situated "alla Pace". Very many views of Rome, including Falda's big map from 1676, indicate this locality. The firm was dissolved in 1738 and its stock became the nucleus of the Calcografia Pontificia then established at Piè di Marmo [210]. Other editions gave the place of origin as "Prope Pasquinum" and "Prope Canestrarum", the latter pointing to Via dei Canestrari, which runs from Navona to the Teatro Valle. Engravings with the style "Al Melone d'Oro" came from the Vicolo del Melone, situated between the theatre mentioned and La Sapienza. The name of the street refers to an inn frequented by peasants bringing melons to Rome from Rieti [211].

Umbrellas, which must be reckoned among papal Rome's most useful and almost symbolic articles, were made in the Via degli Ombrellari, a side-street to Borgo Pio. Their production was relegated to this outer district because it caused an abominable smell. The quarter, with the dome of St. Peter's bulging above it, was full of Vatican flunkeys, apostolic *scopatori* and choirboys, abbots and sceptre-bearers; Ugo Valeri, architect for St. Peter's and "Bernini's last disciple", died in 1786 in the Borgo Pio. A very pious and very mean-spirited district, even today strangely ambiguous in character, thinly varnished with a petit-bourgeois veneer, proletarian without vitality (Pl. 149). It was in this out-of-the-way lane that the cardinal obtained his red ceremonial umbrella, the lady her parasol and the rustics their green gamps, which because of their circumference were called *basiliche*. This last type still survives in comic opera – when Don Basilio in the "Barber" goes off after the last *Buona sera!* he tucks the rolled up contraption under his arm. Dainty slippers for a Rosina or a Donna Rosaura, were on sale in very different surroundings; Via dei Pianellari was a street where shops selling finery would be found, and architecturally seen it was also very exclusive (Pl. 172).

The nicest looking shops were not confined to any special district; they traded in what is so delightfully called *arte bianca,* as they dealt in eggs and flour, meal and macaroni, all pale coloured goods. Set out on the counter they make up, even today, a *nature-morte* in delicate tones that would have gladdened an Oudry. Imagine this artistic display framed by whitish-yellow travertine.

There was once a very short street that took a pride in not specializing in anything. So it was given the name *la Cuccagna,* "Cockaigne". It starts at the south end of Piazza Navona and was formerly "garnished with all the commodities that the heart could desire" [212]. Now there is not much to write home about. The name of the street was, as always in Rome, extremely expressive – later, one found a childish delight in the only little bazaar left; here various fancy goods for sale were all displayed on one tray, and one rather pampered it with this designation. At the time when "Cockaigne" was a fairy land for all to enjoy (as early as around 1700), the Corso had not yet become renowned as the most important shopping centre, as this only happened gradually after the middle of the century. The tourists demanded fashionable goods, souvenirs and reading material. Around 1770 only very few shops of anything approaching a metropolitan character were to be found. Bouchard and Gravier's French bookshop was situated in the new Palazzo Mellini, and this famous firm had a large stock of engravings and topographical literature. Every enlightened traveller was conversant with the attractive corner by S. Marcello, and we know it from an engraving by Vasi [213]. Bouchard was Piranesi's publisher and in the years subsequent to 1746 brought out the splendid series of *Vedute di Roma,* which made the firm and the artist famous all over the world [214]. Piranesi lived for some time in the Corso, *dirimpetto all' Accademia di Francia,* thus not far from Bouchard's, before he moved up to Casa Tomati in the Via Sistina, later to be Thorvaldsen's home. Not far from the fashionable bookshop there were a further six shops to be found in the annex to Palazzo Sciarra-Carbognano [215]. The Palazzo Fiano also housed a bookshop. Further out, the former local agent, now the silk merchant Marino Torlonia – the founder of the noble banking family – ran his shop on a scale equally as modest as that of the first Rothschild, whose small shop in Frankfurt was established as a money changers in 1778 [216]. North of S. Carlo, the Corso faded out and became provincial; the walk through the shopping centre came to a halt, cavaliers and their ladies turned back.

The *Ghetto* was a district which was a caricature of Rome. The Jewish quarter was hemmed in by walls in 1555. The gates were torn down in 1798 to the sound of the Marseillaise, but were raised again during the Restoration after 1814 – to fall forever in 1847. The whole quarter was razed to the ground in the 1880's. Its area between the Tiber and the "Square of Tears" (Piazza del Pianto) was miserly apportioned; the longest stretch along the river was not even as long as the Piazza Navona. Within the walls, the population of a small market town was crowded together (1677: c. 4500 people, 1853: c. 3800) and needed, according to the standard of the time, about five times as much room. This barbarous overcrowding forced the buildings upwards, so that they became gawky and cadaverous. Similar buildings are still to be seen in the old Jewish quarter of Venice, the oldest part of which is an island. By all accounts *la Giudea* in Rome was not merely ugly to look at, but it had a character very much of its own. The houses in the small street nearest the Tiber, the low-lying Via della Fiumara, were plastered with mud by the frequent floods and so took on a most poisonous colour, quite different from the genuine Roman ochre; it may be remembered that the Hebrews had to wear yellow bands or hats. The miserable lanes had names which were quite foreign to Rome. "The Corso" was called Rua in a sort of Portuguese. A little alleyway was called Via delle Azzimelle after the unleavened bread which was produced here. Old photographs show that outside staircases were retained longer in this isolated part of the city than in the rest of Rome. In this respect the ghetto probably resembled small remote mountain villages (as for example Olevano), where the wilderness of steps and burrows and caves can seem like a nightmare. The synagogue, which was a combination of five national schools and temples, also had a large flight of steps. This religious building was cobbled together, having antique columns in front and the seven-branched candlestick in its frieze. No solid ancient monument, no architectural work of quality was to be found within the Jewish enclosure. Only the interior of some houses could in secret boast of valuable Eastern carpets. These were at times hired out to Christian patricians who wanted to make a show [217] – and at every accession to the papal throne, the Jewish community had to deck out the Arch of Titus, their gateway of ignominy, with the deep-dyed hangings of the Orient. Then the ghetto revealed that an older culture than even Rome's, hid its purple and fine linen behind the scabby façade [218].

When the Jews emerged from their prison through the main gate to the Piazza del Pianto, they could not avoid noticing a large building opposite. Its conspicuously broad belt of inscription states in Latin capitals that the house was renovated by Lorenzo Manilio in the year 2221 after the foundation of Rome (i. e. 1468). At that time the ghetto was not in existence. And the noble letters express the cry of victory: *Have Roma.* This Renaissance building still stands. Anybody who has visited the area of the Jewish settlement and by identifying, tried to resurrect the demonic quality of the place, has now only Manilio's house to go by. Marcel Proust once wrote: "There are people of a mystical disposition who believe that things retain something from the eyes that once looked at them, that monuments and paintings only appear to us through a veil which the loving gaze of many admirers throughout the centuries has woven around them." If this highly intelligent reflection has any truth in it, the front of Manilio's house must be absolutely impregnated with hatred. Seen in this light, the building outside the slave gate is the most impressive monument to Rome's ghetto to be found in our search for its bygone days.

Another "seraglio", enclosed by a wall in 1569 [219], the whores' *ortaccio* (with Piazza Montedoro – a resounding name – as its centre point), was, as far as we know, discontinued at the beginning of the 18th century. Its inhabitants of the better sort were moved to the streets near Piazza di Spagna, where the foreigners in particular, sought them with eagerness. By a decree from 1697, the prostitutes were chivvied out to the Via della Vite [220], which even today inspires you with less confidence than do its neighbouring parallel streets (Frattina and Borgognona). Kotzebue tells us that in the evening the Piazza di Spagna swarmed with "willing virgins" [221]. They made less impression on Fernow; he thought the number of "Venus Vulgivaga's priestesses" could only amount to fifty at the most, which seems absurd, and asserted that they practised the mysteries of their goddess without the slightest grace or delicacy, which information is duly noted [222]. The better-looking courtesans must anyhow have graced various bleak façades with their faces. So as far as the aesthetics of the street goes, we must make allowances for the creatures who in those days were called *le donne del primo piano* [223] or *donne di finestra, uve di strada* [224]. "The grapes of the street" – hanging in the close-set lanes which rejoice in the names of the Burgundian, the Grapevine and the flower-painter Mario.

In the course of the 18th century the ancient inns in the Renaissance quarters were going downhill. Most of them were reduced to taverns for the common people and the riff-raff. "Great" and "Small Paradise", mentioned in 1445, and later combined into one osteria under the general term for the heavenly mansions, still stands its ground in the small square called after it (Piazza del Paradiso). This auspicious name was also that of a low-class brothel and tavern in Copenhagen's Vestergade, where Studenstrup was stripped [225]. *"Il Paradiso"* was around 1710 mostly frequented by muleteers from the Piazza Pollarola round the corner [226]; in 1790 the inn is spoken of as being "third class" [227]. Go yourself and look at it – from our plate 141 the reader will sense that the tavern, which is still used, dominates its lively square from beneath the heavy shadow. Roughly contemporary with "the Paradise" was *Albergo Vacca,* mentioned in 1466. The Late Gothic building with the Borgias' bull's head on the signboard still stands at the corner of Via dei Cappellari and Campo dei Fiori and has – in contrast to "the Paradise" – retained its oldest form. The building is not inviting – the symbolic host could have been named Sparafucile – nor is the unpleasant alleyway. The last time the inn gets any mention is in 1697 and thus it is not likely to have given shelter to a respectable full-bottomed wig [228].

The drivers of hackney coaches had their stand in the Via dell' Orso in Holberg's days [229], and at that time the *Albergo dell' Orso* was as yet important enough for Deseine's guide to mention it as very attractive for travellers coming through the Porta del Popolo [230]. This mediaeval inn, one of its guests being Montaigne in 1588 [231], was given a pleasing exterior during the Baroque period. The not very wide front was quietly divided by three windows, of which the highest was set in the centre with a princely view; now the building has been spoilt by an improvement in style [232]. The nearby "Campana" (18, Vicolo della Campana), whose owner, when he died in 1744, was able to leave a large fortune [233], has, on the other hand, retained its worthy appearance. The old building with arcades and fortress-like sloping outer walls is alive behind the plaster and the simple Baroque windows. A side wing facing the yard was probably accommodation for visitors. The inn continued its busy life as late as the 1780's and it is still a restaurant. *Albergo del Sole* (or Montone) in the Piazza della Rotonda also has connections with the past – Ariosto lived here in 1513 and mentioned the inn in his third satire (... *la notte andai sin al Montone a cena* ...); it looks much the same as it did in 1748 when Cagliostro stayed here as "Royal Prussian Colonel" [234]. *Locanda Cesàri* was not nearly as old as the inns mentioned and probably

149. *Glimpse of Vicolo delle Palline.*

151a. *Shop in San Gregorio.*

151b. *Shop in San Gregorio.*

152. *Vicolo del Piede in Trastevere.*

does not date to before 1750. But it was up to date in its appointments and housed in the handsome property on the corner of the Via dei Burrò and Via di Pietra. It can be seen in an engraving by Piranesi from 1753 and has remained unchanged since then, apart from an added storey. The albergo was in a fine position, close to the customs house and the Corso and can be considered as a good example of a middle-class hotel of excellent repute at the time of Goethe. Madama Giacinta, whose husband was granted his licence in 1787, made Stendhal very comfortable [235].

During the 17th century the travellers' main quarters moved eastwards, out to the new and more open part of the city that had grown up between the Corso and Pincio. Artists from abroad had, since about 1600, preferred to have their studios in the rural area of gardens and back premises which were to be found below the Villa Medici, and they have continued to do so. Paul Bril lived in the Via Margutta as early as 1594–1595, as did Rubens 1606–1608, and Pieter van Laer, Claude le Lorrain and Herman van Swanevelt took up residence here in 1625 [236]. The Scandinavians had many a fight in the taverns and painted the bitter reality with romantic warmth. Gradually the many artists took over the whole of the hilly district of Trinità dei Monti. It was about this time that the Corso traffic took society people along the roads by the sloping gardens and introduced it to the European élite. While a traveller from Porta del Popolo formerly turned to the right along the Via Ripetta to get to the old centre of the city, he now turned left and followed the Via del Babuino to the Piazza di Spagna. Here stood the best hotels.

We have a lot of historical information about the inns through which all sorts of famous people passed. Such names and figures are not worth much to us now unless they have some connection with definite premises, and this happens only rarely in literature written by archivists. We want to see the building that carried the sign, we would prefer to be able to touch the door-frame that the hero's cloak once brushed against. So we shall content ourselves with the tales of a few inns that are particularly famous and whose exterior is preserved, or at least known to us from pictures. The reader will follow us with patience as we knock on the doors – perhaps even with a certain amount of excitement, because the Spanish

Square – these two triangles with their pointed ends meeting – possesses stories of the most beautiful days in existence. They are created by every present age.

An unknown artist has portrayed the Piazza di Spagna in a painting which can be ascribed to the period between 1711 (when the depicted *loghetta* in front of the Palazzo Zuccari was constructed) and 1723 (when "The Steps" were started); it is shown here in plate 126. With all the care of the amateur, the painter reveals a group of buildings which must have swarmed with travellers. By comparing this scene with Piranesi's engraving from the 1750's we can obtain a reliable impression of Rome's most elegant hotel district in the 18th century. The painting shows the square which received Holberg, the engraving reflects Goethe's milieu. And the photograph from 1949 (Pl. 138) casts a modern light on the square.

In 1715 Holberg found his first lodging in this neighbourhood in the house of a married couple who let rooms; apparently it was typical of its kind in what it offered the ordinary tourist [237]. The husband was consumptive, the woman drank and was of easy virtue. That the Piazza di Spagna in those days contained rather mixed company, can be seen from the painting. To the left of the slope is a squat hovel hung with washing; in the area behind it stands a small tower which is probably mediaeval. These buildings, together with the pleasant house with a belvedere on the roof, can be identified as the property of the Pozzobonelli family. When it was sold in 1690 to the monastery of Trinità dei Monti "una torretta *medio monti*" [238] is expressly mentioned – as is an area for playing boccia. An amusing detail, instructive too, like the skittle-alley in a Scandinavian hostelry, it brings the place much closer to us. A few steps from this cheerful "place of recreation" – a Roman counterpart to "Black Christian's Bar" in Holberg's Copenhagen – stood the hotels frequented by potentates. The *Albergo Monte d'Oro* was of the very first order. Prince Carl of Denmark, younger brother to Frederick IV, dismounted here in 1698 [239]; in 1704 it is called *locanda nobile* [240]. It was part of the north wall of the square. A note by Valesio from 1704 informs us "that thieves entered the Locanda through the so-called S. Sebastianello gateway and went up to the second floor to a chamber occupied by a man who is major-domo to two Bohemian nobles" [241]. From this it can be deduced: 1) that the building had at least two entrances, one from the square and another – more discreet – from Salita di S. Sebastianello; 2) the second storey, where servants are accommodated, must have been lower than the piano nobile, possibly half a storey. In the anonymous painting, to the extreme left, by the entrance to the Salita mentioned, there is a solid house of two storeys plus a mezzanine, with two entrances. One of them opens on to the narrow street, the other is in the square. A gentleman is approaching this main entrance in which stands a figure waiting to receive him. By studying the picture closer we can see that the latter carries a napkin over his arm, so he must be a *cameriere*. The house is reproduced in a diagonal perspective, not very correctly, clearly to reveal the distinguished façade. It can also be seen in Piranesi, although merely a couple of windows, and it appears in its renovated state behind the palms in the photograph. It will not have been a waste of time to identify "The Golden Hill"; we shall meet old acquaintances on the other side of the ashlared entrance. Count de Caylus arrived here in 1714 and started in a small way on the artistic studies that were later to bring him the name of *un antiquaire acariâtre et brusque* [242]; Joh. Caspar Goethe came in 1740 [243] – and it was a year earlier that the most humorous connoisseur of Rome, our incomparable de Brosses, had unpacked his cases here "in the best, indeed almost the only inn suitable for foreigners" [244]. But his stay was not to be of long duration; the food was very good, but mine host fleeced him and so he moved [245].

House number two from the left in our painting, the corner of Salita di S. Sebastianello, has the Bourbon lilies above the door and must be the hostelry which was called *Lo Scudo di Francia*; Deseine assures us that one was regaled here in the proper French style [246]. After the middle of the 1740's the place was taken over by Roland from Avignon, a former hackney coachman in the square outside, and the name was changed to "La Villa di Londra" and won great renown. Baron Carl Heinrich von Gleichen, later Danish envoy to Madrid and Paris, lodged here in 1753 [247], Casanova in 1760 [248]. Extended and renovated, the "Hôtel de Londres" existed right up to the 1930's (now it is Barclay's Bank) [249].

Further up the Sebastianello side street stood *Margherita's* small hotel which found favour with a number of fastidious Britons – Lord Herbert 1779 [250], Lord Hervey, the Ambassador 1787 [251], the Earl of Bristol with his harem 1788 [252]. In a summer-house, standing by itself on the slope of the Pincio, which belonged to the albergo, Frederikke Brun had her Elysium from 1807 to 1810 and from her windows praised the view down onto the mausoleum of Augustus [253]. Perhaps the excellent landlady is the same as "die Köchin Margherita" from whom young artists in 1769 collected their picnic baskets before going on a day trip to Cappella Sistina to study Michelangelo. They served the cutlets up on the Pope's high altar [254]. We might even go further and suggest she was the little Margherita whom Casanova courted in 1771, when he lodged with her father, the chef at 32 Piazza di Spagna. The adventurer gave *sa jeune hôtesse* among other things, a glass eye [255]. These were her beginnings.

Full of memories, we make our way further into this exciting square and stop in front of the building immediately to the right of la Scalea – this lovely house in faded orange (*rosso romano*) that all lovers of the city know. As far as I can discover, there was a famous lodging-house behind its inviting façades; this was *La Scalinata;* strange that local topographical research has not put up a notice to this effect on the wall [256], for some of the hotel's guests were as charming as the building itself. The fleeced de Brosses, whom we left at the Monte d'Oro, felt more at ease here under Madama Peti's roof where everything was provided, with the exception of bed-curtains [257]. At that time the house had just been built. Alfieri was its guest during his stay in Rome in 1767 and later as well [258], Cagliostro lived here for a few days in May 1789 after his fateful arrival in Rome [259]. The house by the Steps had thus received celebrated personalities before it was ennobled by Keats' presence; his fame has now completely taken it over. When we visit the little corner chamber on the second floor, where the poet expired on February 23rd, 1821 [260] and stand at the window facing onto the square to catch a sight of the sublime picture, we may be standing on the very spot where the president from Burgundy saluted his carefree Rome. In the panels between the beams of the ceiling, gold rosettes are painted on a blue ground. While a fleeting thought is given to Cagliostro in these rooms, it passes as a matter of course to another cosmopolitan and physician with magical powers, who later practised here – Dr Axel Munthe [261].

Yet another hotel in the square can be roughly outlined. It was owned by a retired sergeant named *Sarmiento* and was on the corner of the recessed Piazza Mignanelli (where "American Express" now has its offices). In 1788 Herder described the often changing views from his room; he lived near the back entrance to Trinità dei Monti [262]. The Dowager Duchess Amalie of Weimar lived here too. Furnished rooms could be rented in most private houses around La Barcaccia; about twenty years after Holberg lived near this picturesque fountain (before the Steps), Niels Eigtved arrived, who was later to be the architect for his theatre in Kongens Nytorv in Copenhagen, and moved in with Dr Ignazio Langen [263]. We shall not bore the reader by listing all the lodging-houses in the adjacent streets, only two must be mentioned as being typical of the concept "the cultured pension". One is the *Albergo Pio* in the Via della Croce where Mrs Millar in 1771 was surprised at finding "three or four homely English dishes (thanks to some kind English predecessors who have taught them), such as bacon and cabbage, boiled mutton, bread puddings ..." [264]. The pension opposite offered an apartment of five rooms hung with damask, as well as a kitchen and a servant's room for 18 zecchini a month [265]. A foreigner used to the good things of life, who wanted to run his own household in the Goethean period, the heroic age of tourism, would not find a suitable flat for less than 10 zecchini; in addition there was the payment for the food to be brought in and the hire of a carriage. It is illustrative of the level of rents that the last item mentioned amounted to 15 zecchini a month [266]. According to the standards of the time living was cheap in Rome. Winckelmann has described a good place for eating in the Via della Croce [267]; Moritz, Goethe's friend, has neglected to describe his, but to make up for it, notes that it was situated "just where *Saepta* was" and the consuls were elected [268].

Another commendable small hotel in the Via della Croce was run by the Frenchman *Damon,* an officer in the papal Light Cavalry, a perfect hotelier who presided over the *table d'hôte* with dignity, and in every way assisted his motley company to find their way through the bustle of Roman life [269]. Herder too, was among his customers [270]. It is mostly the people staying in the respectable houses in the side streets who have given us information about Rome; the diplomats and generals who lived in the very expensive places were silent on the subject. I assume that *Roland's Albergo* "by S. Carlo al Corso" belonged to the category which would nowadays be called *maisons de luxe*. It was in an enviable situation here on the corner of the Corso and the Via dei Condotti. Our acquaintance from the Piazza di Spagna had in 1766 given the "Villa di Londra" to a daughter whose married name was Lafont [271], while he himself carried on the new establishment until his death in 1785. The world-famous singer Caterina Gabrielli made her stately entry here in March 1771 [272], and a month later Casanova turned up at his former host's [273]; the Margrave Chr. Friedrich of Ansbach honoured him with a visit at Christmas 1775 [274].

A small problem now arises: on which of the Via dei Condotti's two corners in the Corso did Roland's Hotel stand? When in 1770 he explained to Casanova why he moved, he remarked: *j'ai pris ce palais où j'ai des appartements magnifiques*. Both corner properties were excellent, but only one of them qualifies as a palace on Nolli's map and that is the one to the north (no. 421), the Palazzo della Trinità dei Pellegrini – a well-appointed house owned and let by this hospice. The other (south) corner house (Pl. 135a), which will be discussed later in more detail, also belonged to a religious institution, but to a regular order, namely the Spanish Trinitarians, whose hospice it was. With all due respect to the worldly interests of these brothers, it seems less likely that their religious property was used as a fashionable hotel where notorious prima donnas like *la Cuochetta* stayed. Until we are otherwise persuaded by documentary evidence, we shall continue to believe that it was the palace at no. 421 which bore Roland's signboard; after all, it is said to have been situated "by S. Carlo". We get an excellent impression of its appearance in 1756 from an engraving by Vasi (VII, Pl. 128). We see how the building makes a right-angled re-entrant, thus forming its own little forecourt; this ground plan is still retained. The corner portal had Tuscan, free-standing columns supporting a balcony from which the view of Trinità dei Monti and the Corso's busiest intersection could be admired. And on the wall was a prominent signboard.

When in September 1788 Joh. Fr. von Dalberg, a nobleman and a canon, had to choose a Roman domicile (Damon being the place where he alighted) that would satisfy his snobbish friend Frau von Seckendorf, he eventually found a place to stay which his companion Herder describes in the following words: "einem Palaste (i. e. Ruspoli) gegenüber, und einem Hause *vis-à-vis*, in dem die Favorite des Cardinals Buoncompagni wohnen sollte, es schnitt zwei Hauptstrassen, den Corso and die Condotti, und hatte einen Balkon, um die Ecke laufend, zu beiden" [275]. Is it possible to identify this house with "the palace" used by Roland – or is it the Trinitarians? The decision is tricky, for the property of the Spanish brothers (later the Casa Mengarini) also had, and still has, such a continuous balcony. Unfortunately I know nothing about the residence of the cardinal's mistress, but Goethe may be able to help us out of this dilemma. Informed of Dalberg's ménage he said something to Frau Herder in Weimar, which she passed on to her husband. Goethe, who had a lively recollection of this Roman street, remarked: "Die Seckendorf zeigt einen unsäglichen Verstand in ihrer Einrichtung – es ist das schönste Haus in Rom – mit Eclat und Anstand will sie den Schritt gut machen" [276]. We take note – the house which Goethe has no hesitation in calling "the most handsome in Rome" does indeed deserve to be determined. Could he mean the Spanish hospice? The lover of Antiquity is not very likely to have wreathed a building with such Baroque window pediments with laurels. But the house opposite, as Vasi shows us, was sober in detail, had original form as well as a certain solemn harmony and – it had columns. These were virile, "Etruscan". If this argument holds water, Roland's house on the corner had been given a signal distinction by the poet – three stars. It has since been converted.

The painter Pierre related some time in 1786 what Roman cafés looked like when he was young; he had been a boarder at the Académie de France 1735–1740. "In Rome's beautiful street", by which he must have meant the Corso [277], there were at that time merely three coffee houses and they were fitted up in ordinary shops (*botteghe*) without any

397

special decoration. The furnishings consisted of plain wooden tables and chairs with straw seats. The landlord, dressed up as a Levantine, smoked his pipe and ate an onion for lunch [278]. One of these coffee houses was the *Caffè del Veneziano,* since 1725 situated on the corner of Largo Sciarra and Via Caravita (now a savings bank). It received its name from a Venetian landlord who taught the Romans to drink black coffee in the Turkish style [279], a man in fact to set a fashion in Rome. As in other cafés, lemonade and sherbet were also served. This place was however not Rome's oldest café, as has been frequently stated, for de Blainville visited a coffee house in 1703 [280]. The Venetian in the Corso had a brilliant clientèle, among the regulars were Metastasio and Piccini; literature was discussed, music criticized and the world set to rights in these wretched rooms by the proudest street in the world. Outside, you could both see and hear the carnival. On a snowy January evening in 1731 as Metastasio sat in his room near the Jesuiter Platz in Vienna, he recalled that it was just about this time that the horse-race in the Corso would be starting. He seized his quill and in a letter to the singer Marianna Benti Bulgarini gave a descriptive picture of the sight that had so often rushed past him as he sat in the Caffè del Veneziano (and the windows of the prima donna mentioned): There they come! Here they are! How many horses? Seven! Whose is in front? Gabrielli's but wait, Colonna's is taking the lead. Ah, Jesus Maria, what is this I see? A man falling under the hooves of one of the barbs. He must surely have been killed. His poor mother! Are they carrying him away? No, no ... it was a dog ..." [281].

Across the road from the Venetian *bottega da caffè* was another famous rendezvous "under the Arco di Carbognano", the arch between Palazzo Sciarra and another palace on the opposite corner of the Via delle Muratte. The whole of this picturesque area (now completely rebuilt) can be seen in Vasi (IV, Pl. 67). It was a very cheerful corner for the ill-lit cafés. Pinelli, when very young, spent his time here playing the fool and singing and drawing caricatures of the guests. Like many other writers who have given accounts of the superficial life in the capital (to mention only Gabriel de Saint-Aubain and Fritz Jürgensen) Pinelli learned his best lessons at the tables in the cafés [282]. Further up the

Corso stood the elegant establishment favoured by the Romantic Age, the *Caffè Nuovo,* which was installed in a suite of high-ceilinged rooms on the ground floor of the Palazzo Ruspoli. The beau monde spent leisurely hours here among gilded pier-glasses, silken hangings and busts, sprawling on sofas and playing billiards. At the back was a garden with orange trees where drinks were served.

When in 1786 Pierre was reminiscing about the good old days and then had a look at the cafés of that date, he found them decorated according to the Parisian fashion "and mine host changes the cloth for every meal". Stendhal did not experience anything like that in the Caffè Nuovo and he was far from impressed by the seventeen smoke-filled rooms. The waiters "considered themselves to be the most unhappy beings" when they were forced to put on a clean cloth [283]. European culture had at last arrived in unsophisticated Rome. We can *en flanant* think of the Ruspoli palace as a place of entertainment, not merely the house of an important family. You almost break your neck when trying to get a full view of the enormous latticed windows of the ground floor (Pl. 135a), behind which, gentlemen in Thorvaldsen's days indulged in very small cups of coffee.

Just as the Corso about 1740 only had three cafés, so the much shorter but very fashionable Via dei Condotti had merely a single one. This was under the roof of Palazzo Capizucchi-Gavotti and was visited by Casanova in 1744 [284]. The *Caffè Greco* [285] was probably established in the 1760's and it quickly became popular as the meeting-place for artists, especially the German and Scandinavian; in Thorvaldsen's days it had become quite an institution. Heinse gave it as his address in 1781 [286]. The still existent coffee house has externally retained the original basic features which were typical of the genre: merely a door and the bow-window of the *bottega*. Originally there was only one small dark room, about 8 paces wide, furnished with benches. This was how the composer Mendelssohn described it in 1830, and he found the artists' mongrels detestable [287]; in the same year Berlioz called this café *une détestable taverne* [288]. But Heinse's generation of rough Teutons made themselves at home with their tobacco pipes, talked a lot of drivel about art and spat on the floor.

The Levantine's coffee shop with the rough exterior had for many years a figure standing at the entrance whose appearance was gruesome, entirely in the spirit of Gothic Romanticism. This was the misshapen dwarf "Bajocco". Moritz mentions in 1787 that he stationed himself here to beg from the sons of the Muses, whom he sought to please not merely by his exterior, but also by calling himself "antique" [289]. The painter Grund once witnessed a foreigner about to beat up a crippled midget, whereupon the latter struck a pose and shouted: *Sono Romano!* [290]. This presumably was "Bajocco" holding his own in the same way as he stuck to his post outside the door of the Caffè Greco. We know that the Danish painter Jens Juel painted a full-length portrait of this pitiful oddity, but apart from that, the artist does not seem to have over-exerted himself during his quite long stay in Rome (1773–1776). How typical that this pleasant native of Funen should find the model for his principal work outside his regular haunt – and that he sought a pathetic subject from everyday life, while Abildgaard and Sergel created their exuberant human figures – Philoctetus and Tobias and the fish – by learned studies in the Carracci gallery in the Palazzo Farnese [291]. To me the beggar on Juel's canvas is inextricably linked with the shop in the Via dei Condotti. This human ruin, a mass of grey and brown, was wholly in tune with the character of the place, which was rank and oppressive before the age of the tailcoat made it convivial.

The narrow house in the Piazza di Spagna (no. 88), where the *Caffè Inglese* was situated, is still in existence. The façade is unobstrusive. Practically all the British artists in Rome frequented this place and had their mail sent here – like Richard Wilson in 1752 [292], Northcote in 1777 [293] – but real gentlemen ignored the place. In 1765 Tobias Smollett wrote that no Englishman above the level of artists and guides ever visited a coffee house in Rome – unless he belonged to the Johnny Raws, who posed as *dilettanti*, were *poxed and pillaged* by aged female singers and were led by the nose by art dealers [294]. This was the year that Boswell appeared here, and in 1779 the young Lord Herbert arranged to meet his acquaintances in (or outside) the notorious café [295]. The obnoxious Thomas Jenkins spun his webs from here. He dealt in antiques, fakes, more often than not, was commission agent for various English nobles and ended up a banker [296]. The fame of the Caffè Inglese during the Age of Reason is due not least to the wall decorations in pseudo-Egyptian style, for which Piranesi had made the drawings. Weinlig, who visited the café in 1767 [297], compared the décor with Piranesi's designs for chimneypieces (published 1769); they are terrible. The great lithographic artist was in those days employed in an advisory capacity for the interior decoration in the antique style and as "designer" of all sorts of odds and ends; he provided Dr Burney with drawings of classical musical instruments in 1770 [298]. The interior did of course acquire what is termed an "artistic atmosphere". Here too, as in restaurants of a later age, it was produced with the help of the pastiche; the English coffee house being a pioneer of this dubious genre. In 1776 the painter Thomas Jones described the Caffè Inglese as a dirty vaulted room, its walls covered with paintings of sphinxes, obelisks and pyramids ... more suitable for decorating the interior of an Egyptian tomb than a room for social gatherings [299]. The other Roman coffee shops were unadorned and relied on the atmosphere that some people create around them to contribute to the place.

It was the same with Rome's innumerable taverns. Wherever they were – opposite the Pantheon or in the fusty alleys of Trastevere – they resembled taprooms and were as bare as unused stables. They were timeless, beyond all style, just primitive stores. That was why they were so alive, beloved by all and never out of date. Some unusual wineshops were found near the Porto di Ripa Grande; a Roman tavern is not as a rule thought of as a dockland dive, but when in the summer, people promenaded under the trees along the quay (Pl. 75) and needed a little refreshment, they got into the habit of buying Spanish wine from the boats moored alongside. This had the result that some of the skippers settled on shore and set up taprooms, proper *bodegas* in fact, in Ospizio di S. Michele, where the storerooms behind the entrance arcades were deep and cool. Norbert von Grund mentions these taverns in the 1780's [300]. One of them was to become very popular among artists in Thorvaldsen's time; this was Raffaele Anglada's "Spanish Wineshop", depicted in 1824 in a painting by Franz Catel [301]. Through the open segmental arch, wide as that of a warehouse, the monasteries on the Aventine could be seen across the river. Despite the fact that the premises are thus easily determined, nobody has yet – as far as I can see – searched for the tavern in the building of the hospital itself, where even today it can be located without difficulty. The Spaniard's tavern, which also before Goethe's time smelt of red wine ("even mixed with water it is strong," says Grund), and of *diversi vini stravecchi* (among others probably sherry and the manzanilla from San Lucar so much appreciated by the Swedish poet Bellman), is perhaps the only taproom in Rome whose background has remained unchanged since the siphon went into the bunghole here for the first time.

And now, since our stroll through the city is reaching its end, we must try to retain the impressions through senses other than sight. Let us inhale Rome and harken to its voices.

The streets had the smell that streets have, the various trades adding generously to it all. And it ripened to its fullness, matured as it was throughout centuries. The local odours were mixed with the stagnant atmosphere, common to the whole of working-class Rome – the efflux of rancid oil and sour wine, of garlic and cheese, of sweat and horses, intersected from the open doors by the mustiness which emanates from old clothes crowded between dank stones. We find it at home in church porches, sacristies and mortuary chapels. It was all based on the stink of filth. Where there's trade there's waste. Rubbish stemming from fish, slimy guts, bloated cowpats were reminders long after the market had finished. "The smell of rotten cabbage-stumps pursues and stifles me everywhere," remarked Stendhal [302]. The humans satisfied the call of nature where it was convenient, every nook and cranny was fouled. And every house was saturated with the penetrating strench of cat's piss. Urine flowed in the vestibules of palaces. When the archaeologist Mau, as late as the beginning of the 1870's, surprised a peasant woman in an unmistakable situation behind his front door, she excused herself with the words: *Credevo che fosse un palazzo!* This kind of architecture was reserved for women, the men relieved themselves where they chose [303]. During a survey of the French Academy in the Corso in 1787, the backstairs of the palace turned out to be so filthy that the director's hair stood on end. Not only the people who lived in the academy but also strangers from outside performed on the doorstep of the kitchen, which should have had the result of all the residents in the house getting typhoid [304]. This was the year that Mrs Piozzi, nee Thrale, found it necessary to hold her nose in the palaces she visited; there were faeces on the main staircase [305]. The papal government made well-intentioned attempts to combat the filthiness, but in vain. Water-carts were indeed used, these were barrels on wheels, but only in the Corso and certain other main streets, especially before Sundays and public holidays [306], but apart from that it was left to "Jupiter Pluvius" to clean things up with his showers, the only result being that the muck was spread even further around in a thin porridge of slush [307]. De Brosses thought that the Piazza Navona was even worse than the Place Maubert in Paris [308], and Smollett said that it was just as dirty as West Smithfield, which is the place where cattle was sold in London [309]. It did not improve matters that public middens (*immondezaio*) were established on street corners here and there, as well as in the middle of squares, for the rubbish heaps were left for weeks on end before being carted away [310]. Kotzebue considered Rome clean in comparison with Naples, for the whole of that city was a sewer [311]. A fine souvenir of Roman dirty habits is preserved in the number of inscribed plates which can still be seen on many houses, where they enjoin cleanliness in dignified terms. Examples can be found on Palazzo Crescenzi, Via del Seminario (1743), by "Il Facchino" on the side of Palazzo De Carolis (1748), under a statue of the Madonna on the Palazzo Borgnana opposite Il Gesù (1796). A similar notice on the corner of Via di Mario dei Fiori and Via dei Condotti forbids by a decree of 1733 the dumping of rubbish at this crossroad and directs those intending to do so to the nearest rubbish tips – in the Strada delle Carrozze, at the Fontana della Barcaccia in the middle of the Spanish Square and in the Vicolo della Sirena. The Romans were at any rate able to learn appreciation of good typography from the notices which *il Presidente delle Strada* caused to be set into the masonry. Otherwise they stewed cheerfully in their own juice.

Above the stuffy streets rose a song from young and happy throats in a flood of the charming *ritornelli* (*stornelli*), which were improvised by lovers at the invocation of the names of flowers:

> *Fiore de rosa,*
> *Nun c'è passate più per quella casa,*
> *che la vostra ragazza è fatta sposa.*

which might be translated as:

> Blossoming rose,
> No youth now wanders past the door,
> His love is now a wife whom he did lose.

And the cries of the street vendors shrilled out from dawn to long past dusk. When Holger Jacobaeus was in Rome in 1677 he noted down many of them and thanks to this alert Danish physician, we can still hear an echo of the long drawn-out cries [312]. After sunrise *il padrone* was awakened by the offers of a brandy on an empty stomach: *Robba fina, robba dolce, acquavita!* This pleasant early morning greeting was followed by the short call of the goatherd: *Capra, capra!*, and the maid went down and fetched the milk straight from the udder. The third important character in the house, the cat, was not forgotten – at the sound of the sharp little tune: *Trippa per la gatta!* the pussy-cats streamed out expecting their chunk of chitterling [313]. And so it went on all day long amid shouts, clipped or long drawn-out, carried by metallic voices skilled in the art of phrasing, giving the vowels their full resonance. The conflicting cries advertised the loveliest of things. Listen to this selection and imagine yourself in the yellow alleys: hot chestnuts, strawberries from Nemi (small and sweetly scented, picked in the woods and wrapped in damp leaves), fresh olives, fennel and medlars, oysters, onions and cucumbers, brittle pretzels (included here for dietetic reasons), big lobsters, snails (100 to the quart), knuckle of veal and pigs' heads and quarters of lamb. We shall offer three delicacies with their appropriate cries – first the turtle: *Tartaruga, Tartaru-Tartaruga-a!* Did you hear that? Baked pears, a trayful carried on the head: *O pere cotte calde, o pere cotte calde-e-e!* The heartfelt sound of *O boni fichi, o buoni fichi!* Take notice that the word "good" is given a little extra emphasis the second time.

Street vendors also cried two articles that were alpha and omega in the better-class households (and extremes of colour), coal and snow – charcoal for the braziers in the damp rooms, lumps of frozen snow (from the mountains) to cool the wine. One of these *cris de Rome* which Jacobaeus recorded, has awakened me many a time in the morning; the wording is still the same: *O scope, o scope!* That came from the man who sold brooms, real old-fashioned besoms for brushing the floor – and for beating a back as in the old comedies. In the spring of 1955 I heard a woman selling pigeons' eggs in the Campo dei Fiori recommend them with the cry: *Che belle perle!* Of course the poetry of life did not lack representatives in the choir of the itinerant traders; they sang the praises of crickets in tiny cages, finches and siskins, heroic poems and red flowers. *O rose rosse, o rose ros-se!*

When Shelley in 1819 lived in the Palazzo Verospi, he was stimulated by the Jewish dealers in the Vicolo dello Sdrucciolo, the alleyway that runs up to Largo dell' Impresa, who offered their wares with the cry: *Cénci, Cénci!* This means "old clothes". The poet responded to these cries by writing his poem about the unhappy Beatrice Cenci. It must have been the voice of the city that forced its way into his room.

VII

Most of the buildings in the 18th century were the homes of the third estate and the proletariat (*il basso popolo*). One would have thought that all these houses along the streets, which make up the very city, might have attracted the interest of researchers. This is not the case however. Particular investigations are missing, and we know of neither specialist studies in the type of houses, nor monographs on specific stylistic groups [314]. The survey of the subject, which we shall attempt here, must therefore be expected to have flaws in perspective. Our chronologically fixed points, determined carefully, are placed so haphazardly and are so few in number that a conclusive account can only be presented with reservations. Personal observations may however serve as an interim orientation in this extensive field. A detailed argument for some of the hypotheses put forward concerning the course of development cannot be fitted into this chapter.

The many thousands of buildings, which are our present subject, belong to the genre whose common name is "domestic architecture". But it is difficult to operate with this concept in the Rome of the 18th century. If ordinary house building is characterized by the circumstance of ownership and finance, one is tempted to deny the existence of any "domestic architecture" in the city of the popes. For by far the greatest percentage of all the houses was produced by and belonged to the ruling classes, the Church and the aristocracy. Silvagni calculated that about half the estates in *Ager romanus* was owned by church institutions and the other half by the nobility of Rome [315]. As far as the properties within the city area (*il caseggiato nell' interno della città*) were concerned, the ratio of the possessions of the two powers was however different. Wright reported in 1721 that, according to information given him in the city, of the total number of Rome's houses, about 35 000, c. 23 000 were "clerical", i. e. inhabited by people belonging to religious communities and collectively owned by the Church. Should this be true, asks Wright, then who would dare challenge the city's right to be called *Roma la santa?* [316]. The properties owned by the aristocracy accordingly made up a much smaller percentage in the city than in the country.

We must not forget to point out that Wright's calculation of the Church's town properties also included monasteries and convents, various buildings for the religious orders, probably also certain charitable institutions and so on – quite a considerable collection of units. Nevertheless, however brief and approximate this summary may be, let us accept its estimate as a guide. There is no doubt that the Roman domestic dwelling was usually of very undomestic origin. Since the Church and the State, under papal government, was an absolute entity, in fact synonymous concepts as far as jurisdiction was concerned, it can be suggested that the greatest number of Roman dwellings were not merely State property in the wider sense – but that they had been erected as "civic architecture". This unprecedented phenomenon – only possible in the unique conditions of Rome – was to have remarkable consequences from the artistic point of view as well. As individualism flourishes where the majority of the patrons of architecture are private persons, it was consequently subjected to strict limitations in Rome. By religious orders and institutions employing their official architects to produce plans for the numerous and exemplary domestic buildings to be erected on their land, this architecture became imperceptibly standardized in type and style. There can be little doubt that the aesthetic level of the architecture of dwelling houses, which on the average was high, and the excellent harmony produced in the perspective of the streets in Baroque Rome, were chiefly due to the conditions indicated here.

In short, the State and the other powers' faith in communal living produced a massive building project, very progressive for those days, by investing their capital in properties and having them planned by the leading architects of the period. Late Baroque's most modern blocks of flats were erected by the Church of Rome, otherwise so notorious for its conservatism. And this did not take place under the influence of sociological dogmas. The holy state of Rome built "socially" without intending or realizing it; the Church played its role of reformer in the building market, influenced by firmly based financial and technical considerations. There was a moral in this too. On reflection, it is edifying to consider that *civitas dei* held almost a "State monopoly" in building for the masses and thus – under the banner of the Counter-Reformation and heretics being burnt at the stake – set an example for a system which, with the greatest consequence, was put into practice by Communist Russia three centuries later.

The domestic architecture along the Roman streets at this time, cannot be properly assessed unless it is seen against the background of Antiquity. Tradition from the past emerges even more strongly in the public architecture than in the monumental. The Rome of the Caesars, as the world's most important metropolis, had devised the ordinary multi-storeyed blocks of flats – a cultural achievement, which seen from our "functionalistic" era, almost overshadows Classical temple architecture. Fully developed in the first century of the Imperial period, the multi-storeyed building (*insula*) promoted various types, among which the simple wing with shops and workshops (*tabernae*) included in the lowest storey, was to exert a profound influence on posterity. Rational "lines" of houses where each unit was comprised of only "1 shop + 1 front door" (leading to the inside stairs and the upper storeys) achieved a distinctive rhythm in the grouping of the exterior. The "shop" (*taberna*) did not always alternate with the "door", but 2 shops side by side were frequently followed by 2 doors set close together. Both the plebeian low and long detached block of flats and the impressive block of multi-storeyed flats, used as their basis the *taberna* plan. The question as to what extent and how the principles of this *insula* architecture managed to stay alive in Rome and win new topicality after the collapse of the ancient civilisation, is obviously not for us to discuss here [317]. We must limit ourselves to the following observations on questions of relevance. First, we will deal briefly with the reduction in Antiquity's assets in the form of dwellings which took place after the fall of Rome.

The tenement house of several storeys can be analysed according to its vertical and horizontal divisions. It is in the first instance expedient to break the agglomeration down into its component parts ("shop + door" – "door + shop" etc., with corresponding division of the upper storeys). Such sections will thus, when isolated, appear as houses with two bays. As far as we can see, this type was the predominant one in mediaeval Rome and it became extremely general, indeed the most common form of domestic housing during the Renaissance and Baroque. This is readily understood, for it was simple and straightforward, easily adapted to restricted sites, easy to multiply on open sites. The doubled form became particularly popular – the house with the width of four bays must be reckoned as the second basic type. The axial plan is here very characteristic: the outer bays are moved as far as possible to the sides, the two middle ones kept close together $(1-2-1)$. And so, by the close contact $(1-1+1-1)$, the ancient rhythm appears once again. I ask the reader to note this rhythm well which is so much part of Rome. As an example, we reproduce here a house from about 1500 (Pl. 153). A somewhat older two-bay house, from about 1470, can be seen through the columns of the Pantheon's portico (Pl. 10).

Just take a look at the Campo dei Fiori on plate 155. It shows one side of the square with ten houses between two of the streets that lead into it. Eight of them have two bays each and only the houses on the corners diverge from the norm. If we compare the photograph with Vasi's engraving [318], which shows the square from the same angle, we recognize all the two-bay houses, but every one of them has been increased in height by one storey at a later date. These dwelling houses with their

153. *House in Piazza di S. Giovanni della Malva, Trastevere.*

154a. Terrace house in *Via dei Ciancaleoni*.

154b. The same terrace house.

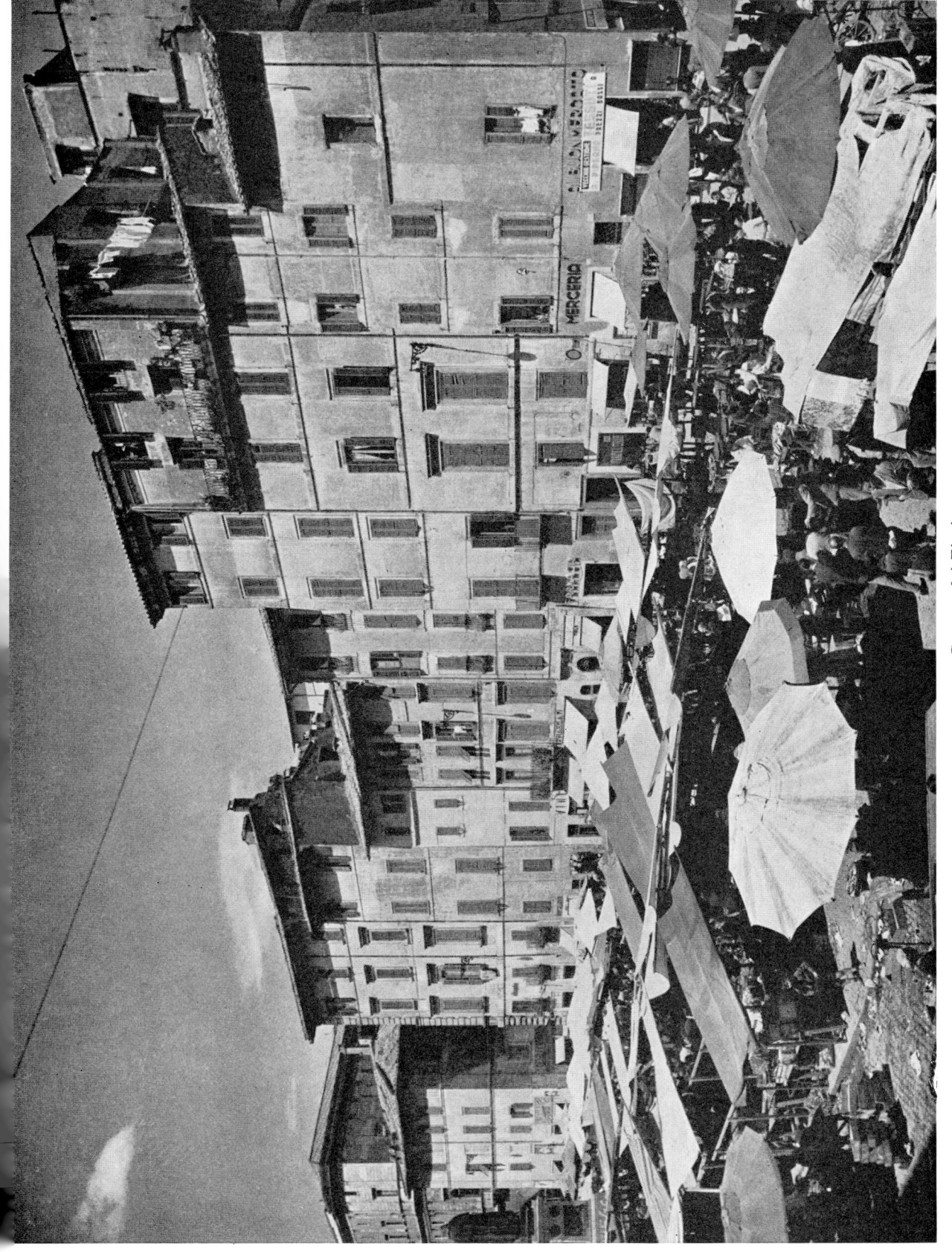
155. *Campo dei Fiori.*

156a. House near S. Eustachio.

156b. House in V[i]a dell'Oro.

157. *Via della Chiesa Nuova.*

159. *Piazza di S. Paolino alla Regola.*

161. *Houses on the western side of Piazza di Trevi.*

163. House in *Via di Campo Marzio* (*Piazza di S. Lorenzo in Lucina*).

164. Cornerhouse between Via dell'Arco della Pace and Vicolo degli Osti.

differing heights belong to several periods between the beginning of the 17th century and the 19th century, but structurally they are identical. The general rule is, that the older the façade, the further the two windows have been moved to the sides, emphasizing the entity of the wall. The earliest Roman Baroque houses of this type, usually three storeys high, are severe and reserved; the lowest section of the walling may even slant like bastions (as found on a house in Vicolo delle Orsoline). A handsome house of the earlier plain type is 17 Vicolo degli Osti, and other examples can be found in the Piazza della Scala in Trastevere.

Among the still numerous characteristic, unadorned two-bay houses from Late Baroque, we must confine ourselves to singling out for special mention a small group in the Via dei Farnesi (Pl. 48), 12–13 Via del Governo Vecchio, 30 and 32a Via Francesco Crispi; 23–24 Via della Vite; late examples of the type – with only slight separation of the windows – are 12–13 Via di Capo le Case and 18–19 Via della Vite. A selection of four-bay houses is not easily made, but 248–251 Via Panisperna may be regarded as the basic type; 30–32 Piazza della Torretta with window pediments in "Régence" style and the houses 36–39 Piazza di Pietra, which probably date from the end of the 18th century, have thin horizontal joints and not entirely balanced spaces between the windows.

In the Via della Purificazione, which since the close of the 17th century has been a low-class street in the foreign quarter, one could until recently observe a collection of predominantly narrow houses. The rather monotonous street wall looks strangely dreary and has probably always done so, partly because it looks as if it were bled white by predatory builders, partly – perhaps especially – because the alley by way of exception is dead-straight (and on a steep slope); the row of small units becomes hopelessly uniform in a perspective without declination. Later neglect increases the impression of poverty. The street with the exalted name was called "The artists' ghetto" in the vernacular, for behind every one of the façades lived people who became well known to posterity. The three-bay house which is reproduced in plate 147 was the sculptor Alexander Trippel's home for a time and he may have executed his bust of Goethe here [319]. Strange to think of the poet (and the freemason Fr. Münter) passing through this door; the street still reeks of proletarians and bohemians. Georg Brandes struggled with death a few steps away from Trippel's rooms, cared for by compassionate people. All these cramped and poverty-stricken houses, how reluctantly we consider them as merely numbers and types.

The year Goethe sat for Trippel (1787), his friend Moritz rented rooms in a house in the Via Borgognona. In contrast to most lodgers in such wretched surroundings he gave some information about his house, which belonged to a religious order and was as narrow as a coffin. The stairs led directly from the street to the first floor, where Moritz was installed; his landlord and landlady made do with the storey above. Each storey consisted of only one room facing the street and a bedroom facing the yard, in which grew a fig tree [320]. In 1780 the Swedish architect Erik Palmstedt, gave a most professional report of this very type of house, the most common in Rome. "Downstairs," he writes, "is a shop with a doorway and a small flight of steps, upstairs at the most two rooms facing the street and one the yard". The lowest flight of steps is usually made of stone, the upper of wood. The yards were laid out as diminutive gardens [321]. This was the architecture for the majority of Romans. The smallest unit of the building was the narrowest possible section between vertical lines that could be made in Antiquity's long, multi-storeyed blocks of flats.

We mentioned above, that the antique *insula* could also be analysed according to horizontal lines. If you divided them up in layers, you got the low, long block with its shops and above that one, and in exceptional cases two, storeys. While two-bay and four-bay houses belonged to confined parts of the city, the long, detached block of flats fitted in naturally in the semi-built-up area on the outskirts. It became a sort of poor people's tenement house, somewhere between the "shacks" of the Middle Ages and the long blocks of flats built for the workers outside the city gates at the beginning of the industrial revolution [322]. How much this interesting type, not previously studied, was used in Baroque Rome is difficult to say. Time has not dealt kindly with it [323]; we can, however, point out two instructive examples. On the east side of the Piazza del Popolo once stood a long "suburban tenement house" like that, and it can be seen in a painting from about 1620 ascribed to Sinibaldo Scorza

[324]. It was built later than 1577, since it cannot be seen in Dupérac's prospect of Rome from that year, and existed until Valadier reorganized the square. The windows were paired two by two. The second example, which has been quite overlooked, is still preserved, a shabby block, well hidden away in Vicolo dei Ciancaleoni behind the Palazzo Cimarra (Pl. 154a-b). The building, which has been condemned, is perhaps the last of its type in Rome and, to tell the truth, seems far more intriguing than many an antique plinth, whose excavation is heralded with a fanfare of trumpets. Here we see the genuine, simple "*taberna*-house" still standing and still inhabited. The linked doors have now been partly walled up, but the system is easily recognizable. A truly Roman monument and an extraordinary sample of historical tradition. For although the long building has the structure of Antiquity, it must have been built after 1676, since it cannot be seen in Falda's prospect (but on Nolli's map). It was, no doubt, erected soon after the Palazzo Cimarra and by its owner, who wanted to make good use of his site.

The types of houses which we have dealt with briefly so far, represent the majority of Rome's domestic architecture up to Late Baroque – the narrow houses make up the great mass, the long blocks of flats are dispersed to the outlying districts. We now turn to another basic type, the large block of flats (*casamento*) of up to six storeys high. It too has its roots in Antiquity, being derived from the fully developed *insula* of the Imperial age. Obviously such large, tall buildings were the part of the city that suffered most by its gradual destruction during the Dark Ages; the smaller houses survived Rome's disintegration and adapted more easily to the city which had grown in such a confused manner. The monumental *insula* did not last through the Middle Ages as a continuing type of dwelling.

The theoreticians of the Renaissance tried to bring it back to life and to include it in their programme for "the ideal city". They had no luck in Rome (but succeeded in Venice [325]). The palaces of the Bramante school, which were constructed on Classical lines and aimed at a reconstruction of the *domus* of Antiquity, should not be conceived as merely an outcome of a "rebirth"; there is a latent tradition inherent in them too. Palazzo Caprini (by Bramante) and Palazzo Dell'Aquila (by Raphael) were erected with *tabernae* on their ground floor, as were Peruzzi's Palazzo Costa and Giulio Romano's Palazzo Cicciaporci [326]. Though there was a desire to re-establish the antique palace, it was more the Classical *insula* which came into existence, smaller and more richly decorated, after its long hibernation. But the few palaces built in the Roman High Renaissance could only stimulate the style, the furthering of a general building of blocks of flats was out of the question. When after about 1600, this began to gain ground in Rome, it had to be influenced by other impulses. These came, not very unexpectedly, from the preserves of the Church. The greatest builder and landowner, *Ecclesia Romana,* considered its greatest non-ecclesiastical field of activity and put into practice the rich experiences gained and tested in monastic architecture since the Middle Ages. Here were to be found not only useful prototypes for the solid large-scale domestic block for the tenement house made up of small units – one might even suggest that the ordinary monastic building in fact was the only available pattern. So we see the monasteries' architectural evolution during the Baroque period running parallel with the great "domestic" building activities and influencing its development at every stage – very crucial in the first phase (especially during Urban VIII's pontificate) and we must not forget that the monastery's architect also erected its tenement houses.

Another source of inspiration for the regular housing complex, especially the smaller ones, was undoubtedly the canonry connected with a church, or the presbytery. In the shape of a flanking building it was controlled by the front of the church, its width and height being in rhythm with the latter's lines. That the monastery became the mother house for domestic tenement houses, is one of the most remarkable feats in Roman architecture. Sober calculation produced this transformation, a halo of unworldly logic surrounds it. And finally – through the religious house composed of cells, the inherent Latin legacy was transferred to the growing city of Baroque. What Renaissance did not succeed in doing out in the open fields, with its gaze fixed on the ruins, was accomplished in successive stages behind enclosing monastery walls. The pope's seat of residence regained the Imperial *insula.*

We can throw some light on this development with the help of a few examples. The square in front of S. Maddalena in Campo Marzio is held together by uniform *casamenti*, dated 1628, which already represent the typical block of flats in its strictest form. S. Eustachio's flanking house (Pl. 156a) reproduced by Cruyl in 1665 [327] has the two-stroke rhythm for its windows, but is otherwise a well-balanced tenement house of medium size, at that time very up to date. A main example of the domestic complex on the largest scale, is the imposing block which according to its inscription was erected in 1675 as a wall in a new street along the side of Chiesa Nuova (Pl. 157). This cube, so powerful in its pure rationalism, was presumably designed by Carlo Rainaldi who replanned the street [328]. The building is completely metropolitan in the modern sense. In Copenhagen this stage was not reached until shortly before 1800. A well-hidden notice [329] designates a couple of Roman tenement houses from 1704, erected for the Augustines following a drawing by G. B. Contini. One is on the corner of Vicolo della Campana and Vicolo Leonetto, the other is no. 42–43 Via dell'Orso. We reproduce the latter (Pl. 156b); it has *botteghe* on the ground floor but otherwise looks like the bare wall of a monastery. Tenement houses observing as strict a rule as this, with no embellishment and purely functional, became fashionable in Rome in Watteau's time, when Rococo was in embryo. You see them in many old streets and hesitate to date them from such a recent time. A characteristic property with close-set rows of windows with shouldered architraves is Casa Guarnieri, 37 Via di Porta Pinciana. It was built by the architect Giovanni Francesco Guarnieri (born c. 1680 in Rome, died there in 1745) presumably after he came back from a stay in Cassel, and was an experiment in this predominantly foreign quarter. The building was a favourite lodging-house for artists until far into the 19th century, Ernst Meyer being one of those who lived here [330]. Of essentially finer quality is the large building on the corner of the Via del Babuino and Via Alibert (Pl. 167) which follows and continues Carlo Fontana's late style and is very striking to the eye. This was deliberate, for the house served in a way as a façade for the elegant Teatro Alle Dame (D'Alibert) in the narrow parallel street behind. Nolli's map of 1748 shows that the main entrance from "the main road" was through the gateway in this building and the corridor to the courtyard, from which a bridge went over the street at the back, to the side door of the theatre. The opera house was built in 1716 by Matteo Sassi (enlarged 1720) [331]. Whether the apartment house was used by a theatre built later; whether it was erected at the same time as the latter to stimulate competition or was adapted to the existing attraction of the place cannot be decided here, but the intimate connection between the two buildings is quite certain and makes the dating to about 1720 seem reasonable. When our friend Moritz in 1787 lay ill in a house next to the large property (he would have been glad to leave), he was plagued every midnight by the noisy crowds that spilled out of the theatre and by the rumble of carriages until about two o'clock [332]. Valadier later had his home in this noisy building on one of the liveliest corners in Rome.

The city scene was changed drastically by the new huge apartment houses which emerged everywhere. They made squares and streets seem more civilized, but also darker, although the façades were made lighter. The whimsical character of the city, which we know from the numerous prospects by Cruyl and Falda, grew less picturesque, but at the same time took on sharper contrasts. Just look at plates 158 and 159; they explain better than any words about the past and the present.

It is interesting to follow in the examples selected, how the two-bay and four-bay houses retained their character down through the 18th century in rivalry with the large tenement house – a contest which the older types were bound to lose. It is quite often kept up by infiltration. If we look at the left wall of the square in front of Fontana di Trevi (Pl. 161) we see three houses, the outer ones each on two axes, the middle one of four bays according to the traditional scheme. They are easy to distinguish from one another; they are not merely a solid block, but form also a free composition with concentration on the middle. This grouping is eminently Roman; the individual parts merge into a voluntary arrangement. Between the simple corner house on the left and the corner in rusticated work, which gradually diminishes towards the top on the right, the whole history of Baroque is fused into a single whole. Piranesi's frontal view of the Trevi fountain shows the mixture as it is today; only the top storey of the middle house and its balcony with "Rococo" windows are younger, and the section right at the top is no doubt very recent.

The property directly opposite the fountain (Pl. 160) is also instructive, consisting of two or three older houses. Hefty columns included in the masonry of the modernized ground floor, date from the early Middle Ages. Whatever inner conflicts the building may contain are concealed behind a front which to some extent follows the scheme 2-2-2; the middle pair stand almost shoulder to shoulder while the outer pairs of windows are accentuated by bull's-eye windows in the very top storey. This excellent house was depicted by Lieven Cruyl in 1666 [333]. In substance it is much like the present one, though the top storey was added later – but before 1756, since Vasi shows it (VII, Pl. 139) – on which occasion the windows below were given their curved pediments and the roof crowned by a belvedere. The house on the right has one too, and a good-sized one at that (also shown by Cruyl). The occupants of these houses by Trevi intended to enjoy their little square. When Salvi's fountain appeared they had the best permanent seats in one of the world's most attractive theatres.

It might be enlightening to compare the properties just mentioned with a private building, which like the others, stands opposite a much appreciated scene, this is the large house in the Via di S. Giovanni in Laterano whose opposite neighbours are S. Clemente and the gardens on Monte Oppio. It is also situated on *Il Possesso,* the route of the cavalcade (Pl. 162). Nolli showed it on his map from 1748. While groups of houses in Rome itself were brought close together by compulsion, this stately building took shape on an open site, so it became homogeneous in its plasticity and symmetry around the axis through the portal and belvedere. As far as form goes, it was subject to the same conditions as an aristocratic country house (cf. e.g. Villa Montalto's "Casino principale" [334], but from the social point of view the building was an unusual example of a "patrician house", which was not only inhabited by "upper class people", but had also been erected by a rich commoner, a bourgeois. In 1769 it belonged to the Merolli family who made their money by commerce and farm rents from the Campagne [335]. The tycoon's house on the erstwhile desolate road between the Colosseum and the Lateran is a real town house, but with the outlines of a defiant fortress.

Turning back to domiciles in cramped conditions, we look at no. 22

Piazza di S. Lorenzo in Lucina which stands at the end of the square (Pl. 163). It also appears in an engraving, not very accurately done, by Vasi [336], and so must be older than the 1750's. The front of the building has a slightly convex bend, the vertical of which is the dividing line; on the left the façade has two windows, on the right it has the axial plan of 2-2. In other words, the front is not composed as one entity, in which case it would be exceptional, yet the windows are distributed on each side of the bend in the wall according to the traditional rhythms. How vital they became in the hands of a builder is shown in a different way at 27–30 Piazza di Firenze (Pl. 165), whose ambition it was to have the loftiest roof above the narrow forecourt – and for that reason this little Roman verse might be fitting:

> *Chi fabbrica la casa in piazza*
> *O che è troppo alta o troppo bassa* [337].

It certainly attracts attention by being a rare example, in the city of that time, of an ordinary house having pilaster strip. Although there was room here for three windows with one on the middle axis, the architect made the obligatory two-windows project. So one could say the anonymous master of his craft built in a headless manner, but not indifferently. Notice also the windows that have been moved right out to the ends of the building.

A narrow façade which juts out like a bastion between two converging streets often has two windows. They are carefully treated as befits such a strongly protruding and isolated front – cf. plate 164 and a house, now no longer extant, in Piazza Montanara [338]. In Denmark for instance, an attempt at three windows would have been made here, or merely one. The pair of doors, linked like a hook and eye, was so common a phenomenon that it was often used as a purely decorative motif (i. e. without any functional pause in the rhythm). Good examples of this can be seen in Piazza della Suburra and Piazza degli Zingari; a house in Piazza delle Coppelle has the scheme: door – 2 windows – door. Let us also look at 82–83 Via dei Farnesi. The bare stretch of wall between two very detached windows at the extreme ends, cried out to be filled in. This was mainly done with the help of circular recesses, sometimes with and sometimes without religious paintings (Pl. 166) or by Madonellas, their frames heralding the Louis Quinze style. Look too at 107–108 Via del Seminario and an admirable house in Piazza della Rotonda (Pl. 135b) which Vasi also shows (II, Pl. 25). The demolished *canonica* at S. S. Angeli Custodi al Tritone had its façade broken up by a stucco relief; its angels and clouds made the whole front shimmer [339]. While we delight in seeing such decorative façades, we should not forget that they were deviations from the norm found here and there. If a permanent carnival seemed to be celebrated in the dark alley, it was after all to the glory of God.

Many of the most impressive tenement houses from the period after about 1720 were of course erected in the city squares whenever room could be found among the churches, abbeys and palaces. Now speculative building and an increasing demand for distinguished-looking houses took place concurrently. As we walk from square to square we come across the most splendid examples of Rome's domestic architecture from Late Baroque to French Empire, as we do in the Corso and the main streets of the foreign quarter. We shall seek out some of the best representatives; in the Piazza di S. Ignazio the collection of good-looking apartment houses from the 1720's has already been discussed, as have the houses flanking la Scalea in the Piazza di Spagna, and we remember that two religious orders were responsible for the building. The large solid house, no. 9 in the Spanish Square was depicted by Piranesi and can still be seen in this form, although increased by one storey (Pl. 138) [340]. The two *piani nobili* have curved pediments and the house was very popular with discriminating people, arbiters of taste and well-off artists. The painter Ph. J. Hackert had his lodgings here (1768–1786) [341], as had the famous carver of gems, Giovanni Pichler (died 1779); Weinlig pointed out the house in this connection when discussing Piranesi's engravings [342]. Goethe bought "fine pieces" from Pichler [343] and Wilh. Tischbein made drawings of antique heads from model casts in his rooms [344]. Finally, No. 9 had the honour, for a while, to house the poet Vincenzo Monti, married 1791 to Teresa Pichler [345]. Nobody regarding the north end of the Piazza di Spagna with a discerning eye and affection can overlook this excellent building, large and vigorous, among the other private houses in the square.

The Piazza Capranica contains a large residence which is particularly impressive here because of the elegant decoration of its façade and its height (Pl. 169). We are able to give it a date and determine its patron by a combination of facts. The Roman journal "Cracas" advertised in 1754 that Goldoni's comedies — two of which were produced that year at the Teatro della Pace [346] — were for sale "in the bookshop bearing the sign of S. Benedetto in Sig. Carlo Giannini's new *palazzina* in the Piazza Capranica" [347]. The obvious supposition that this new building, flattered by the appellation "little palace", is identical with the house reproduced here, is confirmed in an archaeological handbook. The third edition of Venuti's "Descrizione delle Antichità di Roma", prepared in 1824 by Piale, gives the information (II, 125) that ancient ruins were found in 1745 during the digging of the foundations for "Carlo Giannini's house opposite the church" (S. Maria in Aquiro). Since the front of the building faces this church, identification cannot be in doubt. The architect splits up the tall, lanky façade into many divisions in order to control it, and makes use of a section of smooth rustification at the bottom, which was very up to date (cf. Palazzo Macchi di Cellere and Palazzo Boncompagni-Cerasi, both from the 1730's). But the balcony as a centralizing element, is still not able to obliterate the old "domestic" duality; this is established by the paired portals. So it was in one of the shops on either side that people were able not only to buy Goldoni's comedies, but also libretti of the operas performed in the Teatro Capranica across the square, where it stood behind the stern walls of a Late Gothic palace [348].

Another small square, Largo dell'Impresa, contained an impressive dominant feature in the large residential block (now no. 2–4 Piazza del Parlamento), which the Augustines erected in 1748. We know the date from an inscription on the house, in memory of the fact that during the laying of the foundations, an obelisk from Heliopolis was discovered [349]. The dating is valuable, the undecorated *cantonata* shows that Baroque's simple forms flourished in speculative building up to Winckelmann's time. After the site around it was cleared, when the little square was done away with, the property lost the grandeur which it possessed in the enclosed square and among small streets that never saw the light

165. *House in Piazza di Firenze.*

166. House near S. Maria della Quercia.

167. *House in Via del Babuino on the corner of Via Alibert.*

168. *House in Piazza Pasquino.*

169. *House in Piazza Capranica.*

170. *Houses in Via del Corso (nos. 89–91, 93–94).*

171. *House near Tor' de' Conti.*

172. *Via dei Pianellari.*

of the sun. This district, called *la Vignaccia,* was pregnant with the drama of Roman everyday life right up to the roof tops where the cats howled. The papal administration of the lottery (hence the name "Impresa") had its offices in the square, surrounded by apprehension and expectation. Ugo Bassville is supposed to have been murdered with a cutthroat razor by a barber here (1793), Belli spent the wretched years of his youth nearby, and Stendhal, whose address in 1827 was "Largo dell' Impresa della Lotteria", mentions in a letter *la vue infame* from his window. Perhaps his cheap garret was in this very apartment house, which was owned by the Augustines [350].

By going round its corner on Via di Campo Marzio when you enter Piazza di S. Lorenzo in Lucina, you come upon a brighter world, the fashionable square and a pretentious property (no. 31–35) facing the monastery of the Minorites [351]. On the façade all sorts of decorative motifs are misused, from the stucco panels of a Rauzzini to the chunky capitals of a Valvassori; it is a veritable Vanity Fair. It would be unfair to call it "Rococo"; it is "Gründer" style, stucco. Piazza di Pasquino, the booksellers' triangle, was given a slim tenement house (Pl. 168), which in embellishment was very like the Casa Giannini. But here the double beat is kept up by the rhythm of the windows and there are no vertical divisions, thereby making the façade more balanced. The indecisive garlands surrounding shells, which decorate the high-up piano nobile's windows, and the tryglyphs and rosettes in the top cornice reveal the fact that this house, intended on a bigger scale (the vertical toothing on the right hand side indicates this) is fairly late, perhaps from the 1760's [352]. It combines ancient building habits with a dawning Neo-Classicism – in the carefree atmosphere of Rococo.

And now into the main street. The south corner of the Corso with the Via dei Condotti was enlarged 1733–34 with the splendid house which we have discussed above. When the Trinitarians expressed the wish to flank their new church S. S. Trinità degli Spagnuoli with, on one side, a monastery and, on the other, a hospice for laymen, Clement XII gave his permission on the express condition that the monastery was to be sited in the Via dei Condotti, this being considered more fitting; there was nothing against the apartment house facing the Corso. The church's Portuguese architect provided the plans, Giuseppe Sardi was the contractor [353]. Goldoni rented rooms in this pleasant building from November 1758 to August 1759 in the home of Abbate Pinto, a member of the papal court, and had much pleasure from his stay, not least the balcony. The convivial life in the house provided the subject matter for the comedy *Gl'Inamorati* [354]. The Minims from Trinità dei Monti in 1733 bought some houses opposite the Palazzo Fiano in the Corso, so that they could also build a palace for letting [355]. Further along the street, opposite S. Carlo, you can find two typical Rococo houses (Pl. 170), one with the distribution 1–2–1; in the other this rhythm has been abandoned.

We find that many domestic dwellings from the decades before and after 1750 are devoted to decoration pure and simple, most noticeable around the windows, and frequently make use of a coquettish motif such as the wrought iron balcony. It must have been Rauzzini who made this popular in Rome. Excellent examples of such flowery houses can be admired in the Via degli Zingari (from the 1730's) [356], in the Via del Banco di S. Spirito (no. 47–48), in the Via S. Agata de' Goti (no. 6). This engaging ornate fashion was but a fleeting ripple on an otherwise calm surface. Soon the fronts of the houses quietened down again. And taking the monasteries as example, the old rhythm in the arrangement of the windows was eradicated. The large property which Valvassori himself erected in 1750 in connection with S. S. Quirico e Giulitta, opposite Tor' de' Conti, is in every respect refined, benign and compact (Pl. 171, cf. Pl. 69b). This purified Late Baroque, which still characterizes many houses in the district between the Corso and the Piazza di Spagna, was, after the 1770's, cross-bred with Neo-classical trends. The calm surfaces were now hardened and had stiff layers and members added – angular recesses and flat rustication, horizontal entablatures and triangular pediments borrowed from the Cinquecento, dentil mouldings and coronas copied from Antiquity. The large corner house in the Piazza della Rotonda which can be seen behind the obelisk in plate 135b and which was built about 1785 [357], is typical of the type; compare it with the neighbouring façade which has an intimate warmth. Finally we must point out the patrician houses designed by Valadier, the apprentice of the French (e. g. Casa Raffaelli in Via del Babuino, on the south corner of Via Alibert, Pl. 167). And Palladio's Venice attempted in the end to teach Rome the use of columns, but this bore little fruit [358].

The last part of our walk through the ordinary streets which Thorvaldsen saw, will lead us to Via dei Pianellari, one of the loveliest in Rome (Pl. 172). New forms and revived old ones merge here without difficulty into the city's harmony and fade out of sight in the slow curve of the street. One of the façades, very dignified and discreet, carries a little stone tablet with this inscription:

No. 11
Famiglia Canevari
Libera da ogni peso

HOUSES IN THE COUNTRY

The sultry night has given us its comforts,
And morning breezes fresh as crystal water
Stream through the window bearing scented savours
From Rome's lush orange-planted gardens.

I

In Pius IX's time Rome was as yet rather countrified, *una metropoli paesana* [1]. To return from Naples to the lingering tranquility of the papal city was a comforting experience. And people from northern countries were enthralled by the inimitable peace that was such a basic element in the city's enchantment [2]. Inside the walls enclosing Rome there was plenty of space, many gardens and ample quietude. The capital of the Church State seemed like an immense village.

Among the ruins grazed goats and oxen; the Forum Romanum got its familiar name because of this (Campo Vaccino). The temple of Minerva Medica stood among vineyards, like so many other heritages from Antiquity. The Lateran church overlooked a host of vegetable beds. Right up to the 1870's the Piazza Barberini was without paving and covered in weeds [3]. In the spring a wind scented with flowers blew down across the square – the morning greeting that Ludvig Bødtcher recollects in his verse – and mingled with the rank smell of the goats by the Triton fountain. On the outskirts of the city, stables and barns were everywhere; the roads flowed with dung. Where the close-knit city began to thin out, greenery forced its way in. And out among the endless stretches of ruins grew an abundance of flowers; the Colosseum was a happy hunting ground for all the botanists.

Old names of streets tell us where once rural Rome could be found. Via del Boschetto, nowadays a built-up sweet-smelling street between the Via Nazionale and Via Cavour, is a reminder of the sparsely populated outlying district with its many trees which were planted on the Viminal hill's southern slope to keep malaria away [4]. At the end of the 17th century the houses had already advanced greatly, as can be seen from Falda's map from 1676, but many gardens were still found here. Piranesi retired to the rural solitude of this district; he lived "in a little house behind Monte Cavallo at the place called *il Boschetto*. He refused to see anybody here, the more to be able to devote himself to his studies, to meditation and the practice of his art" [5]. Up to the present time this part of the city around "Boscage Street" has retained something of the idyllic *banlieue*. The small Via Clementina contains a country house with a garden wall. A noble Latin inscription on the house states that Clement XII had the street constructed. This tablet was put up in 1734, the fourth year of his pontificate [6]. The house, which must at the latest date from this time, is shown on Nolli's map from 1748. The tall angular house stands on the corner of a crooked lane called Vicolo del Sambuco, Elder Tree Road; the whole atmosphere of the quarter is embodied in this name; the least important of all the shrubs that flower in summer, has lent its scent to these sloping alleys. And this Piranesi inhaled as he went on his nocturnal walks along the Via Clementina, past the country house, which must have put him in mind of his own secluded place.

Via dei Serpenti (Snake Street) and Via degli Zingari (Gypsy Street) close by, suggest by their names an untended and picturesque past. Via del Boschetto's own southern part, the first to be built on, was originally called Via delle Carrette and conjures up the picture of donkey carts laden with fruit and vegetables.

In many other places in the city too, one can still sense a rural quality from the name of the street. This is especially true of the Via dei Fienili (Hayloft Street) which runs along the foot of the west slope of the Palatine, the road from the cattle market (Campo Vaccino) down towards *Forum boarium* (Piazza di Bocca della Verità), for it is the typical backstreet, baked by the sun, deserted and, in spite of the more recent houses, still has an air of grazing cattle about it. Around 1680 this quarter was full of barns and stables; as late as the middle of the 19th century, 26 barns could be found here. Carts stood everywhere by the house walls, the white oxen lay in the dirt, flies buzzed – the whole scene dominated by the jagged ruins of the imperial palaces up on the Palatine. This was what the hinterland of the Roman forum was like. S. Anastasia stands even today with a strange emptiness around it, like the church in a market town during a Sunday afternoon. The square in front of it is hedged in on one side by a row of old houses [7]; broad, low steps lead hospitably up to their fronts and are an invitation to both people and cattle to rest a while. But the carters have gone, no hay-wain creaks any longer through the Via dei Fienili.

On the outskirts of Trastevere, where the terrain begins to rise towards Monte Gianicolo, winds the crooked Via della Paglia (Straw Street). This too is reminiscent of the rural life of the outlying districts. As is the whole of this wonderful part of the city, dilapidated and shabby though it is, with sudden changes from narrow mediaeval alleys to big sites and dumping grounds, from damp vaults to sunlit corners where trees grow. A walk through Trastevere – not following the traffic, but this way and that – is a journey through the original Rome, the real "Eternal City"; for here the cauldron of humanity seethes as ever, here you experience the struggle between history and modernity in as dramatic a form as anywhere in Rome. Trastevere is certainly not a protected area. In this place, where the great portrayer of the life of the people, Bartolomeo Pinelli, was born in 1781 (near S. Gallicano) and found one of his models, a splendid fellow, who deserves to be described as *vero discendente Romano* [8], the stranger feels as if he were being led through a settlement in uproar, where they stare at you malevolently, to the very core of Romanity.

It is possible to find areas of the countrified papal city scattered here and there, if you take time about it and do not shy away from the humblest and most objectionable smelling alleys. Try to find Vicolo del Buco (Oxen Street) if you can. It adjoins Via della Lungaretta and its tail-end runs behind the chancel of S. Salvatore della Corte, also called S. Maria della Luce. The church is nothing much to look at, having an uninteresting façade from the 1820's. But inside, it is splendid, designed by none other than Valvassori, the architect for the Palazza Pamphili. And the church took on this form as the result of a miracle, which fits in well with the district, so we must record it. One day in 1730 a blind man entered a tumble-down house nearby – all the buildings in this neighbourhood are still very ramshackle. When he felt that the hovel was about to collapse onto him, he suddenly regained his sight, saw the Madonna with the Child appear on the wall in front of him and cried: "Light! Light!" The church was therefore rebuilt and called "Holy Mary of Light" [9].

As we move slowly into the shadow of the church, having been fortunate enough to find our way round the wooden struts straining to support falling walls, we too experience a miracle of light. A gateway appears in a corner over which is painted "La Villetta", and we have entered a genre-painting by Ernst Meyer, an idyll by Marstrand, entirely in light-green with sheets of sky-blue at the top and dancing patches of sunlight. A closed courtyard surrounded by low, yellow houses. A flight of steps leading to a fenced-in square, hidden by a pergola covered in vines and wisteria. A stunted tree pushes its twisted branches up through the leafy roof, ivy hangs its garlands on the limewashed wall. People from round about eat their bread and drink red wine at wooden tables; a mason from a site round the corner (a house must be shored up) is wearing a cheeky cap made by "Il Lavoro"; girls are hanging out of the window, carefully watched by an Olympian cat on a barrel of wine (Pl. 173).

Thorvaldsen might have sat at the end of the table, drawing with his fingers in a puddle of wine, the white of his shirtsleeves picking up the moving shadows of the leaves above his head. Hans Andersen would have wanted to draw the subject with childlike strokes. Indeed, even Goethe himself would have felt at home at the rustic wooden table behind Oxen Street. Romanticism's classic osteria in Trastevere, *la Gensola,* bears the name of a plant and had once a lovely pergola. The building, which Marstrand drew, is still in existence and it stands on the corner of the Piazza in Piscinula opposite a Late Gothic palace. But the large taproom, which Blunck depicted in his painting of a festive gathering of Danish artists here in 1838, has been divided up, and both the leafy walk and the scent of flowers will be sought in vain. The improvement along the Tiber has long ago spoilt the rural scenery on the riverbank.

Via della Gensola runs up to a street which is called after the elm-tree (*ulmus*). This stately tree has, with remarkable frequency, given its name to streets and squares in old Rome. The Via dell' Olmata on the Esquiline, which slopes down from the side of S. Maria Maggiore towards a lovely old villa, is now bare, but in Falda's prospect from 1676 you can see a group of trees there, and a papal edict of 1773 strictly prohibits any damage to the elms here and in the church square. The present Piazza Paganica is called Piazza dell' Olmo on Maggi's map from 1625 after one single tree; the Piazza della Pilotta was in those days called Olmo di Trejo (Trevi), no doubt for the same reason. As Salita di S. Sebastianello, the out-of-the-way flight of steps north of Scala di Spagna, was formerly called Elm Slope, we have no difficulty in seeing it shaded by trees like the slope up to S. S. Trinità dei Monti before it became the Spanish Steps. It also seems certain that the Roman places which are called after "the dry elm" (e. g. Piazzetta dell' Olmo Secco in Trastevere) is in recollection of a living tree that brought people pleasure. The Piazza degli Olmi, which formerly ran between Via dei Serpenti and Via del Boschetto, is well suited to its site as is the Via delle Fratte (or Frasche) not far away, and the street in Trastevere that is also called after a thicket (*fratta*), close by the osteria "La Villetta". The reference to a place in the name of a church, S. Andrea delle Fratte, soon shows us the old limits of the closely built-up area at Capo le Case ("The end of the houses").

In some cases one has to be careful about giving a natural background to localities with plant names, as it may be due to an inn-sign. This is probably true of the streets where the promising names of the orange, the fig-tree and the vine (Vicolo dell' Arancio, Vicolo del Fico, Via delle Vite) disguise the cramped reality. But when the word cypress occurs (Vicolo del Cipresso in Trastevere), we believe it was an actual fact, as is the case with the plane-tree, for this glorious tree, now so commonplace along the Roman boulevards and the Tiber, was in the 18th century seen only rarely [10].

Many generations of visitors to Rome have built up a veritable cult around the lone tree, worshipping it in the name of history or the service of a hero. One example is Tasso's oak at S. Onofrio on Janiculum. But it was more likely to be adored as a monument and as an outline in a view; it is "beautiful in perspective". Both the towering, leaning pine in the Giardino Colonna and Tasso's stunted oak-tree were revered by all the tourists. In my copy of Lucio Fauno's book "Delle Antichità della Città di Roma" (1548) Mr Richard Ford, who, according to a note in

173. *Osteria in Trastevere (Vicolo del Buco).*

174. *Portal of Villa Mattei opposite S. S. Giovanni e Paolo.*

175. *Clivo di Scauro seen towards the Palatine.*

176. *The cortile of the Palazzo Borghese.*

177. *Fountain in the courtyard behind the servants' quarters of the Palazzo Santacroce.*

178. *The courtyard of the Palazzo Del Grillo with the steps leading to the garden.*

179. *Part of the garden behind the Palazzo Del Grillo.*

180. *Garden behind the house where Goethe lived in Via del Corso.*

the book, was in Rome in 1840 (and later edited the excellent Cicerone in Spain), has pasted a newspaper cutting which runs as follows: "A storm at Rome has thrown down Tasso's oak and the Colonna pine" – it has the date Oct. 1842 written in by hand. A touching epitaph – the Eternal City was that much poorer, two trees had fallen, two memories were lost. Hans Andersen also uttered a *cri de cœur* in his diary (April 26th 1846): "It looks empty now the pine in the Colonna garden has gone" [11]. But it was on a happy day during his first stay in Rome (January 3rd 1834) that the following was recorded: "Sat by the palm-tree at Pietro in Vincoli and read Thomasine Gyllembourg's "Novels of Everyday Life". I too am becoming familiar with the Roman life." This palm-tree is still in existence, thank God. Rome's first palm-tree was, according to an inscription on the spot, planted in 1588 in the garden of the Genoese Hospital in Trastevere. I wonder if the tiny date-palms that Goethe raised in a garden behind the Via Sistina two hundred years later are still there? The poet sowed the seeds in the hope that the trees would burst into leaf and flourish in his memory.

II

Down in the closely built-up districts on the Campus Martius, plants had little chance to grow, and this is still so. All the same – if you take a closer look you find climbers and flowers everywhere. They spring forth from ancient walls in the same way as nearly overgrown antique capitals sometimes are found breaking loose from centuries of plaster, and the cut-back growth sends out new shoots. There is no alley so wretched where the eye cannot be refreshed by the sight of a flowerpot with red oleander placed here and there on window sills or fastened to door frames. The latticed lights over the doors of the poor are favourite places for growing flowers in crocks and boxes. And however shabby a street may be, it would indeed be strange if it did not allow us more than one glimpse of a small garden in a dark backyard, a garden in the Italian manner, a well by the back wall – perhaps with a stone mask as water outlet – surrounded by foliage plants in earthenware pots, the whole a "formal" design on the smallest possible scale, smelling of earth and dampness as in a grotto. On your wanderings through the sunbaked streets you can easily find such shadowy back-gardens offering you this gift; the Monserrato is particularly recommended for this purpose, for it is one of the loveliest streets in Rome.

Now, as in earlier times, there is a town all on its own above the old Rome. It consists of balconies and terraces, arbours and shelters, a multitudinous creation of pavilions above the roofs, which collectively are called belvederes, for their purpose is to give the occupants below a refreshing view. But also, and particularly perhaps, pure, cool air. Since ancient times the Romans have, in the summer, when the heat made the streets down below feel unbearable, whenever possible, lived and breathed up on the roofs. Here even the poorest person could enjoy the air and the balmy breeze after sundown [12].

This airy city, unseen from the street, is hardly noticed by tourists, yet it is such an important part of Rome's life. The painter Abel Bonnard was happy to live in one of *ces villas célèstes,* where you were as free as a hermit in the mountains. He interpreted their charm in these words: "nothing can compare with this hazy little world high above the palaces of splendour and arrogance" [13]. The Frenchman is certainly right; we remember well the studio of a painter friend that floated above a landscape of sloping roofs, whose weather-beaten tiles bore every shade of pale pink and terracotta, and against this background, the lines of a haphazard village of precipitous cubes, pergolas, all sorts of latticework, sticking out in all directions. Architecture proper is here suspended in the true meaning of the word; this is a playful jest up high on the other side of the top crown of Rome's majestic cornices. Amongst "lookouts" (as they are called in the houses of retired skippers in the Danish towns of Helsingør and Dragør) of all types – from the platform between four pieces of wood holding up a ragged awning to the magnificent belvedere with its masonry arches, a real *palazzina* among arbours – numerous "hanging gardens" thrive. It is worth your trouble to climb up and find a place where you can take in a panorama of this other Rome.

The palaces in the city itself might take pleasure in an espalier up on the belvedere, and their courtyards would nearly always be decorated with plants growing in tubs, or flowers in an ancient sarcophagus, but gardens as such were mostly denied them for lack of space. The finest exception is the *Palazzo Borghese* whose last courtyard, which reaches right down to the Tiber and ends in a small covered terrace, was laid out in 1690 as a *giardino segreto* with voluptuous niche fountains by Carlo Rainaldi [14]. A confusion of statues vies with luxuriant vegetation and tortuous iron lattice-work to create an intimate garden of rare luxury. Prince Borghese's audience chamber on the ground floor faced this garden which, seen through the windows, "had the effect of a fine stage" (*qui lui fait un beau théâtre*) with the large fountain as the focal point [15]. There was originally a parterre here where the finest flowers of the season were cultivated in borders set among stone (Pl. 176).

The garden wall of the Palazzo Borghese borders a street which was once called Vicolo del Melangolo (Merangolo), named after that lovely fruit – the medlar. The explanation of the name has been made by reference to a fruit-tree painted on the palace wall, but as this was an orange tree and the street did not come to be called Vicolo dell'Arancio until later, the interpretation seems to be incorrect [16]. The orange was, after all, far more common than the medlar. Anyhow – the engaging name is like a reflection from the Prince's delightful hidden garden. Which reminds me of a visit to a friendly old lady who lived behind the Piazza di Campitelli; she related with pride that golden fruit often fell down over the wall into her dark yard from her neighbour's, Marchese Spinola's garden. In the same way the narrow street running past Palazzo Borghese must also have been brightened up by the name of this splendid fruit. In the middle of the garden wall there is a picture of the Madonna, with a lantern in front suspended by a cord (Pl. 91a). This lantern's predecessors have no doubt helped at least one dubious character to find his front door – Baron Philip von Stosch, antiquarian and professional spy, paid by the English government to keep an eye on the Pretender James Stuart [17]. Marcus Tuscher, later a court-painter in Copenhagen, was in the service of the shady baron at the time (1726–1731). He lodged in the Vicolo del Merangolo, and must often have taken his bearings from the lantern on the wall when he walked back home at night from his patron's. This street with an atmosphere of its own, can fleetingly remind you of Bollhusgränd in central Stockholm, which became impressive because of the tall wall of the garden behind Nicodemus Tessin's Palace (Överståthållarhuset).

Another large palace on the Campus Martius, the *Palazzo Orsini-Taverna,* has quite a large garden in its courtyard. This enormous and very irregular complex, whose core dates from the Middle Ages and which might perhaps be considered the most romantic aristocratic residence in the papal city, stands on a little hill called Monte Giordano. One can still feel that the edifice was a fortress which gave the Orsini family control over the strategically important Rione Ponte with the bridge to the Borgo quarter and the Vatican [18], for the terrain rises on all sides towards the old baronial castle, that stands like an island in the midst of the confusion of crooked alleys and backstreets. If you risk entering them, you may in the end run up against a wall and that will be the palace. Wretched houses rise along the slope and cling to its foot like a small mountain village with a *rocca* at the top. Nothing can be more exciting when you wander through Rome than to venture into the area surrounding Palazzo Orsini – to push your way along an alleyway leading from Via dei Coronari. This labyrinth – only a few minutes' walk from the Corso Vittorio Emanuele – can feel as stimulating as an adventure story. And in a gloomy passageway called Via del Montonaccio (you are conscious of a slight snarl in the word), which winds its way upwards and ends in a blind alley, gnarled trees stand on the slope. Inside the large courtyard there are now tall weeping willows and this is the garden. Their long swaying branches hang like a framework round a mossy green fountain, its three basins set one above the other [19]. The palace on the little mountain now plays a muted tone. There are merely trickles from the trees and the fountain.

For the people of the Rococo period, Monte Giordano was nothing but an antiquity, defying all the laws of taste and scorning every comfort. This the French Ambassador, the Duc de Nivernois, found to his discomfort, when in 1751 he was to pay a visit to Cardinal Domenico Orsini, for as six horses could not pull the coach up the hill, the Duke had to get out and make his laborious way up on foot, where, weighed down by his gold-embroidered attire, he arrived in the apartment of the Prince of the Church "covered in sweat" (*tutto in acqua*) to the commiseration of everybody. The anecdote comes from Benedict XIV himself [20]. I wonder if the weeping willow was there at the time (Pl. 102).

When you walk along the Via di Pallacorda towards the north in the direction of the Piazza Borghese, you go past a long wall on the right hand side which conceals the large garden behind Palazzo di Firenze. You will be rewarded if you look up to the left, away from the line of the wall. You find to your delight a little grove on a terrace, wedged in high up in a large building, the *Palazzo Cardelli*. The three walls around this suspended flower garden are richly decorated with sculptures, particularly the wall through which you pass to get to the terrace from an adjacent apartment. I have been fortunate enough to visit this enchanting spot, a salon under the open sky, sheltered by yellow walls and kept cool by the plants. To get to this place you have to climb ringing steps under cavetto vaulting [21] and walk past a number of rooms, one of which has dark forested landscapes painted *al fresco* on the walls. The transition from these proud and melancholy salons to the whimsical terrace was as abrupt as the gap between a *Folie d'Espagne* and a *Siciliano*.

The *Palazzo Santacroce* too, has a surprise waiting for the wanderer who goes round the back by the Vicolo dei Catinari. At the beginning of the 1800's it was called "Stable Lane" because it separates the palace from its annex for *familiares,* servants and horses. Facing the portal to the palace, you find a little courtyard with a fountain set near the back wall [22] (Pl. 177), and, on the other side of the street, a bridge has been built leading from the prince's apartments to a roof garden on top of the building opposite. When the Prussian envoy, in Rome one day in 1864, visited Principe Santacroce, he was taken by his host straight from a salon to the secret garden and told that it was called after Cardinal de Bernis "who had a *liaison* with my beautiful grandmother" [23]. The arrangement must have been very convenient for the soulful meetings between the princess and her purple-clad admirer, all the more so since he was a poet; he was a devotee of Armida's hanging gardens.

There is something romantic about bridges that, way above the heads of people walking in the street, are direct connections between a room and a garden. You could call it the triumph of luxury in the midst of a crowded city. The arched bridge (*arco, cavalcavia*), which since the Middle Ages was an ordinary occurence in Rome as a closed passage between interdependent buildings each on its own side of the street, could, especially as a ramification of a palace to its garden, become a splendid architectural motif. According to Vasari [24] Michelangelo had planned an axial link between the Palazzo Farnese and the Villa Farnesina at Lungara (Trastevere) across Via Giulia and the Tiber. A rudimentary part of this grandiose plan is the arch which forms a bridge from the side wing of the palace to the stable building in the Via Giulia (Pl. 89). There was originally a garden with four "pleasances" between this latter building and the bank of the river.

The most elegant presentation of this idea was carried out at the Piazza Colonna. In contrast to the aristocratic houses previously discussed, this one is situated on the outskirts of the closely built-up area of Rome, where it changes to become the territory of the large villa gardens, and it has the slope of the Quirinal hill behind. Up this slope the *Giardino Colonna* was given its enviable position, an arrangement of terraces with a magnificent view over the city from the uppermost plateau, the access to which is through a gateway (by Vincenzo della Greca, 1618) in the present Via XXIV Maggio. The garden of the Colonna family dates right back to the Renaissance, when the Temple of the Sun was thought to be located here, indeed even Nero's palace, since remains of ancient steps and various antiquities were found on the slope down towards the Piazza di S.S. Apostoli [25]. The lower part of this, a fairly narrow rectangle parallel with the back of the palace, was laid out as a parterre; at the back, it rose in terraces ending with a retaining wall. In this form, the main features of which are still preserved, it is shown in Falda's bird's eye view from 1676. But the garden did not take on its final form and elaboration, under the supervision of Paolo Posi, until the middle of the 18th century. The parterre was enclosed on the north side by a casino, built in two storeys, the roof of the lower being the balcony of the upper.

However, this "secret garden", concealed behind a high wall, is separated from the Palazzo Colonna by a street, Via della Pilotta. This name refers to a ball-game (as do the words *palla* and *pallone*) and we know that this quiet street between naked walls – for the palace too turned its back on it – provided excellent opportunities for games. The chronicler Valesio, mentions in 1740, that the game had become popular here again after an interval of forty years. Prince Colonna and his family naturally had to be able to get from their house to the garden without setting foot on the street and being molested by the sporting activities of young louts. For this reason, two bridges were built over the Via della Pilotta, one at each end of the palace; Don Filippo Colonna was given permission for this by Pope Innocent XII (1691–1700). It was probably in the 1750's that two more bridges were added between the old ones [26]. As can be seen from plate 92, which shows the one to the south at the entrance to the Via della Pilotta, the original arcades curved in a gentle arch and had a railing borne by balusters, all in straw-yellow travertine. The canting arms of the Colonna family, a crowned column (*colonna*), can be seen carved on the plinth above the keystone of the arch. This pleasant quiet street, which still has such a private character, is now gaily decorated by the figures of seminarists clothed in all the colours of the rainbow on their way back and forth to the Gregoriana University nearby. Showing above the garden wall are the stone pines and cypresses, the unrivalled supporters of the Roman villa. The Colonna pine on the top terrace we have dealt with before.

As befits a wanderer studying the streets, we have up to the present only looked at the bridges across Via della Pilotta from pavement level and considered their side view. But this was not how the Colonnas saw them. They only regarded the bridges as passages and lines in a straightforward view from palace to garden. The arch that we reproduce had the most important function of them all, for it forms a continuation of the large gallery and is adjacent to a room at the end of this. When you open the tall glass door, the way leads straight across the street to the parterre, and it finishes up at a piece of architectural stage scenery which has a statue of the naval hero Marc' Antonio Colonna set in the middle niche flanked by columns. This setting erected in honour of the family's great man, the victor of the Battle of Lepanto, was put up by Don Filippo Colonna in 1713. The other bridges too, ran directly into the garden, the fourth, the one furthest to the north nearest the casino, directed the gaze to the ascent of a steep flight of steps. All this can clearly be seen in a watercolour by Napoleon's architect Charles Percier [27].

It is not difficult to conjure up an evening entertainment in this wonderful parterre with a wall of clipped hedges on one side and the illuminated piano nobile of the palace in front, separated by the Via della Pilotta, crossed as it is by pathways hanging in the air. When Innocent XIII in 1721 succeeded to the throne of St. Peter, Prince Colonna arranged a musical entertainment in his magnificent open-air theatre. The English traveller Wright, who was present, relates that small orchestras sat on the two bridges across the street. The orange-trees were festooned with candles set in hollowed-out oranges hanging like real fruit in the foliage. When the music stopped for a while, fireworks were let off at both ends of the garden [28]. This fairy-tale *serenata* reminds us of Don Giovanni's nocturnal party in his villa, where ensembles of wood-wind players played country dances and minuets completely at random. Down in the Via della Pilotta stood an expectant audience and stared upwards. Somebody probably received an undesirable present into the bargain when trumpets were drained over the balustrade, but people were accustomed to be spat upon from the gallery in the opera house. And the framework for this garden party, one of many, in fact the whole of this entrancing work of art does still exist. A Colonna can illuminate it even today, can people the great stage and strike up the music. But modern barracks towering in the neighbourhood can stare down into this enclosed world of beauty. Looking out from the Danish ambassador's home, which can pride itself on having obtained the highest perch among these architectural upstarts in the district, you have a splendid view into yet another enclosed Colonna garden, this one situated in the great courtyard furthest away from the palace, completely shut away behind the wing facing Via della Pilotta. Tessin, who saw it in 1687, found it a "considerable plantation of nothing but tall orange-trees" [29]. In 1713 Deseine mentions lemons and pears as well [30].

If you want to find out what the entrance to a real "secret garden" from the Baroque period looks like, you should make your way down the Vicolo Mazzarino and pass imperturbably through the portal to the *Palazzo Rospigliosi*. On your right you will see the hermetically sealed front to the special garden set between high walls, which are like a rectangular building without a roof – and will continue to be *segretissimo*. Nolli's map shows that the flight of steps, shaped in an oval immediately inside the gateway, led down to the parterre arranged around a pool. The princess used it for entertaining on summer evenings [31]. As in Guido Reni's "Aurora", the dawn arose from the darkness to look down upon the guests.

Another curving flight of steps runs into the most charming of all Rome's hidden gardens. It lies behind the *Palazzo Del Grillo* on a terrace carved out of the slope of the Quirinal hill and is connected to an inner courtyard that in height corresponds more or less to the piano nobile (Pl. 178). Everything here is pure theatre; the shallow steps seem intended for progress on high heels, they form a bridge between the stalls of the cortile and the stage in the garden. In this way, the floor of the auditorium during an evening's entertainment in the opera house might be connected with the stage by covering the orchestra pit with an engaging flight of steps. We are reminded of Francesco Guardi's painting (1782) from the Teatro S. Benedetto in Venice. But Del Grillo's stage-setting is far more elegant – and has permanence. The steps from the garden continue down to the corners of the courtyard in gentle curves of stone and end there in shell decoration. The scenic architecture positively undulates and can be appreciated from all sorts of angles, for in theory it is based on a three-dimensional scroll. A style such as this might well be called frivolous, but that is not the case here – its sweeping outline is logical in all its members; the structure yields, but is not strained beyond its limits.

Up in the narrow garden other decorations are revealed. On the right hand side at the end of the long garden is a fountain, where two naked youths stand on close-set pedestals, holding up a basin. The whole sculpture is redolent and sensual, one is hardly aware of what is the flora of stone and what are the real flowers. Facing this scenic arrangement, at the opposite end of the garden, is a sunken garden set transversely. Going down a few steps, you find gates with the curling tendrils of the vine made in wrought iron; this is an open-air salon surrounded by the swirling lines of wall set with stone seats, made for very small bottoms – or were they perhaps reserved for figurines which never materialized?

Scrolled consoles such as these garden seats were usually the place for knick-knacks or birds made in faience (Pl. 179). It is in fact a nymphaeum looking like an altar piece, crumbling sculpture, dripping water, pillows of moss, touchwood and toadstools, and white magnolias. In short: "Act III, scene 2. Towards evening. Silvia at the spring. Enter Lelio...".

The whole thing is extraordinary, for the setting recalls scenes of lyrical theatre by Pergolesi and Scarlatti that have long since vanished. The artistic effect is not in itself surprising but the intrinsic value certainly is. The stylistic plants inflate the ornaments, the contours are lush and expand under the open sky, rising with the spirit and joy of a *coloratura,* the rock-work grows out of the grotto's tufa like acanthus from the soil. And the trappings of a burlesque which we otherwise only see in old engravings or for a short time recreated on modern stages (many people may remember the tip-up seats in "One Servant and two Masters") can here be used every day. The concept *rocaille* comes into its own in this secret pleasance, if anywhere. The play of Rococo has left its imprint in the substance of the garden and the rhythmic plan.

We do not know the name of the artist who produced this setting or when it took place. On Nolli's map, where we find indications of sculptural decorations in the Giardino Colonna, the Del Grillo garden is only an empty space. From this we can at least deduce that the arrangement of the garden is subsequent to 1748, which for stylistic reasons also seems probable. If this is so, it must have been carried out for Marchese Onofrio Del Grillo, who took over the palace after his uncle Bernardino around 1750. He is mentioned as living *all' Arco Del Grillo* in 1757 and died in 1787 as the last male of his line [32]. The sculptor was certainly familiar with French ornamental engravings; the fountain in particular, with the two slender male figures, is very reminiscent of a design by Oppenordt [33]. He had made up his own style, and from this created Rococo, by sketching happily in the Baroque gardens of Rome. A part of this borrowing was here repaid with a handsome interest.

The banks of the Tiber were, apart from the terrain beyond the Castel Sant' Angelo, so closely packed with buildings, that not much space was left for gardens here. The smelly river was not exactly tempting to have as a neighbour when entertaining out of doors. An engraving by Vasi shows a pleasance at Bocca della Verità. The retaining wall down in the muddy water was crowned with flower-pots, but it was also pierced by the outlet of the *cloaca maxima*. The guests who assembled in the *Vigna Cenci*'s small casino [34] right on the Tiber must have had the doubtful pleasure of the evening breezes wafting over them. The *Palazzo Falconieri* in the Via Giulia had the advantage of possessing a terrace out to the river which was placed sufficiently high. Flowers were cultivated here in a tolerable air [35]. Behind the *Palazzo Spada a Capo di Ferro* you can still find a long, narrow garden with entrance from the Via Giulia that is as fascinating as it is difficult of access.

Across the river on the opposite bank there is in Trastevere quite a large garden which is open to all and sundry, provided they can find it, which is not all that easy. In its original form the park was elegant, having fine flower-beds, avenues with arches of espalier-trained trees, orange-trees and all sorts of rare plants. It was created by Cardinal Francesco Maidalchini, Donna Olimpia Pamphili's brother's son. She was Innocent X's sister-in-law and evil genius. The memory of this domineering lady hung for a long time over the Pamphili garden "with its lovely views across the Tiber" [36]. As late as 1770, Volkmann only mentions "the pleasant casino" because of the ill-repute the place had had since the days of Donna Olimpia [37]. The Romans in fact considered that there was a curse on the casino [38]. It was removed about a hundred years ago by this same family, which had acquired enormous wealth with the help of Donna Olimpia, for Don Carlo Doria Pamphili in 1860 founded a sanatorium for incurables on the site of the old garden. Above the entrance we can read: *Morbis Chronicis Curandis Xenodochium Ab Auria Pamphilianum*. The parterres of the Baroque garden have now been turned into vegetable beds, encircled by vine-covered pergolas. A high wall on the river side excludes this oasis from the clamour of the world. French nuns of the order of St. Vincent de Paul, dressed in blue and with large white wimples, move quietly among the wretched sufferers, and look after the tomatoes with equal concern. During my first visit here, one of the sisters, a large, round and red-faced peasant-girl from Normandy, said these simple words: *Nous sommes tellement heureuses ici, il y a si calme sous les arbres* . . . Thus peace came to the garden of the haunted house. Anyone wishing to find the place should set out from S. Cecilia and follow the Via dei Genovesi in the direction of S. Maria in Coppella, at the side of which Giardino Maidalchini lies like a cloister garth.

The big religious houses in the middle of the city had, in some cases, quite large gardens in the form of cultivated courtyards – places of repose squeezed in between dark wings – as at the convent of the Augustinians at S. Maria delle Vergini and the Jesuits' monastery next to their principal church of Il Gesù; here were four "pleasances" with a fountain and basin set in the middle [39]. The Dominicans' largest *chiostro* (at S. Maria sopra Minerva), whose acreage is about that of Palazzo Colonna's cultivated courtyard right at the back (before c. 1750), is even today a fine quadrangle with tall trees. In the less built-up areas of Trastevere, a number of monasteries and churches had particularly large vegetable and flower gardens, such as S. Francesco a Ripa and S. Maria dell' Orto, its name ("Holy Mary in the Garden") being very eloquent. The guild of fruiterers and greengrocers (*l'Università de' Fruttaroli e Pizzicaroli*) in fact owned the last mentioned church. *S. Cosimato (S. S. Cosma e Damiano)* too, had a large garden which like the others has now been built on. But the large monastery complex whose reserved façades have to an increasing extent been taken over by highly secular places, such as motor repair shops, conceals a lovely *chiostro* from the Renaissance, quiet arcades around fertile flower beds. In 1731 a handsome fountain was erected in another courtyard [40].

The nuns of S. Cosimato's convent were, in those days, famous for their manufacture of artificial flowers, a species which in richness far surpassed Trastevere's natural flora, as they did in popularity. For Roman ladies had an unconquerable aversion to the scent of flowers; a remarkable thing, but attested to by numerous witnesses. While Romans of the female sex, even of the upper classes, were completely impervious to the stench of urine prevailing everywhere – "people answered the call of nature in alleys, under the arcades of palaces, on stairways, in corridors, even at the door of the anteroom" [41] – and felt no disgust at anointing their hair with candle-grease, thus surrounding themselves with a noisome smell, instead of using the many pomades produced in Rome, they could endure neither the scent of perfume nor the sweetest-smelling flowers. An English lady, married to an Italian, expressed her surprise that Roman ladies were so greatly averse to *odori* that even a drop of lavender water on a handkerchief or a corsage of roses could give them the vapours [42]. The answer may be found in the fact that the smell of urine was supposed to prevent fever and that the scent of flowers was injurious to health, but of course affectation was also part of the game and it was *bon ton* to swoon over a violet. However that may be, artificial flowers were worn by everybody and resulted in the development of quite a little industry. From S. Cosimato's nuns you could buy a bouquet of 30 or 40 splendidly imitated flowers for about two guilders and a delicious rose for three paoli [43]. When we see a portrait of an Italian Rococo beauty with carnations in her powdered hair and orange blossoms at her bosom we must keep sentimental associations in check and merely take pleasure in the *bouquet* produced by the paintbrush, which should be sufficient. For the flowers are made of fabric. Don Giovanni's famous lines (in Mozart's opera): "I seem to detect the scent of ladies" (*mi pare sentir odor di femmina*) adds a new and surprising nuance to the asmosphere hinted at here – was Donna Elvira's ambiguous appearance announced by the smell of tallow wafting from her curly locks?

Looked upon in the proper light, this little excursion to the workshop by S. Cosimato's gardens has opened our nostrils to certain *parfums de Rome* which not even Veuillot sensed, and caused us to suspect from this quick airing that the Roman feeling for nature was suppressed by conventions in the 18th century. We shall go into it later more fully.

The princely monastery of the Augustinians, rebuilt by Vanvitelli, was given a fountain for its courtyard in 1750. The entrance to this is from the Via dei Portoghesi. The fountain is the sculptured figure of a boy with a goose, thus a similar motif to that used by Le Clerc for his group from 1739 in the Copenhagen Royal Garden (only this sculptor preferred a swan). Shady plants surround this rural subject in the Fathers' grandiose arcaded courtyard. A Latin inscription on the front of the fountain informs us that Benedict XIV in the jubilee year gave the monastery an abundance of water from Acqua Vergine [44].

A palace in the Corso itself, although in the northern part, which in the second half of the 18th century was still pretty rural, shows the period's most recent cultivated quadrangle, the last work in the series whose first monument is the garden behind the Palazzo Borghese. Here again, water forms the important element and the fountain is the real centre of the scene. In 1764 the Marchese Giuseppe Rondinini provided the back wall of his large *cortile* with a decoration centred round a niche fountain. Goethe must have seen this nymphaeum in Neo-classical style when he went on his pilgrimage to see the mask of Medusa in this same palace. But he does not mention the Bacchus fountain in his Roman journal. Perhaps it did not occur to him that it had any style. The rest of us consider it emotionally as a set-piece in the Roman world of the Hellenist. Goethe himself went straight to the point, and the smallest fragment of nature became a wealth of lasting beauty; he found his roots in the garden behind his lodging which was in a quadrangle surrounded by high walls opposite the palace (no. 18 Via del Corso), and here met with greater gods than the Marchese's fungoid Bacchus. "In our garden an old priest looks after well-kept lemon trees, of moderate size, planted in ornate pots of baked clay" (April 1788). And from his room right at the top of the house he was delighted to see a paradise of growing flowers on the balconies of mean houses. The courtyard still has its flora. Under the leaves of the potted plants wanders a tortoise feeling small amongst the giant vegetation (Pl. 180). We too, find here a luxuriance of plants that the poet never experienced.

III

It is now time to leave the gardens inside Rome itself and make expeditions further out. Well over two-thirds of the area behind the walls had not yet been built on, in the period we are dealing with here, and for even longer than that, in fact right up to Pius IX's days. It is particularly the city's east and south sections, the undulating terrain which includes the hills with such musical names as Pincius, Esquilinus, Viminalis, Caelius, Palatinus, Aventinus and Janiculum which lies west of Trastevere. And this is the mighty realm of the ancient ruins. Between the remains of the ancients' buildings, overgrown and rugged, vegetable plots, vineyards, country houses and villas grew up quietly, some in the valleys, some on the slopes of the hills. Immediately outside the gates the countryside of the Campagna stood ready for large gardens to be constructed along the ancient roads emerging from the city.

As a bird's eye view, this uninhabited part of Rome and its border area on the other side of the walls might seem like an enormous "green belt", encrusted with the colours of the sun-dried ruins and brown bricks. But the man who fought his way through the low-lying, rugged wilderness of gardens, fields and common-land, had little occasion to extol a thriving landscape. His progress along the dusty roads was hedged in by endless walls. Only now and then did a wrought-iron gate or a wicket afford him a fleeting view of a gravelled path between hedges, of a row of vines or vegetable beds. Only the tops of the trees towering up over the walls betrayed the avenues of the rich, jealously hidden from the traveller who made his way along in the insignificant shadow cast by the walls. There must have been something intriguing about this ceaseless traffic going in all directions between unrelenting walls; a compact system of closed-in roads spread over the silent area forming a labyrinth, which was tiresome in the heat of the day, full of danger after darkness fell. You can follow the irregular lines of the network of passages and the relief of the walls in the perspective maps of Rome from the Baroque period (Tempesta, Maggi, Falda). And what is even better, you can nowadays still experience the stern architecture of the lonely roads along the gardens. But – you must hurry. In a few years time this Roman epic too, will have come to an end.

We started this book by bringing the reader to Rome by the most beautiful road, the Via Aurelia, the inner part of which heads towards the Porta di San Pancrazio, following the wall of the Villa Doria-Pamphili and other country estates. The stretch of the Appian Way, which is now called Via di Porta S. Sebastiano and runs from this city gate to Caracalla's thermae and S. Sisto, has also preserved the solemnity of former days, and one still has to pass a continuous line of garden walls on both sides. Here we find Cardinal Bessarion's country house (erected c. 1460), noble in its simplicity, situated beside nameless vineyards. This little summer residence, the oldest Renaissance villa in Rome, and the vineyard at S. Cesareo belonging to it, was presented by Clement VIII in 1604 to the Somaschi, those erudite teaching fathers who ran Collegio Clementino [45]. They owned the vineyard throughout the whole of the 18th century and excavated many interesting antiquities on the land where Bessarion, the humanist, had in earlier times assembled literati and aesthetes for Greek symposia. The discovery of a columbarium with all sorts of goods from graves in July 1732, resulted in a succession of archaeologists turning up behind the sun-baked wall. Ficoroni was the first to arrive [46], but apart from that the traffic on the road was mostly asses pulling tumbrils full of grapes.

On Monte Celio there is still a stretch of classical road of great beauty. It is not very long and is beyond compare even in Rome; for several centuries it has provided subjects for artists without losing anything by it. Its entrance is through the Arch of Dolabella (close to S. Maria in Domnica), a fine mass of masonry from Cicero's time, and it ends at S. Gregorio Magno with the Palatine in the background. The first half of the road is enclosed by walls, those on the left protecting the Villa Mattei (Celimontana). There is little traffic here. The last time I went along this narrow, greyish-yellow place, the perspective was dominated by a solitary man who must have been madly in love. He stopped every tenth step or so, remained like a statue with bowed head, then went on with staggering steps. When I overtook him, I heard passionate outbursts about *amore* as I went past. This tragic figure was entirely in the spirit of the place. About half-way along the road, a small square appears in front of S. S. Giovanni e Paolo and its adjacent monastery. It is now a parking space for opulent cars. But Villa Mattei's portal has retained its elegance. It was erected c. 1600 for Duke Ciriaco Mattei, probably by the architect Jacopo del Duca [47] and provides the enclosing wall of the villa with an impressive corner in this little sloping church square (Pl. 174). You should stop in front of it and look back on the picture of the empty road as it runs down towards Arco di Dolabella.

The rest of this back way to the gardens continues under the flying buttresses of S. S. Giovanni e Paolo. The historical perspective from here goes back a long way; set into the church's side wall on the right is a house from ancient times [48] and the descent of the road itself is none other than *clivus Scauri* of Antiquity (Pl. 175). The pictorial perspective is equally fine. At the end of the road you have to turn round; from here the whole of this group of buildings and trees is dominated by the apse of S. S. Giovanni e Paolo, surmounted by its columned gallery. Many painters have immortalized this motif in their sketch-books, Claude le Lorrain above all [49].

Up on Pincio there are a couple of roads which were formerly completely enclosed by garden walls and which still retain something of their earlier rustic character. The Via di Porta Pinciana rises abruptly from Capo le Case, a typical exit road from the noisy city down below to the quiet countryside of villas up here, with its beneficial air. On the right hand side immediately after the Via Sistina, the old built-up area stops and the last house can be singled out, the Casa Guarnieri; this was the boundary in Goethe's time. Then comes a massive wall hiding S. Isidoro's monastery. Standing on this spot we have, on the right, the modern district which has replaced the Villa Ludovisi, one of Rome's largest and most splendid parks. The road is as it were split lengthwise, for the left side right up to the Porta Pinciana is still a good, old road, the fashionable blocks of flats have more or less the same neighbours across the road as Prince Ludovisi's villa. If tomorrow, Thorvaldsen tried to make his way up the now heavily trafficated street and screened his right eye, he would feel quite at home – in spite of everything. Opposite the corner of the S. Isidoro garden, the eye is arrested by a rustic gateway (c. 1600) to the Villa Medici; this is the original entrance and gave access to the casino on Monte Pincio through an avenue of orange trees [50]. Under the gateway's arch, now closed, the carriages of cardinals and other important people drove up to the famous villa, whose owners (up to 1787) were Grand Dukes of Tuscany. The eye now follows the long wall curving gently in front of the Villa Medici's vegetable gardens. About midway, the stretch of wall is interrupted by a simple yellow house, whose clean-cut proportions look fine. It can be seen marked in Falda's plan from 1676. Not only Thorvaldsen, but also Piranesi must have seen it on the way up to the antiques in the Villa Borghese. Modern times look upon it as a monstrosity, this simple gardener's house, which was once the only dwelling in the quiet road of the gardens (Pl. 183a).

In other places too in the Ludovisi district, now so commonplace and fashionable, we find relics from the past, such as the Via degli Artisti, which formerly ended up as a blind alley at the little square in front of S. Isidoro. You can still see the line marking the junction with its continuation. A corner house by the stepped alley down to Via Veneto and the Capuchin church has held its position as outpost since the 17th century — and as the finest piece of architecture in this seriously threatened street, formerly so idyllic. A witness from Holberg's time says of it "that it is a lonely place full of gardens and inhabited by those who like a solitary existence, such as scholars" [51]. The name of the street indicates that later — like the whole of the adjacent part of the city — it was preferred by artists, for the rural surroundings, the air and the walks in the Villa Ludovisi attracted them up here. The Danish sculptor Carl Frederik Holbech, who carried on the tradition from Thorvaldsen's Roman studio right up to Bergsøe's time (in whose "From the Piazza del Popolo" he has an important subsidiary role as the last real Old Roman), lived in Via degli Artisti [52].

On the Esquiline hill the Via delle Sette Sale (called after the remains of cisterns from Nero's "Golden House") still retains some of the atmosphere of this district's past as *banlieue*. It winds its way in behind S. Pietro in Vincoli's chancel in the direction of S. Martino ai Monti. Gardens and areas of ruins on the south side now form an open parkland (Parco Oppio), but the north side along the slope down towards Suburra still has the character which old boundary walls lend. In the Galleria Doria there is a vedute from 1711 (by H. van Lint), the subject of which has not so far been identified. But it should be easy to prove that the prospect represents the area behind S. Pietro in Vincoli and provides a magnificent impression of this district when it vegetated among scattered monasteries. The two mediaeval towers, seen on the extreme left in the painting, are still there, the tallest being incorrectly called the Borgias' tower [53] (Pl. 182).

The Palatine hill stood like an island in the enchanted garden, lofty and sweet-smelling, and it was as enticing to all lovers of beauty as Circe's headland. You entered this country paradise by lovely steps and ramps, past the cool nymphaeum and two airy aviaries; became enraptured by the lofty architecture which Vignola had created for Paul III Farnese

181. *Portal in the garden wall in front of S. Sabina on the Aventine.*

182. *The country around S. Pietro in Vincoli. Painting by H. van Lint (Palazzo Pamfili-Doria).*

183a. Old gardener's lodge in Via di Porta Pinciana.

183b. Garden wall in Via dei Riari; to the right in the background the Palazzo Corsini.

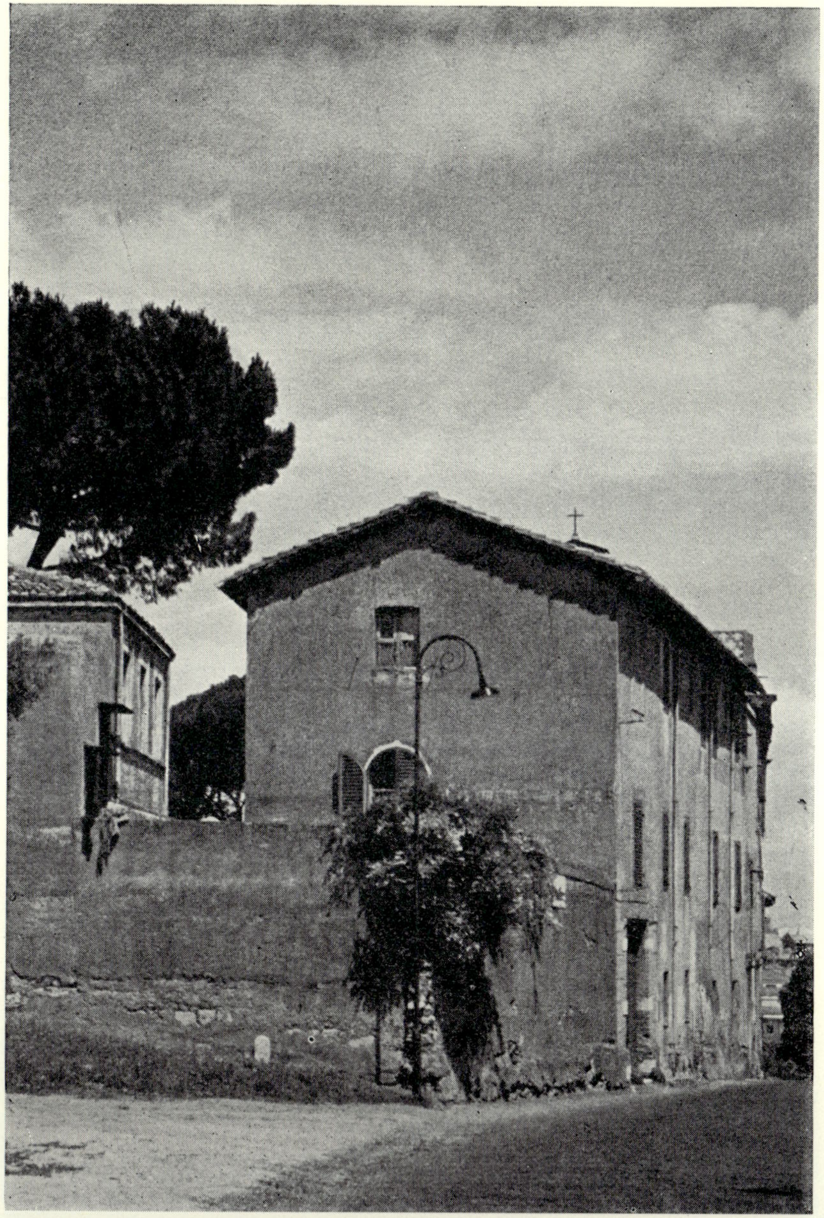

184a Old buildings [illegible] the Aventine

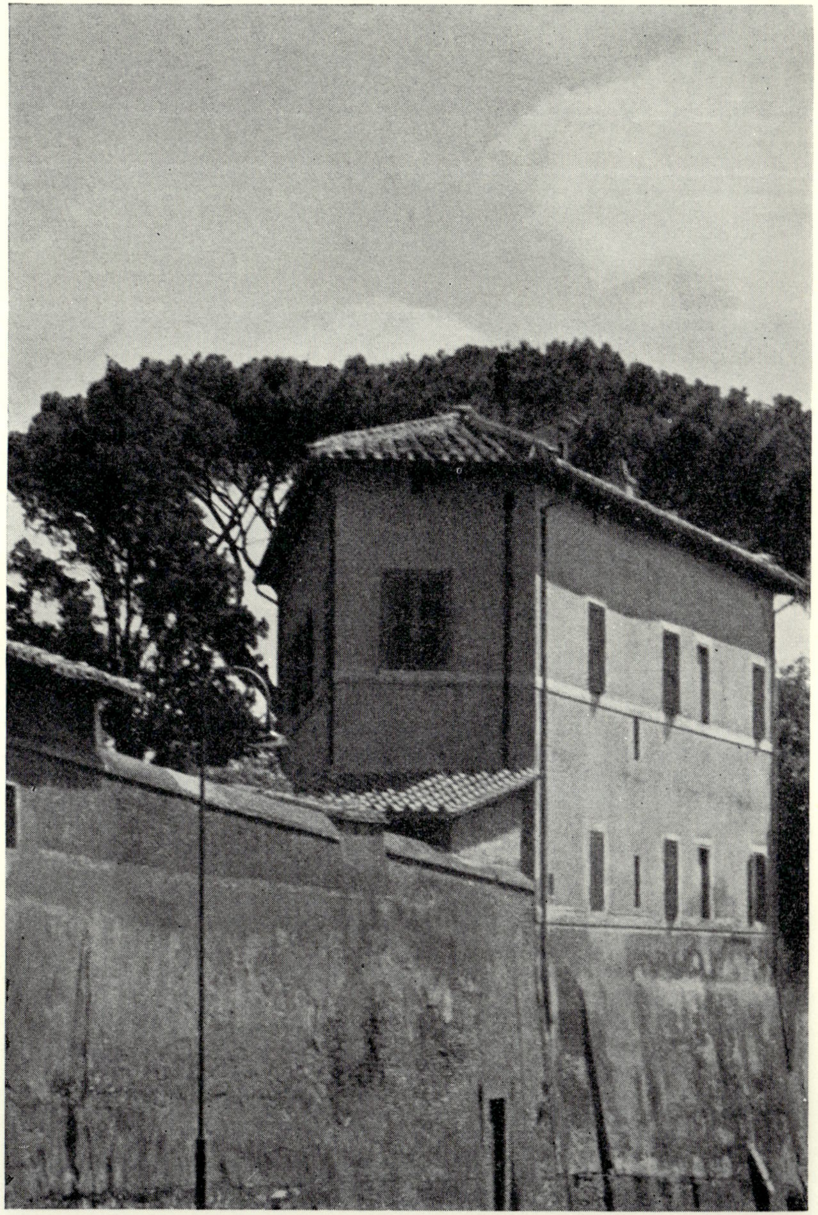

184b Farmhouse on the Aventine

185a. *Workshops in Via delle Fornaci, at the foot of the bastions of Gianicolo.*

185b. *At the back of the Jesuit vineyard on the Aventine.*

186. *Villa Altieri. Engraving by Vasi.*

187a. *The flight of stairs of Villa Altieri seen from above.*

187b. *Obelisk in front of Villa Altieri.*

188. *The terrace between Acqua Paola and S. Pietro in Montorio (detail of view by Vasi 1765).*

and which has often inspired artists to romantic fantasies of nature [54]. The Baroque period gave the site its particular, captivating atmosphere which stems from the profound mystery of decay. And for the people of the Rococo period, this terrain was a pastoral landscape, for where else could you find an arcadia with such approved relics as this place? The Palatine was enveloped in the most magnificent pagan legends which every cultured traveller knew by heart. On yonder plateau you could, if anywhere, imagine these famous mythological figures enact their parts. When Hercules graced the Palatine with his very presence it was on this hill that Evander, the Arcadian, raised an altar to him. "What a pleasure it would be to find *Ficus Ruminalis* with the two little boys (Romulus and Remus) clinging to the teats of the she-wolf," sighs de Brosses [55]. But that figtree did not present itself and he had to be content with box trees and pines. The weathered shafts of columns flung about in disorder provided the décor for well-read cavaliers, and it was all very suitable for picnics. The painter Charles Natoire, director of the French Academy in Rome, in 1759 sketched a view from the Palatine in which the foreground is taken up by a girl unpacking a luncheon basket, a young man playing the bagpipe, as well as an affectionate child and divers goats [56]. In this way the Farnesi garden experienced an Indian Summer with all the features of a pastoral play.

So far the axe was only laid at the tree's root. Around 1700 the greater part of the area was still untouched. Addison was certainly right when he said there were many "promising spots of ground" [57]. In the 1720's people began to explore the palace ruins of the Caesars [58] and to rummage around for antiquities, which were soon put away. Cardinal Polignac obtained some of the items for his famous cabinet [59]. Bianchini tried, by excavating, to obtain more facts about the layout of the Imperial palaces and left a paper on them, printed in 1738 [60], but it was not very good, for he knew too little and was too easily taken in. When somebody once asked Cardinal Davia if he knew the ancient palaces on the Palatine, he received the answer: "Do I know them? I built some of them." There was some truth in the statement, for after Davia the connoisseur had seen the archaeologist's plan of the ruins, he remarked: "Signor Bianchini, there you go constructing a palace *à la française*, when you know perfectly well that the Romans never failed to provide their buildings with porticoes where they spent most of their time," whereupon Bianchini to the best of his judgment added a few porticoes to his reconstruction [61]. Polignac related the anecdote to Montesquieu during a walk on the Palatine in 1729. About ten years later de Brosses expressed his amusement at the many obstacles Bianchini had come up against during his time as archaeologist [62]. But it was more than a century after Natoire's picnic, before antiquarians instigated systematic examinations which, up to this day, have continued with varying intensity. Vignola's park had in the end to pay the penalty for the fact that it stood in all its beauty on the most Classical of soils.

And yet – in spite of all the efforts of the scholars, the remains of the *Orti Farnesiani* are still able to excite you as you wander round the Palatine. The Nymphs and Graces have not been frightened away, but play among the oleander bushes well away from the exposed ruins. In earlier times they had another domain beyond the Farnesi sphere in a villa which was built in the 16th century by the Mattei family, later to change its name to Spada and Magnani [63] before being bought by Abbé Rancoureuil in 1770. He had thorough excavations carried out and discovered a part of *Domus Augustana* [64]; *Miranda* saw "three large rooms" in 1785 [65]. It was not quite so momentous that the vineyard was acquired in 1818 by Colonel Charles Mills who had returned from India "with a burnt-out liver and heavy money-bags" [66]. This gentleman turned his large and lovely piece of the Palatine into a "Tivoli Garden" by building his casino in a semi-Gothic, semi-Moorish style and hoisted a swallow-tail flag above one of the towers. But this could be remedied. Not long ago, the Englishman's castle on top of the palace of Augustus was razed to the ground; in its ruinous state it finally attained to a sort of dignity and was, I regret to say, even more picturesque than the genuine ruins, which are pretty crude. Now this whole corner has been cleared (it sounds like a scorched earth policy). The dryads seek a needy shelter by the S. Bonaventura monastery (Pl. 72), where Küchler venerated the genius of art to the very end. "They say they are going to excavate here," complained the old man to M. Galschiøt, "these days they tear down monasteries to dig up walls . . ." [67].

All the same – if a present-day traveller to Rome wants to experience the Palatine as the hill of lovely gardens and be alone in a vineyard, his desires can still be fulfilled, but he must trespass on private property. North of the monastery and its *via crucis* lies the *Vigna Barberini,* surrounded by a tremendous wall some of which goes back to Antiquity. The large area is immaculate, an honest kitchen garden. The gable of S. Sebastiano al Palatino is the centre of the scene, with a cypress next to it; both are equally Classical. Fragments of ancient masonry project outside the enclosing wall, cauliflower and lettuce are cultivated inside. A hoe lies on the ground; the gardener is having his siesta. The Palatine has preserved its priceless tranquility here.

An ancient weathered arch at la Marmorata, on the slope below the villa of the Knights of Malta, has, since the Renaissance, been called "The Arch of the Seven Wasps". The name is ominous. Nearby stood a little oratorium where alms were collected for the lepers. The hill at the back of this was known as the "Hill of Snakes" by the man in the street. *Arco delle Sette Vespe* and *Monte del Serpente* – these expressive names demonstrate that here was once an area outside the civil law, abandoned to loneliness, weeds and all sorts of vermin. This was how it had existed since time immemorial.

The Aventine is the Roman hill that was allowed to remain untouched longest, like a reserve behind silent walls. Merely two generations ago this enclave was more or less unexploited and its general aspect differed little in essence from what Addison, Montfaucon and Holberg had contemplated. Only a narrow strip along the edge of the steep slope down towards the Tiber had a continuous row of monuments: S. Sabina, S. Alessio, Priorato di Malta – this crown, whose silhouette is a delight to everybody. Gardens lie among the churches and monasteries (Pl. 181) and the whole group is flanked by such: furthest to the west the belvedere belonging to the Knights of Malta, to the east – nearest the approach from the Circus Maximus valley – a garden which in the middle of the 18th century was owned by the Ginnasi family. The ecclesiastical and literary society *degli Infecondi* held its meetings in the casino for a period and during this time was able to look down on Rome's other academies [68]. The area, which later belonged to S. Sabina's religious house, is now (since 1933) laid out as a public park and provides a magnificent view from the terrace.

But behind this northern fringe development, the Aventine was an undulating common covered with an irregular network of large and small vineyards, most of them belonging to Roman patrician families. Here were no aristocratic villas; only three early Christian churches (S. Saba, S. Prisca, S. Balbina) stood in this region and emphasized its remoteness from the world. Melancholy wayfarers had all the peace they could desire and here the Jews visited their miserable cemeteries. It was so serene and silent on the Aventine in the old days, very little tolling of bells, a lot of singing by the lark, braying of mules and the piercing melody of cicadas. Narrow desolate paths, sleepy vegetable gardens; a peasant with his creaking cart, monks on evening walks.

Now there is only a single noble monument left from the dreamy Aventine of Baroque and Romanticism, set in its very middle, and this is in my estimation, worth far more than a fragment of masonry from the earliest days of Rome. A large country house has as if by a miracle remained standing, with an imperceptible air of isolation and the smell of manured earth surrounding it. An irregular building, apparently cobbled together, the main house simple and strong, with a loggia on its roof. From end to end a true *casa in campagna*. It can be seen on Falda's map from 1676 and must even then have been advanced in years, although it is difficult to ascertain the date [69]. In the 18th century and later [70] it belonged to the Jesuits' *casa professa* (Pl. 185b).

The garden at the back is a wilderness, the last defiant outburst of nature on the Aventine of today. When this corner has been tidied up and the neglected buildings razed to the ground, which will soon happen, the desirable residences, with which this area has recently been dotted, will have won a decisive victory over the land of the past. Only the Jesuits' vineyard stands in the way. Other country houses of more recent date, but definitely from "the good old days", reliable and strong, can be visited and inspected with pleasure; they fit in perfectly with the hill. There is nothing fancy here (Pl. 184a–b).

It was the Palatine's fate to become hallowed ground because of the ancient ruins. Monte Aventino escaped this danger, and for this very reason it enjoyed a longer life without being spoilt. Latin writers could show were temples had stood on this hill too, but the bare bones did not stick up out of the ground [71] – the only striking ruin is from the Middle Ages, and that is the castle of the Savellis. Frederikke Brun, the indefatigable, of course made her own Aventine pilgrimage. She was stimulated by the memory of the giant Cacus who stole Hercules' cows up here, so she searched – like other well-educated tourists – for the unfortunate grotto in which these cattle had rested, but got little return from her hunt for beautiful *rudera,* although Zoëga was her guide [72]. The Vigna Cavalieri too, on the south-east slope of the Aventine down towards Caracalla's thermae, received a visit, and a grave mound was contemplated with a shudder. The lady was not to know that in the Vigna Maccarani, not far from this place, there languished a splendid fragment of the city wall, which bears the name (without reason) of Servius Tullius, but nevertheless is of respectable antiquity [73] – and that the owner of this land took a lot of trouble to demolish it on the quiet. Bergsøe tells an intriguing story about it [74].

The slope of Monte Gianicolo down towards Lungara is as yet full of gardens, in particular of course the Giardino Corsini [75], and the district's narrow, steep little alleys have still the provincial atmosphere of a suburb (Pl. 183b).

But in fact, the concept "suburb" was practically unknown in Rome's earlier times; the city did not slowly tail off outside the walls. The Campagna and fever prevented scattered houses being built along any of the main roads, and no working-class proletariat was pushed out to the outlying districts. The only attempt at a suburb, as we understand it, could be found in the valley west of Gianicolo, where most of the Roman bricks were made. The back road, which drops down from the Via Aurelia Antica beyond the Villa Doria-Pamphili and winds down towards the Borgo, not only bears the name of these brickworks (Via delle Fornaci), but there are remains of the old workshops, albeit in a very dilapidated state (Pl. 185a). It is difficult not to feel a shadow hovering over this road which until recently has remained deserted, for here, dwellings of extreme poverty stood in a constant change between mud and dust. Significantly enough this industrial district was called "The Valley of Hell"

(Valle dell'Inferno), and that is still its name. That the church Madonna delle Fornaci was built for the Trinitarian monks, whose most important task to buy the freedom of slaves, has no connection with the kind of people who lived here.

In those days the tourist would look in vain for a Roman suburban area that, with the feigned sweetness and frivolity of the working-class district outside the city limits of Paris, abounded with tavern gardens and *guingettes*. The Via Flaminia between Ponte Molle and Porta del Popolo had, it is true, several hostelries, some being patronized by the better-class people from the city [76], and the Villa di Papa Giulio functioned moreover as an official hotel, the last place for envoys of foreign powers to rest before they made their *entrata della campagna* [77]. But a wild night-life like that of the Porcherons or La Courtille of the 18th century, which took place amid swing-boats, dance halls and pleasure pavilions, was inconceivable outside Rome's main gate. The whores, who had been banished to the area beyond the Porta del Popolo in Benedict XIV's time from the L'Ortaccio district ("the neglected garden") near Ripetta [78], plied their trade indoors. Vineyards, not wineshops, had after all the upper hand here. It was the peasants' merriment that Goethe heard here and recollected:

> Hörest Du Liebchen! das muntre Geschrei
> den Flaminischen Weg her?
> Schnitter sind es, sie ziehen
> wieder nach Hause zurück ... [79]

The endless enclosure of walls, which made the roadway into a dried-up canal, covered with clouds of dust when carriages, during the time of the Corso race, rattled on their way to the Ponte Molle, was interrupted at times by gateways to aristocratic country estates. The families of Cimarra, Cini, Boccapaduli had vineyards within easy reach here, the last-named casino (from 1725) having the honour of a visit by Benedict XIV in 1748. Don Livio Odeschalchi's estate, its main building standing on the slope of Monte Parioli, was used for a time as the meeting place for a literary academy which was in competition with the Arcadian Academy [80]. Among the modern blocks of flats in Via Flaminia you come across a simple two-storeyed house, which belonged to Vigna Sinibaldi, and in 1750 a niche fountain was built into it with an upright shell above the basin. We know of equally fine and very natural shell-basins from Jardin's buildings in Copenhagen ("Christian's Plejehus" in Store Kongensgade, Andreas Bjørn's house in Strandgade in Christianshavn), which are like a greeting from Rome. On the Flaminian Way an inscription in ringing Latin announces that the fountain "was put in order for the pleasure and use of many". In the same jubilee year the fountain in the small corner of Pius IV's casino nearby, which at that time belonged to Don Fabrizio Colonna, was restored as well. His father too, Don Filippo, is remembered on the handsome monument. His ducal hat shadows a bearded, water-spouting face. The hinterland of the Parioli heights and up towards Acqua Acetosa was a labyrinth of enclosures and orchards. Here, even Frederikke Brun lost her way, after having knocked in vain on many a garden gate. In the end a woman appeared who shouted for her husband: "Arlecchino! Arlecchino!" [81]. She waited expectantly to see him, as if he came straight out of the Commedia del Arte.

The Via Salaria, the road to the Villa Albani, was described very briefly by Bergeret in 1774 as "a narrow lane between two walls" [82]. Nowadays this is true of only a short distance (by Villa Lancellotti). But in earlier times it held good for nearly all the main roads that went through the silent part of Rome, this metropolis of gardens and ruins. Along the Strada Pia (Via 20 Settembre) there were "practically only churches, walls and gardens" [83]. The Via di S. Giovanni in Laterano – a stretch of the papal triumphal route itself – was more or less uninhabited around 1770 [84]. And Zoëga wrote on March 19th 1785 to his father: "At the beginning of February I left my lodging near the Rotunda (Pantheon) and now live in the garden district, in the Strada Gregoriana, with a view across the whole of this proud city, almost in the country..." [85].

The last words are significant in the papal *città paesana*. Bonstetten, the good friend of Frederikke Brun, has left us the following reflection: "When one speaks of a city, one imagines streets, houses, families. But in Rome one must rid oneself of any such vulgar ideas" [86].

IV

The Roman *villa suburbana,* the country estate inside the city wall or a little way outside, is solidly fenced in. The enclosure disdains any approach, is a fortified piece of nature, which does not attempt, like the French Classical gardens, to dominate the terrain around it by long views through avenues, and would not be able to either, for no estate extends very far behind its gateway. The enclosing walls, which are a prerequisite for the existence of the villa, are often extremely high and substantial, and are in fact the gardens' most impressive architecture. The outer walls around the Villa Borghese had a total length of five Italian miles, and every year 4000 scudi were needed for their upkeep [87]. In some places where the countryside is very rough, the gardens on the outside look practically like fortresses with bastion-like parts (e. g. Villa Massimo and Villa Aldobrandini at Magnanapoli). A walk along the flanks of the Quirinal garden, straightened by Urban VIII [88], is like a tour of the walls of a Jericho that cannot be brought down. In the depth of the curving Via dei Giardini one is completely daunted by the enceinte of the garden citadel high above. The villa can be defined in a few words as a silhouette of barrier walls with a cultivated green area inside. On this ground stands a main building called *casino* or *palazzina,* described by non-Italians as "the villa" itself. This is not correct – the building is a secondary factor, the boundary of the garden defines the villa.

The Roman villa is furthermore distinguished by costly appurtenances, which are not merely richer, but also of far greater merit than the usual sculptural works in French gardens, for they consist of the treasures of Antiquity – busts and statues, hermae and reliefs, obelisks, sarcophagi, fragments of buildings yielded up by the good, inexhaustible earth. Some Roman gardens are indeed situated on land used for the same purpose in ancient times, like the Villa Ludovisi and the Villa Medici. It is really wonderful that a *villa suburbana* need not be decorated with artistic articles made to order; it is supplied with gifts from deep down in its own countryside. And above all – the Italian appreciates the large scale harmony in his own small part of the landscape; he is less likely to violate the special tone of his land than is the Frenchman, but prefers to emphasize its own peculiar characteristics, both the relief of the terrain and the type of vegetation. An old pine grove is lovingly preserved, and ever since the Renaissance it has been the custom to add a stretch of unfenced woodland (*selva, bosco*) and grassy meadows (*prati*) to the formal parts of the villa – the Campagna was brought right in. Instead of fighting against the conditions of a temperamental climate, the gardens gloried in them. De Brosses notes: "Evergreen trees, grass rather than gravel on the paths, narrow passages between high hedges which always provide shade in this hot country." Walls of clipped trees cannot be going against nature among a people who ennoble all naked walls and venerate every towering shade. After having compared the villa with a retreat in the warm season, an English observer added that this was the reason why many large shady trees and tall hedges were included in the gardens [89]. De Brosses also remarked that constant dampness underfoot "apparently is not so unwelcome to the Italians as it is to us" [90]. Even from the sour soil things were encouraged to spring forth in the Roman garden; the Parisians covered it with sand and raked it over.

Wishing to delve even further into the superficial scheme of these villas, it is necessary to turn up some of the hidden layers of culture on which they stand. Unexpected discoveries can then be made. The most important one will take only one sentence: the aristocrat in Rome used his suburban villa very little. The town house, so aloof and reserved, was his true background and real home for the greater part of the year. It was not the same in France and England (nor in Teutonic countries). Apart from the narrow circle of French noblemen who could only thrive in the hothouse atmosphere of the court and considered it a death sentence "to have to withdraw to their estates", the aristocrat in Louis XV's time was first and foremost lord of his castle; he moved to his mansion in the Faubourg Saint-Germain for only a few winter months [91]. As far as the English are concerned, Wright in 1721 gave as his opinion that the nobility in England lived in great style on their country estates and spent no more than was absolutely necessary in town, but in Italy it was exactly the other way round; the town residence was far bigger and always far more splendid than the villa, which was only designed for short stays in the hot season [92]. Some twenty years later, Nugent made the same assertions [93]. No court in the Versailles sense of the word kept the aristocrat in Rome, but his father's house did. He was a metropolitan from top to toe, miles removed from "the squire", from *le gentilhomme campagnard* and from all the fine landed gentry wherever they had their roots. The Roman patrician had a cavalier attitude to his country estates and castles far away, he accepted the rents, collected feudal titles and left the castellans to do the rest. He might of course take up residence in his principality over a period, here where he was the central figure – we are likely to meet a Rospigliosi in Zagarolo, a Pamphili in Valmontone, a Colonna in Paliano, a Chigi in Ariccia, a Cesarini in Genzano, for all these were modern palaces – but he ignored most of his castles set in the loveliest countryside, and some he never visited at all. According to Lady Morgan, three generations of the Borghese family had not set eyes on their magnificent country seat in Palestrina. When she expressed her surprise at this to the then *principe,* he answered that the post-horses were not good enough and that the trip up there was a bit too far for his own carriage horses [94]. But a villa was suitable for a society gentleman. No farming was done, no feudal duties had to be carried out, it was usually comfortable and of recent date and furthermore situated at a reasonable distance from Rome. So it was only used for recreation. The so-called *villa rustica* further out, preferably in the Albani mountains, was reserved for *villeggiatura,* while the suburban country house was used for short stays in the country.

Having now encompassed the sites we are going to deal with, we then ask without further ado: what was the owner's purpose in visiting them? In other words: how did he spend his holidays? The answer is not as simple as it seems. If you imagine that he stayed in the country to devote himself to nature, you are very much mistaken; he was not going to sit and rest on fallen tree trunks or recline on the grass. The most important reason for visiting his villa was the climate; he was of course drawn to his garden to breathe better and cooler air. Paradoxically enough it was this same country atmosphere that drove him back to the city again. It cannot be too strongly emphasized that the use of Rome's villas was very limited for fear of malaria. This circumstance was in reality decisive for their fate. The villa garden on the outskirts of city was full of danger, especially after sundown. On a day in June 1714, Clement XI paid a visit to the Queen of Poland; he made his entry through her garden on the slope of Pincio (behind the Via Sistina), but as darkness had fallen at the time of his departure, he was afraid to go back the same way [95]. Berkeley wrote at the time, that it was very inconvenient for people of standing that they never dared spend the night in their villa for fear of *aria cattiva,* and so they only occasionally drove out to their gardens in the daytime to do some shooting or have some fun [96].

It cannot be set out more clearly. The nobleman visited his nearest villa as does the ordinary man his allotment these days. He enjoys the cleaner air, the city is within his reach and its rhythm in his blood. The garden was a place for games. Innocent XII drove out to the Villa Pinciana (Borghese) "to see the fallow deer running in large herds" [97]. In 1740 Thomas Grey saw "the two lads", little Prince Charles Edward Stuart and his brother Henry, shooting them with sporting guns [98]. But otherwise the pleasures of country life were mostly indoor ones; the company continued the habits of city life, people slept until nearly noon, spent long hours at the table, even longer at the gaming table, held concerts, danced and acted in plays [99]. When a witness reports that the Duke of Montelibretti and his family often spent the evening as well, at the Villa Barberini, situated high up on the bastion south of St. Peter's Square, he adds the very significant remark: "There is a very good billiard-room" [100]. Clement XIV rented the Villa Sacchetti immediately outside Porta Pia for the particular reason of being able to relax at this game [101]. We need not take the trouble to evoke elegiac *fêtes-champêtres* in the spirit of Watteau or Lancret behind the Roman walls of those days. The social gatherings took the air for a few hours by open doors.

How little feeling the aristocrat had for nature, in comparison with his respect for fashion, is all too evident from the fact that he did not make certain to leave Rome at the height of summer, for the hottest time of the year was also a "season" to some extent. Then the parade on the Corso and out to the Ponte Molle was given a special impetus, because the theatres were closed; the fashionable set was carried back and forth in great throngs to show off their attire and equipages – "without even a pretence of taking fresh air" [102]. The urge to take part in collective pleasures was stronger than the dread of fever; the discomfort of sweating in a heavy atmosphere and amid swirling dust was of no importance. A truly "baroque" example of a Roman relaxation for the upper classes during the summer was the "Water Corso" which took place in the Piazza Navona every Sunday in August. After vespers the fountain's outlet was stopped up and a couple of hours later the square was flooded to a depth of one and a half to three feet, and the carriages then set out on their circular tour splashing through the water to the sound of orchestral music. The street-urchins were naturally in the seventh heaven, ducking each other and spattering the wigs with water. The ancient circus and sea-fight (*naumachia*) were brought back in this *lago estivo* and were popular from 1652 to 1866 (with a break 1676–1703) [103]. While the elegant games attracted the aristocrats to the sweltering streets, the villa gardens were empty.

The social habits outlined here affected the suburban country house in a strange way. The owner's way of life and his use of the villa as nothing more than a *pied à terre* isolated it; it was, as it were, pensioned off and life passed it by. One can, by arguing historically, understand to some extent why the barons, who owned too many of the good things in life and who had acquired an inflexible style, did not make full use of their delightful rural estates so close at hand – thus the Villa Doria-Pamphili, the most beautiful of them all, was in the 1780's only rarely honoured by the presence of the young Prince Doria [104]. But were these magnificent places of pleasure to anybody else? The good citizenry, the mass of the people, romantic young people, tourists and artists perhaps? It could happen, but to a surprisingly limited extent. The personal unapproachability of the owners was an even greater obstacle than the walls themselves – it was a great favour, rarely granted, to be let in. The Villa Ludovisi, in particular, was for a very long period notorious for its barred gates [105]. By the 1840's only a small number of foreigners, and indeed perhaps of the younger generation in Rome even, could boast of having visited it [106].

While people from the city had to petition for a graciously given admission, the traveller had to pay for it. This was an advantage to the wealthy, but not so for artists and scholars [107]. Winckelmann complained that tips to the doormen made his studies expensive, half a thaler per visit [108]. And at times he found it necessary to resort to cunning; he only got into the Villa Giustiniani by pretending to want to buy fruit. In the end people began to notice him and watch where he went. "When I arrived there the last time and knocked, I was stared out of countenance by a man through an opening in the door. A voice shouted from inside the vineyard: *Chi e?* The answer was: "It is the Englishman." "Which Englishman, the wizard (*Il necromante*)?" replied the man at the door. "Keep the heretic out (*Lasciatelo stare l'eretico*)". "That is how I was stopped" [109]. The anecdote could be true of a large number of abortive assaults. Touchy owners united with malaria to ensure the large gardens an unassailable peace and quiet [110].

These special circumstances are closely connected with the fact that Rome's large Baroque gardens were neglected and had been from early on. It would be difficult to state which was cause and which was effect in this affair, for a garden that is not used much falls into decay and nobody cares to show off an untended park. By and large, infrequent use must no doubt have been responsible for the progressive deterioration of villa gardens. Burnet noted in the 1680's that apart from the Villa Pinciana, the gardens were even worse looked after than the palaces [111]. The oldest of the estates that were famous for their Classical style, Villa Montalto-Peretti on the Esquiline, was sold in 1696 to Cardinal Giovanni Francesco Negroni [112]. After his death in 1713 his reputation was summed up as follows: "He was well advanced in age and very rich and very mean. So he is missed by nobody" [113]. Like an executioner of old he tortured the life out of the villa that had fallen into his greedy hands; he stopped the hundreds of fountains flowing by selling the lead pipes, and he planted cabbages in the finest parterres. "You have never seen such neglect, and no wonder everybody is denied access," the little bookseller Deseine ventured to assert about the still-living prince of the church in a guide he wrote [114]. Negroni's heir sold off most of the sculptures [115] and before 1780 the axe had made clearings among the cypresses and pines; the garden was like a desolate ruin [116]. Shortly after 1700 the Villa Doria-Pamphili was described as neglected and its statues defaced [117]. The Villa Ludovisi too was in disrepair; it was said (1707), that it would have been one of Rome's finest gardens had it been better looked after [118]. De Brosses was polite and said that it was "the least badly looked after" [119]; in the eyes of Kotzebue it was purely and simply "nothing but a field hospital for antiques" [120]. About 1770 nobody felt any shame when the pine grove which was the pride of Villa Mattei was cut down [121]; the finest of the statues were sold and most of the remainder were damaged by neglect. The gardens behind Villa Medici were also in danger of falling into decay [122], but the Grand Duke of Tuscany had them put in order in the 1760's and even opened them to the public. It was due to a foreign country (and an Archduke of Austria) that Rome was given its first public park [123].

This event makes us stop for a moment to consider the matter once again. We have seen that the gardens near Rome were neglected and we have discovered the direct causes of it. The pertinent question now is whether the interpretation of this strange situation should not be gone into more deeply. When all is said and done, one is forced to assume that the miserable state of the gardens is a result of a contempt for nature. The Italian is not interested in "going hiking". If the Romans' feeling for natural beauty were more highly developed, it would bring about a demand from the population which could not be contained. But there is nothing to indicate that there was any particular urgent need for such accessible pleasure grounds, at least not until about 1780, when the gospel of nature worship eventually reached Rome. Duclos noted that although the Villa Medici had recently been made freely available to the public, he met only foreigners there, the Romans having not yet developed the taste for going to the parks. Ordinary people, meaning the overwhelming majority, looked for their summer pleasures either in short excursions outside the city gates or in the city itself. Trips to the country were determined by the season, the greatest exodus being in May and October (*le Ottobrate*) [124]. A favourite destination was also the nearest one, the meadow with scattered trees, Prato del Castello or "del Popolo Romano" at Monte Testaccio, in whose grottoes people cooled the new wine; lunch baskets were unpacked and served on simple wooden tables; the gaiety was boisterous, the saltarello's chain weaved along the bank of the Tiber

[125]. We find Casanova out here in 1744 taking part in a family excursion, which in its cheerful atmosphere could compete with any contemporary woodland picnic north of the Alps [126]. People also liked to make their way out to the Villa Madama, "where we enjoy our bacchanalian revels with the girls at times" wrote Sergel in 1769 [127], and all the hostelries outside the city gates were well patronized. Only well-to-do citizens found lodgings in the villages of the Albani hills or contented themselves with a winegrower's *vignate* in this area.

But in actual fact the population of Rome enjoyed the summer in an inspired fashion out in the streets. During the evening and at night they met at the fountains, the streets resounding with serenades, refreshing drinks were on sale all over the place and there were lively goings-on until dawn [128]. The delight of the Italians in making fun of themselves came to the fore in the warm darkness. They had a fondness for dressing up in cool linen smocks and straw hats with turned-down brims to pretend to be peasants, "and in this disguise, which was assumed under the pretext of greater comfort, all sorts of tomfoolery could take place and anyone do whatever he felt like under the cloak of his incognito" [129]. This was a summertime carnival without the help of masks [130]. And it was an entirely different kind of witchery than that of the Nordic young men's flight from the sylph maidens. No *Romano di Roma* in his right mind sat dreaming of nymphs in empty enchanted gardens. Midsummer Eve was not celebrated in the countryside, but by eating snails in the streets near the Lateran – as is still done. The Spanish Steps became the perfect stage for the Romans' nocturnal activities during the summer. Impromptu singers lifted up their voices, small bands of wood-wind players gave concerts, the steps themselves were crowded with reclining clusters of people. A vague chiaroscuro gave the scene a magic atmosphere [131]. Up in his room near the Piazza Pollarola, Winckelmann moaned; he could not sleep because of the noise of the late-night revellers [132].

We now begin to understand the loneliness and decay of the villas. The Roman was deaf to the blandishments of nature; he played tarot in the salon or strummed a tune in the alley, but he was not aware of the pipes of Pan.

Contrary to all expectations the time arrived when amends were made to the old parks in the most surprising way. It did not fall to the lot of the Romans to bring this about, for their guests, including poets and painters, were the reformers. When after Rousseau, the passion for nature had captured everybody and the crusade against the French garden had successfully been brought to a close throughout Europe, the time was ripe for the Roman garden; it had then reached a suitable minimum of maintenance. Austere grounds were now in a wonderful state of dissolution, lines had been softened, shapes broken up, planes torn asunder. Most villas rejoiced in ruins of all kinds. At this point in time, when tender hearts longed for a ravaged garden in which to sob, as if it were a churchyard, the Roman garden was at its lowest ebb, ready for commiseration and charity. Rome's horticultural bankruptcy was to inspire the whole world. The artists who managed to get into the gardens' wilderness filled sketch-books with their impressions of collapsing steps and damaged vases. What pitiful bushes and trees with wild creeper like mourning crape fluttering from the branches! Thistles and nettles had taken over where previously ungainly tidiness held sway. In the same way as the ancient building profited by its ravaged condition, so the architecture of the garden was glorified in the hours of its ignominy.

Now there was a complete change of tune; what had been censured yesterday was lauded today. Already in 1770 it was said of the Villa Mattei that its sublime character was rooted in "die schlechte Unterhaltung" [133]; it was this that helped to fill the painters' heads with pictures of *des fêtes agréables sur le tableau* [134]. The avenues had a "melancholy but noble appearance" [135]. Of the Villa Negroni, whose destroyer had been publicly reproved in 1712, it was said seventy years later: "The negligence of the present owners through many years has again established nature to its former rights; it now gives us true pleasure." Its character is depicted thus: "From the green jaws of a moss-grown lion trickles a thin stream of water with a monotonous sound; and at the same time as this lulls my soul to meditate on disappointed plans, false desires and forlorn hopes, the turtledove coos at my side..." [136]. The Villa Ludovisi itself was now picturesque, meaning that nobody paid any attention to it, which was not what Lenôtre had had in mind [137].

The Villa Doria-Pamphili too, was a source of great inspiration for artists, and soon in fact, every garden was echoing with *les exclamations des peintres* [138]. The loudest cries of rapture at the sight of melancholy views were voiced by Hubert Robert, Fragonard and Richard Wilson [139].

Perhaps Chiswick Park was the earliest example of an English landscape garden, laid out shortly before 1717 by Lord Burlington after his return from Italy [140]. Its ideal background would have been Claudesque scenes from the beautiful countryside by Lake Albani. With impressions from his "grand tour" still fresh in his mind, Addison in 1712 printed his epoch-making letter in the "Spectator" [141], from which we quote the following passage: "... our English Gardens are not so entertaining to the Fancy as those in France and Italy, where we see a large Extent of Ground covered over with an agreeable Mixture of Garden and Forest, which represents every where an artificial Rudeness, much more charming than that Neatness and Elegancy which we meet with in those of our own Country". The subsequent development of the landscape garden in England took place amid an unbroken series of Italian impulses; travelling gentlemen spread the gospel of the picturesque taste in the country where the holm oak spreads its branches over the carpet of the greensward. The *prato* in the villa can be construed as the progenitor of the English lawn with free-standing trees, and the morbid idyll, nourished by decay, stimulated by fallen columns and trees blown down by the wind, found all too fertile soil on the English country estates. In the second half of the 18th century the game of "the English Garden" had been won by the nation which was to give it its name. English country gentlemen could lob the ball back over the net, for now it was they that walked in the Roman parks giving instructions in the art. Wherever they went they tried to make comparison with what they had at home; they gave the villas good advice and almost considered a seedy park near the Tiber as a poor copy of gardens by the Thames – *Georgian England revisited*.

Young Lord Herbert, (whose great-grandfather the 9th Earl of Pembroke (The Architect Earl) had, in 1737, himself produced the plan for the Palladian bridge in Wilton Park and turned it into an Elysium) walked around in Roman gardens in 1779 and looked upon them as a kind of offshoot of the Italy back home, which Richard Wilson had depicted in his views. The glades at the Villa Borghese, he remarked, were in the English style, but the grass was not green enough [142]. Mrs Millar was in 1771 extremely pleased with the Villa Mattei whose garden she considered better at that time than previously, when it had been kept up; the trees had outgrown the shapes which Roman gardeners' shears had pitilessly forced upon them. The ground showed much promise, and she thought that if an Englishman were to buy the villa he could at little expense provide the Romans with a prototype which they could copy in their gardens [143]. She also praised the Villa Barberini; the trees here had not been very ill-treated and the so-called "Coffee House" would, in the neighbourhood of London, have been appreciated as a handsome pavilion [144]. Fr. Münter's observation on the Villa Chigi in Ariccia is priceless. The park, he wrote in 1785, is completely wild, "just as nature created it" – and it still is. But that was not enough, "merely at the expense of cutting a few footpaths through it would turn it into the most beautiful English garden" [145]. The naturalness was not sufficiently artificial to be quite natural. Prince Chigi probably did not understand one word of this sophistry, he left things to themselves.

Now it was the turn of the poets to come into the garden and absorb its noble style. The parts which the owner regarded as superfluous, remote places for shooting, empty areas bearing witness to the excess of the rich, became an Arcadia for poets. Decay was a sign of innocence, the meadows were as if laid out for "the spirits of the dead" in Gluck's "Orpheus", the solitary tree awaited Daphne and Chloe at its root. The large *prato* at the Villa Doria-Pamphili became a leading motif in Goethe's Classicism, more influential than any text that the history of literature can produce. Was it not the reality of a dream? Goethe walked out to this place one day at the end of November 1786 and remained until late in the evening. He wrote to Frau Stein about it: "Eine grosse mit immergrünen Eichen und hohen Pinien eingefasste, viereckte, flache Wiese war ganz mit Masslieben übersäet, die ihre Köpfgen alle nach der Sonne wendeten ..." [146]. Moritz, who together with some artists had accompanied the poet, gave a fuller description: "Shady laurel groves in which you lose your way, broad clearings where you find it again; sunlit hills which you climb, pleasing (angenehme) valleys where you lie in the shade; woods encircling fields ..." [147]. This last picture, with an "altar" from pagan times into the bargain, is reproduced in plate 207.

Then Moritz summarizes his impressions: "There is something new and unusual about all this; *die Idee vom Garten verschwindet ganz.*" The Greek landscape of Iphigenia and Mignon rose up in the desolate Roman garden. Its apotheosis, created with the same artistry as a funereal tableau on the stage, in honour of a beloved actress who has died, we shall visit later, in the Villa Borghese.

Before then we must wander around those villas which were newly built in our period and had not yet been neglected. Their architecture belonged to the age – and the nature of the gardens was entirely contemporary.

V

The Altieri family owned a large vineyard between S. Maria Maggiore and S. Croce, its main entrance being in Strada Felice. It is very unlikely that Clement X Altieri himself had any wish to provide his family's vineyard with a stately main building; anyhow the *Villa Altieri*'s new casino was not built by the time the Pope died in 1678, for it cannot be seen in Falda. The building was probably erected by the Pope's relation, Cardinal Paluzzi Altieri or by Don Gaspare, at the same time as the family's palace by the Gesù was rebuilt and extended. Giovanni Antonio de Rossi was the architect for the villa as well [148].

The main building of this is a work that has been ignored [149], which is rather remarkable considering that the number of large Baroque villas in Rome is very limited. It is hard to believe that the building is still there, which is the case, although in a much neglected condition and with its existence threatened by modern flats. Prince Altieri's casino deserves close attention, not merely as a historic monument, but also because of its architecture. This imposing house, impressive by its weight alone, is a model of its kind, a classic of Late Baroque created to become a pattern for later and smaller villas. The façade of the building is a solid block, the topmost horizontal feature of which is crowned by a belvedere with arcades (Pl. 186). A horseshoe-shaped external flight of steps leads up to the portal in the *piano nobile* and it gives the massive house an agreeable and much needed spatial extension forward (Pl. 187a); the cube welcomes and absorbs it without making any concessions. Down between the enclosing arms of the stairway an example of Baroque's gloomy nature has been preserved; rough cliff-like masonry forms a grotto in which statues of wet gods vegetate. Behind this nymphaeum is the entrance to the large cool parlour (*sala terrena*). The two obelisks bearing the Altieri star, still stand in front of the building (Pl. 187b), as do the remains of imaginative rock fountains at its sides, along which the paths led down into the garden. From this side view, the casino has two short side wings; above the terraces the block of the building is opened up. While this type of rear elevation is reminiscent of the Danish Frederiksberg Castle's garden-side, there is also a similarity between the casino's façade and the more or less contemporary Sofie Amalienborg in Copenhagen [150]. The Villa Altieri had become typical of its genre and the one hundred years' tradition since the Villa Montalto had settled down in this building, which was once seen by all the important members of society but is now hidden and forgotten. Indoors, antique wall-paintings, found "about 1675", could be admired [151] while in the garden stood the most beautiful umbrella pine [152].

By the Via Aurelia, immediately outside Porta di S. Pancrazio, Mgr. Lorenzo Corsini (at the time treasurer, later Pope Clement XII) bought an enormous tract of land on which to establish a villa. It was a fortunate purchase, the view was without equal and when in 1697 work was being carried out in the garden, an antique columbarium of great archaeological value was discovered. The casino had just been finished at this time, and Francesco Bartoli, who had been in charge of the excavations, depicted it in an engraving in his work "Gli antichi sepolchri", 1697 [153]. The building, which was called *Casino dei Quattro Venti,* was given its name for a good reason. High winds blew round it from all the points of the compass and four portals in the rectangular block opened into the large square hall, which took up all the space of the inside.

Corsini's pavilion was constructed as one large belvedere raised up by a tall terraced building with balustrades; above the main cornice an attic storey appeared, topped with vases that seemed to sway in the wind. But clearly there was Classical substance in this casino, which has risen above the graves of the ancient Romans. In plan and structure this symmetrical piece of architecture is reminiscent of the Arch of Janus, in those days often called the temple of Janus Quadrifrons; the four portals were supposed to symbolize the seasons of the year [154]. One could well believe that the idea would have appealed to a bibliophile like Corsini, and its execution should have been child's play for a pupil of Fontana. The architect might have been a disguised Classicist from his circle. Specchi later showed an interest in the conservation of the Arch of Janus [155]. All the same it is not improbable that a Florentine architect was employed; a certain daintiness in the style and the fuzziness of outline – small capricious pinnacles were added [156] – might be an indication of this [157]. The casino of the four winds had to pay the penalty for its bold elevation, for during the fighting outside Porta di S. Pancrazio in 1849, Garibaldi used it as an observation post and it was shot to pieces. In its place now is the entrance pavilion to the Villa Doria-Pamphili.

The *Villa Carpegna* stands as the principal of its kind in Rome. This patrician country house is now (1951) the most authentic example of a suburban villa from the period of Late Baroque. It certainly bears the scars of neglect but has not suffered serious damage, nor has it been prettied up. Topography has recorded this important building [158], but history of art has not. So we will try to interpret on our own. First a brief description. The rather limited space on the hill by S. Maria del Riposo behind St. Peter's, is surrounded by a wall on the top of which two strange free-standing window pediments appear. They indicate that the garden walk behind comes to an end here. The casino, which stands further out in the grounds, is connected to the barrier wall in front by three paths lined with hedges, the middle one being the axis that joins the house with the main gateway. The other two radiate from the middle of the building and run diagonally out to the wall.

So this *patte d'oie* does not follow the basic pattern in the Villa Montalto-Negroni, for here the situation was the other way round: the paths in that trifurcation diverged from the entrance to the garden and included the casino in their spread. The system in the Villa Carpegna is after all French (Vaux-le-Vicomte; Versailles) but need not necessarily have been imported. For the arrangement at Montalto is suitable only for a large site where the palazzetto was extended on the transverse axis with *giardini segreti* and was therefore wide enough to include such a spread. The Casino Carpegna is on the small side and has no arms to extend. But the French plan with its points towards the entrance can be shortened whenever necessary, although it is of course used to its best advantage on a large site.

Behind the main building a middle axis runs down a slope to a "circus" which is surrounded by palms and has a basin in the centre; this is further kept together by stone seats (Pl. 191a). Projecting from this *rondel* is a semicircular podium from which there is a view towards the main avenue, across a falling, then rising terrain (Pl. 190). Along the podium's curved retaining wall are set symmetrical steps, and there is a small nymphaeum at the base of the wall's apogee (Pl. 191b, 193). In its moderate decay, this sight is particularly characteristic of the architecture of a genuine Baroque garden. As we leave the crumbling fountain and walk along the undulating path, we are drawn towards a grotto-like structure which forms the end of the perspective. It is faced and lined with artificial rock, porous as tufa; the room inside is cool and tart, like a cellar. Here again, curving steps along the side of the building lead up to a platform decorated with huge antique urns, most of them in fragments (Pl. 190). From here the reverse view can be enjoyed.

Everything in this comparatively small and simple garden, both the plan and the details, has been fashioned according to old and tried customs. We recognize it all, but indeed with quiet happiness that it has been one's lot to experience this wholly exemplary and completely normal sight. And the grounds are also in such a condition that you feel you are looking at the genuine past. No matter that this work of art has some cracks in it, that it has been patched up here and there – its form is nevertheless undamaged, and its substance has taken on a new and perhaps greater splendour by being worn by time. One might regard it from two points of view as living history. The Villa Carpegna gives us a valuable insight into a garden such as was created in Holberg's time – and also how it changed by the decay into which Baroque's old gardens fell during the following century. I should think that the forgotten country house near S. Maria del Riposo is now the only park near Rome that is still extant which Hubert Robert would love and believe he had seen before.

The modest casino is well suited to its garden, both rustic and decorative, a neatly shaped little mass. A belvedere rises above the centre of it and there are squat towers at the ends (Pl. 192). The great motifs from the Villa Altieri and Villa Borghese have been reduced to pocket size. The window frames above the entrance are scribed all in one with an arid flourish. So now we want to find out the two signatures, that of the builder and that of the architect, as well as a date for the erection. The casino itself gives nothing away, no inscription, no Latin. The builder could certainly wield a pen and was entitled to put a coronet above his name. This was Gasparo Carpegna, member of a noble family who enjoyed feudal rights in Umbria; who became cardinal in 1670; Bishop of Sabina (one of the seven *Sedi Suburbicarie,* reserved for the highest rank of the Holy College) from 1698; cardinal vicar in Rome in 1704, died 1714, thus one of the leading paladins of the Church. He was an antiquarian like his colleague Aless. Albani, owned a fine collection of glyptics, was a highly regarded numismatist, and when he died left many *anticaglie,* these became part of the Vatican collections and filled a cabinet of their own [159]. The theatre also enjoyed his favour [160]. This man, raised to the purple, who in the end became regent for the capital, clearly wanted to live in a very retired manner when he sought recreation on his hill. The contrast between Carpegna's power and the simplicity of the house, may well be a reflection of his refined humanism. As with Horace, this unsophisticated "Sabine" country house appealed to the patron of the arts. Carpegna was also an "Arcadian", the first cardinal in Queen Christina's academy.

We have reason to believe that the architect was of a high order; the villa certainly is. Giovanni Ant. de Rossi is known to have worked for the Carpegna estate, and in his will he made Cardinal Gasparo his principal executor, which cannot but indicate a close connection between the two men [161]. Carpegna was related to the Altieris, whose villa it will be remembered, was built by de Rossi, and he had a close kinship with Clement X who made him datary and cardinal. However, since Pascoli, to whom we owe the information about the relations between de Rossi and Carpegna, does not include this villa in the comprehensive list of the architect's works, one hesitates to regard him as the villa's originator [162]. Unless of course a project by de Rossi was not executed until after his death in 1695. If the cardinal's building activities were subsequent to this, it would have been more natural for him to employ Carlo Fontana, who was the principal architect of the Curia. The wavy ornamentation with side volutes above the balcony window of the Casino Carpegna has some analogy with Fontana's drawing for the S. Michele hospice [163]. But all the same, the building cannot be ascribed to him on such a fragile basis, however probable it could seem. The date of the erection was very likely before 1710, for by that time Carpegna was over eighty-five. An excellent artist, competent in his profession, assisted him. It might have been yet another man.

The Maltese *commendatore,* Guido Vaini, was in 1697 raised to the rank of prince by Innocent XII [164]. A few years later the newly fledged *principe* began to build a villa on a site just below the terrace in front of the Acqua Paola on Janiculum (Pl. 188). Work was in progress in 1703 [165]. The casino which still rejoices in its sunny position, although somewhat altered, is absolutely unique among Roman villas, in that this little building is provided with a broad and gently curving apse in the middle of the façade. It is obvious that the architect, Carlo Fontana himself, in this case let himself be influenced for once by the latest French country houses (*maisons de plaisance*), such as the Château de Montmorency which dates from roughly the same time; in Denmark, Bernstorff Palace is a later scion of the type [166]. It was without doubt the client himself who suggested French models, for Prince Vaini had visited Paris in the middle of the 1690's and was a sworn adherent of the French party in Rome. On June 7th 1699 he arrived in Versailles to receive the Order of the Holy Spirit from the hand of Louis XIV [167]. Before this audience, the Prince had lived for two months in Paris and had then had the opportunity to visit the fashionable country houses of his social equals in the surrounding districts. When he returned home to Rome, basking in the favour of both the Pope and *le Roi Soleil,* he was very conversant with what a summer residence *à la française* should be like. Perhaps his luggage included plans and engravings?

The Casino Vaini stands not far from the *Orti D'Alibert*, which is also situated on the slope of Janiculum, right at the top of a small street coming from Lungara, but as far as style goes, the two buildings are miles apart. The Maltese knight's country house is an unobtrusive little product which would not be out of place on a hillside near the Seine. The other villa on this side of the Tiber is Italian enough, but it borders on the limits of Roman good taste. This might be due to the builder's own eccentric position. A definition of the Alibert summer residence is indeed not easy, for as far as I am aware nothing certain about its origin is available, neither the year of its erection nor its architect [168] and strictly speaking, not even the name of the man who built it. The choice lies between two Counts D'Alibert, father and son. Both were interested in the theatre. Giacomo D'Alibert (1626–1713), of a noble Orleans family, came to Rome c. 1657 and became secretary to Queen Christina. He showed great talent as *maître de plaisir* and had plenty of knowledge of the theatre in general as well, and as far as the latter was concerned, he became the guiding star to the whole city. He erected Rome's first opera house, Teatro Tordinona (1670), and had the contract for running it; at the same time he planned theatres for both the Corso and the Via Margutta [169], gave concerts and marionette shows and had a hand in practically all the private theatres in the city. Despite his flair and intrigue he foundered somewhere along the line, like many other theatre impresarios. In the game of hazard, too, luck deserted him; Innocent XII gave him the coup de grâce by ordering the demolition of the Teatro Tordinona in 1697 [170].

Antonio D'Alibert followed in his father's footsteps. In 1716 he built the large "Teatro alle Dame", which also bore his own name, as did the narrow street leading to it (Via Alibert). But although this new opera house was well attended and had a number of successful seasons – Caffarelli and Farinelli made their début here – Count Antonio finally had to throw in his hand too. In 1725 his creditors took over his theatre [171]; the next year he had a stroke, was admitted to the S. Spirito hospital and died on January 31st 1731 in Casa Turci, the picturesque little Early

Renaissance palace opposite Governo Vecchio [172]. If nothing else, the two theatrical counts left behind a couple of street names in Rome – apart from the one just mentioned, there is also the "Vicolo Alibert" which is the name of the road to the somewhat enigmatic pavilion situated near the Palazzo Riario (Corsini), Queen Christina's residence. Presumably the land was originally hers. Which of the two gentlemen authorized the building? It seems obvious to try and discover it from the house itself, but its style is so ambiguous that it could only provide very dubious answers. The best basis for a dating might be the shape of the cartouches around some reliefs of arms. Their lines are very close to the style of Bérain's arabesques and is a definite indication that it was made after 1700. So, if Giacomo D'Alibert built the casino, it must have happened in the period of his decline, after the fall of Tordinona, which is not very likely, if not completely out of the question. It seems far more probable that Count Antonio built the country house in his flourishing period around 1720. He was so successful that King John of Portugal is said to have required him to come to Lisbon as director for the opera [173].

From the point of view of style the dating of the building to this period is perfectly acceptable. There are no surprises in the plan, a wing at the top of the garden turns its back on a terrace and two short wings at the ends project towards the descending terrain (Pl. 189). But the decoration does surprise. Its most important feature is the twin pilasters whose heavy lengths have been carved open and the fillets turned outwards. Forms without reason behind them, plucked from nature or engendered under the footlights. Very similar things appear in the drawings for décor by the greatest scenographers of the time, the members of the Galli Bibiena family [174]. We do know that Francesco Galli Bibiena in 1720 produced the scenery for Teatro D'Alibert [175] and that in 1721 he decorated the courtyard in the Collegio Clementino for a reception in honour of Cardinal Pereira who had been made the King of Portugal's minister [176]. The conclusion seems to be that Count D'Alibert as an impresario employed a theatre architect when he built his country house.

The garden was picturesque, one can just make it out in Vasi's prospect (1765) of Gianicolo. Now the wall hides a poor, ill-kept vegetable garden that is completely overshadowed by a large fig tree. At the end of the garden wall, nearest to Lungara, stands a two-storeyed house with four bays, which bears the same emblem as the casino (a crescent above five hills; cf. the Chigi arms) [177]. The very low mezzanine was well suited to be the hiding place of a bankrupt – could this building in the Vicolo degli Orti D'Alibert have been the part of the property that Count Antonio owned at his death? There is a temptation to give too full a rein to one's imagination here, for this place still seems to reflect the aura of the world of the opera that these Roman princes moved in – and this in itself is a charming vista of the South. Can you imagine better décor for the first scenes of Don Giovanni? In the gateway to the garden on the left, Leporello stands on guard, Don Giovanni and Donna Anna rush out of the house down the shallow steps, the commandant falls amid lamentations where the tree casts its shadow ... but we are forgetting where we are.

We now proceed to a couple of less pleasing villas which have since disappeared. *Villa Casali* was situated opposite S. Stefano Rotondo; the not very important casino was designed by Tommaso Mattei probably at the beginning of the century. Like D'Alibert's country house, it had two short pavilions. Wright visited it in 1721 and praised the excellent antique statues, some of which were set in the middle portico and had been excavated in the grounds here. The famous Casali sarcophagus finally ended up in Copenhagen's Glyptotek [178]. *Villa Patrizi* outside Porta Pia was built 1717 for Cardinal Giovanni Patrizi, with Sebastiano Cipriani as architect [179]. The building, traditional in type, had a belvedere in the centre which emerged from the body of the house with some difficulty and stretched the main cornice to breaking-point. The steps were very elaborate – a plan for the Spanish Steps is also ascribed to Cipriani [180] – and the view especially famous. Goethe came out here one evening to see the sun go down over the Campagna [181].

The Arcadians' garden, the mere name of which is a poetic dream, was a reality in Rome, and still is. Only here could it flourish, tended by pastoral enthusiasts who followed the trail of Gods and Muses among the seven hills. The literary society called *l'Arcadia* was established in 1690 as an offshoot of Queen Christina's Academy. The Swedish Pallas

Athene had died the year before. The meetings took place in a monastery garden by S. Pietro in Montorio, and right up to this very day the Arcadians meet in natural surroundings, for their vocation was to instil into Italian literature a fresh spirit from the Greek garden. This, unfortunately, became rather coy, coming as it did mainly from sweet bucolic idylls of Late Antiquity. The poets were organized in an extremely Classical manner, the president being called *Custode,* while the members assumed Hellenic names, and as shepherds, had pastures in Boeotia or Epirus allotted them. The pipes of Pan were the society's emblem, "Olympic Games" were envisaged, and the actual scene for literary manoeuvres was always a grove, called *Bosco Parrhasio,* where there was only standing-room for dryads.

Consequently the physical activity of the Arcadians took the form of a traveller's tales, for they went from one garden to another. In 1691 they settled in Giardino Riario (Corsini); in 1693 the Duke of Parma gave them shelter up on the Palatine, where Evander himself, prince of the real Arcadia, is thought to have practised his arts. It was not long before the shepherds wandered down to the garden behind Palazzo Salviati (near Lungara); in 1705 they transported themselves and the "Tablets of the Law" to the Villa Giustiniani (outside the Porta del Popolo); Prince Ruspoli called them to his garden on the Esquiline in 1707 and built them an amphitheatre here (1712). Eventually the poets' roving life was over, for the generous John V of Portugal gave them money for a piece of land on Janiculum, where, in 1725 they laid the foundation for the literary scene which still belongs to them [182]. On September 9th 1726 Valesio noted: "Today Arcadia held its first meeting in the new place by Salita del Gianicolo; this meeting place has turned out to be very cramped."

This last remark may be true, but the situation could not have been better. This was after all the hill where the Academy had been founded. And Monte Gianicolo had already been poetically initiated. Tasso died in the monastery at S. Onofrio and was buried there, his oak tree was an object of inspired veneration. Below the place where it stood S. Filippo Neri had (c. 1620) laid out his open-air oratorium, a graceful park with curving and rising rows of stone seats among the cypresses. It can be seen

189. *Orti D'Alibert.*

190. *Villa Carpegna. The central axis of the garden seen towards the grotto.*

191a. *Villa Carpegna. The Rotunda.*

191b. *Villa Carpegna. Staircase.*

193. *Villa Carpegna. The Nymphaeum.*

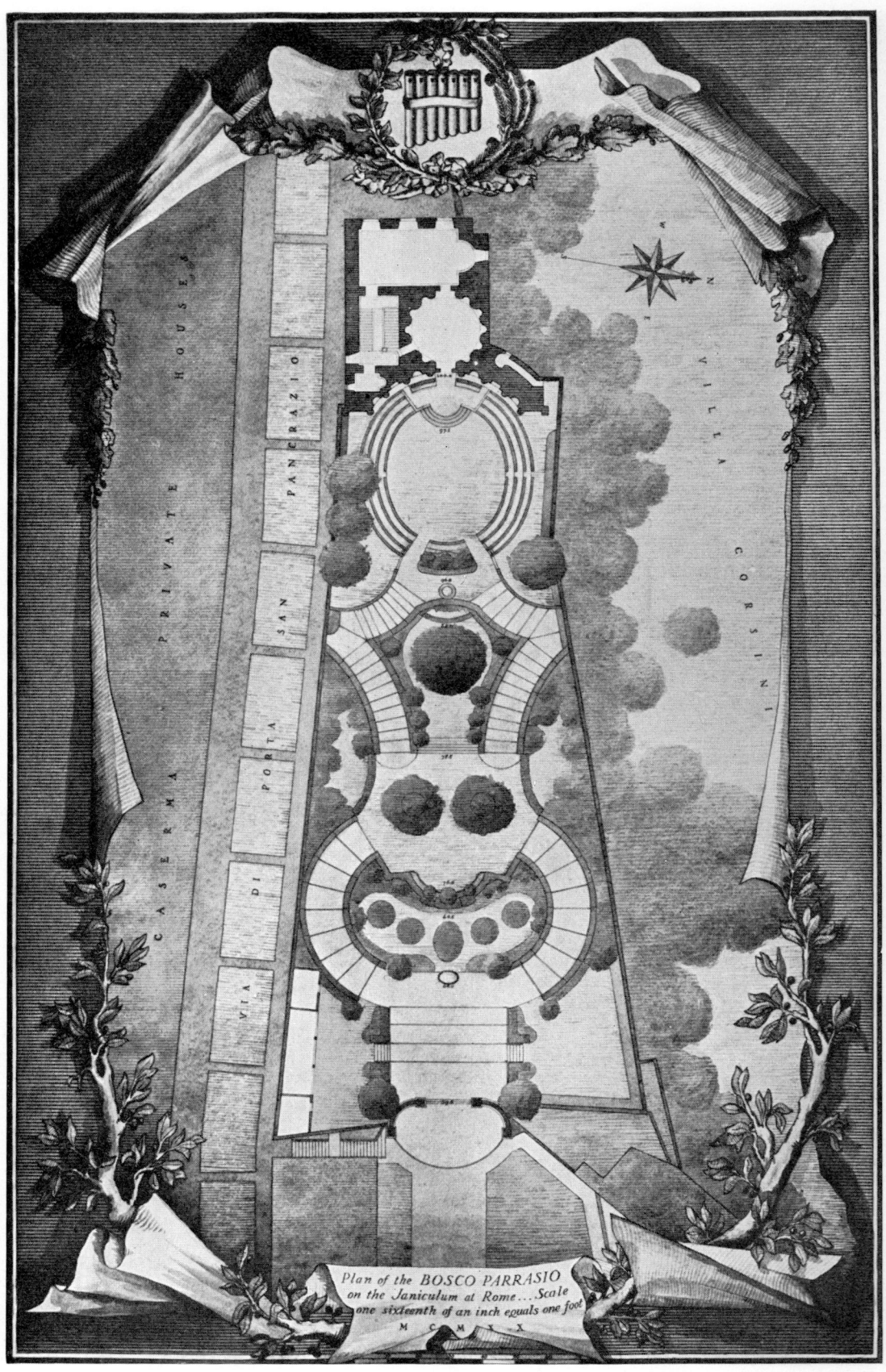

194. *Plan of the Arcadian Gardens (Bosco Parrhasio).*

195a. *The Arcadian Gardens. The Theatre.*

195b. *The Arcadian Gardens. Flight of stairs.*

196. *Villa Albani. Engraving by Piranesi.*

197. The pavilion in the Quirinal Gardens. Painting by Pannini.

198. *Plan of Villa Chigi.*

199a. *Villa Chigi. The garden seen from the back.*

199b. *Villa Borghese. Entrance to the Separate Garden.*

200. *Villa Borghese. Casino Dell'Orologio.*

on the extreme left in Vasi's prospect of Rome from 1765 (where it is called *Teatro de' pii trattenimenti*), and is still preserved.

The design for the Bosco Parrhasio was executed by Canevari, of whose connection with the king in Lisbon we know. In a monograph concerning the foundation of the Academy, published in 1726, is an engraved prospect of the layout which corresponds pretty closely to the plan given here (Pl. 194) [183]. The grounds of the garden form a very pointed triangle wedged in along the Via di S. Pancrazio on a steeply rising terrain; the entrance is on the left-hand side of the Assunta institution, a little further up (Pl. 70). As the architect had to include an open-air theatre on this awkward site, there was only one way to do so: to set it out as a flight of steps with close-packed modulations in as varied a form as possible. Canevari did his job well. Not only in the basic outline, but throughout the terrain itself, his work pulsates in splendid rhythm. It begins with a row of steps in front, and then concave flights of steps flow up past a nymphaeum with fountains. After this bulge, a constraint of narrower flights is introduced on both sides in elastic convex curves. Where they meet the enclosing wall on the higher level, they are tensed almost like two springs and held in place by the next lot of steps going in the opposite direction, until at the top they are released in the soft ellipse of the arena, which is the highest and deepest plane. We have now reached the stage which is truly Classical, edged with stone seats, spread out before an altar (Pl. 195a-b). Recitations were performed here.

The affairs of the Academy on the beautiful steps changed during the 18th century, when its fame suffered a sharp decline. It had shrunk to "eine Armseligkeit", which was Goethe's opinion in 1788, after he had accepted membership [184]; it consists mostly of sonneteers, hissed Archenholtz [185]; *un mot sur l'académie des arcades: c'est un nom*, maintained Mercy Dupaty [186]. And Baretti poured scorn in bucketfuls on the shepherds of Janiculum. We can agree that they were not all great poets. But the contempt expressed by the beaux-esprits of the pre-Romantic period was due mostly to the theatre of Bosco Parrhasio itself. Inspirations from Antiquity could not possibly displease pupils of such an expert on Alexandrines as Winckelmann, but Baroque flights of steps were beyond the pale; they were playthings, unaesthetic. A true "Götterhain" must be full of gravity and soughing.

Let us beware of believing the most celebrated truths. Rococo's empirical imitation of classical style contained a sensitivity which was perhaps a more genuine affectation. We must allow that the people of the Mediterranean countries were closest to the sources of Antiquity. Their odes and lyrics are sweet as honey from wild bees, with a tang of mint. Metastasio was prince of poets in this Arcadia, and I dare say its gentle glow exceeded the temperature in Weimar and Göttingen. A Corelli, an Alessandro Scarlatti – both shepherds from the Bosco Parrhasio – rejoiced in a breath of sensual Hellenism, such as was invoked in vain by Gluck and which was never revealed to Beethoven.

Nor must we forget that the ingenious architecture on the poets' hill weaved its way through rampant foliage. Laurel was not the only vegetation; violets and white roses grew here too. A love-sick poet found consolation in this *solitario bosco ombroso* [187] – and Monsignore Albani (later Clement XI) found inspiration in the society's gardens to compose sonorous stanzas on the coming of spring:

> *Vaghi fiori, già sparsi di gelo,*
> *Fanno pompa di rara beltà*
> *E di perle cadute dal cielo*
> *Ogni rosa conchiglia si fa.*

In less melodic English it might run something like this:

> Freed from the frost now the flowers' confusion
> Blinding in beauty their petals unfurl,
> And by the dewdrops in Heaven's profusion
> Roses are lacquered with mother of pearl.

In the Villa Doria-Pamphili, also called *Belrespiro,* alterations of the oldest casino were undertaken in the 1730's, which is included in the wall along the Via Aurelia. The prince stayed here very occasionally, while the famous main building (c. 1650, by Algardi) was reserved for entertainments. The modernization, which was supervised by Valvassori, (after 1739 by Ameli) [188], has enchanting details; out here he could design more delicately than had been the case with the façade of the Corso palace, which had been done under various pressures. The architect carved out a row of windows in a barrier wall with the delicacy of a cabinet maker and supplied them with a lacework of lattice [189]. His walls around a special garden, the grove of cedar trees, have again a finely calculated texture; they are distinguished by panels of tufa, spongy as moss; a fountain with the recumbent statue of "the Tiber" adds lushness to the decoration. The *Villa Corsini* was situated very close to the Pamphilis' country estate and was later included in this. The palazzetto was probably built in the 1730's for the princely family, the most important member of which was the reigning pope. It was a building of the orthodox type, a block with a high middle section. The decoration of the façade, with busts in circular niches above the windows, was derived from "Belrespiro". Simone Salvi is said to be the architect, and Fuga too has been mentioned [190], the latter for no good reason; the former is an unknown quantity.

A couple of casinos elsewhere date from Benedict XIV's days. They are of rather more brittle stuff than the older ones. This is especially true of the Pope's own pavilion in the Quirinal garden, the so-called *Cafféous*, built 1741–43 by Fuga [191]. The name was very apt, for this was the place where Papa Tabaccone liked to have his after-dinner coffee in the company of intimate friends and specially favoured guests. This was the time for all etiquette to be set aside; "he fooled around and cracked jokes and laughed as if he were not a pope" [192]. When in November 1744 Carlos III passed through Rome on his way to Naples and his new kingdom, Benedict desired to meet him without any ceremony in this secluded casino, but the Spaniard spoilt it all, for hardly had the Pope's bulky figure loomed up at the end of an avenue, before the King hastened forward and knelt down. Lambertini got annoyed and shouted: *Che coglione!* [193]. This outburst announces the same desire for rural peace as Bernstorff's *honesto inter labores otio sacrum*, although that was expressed in the private individual's accent of irritation. The official picture of the meeting with the King is given i Pannini's painting (Pl. 197). Like Louis XV, the Pope liked to have a *Monrepos* near at hand, so he could make himself scarce whenever he wanted to. "The Coffee House" is French in character, almost so in style, but the English name refers mainly to the beverage [194]. The casino consists simply enough of a

475

closed portico in the middle (with French windows) and two short pavilions at the ends, each containing a small room. There were very up to date pictures on the walls, among them paintings by Pannini of S. Maria Maggiore and Monte Cavallo with the new Consulta palace [195].

The building is stiff, so we could suspect it of having been finished before the Neo-Classical period [196]. Perhaps it merely solidified under a frosty influence from Paris, for here this type of building was common among upper-class country houses. The casino which Cardinal Valenti built c. 1750 immediately outside Porta Pia, is said to have been designed by Pannini, but the French engineer Maréchal was in charge of the erection [197]. The building which has been greatly altered and is now completely inaccessible, seems in the interior too, to have proclaimed Louis XV's style where it was suitably blended with chinoiserie and antiquities *à la mode*. The Secretary of State, like a good diplomat, was so civilized that he could oblige in all directions. His colleague, the Treasurer Cardinal *Mario Bolognetti,* employed Nicola Salvi in 1743 to build a country house in the Via Nomentana. To judge from old surveys [198] it was a trifle stilted, the architect's leaning towards Classicism is unmistakable; the result was a companion piece from its time to the Villa Pia in Vaticano – "Neo-Antiquity" is meant to emerge in precise forms and in a propensity for peristyles. The manner of the style is as clean as plaster, which can be seen from the pavilion which still stands at no. 345 Via Nomentana.

Perhaps Cardinal *Ferroni's Casino* was the last suburban villa of the old bluff type, the box with a balcony on the roof. It was erected in the 1760's and stood in the vicinity of "Belrespiro". It was indeed strikingly old-fashioned, for it had crypto-ressauts between heavy rusticated pilasters. It is still in existence, although altered out of all recognition [199].

About this time Rome was already in possession of a villa which was meant to be the great exception to the norm and was the subject of conversation for all people of taste. Its builder, Alessandro Albani, was born lucky, one might say. He came into the world with a taste for aestheticism and his uncle on the maternal side became pope when Albani was eight years old. Even as a child he was an antiquarian and spoilt into the bargain; as a Colonel of Dragoons, almost before he started to shave, he became a collector. Throughout his life he idolized Antiquity and tried to improve on it, for he was deft with his fingers and was methodical. When he attained power and wealth he was regarded as an oracle among those who cultivated the art of Antiquity; his knowledge of these matters was indeed unsurpassed. In the years following 1717 he started excavations in Nemi, Tusculum, Palestrina, Tivoli and many other places; he turned the Campagna inside out and had his spies keep him informed. Addison has given an amusing picture of the Roman *scavatori* in action, how they purchased the rights to turn fields, gardens and vineyards which promised any yield, upside down and how they paid in proportion to the size of the acreage, after first having made trial digs "as they do for coal in England"; they foraged in the most promising places [200]. The result of Albani's zeal was a huge collection. Wright has provided a description of his "cabinet" in 1721 [201]; this was the year this archaeological man of the world was made cardinal.

Albani however, cultivated pleasures others than those of procuring a series of busts of emperors, for he was also a connoisseur of female beauty and poured out money like water. During Clement XII's pontificate, he had to get rid of most of his treasures, many of which went to the Capitoline Museum, where de Brosses in 1739 saw them lying around in great disorder [202]. Then Cardinal Alexander started all over again. He went ahead regardless, using all the powers at his disposal without any scruples at all [203], and within a few years he had acquired an even more splendid collection which made his palace at Quattro Fontane burst at the seams. So Albani, when 63 years old, decided to build a villa for himself and his antiquities, outside the Porta Salaria. The basic outlines of the project were according to his own design [204]. The architect was Carlo Marchionni and the garden was designed by Antonio Nolli. The two antiquarians, Ridolfino Venuti and Winckelmann, the latter having become His Eminence's librarian in 1758, worked behind the scenes. It is most unlikely that the astute Prussian had anything to do with the building activity, but as far as taste was concerned, he was Albani's right-hand man and evil genius. Winckelmann's spirit loomed ever more menacing as the building grew, and like a sorcerer's apprentice, he made the old collector's brooms dance in a magic ring around the building and could not put a stop to it – and it still weaves its spell round the world, through academies and museums.

If we are to make up our minds about Villa Albani, an extremely problematic work, the wisest thing to do is to look at it from various angles. First we must consider it while building was in progress. Strange as it may sound, this very famous house is frequently inaccurately dated [205]. It is as important to determine this exactly, as it is easy to find out. The following inscription can be read in large letters: *Alexander Albanus Cardinalis Romano Animo Instruxit A° 1757*. In other words, the building was regarded as being started in the year indicated. This must mean the construction of the walls. Winckelmann wrote on March 9th of that year: "Albani is now building a villa, a miracle of art in everybody's eyes" [206]. The foundations must have been laid 1755/56, for Winckelmann remarked in a subsequent letter [207], that he had seen this in progress, and as we know, he arrived in Rome on November 1755. When he therefore writes on September 25th 1756, that all discerning people hoped that the Cardinal would live long enough to complete his villa, he conjures up the picture of an old man who has viewed the newly laid foundations [208]. On February 1758 the same excellent authority notes: "Albani has now finished building", i. e. the rough outline is completed; the many columns "looked like a (felled) forest before they were set up" [209]. Then followed the interior decoration. Rafael Mengs' fresco on the ceiling in the great hall was begun in June 1760. Casanova saw the work in progress the following winter [210]. Winckelmann gave his opinion of it in March 1761 [211]. Clement XIII visited the Villa Albani in July 1763. The building was then ready. Work was continued on the interior and in the gardens up to just before 1770 [212]. The owner died in 1779 (Pl. 196).

Now that the casino has been built, we will go round it in the company of a number of reliable eye-witnesses to find out how its own era and the age immediately following evaluated the architecture. What did people see in this house that was to mark an epoch? We shall start with the evidence of our principal witness, Albani himself. In the inscription we quoted he states that the building was erected "in the Roman spirit" (*Romano Animo*), whereby a taste for Antiquity is postulated. These words form the first tenet in the house's credo, proclaimed in Latin capitals above the portal. Interestingly enough, we have a commentary to it from Albani's own lips. In 1758 the villa was visited by Grosley, and the owner was his guide. When after this tour the Frenchman described the casino as *un palais dans le goût de l'ancienne Rome,* we detect an echo of the Cardinal's personal interpretation. But we can also hear a direct utterance. After having received his guest's compliments "he smiled maliciously" and retorted: "It has not been created for eyes accustomed to seeing the marvels of French architecture. The idea may seem extravagant to you and its execution abominable" [213]. The builder meant that his Roman style was intended to shock; the villa was revolutionary.

For the time being, it was permitted to rest in the noble shadow of the past. Winckelmann's name and personality created the necessary hypnotic atmosphere. He asserted in March 1765 that the villa was superior to all other works – except perhaps St. Peter's [214]. Abbé Richard, who visited the villa several times in 1762 and gained much benefit from the Cardinal's learned instructions, compared the casino with a description of an ancient country house in Pliny the Younger [215]. Ten years after Grosley's visit, Weinlig arrived (January 1768) and was shown round by Winckelmann. It turned into downright idolatry; he admired the Antinous relief "with dedicated solemnity", only an Iroquois savage could have seen it without being moved [216]. However – the villa and its architecture lost its attraction a few years after its antiquarian guardian angel had been murdered (1768). It was an ominous sign that Guidi in 1773 demonstratively gave prominence to the frames round the paintings and the pedestals under the sculptures, and to the fact "that everything was in its right place" [217]. At the same time Bergeret bluntly referred to the architecture as "being of the worst sort" and the garden as "quaint", in this way confirming the Cardinal's premonitions of French criticism [218].

From now on, its Classical reputation quickly deteriorated. In no other place has so much restoration and labelling been done as here, wrote Roland with obvious loathing [219]. Adler thought (1782) that it was more like a school than a garden [220]. Heinse was completely unsparing (1783): he regretted the total lack of spirit of the site; it looked dried-up and disconsolate, as it would have "if a blind man and a librarian had lived there and were still in residence" [221]. It was the same year that Kotzebue's guide here avowed that Winckelmann had been *un galant'uomo,* a rather poor recommendation [222]. And Ramdohr lamented: "A pity that the taste shown in the building is not more refined" [223]. We can conclude with Reumont's resigned estimate: the Villa Albani has an insipid taste, but it is preferable to that of the contemporary buildings [224].

As we have found, the ancient Roman style of the Villa Albani was only recognized without reservation by its builder, who was more than half blind and a brilliant faker in the field of restoration, and by his learned assistant, who was more credulous than observant, in architectural matters. At the moment when a truly Neo-Classical architecture, practised by experts and based on research, had reached its first maturity, Villa Albani was dismissed as – Baroque.

And so it is. Regarded from yet another point of view, that of the critical historian, Albani's casino was certainly "in the Roman spirit", but traditionally so. The isolated cube is not even without its small belvederes on the roof. If, in spite of everything, the house differs from others of its genre, this is because the Cardinal sought his inspiration in an early Roman Baroque, which was "classic", and discovered it in a work whose actual function anticipated the essential task of his villa. For the Casino Albani was conceived and built, not merely as a home of the Muses, but as a museum purely and simply, which is something completely different. The only buildings in Rome, that around 1755 served as official mantles for collections of antiquities, were the two side palaces on the Capitol, of which that of the Conservatori was the first to be made into a museum by Cardinal Albani's uncle Clement XI. The decorative background for the statue of "Roma" in the cortile was designed by Specchi in 1720 [225] (Pl. 211a-b).

A leading motif, and the only one that is actually new, is the portico that takes up the whole of the lowest storey and was intended as a gallery for statues. Loggias placed in the middle of the façade looking on to the garden had long been used for exhibiting sculptures (e. g. Villa Medici, Villa Borghese, Villa Casali), but a continous portico opening up the whole of the house at the bottom, was markedly novel for the luxurious country house. The idea for this was borrowed from the Capitoline palaces [226]. Arches of the "Palladian" type go back to Specchi's arcade in the courtyard of the Conservatori palace, and in an indirect way to the middle arch in the garden façade of the Villa Medici. Also, the sunken parterre has a local model from the Baroque period in the Villa Doria-Pamphili, but it was touched up in the French manner with neatly set out beds. The casino's external decoration is vapid in other respects. It could be that "the antiquarian" in actual fact is out of date mannerism and that "the modern" is feeble art. No less do the expensive, yet so sad interiors open our eyes to the fact that the Villa Albani is debased. Everywhere the pastiche has taken over. His Eminence's own bedchamber is decorated in a mixture of antique grotesqueries, vines *à la* Bérain – fashionable when Albani could not yet button his own trousers – and imitation Chinese lacquered paintings. Pilasters with mirrors are reflections from Louis XIV's Versailles, the glazed tiles show Dutch scenes. The whole colour scheme is redolent: golden, pale pink, ocean blue, chocolate brown. The connoisseur had savoured too many tastes in his time. His brother Annibale's background is certainly different. He lived during the summer in a palace (by Vignola) in Soriano nel Cimino (east of Viterbo) and had furnished it himself. I have visited his rooms, which are still roughly as he left them [227]. They are distinguished, not over-filled and truly Olympian. The armchair with his emblem seems created by talented and unorthodox people; we find a few engravings of ceremonies that took place under his patronage, but not even a poor relief from the Late Roman Empire. The most impressive ornament of the interior is the inscription over every door: ANNIBAL CARD. ALBANUS – this being the name of "the best brain in the Holy College and the most evil-minded man in Rome" [228]. But returning once again to the villa in the Via Salaria we realize that, although it marked an epoch, it was at the transition from a taste for harmony to a discordant one.

Directly opposite the casino stands that of the villa's lesser building, which is most successful in trying to be a work from Antiquity, namely the so-called *Canopus,* a portico on a semicircular plan. The statues were on show in the arcaded walk in 1764 [229]. As both the name and plan show, the Cardinal intended here to imitate the Egyptian-like structure (with the Temple of Serapis) in Hadrian's Tiburtine villa; this was the place where Albani had made some of his best discoveries, such as the Antinous relief. Based on the Emperor's freely adapted construction, he now built his own [230]. When Cancellieri called him "the Hadrian of his age" it was quite apt in a narrow sense. Commonly, Albani's "Canopus" went under a more familiar name: "the Coffee House". We hope the Classical illusions were not destroyed. But the coffee must have got cold here; in Papa Lambertini's enclosed house it steamed happily.

The period of sincerity came before Winckelmann. So we find that only in those parts of the garden that lie outside the oppressive view from the casino to the Coffee House is there a simple dignity, indeed impressive style. The man who designed the garden was not deceived by philologians; he learned from the old Baroque and built with green walls while carving out clear spaces filled with landscapes – and the Albani hills beyond [231]. Nature is Classical in stature here, as in the avenues of the Villa Ludovisi. The Neo-Classical element is the slim pedestals with busts, projecting above hedges, and solitary columns and hermae along the path. Things which were benumbed in the galleries of the museums seemed here to take root and come to life in the sun. If all these shafts are conceived merely as polled trees among trimmed bushes, thuya and yew, we see the meaning behind it and realize their beauty. Jardin and Wiedewelt, who learned a lot in Rome, introduced a similar ornamental gardening into Fredensborg Park in Denmark [232]. Here, the "columna rostrata" and the "enigmatic antique" [233] fit into the woods round Esrom Lake as calmly and majestically as do the monuments beneath Albani's pines. Eckersberg and Constantin Hansen could make their sketches in the Cardinal's grounds as if faced with one large sculpture.

The conflict which now developed between Baroque's vigorous style and mannerism based on archaeological discovery, emerges very dramatically when we compare two contemporary works, which are just a few years younger than the Villa Albani. One is the gatehouse in front of the *Priory of the Knights of Malta* on the Aventine, erected c. 1765 and designed by Piranesi. The façade shows a varied collection of heraldic and antique items, which are all over-dimensional. This officious exhibition has little to do with architecture. *Villa Chigi,* on the other hand, is real architecture, nothing original or robust about it, but superior all the same, without boastfulness and caprice. It is situated outside Porta Salaria and so far is still intact, Cardinal Flavio Chigi being the originator (Pl. 198); the casino was erected 1763–1766 and designed by Tommaso Bianchi [234]. The delicate, pale-coloured main building, in the subdued light beneath the trees, has Rococo's gentle touch around the gateway and the wide window in the side wing. In spite of its charming lassitude, the house is in complete control of its grounds; at the sides lies the parterre garden with low hedges, shallow steps; even in its lines it seems to lose heart – but further out the terrain takes over, a gently rolling downland. It is subjected to straight lines; one axis is at right angles to the casino's portal, the others are the enclosing avenues which form an irregular figure. The intersections of the bowery walks have monuments with smooth backs and remind you of Wiedewelt's monuments at Jægerspris in Denmark. Seen from the neighbouring vegetable gardens, these arrogant stone backs look perfectly delightful, with the landscape of the Campagna behind them forcing its way into the garden (Pl. 199a).

This part of the Villa Chigi with its unobstructed view is a very fine example of Neo-Classical ornamental gardening as it was in its early and still innocent state; here nobody is trying to ram anything down your throat. The antique set pieces are neither altars nor confessionals, only soothing scenes of a pastoral nature which ageing Baroque had regretfully relinquished.

While Cardinal Albani, much advanced in years, stumbled around in his garden palace, raised on wasteland and based on an obstinate idea, the richest man in Rome, Prince Marc'Antonio Borghese began to transform his almost 175 years old villa. Here, unique opportunities presented themselves. The impressive casino, erected 1613–1616 by Vasanzio, was of course to be made into a museum for antiquities and to surpass Albani's. The alterations (by Antonio Asprucci), which made the main façade banal, removed part of the back and completely renovated the interior, were already in progress in 1779. One day in September of that year, Lord Herbert was on the site walking among the scaffolding; in the vestibule (*il Salone*) Mariano Rossi's ceiling had been finished; over the portal could be seen the relief of "Curtius on horseback jumping into the abyss". The critical sporting gentleman was dissatisfied with the Roman hero's steed and with the decoration of the walls, which he described as being in the same style as "The English Coffee House", but quite unsuitable for a palace belonging to Prince Borghese [235]. It is an amusing observation; this hostelry in the Piazza di Spagna (no. 88), decorated by Piranesi in Egyptian style, was a meeting place for the dilettanti. A crowded restaurant is not the place for learning aesthetics, you eat there; the aristocratic salon must hold on to the ideals. However costly Borghese's interiors were, resplendent with marble and porphyry, they displeased the Englishman all the same; he found them to be without taste. It is delightful to learn that Don Marc'Antonio, with whom he was personally acquainted, himself admitted that he had no taste; and Herbert felt Borghese might at least have conferred with somebody who did, as he would have done in his place. This is the Casino Borghese, the Classical museum, evaluated by a cultivated man from the Regency period. We fully agree with him [236].

Justice ordained that to be fair the rejuvenated Villa Borghese must be assessed primarily by Britons, for the layout as a whole concluded the great Roman tradition by breaking with it and following English trends. The park's extensive grounds had from the beginning been principally a deer park; there were special enclosures for the deer; peacocks and ostriches strutted around beneath the myrtles; lions roared in their *serraglio;* there were birds swimming on the ponds, fish preserves, even a place for tortoises. Only the areas nearest to the casino, the *giardini segreti* with aviaries and orangeries (Pl. 199b) and the shrubbery behind hedges, were in formal Baroque. Groves were spread all over the area; "the thousand pines", which Zoëga loved [237] gave the landscape of these grounds magnificent contours. In Addison's time, one of his compatriots called Villa Borghese "a perfect country" carved out into a variety of pleasant scenes [238]. This happy soil awaited its perfect, its English park, and only a few changes were necessary to make it so [239]. Around 1770 the English were given kind permission to play cricket and football twice a week in the garden, where once the little Stuarts played. This was the introduction to a new era [240]. A few years later, about the time that the main building was given its antique character, the progress began which was to turn the Villa Borghese into an internationally known Romantic garden.

It is not generally known that this was carried out by a Scotsman, the landscape painter Jacob More [241]. Rome's most famous garden is basically a British affair. More, who lived for many years in Rome until his death in 1793, was in his time highly regarded as an artist, particularly by English collectors, who considered him quite a dangerous rival to Claude le Lorrain. Anyhow, he painted stirring views from the countryside around Rome, à la Claude, and has been commended for his original subjects. In a series called "the Four Elements", painted for Lord Bristol, the eccentric Bishop of Derry [242], fire was represented by Vesuvius in eruption, with the added effect of Pliny's death. More also specialized in moonlight [243]. Prince Borghese could make good use of this fashionable virtuoso, who very aptly lived above the English Coffee House [244].

Villa Albani's garden, hardly twenty years older than Villa Borghese, had been modelled by a Roman gardener. This time the park was designed by a painter from Edinburgh, which was very appropriate for this epoch. Richard Wilson once told a friend that it was possible to take a walk in Claude's pictures and count up the miles [245]. More and his assistants turned the villa outside Porta Pinciana into a series of veduti, of which you could never weary. Pope had already reasoned that all landscape gardening was landscape painting. Stowe Park, by William Kent, was with justice called "that fine Landscape of Albano"; the cascade at Bowood was designed from a painting by Gaspard Poussin [246]. More, who had proved himself competent in this genre on canvas (he also provided Prince Borghese with paintings), could now compose with groups of holm oaks, with clearings and valleys. In contrast to the other famous gardens, Villa Borghese did not gain its beauty from decay but by painstaking attention. So in the end, what every gentleman had wished for with regard to his real old garden, which was merely Roman, had come to pass. The spade and the axe, by being skilfully handled, helped nature to win through. This made it Romantic.

Things were added and subtracted – a lake was constructed in the special garden (*il Giardino del Lago*), arbours of various kinds were put where they could promote sensibility. A cylindrical pavilion with columns (by Asprucci) bearing Diana's name is classic in the sense that this was the type used all over the place in Neo-Classical gardens; they were in a direct line from the Sibyl's temple at Tivoli and kept the Claudesque round temples in mind. It is possible that Sir John Vanbrugh's rotunda at Stowe Park stood sponsor for Borghese's *tempietto* [247]. Other garden pavilions that conjure with Antiquity, will be discussed in an epilogue – but "the hippodrome" must not be forgotten here. This racetrack too was a pastiche, but – it was in actual use and in a manner particularly characteristic of this villa. The secret gamekeeper's hut was only a decoration in a picture meant for solitary dreamers, but Don Marc'Antonio had the masses in mind too, so he held public celebrations. Archenholtz insinuates that he wanted to subdue widespread disaffection with his heavy-handed management of the estates by currying favour with the masses [248], and this is very possible, for the family was always very enterprising. *I Borghese sono sempre borghesi* was one of Pius IX's puns. The host probably imagined himself in the role of an old Roman senator, who gave his needy fellow-country men a little bread and a lot of circuses.

In his *Invito a Nice* the poet Vincenzio Monti has described the tournaments, races and serenades that were arranged in 1779 [249]. In later years, the Prince invited the general public to come every October and enjoy the swings and riding at the ring. The steps of the long arena were utilized, there was sailing in lantern-lit boats on the lake and concerts were given [250] – the poor man's recreation in a park that owed a lot to the original Tivoli. *C'è la villeggiatura dei miserabili,* said the wealthy Romans [251]. All very charming – the owner moved graciously around and talked to the joyous crowd, says Meyer [252]. And Fernow felt that the Roman people owed this aristocrat, who had been recalled in 1800, a memorial column because he had opened his villa to the people, granted them harmless amusements and brought Roman landscape gardening back to life after a century of hibernation [253]. But most of this was pure humbug. Borghese rarely visited the villa himself, he preferred, I suppose, to drive back and forth on the road to Ponte Molle [254], and before 1800 the influx was kept to the minimum. Most of the hours of the day, the grounds were silent. This was the time for noble houses such as the Casino dell' Orologio to come to life (Pl. 200).

The spirit in the woods is no longer there, Pan has been driven away by the multitude of people. The noble masquerade is sometimes revived, and I saw it once. Eight white horses were dancing in the arena – the riders were dressed in cinnamon-coloured coats and wore black hats like Napoleon's. Don Marc'Antonio, father-in-law of Pauline Bonaparte, is believed to have sent for the Spanish Riding School to come to his circus. The tails of the Lippizaners swayed as lazily as the cypresses in the summer breeze.

THE CALL OF THE RUINS
AN EPILOGUE

Every period in the history of Roman life and art is bound up with antiquity in a visible form. Nothing like that is valid for Paris or London. This constant contrast between the ruins of the past and the growing city makes architecture in Rome exciting in its own special way. Whether the prevailing style of a period is of the old school or reacts against its ideals, its dialogue with the past is always characterized by the menacing presence of the other. No wonder that other periods have had to bluster rather loudly from time to time, for antiquity has a stentorian voice.

Our introduction to this work touched on the broad outlines in Rome. As will be remembered, the tangible inheritance from the period of antiquity was not included. That is too great a theme to be part of a prelude. Only at the conclusion of our text can the most important of all Roman motifs strike its own chord.

During the period between Bernini and Thorvaldsen, ancient Roman architecture was always highly revered. But this reverence expressed itself in many different ways. The self-satisfied Baroque's way of showing its respect for Olympian art was to oppose it violently with all due respect. After putting up a good fight, such as we have witnessed in earlier chapters, the architecture of the present finally surrendered to the past, and this happened in the period just prior to 1780; it capitulated out of pure veneration. The beauty of friezes, the precision in the way the stone was cut, the elegance of antiquity and classical emphasis can be a source of great pleasure to many people, and may even refine their taste. When all is said and done, such a "renaissance" is really only a game played by architects, applauded by an audience. But what happened when Neoclassicism and Romanticism breathed life into the cornice and embraced it with ardour? It became too much for them both. If one really wants to understand the relationship between the latter part of the Age of Reason and antiquity, particularly within the walls of Rome, one must eschew the high road of formal art history and find the way to the outskirts of human illusions, to the area where stones become an inspiration and a reality. Sentimental Neo-classicism is by its nature a sort of animism. We must draw closer to the art that has become history and which has been interpreted for us all by the poets as an incantation. Any yardstick should be left behind, and it would be a great help in our scrutiny if we could manage to keep a cool head.

After these introductory remarks it will be understood that our concluding survey of antiquity in Rome is seen from the human angle, not as an attack from the point of view of the history of style. Antiquity is first of all what you make of it, and then what its use is. So let us see how Rome's ruins were idolized in the days of Voltaire and Goethe. These names denote two stages in the history of the cult as a European phenomenon. Antiquity as an artistic motif shows a very special dramatic development in the century we are dealing with here. We have already touched upon the conflicts inherent in it on a number of occasions. It has earlier been described more fully by others [1]. It is not the intention here to summarize the progress of the development from generation to generation. As a conclusion we merely wish to examine a subject which has so many facets, and to try to give it plastic form by illuminating it from different angles. The classical ruin is to be confronted with various forces – with the Romans, with the Latin text, with nature and with ethos. And at every meeting the question is raised: "What's Hecuba to you – or you to Hecuba?"

Antiquity became a part of Roman everyday life. The ruins were usable, and that is perhaps the greatest compliment that could be paid to these famous remains. The Romans saw no reason to stand and gape at the relics of buildings when they could put them to use. The daily round was bound up with what was left over from Caesar's time. Both the workaday and the holiday rhythm were caught up in them. Goethe's father noticed that le Colonnacce, the twin columns in Nerva's forum roofed with its heroic architrave, contained a booth selling oil and radishes [2]. A hundred years later you could find a popular bakery in its place [3]. In my own young days the lower arcade of the Marcellus theatre was still crammed with market stalls, forming the veritable shopping centre of the Piazza Montanara [4]. The Via delle Botteghe Oscure got its evocative name from the workshops and stalls, dark as caves, which were hidden in the vaults of the ruins long since gone. Around 1770, a barber could be found plying his trade in the half-ruined Septimus Severus arch [5]. The customers of the barber were dealt with outside the door and their attention was centred far more on the razor than on the forgotten triumph of the emperor [6]. And once the fish-market occupied Octavia's Porticus and filled it with loud-mouthed harridans and stench [7]. Caracalla's thermae serve no other purpose, says Volkmann, "than to entertain the pupils from the Seminario Romano during their holidays by letting them enjoy ball games and other exercises" [8]. Augustus's Mausoleum was used both as a coach-house by a cabby and as a circus with wooden benches for the spectators. Here the audience could bellow at bull fights [9].

As mentioned earlier, Diocletian's thermae were divided up into barns, monks' cells and barracks for the cavalry. The temple of Vesta resembled a clearing-house in the local haymarket, where all the carriers congregated [10]. The cattle-market (Campo Vaccino), the Forum Romanum itself, was like a common, the Via Sacra had trees dotted about and looked more like a cattle-track; on market-days the butchers tied the livestock to the columns of the temple called after Jupiter Tonans and Jupiter Stator [11]. The senatorial Palace on the Capitol "where in earlier times trophies from conquered nations were set up" was now beflagged with washing [12]. And if in 1765 you had wanted to find the Tarpeian Rock, you would need to pass through the house of a tailor and then traverse lengthy haylofts before ending up on a small roof balcony. It was then possible to enjoy the sight of the gruesome abyss framed by backyards. "I have a suspicion," says Lalande, "that nobody has had the nerve to conduct Madame du Boccage through the lofts mentioned, and that is probably the reason why in her "Italian Letters" [13] she says that it is easy to jump down from the Tarpeian Rock" [14]. Need we repeat the names of those houses of God that had usurped the heathen temples? Or mention addresses of authorities and grandees in the demolished buildings of the ancients.

The writer Mercy Dupaty expressed the opinion of every indignant traveller when he accused the Romans of profaning their proud heritage. According to this gentleman, they did not preserve the relics of antiquity out of respect for them but simply out of cupidity. "The Italians look after their ruins for the same reason that beggars look after their sores" [15]. But the Frenchman was mistaken. Like most half-educated tourists, then as now, his own vulgarity flourished more noticeably in foreign soil, and he condemned what he could not be bothered to understand. One of Mercy Dupaty's countrymen tells an anecdote – it dates from about 1760 – in which the narrator without realizing it comes close the knowledge of truth and shows himself up. The story goes as follows: "One day when I was engrossed in the remains of the Concordia Temple, where the senators often congregated, some beggars under the colonnade asked for alms. I said to a couple of Romans with whom I was walking, "It was here the senate made kings wait while they deliberated on their fate. What is left?" The Romans would be the first to joke about such things, provided that you admire their antiquities, and moreover they are flattered" [16]. Abbé Richard failed to understand that the inhabitants of Rome could make a joke of it, let themselves be insulted by a visitor and yet smile. This reaction – one can see the accompanying slight shrug of the shoulders – expresses a true, a justified superiority. The Roman knows better. Rome not only belongs to him, but imparts to him his ancestors' secrets.

On the same occasion Richard sneers at the Romans' veneration of the Capitol, "which is now their town hall and nothing more than that". But that is surely something! "When they enter the halls adorned with statues of the Scipios, of a Marius, a Sulla, a Pompey, a Caesar they pretend they are in the senate and when they leave, they are imbued with such a feeling of noble pride, that it seems to raise them above the rest of us mortals." It was quite right that the contemporary Romans should take it as a matter of course that the Capitol was not just a hollow shell, but the meeting place for their patres conscripti. They did not care that the heroes of European civilization, the ancient sons of the city, were ensconced upon the hill – but this annoyed others. It did not occur to the Romans that Caracalla was being profaned because schoolboys played marbles among the ruins of his baths; after all the emperor himself had been a Roman, although long ago. Continuity was all that mattered for the people of the seven hills, the knowledge of belonging as citizens to a classical soil was deeply rooted in all whose cradle had been rocked beside the Tiber. And like all of ancient stock they more often thought than talked about it, for they are the most urbane people on earth. What has Rome not experienced? What is left for the Romans to be impressed by? Their weary smile to the uninvited, rough-diamond guest is charming. On one occasion in the 1770's it so happened that the Queen of Naples drove across a Roman market-place, a crowd gathering to gape at her. Suddenly a woman at her vegetable stall loudly voiced the city's thoughts: "What has Rome come to! Once Queen Zenobia was driven past here in chains. That was a bit different from this poor fish of a queen!" (*roba tutta diversa di questa reginuccia*) [17]. The moral of this episode should not be misinterpreted. The vegetable seller was far from whining about the decline of Rome. She merely emphasized that the Eternal City was used to the best of everything, and deserved to be. It was not impressed by trivialities.

A similar feeling was expressed in a remark let slip by Carlos III of the Two Sicilies, for when he was informed of the discovery of the splendours of Paestum, he mumbled: "Why fuss about one old temple more or less?" (*Che mi fa un tempio antico più o meno?*) [18]. The remark has an unpleasant overtone of arrogance – the man was extremely unintelligent and an absolute monarch to boot – but all the same even when making allowances for these characteristics, it indicates the king's pleased but blasé state of mind with regard to the abundance of wealth, rather than any contempt for his heritage. In any case he was a Spaniard, not a Roman.

The true descendents of the Latins who surrounded the Imperial Throne felt at home with the ancient buildings, in a way which was both intimate and off-hand. Familiarity does this sort of thing. We must accept this fact and use it as the background for what now follows.

We have no need to emphasize that the foreigner's ideas of the Roman ruins were quite different from those of the city's own sons. On the other hand, we must remember that the great majority of the visitors were men of wide reading. For the above mentioned woman in the market-square, Zenobia was a local legendary figure (comparable with Lady Godiva in England), but for the educated tourist she was a historical figure worthy of commentary and note. In the same way as the myth of "the Land of Classicism" was created by those barbarians who holidayed on the Mediterranean, so the cult of the ruins was initiated by philologists whose heart was set on doing their revision on the spot and seeing for themselves.

The whole thing was set in motion during the Renaissance and was revived in the 18th century with even greater fervour but with less artistic merit. As we all know, true gardening enthusiasts notice only those plants which they can readily put a name to, preferably a Latin name. The same thing happened with Rome's ruins. On his daily round a greengrocer from the Via del Boschetto rarely took any notice of the acanthus tendrils sprouting on a capital at a street corner – "retiring little plant, its sweetness does enchant, unremarked and shy" – but the savant, possibly from Göttingen, did not rest until he had given the fragment a name and had confirmed it. Then he felt justified in paying homage to it. Nomenclature became a matter of the most extreme importance. The classical authors were constantly referred to; the texts were browsed through, and then the field sampled.

To some extent, this procedure was as understandable as it was harmless. Nor can it be suggested that there was any lack of incentive. Many, in fact the great majority, of these foreigners whose one idea was to get to the Capitol, were a kind of Romans in partibus infidelium, visiting their spiritual home, whose present was in a state of suspended animation. They had imbibed Latin almost with their mother's milk, in their dame schools they had followed Caesar's legions, had shuddered at Brutus and Catiline, admired Mucius Scaevola. They learned sagacity from Cicero, wordly wisdom from Horace, laughed with Terence, sweated over Tacitus. Their path through life was paved with Roman maxims, their imaginations peopled with toga-draped figures. When they opened a book, laurel-crowned heads emerged from its pages, when they went to the theatre the steely voice of a Cinna resounded, when they sought diversion at the opera they were roused by Cato of Utica, when they banqueted they enjoyed soup beneath Juno's peacock on the ceiling, and their conversation was distracted by Leda and the swan over the mantelpiece. The general was acclaimed as an Alexander the Great after a glorious career, the pastoral poet could expect to be called a Flaccus, every private tutor a Mentor, the much sought after lawyer a Hortensius, the overthrown politician a Belisarius, a doctor with a large practice became a Hippocrates, the matron with lovely children ran the risk of being compared with the mother of the Gracchi when she fell ill and if her husband was a man of substance. Whatever the difference in all these well brought-up people of the period, in Edinburgh, Grenoble or Stuttgart – the pictorial world of the Latin authors enveloped them. At last they came to the genuine Roman scene. Texts were part of the luggage, small, handsome books bound in calfskin with gilded edges. There was to be a reading and a sight-seeing, a discovery of the famous characters, famous places provided with inhabitants.

In 1785 the Spanish scholar Juan Andres once asked Abbate Lanzi which was the largest population of Rome, that of the living or of the dead, of people or of statues. After some hesitation Lanzi answered that if not only life-sized figures were included, but also busts and heads and reliefs, the total of all these individuals would by far exceed the whole of Rome's population of about 170,000 souls [19]. Ficoroni, the antiquarian, stated in 1721 that he had counted just over 11,400 antique statues [20]. Although this number can be taken with a pinch of salt, there were all the opportunities in the world for high-flown conversations with marble Romans, once one could get a hearing. The tourists introduced themselves by using editions of the classics as phrase-books.

The Irishman Sherlock writes that it was a great joy for a lover of literature always to have his Horace in one pocket and his Virgil in the other when out walking, and to observe the thousand objects depicted by these masters [21]. No doubt most tourists restricted themselves to one volume at a time, although the pockets in both the swaying frock-coats of the Rococo period and the tail-coats of the Werther period were well able to hold a number of Elzevir editions. As we are now taking a bird's eye view of the world of Roman ruins, small figures can be observed moving around charily, all carrying a duodecimo in their hands or having bulging outside pockets. They stop, look something up in their books and take a seat on the sacred soil. "With my Livy I sit under the trees by the old Via Sacra," says Moritz – and lifts his eyes from his crabbed handwriting: "On the spot where now three columns stand Romulus raised his thoughts to heaven and promised Jupiter Stator a temple if his warriors stood fast" [22]. Whereupon Moritz rose and examined those parts of the temple that still existed. Mannlich, the German court-painter, set out with Plutarch [23], Bonstetten took Horace with him on his walk to Albano [24]. At Egeria's fountain, Moritz found it most suitable to read Juvenal [25]. Gibbon consulted Tacitus on the Capitol [26], Stendhal climbed over the masonry of Caracalla's thermae with a volume of Gibbon in his hand [27], a certain art-historian has read Stendhal on the same spot without realizing the significance of his recreation. Shelley had his portrait painted by Severn in Caracalla's baths with his finger stuck in a classic [28].

Convenient pocket-editions sold like hot cakes; they could always be had cheaply from the second-hand booksellers on the Corso [29] – "The ancients themselves loved such small editions," it was said, to encourage the cultured readers even more. Goethe presented his friend Moritz with a diminutive Livy [30] and wrote on the flyleaf:

> Ein wenig Pergament umschliesst den weitumfassenden Livius,
> der meinen ganzen Bücherschatz aufwiegt.

In the light cast by such cicerones – who all overshadowed the ordinary tourist guides like Misson, Deseine, Nemeitz, Volkmann, Vasi etc. [31] – the ruins revealed their secrets and the figures moved about in the noble theatre of illusion. Addison writes that a person in Rome can hardly glimpse an object which does not call to mind a passage in a Latin poet or historian [32]. Holberg, undaunted, hunted for the triple gateway (porta trigemina) of the Horatii – and found it [33], although it does not exist. "To stand there, where once the Romans stood, what a precious experience, the soul overflowed with Hochgefühl" [34], – to step upon "particles of the ephemeral, cold dust, which 2000 years ago was once Octavian" [35]. But best of all: the dear-departed personalities appear in bodily form in sculptures, weakened by the fragility of age, but they have the use of language, words can be exchanged with them face to face, they have at last risen from the mysteries of the written word. "To see emperors, consuls, generals, orators, philosophers, poets and other great men whose fame in history rather than anything else captivated our senses, to see them now in flesh and blood before us ... the past is made present. Although we are debarred from hearing Paul preach, we can see Tullius (Cicero) declaim and Caesar dictate, we can behold the beauties of the distant past – Faustina, Livia, Plautilla", and this against their authentic decorative background – this was the sightseeing of a British gentleman in Holberg's time [36]. Gibbon must have been deeply moved by standing where Cicero orated, and wrote his Decline and Fall of the Roman Empire after being inspired by the ruins of the forum [37]. And when Boswell saw the place on the Palatine where Cicero's house is believed to have stood, the spirit moved him – I began to speak Latin [38].

For the select few, life here was one long intoxicating voyage of discovery. The happy individual cast aside all his native superficialities, only the purified ego dared cross swords with antiquity and become – as Goethe magnificently expresses it – "ein Mitgenosse der grossen Rathschlüsse des Schicksals". The scholar and the artist were best fitted to conquer that wonderful imagined world. The prudent people chose to follow the examples of the freeborn and assume the parts they played – for without imitation, it seemed impossible to believe one was in classical Rome. Winckelmann, who came here on 18th November 1755, immediately adapted himself to the student atmosphere, "I am poor and own nothing, but I enjoy a proud freedom which I would not exchange for all the treasures in the world". Soon after his arrival he wrote home: "I live like an artist, and am taken for one." He always wore rocquelaure, this modest garb being the fashion among young intellectuals [39]. The immensely wealthy financier Bergeret, the patron of Fragonard, was, as a young man, a dilettante artist [40], and Goethe thus followed a tradition when he spent his time in Rome playing at being an artist. In pictorial art he had little talent, which his sketches show, but nobody before or since has felt the artistry of Rome so intensely as he did. Heinse lived like a vagabond in order to get to know that side of the conflicting city.

The pioneers often ran great risks before they succeeded in creating harmony between the texts and the monuments. Classical archaeology was dangerous, literally so. An arch collapsed on Bianchini on the Palatine; his spine was injured, and this eventually led to his death [41]. Piranesi carried out his studies of the ruins with death hanging over his head. The French architects Moreau and de Wailly showed great daring when in 1757 they measured up Diocletian's thermae, fumbling their way around subterranean rooms and balancing on crumbling ledges [42]. Hubert Robert performed a real balancing act conquering the heights of the Colosseum [43]. Archaeologists could not even feel safe in the forum; when there was a cattle-market in warm weather the bulls became uncontrollable, and people were quite often savaged by these beasts [44]. In remote vineyards it was a daily occurrence for mongrel dogs, as wild as wolves, to attack innocent pundits [45]. Sculptures too, had to be treated cautiously in the neglected gardens. Winckelmann just escaped with his life after nearly being crushed beneath a statue in the Villa Ludovisi when he was examining it at close quarters [46]. All such dangers had to be faced stoically. When Piranesi was at his last gaps he refused medicine and asked for a Livy, for this was far more efficacious than all medical remedies [47]. Normal Romans shook their heads at the madmen swarming around their peaceful ruins.

Sedate travellers, however, were held in far higher esteem, for after all they did drive in carriages. This whole army of distinguished visitors to Rome broadened the trail broken by the zany enthusiasts. They took up this new subject and reduced it to the level of prejudice. And this was easily done, the cicerones saw to that; they tarnished the coin and spoiled the holiday trips of many generations with their pompous drivel. Next to Europe's pedagogues of the "grammar" schools, this corps of town-criers bear the greatest responsibility for the spread of a false and poisonous classicism – false because it was the skimmings of erudite guessing, poisonous because it taught a whole century of people the disastrous belief that the art of antiquity must always be the standard of the contemporary. We can still detect the after-effects of the drastic remedies administered by these guides with their ever-superior knowledge. There is a field of study known as "Classical civilization" . . .

Everything, after all, is a matter of degree. Some of Rome's professional guides during the chocolate-box period in the cult of the antique, were, or had been, honest scholars, even leading ones. Old Ficoroni ended up as an eccentric. Deaf and poor, he daily drove foreigners to distraction, at a sequin a head, with his never-ending palaver [48] and had to put up with some rough treatment [49]. At one time he had been a man of letters whose words carried weight [50]. Men like Hirt and Reiffenstein were deservedly and rightly esteemed. The latter, living in Rome from 1762 until his death in 1793, was among other things also Goethe's guide [51]. Winckelmann's appointment in 1763 as prefect to the Apostolic court for Rome's ancient monuments gave him the official position which raised him far above the minions of the profession whose work was in the highway and byways. It matched the fame he enjoyed throughout Europe; he was in very truth l'antiquario nobile. Another celebrity, a Dane named Georg Zoëga, who is the true founder of scientific archaeology, was not spared the donkey-work. Plagued by pecuniary difficulties, he had to waste his valuable time guiding tourists, of whom only very few – some of these being Frederikke Brun and Elisa von der Recke – were able to appreciate his great integrity as topographer and his very fine character. It is pitiful to read Zoëga's letter to his friend Engelbreth in Denmark (19th Aug. 1797): "If I could sing I would ask you to look for a job as parish clerk for me in your neighbourhood, for I would rather be a parish clerk in the country than a guide in Rome" [52]. Friedrich Müller too, fell upon evil days when he was old, "Once a poet and a painter, Müller's muse has slumbered for many years" wrote Fernow, "his job is now that of a peripatetic antiquarian" [53].

Particularly after 1750, when anticomania got into its stride, Rome was flooded with the most dishonest charlatans ever to be in the pay of the fashion for antiquity. "All Europe's antiquarians are rolling up," wrote Barthélemy in 1757, "we are smothered with brochures about medallions and inscriptions by people who have merely a superficial knowledge and yet make names for themselves" [54]. The majority of the native cicerones came from the proletariat, empty phrases being the sum total of their learning. Princes and cardinals kept such people as pets, and they were well suited to be spies, newsmongers and intermediaries in shady deals. Here is a snapshot of a cicerone in action among the ruins he is describing to an Englishman: Ecco le rovine del famoso, del superbo, del maestoso tempio di Vesta! The young Briton objects that the goddess mentioned ought to have a round temple, the one shown being square. Sicuro, Eccellenza, ma queste pure sono le rovine etc. etc. Capisce? "Quite right, your Excellency, but all the same this ruin ..." etc.; the Englishman: Very well [55]. Most of the guides, with self-awarded academic qualifications, ranked in Duclos's opinion no higher than waiters from a hotel garni [56]. If they were not obtained by the proprietor of the albergo or did not advertise themselves impudently on street corners, they could be sought for in special cafés. Here the most grotesque characters could be found, threadbare priests and Cheap Jacks argued heatedly about whether a bust depicted Caius Gracchus or his brother Tiberius Gracchus, flinging scraps of Latin, misunderstood quotations, fake fragments of pottery about, coming to blows in their disagreement and then, with the clear conscience of scholars, leading honest folk by the nose [57].

This happened systematically when actual courses were held. A "good" one, according to John Moore, lasted six weeks with a daily assignment of three hours. Churches and the art collections of palaces were included in the bargain [58]. Naturally, the sort of conducted tour, that started punctually and was rushed through, did more harm than good, then as now. Surprisingly enough, highly enlightened, or at least cultivated people, participated in such arrangements; they had after all both time and money enough to make their own plans and could expect to obtain first-hand experience on their own initiative. The wife of the ambassador of France, the Duchess of Choiseul, followed her cours d'antiquité in the 1750's under Abbate Venuti [59], who was Winckelmann's predecessor in the post of Prefect of Antiquities (which did not prevent the grandiose German from calling him "a little imitator" on one occasion [60]. And even Herder went on a "curs" in 1788 under the direction of Hirt, who was so intolerably long-winded that the party controlled by his pointer was sick to death of the process before they got half-way through the programme, and in the end did not turn up at all. The Duchess of Weimar, "the Athena of the North", also played truant like a schoolgirl. On a particularly fine day Hirt trudged around with Herder over a distance which in the end amounted to 12–13 migli [61]. The German prophet departed from Rome with a deep sigh of relief. William Beckford was able to make better use of his time in the Eternal City and categorically refused "to be conducted by a prattling antiquarian from one fragment to another", and preferred, a sturdy individualist to the bitter end, "to straggle and wander about, just as the spirit chuses" [62]. A few upright souls, who otherwise pursued their courses with industry and did not doubt the sacrosant greatness of antiquity for a single moment, sometimes heaved an unwitting sigh. Goethe is to be commended for this note from 5th November, 1786: "Gestehen wir jedoch, es ist ein saures und trauriges Geschäft das alte Rom aus dem neuen herauszuklauben, aber man muss es denn doch thun . . .". We are able to supplement this Olympian's frank admission with evidence from the worldly Lady Morgan, who did not spare herself either, but all the same maintained her common sense throughout her whole campaign in Rome. She writes, without beating about the bush, that the greater part of the mutilated masses which are generally called ancient monuments are nothing but ruins of ruins. The guide described them with enthusiasm, the visitor listened and marvelled, but his doubts grew with every step he took; finally, when at long last the evening came, he returned home weary and disgruntled [63].

Whether the visitor approached antiquity in Rome with the impetous pace of the infatuated, with the tentative footsteps of a scholar or harnessed to a leading rein, he might consider the Promised Land as merely a pundit's playground. What was visible along the paths between lessons was positively encumbered by disputatious texts. That dedication to the marvels of classical Rome was not stifled by sheer *amoenitates philologicae,* was due to a very special and very fortunate circumstance. The people of that time had a great advantage over those of our day: they had matured within a harmonious culture based upon taste, whatever name the style was given. Hidden beneath their classical development there was a ferment. In those days it was called "taste". An inherent sense of beauty was included in this concept, or – if you like – aesthetic talent. Because of the presence of this miraculous ferment, the observant person required of a ruin that it should be beautiful. It was not enough that it occupied the imagination and stimulated the intellect, but it should also delight the mind in its physical form, as if it were a work of art. To be beautiful the ruin had to fulfil two conditions: to be in beautiful surroundings and to be to some extent complete.

It may be put forward that the true, the classical Roman ruin, could only be found as part of a landscape. The Pantheon can be regarded as the great exception, but then, it is not a ruin. Just as an ancient building in a dilapidated condition only stimulated the mind by its historical context, it only satisfied the requirements of beauty by fitting in with conventional natural surroundings. The composition of paintings since Poussin and Claude le Lorrain are to be equated with the Latin texts. A fragment of masonry is in itself ugly, untidy. The Latin part of it makes it interesting, Nature makes it picturesque. We can continue the parallel. The practice of classicism progresses as an unbroken series of verifications in the field, eagerly sought and often found; while on the one hand, the devotees of texts determine that yonder remains are substantiated by a passage from Suetonius and brought to life by a character in Polybius, the aesthete maintains that this building has the same natural surroundings as a temple in a painting by Claude. And because he recognizes it, he is thrilled [64].

But the Neo-classical observers were also provided with spectacles of a colour different from those of the painters. They saw the subjects well enough, but for them the motifs faded in a dim literary haze. There were no sunglasses and the glare of the monuments in the open were toned down by the delicately coloured stained-glass windows of elegy and idyll. In travelling bags, little books of verse were paired with pocket classics and if the tourist lacked literary nourishment on the spot, then he could obtain it from the booksellers of the Corso, the neat volumes being displayed on the counter next to Vasi's Itinerario and Piranesi's etchings. We can join Mercy Dupaty one day in 1785 and look over the bookshop's poetic best-sellers. In the front row we find Thomson's The Seasons (first published 1726–1730), Saint-Lambert's Les Saisons (1765),

Delille's Les Jardins (1782) – that lovely poetic cycle on English gardens – and a suitable ornamental figure in the landscape of ruins, is presented in *ce drame si touchant de Philoctète, qui nous rend Sophocle* ... [65]. For Abildgaard the meeting with this tragic Greek in Rome led to the creation of his classical major work "The wounded Philoctetes" (1774–1775). Fortunate visitors to Rome! They read, and their liberal reading matter made them sensitive. Gessner's silver-toned songs of antiquity among the roses soothed their eyes in the flicker of sunshine between the pines, and from time to time the landscape was darkened by Shakespeare's thunderclouds. They were reminded of Rubens by looking at the truncated, threatening outline of the Palatine, and felt the pathos of the imperial mount in the darkness around Coriolanus. Their overtures to the incomparable city, started in books, played out in natural surroundings, were, as the years went by, ennobled into the precious Souvenirs de Rome.

It is a well known fact that what people obtain from travelling is in direct ratio to their spiritual luggage. The more tourists bring with them, the more they take away. The less well equipped return like a rumbling barrel. The followers of Neo-classicism and Romanticism crossed the Alps and lost themselves in the scenic beauties of Italy with a firsthand knowledge of its ideal character. They knew not only a classical Italy from paintings and descriptions, from accounts of journeys and poems, but were also familiar with its features from the "English" landscape garden [66]. Although this was created north of the Alps, mainly from etchings and painted views, in Italy the soil gave forth its scent, the trees were alive. The waterfall among the myrtles in the grove filled the ear with its music, and the white temple beyond the lawn was a real habitation, a summer-house, and the marble statue by the cypress was an intimate friend in Sussex and on the Island of Funen. It was once more the destiny of the traveller to prove that his Arcady really existed. He made a pilgrimage to the real temples in Rome's huge and silent garden, recognized them, called them by name and absorbed with intense emotion the sun-warmed spirit of the plants at their foot. The ruins were beautiful for they existed among growing things, embraced by tendrils. It was as if the ruins themselves were growing. Thus it was that the Latin in the buildings of the ancients flourished anew, now being interpreted through a profusion of blossoms.

Young artists had presented antiquity as the world of the enchanted garden. It was about 1600 that this was started by the members of the Netherlands artists' colony in Rome, with Paul Bril at their head [67] and that brilliant German, Adam Elsheimer. But the highroad to the pastoral and heroic Atlantis was made by Claude and Poussin. These Romantics obtained their richest inspirations out in the mountain towns, near Lake Albani and Tivoli, where the scenery was particularly picturesque, but soon the whole of Rome was included in the magic circle – indeed the prospect of ruins in a lyrical light became a part of the syllabus of the École de France; at this conservative school, art students generally drew from plaster models and copied Raphael or Carracci. The break-out into the open air took place around 1730. Vleughels, "who was enamoured of this country's lovely views", made an excursion with his disciples in 1724 to cleanse their eyes and make them perceptive of the Elysium close at hand. He said "that the bizarre in Nature, her remarkable situations, arrangement of divers buildings and suchlike will liberate the talent of the young people and teach them to compose in an ingenious manner" [68]. They learnt the lesson thoroughly, as decorative items the ruins were posed magnificently against a landscape background, and the bizarre lost nothing by it; Pannini and his successors, even Canaletto, distributed the monuments of antiquity on the canvas with sovereign contempt for topography. This was not important as long as the colonnades and pyramids were given a fine, realistic natural setting, and they were. Hubert Robert approached the subjects in a better way. More than any other artist, he contributed to making the veduta of Roman ruins not merely reflect an ideal landscape gardening, but also kept them under control. Where Piranesi used the pruning knife and laid his ruins bare, Robert made them hide behind rustling leaves.

The ruin was enticing when seen at a distance, kept in equilibrium by an arched shrubbery and proclaimed by a pine. But it was completely irresistible when it included a human being. Then plants and masonry closed above his head, and it was as if a magic mountain enclosed a dreamer. "The wild fig-tree splits the marble of Messala" – now Martial's prophesy was seen in all fulfilment. The contest between stone and plant was a lover's tussle, the young grass sprang forth from the cracks in the weathered masonry, "a golden harvest is ever brought forth" [69]. Archaeology too, found its studies ennobled behind greenery. Hardly anybody in this field has acknowledged this in warmer words than the austere scholar Zoëga. On the 2nd August 1780 he wrote to Esmarch: "You see in all the gardens how the vines are entwined in the temples of the gods and provide new leaves for their defoliated columns ... and oranges gleam in the evening sun more vividly than the gold once did in their ornate halls" [70]. If only this inspired view of ancient works of art could be reborn and sculpture could win back its innocence and get down to earth! This is more easily done in the greenhouse and the park than in the lecture room of a museum.

When the painter Wilhelm Tischbein sent Goethe a collection of water-colour sketches for the "Idylls" in 1821 and asked his old Roman travelling companion to write a verse for them [71], the memories of the old man in Weimar were revived. He saw the Imperial City in ruins before his inner eye – but remembered also that Rome is rooted in an ever fertile Nature:

> Dann beginnt das Leben wieder,
> Boden mischt sich neuen Saaten,
> Rank' auf Ranke senkt sich nieder,
> Der Natur ist's wohlgeraten.

His own Roman idyll in 1786 and his meeting with antiquity, were seen in retrospect beneath heavy luxuriant foliage.

Even a humble Danish observer in the days of Frederick VI understood the fine art of assembling the *disjecta membra* of antiquity into a harmonious whole when he came upon them in natural surroundings; here they were not just ciphers but organs. A. C. Gierlew, a theological student from Borch's College, saw the residual fragments on the Palatine become a work of art again when he visited Rome in 1803. He did not try to imagine these pieces assembled into a dusty reconstruction, but enjoyed the pattern they made on blessed soil. Here there lay "in some places huge blocks of marble, in others the shaft of a column, elsewhere its capital, again its frieze or architrave" – he saw "the broken greatness of this palace strewn around among the fertile vegetation", but it was all as pure as a gospel to him, "for Nature conquers art" [72]. Everywhere on his lonely path, the human being could observe how the Creator exalted the fallen. The crooked avenue of the Campo Vaccino could be appreciated as the cool winding path of a Romantic landscape garden [73]. It had now become a Via Sacra in a different sense, and on the top of the "temple of Peace" itself (Constantine's basilica), there grew an arbour – but you had to be careful how you moved around up there, says Lalande, ever considerate [74], so as not to fall through a hole in the vaulting. On the ground, impressions of antiquity constantly alternated with impressions of the flora, each enhancing the other. The moss made the tiles more venerable, in place of antiquity's wilted festoons of fruit, the garlands of ivy were entwined by Nature. Myrtle and laurel are also antiquities. When the dear Mrs Millar once wandered along the grass path of a villa garden in 1771, her excursion pleased her very much because of the classical cinerary caskets which lined her path on both sides (possibly in the Villa Mattei). These sentimental trappings were just as effective as the melancholy holm oaks and the lichen, grey with age, spreading over the pedestals. "What a fine evening's walk would not this have been for our famous Doctor Young!" [75]. Any moralist could here find on his evening walk evidence of resurrected life in nature.

And now, as often before, we must call upon Goethe. He shows us the most vivid and detailed picture of the human being in a down-to-earth relationship with ruins, in this case "Nero's Palace". He says: "... we went through recently weeded fields of artichokes and could not help filling our pockets with small fragments of granite, marble and porphyry which lay here in their thousands" (Ital. Reise, 18. Nov. 1786). The mineralogist collected, but the Classical scholar also plucked the past from among the vegetables, the poet gave antiquity's enchanted visions a foothold, where the gardener's hoe left its trace. And he went home with dirty fingers and a joyful heart.

There are now few such classical field-paths in Rome and those that are left are seldom trodden by strangers. The time will soon come when nobody will be able to find old monuments planted among artichokes. The hill path down to Egeria's grotto passes through broad fields covered with the above mentioned delicacy, but within the area of the city, I can think of only one place where the antique emerges from a kitchen garden and reigns over the cabbages and thistles. When I last visited the area (1950) the blackbird was singing tenderly in an elder bush, set in his poor domain of vegetable beds. A sheepdog slunk around growling, as shaggy as the carrot-tops. The site lies behind S. Costanza and a large isolated exedra from the Late Antique period. Bartolomaeus Breenbergh made a drawing of the subject in the 1620's [76], Nicodemus Tessin the Younger reproduced it in a sketch half a century later [77] (Pl. 202). We have a view dating from the 1780's by Franz Caucig [78], and Goethe drew the scene at the same time. We can see in our photograph (Pl. 203) how the motif appears on these pages. Time has not left any marks worth mentioning on its beauty. Even Raphael would feel at home in this picture of the homeland of ruins.

As the reader will remember, we put forward above two conditions for a ruin to possess beauty and to be recognized a worthy in the eyes of the observer. The first of these, a matter of landscape, has just been discussed. It is now our task to reflect a little on the second condition: ancient monuments must only be ruined within certain limits. It is necessary – partly at any rate – that they should keep their original form. In the present day everybody falls into ecstacy over the most trivial fragments in an excavation which is later to contain the foundations of a concrete building – and this they do without being able to quote a single Latin tag. It was not like this in the days of Voltaire or Goethe. People were after all only enthusiastic about remains with an architectural value. Three upright columns are also a building; the bare foundation stones are merely postulates.

It is important to recognize this way of looking at things by the people of those days, because side by side with the requirement for a rustic setting, it provides a very true explanation of their enthusiasm for ruins. So basic was the actual aesthetic feeling in those days that people could not regard anything amorphous as beautiful merely because it was historically interesting. Who can write odes inspired by a vivarium, that silly, artificial empty space with broken stones at the bottom? A rubbish dump, yes, this can have a soul, but not a glass tank with a layer of rubbish. Think of the area of ruins of the Piazza Argentina, which is not even inhabited by a cat. During the Classical period people may have regarded the ruins as evidence of the epic of antiquity, but they only wove garlands for the monuments that were based on a firm aesthetic foundation.

In 1696 Oppenordt had surveyed the church of St. Ignatius, a modern work. In his introduction the director of the French Academy wrote the following apologetic words to his superior in Paris: "I am convinced that the public will obtain just as great an advantage from these drawings as from ancient buildings that have been surveyed, for apart from the Rotunda we have had merely time-worn ruins (*des ruines bien usés*) handed down to us" [79]. La Teulière's summarized judgment of the classical monuments is very instructive. He looked upon the ruins as architecture and took it upon himself to grade them according to their artistic merit. Completely disfigured works were not edifying, for they were lacking in taste. Poerson, the successor to La Teulière, had the same attitude in 1707: "With the exception of the Pantheon, the Colosseum and a few columns Antiquity (here) has not bequeathed to us any work important enough for the edification of scholars" [80]. The statement has perspective. It was addressed to J. Hardouin Mansart, the great leading Court Architect of Louis XIV responsible for Les Invalides.

"And a few columns – ". An off-hand reference. The group comprises the most famous pieces in ancient Rome, these columns – one, two, three or more – whose isolated outline against the sky was the very symbol of the age of the Caesars and is the delight of all tourists. In the Forum Romanum could be seen the column of Phocas, Vespasian's temple, which in those days was believed to be dedicated to Jupiter Tonans or Jupiter Stator (three columns square), the temple of Castor and Pollux (three columns in a row), the temple of Saturn, called "Concordia's temple" (eight columns in all, six in front, two at the sides). Furthermore, the two columns (*le Colonnacce*) by the temple of Nerva. The first mentioned example in this group was and is purely a memorial, the remainder being highly venerated strictly as architecture. Although they were destroyed, they were respected as buildings which were once entities. It did not minimize their prestige that they could be restored. The fragment itself was complete, cast in one piece, finished, classical. The cult of columns gained more and more momentum in the course of the 18th century. Firmly rooted and unencumbered, they were sufficient to form a building on their own. The remains stood as a complete cella in "the baseless fabric of the soul" and filled the observer with a sense of beauty. "Kennst du das Haus, auf Säulen ruht sein Dach" – with these words the picture is complete, the ancient house is erected before our eyes as a plurality of slim columns [81]. Connoisseurs before c. 1760 required no roof; architrave and frieze were enough for them. The enormous disengaged column which originates from the "Temple of Peace" and stands in the square south of S. Maria Maggiore, was according to de Brosses "the finest piece of architecture in the world", and accorded him "greater pleasure than any other complete building from antiquity or modern times, because it gave the idea of ultimate perfection" [82]. Not until Goethe's time was the lack of a roof above columns thought to be regrettable. Radical Classicism viewed antiquity as a strictly functional architecture, and according to Laugier ("Essai sur l'Architecture", 1753) a column must always support something. If this is not the case, it fails in its task and outrages moral standards. In 1785, Moritz called a column without a load on its head "mehr eine Spielart des Geschmacks" [83]. This view won the day, and therefore the broken column was banished to the churchyards and the memorial parks of the Empire period, where it stood as a sermon in stone on corruption. If it was seen in the natural surroundings of Rome itself it was merely a heap of stone (Pl. 208). The obelisk was a different matter altogether, from its first conception fully developed as a very slim pyramid, an entity to the very last detail. However, only very doctrinaire arbiters of taste found any fault with the Roman column, which merely rose into the sky. Its body was loved without inhibition, even when it lay sprawling on the gravel. Ida Brun embraced a fallen column drum [84]. Every ornament was sketched and caressed, the rosettes and bull's skulls in the frieze, the foliage of the capitals, the lovely flutes of the shafts.

Those monuments whose tops had come within easiest reach, thanks to the strata of soil laid down through centuries, enjoyed a particular favour. "Le Colonnacce" must certainly be visited, enjoins Bergeret, for

201. *The Rotunda. The Pantheon.*

202. *The country behind S. Agnese fuori le Mura and S. Costanza. Drawing by N. Tessin the Younger.*

203. *The same motif as above.*

204. *Egeria's Grotto.*

it is so easy to get a close view of them [85]. The same was true of the three Corinthian columns of the temple of Jupiter in the Forum. Piranesi praised them highly for their select elegance of detail, and emphasized *la maëstà della fabbrica*. The temple was considered to have been built by Augustus. The deeply carved curls of the acanthus on the magnificent columns, which emerged from the damp soil like giant plants from the Underworld, weighed heavy on the imaginative observer's head. Strangely enough, the ruin had the name of "the grammar of the architects". An Englishman wrote in 1721 that it was not very likely that it would all remain standing for very much longer [86].

If we take stock of the ruins, we are struck by the fact that the group of monuments most admired in the 18th century is not identical with that of modern times. There are a number of ancient monuments in and around Rome, which were greatly esteemed by our great-great-grandparents and even earlier generations, but nobody thinks very much of them in 1950. Their fame was due to factors which are no longer valid. It may well be apt here to provide short analyses of the position of a few of the monuments in the history of taste, four in all but selected with care; two of these are very renowned, the other two were at one time. Each example should be able to provide an aspect typical for mature Neo-classicism. All the works had the strongest attraction for the people of those days. Why?

The Pantheon was regarded purely and simply as the unattainable pattern for a sacred building. All the virtues which the followers of Classicism ascribed to the ideal temple of ancient times were seen to be united here. In the first place the building is circular – the cylinder was considered the noblest form – and therefore "the Rotunda" was the Pantheon's honorific name [87]. Furthermore, it has a portico which beneath its triangular gable stands out in itself as the most sublime peristyle temple. By the cylinder and the colonnade being joined together, a supreme prototype of the temple of the ancients is produced. At first sight, the building seems to proclaim the most complete and solid rotundity, then the projection of the colonnaded hall becomes visible and can be surveyed both laterally and diagonally – finally to appear solid and wide, when seen from the front. One could easily compare the portico with *"un beau vers de Corneille"* [88], altogether the Pantheon was a heroic drama.

The number of its ecstatic admirers is boundless. We shall be content with seeing the reaction of two Danes to its front. Wiedewelt declaims with raised forefinger: "At the first glance I found ... in the Rotunda a vision of a temple" [89]. Zoëga dreams that he looks out of his window into the darkness and sees the dim pronaos become even deeper, behind the flickering gleam of the lanterns carried by nocturnal wayfarers [90].

Finally, the Pantheon is a building of exceptional strength, with a dome like the vault of heaven [91]. To stand in the centre of this hall of the gods gives the sentient person a feeling of tremendous expansion of the ego. "The moment one enters one begins to float, one is in the air, and the earth disappears" – this was Heinse's experience, on his very first evening in Rome. Hardly had he unpacked in his lodging in the Spanish square before off he went hotfoot to the Pantheon, which received him "in the blissful light of the setting sun" [92]. Indeed, every discriminating traveller saw the portico in a transfigured light. And he himself became a statue beneath the dome – Beckford stood in the centre with his arms folded [93], the composer Rudolph Bay took up the same plastic posture in harmony with the body of the hall (and with his own personal embonpoint) [94]. For Goethe, the Rotunda was "der inneren Grossheit nach", unconditionally the greatest work that he had met with in Italy.

The temple now called Minerva Medica is situated between Porta Maggiore and S. Bibiana, in depressing surroundings near the railway. But in the old days this imposing ruin stood in a vineyard and had space and silence all around it [95]. The building, which is neither spoken of in ancient literature nor mentioned in inscriptions, has nevertheless given imaginative antiquarians much to think about, and has changed its name innumerable times. The designation "le Galluzze", a corrupt form of basilica Caii & Lucii, was in fashion among antiquarians in the first half of the 18th century, and was also used by the architect Nicolas-Henri Jardin [96]. The philosopher George Berkeley was keen-sighted enough (in 1717) to reject this interpretation, for in his opinion the decagonal central building with its dome could not possibly be comparable with the style of a basilica [97]. Also the definition of the ruin as a temple dedicated to Minerva Medica was untenable [98]. All this learned rubbish could however cheerfully be ignored, for the work itself had unique qualities.

Its renown was based in the first place on being a circular building, thus belonging to the same élite as the Pantheon, when taken as an ideal. But while the Rotunda was plainly marred by the urban confines of its neighbourhood, "Minerva Medica" enjoyed rustic freedom. This building on the outskirts also had the great advantage of being just dilapidated enough – only to such a small extent that the dome still retained its full outline (up to 1828), yet so much that the monument really looked like a ruin. "Minerva Medica's temple" could thus be placed on the same footing as such classics as "The Temple of the Sun" by the Tiber and the temple of Sybilla in Tivoli, those famous round temples set in the most venerated landscapes. The epicure de Brosses, expressed the idea of his time with his usual ease when he called the ruin "good enough to eat" [99]. The poet Thomas Gray pictured at this time (1740) what a wonderful "English garden" could be laid out on this spot, for the most important elements were at hand; well tilled soil, blue mountains on the horizon, an overgrown ruin with a dome, and subterranean grottos, full of the graves of the ancients, nearby [100]. Cultured people of the propertied class immediately found the site intriguing [101], since the park had the necessary trappings. This unsophisticated interpretation of the ruins by men of the world was really quite correct. In contrast to the bookworms, they estimated the whole thing as an example of landscape gardening. Present-day archaeology regards "Minerva Medica's temple" as a nymphaeum from the 3rd century A.D., perhaps belonging to the Horti Liciniani [102]. Stendhal hit the nail on the head when he called the building a "pavilion built by a rich Roman in his park" [103]. Tourists who now catch a glimpse of the famous ruin – perhaps inadvertently or merely from the window of a railway carriage – will perhaps think that it is nothing to write home about. Nor is it. This is merely a rough, barren heap of stones.

Up to a few years ago Egeria's Fountain enjoyed peace and quiet and was rarely visited by travellers to Rome. But in the past it was one of the most favoured shrines. And this is easily understood. Educated travellers recognized here a situation which poetry had taught them to love. The cult of fountains in Classicism and Neo-antiquity is after all a literary phenomenon. The running water, which springs forth in all its mystery, is divinely animated and artistically inspiring. Who did not remember the springs of Castalia on Mount Parnassus itself, from whose flowing stream poets drank inspiration – or the Hippocrene on Mount Helicon of the Muses, which sprang forth where Pegasus had stamped his hoof on the ground? Apollo and his company had consecrated the springs and given them power. Everybody could quote Horace and invoke the Sabine spring – O, fons Bandusiae, splendidior vetro [104]. The fountain poetry of the 18th century overflowed all book shelves, gurgled in slim poetic volumes, dripped through albums.

If this were not enough, from Holberg's day onwards, the poetic cult of the fountain also assumed visible form in gardens; aesthetes had an antique grotto built, called forth water in it and grew lyrical to the music of gently running water. Pope's founted grotto in Twickenham, which enchanted Addison and even Dr Johnson, had offshoots everywhere in the Romantic gardens of the age of sensibility. Goethe had a number of grottos with fountains built near Weimar and celebrated such a shrine in lovely Sapphic strophes. Wiedewelt, who had seen Pope's grotto during his visit to England, planned an imitation of it in the palace garden of Fredensborg Castle (first erected 1777), and in the 1780's Søndermark Park and the gardens of Frederiksberg Castle in Copenhagen, were enriched with grottos which are still extant, and in which running water assuaged tender hearts and filled the picnic kettles [105]. Fauns and nymphs were assumed to be romping outside in the bushes.

Since at this time, well-read people, also ladies, came to Rome with these idyllic pictures engraved on their souls, they longed to drink water from a fountain whose noble past was certified by the best classical authors and which rejoiced in an especially choice ornamentation. The grotto and fountain of Egeria fulfilled all expectations. According to Juvenal, the deity of the place, the nymph Egeria, had given King Numa Pompilius good advice. This was an excellent subject – the ruler in a period of Latin legend, listened to a lovely girl who was just as spirited as Sybil and Grace and Louise at home under the poplar trees. At the sight of a stream in Holstein, Baggesen dreamed of being "In Numa's sacred grove, harkening to Egeria's wisdom". And the young, soulful Thorvaldsen chose the subject for a relief (1794), very sensitively done. It was impossible to be disappointed when the reality was revealed.

The surroundings of the grotto were lonely, and deep silence lay upon this hill and vale in the Campagna near the Via Appia. You passed by an antique temple in the Vigna Caffarelli (later S. Urbano Church), that was so well preserved that it could serve as a pattern for a summerhouse – and on a ridge forming the background to the scene could be glimpsed the sacred grove, a bosco sacro, raising its low domed crest. A generation ago it stood as shown in pl. 206, which is an old photograph, but now only a few spindly trees remain. The landscape was entirely classical, Nature in epic mood. Down in a dip, surrounded by Prince Torlonia's fields, is the grotto, decayed and overgrown. We can remember how poignantly beautiful it was (Pl. 204). The water was fresh, the plants juicy; there was a green smell of summer. The ancients were right –

> Hörbar walltet im Quell der leise Fittich
> Segnender Geister ...

An incalculable number of sensitive people picked flowers in front of the built-up niche with Egeria's broken statue, and never forgot it. Wright visited "the cave" (la spelunca) in 1721 [106]. D'Orbessan relates that on the first Sunday in May 1750 he betook himself to this vale to witness rustic festivities in honour of spring, and the beauties of the place always attracted great crowds in that lovely season of the year [107]. Both Lalande [108] and Volkmann [109] have reported that numerous artists sketched there. That steadfast lady Mrs Millar could not resist seeing the spot "where Numa had his rendez-vous with the nymph" and was, as always, a mouthpiece for contemporary widely held opinion: It is ... a most charming romantic spot, where one might indulge in contemplation –

> *Of forest and inchantments drear*
> *Where more is meant than meets the ear.*

As could be expected, she is quoting Pope [110]. Here even the peevish Kotzebue capitulated, when in front of the grotto he saw a quail hastily break away from a moorhen and fly off towards Rome, while its partner scurried under a block of stone: "If you believed in the transmigration of souls you might imagine the presence of Numa and his beloved" [111]. Moritz did not leave the spot until he had persuaded the artist Hr. Lütke to make a drawing of it, reproduced as the titular engraving in his "Reise eines Deutschen in Italien", volume III (1793); Münter extemporized in delight about the grove of the Muses and the Temple of Bacchus [112]. Mercy Dupaty had difficulty in tearing himself away after wishing that the site could be transferred to a region where herds of sheep could drink from the spring and shepherdesses lose themselves in reverie to its murmuring [113]. One would have thought the rustics would have been good enough, preferably on horseback. Miranda, visiting this place in 1785, missed the figures of the Muses in the side niches [114], Molbech enjoyed the full moon [115].

"I would that I could describe with the pen of a Pope or a Delille what I have seen lately," sighed Adlerbeth on the last day of the year 1783, after having appraised the greatest monuments of ancient Rome [116]. He certainly needed the pen of the literati mentioned when it came to describing idylls such as the Fountain of Egeria. Faced with the Pyramid of Cestius one reached for one's charcoal. This monument lived under black clouds, it was glorified, a sombre elegy. The dark side of the world of fantasy in those days and the prevalent elegiac poetry [117] prepared people to be pleasurably frightened here. Everything around the great tomb shocked the soul, no decor for a tragedy at the theatre could compare with this fearful stage. The pyramid itself was Egyptian, thus shrouded in mystery – like the temple with "the sacred halls" in Mozart's "Magic Flute" [118]. It was the symbol of eternity. And its triangular faces must have stimulated all Freemasons to speculate, like the two columns which Alexander VII had reconstructed outside [119]. Lalande, who was a keen Freemason and Grand Master in Paris [120], praised its elegant proportions and imagined that the region here near Monte Testaccio resembled the land of the Egyptians [121]. The shape of the pyramid had long been used as a principal motif in the mausoleums and catafalques for princes all over the world. Ewald's poem "Now cease, o tears, your flowing..." has its visible counterpart in the castrum doloris erected above Frederick V of Denmark, to which Jardin gave a pyramidal form [122]. The tomb of Cestius however, had antiquity on its side and was pregnant with fate for the young architects of Classicism, who followed the teachings of Piranesi and had their heads "stocked with pyramids" [123]. One of Robert Adam's earliest works, the plan for a monument to General Wolfe in Westminster Abbey (1760), misuses the lines of the pyramid [124]. The colossus in Rome was something more than plastic art. It was partly veiled in "a picturesque drapery of moss and ivy", thus a recognized sepulchral vegetation, and on the other side of the open space in front of the pyramid, stood a wood of oak-trees [125] – a grove of those huge, decaying trees which infatuated all Northerners during the "Sturm und Drang" period. Zoëga had listened in fear and trembling to the cry of the ravens in an old forest of oak-trees near Kerteminde before he was bemused by black melancholy beneath Roman holm oaks [126].

Furthermore, in 1765 the tomb of Cestius had been joined by a neighbour of particular virtue [127], namely the Protestant cemetery, a miserable field of weeds. This "God's Acre" for heretics, bordered the meadows (Prati del popolo Romano) near Monte Testaccio, where the people caroused under the chestnut trees. This clash between the hubbub in the Romans' playground and the silence among the poor graves of the heretics was rather dramatic [128]. "The greatness of antiquity overshadows the pettiness of the present" wrote Gierlew, and criticized those in the land of the living who were not put off their pleasure in a full mug, by the proximity of the departed Roman's monument and the tombstones of the ungodly [129]. As if the cup of terror here were not filled to overflowing, the burial of Protestants always took place at night. The corpses were brought out in secret, the coffins, contrary to custom, had the lids nailed down, and closed carriages made up the cortège. These hasty funeral processions, with only a few torches and escorted by mounted sbirri, were horrific. The travellers of those days, who got goose pimples from reading ballads of ghosts and trolls – such as Bürger's "Lenore", Robert Burns' "Tam o' Shanter", Goethe's "Erlkönig" – could not look upon the Pyramid of Cestius as just a mere antique, for in their eyes it was a temple of tragedy. Not until the gravediggers had filled the graves with earth, and the circle of mourners in long cloaks had broken up in silence and the torches had been extinguished, did a sight of gruesome effect disappear. "Treated by a clever specialist in night-pieces," asserts Fernow [130], "the scene would make an interesting picture."

The terrain can be viewed in Vasi's great panorama (Pl. 188), dating from the same year as the Protestants' churchyard was established. Our own plate (No. 205) shows that the site still has a natural charm and sublimity. Wild strawberries grow among the tussocks. Shelley was deeply moved on seeing the graveyard which was soon to be his own resting place. He wrote in a letter that the green hillock outside the city wall was "the most beautiful and solemn cemetery I ever beheld". He heard the wind whisper around the pyramid, and thinking of the graves of the young "one might, if one were to die, desire the sleep they seem to sleep" [131]. His mood developed into magnificent music in "Adonais".

Now that we have explained the cult of ruins by giving examples of its different forms in Rome, we can go on to outline an assessment of their ethos. Without doubt it had great positive features. The people of that time cherished a close, almost loving relationship to the classical ruins. An intimate knowledge of the long-vanished period of greatness of these ruins and an enjoyment of what was left of them in natural surroundings, made the observers in those days privy to what was best and most beautiful. Antiquity had for them a destiny which was of immediate importance for the ego, not merely history. This genuine humanitarianism, refreshed by sentiment, has long ceased to exist. Various eccentrics try to keep it alive artificially within their professional fields, but asocial individuals have no standing. Nowadays the cult is replaced by investigation: first the work must be dated, at the end it must be authenticated, and in the middle, the type and style must be discussed. No human soul seeks the soul of the monument, nor wishes to foist a genuis on it or provide it with a myth. Its interpretation is done much better without the help of the spirit, it must be resigned to the cautious pursuits of the intellect.

Vitruvius quotes a delightful myth about the origin of the Corinthian capital. A young woman's grave was decorated by her maid with a basket, in which the personal effects of the dead woman were placed covered by a tile. Then an acanthus grew up under the basket and embraced it with its laciniate leaf-stalks. An artist went past, was moved by the sight – and sketched a new capital based on this poetic motif. Just as the tile was here entrapped by the wild plant, so was the mass of the ruins conquered by the vegetation, and a new art arose. The Danish sculptor Wiedewelt, who could be said to be a man of extensive learning, sketched a monument for the gardens of Fredensborg Castle in Denmark inspired by this ever-fresh myth. Some fifty years after his death (1802), the spirit of such old fables had lost all food for thought, as far as antiquarians and laymen were concerned. Flowers were not to be included in the archaeologists' harvest. "The poor man, the poor men ..." We can imagine a cultured tourist in modern times pass by the fine stump of a column on the Palatine, which is reproduced here (Pl. 208). At best he will have taken note of it as a relic from the palace of the Flavii, a chance isolated object without particular character – and would go on his way. But a person in the Goethe period could be awakened by the fragment. Its importance lay in its appearance and the reflections it called forth. The garden of the Marquis de Girardin in Ermenonville, the scene of Rousseau's last days, contained a monument in the shape of a broken column. Its inscription ran: *Falsum stare non potest* [132], "the false cannot stand upright". That the column was an imitation did no harm to the moral, and in this case the truth was loudly proclaimed: "Let fall what cannot stand". The broken column on the Palatine was also the symbol of a fall, in truth a tragic one: the decay of the culture of antiquity. Any enlightened person in 1780 or 1820 would at once understand the column's terse message. And it was good to be able to. The stones had something to tell which came from their very core – the intuitive felt it too.

However – beneath its warm lyricism, the cult of the ruins concealed dangerous, indeed destructive characteristics. They were inherent in its nature. For the cult was not merely a rite in the name of aestheticism and history, but also a part of a veritable religion: the idolization of the whole of antiquity.

Now that its deities were practically extinct to its followers, always a difficult predicament for any congregation, the whole trend of belief had to become chimerical. And because its temples had for the most part crumbled into ruins, the cult was constantly reduced to erecting houses of prayer in their imagination and seeking out fallen altars. The style with the high ideals and beautiful feelings is the art of the tomb, the name of the god of the anticomaniacs was really corruption. And the ruin became its proper shrine. A religion of taste, the base of which is cracked by such fearful internal stresses, must regard the urge for artistic expression at the time in question, with fear and trembling, and must as a result, entrench itself behind an overriding intolerance. Never had such a worm-eaten faith been seen. It wished to construct by emphasizing destruction, it eulogized amid floods of tears.

Here it is both necessary and instructive to follow the characteristic train of thought lying behind the cult, and to give the reasons for its opinions. An excellent analysis of the ethical attitude of the visitors to Rome is given by Duclos (1767). According to him, the ruins call forth a spontaneous melancholy, "which is not sadness"; they also provide food for thought about the decline and fall of empires. Such reflections finally encourage the human being to remember his own self and "reminds him to take pleasure" (*et l'avertissent de jouir*) [133] – to take pleasure with head held high that fate is immutable for great and small (a common shipwreck does not engender *tristesse,* only melancholy is fitting), to take pleasure in being alive, to take pleasure in taking pleasure. The thoughtful man thus tutored by the ruins, became a conscientious moralist, although draped with crepe – so he believed. He could at times be confused with a sentimental pharisee.

This is baroque. People went around here in a Rome that had never been more beautiful before, and were downcast. They drew attention to the perfection of a city and a culture that no longer existed – *Roma fuit*. This constitutional melancholy was frequently expressed in petulant jeremiades, when they discovered that life was laying violent hands on the sacred relics. The temple of Fortuna Virilis "is said to have been built by King Servius Tullius, Rome's 6th king" – this is madly interesting (although incorrect); the building is handsome – how magnificent! "Now Armenian Christians live out their lives here" – doubly scandalous

[134]. Canon Meyer wandered in the Forum, saw the sublime subjects and ought to have been delighted, but was interrupted at every moment "by bellowing cattle, bawling hawkers and by the quarreling of the mob". He went away embittered; the great moment was ruined, a lovely morning sullied [135]. Heinse, that impressionable man, went to the Capitol. Was he engrossed by that grand work of art, Michelangelo's square, which surrounded him? Not in the least – "My spirit was filled with the triumphs for the Scipios and the Caesars". In spirit he razed the three palaces to the ground and the site echoed with his cry: "Proud little hill, compared with which the highest mountain of every realm in the world is only flat land . . ." [136].

The Roman cult in the era of Neo-classicism and Romanticism introduced a particular way of walking for its participants. The rhythm became slow, one moved with a dragging step, weighed down with responsibility and sorrow, paused many times and often had to clutch at some support so as not to be overcome by impressions. Beckford said [137] that while he went home at his leisure and passed by the Campo Vaccino, he leaned for a moment against one of the columns in Jupiter Stator's temple. Mercy Dupaty could not make his way across the Forum Romanum without bracing himself in ritual postures: "Leaning against the wall where the tablets of the law were set, standing above the prison to which Catilina's accomplices were led to die after Cicero had spoken, supported by the shaft of a column in the temple of Jupiter Tonans . . . I contemplate –" [138]. The Roman via dolorosa of the pilgrims and tourists, was in truth a tender and enchanting experience, unfolding from morning to evening amid sun-warmed walls and departed spirits. It could be a serious game, smiling beneath the tears, now and again childish too; only wholly creative for the great – a Piranesi, a Goethe – who were driven on by demons. But for the average crowd, even the artists, the experience of Rome's ruins was a fateful test. Only very few passed it. While the melancholy lovers of antiquity made for the halls of the blessed, they were very inclined to cast aspersions on contemporary buildings. In architecture they saw and honoured virtue and the sole truth, yet at every step they took, they were in danger of being fooled by deceptive appearances. No style, not even the Renaissance, brought such serious sacrifices to illusion as mature Neo-antiquity. How could it be otherwise, when even its great revelation was a delusion and the guidelines for its taste were laid down among fragments? Deepest down in the soul of the classicists lay fear for, and hatred of the living and their rights. The removal of the last layer above the psychology of the worshippers of ruins reveals their inherent ineptitude to create anything independently and of value on hallowed ground.

We have frequently emphasized in the foregoing, that building stagnated after 1760 and in the wider view, came to a standstill c. 1780. Nevertheless, there was something created on the basis of the new ideals. The most characteristic works are not to be found among churches or palaces. The original achievements are only the artificial ruin and the modern museum.

One would have thought that an artificial "ancient ruin" would have been impossible in Rome. The milieu itself would laugh it to scorn. On the contrary – faked ruins actually produced a brilliant effect. One could be certain when ruined temples were erected from the ground up, that they honoured all justified demands with regard to location and artistic arrangement. The sight of them alone could remove from the mind any memory of less successfully composed relics and thus raise the standard. Who said humbug? Nobody would let such a word pass his lips and certainly nobody would admit that the term was really applicable in this respect. The boundary between the artificial and the genuine was constantly being overstepped in this Mecca of the antiquarians, where the world's most capable restorers lived and had their being. Even Alessandro Albani was eminent in this field. When therefore he had a complicated and tragic ruin erected at his villa – it still exists – he could reckon with the applause of all beaux-esprits. The audience was convinced that it was at least accurate, although its authenticity could be challenged. The learned expert in antiquity, Juan Andres, saw it in 1785, "a little half-ruined building, which resembles a demolished temple with columns and pieces of marble fallen to the ground", and, he adds, "it looks very nice" [139]. The arrangement is indescribable. It is well known that when marbling by means of a brush is rough enough to be bad as an imitation, it can be good and fine; this antique falsification is not even bad enough as such to be pleasant in its crudeness. We cannot believe that Cardinal Albani really ever had this in view – it must have been erected after his sight had completely deteriorated. But the ruined temple suits His Eminence's garden very well all the same, and had some meaning here. A serious old scholar relaxing by building with toy bricks.

In the Villa Borghese, there is a complete lack of background for faked antiquity, but the landscape is used in a particularly ingenious fashion to make up for it. For Don Marc'Antonio spurious temples, in toto or in pieces, were merely modern objects which were indispensable in a proper "English garden". They were imported. However paradoxical it may sound, it must be stated that no decoration can be more un-Roman than the examples which Prince Borghese had erected in his park and given classical names. The "Temple of Aesculapius", which was completed in 1786, after a drawing by Antonio Asprucci [140], is just as bad a decoration as found on any sentimental site in Europe at that period. Many temple buildings were better, even in Denmark. More acceptable is the feigned ruin which unashamedly is given the name of the "Temple of Antoninus and Faustina" (Pl. 209). Merely a piece of airy scenery silhouetted against the sky and making no attempt to impress anybody. The inscription is so impudent in the city where the original stands that "the ruin" itself repudiates it. And may perhaps even be a joke.

We might be wrong in thinking this. There are two sides to the question. We can of course dismiss these pieces of garden architecture as toys which do not merit further attention. This is wrong. Although no enlightened person would consider these works classical, nevertheless they were taken seriously as classical ornaments. The material is still false, on the other hand the effect is genuine. Buildings which have enjoyed the respect of the greatest minds of the time in their halcyon days, are not entirely absurd. Two days after his arrival in Rome, Goethe went out to the Villa Borghese [141], which completely won his heart and gave him rich poetic inspiration. As far as I can see, he did not speak directly in his letters of either the Temple of Aesculapius or of Faustina, but his friend Moritz, his escort on many a walk in this park, has described with enthusiasm the milieu around the first mentioned shrine by the lake, and without doubt these scenes also appealed to Goethe. We are justified in imagining that he observed and appreciated artificial antiquity. He completed "Iphigenie", his purely classical work (January 1787) at the Villa Borghese [142], the witch scene in "Faust I" was also written here, and "Egmont", which was reported as being finished on August 11th of the same year, was partly composed under the pines out there. After an evening walk around the villa he wrote to Frau von Stein: "Gleich vier herrliche Tableaux habe ich gefunden, die man nur abschreiben dürfte, wenn man's könnte. Auf eben dem Spaziergange machte ich Anstalten Egmont zu endigen" [143].

The "tableaux", meaning picturesque scenes in the garden, which Goethe found good enough to write home about, were presumably composed by More (whom the poet visited) [144]. "Erhabener Geist, Du gabst mir, gabst mir alles, warum ich bat" – the magnificent monologue in "Faust" – was written in Rome. If it is true that this was conceived in the atmosphere of Prince Borghese's park, which had been laid out by a Scottish painter and was enlivened by very artificial temples, it is rather amazing. Many years later, in 1804, Goethe received a letter from his friend Karl Wilhelm von Humboldt, who at that time lived in the same house in Rome as Thorvaldsen. The Prussian scholar wrote that he often had to bite back his anger when foreigners expressed surprise that the Romans did not lay out more "English gardens", and when the only reason they put forward for giving the area around the lake at the Villa Borghese its due, was "because, after all, there are artificial ruins there". The aversion to a sentimental atmosphere in parks – says Humboldt caustically – is just "one of the most striking instances of the Romans' healthy common sense" [145]. If the city's own sons did not appreciate simulated antiquity as much as their guests did, it was because their tact was better developed than the latter's "taste". Perhaps it is more reverent to sell oil in a ruin than to fake columns and write poetic elegies about them. However, the foreigners performed the miracles of love and made even the banal scintillate. We are reminded of the process in the psychology of passion which Stendhal calls *cristallisation*.

Once when the young Thorvaldsen strolled along the side of the lake at the Villa Borghese, he met Frederikke Brun and the sweet Ida. The artist had both the ideal landscape and the antique temple at hand – and

205. *The Pyramid of Cestius.*

207. *Clearing in Villa Doria-Pamphili.*

208. *Broken column on the Palatine (Palazzo dei Flavi).*

now a muse came along! Straightaway he lifted Ida up on to a branch and made her assume graceful attitudes. She wanted to get down again, but Bertel did not want to lose his tableau and pleaded: "Oh, just a few more poses . . ." [146]. The founder of Neo-classicism's pure plastic art was delighted by a bogus temple and an insipid girl. The style was so overwhelming, for better or for worse. When Oehlenschläger remembered Rome when he was back home enjoying the Danish summer, it was mainly the Villa Borghese which came into his mind – and he mentions the two seductive temples as the principle works in the park, and indeed as the main monuments of the city. This is done in the poem "Retrospect of Rome". While he gazes upon his own beloved garden beneath the beech-trees, he finds something missing all the same:

> No pale and shining statue in the boscage,
> No temple to Asklepios, he whose aspect
> Can heal the broken heart by mere observing.
>
> Nor see I loving memory of Faustina,
> Of Antoninus, no tall columns rising,
> No lovely ruin to stir a deep emotion.

But he did have a temple to Apis.

The "Egyptian pylons" at the Villa Borghese were quite new when Eckersberg described them (1814). He, who had revelled in Denmark's Romantic gardens – Liselund, Sanderumgaard, Enrum – and had sketched a "ruined" colonnade in the Parc Monceau, now stood with the same gravity before the Egyptian pastiche as in the arcades of the Colosseum and by the Pyramid of Cestius. Eckersberg was not easily impressed but for him the pylons possessed an objective truth, for they were solid, well formed. He might well have made a painting of "The Mediaeval Citadel", actually the Villa Pinciana's most genuine curiosity in architecture (Pl. 212). Its fortificatory style has some similarity with the barrier walls of the villa, and the moss-grown stucco harmonized well with the greensward, the fallen cones from the pines above, crunching in the grass. Perhaps the castle housed wheelbarrows and such like. Artists have since, to this very day, used it as a studio and thus filled it with new illusions.

The perfect masterpiece in delusiory antiquity was the creation of the museum as an independent structure. In contrast to the construction of summerhouses, this process was entirely Roman and on a grand scale. Its historical development is well known [147], but an interpretation of its ideas is called for. We must feel our way into the concepts which brought about the classical monument of the genre: the Vatican Museum. Here too, development was determined by changes in the nature of the cult.

It would hardly be wrong to say that every Roman of standing at that time possessed antique sculptures; in many cases they could be dug up from the ground he owned. The sculptures of antiquity were highly valued by aristocrats because of their age and their excellent decorative features. Therefore they found their proper setting in the yard and vestibule of the palace, in corridors and on the main stairway – not to mention the villa garden. The best collections of antiques in the Renaissance period were housed in the courtyard of the palace and the garden behind [148], and this tradition was continued. Statues of toga-clad figures in the vestibule were just as feudal as the coat of arms over the portal, and it was elegant to cover the walls of the courtyard with fragments of friezes, with sarcophagus reliefs and inscriptions (cf. Pal. Mattei di Giove); similarly the walls of the finest rooms of the palace were hung with close-set paintings. These paintings and sculptures were regarded by their patrician owners as furnishings rather than actual collections of objets d'art. Rarely was any attempt made to classify the items by grouping, and in general the owner's knowledge of their artistic merit was slight. He paid a *guardaroba* to know what was necessary. Only the foreigners who managed to get into the palace took the works seriously. But they were odd.

No normal person bothered about style or school, and the cultured amateurs tried merely to recognize ancient myths or fables in the reliefs and to identify portraits of famous historical figures – in so far as they fixed their attention on individual pieces at all, and were not merely satisfied with seeing them *en gros* as a picturesque decoration. The numerous antiquities, both in private as well as papal possession, were visual aids in a course for philologians. Men of the world – who were always the majority of visitors in those days – experienced pleasure by looking at the imposing spread but were otherwise content to reiterate a few of the particularly illustrious names of emperors and generals to be found among the busts. The owner of the palace was of course able to appreciate the statue of a Pompeius Maximus, for it was the symbol of his own family's power and was reckoned among the penates of the house in a wider context. The Jutland squire in the days of Christian VI was similarly proud of a bird of prey nailed to his gate, or of a successful stallion from his own stud – people wanted to see it.

In short, the Roman collections of antiquities had a cultural position which was determined by feudal attitudes from above, by academic ones from the side. They were credited as decorative jewels inherited by the family, and were revered as evidence of a glorious past in the history of mankind. But – the sculptures were also art with a capital A. When this was realized, it proclaimed the ideal. This unique event, motivated by Winckelmann, was in the 1760's the ultimate revelation of truth. Accordingly there was only one god, and only one prophet: the man with the text and the spade. The fortuitously growing collection of antiquities could now expect to be ennobled to the status of a *"Museum"*. This very word contains the elements of a mission, a call, which the word "Collection" lacks. Once the idol was set up, the priests of the cult present, and the congregation constituted, the museum quite logically became a temple. And this was a revolutionary event. Up till now pictorial art had been localized to an aristocratic interior – under a roof or under the open sky – in which one lived ceremoniously, possibly enjoyably, to the accompaniment of painting and sculpture – or which one merely took for granted. Now the visitor had a weighty responsibility and was kept on his toes. In the museum, life meant looking at art. And laughter was out of place.

The function of the museum as a temple, housing antiques, brought with it a correspondingly new form of building. We have previously mentioned (p. 486) that the portico is the archetype for museums exhibiting Roman sculpture. As a loggia it faced a garden or courtyard. The detached arcade is a showcase, open to the light, protective in bad weather, in which the selected object is placed only to be viewed from the front. During the extension of the papal collection of antiques in the

Palazzo dei Conservatori on the Capitol, the motif of the arch was used symbolically, as it were officially, in the portico, which according to the inscription was erected in 1720 as the back wall of the courtyard. The following year the Egyptian statues, unearthed in a vineyard near the Via Salaria in 1715, and the "Roma triumphans", [149] were brought here. Along with the portico the nymphaeum was often used for the exhibition of ancient sculpture, both types of building being extremely decorative, even "profane", emphasizing works of art as if by the grace of God. Immediately after Clement XI had erected his Capitoline portico, his nephew Alessandro Albani had the above mentioned nymphaeum built around a statue of Caesar in the courtyard of the Collegio Nazareno. The next step in the development was made by Clement XII, the founder of the *Museo Capitolino,* when he closed the courtyard of the palace with walls containing a niche in which the river god "Marforio" reclines behind a fountain. Here the nymphaeum motif is reinterpreted as a memorial for this popular figure. Pasquino's collocutor was not merely an antiquity but also a Roman folk-hero on the Capitol. The rooms in the palace were soon crowded, thanks to the abundant acquisitions of Benedict XIV. "I have spent a couple of hours here," wrote Barthélemy in 1755, "and I have seen nothing. The enormous accumulation destroys all pleasure" [150]. A depository indoors, decorative memorials to ancestors in the courtyard. Feudalism was still present even in the public exhibition of antiquities; the museum was as yet not ready for the innovation of a complete building to house the cult around its ideas, to escape from the exteriors of an old palace to an architecture with its own centre of gravity. Even the new Villa Albani was, in spite of everything, the summerhouse of a grand seigneur ornamented with anticaglie; Smollett complained that in its core there was nothing to be found but "carving and gilding, which is a kind of gingerbread work" [151].

But the idea of the pure, austere museum was developing [152]. It was first given concrete form when ancient fragments were collected together and were given sanctuary in a reconstructed ancient building. "The temple" in the figurative meaning of the word sought and found a temple in the tangible sense. When Montesquieu was in Rome (1729) he reflected as follows: "An academy of sculpture (une école de sculpture)

209. *"The temple of Faustina and Antoninus" in Villa Borghese.*

210. *The Capitol, illuminated.*

211b. *Central arcade in the Casino of Villa Albani.*

211a. *Portico in the courtyard of the Palazzo dei Conservatori.*

212. *The Gothic Citadel in Villa Borghese.*

needs a space such as that of the Pantheon, where a large number of statues could be set up requiring only light from above" [153]. This is an important pronouncement; "the Academy in Rome", the ideal museum, should be a Rotunda, that is a temple of the most superior type, with majestic authority, completely shut off from the bustle of the world, only with light from on high. This very beam of light penetrating down into the cylinder was highly suggestive, making both the statues and the public interesting – both types of figures took on a completely different aura which was almost an apotheosis. Smollett as a practical man would naturally have wanted the hole in the ceiling covered with a glass pane, but otherwise he found the interior of the Rotunda "more and more gloomy and sepulchral" each time he visited it [154]; such a chiaroscuro fitted a temple to the art of the ancients perfectly. Harsdorff, who went to Rome shortly before Smollett, made a drawing of the Pantheon's interior which strongly emphasized the dramatic effect of light which he saw as Piranesi saw it. Another artist, Norbert von Grund, declared straight out that the Pantheon was principally visited by the fair sex because of the flattering effect of its light, for faces became much more beautiful inside it [155]. Certainly, the Rotunda had all the qualities favourable for a museum.

Ten years after Montesquieu had put forward his ideas, de Brosses suggested in a letter that the papal collections of antiques should be removed to the Vatican, where they could join the statues in the courtyard of the Belvedere [156]. And this is exactly what happened. The private wishes of both these intelligent Frenchmen echoed the feeling of the time, and were fulfilled, because the idea about the "Rotunda" also became a reality. *Museo Pio-Clementino,* the main part of the world's greatest museum of antiquities, was founded in 1770 by Clement XIV with Cardinal Braschi as the driving force. After his accession to the papal throne in 1775 Braschi (Pius VI) completed this great work. A start was made by establishing a gallery for statues in Innocent VIII's villa behind the Cortile del Belvedere, the hall being divided up by arches borne on columns of the type known from the Capitol and the Villa Albani. Also the courtyard of the Belvedere was given an inner portico of arcades and four corner chambers in which the most renowned works (such as the Apollo Belvedere and Laokoon) were given the place of honour. "The premises are not sufficient," wrote Roland de la Platière after paying a visit there in 1777, "and extensions are now being made" [157]. As the existing structure was nearly bursting at the seams, the job of putting up new building units was tackled – a strange group of well-formed members, each one constituting one room of a museum, each a temple on its own. We can list these premises, which have greater fame than cathedrals. There is the *Sala a Croce Greca,* built in the form of a cross with equal arms; the *Sala delle Muse,* octagonal; the *Sala Rotonda,* the domed main hall – all designed by Michelangelo Simonetti – also Camporese's *Sala della Biga.* The two last interiors were called by contemporaries "the two Rotundas" – thus being classified as among the most noble [158], for their close relationship with the Pantheon was acknowledged.

Now the goal had been reached, the classical museum arisen. It was composed of rooms given an antique character, all of which had the reputed correctness of a pastiche and also boasted genuine fragments included in their structure. Connoisseurs and enthusiasts were thrilled, for here was peace and no conversation, nothing but study and worship. In 1785 the "Sala Rotonda" aroused awe in Juan Andres by its majesty, but he had to admit that the height of the room detracted from the "colossal statues" as they seemed dwarfed by it [159]. Nemesis was on the heels of the antiques; they were being overworked by having to be ideals all the time and having to react to the pretentions of the milieu by being in better taste. How tiring it must have been for the canonized statue always to be alone in its chapel, like a lion in a cage, when once it had stood amid bustling people in the market-place or under the cedar trees of the park! How sad for the bust of an out-and-out original to have to be eternally put on show on a shelf and jostled by copies. The goal was not merely reached, it was overrun. These new temples in the Vatican, gleaming white in Carrara marble, polished to perfection, were the real religious buildings of the mature Classicism of that period. They were draughty. In actual fact they introduce a new era into the history of culture.

While church building was on the wane – in Rome! – this museum propaganda began to have its effect. In the long view it was far more dangerous than the activities carried on from the Missionary College in the Piazza di Spagna, for the idols of taste do not have the constancy of a living god. Now priests and monks were to be sent to the collections of antiques, willy-nilly.

Let us look at a contemporary genre picture from 1787, described by Moritz: "The monks can always get in free. I have often seen a flock of Franciscans wandering here with their shepherd. They always paused longest at the figures of animals and could not admire a skilfully executed ox enough, and then they moved off" [160]. The antique animals arranged in the *Sala degli Animali* were not authentic. New temples for old – just schoolrooms. We are justified in this opinion, but we must not forget that immortal works of art were also found here, and that it gave mature people of standing great pleasure to see them.

Once again we perceive this dualism of false and genuine in Neo-antiquity. For what was absurd in the cult, and this was all too visible when looked at dispassionately, became dimmed by the contemporary atmosphere, quite literally – and was dissolved in the chiaroscuro conjured up around the sculptures. An essential part of the secret of man's profound infatuation with the art of Antiquity was, in our opinion, that he did not always see the rooms of the museum in the ordinary light of day, the soberness of which was hostile to all illusions. He wanted a phenomenal light, the glow of the sacrificial fire and the flame of the altar. When these were lit, the circular domed hall became indeed a temple, warm and living. Right from the earliest times of the Vatican Museum it was a practice that visitors frequented it after darkness had fallen and saw the sculptures by the light of torches. Tourists made up small parties to experience the nocturnal magic of the museum together. They performed their devotions in the "Rotunda" and felt that the classical figures were now more intimate, that they had passion, humanity, life, and were not merely fragments and stones. And before the hour of departure from Rome, all people of sensibility went to the Vatican for a farewell celebration by torchlight.

This pleasant and wise custom was no doubt started in artistic circles. They were accustomed to drawing their models in artificial light. This old practice, used in the ateliers of sculptors and small academies, was now transferred to the service of high ideals. Round about the same time, in the second half of the 1770's, the *Moccoli* festivities were instituted on the last evening of carnival. The swarm of people on the Corso lit small wax tapers, which flickered in their thousands. It was as if the Romans followed the masquerade to its grave, with shimmering lights [161]. In those days, the age of tense and overflowing feelings, candles were always lit whenever something unusual was to be witnessed. To its traditional torchlight festivities, Rome now added others that seemed to be mystery plays, rather than entertainment. When the catacombs of the past were visited, this took place by the sombre light of torches. The graves of the Scipios were a great attraction, having been discovered in the Vigna Sassi in 1780 near the first stretch of the Via Appia [162]. Climbing down into these grottos, filled with magic miasma, was a pilgrimage to heathen crypts.

Zoëga had seen the Museo Pio-Clementino by torchlight in 1781. It was in this place in 1783 that Meyer discovered that the works of art gained a great deal by being seen in artificial light, showing themselves thus in their greatest beauty. The marble seemed to come alive in the glimmering glow, Apollo soars, the muscles move in Laokoon's tortured body – "nothing stimulates the imagination so much as the sight of this suffering man at a late hour of night" [163]. Not merely the sculptures, but also the chilly halls came to life. Ceilings and domes rose high in the darkness, strange shadows were cast on the walls. Münter too, took part in this cult. On one occasion in March 1785 he trudged to the Vatican with a large party of Danes to enjoy the great experience, but to his annoyance he found "alles schon besetzt" by the Russian ambassador. They had to return home in foul weather without having accomplished anything [164]. But at other times he had more success there, and discovered that the Apollo Belvedere regained his full, blooming youth, like a vision beneath the restless light of torches [165]. Statues must always be looked at in this way, decided Moritz [166]. Goethe convinces posterity of this by his words on the subject – the great works of art are interpreted in the chiaroscuro "as a dream which gradually dies away" (wie ein nach und nach erlöschender Traum) [167].

In this way, life came to the temple and light to the museum. The gifted sculptors were the high priests of the cult. Madame de Staël persuaded Canova to show his works to Corinna and Lord Nelvil in his studio by candlelight [168], Sergel showed Francisco Miranda the same courtesy (1787), both among the casts in the Stockholm Academy of Art as well as in his own studio [169]. Thorvaldsen himself used candlelight in the Roman museum and in his "Studies" at the Piazza Barberini [170]. The custom lived on in Rome down to the time of Pius IX.

Scenes from antiquity took on a pulsating life in the half-lit darkness, and in an aura which the age craved to see around them. It was the human being himself who had animated the clay, because he had learnt to see as an artist. In the same spirit, people had made a harmonious whole of the fragment beneath wild plants and had ennobled ruins by giving them a landscape. These strange people of the decade before the Revolution could halt the pulse-beat of architecture in Rome and poison an optimistic art with utopias. But as poetic interpreters of the past they were creative. These everlasting dreamers made Rome a world stage, where, surrounded by ancient ruins, the spirits of light strove against the powers of darkness. The Colosseum was made to glow beneath the fiery clouds like a magic mountain to prove its bygone virility. The Capitol was illuminated with blazing barrels of pitch (Pl. 210). The palaces and steps thus gained a majesty which can only be compared with a vision. At night the shades of the ancient Romans met with Michelangelo and the godless one himself.

Goethe's farewell to Rome was preceeded in a particularly solemn manner by three nights of clear moonlight [171]. On the fourth night he went out into the city. "After wandering along the whole of the long Corso, probably for the last time, I went up to the Capitol, which stood there like a fairy palace in the wilderness. The statue of Marcus Aurelius reminded me of the commandant in Don Giovanni, and made the wanderer understand that he was doing something uncommon."

BIBLIOGRAPHY AND NOTES
INDEX

BIBLIOGRAPHY AND NOTES

THE GREAT MOTIFS

[1] Michel de Montaigne: Journal du voyage en Italie, ed. Edmond Pilon (Paris 1932), 155. – [2] Francesco Scotti: Itinerario ouero Nuova Descrittione de viaggi principali d'Italia (Rome 1650), 160; on Baccano's bad reputation cf Edoardo Martinori: Via Cassia antica e moderna (Rome 1930), 25-27. – [3] Nouveau Voyage d'Italie, fait en l'année 1688 (the Hague 1691), II, 122. – [4] Ludvig Holbergs Memoirer, ed. F. J. Billeskov Jansen (Copenhagen 1943), 61, 265. – [5] Des Präsidenten De Brosses' vertrauliche Briefe aus Italien an seine Freunde in Dijon 1739-1740, ed. W. Schwartzkopf (Munich 1918), I, 274. Several editions of this classic book have been consulted, but in the following is referred to the splendidly annotated German edition. – [6] Voyage en Italie, ou Considérations sur l'Italie (Lausanne 1791), 36. – [7] Italienische Reise, Oct. 27. 1786. – [8] Letter to M. De Fontanes Jan. 10. 1804, quoted from Chateaubriand: Voyage en Italie, Edition Mermod (Lausanne 1944), 153. – [9] Corinne ou L'Italie (Paris 1807), II, 170. – [10] The expression is attributable to Stendhal, cf Correspondance de Stendhal, edd. Ad. Paupe et P.-A. Cheramy, II (Paris 1908), 397. – [11] Improvisatoren, Kap. V (Campagnen). – [12] Romerske Dagbøger, edd. Paul V. Rubow og H. Topsøe-Jensen (Copenhagen 1947), 15 (Oct. 26. 1833). – [13] Pictures from Italy (London 1846), 163. – [14] On the Campagna in general see Friedrich Noack: Die römische Campagna (Rome 1910); M. Mackeprang in "Rom og Danmark", III (Copenhagen 1942), 1-24; Silvio Negro: Seconda Roma (Milan 1943), 55-82; Carl Fries: Vägen till Rom (Sth. 1953), 132-204. – [15] Johann Caspar Goethe: Viaggio in Italia (1740), ed. A. Farinelli (Rome 1932), I, 124. – [16] Thus Labat (Voyage en Espagne et en Italie, IV, Amsterdam 1731, 116-120), and A. C. Gierlew (Breve over Italien og Sicilien, II, Copenhagen 1807, 102). – [17] On these (ruins of Iseum and Serapeum) see Vilh. Lundström: Undersökningar i Roms Topografi (Göteborg 1929), 127 ff. Characteristic, because of the name too, is also Vicolo del Monticello between Piazza della Pilotta and Via dell' Umiltà. – [18] Louis Madelin: La Rome de Napoléon (Paris 1906), 236. – [19] An outline of the floodings of the Tiber in C. St. A. Bille: Erindringer fra Rejser i Italien (Copenhagen 1878), II, 376-379. Cf also A. von Reumont: Römische Briefe von einem Florentiner, II (Lpz. 1840), 317-318, and L. von Pastor: Die Stadt Rom zu Ende der Renaissance (Freiburg im Br. 1925), 25-26. – [20] Pietro Romano: Roma nelle sue strade e nelle sue piazze (Rome c. 1950), plate between p. 458 and p. 459; a number of watercolours by Roessler-Franz in Museo di Roma. – [21] Read F. Gregorovius' (1853) monograph on the ghetto in Wanderjahre in Italien, ed. Schillmann (Dresden 1925), 265-318, and Vilh. Bergsøe's excellent novel "Nemesis" (1911), which in part adapts impressions from this district on the river. – [22] Reproduced in Henrik Schück: Rom. En Vandring genom Seklerna (2. ed.), II, Stockholm 1923, Fig. 29. – [23] Christian Elling: Jardin i Rom (Studier fra Sprog- og Oldtidsforskning Nr. 193, Copenhagen 1943),

18-20. – [24] A couple of beautiful drawings by N. Tessin the Younger in Nationalmuseum, Stockholm. – [25] Mentioned on Nolli's map 1748; depicted on an etching by Bart. Pinelli. – [26] Burnet: Voyage de Suisse, d'Italie et de quelques endroits d'Allemagne ... fait ès années 1685-1686, 2. ed. (Rotterdam 1688), 399. – [27] On the fountains of Rome see M. Guidi: Le fontane barocche di Roma (Zürich 1917); Emil Zilliacus: Romerska Vandringar (Sth. 1950), 11-41. – [28] On the art of Roman town planning after the Renaissance see particularly Gustavo Giovannoni: Il quartiere romano del Rinascimento (Rome 1946); P. Romano: Il quartiere del Rinascimento (Rome 1938), 5-23; Piero Tomei: L'architettura a Roma nel Quattrocento (Rome 1942), 5-29; Hans Rose's monograph "Stadtanlage" in the 4. ed. of H. Wölfflin: Renaissance und Barock (Munich 1926), 216-244; Ragnar Josephson: Hur Rom byggdes under Renässans och Barock (Sth. 1926); subtle esthetic observations in Marcello Piacentini: Il volto di Roma (Rome 1944). – [29] Guglielmo Matthiae: Piazza del Popolo (Rome n. d., c. 1948), 9-10. – Lione Pascoli: Vite de' pittori, scultori ed architetti moderni, II (Rome 1736), 557. – [31] Cf H. Wölfflin: Renaissance und Barock, Chap. III. – [32] Promenades dans Rome, Nov. 17. 1827. – [33] Tagebuch des Herrn von Chantelou über die Reise des Cavaliere Bernini nach Frankreich, ed. H. Rose (Munich 1919), 60. – [34] Ibid., 213. – [35] Anatole France: Le Génie Latin (Paris 1917), the Preface. – [36] Resa till Italien, ed. Gunhild Bergh (Sth. 1925), 150, 152. – [37] Christian Elling: Det klassiske København (Copenhagen 1944), 74. – [38] Italienische Reise, Feb. 2. 1787. – [39] To regard the convex façade as a manneristic phenomenon is untenable; I am preparing a monograph on the motive as a phenomenon of the Roman Renaissance. – [40] Rome, Naples et Florence, edd. P. Arbelet & Ed. Champion, I (Paris 1919), 43-44. – [41] A View of Society and Manners in Italy, II (London 1783), 63-64. – [42] Observations sur l'Italie et sur les Italiens, II (Paris 1764), 366. In direct support of Grosley Stendhal states in his diary 1811, Sept. 20. about the Italians: "Ils sont très réservés et d'une politesse encore cérémonieuse". See also Giuseppe Gorani: Mémoires secrets et critiques des cours, des gouvernemens, et des moeurs des principaux états de l'Italie, II (Paris 1794), 138-139, and I. W. von Archenholtz: England und Italien, II[1] (Lpz. 1785), 207-212. – [43] Voyage en Espagne et en Italie, III (Amsterdam 1732), 150. – [44] Voyage d'un François en Italie, V (Paris 1769), 126 ff. – [45] An Account of the Manners and Customs of Italy, I (London 1770), the Preface. – [46] Lancelot Temple: A Short Ramble through some Parts of France and Italy (London 1771), 9-10. – [47] William Stewart Rose: Letters from the North of Italy (London 1819), I, 202. – [48] The expression is attributable to Paul V. Rubow. – [49] Hans Rose in H. Wölfflin: Renaissance und Barock (Munich 1926), 201-215.

THE CAPITAL OF CHRISTENDOM

[1] Ludvig von Pastor: Geschichte der Päpste, XV (Freiburg im Br. 1930), 356. – [2] Goethe: Ital. Reise, Sept. 17. 1786. – [3] K. L. Fernow: Sitten- und Kulturgemälde von Rom (Gotha 1802), 76-77. – [4] Particular attraction had the Del Divino Amore pilgrim's church, built in 1744, near Castel di Leva, Via Ardeatina (Edoardo Martinori: Lazio turrito, I, Rome 1933, 139-142; Pastor: Gesch. der Päpste, XVI[1], 106). – [5] Gonippo Morelli: Le corporazioni romane di arti e mestieri dal XIII al XIX secolo (Rome 1937). – [6] David Silvagni: La corte e la società nei secoli XVIII e XIX, 3. ed. (Rome 1884) I, 50-53. – [7] M. D'Armailhac: L'église national de Saint-Louis des Français à Rome (Rome 1894). – [8] J. Schmidlin: Gesch. der deutschen National-Kirsche in Rom, S. Maria dell' Anima (Freiburg 1906); G. von Graevenitz: Deutsche in Rom (Lpz. 1902), 101-103; Fr. Noack: Das Deutschtum in Rom

(Berlin & Lpz. 1927), I, spec. 149-156, 249-255. – [9] Carl Justi: Diego Velázques und sein Jahrhundert, Ed. Phaidon (Zürich 1933), 284, 288. – [10] Cf M. Loret: Gli artisti polacchi a Roma nel Settecento (Milan 1929). – [11] F. S. I.: La questione di S. Girolamo dei Schiavoni in Roma (Rome 1901); Pietro Paolo Trompeo: Piazza Margana (Rome 1942), 28-35 (Ricordi di Schiavonia). – [12] Oreste Tencajoli: Le chiese nazionali italiane in Roma (Rome 1928). – [13] Pietro Romano: Il quartiere del Rinascimento (Rome 1938), 83-84. – [14] The present façade, in cold pseudo-renaissance, is built in 1853, according to the inscription by Ferdinand II of the Two Sicilies; cf also Tenjacoli: Le chiese nazionali, 104. – Juvara made a design in 1709 which was not executed. – [15] Aristide D. Trani: Gli ordini religiosi a Roma (Rome 1931); I have often consulted Hippolyte Hélyot: Ausführl. Gesch. aller geistlichen und weltlichen Kloster- und Ritterorden, I-VIII (Lpz. 1753-1756). A short survey in Peter Schindler: Vesterledens Munkevæsen, III (Copenhagen 1939), 73-107, 327-332. – [16] An old photography of Piazza dei Cappuccini, which has fallen a victim to Via Vittorio Veneto is reproduced in Silvio Negro: Seconda Roma (Milan 1943), plate facing p. 352. – [17] Voyages du Père Labat, III (Amsterdam 1731), 198. – [18] Hartmann Grisar S. J.: Das Missale im Lichte röm. Stadtgeschichte. Stationen, Perikopen, Gebräuche (Freiburg im Br. 1925). – [19] P. Romano & P. Partini: Piazza Navona (Rome n. d.), 160. – [20] W. Müller: Rom, Römer und Römerinnen, II (Berlin 1820), 38 f.; C. St. A. Bille: Erindringer fra Rejser i Italien, II (Copenhagen 1878), 245; Vilh. Bergsøe: Under Palmer og Pinier (Copenhagen 1905), 50-51; Louis Bobé: F. Brun og kendes Kreds hjemme og ude (Copenhagen 1910), 113. – [21] Works, IV (London 1871), 525. – [22] Ital. Reise, Jan. 18. 1787. See also Fr. von Matthisson: Erinnerungen, IV (Zürich 1815), 215-218; Fr. Brun: Prosaische Schriften, III (Zürich 1800), 214 f.; H. C. Andersen: En Digters Bazar (Saml. Skr., 2. ed., VII, 111-112); Carsten Hauch: Minder fra min første Udenlandsrejse (Copenhagen 1871), 282; L. Bobé in "Rom og Danmark", I (Copenhagen 1935), 334-335. – [23] On the "Bocca della Verità" see a chapter full of detailed and flurried wisdom in G. M. Crescimbeni: L'Istoria di S. Maria in Cosmedin (Rome 1715), 27-37. – [24] Cf Labat, III, 194-195. – [25] Reisen der Lady Morgan. Italien, IV (Lpz. 1823), 9-10. – [26] Em. St. Hermidad [Vald. Thisted]: Romerske Mosaikker (Copenhagen 1851), 28-30. – [27] On Festaroloes see Labat, III, 126; Nic. Zabaglia: Contignationes ac pontes (Rome 1743); Lalande, IV, 547-548. On Zabaglia see also: [J. Russel:] Letters from a young painter (London 1750), 133-135. – [28] Sam. Sharp: Letters from Italy in the Years 1765 and 1766, 2. ed. (London 1767), 202. – [29] The excommunication was brought to an end during Clement XIV in 1770 (G. G. Adlerbeth: Gustaf III's Resa i Italien. Anteckn., ed. H. Schück, Svenska Memoarer och Bref V, Sth. 1902, 176; J. J. Volkmann: Hist.-krit. Nachrichten von Italien, II, Lpz. 1770, 699; cf Sharp op.cit., 201). – [30] The procession in the colonnade is depicted on a painting by Luigi Fioroni in the Thorvaldsens Museum; François Deseine: Rome moderne, V (Leiden 1713), 1357-1366. – [31] Epistola CCLXIII (L. Holbergs Epistler, ed. F. J. Billeskov Jansen, III, Copenhagen 1947, 281). – [32] Wm. M. Cooper: Flagellation and the Flagellants. A History of the Rod (London n. d.), 117-118; J. C. Goethe, I, 247. – [33] Labat, op.cit. IV, 66 (Naples). – [34] [De Blainville]: Voiage historique et politique, II (Frankfurt 1737), 162. – [35] Correspondence of Thomas Gray, edd. Paget Toynbee & Leonard Whibley, I (Oxford 1935), 147. – [36] Santo Domingo: Rom wie es ist (Lpz. 1825), 43-48; J. G. Keyssler: Neueste Reisen, I (Hannover 1740), 619. – [37] Richard: Description histor. et critique de l'Italie, V (Paris 1766), 250. – [38] Ridolfino Venuti: Descrizione topografica e istorica di Roma moderna (Rome 1766), 398. – [39] Charles-Louis Baron de Pöllnitz: Mémoires contenant les observations qu'il a faites dans ses voyages, 2. ed., III (Amsterdam 1735), 65-67; Venuti, 401; Keyssler, I, 698. – [40] Venuti,

229. – [41] Aug. J. C. Hare: Walks in Rome, 5. ed., II (London 1875), 175 (Citat by About). – [42] Cf H. C. Andersen: Romerske Dagbøger, Jan. 24. 1834. – [43] Keyssler, I, 640; Lalande, IV, 133. – [44] Voyages de Montesquieu, ed. A. de Montesquieu, I (Bordeaux 1894), 217. – [45] Labat, IV, 20. – [46] Ibid.; cf Goethe: Ital. Reise, Dec. 24. 1786; Christopher Hervey: Letters from Portugal, Spain, Italy and Germany in the Years 1759, 1760, and 1761, II (London 1785), 525, 535, III, 282; F. J. L. Meyer: Darstell. aus Italien (Berlin 1792), 181-184; K. Ph. Moritz: Reisen eines Deutschen, II (Berlin 1793), 203. – [47] Guidi: Lettres contenant le journal d'un voyage fait à Rome en 1793, II (Genève 1783), 135. – [48] On this idea see Christian Elling: Operahus og Casino. Studier i det ital. Logetheater 1670-1830 (Copenhagen 1942), 40-44. – [49] G. Baretti: Les Italiens ou moeurs et coutumes d'Italie (Genève & Paris 1773), 292-294. – [50] J. W. von Archenholtz: England und Italien, II^1 (Lpz. 1785), 227-228. – [51] Lione Pascoli: Vite de' Pittori, Scultori ed Architetti moderni, I (Rome 1730), 324. – [52] Pastor, XIV^1, 626. – [53] "non avesse gran ingenio alle fabbriche" (Pascoli, I, 311). – [54] Ragnar Josephson: Barocken (Sth. 1948), 192. – [55] Fil. Baldinucci: Vita des G. L. Bernini, ed. A. Riegl (Vienna 1912), 230. – [56] Pascoli, I, 311. – [57] Pascoli, I, 323; Tagebuch des Herrn von Chantelou, ed. Hans Rose (Munich 1919), 210, 368. – [58] Tagebuch des Herrn von Chantelou, 210. – [59] Ugo Donati: Artisti ticinesi a Roma (Bellinzona 1942), 264. – [60] M. de Rossi had then, according to Pascoli, been 25 years in Bernini's service. – [61] Ed. Coudenhove-Erthal: Carlo Fontana und die Architektur des röm. Spätbarocks (Vienna 1930), 133-149: a very painstaking monograph. – [62] Donati: Artisti ticinesi, 263. – [63] Ragnar Josephson: Tessin, I (Sth. 1930), 52-55. – [64] Osvald Sirén: Nicodemus Tessin d. y.'s Studieresor (Sth. 1914), 47. – [65] Pascoli, I, 317. – [66] G. Donati in "L'Urbe", 1940, 20-26. – [67] For the last mentioned family he built the beautiful church on the square in Vignanello (dated 1723 on the façade); the high altar in S. Venanzio, which he designed, was paid for by Marchesa Girolamo Ruspoli (Venuti, 344). – [68] Vite, II, 557-558. – [69] He lived his last years in Vicolo del Governo Vecchio, on the corner of Strada Papale, opposite the Governor's Palace (P. Romano: Roma nelle sue strade, Rome n. d., 241). – [70] Hans Sedlmayr: Fischer von Erlach der ältere (Munich 1925), 3. – [71] Bruno Grimschitz: J. L. v. Hildebrandts künstl. Entwicklung bis zum Jahre 1725 (Vienna 1922), 72-73. – [72] Coudenhove-Erthal: Carlo Fontana, 140. – [73] Christian Elling: Tegninger af Oppenordt i Marselis' Studiebog (Architektens Maanedshefte, 1930, 92-104). – [74] Fr. Weilbach ibid. – [75] Correspondance des Directeurs de l'Académie de France à Rome avec les Surintendants des Bâtiments, edd. A. de Montaiglon & J. Guiffrey, II, Nr. 934. In the following quoted: Corresp. – [76] N. Tessin d. y.'s Studieresor (Sth. 1914), 43. – [77] Bart. Nogara: S. S. Ambrogio e Carlo al Corso (Rome n. d.), 14-15. – [78] Deseine remarks (I, 36) that "two palaces symmetrically arranged" on both sides of S. Carlo endow this with much grace. The French bookseller realizes these contraposti and perceives, in accordance with his age, a unity in the layout; a point of view which is now forgotten is revealed in his cliché. – [79] Pastor, XIV^2, 691; Roma moderna (1727), 219; Deseine, IV, 886-887; Venuti, 404. – [80] Deseine, I, 52; Venuti, 173. – [81] Venuti, 265. – [82] Donati: Artisti ticinesi, 274. – [83] Coudenhove-Erthal (op.cit., 51) is talking about "ein Janusgesicht des Kunstwollens Fontanas". – [84] Cardinal Gastaldi's sister was prioress of the convent (Deseine, IV, 914). – [85] Zeitschr. für Kunstgesch., III (1934), 305. – [86] Cf a fine analysis in Vilh. Wanscher: Architekturens Historie, III (Copenhagen 1931), 314. – [87] Coudenhove-Erthal, 53; Donati: Artisti ticinesi, 274. – [88] Cf also Pietro da Cortona's project for an exedra-building on Piazza Colonna (Antonio Muñoz: Pietro da Cortona, Bibl. d'Arte illustr., 1. series, part. 6, 15). – [89] Coudenhove-Erthal, 52. – [90] Francesco Milizia: Memorie degli architetti antichi e moderni, 4. ed.,

II (Bassano 1785), 216 ("di pessimo gusto"). – [91] Bruno Massi: Le chiese dei Serviti (Rome 1941), 33-34. – [92] Nationalmuseum, the Tessin-collection; published by Josephson in Tessin I, fig. 51. – [93] Coudenhove-Erthal, 21-22; according to Donati: Artisti ticinesi, 265. – [94] G. Giovannoni in "Capitolium", V, 1929, 594 ff. – [95] Coudenhove-Erthal, Pl. 2, cf Fig. 8. – [96] Pascoli, I, 317; G. Vasi: Delle Magnificenze di Roma antica e moderna states 1685 as the year of building; Letarouilly: Les édifices de Rome moderne, III, Pl. 279. – [97] Labat, III, 102. – [98] Pastor, XV, 8. – [99] Ibid., 373. – [100] Corresp. III, No. 1086. – [101] Donati: Artisti ticinesi, 378-380. – [102] F. Clementi: Il Carnevale Romano, I (Rome 1939), 635. – [103] See also Ths. Ashby & S. Wesh in The Town-Planning Review 1927. – [104] Corresp. VI No. 2607; was architect for Rioni Monti, Trevi and Ripa (H. Egger: Röm. Veduten, II, Vienna 1931, 29). – [105] Clementi: Il Carnevale Romano, II, 6. – [106] Corresp. III No. 1158; a member of the S. Luca Academy 1696; U. Valeri: L'ultimo allievo del Bernini, Antonio Valeri, 2. ed. (Rome 1946). – [107] Not even mentioned in Thieme & Becker; the following information is given in Labat, IV, 50-51; see also V. Golzio: Il Seicento e il Settecento (Turin 1950), 151. – [108] Mortier: Histoire des Maîtres Généraux de l'Ordre des Frères Prêcheurs, VII (Paris 1914), 71-75. – [109] P. Romano & G. Partini: Piazza di Spagna (Rome n. d.), 68. – [110] On R. see Furio Fasolo: Le chiese di Roma nel Settecento, I (Rome 1949), 121-122 and elsewhere. – [111] Ibid. – [112] Ibid. – [113] He patronized Andrea Pozzo (Pascoli, II, 265). – [114] "Filippo Juvara", I (Milan 1937), Pl. 31. – [115] Aug. Telluccini: L'arte dell' architetto Filippo Juvara in Piemonte (Turin 1926), Fig. pag. 7. – [116] Correspond. III, No. 1343, 1350; on J.'s employment with Ottoboni see also No. 1363, 1382, 1385, 1390. – [117] Ludvig Holbergs Memoirer, ed. F. J. Billeskov Jansen (Copenhagen 1943), 73. – [118] J. Addison: Remarks on several Parts of Italy in the Years 1701, 1702, 1703 (London 1753), 211. – [119] Ibid. 110. – [120] Mentioned by La Teulière in 1696 (Coudenhove-Erthal, 88). – [121] Egger: Röm. Veduten, II, 19. – [122] Bernini's opinion of the Colosseum: Tageb. des Herrn von Chantelou, 15, 16, 108, 213; on Fontana's project: Coudenhove-Erthal, 97-102, Pl. 41, Fig. 35. – [123] C. Elling in "Artes", VII, 1939, 67 ff. – [124] Roma moderna (1727), 210, with an etching of the church after the rebuilding; Cecconi: Memoire storiche della diaconia di S. Teodoro Martire (Rome 1716). – [125] Pastor, XV, 375. The Pope also visited S. Teodoro on Nov. 10. 1703. – [126] Titulus S. Clementis was already mentioned in the time of Constantine (Chr. Huelsen: Le chiese di Roma nel Medio Evo, Florence 1927, 238). – [127] Ph. Rondininus: De S. Clemente Papa et Martyre eiusqve Basilica in Urbe Roma (Rome 1706), dedication on pag. XV ff. – [128] Donati, 378-379. – [129] Labat, VII, 46, (leaves Civitavecchia); III, 197. – [130] Lalande, IV, 526-527. – [131] Fasolo: Le chiese di Roma nel Settecento, 92; Roma moderna (1727), 134. – [132] Reproduced in Coudenhove-Erthal, Fig. 38-42. – [133] Emile Mâle: Rome et ses vielles (Paris 1942), 202-205. – [134] Venuti, 432. – [135] Lalande, IV, 354. – [136] Edward Wright: Some Observations made in travelling through France, Italy, etc., in the Years 1720, 1721, and 1722, 2. ed. (London 1764), 212; Venuti, 139. – [137] C. Bildt: Svenska Minnen och Märken i Rom (Sth. 1900), 34-37. – [138] Deseine, II, 465; Adlerbeth: Gustaf III's Resa, 196, states 1706. Described in J. J. Björnståhl: Briefe auf seinen ausländ. Reisen, 2. ed., II (Lpz. & Rostock 1780), 110-114. – [139] Vasi: Delle Magnificenze, IV, Fol. 36. – [140] Axel Boëthius: Bland svenska Minnen i Rom (Göteborg 1946), Frontispiece. – [141] Gustaf III's Resa i Italien, 196. – [142] Mélanges de la Faculté orient., V (Beyrouth 1910), 1-36; Venuti, 507. – [143] "Filippo Juvara" I, Pl. 78-99. – [144] Donati: Artisti ticinesi, 373. – [145] Roma mod. (1727), 204-205; Donati, 379; Vasi: Delle Magnif., III, Pl. 53; Lalande, IV, 421; Corresp. VI No. 2431 (examined by the Pope in June 1722). – [146] Venuti, plate facing p. 399. – [147]

Donati, 373-374; Pastor, XV, 379-380. – [148] Donati, 392. – [149] "Sor Maria Arcangela Muti Abbadessa nell' anno terzo del suo Abbadessato che fu l'anno MDCXCIII fece fare tutto questo nobile lavoro di volte e loggie ..." – [150] Cf Pl. 64*b* in this work. – [151] Lalande, III, 611; also Vasi, VIII, Fol. 32. – [152] Pastor, XV, 379, Note 7. – [153] Vasi, VII, Pl. 132. – [154] A. E. Brinckmann: Baukunst des 17. u. 18. Jahrh.'s in den roman. Ländern, 4. ed. (Berlin 1919), 116. – [155] Fasolo, 124-135. – [156] De Brosses, II, 122, also Lalande, IV, 358. – [157] G. M. Crescimbeni: L'Istoria di S. Maria in Cosmedin (Rome 1715); here, at p. 61, an engraving of the original façade of the church; G. B. Giovenale: S. Maria in Cosmedin (Rome 1927). – [158] F. Ex. Soria's S. Maria della Vittoria (Balustrade) and C. Fontana's S. Maria ad Nives. – [159] E. Hannover: Maleren Constantin Hansen (Copenhagen 1901), Fig. 34. – [160] Corresp. VI No. 2537. – [161] Ibid., No. 2550. – [162] Ibid., No. 2457. – [163] Ibid., No. 2455; the restauration was at work in 1723 (Pastor, XV, 459); Deseine, II, 314-315. – [164] On a façade from the time of Clement VIII cf Egger: Röm. Veduten, II, Pl. 97, pag. 40. – [165] "Fil. Juvara", I, 128. – [166] Corresp. VI No. 2499. Canevari was also sent for from Portugal, "but returned with his tail between his legs" (Milizia: Memorie, II, Bassano 1785, 251); cf E. Lavignino: Gli artisti ital. in Portogallo (1940), 94. On C.'s later work in Naples see Roberto Pane: Architettura dell' età barocca in Napoli (1939). – [167] Pastor, XV, 410, 416. – [168] Corresp. VI No. 2339. – [169] Vasi, VI, Pl. 113, Fol. 37. – [170] Venuti, 224; "Le Chiese di Roma" XXX. – [171] C. Gurlitt: Gesch. des Barockstiles in Italien (Stuttg. 1887), 388-389; G. Zucchini: Edifici di Bologna (Rome 1931), 78-79. – [172] Vasi, VII, Pl. 131, Fol. 46. – [173] Fasolo, 121-122. – [174] J. H. Fokker: Roman Baroque Art (Lond. 1938), I, 295. – [175] Le Vite, II, 554. – [176] Memoire, II, 251. – [177] Nina Caflisch: Carlo Maderno (Munich 1934), 17. – [178] Fokker loses himself in discussions on Early Baroque contra High Baroque contra Late Baroque. – [179] Roma moderna (1727), II, 250. – [180] Venuti, 225. – [181] A. Telluccini: L'arte dell' arch. F. Juvara in Piemonte (Turin 1926), Pl. 6, pag. 44. – [182] "Fil. Juvara", I, Pl. 66, pag. 125. – [183] M. Paroletti: Turin et ses curiosités (Turin 1819), 152. – [184] "Fil. Juvara", I, 76. – [185] C. Elling in "Tilskueren" 1931, II, 218-227. – [186] Voyages de Montesquieu, I, 214. – [187] Corresp. VI No. 2852. – [188] Ibid. No. 3067. – [189] Pastor, XV, 604. – [190] Voyages de Montesquieu, I, 211. – [191] Pastor, XV, 475-476. – [192] P. L. Duchartre: The Italian Comedy (London 1929), 212. – [193] Mario Rotili: Filippo Raguzzini e il Rococò Romano (Rome n. d. c. 1952), 11 ff.: concerning the following see also M. Loret's basic treatise in "Boll. d'Arte", XXVII, 1933-1934, 312-321, and V. Golzio in "Archivi d'Italia, 1933-1934, 144-149; my conception of R's stylistic development diverges much from these scholars'. – [194] Rotili, 17-21. – [195] Reproduced in "Europas förstörda Konstverk" (Sth. 1946), Pl. 115, 116. – [196] Voyages, I, 199, II, 56. – [197] Valesio's Journal; these notes are published by E. Scatassa in "Rassegna bibl. dell' arte ital.", XVI, 1913, 111-119, 156-161; XVII, 1914, 138-140. – [198] Labat, VI, 148. – [199] Fx S. Giuliano in Via del Sudario, S. Stefano del Cacco, S. Brigida. – [200] See Alfonso Capecelatro: La vita di S. Filippo Neri (Rome 1889), II, 563-568, and La Spettacolarità del "Gaudium" di Andrea Lazzarini e la visita filippina delle sette chiese del P. Carlo Gasbarri (Rome 1947), 59, Pl. IV and V. – [201] Benedict XIII visited the church in June 1724 (Corresp. VII No. 2768). – [202] Venuti, 521. – [203] Valesio, June 22. 1728. – [204] Unless Rotili (op.cit. 38) alludes to "la chiesa del convento francescano". – [205] Deseine: Rome moderne, IV, 994. – [206] Lina Montalto: Il Clementino 1595-1875 (Rome 1939), 63. – [207] Corresp. VII No. 2931. – [208] Keyssler: Neueste Reisen (1740), I, 621. – [209] Rotili, Fig. 1. – [210] Voyages, II, 32, 34. – [211] Ibid., II, 6, 9. – [212] It still occurs sporadically in Venezian Baroque (for instance in Pal. Rezzonico). – [213]

Thomas-Simon Gueullette: Notes et souvenirs sur le Théâtre-Italien au 18e siècle (Paris 1938), 27, 36, 63. – [214] Franz Haböck: Die Kastraten und ihre Gesangkunst (Berlin 1927), 468-470. – [215] Briefe, ed. Dassdorf, I, 228. – [216] B. Grimschitz: J. L. v. Hildebrandts künstl. Entwickl. (Vienna 1922), 12. – [217] Dagobert Frey: J. B. Fischer von Erlach (Vienna 1923), 107. – [218] H. Sedlmayr: Oesterreichische Barockarchitektur 1690-1740 (Vienna 1930), 75, Fig. 63. – [219] "Wahrhaftes Kriegs- und Siegeslager des Printzen Eugenii Francisci" (Vienna 1731 ff.). – [220] Corresp. VI No. 2394. – G. Giovannoni and others: S. Agata dei Goti (Rome 1924), 103, 122-124. – [224] Venuti, 144. – [223] Vasi: Magnif., VI, Pl. 106; Nolli 447. – [224] Venuti, 126-127; Golzio in "L'Urbe" 1938. – [225] A. Cametti: Il Teatro di Tordinona (Tivoli 1938), I, 127. – [226] Venuti, 410. – [227] Valesio, Feb. 5. 1728: "la fabbrica la fanno i maëstri beneventani" (Scatassa); Fasolo, I, 57. – [228] Corresp. VII No. 3151. – [229] Ibid., IV No. 1543, VII No. 3113, 3160; Noack: Deutschtum in Rom, II, 202. – [230] He was closely associated with Mengs and his circle, cf Martin Olsson in "Fem stora Gustavianer", ed. S. Strömbom (Sth. 1944), 68-69. Lalande (III, 331) called S. Claudio "lean". – [231] Cf Frithiof Brandt: Maximer og Sentenser (Copenhagen 1945), 63. – [232] Voyages, I, 211. – [233] His influence on the Roman building of the period (the Rococo) is greatly exaggerated by Rotili (op.cit. 95-104). – [234] Corresp. VII No. 2896. – [235] Lucie Ceconi: Unsterbliches Rom (Zürich 1948), 93; on Clement XII's building activities in general see Guilio Pisano in "Roma", XII, 1934, 195 ff, 261 ff. – [236] Corresp. IX No. 3758. – [237] Ibid. No. 3931. – [238] Ibid. VIII No. 3632. – [239] Pastor, XVI[1], 101; Tommaso Valenti: Papa Lambertini umoristico (Rome 1938), 204. – [240] Corresp. VIII No. 3596; cf Milizia: Memorie, II, 249. – [241] Milizia, op.cit. – [242] F. Kimball in Royal Inst. Brit. Arch. Journal XXXIV, 675-693; Martin S. Briggs: Men of Taste (London 1947), 145-152. – [243] Corresp. VIII No. 3596. – [244] "Fil. Juvara", I, 97. – [245] Benedetto Croce: Aneddoti e profili settecenteschi (Milan 1922), 150-151; plate. – [246] Guglielmo Matthiae: Ferdinando Fuga e la sua opera romana (Rome n. d.), 69; concerning the following is also referred to this fine monograph. – [247] Vilh. Wanscher in "Artes", II (1933), 13. – [248] Milizia: Memorie, II, 251. – [249] V. Moschini in "Roma", 1929. – [250] G. Donati i "L'Urbe", 1940, Aug. – [251] On V. see M. Loret in "Illustrazione Vaticana", IV, 1933, 428 ff., A. Ravà in "Capitolium, X, 1934, 33 ff.; Zeitschr. f. Kunstgesch., IV, 1935, 252. – [252] Corresp. VIII No. 3689. – [253] Ibid. VI No. 2606. [254] Ibid. VIII No. 3733. – [255] Pastor, XV, 751. – [256] "Fil. Juvara", I, 95-96. – [257] Corresp. VIII No. 3541. – [258] Ibid. VIII No. 3543. – [259] Ibid. 3552. – [260] Ibid. 3596. – [261] Ibid. 3552, 3560. – [262] Memorie, II, 264. – [263] A project by Vanvitelli has recently been published by A. Schiavo in "Palladio", IV, 1953; project by Rotili has been attributed to Rauzzini (op.cit., Pl. 19); I find this to be a matter of doubt. On Dérizet's participation see Prandl in "Roma", 1944. – [264] Corresp. VIII No. 3572, 3583. – [265] Ibid. 3588. – [266] Ibid. IX No. 3763. – [267] Pastor, XV, 752. – [268] Déscript. de l'Italie, V, 408. – [269] II, 264. – [270] III, 373. – [271] Aus den Tagebüchern Friedrich Münters, ed. Øjvind Andreasen, II (Copenhagen & Leipzig 1937), 131. – [272] The expression is used derogatively by Hans Rose in his ed. of Wölfflin: Renaiss. u. Barock (Munich 1926), 323. – [273] Voyage en Italie, 6. ed. (Paris 1889), I, 309. – [274] Briefe aus Italien (Bonn 1922), 250; also Gurlitt rated this work highly (Geschichte des Barockstiles in Italien, Stuttg. 1887, 524). – [275] Emphasized by Golzio: Il Seicento e il Settecento (Turin 1950), 613. – [276] Costantino Baroni: Bramante (Bergamo n. d.), Pl. 120. – [277] Assumed most recently in A. De Rinaldis: L'arte in Roma dal Seicento al Novecento (Bologna 1948), 51. – [278] Christopher Hussey: English Country Houses. Early Georgian 1715-1760 (London 1955), 17. – [279] Ibid. 16, 19. – [280] Concerning the historical circumstances see Pastor, XV, 752; Corresp. VIII No. 3531,

3533, 3583, 3591, 3597, 3615, 3619; IX No. 3795, 3897. – [281] Ibid. VIII No. 3524. – [282] De Rinaldis, op.cit., 51. – [283] Egger: Röm. Veduten, II, Pl. 93-94. – [284] Corresp. VIII No. 3537. – [285] Le Vite, ed. Frey, I (Munich 1911), 37. – [286] Corresp. VIII No. 3583. – [287] Ibid., No. 3588. – [288] Ibid., No. 3615. – [289] Matthiae: Ferd. Fuga. 72. – [290] Ibid., 17-18. – [291] Ibid., 72. – [292] Concerning the type of façade cf S. Lorenzo in Piscibus, Piazza Rusticucci, rebuilt in the 1730'es by Navona ("Arch. min. in Italia. Roma", II, Pl. 19). – [293] V. Golzio in "L'Urbe", July 1938. – [294] Fasolo: Le chiese di Roma nel Settecento, I, 56, 57, 67. – [295] Reproduced from an old photograph in "Arch min.", I, plate 46. – [296] Fasolo, 56-57; P. Romano: Roma nelle sue strade, verbo "Gensola". – [297] Vasi: Magnif., VI, Pl. 108, Fol. 27. – [298] Fasolo, 177-186. – [299] Deseine, I, 133. – [300] V. Golzio in "Dedalo", XII, 1932, 58, 64, 70 f., 100 f., 181; also in "L'Urbe", 1938, July; Zeitschr. f. Kunstgesch., III, (1934), 305. – [301] Vasi, VII, Fol. 67. – [302] M. Loret's critical article on Sardi in Thieme & Becker. – [303] Le chiese del Settecento, 117. – [304] Viaggio in Italia, ed. Farinelli, I (Rome 1932), 200. – [305] Malerische Reise eines deutschen Künstlers, II (Vienna 1789), 70. – [306] Which happens in Golzio: Il Seicento e il Settecento, 625-626. – [307] Tom. Valenti: Papa Lambertini umoristico, 204. – [308] B. Bernardini: Descr. del nuovo ripartimento de' rioni di Roma (Rome 1744). – [309] Alfredo Petrucci: Le Magnificenze di Roma di Giuseppe Vasi (Rome n. d.). – [310] Pastor, XVI[1], 114. – [311] Ibid., 115. – [312] Tom. Valenti: Lambertini umoristico, 209. – [313] Ibid., 333. – [314] See now R. Chiarelli in "Emporium", 1954, 104 ff. – [315] U. Valeri: Antonio Valeri, 2. ed., Rome 1946. – [316] Corresp. IX No. 4038. – [317] A. Ravà: I teatri di Roma (Rome 1953), 131. – [318] Golzio in "L'Urbe", 1938, July. – [319] Ravà, op.cit., 25; on the relationship to Gregorini see Cametti: Teatro Tordinona, I, 127. – [320] "Fil. Juvara", I, 70. – [321] Corresp. VI No. 2502. – [322] Mémoires de M. Goldoni, ed. H. von Loehner, I (Venice 1883), 285, 294, 363. – [323] G. Casanova: Mémoires, ed. R. Vèze, II (Paris 1924), 282; cf a hardly noticed passage in Michael Kelly: Reminiscences, I (London 1826), 102. – [324] Winckelmann und seine Zeitgenossen, II[1] (Lpz. 1872), 147. – [325] In 1731 he drew a plan of Campo Vaccino (Egger, II, 15). – [326] Corresp. XI No. 5067; cf No. 5570 (sale of his paintings). – [327] Cf H. Olsen in Kunstmuseets Aarsskr. XXXVIII, 90-97. – [328] Luigi Càllari: Le ville di Roma, 2. ed. (Rome 1943), 321. – [329] II, 317. – [330] Mémoires, ed. Vèze, I, 204 ff. – [331] Valesio's Journal, Aug. 8. 1741 (Golzio in "Archivi", 1936, 123). – [332] D. Taccone-Gallucci: S. Maria Maggiore (Rome 1911), 83; Pastor, XVI[1], 113-114; Matthiae: F. Fuga, 33-38, 75-76. – [333] Egger, II, Pl. 64-65, and texts. – [334] III, 420. – [335] Richard, V, 423. – [336] Tagebücher, II, 132. – [337] Briefe über Italien, Weimar 1785, quotation from: Skizzen von Italien, II, 1790), 135. – [338] "Fil. Juvara", I, Pl. 206, 210, 212; cf his sketch plan of the Lateran church ibid. Pl. 74. On Gregorini and scenography see H. Tintelnot: Barocktheater und barocke Kunst (Berlin 1939), 128. – [339] Pastor, XVI[1], 115. – [340] Donati: Artisti ticinesi, Pl. 258. – [341] P. Romano: Roma nelle sue strade, verbo "Fontane secca". – [342] Venuti, 445. – [343] Fasolo, 118. – [344] Le Chiese di Roma, XXXIII (Ist. di Studi Romani). – [345] Roberto Longhi in "Paragone", May 1954, 28-39. – [346] Fil. Titi: Descr. delle pitture e architetture ... in Roma (Rome 1763), 60. – [347] Matthiae, 47-48. – [348] Fasolo, 165. – [349] H. Hélyot: Gesch. aller Kloster und Ritterorden, III (Lpz. 1754), 519. – [350] Richard Ford: A Hand-Book for Travellers in Spain, 2. ed. (London 1847), 264-265. – [351] Venuti, 288. – [352] Luigi Zambarelli: S. S. Bonifacio e Alessio all' Aventino (Rome n. d.), 14, 33, 34. – [353] Vilh. Wanscher: Michelagniolo. Nye Studier (Copenhagen 1944), 102-103. – [354] Le Chiese di Roma, No. XXVIII; Venuti, 28. – [355] Golzio: Il Seicento e il Settecento, 630. – [356] C. Justi: Winckelmann, II[1], 147-148; Pastor, XVI[1], 122-123; Egger: Röm. Veduten,

II, Pl. 38; Münter: Tageb. I, 263. – [357] Lettres de Madame Du Boccage contenant ses voyages ... 1750, 1757, 1758 (Dresden 1771), 180. – [358] Ibid., 204-205. – [359] Francesco Fichera: Luigi Vanvitelli (Rome 1937), 67. – [360] A description of the removal of these canvasses from S. Pietro in [J. Russel:] Letters from a young painter, II (London 1750), 135. – [361] On the rebuilding see Titi (1763), 285 ff. – [362] Cf H. Rostrup: J. A. Houdon (Copenhagen 1942), 16 ff. – Cf Duclos: Voyage en Italie ou considérations sur l'Italie (Lausanne 1791), 122. – [364] Freschot: Nouvelle Relation de Venise, II (Utrecht 1709), 168-169; Giulio Lorenzetti: Ca' Rezzonnico (Venice 1951), pag. VI-VII. – [365] Corresp. XII No. 6148; cf No. 6240. – [366] II, 104. – [367] Justi: Winckelmann, II^2 (Lpz. 1872), 15. – [368] J. J. Björnståhl: Briefe, 2. ed., II (Lpz. and Rostock 1780), 96. – [369] Pastor, XVI^1, 463; Clement's own death is told to be due to excessive eating of sturgeon (Ein deutscher Maler und Hofmann. Lebenserinnerungen des Joh. Chr. v. Mannlich, Berlin 1910, 152). – [370] Cf for instance the list of guests at Cardinal de Bernis' (F. Masson: Le Card. de Bernis depuis son ministère, Paris 1903, 284-285) and Justi: Winckelmann, II^2, 34-57. – [371] V. Thorlacius-Ussing in "Rom og Danmark", I, 154. – [372] C. A. Ehrensvärds Bref, ed. G. Bergh, I (Sth. 1916), 23. – [373] Henri Focillon: G.-B. Piranesi (Paris 1918); A. Samuel: Piranesi (London 1910). – [374] According to a letter of May 12. 1756 from Barthélemy to Caylus (Barthélemy: Voyage en Italie, Paris 1801, 132). – [375] C. Elling: Jardin i Rom (Copenhagen 1943), 14-15. – [376] Casanova: Mémoires, ed. Vèze, VII (Paris 1928), 191. – [377] Mémoires de M. Goldoni (Paris 1787), II, Chap. 37. – [378] Corresp. IX No. 5696. – [379] Mannlich, 153. – [380] Luigi Ruggeri: L'Archiconfraternità del Gonfalone (Rome 1866), 162-165. – [381] Max Lamberg: Le Mémorial d'un Mondain (Frankf. a. M. 1775), 97. – [382] Rudolf Zeitler: Klassizismus und Utopia (Sth. 1954), 50-52; W. Körte in Zeitschr. f. Kunstgesch., II, 1933, 16-33. – [383] [Mrs. Millar:] Letters from Italy ... in the Years 1770 & 1771, III (London 1776), 166. – [384] Bergeret: Voyage d'Italie 1773-1774, ed. J. Wilhelm (Paris 1948), 77. – [385] [Roland de la Platière:] Lettres écrites de Suisse, d'Italie, de Sicile et de Malthe, V (Amsterdam 1780), 197. – [386] Focillon: Piranesi, 116. – [387] Fr. Weilbach: Architekten C. F. Harsdorff (Copenhagen 1928), 18. – [388] Corresp. XII No. 6233. – [389] C. V. von Bonstetten: Reise in die klass. Gegenden Roms, I, (Lpz. 1805), 173-174. – [390] "Rom og Danmark", I, 322 (L. Bobé). – [391] C. Elling: Den romantiske Have (Copenhagen 1942), 101-110. – [392] Ital. Reise, 1787, Feb. 2. – [393] Reisen eines Deutschen in Italien in den Jahren 1786 bis 1788, I (Berlin 1792), 207. – [394] The Travel-Diaries, ed. G. Chapman, I (Cambridge 1928), 190. – [395] F. J. L. Meyer: Darstellungen aus Italien (Berlin 1792), 174. – [396] Tagebuch, I, 338, cf 263. – [397] C. Gabillot: Hubert Robert et son temps (Paris n. d.), 284; cf Roland de la Platière, V, 231, and Wilh. Heinse: Briefe, II, 142 (Sämmtl. Werke, X, Lpz. 1910); also Barthélemy, 389-390, and A. v. Kotzebue: Erinnerungen von einer Reise ... nach Rom u. Neapel, III (Berlin 1805), 50. – [398] M. had also made a design for the rebuilding of Teatro Argentina (1763, now in Villa Albani), cf A. Ravà: I teatri di Roma (Rome 1953), 37, Pl. VII-IX. – [399] Erik Palmstedt: Resedagbok 1778-1780, ed. Martin Olsson (Uppsala 1927), 110. – [400] Heinse: Briefe, II, 147; Münter: Tageb., II, 251; Meyer: Darstell., 106; Norbert von Grund: Maler. Reise eines deutschen Künstlers nach Rom, II (Weimar 1789), 25. Also Corresp. XIII No. 6979 and XV No. 8985.

CONVENTS AND MONASTENES

[1] Deseine, V, 110. – [2] V, 127. – [3] In 1753 Elsinore had only 3400 inhabitants; not until about 1800 did it have about 6000. During Pius IX there were just under 2500 monks and

about 2000 nuns in Rome (Negro: Seconda Roma, 156). – [4] Eugène Briffault: Le Secret de Rome (Paris 1846) is typical; also Zola's "Rome" belongs to this genre. – [5] Labat, IV, 63. – [6] Duclos, 107; in 1779 the number was c. 400 (The Pembroke Papers, ed. Lord Herbert, London 1942, 275). – [7] Pastor, XVI[1], 217. – [8] J. Gorani: Mémoires secrets et critiques, II (Paris 1794), 11. – [9] Tageb., I, 300. – [10] Les Recréations des Capucins (the Hague 1738). – [11] M. Heimbucher: Die Orden und Kongregationen der kathol. Kirche, I (Paderborn 1907), 485. – [12] K. von Schlözer: Röm. Briefe (Stuttg. 1913), 236; cf Beckford: The Travel-Diaries, I, 286-287. – [13] Heimbucher, II, 241; Johs. Jørgensen: Den hellige Ild (Copenhagen 1907). – [14] On Chartreuse-Romanticism see Yrjö Hirn: Eremiter och Pilgrimer (Sth. 1924), 96-111. – [15] Labat, IV, 123; De Blainville, II, 174. – [16] Archivo del General Miranda. Viajes, Diarios 1785-1787, II (Caracas 1929), 62-63. – [17] Cf Moritz, III, 97; Alma Söderhjelm: Gustaf III's Syskon (Sth. 1945), 145. – [18] Rome, Naples et Florence, ed. D. Muller, I (Paris 1919), 55. – [19] Ibid., I, 346. – [20] Cf for instance Stendhal: Promenades dans Rome, April 18 1828. – [21] Voyage en Italie, 6. ed., I (Paris 1889), 291-296. – [22] P. Tomei: L'architettura del Quattrocento in Roma (Rome 1942), 255 f. – [23] On murals with landscapes from the 18. century see A. Rossi in "Boll. d'Arte", 1907; Aug. C. J. Hare: Walks in Rome, 12. ed. (London 1887), I, 289. – [24] Heimbucher, I, 397. – [25] Delle Magnif., VIII, Fol. 42. – [26] Emma Amadei in "L'Urbe", 1940, March, 18-23. – [27] Reproduced in Vasi, VII Pl. 143. – [28] Alfr. von Reumont: Röm. Briefe von einem Florentiner, III (Lpz. 1844), 254. – [29] Brigante Colonna: Ottocento Romano (Rome 1944), 21. The author was born in 1837, died in 1933. – [30] Ibid., 19. – [31] Les Italiens ou mœurs et coutumes d'Italie (Genève & Paris 1773), 221. – [32] V, 266. – [33] Lalande, III, 442. – [34] Vasi, VIII, Fol. 24. – [35] Corresp. VII No. 3045. – [36] Ibid. VI No. 2371, cf 2359 (S. S. Dom. e Sisto). – [37] Clementi: Il Carnevale Romano, II, 11. – [38] Valesio's Journal. – [39] Emma Amadei: Roma turrita (Rome 1943), 33; cf P. Romano: Roma nelle sue strade, 280, which states 1752. – [40] The monastery also possessed a Vigne outside the city walls, near Circus Maximus (Nolli 953). – [41] Schlözer, 263. – [42] III, 66. – [43] D'Orbessan: Mélanges historiques, I[2], (Paris 1768), 559. – [44] Labat, III, 192. – [45] Luigi Càllari: Volti tragici e comici della Roma papale (Rome 1944), 176-177. – [46] Heimbucher, II, 305; Deseine, IV, 942. – [47] E. Hempel: Francesco Borromini (Vienna 1924), 122 f. – [48] Hans Sedlmayr: Die Architektur Borrominis (Berlin 1930), 69, Note 2. – [49] Brigante Colonna: Ottocento Romano, 215. – [50] Mortier: Hist. des Maîtres-Généraux de l'Ordre des Frères-Prêcheurs, VII (Paris 1914), 389. – [51] Labat, III, 72. – [52] J. J. Volkmann: Histor.-krit. Nachrichten von Italien, II (Lpz. 1770), 784-785. – [53] Hélyot, VII, 349. – [54] P. Romano: Roma, 35. – [55] Enzo Petraccone: Cagliostro nella storia e nella leggenda (Milan) 1937, 110-111. – [56] Hare: Walks, 12. ed., I, 491. – [57] Hélyot, VII, 250; Venuti, 37; Heimbucher, II, 488; Nolli No. 67. – [58] Delle Magnif., IX, Pl. 169. – [59] On Labre see Corresp. XIV No. 8382, 8391, 8404, 8427, 8449 and elsewhere; Münter: Tageb. II, 157-158 ("The idol of the Mob"); Meyer: Darstellungen, 197, 215 ff. – [60] Nouveaux Mémoires ou Observations sur l'Italie, II (London 1764), 411. – [61] Clementi, II, 5. – [62] Labat, V, 144. – [63] Venuti, 412; on the strict Regina Coeli convent see Deseine, IV, 945. – [64] L. Madelin: La Rome de Napoléon (Paris 1906), 325-326. – [65] Lettres contenant le journal d'un voyage fait à Rome en 1773, I (Genève & Paris 1783), pag. VII-IX, and Note 1. – [66] Madelin, op.cit., 328-329. – [67] Deseine, I, 219; Pascoli, I, 327. – [68] Vasi, VIII, Fol. 24; Donati: Artisti ticinesi, Pl. 279. – [69] R. Bay: Musikalsk Rejse 1842-1843 (Memoirer & Breve XXXIV), 63. – [70] Labat, III, 122; on the monastery see also Giov. Baglione: Le vite de' pittori, scultori et architetti (Rome 1642), 181; Venuti, 273; Volkmann, II, 457. – [71] For instance Vasi, VII, Pl. 102,

VII, Pl. 127. – [72] The monastery was built in the beginning of the 17. century by Francesco Pozzi; Vasi, V, Pl. 92. – [73] By the former, among others, the convents at S. S. Apostoli, in the 1590'es ("Artisti ticinesi", 29) and at S. Sabina, of the Maderno Convertite convent at the Corso (ibid., 109); other monumental works are the convents at S. Carlo de' Catinari (reproduced in "Arch.min." II, Pl. 111) and at S. Basilio (ibid., II, Pl. 75). – [74] Especially the convent at S. Carlino and the convent of the Philippines. – [75] See p. 412 ff. – [76] And also concerning certain public civil buildings, cf C. Elling: Function and Form of the Roman Belvedere, 34, Note 70. – [77] See for instance "Arch. min.", II, Pl. 6. – [78] Baglione, 339. – [79] Ibid.; "Arch. min.", II, Pl. 128. – [80] Egger: Röm. Veduten, II, Pl. 91. – [81] A typical example is the monastery at S. Paolo fuori le mura (Vasi, V, Pl. 100). – [82] Cf a building on the Tiber (Vasi, V, plate 90) where the window leaves an imprint in a segmental arch. – [83] Wölfflin: Renaiss. u. Barock, 4. ed. (1926), 129 f., and C. Elling: Function and Form, § 4. – [84] Venuti, 511. – [85] "Arch. min.", II, Pl. 76; Vasi, III, Pl. 48; Deseine, III, 702. – [86] A typical example is a wing of S. S. Domenico e Sisto (Vasi, VIII, Pl. 149). – [87] See for instance Vasi, III, Pl. 47; VII, Pl. 132; VIII, Pl. 144, 147, 152, 154. – [88] Labat, III, 74. – [89] Vasi, VII, Pl. 131; "Arch. min.", I, 90-91; E. Hempel: F. Borromini, 35. – [90] Adrien Schoonebeck: Courte description des ordres des femmes et filles religieuses (Amsterdam c. 1691), Pl. 38. – [91] G. Giacoletti: Compendio della vita della ven. Donna Camilla Borghese (Rome 1842), 59-60, 93-96. – [92] Pascoli, II, 554. – [93] Vasi, VIII, Fol. 12. – [94] Venuti, 273; a characterization of Cloche in Corresp. IV No. 1900 and in Hist. des Maîtres Généraux, VII, 207 ff., 301. – [95] Luigi De Gregori in Rivista d. Accademie e Biblioteche, II, 1928, No. 2. – [96] Described in Labat, III, 67 ff. – [97] Corresp. VI No. 2418. – [98] In 1877 the inscription was conveyed to the interior vestibule of the church. – [99] Heimbucher, III, 285-287. – [100] Mentioned in this work p. 426, reproduced on Pl. 171. – [101] Venuti, 147. – [102] Vasi, VI, Pl. 105. – [103] Pascoli, II, 549; M. Amici: Memorie istoriche intorno S. Camillo de Lellis (Rome 1913), 43. – [104] Valesio, Diario, 27. Febr. 1738. – [105] Venuti, 160. – [106] Heimbucher, III, 323. – [107] See for instance Labat, VII, 18-29. – [108] Donati: Artisti ticinesi, 381; Venuti, 155. – [109] Pascoli, II, 547, 550. – [110] Vasi, VIII, Fol. 39. – [111] Clementi, II, 192. – [112] See p. 425 and Pl. 135a. – [113] Fasolo, 177-186. – [114] Lalande, IV, 89; Vasi, VIII, Fol. 15; Volkmann, II, 380; G. Donati in "L'Urbe", 1940, Aug., 20-26. – [115] F. Fichera: Luigi Vanvitelli (Rome 1937), 72-79. – [116] To be seen on a watercolour by A. Acquaroni (1825) in the Thorvaldsens Museum (reproduced in C. Elling: Breve om Italien, Copenhagen 1945, plate facing p. 80). – [117] Pastor, XVI, 2; Deseine, III, 802. – [118] Ibid., XVI[1], 230; there is a description of S. Leonardo as a missionary in Rome in [J. Russel:] Letters from a young painter, II (London 1750), 317-319. – [119] According to Moritz (III, 151) the original paintings were "miserable"; cf Venuti, 394-395. – [120] Moritz, ibid. – [121] He published a "Götterlehre", Berlin 1791. – [122] Corinne ou l'Italie, I (Paris 1807), 188. – [123] Romerske Dagbøger, May 1. and 20. 1861 (the palm isn't mentioned specially, but the view is). – [124] Röm. Briefe von einem Florentiner, III (1844), 29. – [125] Vilh. Wanscher: Arch. Hist., II, 526 f. – [126] Thereafter it was left to the Passionists. – [127] At any rate he rebuilt the church (Venuti, 394). – [128] Correspondence of Thomas Gray, ed. P. Toynbee & Whibley, I (Oxford 1935), 161. – [129] Tageb., II, 189. – [130] Vasi, VIII, Fol. 40. – [131] C. Elling: Function and Form, Pl. 27 a. – [132] Venuti, 279. – [133] Measured up by Letarouilly: Edifices de Rome moderne, II, Pl. 152. – [134] Ed. Martinori: Lazio turrito, II (Rome 1934), 54; Heimbucher, III, 309-310. – [135] Heinse: Briefe, II, 189; on a project in 1786 for an Eremitage on the ruins of the Temple of Jupiter see Corresp. XV No. 8810.

THE COMMON WEAL

[1] Egger: Röm. Veduten, I, Pl. 70, 74-76. – [2] I doubt whether Coudenhove-Erthal, op.cit., 69, has evaluated completely the importance of the situation as to the design. – [3] Pascoli, I, 327. – [4] The medaillon-inscription was put up before November 1694 (Corresp. II, 78). On the financing see Volkmann, II, 315. – [5] Corresp. II No. 730. – [6] Coudenhove-Erthal, 70. – [7] Vertrauliche Briefe, II, 18-19. – [8] Index librorum prohibitorum Benedicti XIV (Parma 1783), 195. – [9] Voyage en Italie (Lausanne 1791), 43; also Winckelmann had books confiscated here (Briefe, ed. W. Rehm, I, Berlin 1952, 190). – [10] Guidi: Lettres, I, 206. – [11] Reise ... i Aarene 1819 og 1820, III (Copenhagen 1822), 204. – [12] On the Curia in general see N. Del Re: Le curia romana (Rome 1953); D. Redig de Campos: Raffaello e Michelangelo (Rome 1946), Pl. 3. – [13] Ant. Fonseca: De Basilica S. Laurentii in Damaso libri tres (Fano 1745); Corresp. V No. 2096; Lalande, IV, 95. – [14] Justi: Winckelmann, II[1], 114. – [15] IV, Pl. 74. – [16] A. Petrucci: Le Magnificenze di Roma di G. Vasi, 48; Canova stayed in Pal. di Venezia when he first came to Rome. – [17] The younger Fischer's part in the work is discussed in H. Sedlmayr: Fischer v. Erlich d. ä., 67-69. – [18] G. Pisano in "Roma", XII, 1934, 195 ff., 261 ff.; G. Matthiae: F. Fuga, 70-71; cf Corresp. VIII No. 3591. – [19] II, 255-256. – [20] Lalande, III, 567; V, 21. – [21] Ermanno Ponti: Il Banco di S. Spirito (Rome 1941), 87-92. – [22] For instance Falda's, reproduced in Donati: Artisti ticinesi, Fig. 220. – [23] Eberh. Hempel: Borromini, 176-177; Donati, 186. – [24] Rose in Wölfflin: Ren. u. Barock, 4. ed., 226-230. – [25] N. Caflisch: Carlo Maderno, 95. – [26] Mario Tosi: Il Sacro Monte di Pietà di Roma (Rome 1937), 131-132. – [27] F. J. L. Meyer: Darstell., 192; Moritz, III, 272. – [28] Henri Focillon: G. B. Piranesi (Paris 1918), Pl. XVIII, XIX. – [29] Corresp. XI No. 5669; Pastor, XVI[1], 467. – [30] Neueste Reisen, I, 604. – [31] Volkmann, II, 748. – [32] N. Brooke: Voyage à Naples et en Toscane (Paris 1798), 257. – [33] Corresp. XII No. 6483. – [34] VII, Pl. 159. – [35] G. Stenius: Bag Vatikanets Mure (Copenhagen 1949), 80. – [36] Has now been reconstructed ruthlessly. – [37] III, 180. – [38] Letters from Portugal, Spain, Italy, and Germany (London 1785), III, 209. – [39] Grosley, II, 312. – [40] Deseine, V, 1207. – [41] Volkmann, II, 438; Venuti, 209; cf Silvagni, 1, 204. – [42] S. Negro: Seconda Roma, 151, 162, 434. – [43] Rom under Pius IX (Copenhagen 1877), 357-359. – [44] Volkmann, II, 479. – [45] Reumont: Röm. Briefe, I, 49. – [46] H. C. Andersen: Rom. Dagb., Jan. 16. 1834. – [47] See Piranesi's etchings, for instance reproduced in "Rome past and present" (The Studio, 1926). – [48] E. Petraccone: Cagliostro (Milan 1937), 111-122. – [49] H. Schück: Rom. En Vandring genom Seklerna, II (Sth. 1923), Fig. 137. – [50] John Howard: The State of Prisons, 4. ed. (London 1792), I, 112. – [51] The Maestro Generale of the Dominicans still has ex officio seat in the Inquisition's Congregation, cf "Annuario Pontificio" and Stenius, 75. – [52] Labat (III, 275) calls him a "peintre de réputation"; he was, though, only an imitator of his famous father, Baptiste M. (died in 1699). – [53] Corresp. VIII, 92; cf Montesquieu: Voyages, I, 236. – [54] Voyage, III, 79-81. – [55] Howard: The State of Prisons, I, 112. – [56] Les aventures de Joseph Pignata, échappé des prisons de l'Inquisition de Rome (Cologne 1725). – [57] Ibid., 42. – [58] Emma Amadei: Roma turrita (Rome 1943), 82-88. – [59] Deseine, II, 439. – [60] Nicola Bonfiglio: Il Museo criminale di Roma (Rome 1950); E. Rossi in "Roma", April 1930, 169-76. – [61] "Justitiae Et Clementiae ... Novum Carcerem Innocentius X Pont. Max. Posuit A. D. 1665". – [62] See for instance George Kennan: Sibirien, 2. ed. (Kristiania c. 1891). – [63] Reumont: Röm. Briefe, III, 160; also Howard. – [64] Reumont, III, 180; Pastor, XV, 361; Labat, III, 64-67; Russel: Letters, II, 199-200. – [65] Reumont, loc.cit. 181-182. – [66] G. Pisano in "Roma", XII, 1934, 270. – [67] Romano &

Partini: Piazza di Spagna (Rome n. d.), 14 ff. – [68] Voyage de Suisse et de l'Italie, 2. ed. (Rotterdam 1688), 393. – [69] Pastor, XIV², 679. – [70] Roma moderna (1727), 267 (completed in 1685). – [71] Donati: Artisti ticinesi, 285; S. Tommaso was restored hideously in the 1860'es (K. v. Schlözer: Röm. Briefe, 294). – [72] Corresp. XII No. 6428, 6436. – [73] In 1818 A. Tadolini's studio was here according to J. Hartmann. – [74] Lina Montalto: Il Clementino 1595-1875 (Rome 1939). – [75] Björnståhl: Briefe auf seinen ausl. Reisen, II, 143. – [76] P. Vannucci in "L'Urbe", 1950, March-April, 3-10. – [77] Fernow, 143. – [78] Nino Valeri: Pietro Verri (Milan 1937), 19. – [79] Vasi, IX, Pl. 168. – [80] Volkmann, II, 316; Clementi, II, 30. – [81] Vasi, IX, Fol. 20. – [82] Rotili: F. Rauzzini, 43; here the year 1724 is stated as the year of building. – [83] Brigante Colonna: Ottocento Romano, 22-23. – [84] Venuti, 280; cf Richard Lassels: Voyage d'Italie, I (Paris 1671), 304; Grosley, II, 376; Heimbucher, III, 287-291. – [85] Fernow, 140-143. – [86] On P. Corsini, the general of the Scolopis see Barthélemy: Voyage en Italie (Paris 1801), 137; Winckelmanns Briefe, ed. Rehm, I, Reg. – [87] Anders Österling: Jacob Jonas Björnståhl (Sth. 1947), 54. – [88] Münter: Tageb. I, 364 and elsewhere. – [89] Briefe, ed. Rehm, I, 290-291. – [90] Reise in die klass. Gegenden Roms, II (Lpz. 1805), 16, 20. – [91] Guidi: Lettres (Genève 1783), II, 135; on Rome's wellfare institutions in general see Carlo Luigi Morichini: Degli Istituti di Carità ... in Roma (Rome 1870). – [92] Deseine, II, 472. – [93] Clementi, II, 38. – [94] The Pembroke Papers, ed. Lord Herbert (London 1942), 272. – [95] J. W. von Archenholtz: England u. Italien, II¹ (Lpz. 1785), 228-230. – [96] The Pembroke Papers, loc.cit.. – [97] Philip von Zesen: Beschr. der Stadt Amsterdam (Amsterd. 1664), 516. – [98] A. E. D'Ailly: Histor. Gids van Amsterdam (Amsterd. 1949), 94. – [99] By Giovanni Fontana; Clement XI had a carillon put up (Vasi IV, Fol. 30). – [100] Olof Celsius: Diarium öfver sin resa i Italien, ed. E. Lundström (Gbg. 1909), 63. – [101] Deseine, V, 1417. – [102] Pastor, XIV², 692. – [103] Ibid., 690. – [104] Coudenhove-Erthal, 117-119. – [105] Ibid., Pl. 18. – [106] On the hospits see also De Blainville, II, 265, 268; Deseine, IV, 902, V, 1255; Corresp. VI No. 2495. – [107] De Blainville, II, 265. – [108] Pastor, XVI¹, 111. – [109] Corresp. IV No. 1526; cf No. 1794. – [110] Montesquieu: Voyages, II, 64. – [111] Lalande, IV, 518-519. Also De Brosses missed quays. – [112] Venuti, 166; Deseine, I, 72; Valesio April 1. 1728 (the chapel is consecrated). On orphanages in general see: Labat, III, 62. – [113] Deseine, III, 777. – [114] Labat, III, 63. – [115] Venuti, 413. Casanova has mentioned an orphanage like this in his memoirs (ed. Vèze), XII, 22 ff. – [116] Venuti, 439. – [117] VIII, Pl. 159. – [118] Röm. Leben, I, 133-135. – [119] Pictures from Italy (London 1846), 216. – [120] Donati: Artisti ticinesi, 361-362. – [121] Reumont, I, 162. – [122] L. Bobé: F. Brun, 110. – [123] Fernow: Sitten- u. Kulturgem. Roms, 118. – [124] Weinlig: Briefe, I, 43; cf Albert Babeau: Paris en 1789 (Paris 1889), 440. – [125] Briefe, II, 147; less favourable opinions in Brooke: Voyage à Naples et en Toscane, 218-219; see also F. Brun: Röm. Leben, II, 49 (1803). – [126] M. Besnier: L'Ile tibérine dans l'antiquité (Paris 1902). – [127] Vilh. Bergsøe: Fra sollyse Strande (Copenhagen 1886), 40. – [128] Egilberto Martire: L'Isola della Salute. Dal tempio romano all' ospedale di S. Giovanni di Dio (Rome 1934), 53-55. – [129] On the relationship between Belli and Pinelli see Valerio Mariani: Bart. Pinelli (Rome 1948), 126-129. – [130] Morichini: Degli Istituti di Carità, 163-164; Vasi, IX, Pl. 174; Venuti, 429; Mario Rotili: Fil. Raguzzini, 34-37, 67. – [131] Thus Rotili, op.cit., 35. – [132] IX, Pl. 174. – [133] Rotili, 42; Valesio, Feb. 13. 1727. – [134] Roma moderna (1727), 430. – [135] The hospital was demolished in 1910. – [136] Johs. Jørgensen: Den hell. Frans af Assisi (4. ed., 1942), 19. – [137] Bruno Cassinelli: Histoire de la Folie (Paris n. d.), 332. – [138] Mémoires de M. Goldoni, ed. Loehner, 36. On Lancisi see Pastor, XV, 367, 380; Antonio Bacchini: La vita e le opere di G. M. Lancisi (Rome 1920). – [139]

Lalande, IV, 558. – [140] P. Tomei: L'architettura del Quattrocento, 142. – [141] T. Valenti: Lambertini umoristico, 221. – [142] Venuti, 515-516; Pastor, XVI[1], 114; Reumont, I, 157-160; Matthiae: Fuga, 43-44, 79. – [143] "Arch. min." I, Pl. 138. – [144] The older building is partly to be seen in Vasi, I, Pl. 15. – [145] Reumont, I, 165. – [146] Dorothy George: London Life in the 18th Century (London 1925), 42-44. – [147] G. Matthiae: Ferd. Fuga, 79. – [148] Duclos: Voyage, 107. – [149] Archenholtz, II[2], 120. – [150] L. Madelin: La Rome de Napoléon, 70-71. – [151] Reisen eines Officiers durch die Schweiz. u. Italien (Hannover 1786), 224. – [152] Gorani, II, 259-260. – [153] Concerning the papal fighting services cf Deseine, V, 1243 f.; Labat, IV, 202; Grosley, II, 290; Lalande, V, 69-70; Corresp. VII No. 2806. – [154] De Brosses, II, 255. – [155] Silvagni, I, 219. – [156] The Pope, however, didn't die until 6 months after this incident; the rumors of his death were innumerable, many believed that he had been poisoned. – [157] Adlerbeth, 191. – [158] De Brosses, II, 255. – [159] Montesquieu, I, 219. – [160] Labat, IV, 125. – [161] Moritz, III, 79. – [162] Reisen eines Officiers, 236. – [163] Clemens XIV, by the way, fell from his mule during the Possesso-cavalcade; the groom ran away when the mule got restless. – [164] Moritz, III, 93-94. – [165] Mercy-Dupaty: Lettres sur l'Italie en 1785, II (Rom & Paris 1788), 83. – [166] Vasi, II, Fol. 42. – [167] See Pl. 76. – [168] Corresp. IX No. 4013. – [169] G. Matthiae: Piazza del Popolo (Rome n. d.), 103; Pl. XXIV. – [170] Corresp. de Stendhal, edd. Paupe & Cheramy, II (Paris 1908), No. 423; cf P. P. Trompeo: Sulle orme di Stendhal (Rome 1924), 242 ff.

THE PALACES

[1] There is a useful survey of the Roman nobility in Alfr. von Reumont: Römische Briefe von einem Florentiner, I (Lpz. 1840), 207-218, 417-434; on its condition at the beginning of the 18. century see Deseine: Rome moderne (Leiden 1713), V, 1221-1234. Also Silvio Negro: Seconda Roma (Milan 1943), 117-148. – [2] This applies to towns like Paliano and Genazzano (the Colonna family), Zagarolo (Rospigliosi), Ariccia and Campagnano (Chigi), Genzano (Cesarini), Vignanello (Ruspoli), S. Vito Romano (Theodoli), Poli (Conti); the author knows these localities from personal experience. Cf the monographies in question in Edoardo Martinori: Lazio turrito, I-III (Rome 1933-1934). – [3] David Silvagni: La corte e la società romana nei secoli XVIII e XIX, 3. ed., I (Rome 1884), 95-125 and elsewhere; Carlo Bandini: Roma al tramonto del Settecento (Rome 1922), 149-185; Kasimir Chledowski: Rokoko-Människorna i Rom och Italien (Sth. 1922), 342-345; Abbé Richard: Déscription historique et critique de l'Italie, V (Dijon & Paris 1766), 132-145. – [4] Richard, V, 151. – [5] Giuseppe Gorani: Mémoires secrets et critiques des cours, des gouvernemens et des moeurs ... de l'Italie, II (Paris 1794), 24. – [6] Christian Elling: Operahus og Casino. Studier i det italienske Logetheater 1670-1830 (Copenhagen 1942), 38-40; in this work is also an analysis of the conception of conversazione, 44-51. – [7] Carlo Bandini: La galanteria nel gran mondo di Roma nel Settecento (Rome n. d.), 103-112. – [8] Richard, V, 143. – [9] Roland de la Platière: Lettres écrites de Suisse, d'Italie, de Sicile et de Malthe ... en 1776, 1777 & 1778 (Amsterdam 1780), V. 55. – [10] Bergeret de Grancourt: Voyage d'Italie 1773-1774, ed. Jacques Wilhelm (Paris 1948), 58. – [11] Mme de Genlis: Mémoires (Paris 1825), III, 35. – [12] Gorani, II, 154. – [13] Voyage d'un François en Italie fait dens les années 1765 & 1766 (Paris 1769), V, 130. – [14] Guidi: Lettres concernant le journal d'un voyage fait à Rome en 1773 (Genève 1783), II, 132; Corresp. of Thomas Gray, I, 149: Grosley, II (1764), 435. – [15] Richard, V, 131; Masson: Le Card. de Bernis, 128-129; Brooke: Voyage, 73; Fernow, 54. –

[16] For instance Pal. Giustiniani and Pal. Nunez in Via Condotti (C. Elling: Function and Form of the Roman Belvedere, Pl. 31, 32). – [17] Emma Amadei: Roma turrita (Rome 1943), Pl. XVII. – [18] The expression is due to Pöllnitz (II, 281). – [19] On the Pal. della Famiglia Borghese see Elling, op.cit., 13. – [20] Roland de la Platière, V, 33. – [21] Corresp. VIII, 223. – [22] G. Maugras: Le Duc et la Duchesse de Choiseul (Paris 1924), 36. – [23] Christian Elling: Operahus og Casino, 51-55. – [24] Richard, V, 56. – [25] Archenholtz, II^2, 74. – [26] Silvagni, I, 102; Clementi: Il Carnevale di Roma, II, 125, 164. – [27] Baretti: Les Italiens, 306-307. – [28] Lalande, V, 59. – [29] Pöllnitz, III, 55. – [30] On the formidably rivalry among coachmen concerning positions in processions see Blainville, II, 157; Corresp. III, p. 434. On luxurious horses and famous coachmen cf Peppino Partini: Della Carrozza alla "Botticella" (Rome 1940) 29-43; also Silvio Negro: Seconda Roma, 141 ff. – [31] Old photograph reproduced in "Arch. minore", II, Pl. 95. [32] Delle Magnificenze di Roma, IV (Rome 1754), Pl. 62. – [33] "Rom og Danmark", II, Fig. 42, 43; old photograph in Negro: Seconda Roma, facing p. 272. – [34] According to Pascoli (I, 327) the portal of Pal. Altieri's posterior façade "e ancor la stalla" was executed by Mattia De Rossi. – [35] Burnet, 383. – [36] Vertrauliche Briefe, II, 14; this passage is also found in Lalande (V, 138), who consequently must have had access to a copy of De Brosses' manuscript, not published until 1799. – [37] The Grand Tour, III (London 1756), 16-17, 245. – [38] Rome, Naples et Florence, ed. D. Muller, I (Paris 1919), 40-42. – [39] Corresp. de Stendhal, edd. Paupe & Cheramy, II (Paris 1908), 194; H. Jacoubet: Stendhal (Paris 1943), 77; M. Josephson: Stendhal (New York 1946), 364-365; Henri Martineau: Le coeur de Stendhal, II (Paris 1953), 303. – [40] In the 1740's it belonged to the Ferrini family (Pietro Paolo Trompeo: Nell' Italia romantica. Sulle orme di Stendhal, Rome 1924, 291). – [41] The extinct Muti family's name was continued by Marchese Paolo Muti-Bussi, whose mother was Cecilia Muti. The Bussi family was ennobled in 1746 (P. Romano: Pasquino nel Settecento, 44); cf Trompeo: La Scala del Sole (Rome 1945), 206 ff. – [42] Pastor, XIV, 626; on the A. family see Silvagni, II, 223; Clementi, I, 582; Reumont: Röm. Briefe, I, 425. – [43] Rome moderne, I, 254. – [44] Coudenhove-Erthal, Fig. 10. – [45] Nat. Mus., Sth. – [46] C. Elling: Function and Form, 44-45. – [47] Coudenhove-Erthal, 44-45; Donati: Artisti ticinesi, 272; Pascoli, II, 543-544. – [48] C. Elling, op.cit., 15. – [49] D. Angeli: Storia romana di trent' anni (Rome 1931), 84 ff.; Gorani: Mémoires, II, 238 f. – [50] Promenades dans Rome, Dec. 11. 1827; cf Reisen der Lady Morgan, III (Ppz. 1823), 363-364, and F. C. Hillerup: Italica (Copenhagen 1829), I, 185 ff. – [51] S. Negro: Seconda Roma, 135; A. Zucconi: Lodovico innamorato (Milan 1944), pass.; Iris Origo: The last Attachment. The Story of Byron and Teresa Guiccioli (London 1949), 397, 493; Joh. V. Jensen & Aage Marcus: Thorvaldsens Portrætbuster (Copenhagen 1926), 103, Pl. 64. – [52] T. H. Fokker: Roman Baroque Art (London 1938). – [53] Avviso Marescotti, Nov. 19. 1689 (Pastor, XIV^2, 1056). – [54] Primi Visconti: Mémoires sur la cour de Louis XIV, ed. J. Lemoine (Paris 1908), 22; he was a brother to Louis XIV's mistress, Maria Mancini, who was married to Lorenzo Onofrio Colonna (Clementi, I, 545). – [55] Voyage en Italie, 42; cf Titi: Descr. di Roma (1763), 321. – [56] III, 593; cf Volkmann, II, 293. – [57] O. Celsius d. ä.'s Diarium öfver sin resa i Italien 1697-1698, ed. E. Lundström (Göteborg 1902), 50. – [58] Silvagni, II, 268. – [59] Rome moderne, III, 559. – [60] E. Hempel: Carlo Rainaldi (Munich 1919), 92-94; two doors are depicted in Dom. De Rossi: Studio d'architettura civile, I, 1702. On the Del Grillo family cf C. Elling in Festskr. til L. L. Hammerich (Copenhagen 1952), 112-115. – [61] Briefe, ed. Rehm, I, No. 143. [62] Is going to be discussed by the author in a monograph. – [63] "Fil. Juvara", I, 51. – [64] Clementi, I, 654; Corresp. V No. 1333. – [65] On the R family see A. Mauceri: Messina nel

Settecento (Milan n. d.) 68, 76 ff. – A similar palace was owned by Marchese Galli and was situated near the Cancelleria (Vasi, IV, Pl. 74). – [66] Newman Flower: Handel, his personality and his times (London 1947), 89-91. – [67] Donati, 264, Fig. 230. – [68] Performed by young Danish architects in 1952, published in "Arkitekten"s Maanedshefte, 1952, 158. – [69] Pastor, XV, 629, 633, 679. – [70] Silvagni, II, 364-365; Nino Valeri: Pietro Verri (Milan 1937), 147 ff. – [71] Pascoli, II, 549. – [72] Deseine, VI, 1510; Pastor, XV, 251. – [73] Corresp. IX No. 3740. – [74] Neueste Reisen, II (1741), 78. – [75] Corresp. VII No. 3079. – [76] P. Romano: Tre secoli di vita romana (Rome 1941), 85. – [77] Reproduced in Vasi, III, Pl. 44. – [78] P. Romano: Roma, verbo "Marcello". In Roma moderna (1727), 387 the Pal. is said to be finished; on interior decoration see Pascoli, I, 214, 231. – [79] Corresp. IX No. 3740. – [80] Vertraul. Briefe, II, 68, 176. – [81] Valenti: Papa Lambertini umoristico, 140. – [82] Corresp. XII No. 6430; cf Grosley, II (1764), 375. – [83] F. Masson: Le Card. de Bernis (Paris 1903), 125-130. – [84] Reproduced in Coudenhove-Erthal, Fig. 1. – [85] Corresp. VIII No. 3247; Pastor, XV, 740. – [86] Nolli No. 230. – [87] A. E. Brinckmann: Bauk. des 17. u. 18. Jahrh.s in den roman. Ländern, 4. ed. (Berlin 1919), 98. – [88] Mémoires, II (1735), 274. – [89] Golzio in "L'Urbe", July 1938 (Note by Valesio). – [90] II, 87. – [91] Reumont: Röm. Briefe, I, 423. – [92] Roland de la Platière, V, 336; on a ball in honour of Joseph II see Mannlich, 160; interesting information about the creation of the gallery in Corresp. IX No. 3862, 3864, 3869, 3955, 3963. – [93] Lalande, III, 600-601; donated to S. Agnese by Camillo Pamfili (Titi, 1763, 132). – [94] Copy in the Library of the Kunstindustrimuseum. – [95] Richard, V, 68; Masson: Bernis, 137. – [96] C. Elling in "Artes", V (1937), 145; on this feast see also Corresp. III No. 1054; Hervey: Letters, III, 305; Grosley, II (1764), 408; Bergeret, 122; Moritz, III, 268; Meyer: Skizzen von Italien (1789), I, 143-164; Stendhal: Rome, Naples et Florence, ed. Arbelet, II, 390-391; Pastor, XV, 413; P. Zucker: Barocktheater u. barocke Kunst (Berlin 1939), 289-291; G. Ferrari: Bellezze arch. per le feste della Chinea in Roma (Turin 1920). – [97] Donati: Artisti ticinesi, 376; Fokker, I, 177, 188; cf Il Mercurio errante (Rome 1693), I, 47 (the gallery was in progress) and Deseine, I (1713), 210 (the decoration not completed). – [98] Vasi, IV, Pl. 63, Fol. 14. – [99] Ettore Lo Gatto: Gli artisti ital. in Russia, II, 50-52. – [100] Corresp. VIII No. 3281; A. Ravà: I teatri di Roma, Pl. 15. – [101] Corresp. VI No. 2594. – [102] Lalande, III, 569-570. – [103] The residence was often removed to the Vatican during Easter because of the many and lengthy functions in the Basilica (Coyer: Reise nach Italien u. Holland, Nürnberg 1776, 128). – [104] Cf C. Elling: Function and Form, 20-31. – [105] Matthiae: F. Fuga, 8. – [106] Pastor, XV, 747. – [107] Valesio Nov. 22. 1730, cf Scatassa in "Arte e Storia", 1917, 18. – [108] Milizia: Memorie (1785), II, 287; Matthiae, 8. – [109] Matthiae, 7-10, 70. – [110] II, 155. – [111] Golzio: Seicento e Settecento, 619; H. Bergner: Das barocke Rom (Lpz. 1914), 78. – [112] Matthiae, Pl. XII, 1. – [113] Brinckmann, op.cit., Fig. 139. – [114] C. Bildt: Svenska Minnen och Märken i Rom (Sth. 1900), 100-104; Matthiae, Pl. IX, 1. – [115] P. Romano: Roma nelle sue strade, verbo "Lungara"; concerning the historical circumstances see Matthiae, 73-74. – [116] Grosley, II (1764), 436, 440. – [117] On the library see among others Adlerbeth, 165; Björnståhl, II, 60; Kotzebue, III, 38; Juan Andres: Reise durch die verscheidene Städte Italiens, I (Weimar 1792), 117; Justi: Winckelmann, II[1], 145; Winckelmann: Briefe, ed. Rehm, I, 194; Agata Lo Vasco: Le biblioteche d'Italia nella seconda metà del secolo XVIII (Milan 1940), 62, 65-66. – [118] Silvagni, I, 472. – [119] Ugo Boncompagni Ludovisi: Lettere di una signora romana del secolo XVIII (Rome 1935). – [120] Gesch. des Barockstiles, 408. – [121] Baldinucci's Vita des Bernini, ed. Riegl, 184-185. – [122] I, 311. – [123] Milizia: Memorie (1785), II, 254. – [124] T. H. Fokker: Roman Baroque Art, I, 314-

15. – [125] Ibid., 314. – [126] Calza's name for an Old Roman type of storeyed house. – [127] Armando Schiavo: Villa Doria Pamphili (Milan 1942), Note 2. – [128] Matthiae, 79. – [129] Silvagni, I, 17, 25; the Petroni family died out in 1771 (L. Càllari: I palazzi di Roma, Rome 1944, 438). – [130] In 1738 Mellini returned to Rome from his nunciature in Vienna and in 1748 he became Imperial Ambassador to the Holy See (Noack, II, 392). According to Vasi, IV (1754), Fol. 21, the palace was rebuilt "ultimamente", cf Titi (1763), 325. – [131] Venuti, 221 ("l'odierno principe ha rifarcito ed ampliato verso la piazza di S. Carlo a' Catinari questo palazzo"). – [132] Hare: Walks in Rome, II, 183. – [133] C. Bandini: La galanteria nel gran mondo di Roma (Rome 1931), 391. – [134] Corresp. VII No. 2987. – [135] Venuti, 237. – [136] Brigante Colonna: Ottocento romano, 12 ff. – [137] Ibid., 13-14. – [138] E. Petraccone: Cagliostro (Milan 1937), 113. – [139] Silvagni, II, 231. In 1747 the Marchese G. Rondinini had presented Benedict XIV with an antique sarcophagus (Pastor, XVI[1], 157). On Goethe's visit to the palace see "Ital. Reise" Nov. 8. and Dec. 25. 1786, on Münter's see Tagebuch I, 352. – [140] See Donati: Artisti ticinesi, 617-620. A short history of the palace by Carlo Pierangeli in "L'Ossevatore romano" 1952, No. 124. – [141] Giuseppe Ceccarelli: I Braschi (Le Grandi Famiglie Romane VII, Rome 1949), 33, 40; Gorani: Mémoires, II, 399-400. Concerning a design for Pal. Braschi on the Corso see Adlerbeth (Gustav III's Resa i Italien, ed. Schück, 1902), 72. – [142] Röm. Leben, II, 169-170.

SQUARES AND STREETS

[1] H. P. L'Orange: Romersk Idyll. (Oslo 1952), 57-71. This fine study contains analyses of profound significance on the structure of Roman townscape. – [2] Il volto di Roma (Rome 1944), 90, cf 87-89. – [3] Ibid., 96. – [4] Coudenhove-Erthal, 91, 96; Pl. 39. – [5] During the reign of Pius VI Cosimo Morelli designed a project which developed Fontana's idea (depicted in Donati: Artisti ticinesi Pl. 515); Napoleon is said to have wanted it brought into being. F. J. L. Meyer warned (1783) in profetic words against such a solution: "Ob ein solcher Plan jemals gemacht ward, weis ich nicht – gewiss aber würde die Ausführung grosse Schwierigkeiten finden und doch immer der Erwartung davon nicht entsprechen"; he preferred the sudden view of S. Pietro (Darstell. aus Italien, 97). Cf V. Wanscher's reflections in "Tilskueren", 1937, I, 344-47. – [6] Venuti, 124. – [7] Old photograph published by Arturo Bianchi in "Capitolium", X, 1934, 41-43; Venuti, 208. – [8] Pastor, XIV[2], 1056. – [9] Hans Rose: Spätbarock (Munich 1922), 27. – [10] A. Ravà: I teatri di Roma (Rome 1953), 127-128. – [11] Edw. Wright: Some Observations made in Travelling through France, Italy, etc., 2. ed. (London 1764), 281. – [12] Corresp. IV No. 1644. – [13] Ibid., VII No. 3093. – [14] H. Tintelnot: Barocktheater u. barocke Kunst (Berlin 1939), 139, Fig. 105. – [15] Clementi, I, 550. – [16] Ibid., II, 172. – [17] Titi: Descr. delle pitture, etc. (1763), 196. – [18] Keyssler, II, 61-62; J. C. Goethe, I, 234. Monument reproduced in "Arch. min.", II, Pl. 175. – [19] "Fil. Juvara", Pl. 12-17. – [20] Coudenhove-Erthal, 96-97, Pl. 40. – [21] Roma vetus ac recens (Amsterdam 1695), Pl. facing pag. 207. – [22] Hélène Leclerc: Les origines italiennes de l'architecture théâtrale moderne (Paris 1946), 204-207. The identification (p. 206) of a project of Fontana in the Soane Museum in London is not satisfactory. The drawing in question does not concern "l'emplacement d'un palais pour une Société de gens de lettre", the mentioned "case antiche de'letterati al Corso" must be the buildings of the letterati-orphanage (see p. 228). In which case Fontana's project may be related to Giacomo d'Alibert's plan of building a theatre "nel luogo ... presso S. Silvestro in Capite, già ricovero pei fanciulli abbandonati fondato da Lionardo Caruso, detto *il Letterato*"; the plan however was not carried out as

Innocens XII handed over the site to the convent of S. Silvestro (A. Cametti: Il Teatro di Tordinona, Tivoli 1938, I, 19-20). – [23] P. P. Trompeo: Piazza Margana (Rome 1942), 28-35. – [24] Pastor, XV, 380. – [25] Rome moderne, I, 71. – [26] A project of Teatro Tordinona is attributed to Specchi (Leclerc op.cit., 204). – [27] Weinlig: Briefe über Rom, I (Dresden 1782), 31-32. – [28] Pastor, XV, 381. – [29] Mémoires, ed. R. Vèze, I, 216. – [30] Goethe: Ital. Reise, April 1788; Jul. Vogel: Aus Goethes röm. Tagen (Lpz. 1905), 281-282. – [31] De Blainville, II, 58 ff.; Labat, III, 180; De Brosses, II, 39; Lalande, III, 629-632; Pastor, XV, 370-371. – [32] Constanza Gradara: Pietro Bracci (Milan 1920), 77. – [33] Voiage histor. & polit. de Suisse, d'Italie et d'Allemagne (Frankfurt a. M. 1737), II, 63-65. – [34] Ant. Muñoz: P. da Cortona (Rome n. d.), 15 (Fig.). – [35] On Mignard's project see Ragnar Josephson: Kungarnas Paris (Sth. 1943), 139-141. – [36] Pio Pecchiai: La Scalinata di Piazza di Spagna. Villa Medici (Rome 1941). – [37] Christian Elling: Villa Pia in Vaticano (Copenhagen 1947), 31-32. – [38] Pecchiai, 30. – [39] Ibid., 23-24. – [40] Ibid., 24. – [41] Reg. Blomfield: A History of French Architecture 1661-1774, I (London 1921), 65-66. – [42] Eberh. Hempel in Festschrift Heinrich Wöfflin (Munich 1924), 277; an outstanding monograph. – [43] Pecchiai, 26. – [44] Josephson (Barocken, 232) has mentioned, though, that Benedetti has had contact with Bernini at a certain occasion. – [45] Mémoires de ma vie, par Charles Perrault. Voyage à Bordeaux (1669), par Claude Perrault. Ed. Paul Bonnefon (Paris 1909), 57-58. – [46] M. Mayer: Villa Benedetta (Rome 1677); on Benedetti's later artistic activity in Rome see also: Corresp. VI No. 2636, 2643, 2685 (1687). – [47] Nic. Tessin d. y.'s Studieresor, ed. O. Sirén (Sth. 1914). – [48] The mentioned diary is now in the possession of Dr. Carl David Moselius (Sth.), who has kindly allowed me to consult it. – [49] Sirén, op.cit., Pl. 50; R. Josephson: Hur Rom byggdes under Renässans och Barock (Sth. 1926), 57 (fig., drawing at Fullerö); also: Tessin, I, 51-52; also: Barocken, 232. – [50] Hempel, loc.cit., 279 f.; Pecchiai, Pl. III. – [51] Memorie (1785), II, 241. – [52] loc.cit., 281. – [53] "Fil. Juvara", I, 68-69. – [54] loc.cit., 44. – [55] "Fil. Juvara", I, 20. The regular ecclesiastic to whom J. is said to have delivered his design was the Provincial of the Minims in Turin. – [56] For instance a project reproduced ibid. Pl. 114. – [57] Corresp. VI No. 2408. – [58] Ibid., No. 2428. – [59] Ibid., No. 2464. – [60] Ibid., No. 2483. – [61] Ibid., No. 2499. – [62] Is, for example, cognate to Castel Fusano at Ostia, built after 1620 (Ed. Martinori: Lazio turrito, Rome 1933, I, 132-134). – [63] In the possession of Duke A. Torlonia, Rome; reproduced in Mostra del giardino italiano, 2. ed. (Florens 1931), Pl. 50. – [64] It is possible that certain family connections, which are quite unknown, might have explained a few secrets of the career of the architect; he has probably enjoyed a special patronage. A few persons with French connections bore the name of De Santis. A Marchese (later Count) D. S. was the Duke of Parma's ambassador in Rome in 1722 and 1723; a certain Mr D. S. was secretary at the French Embassy in Rome during the reign of Louis XIV (Corresp. I, 90-93, VI No. 2329, 2397, 2482, and elsewhere). Giuseppe De Santis, the wellknown adventurer and one of the fellows in Casanova's entourage, gave himself out to be – and maybe rightly – "a Roman gentleman" (Ch. Samaran: Jacques Casanova Vénitien, Paris 1914, 322). – [65] Pecchiai, 44. – [66] Corresp. VI No. 2416. – [67] Ibid., No. 2531, cf 2534. – [68] Ibid., No. 2539. – [69] Ibid., No. 2544. – [70] Pierre Paul: Le Cardinal Melchior de Polignac (Paris 1922), 364. – [71] Corresp. VI No. 2551. – [72] Ibid., No. 2550. – [73] Ibid., No. 2554. The audience took place on Oct. 15., the dispatch is dated Oct. 19. – [74] Published by Hempel, as mentioned above, Fig. 6. – [75] Corresp. VI No. 2562. – [76] Ibid., No. 2575. – [77] Ibid., VII No. 2889. – [78] Pecchiai, 53 ff. – [79] Journal de voyage en Italie, I, 207. – [80] Pecchiai, 83-84; on the restauration see Corresp. VII No. 3388, 3399, 3470, and elsewhere. – [81] Pecchiai, 80-83. –

[82] Ibid., 57. – [83] loc.cit. – [84] Hempel, loc.cit., 286. – [85] Pecchiai, 40. – [86] Ibid., 45 Reference to Bom Jesus). – [87] Corresp. VI, No. 2586, 2593. – [88] Ibid., VII, No. 3014. – [89] Pöllnitz, II, 231-232. – [90] Romano: Roma nelle sue strade, verbo "Ignazio". – [91] Rotili: Fil. Raguzzini, 51-54. – [92] For instance in Villa Marlia at Lucca (Fot. Alinari No. 41390, 41392). – [93] Architekturens Hist., III, 463. – [94] Cf the designs in Brinckmann, Wanscher and Fokker. – [95] On the meaning of this street name see P. P. Trompeo: Piazza Margana, 47-53. – [96] I, 323. – [97] Trompeo: La Scale del Sole, 216. – [98] Ibid., 221. – [99] Egger: Röm. Veduten, II, 32-33. – [100] Baldinucci-Riegl: Vita del Bernini, 30-31. – [101] Egger, II, Pl. 78. – [102] Corresp. VI No. 2359. – [103] Ibid., No. 2367. – [104] Ibid., No. 2531. – [105] Ibid., No. 2606. – [106] Pastor, XV, 749; Benaglia, however, did supply some sculptures to Salvi's fountain, cf Corresp. VIII No. 3583, 3591. – [107] Costanza Gradara: Pietro Bracci (Milan 1920), Pl. XXVII; F. Fichera: Luigi Vanvitelli (Rome 1937), Fig. 13. – [108] Gradara, Pl. XXIX. – [109] H. Thirion: Les Adam et Clodion (Paris 1885), 56; A. Roserot: Edme Bouchardon (Paris 1910), 27; Corresp. VIII No. 3367. – [110] Pastor, XV, 750. – [111] II, 46. – [112] Millizia: Memorie, II, 254. – [113] Gradara, 98. – [114] Mario Dell'Arco in "Studi romani", I, part 2, 156. – [115] Silvagni, I, 387. – [116] Rom. Dagbøger, Jan. 4. 1834. – [117] Albert Besnard: Sous le ciel de Rome (Paris 1925), 84. – [118] Lettres (1711), 177. – [119] III, 507. – [120] Lettres concern. un voyage fait à Rome en 1773, II, 119. – [121] Sämtl. Werke, VII (Lpz. 1909), 85. – [122] Ueber Mahlerei in Rom, III (Lpz. 1787), 366. – [123] Reise III, 201. – [124] Cf the cold reference in Reumont (Röm. Briefe, I 126). – [125] Keyssler, I, 712; Lalande, IV, 358; G. B. Giovenale: S. Maria in Cosmedin (Rome 1927), 372. – [126] Egger, II, Fig. 22. – [127] Corresp. IV No. 1540. It can be added that the fountain in front of S. Maria in Trastevere was renewed in 1694 by C. Fontana (Lalande, IV, 531) and that the well in Piazza Montanara was restored "into better form" in 1696. (Venuti, 348). – [128] Lalande, III, 630; Venuti, 131; Pastor, XVI^1, 121; reproduced in Vasi, II, Pl. 23. – [129] Nugent: The Grand Tour, 2. ed., II (London 1756), 239; Corresp. VIII No. 3663; Lalande, III, 392; Venuti, 16. – [130] Vasi, II, Pl. 34. – [131] Pastor, XV, 748. – [132] Clementi, II, 62. – [133] Vasi, II, Fol. 18. – [134] Volkmann, II, 357; Lalande, IV, 58. – [135] P. Romano: Il quartiere del Rinascimento, 82. – [136] Ibid.: Roma, verbo "Monte di Pietà". – [137] Venuti, 22; Pastor, XVI^1, 120. – [138] On Canova and Bonaparte cf F. Brun: Röm. Leben, II, 30-32. – [139] Abh. über die Litt. und Kunstwerke des Alterthums (Lpz. 1776), 59. – [140] R. Venuti: Descr. top. di Roma, 3. ed., I, Rome 1824, 153. – [141] Münter: Tageb., II, 133-134. – [142] A. C. Gierlew: Breve om Italien (1807), I, 419. – [143] Ital. Reise, Sept. 1787. – [144] Corresp. VIII No. 3663. – [145] Pecchiai: La Scalinata, 95-103. – [146] Goethe: Röm. Carneval; the obelisk is judged severely: Corresp. XV No. 8997, 9001. – [147] Ital. Reise, Feb. 13. 1787. – [148] Mercuri: Nouv. Descr. de Rome (Rome 1853), I, 61-63; Volkmann, II, 327; Münter: Tageb. I, 328-329; Ital. Reise, Sept. 3. 1787; the uncovered obelisk is reproduced in Vasi, II, and in Russel: Letters from a young painter (1750), II, Pl. III. – [149] Münter, II, 132-133. – [150] N. Schow: Georg Zoëgas Liv og Fortienester (Copenhagen 1809), 31; Fr. Gottl. Welcker: Zoëgas Leben (Klass. der Archäol., Halle 1912), II, 43, 44, 46, 47 and elsewhere; K. Friis Johansen in "Rom og Danmark", I, 248-250. – [151] Welcker, 51. – [152] Vasi-Nibby: Itinéraire de Rome, I (1818), 216; Joh. Ph. Siebenkees: Handb. d. Archäol. (Nürnberg 1799), 323; also Wright: Travels, 196, 273. – [153] Corinne ou l'Italie, I (Paris 1807), 316. – [154] Ital. Reise, Nov. 3. 1786. – [155] Rudolf Zeitler: Klassizismus u. Utopia (Sth. 1954), 242; in 1788 the French Academy in Rome wanted to acquire a cast of one of the Dioscuri (Corresp. XV No. 8902). – [156] Rik. Magnussen: Thorvaldsens Livsanskuelse (Copenhagen 1936), 58. – [157] Th. Oppermann: Thorvaldsen. 1797-1819 (Copen-

hagen 1927), 32. – [158] C. L. Fernow: Röm. Studien, I (Zürich 1806), 198; cf C. Elling: Thorvaldsen (Copenhagen 1944), 11-12. – [159] G. Matthiae: Piazza del Popolo (Rome n. d.), Pl. VIII, IX. – [160]. I.e. through the projects by Berthaults, the Imperial architect; a precise evaluation of the place in R. Josephson: Hur Rom byggdes, 152-153. – [161] Nolli No. 215, "guglia giacente nel cortile". – [162] Matthiae, 126. – [163] Nino Valeri: Pietro Verri (Milan 1937), 19. – [164] Briefe, I, 226. – [165] Ital. Reise, Dec. 13. 1786. – [166] Cf C. Elling: Det gamle København (Copenhagen 1948), 11 ff. – [167] Claës Lagergren: Efterlämnade Dagboksanteckningar, I (Sth. 1940), 133. – [168] P. P. Trompeo: Piazza Margana, 18-22. – [169] Casanova: Mémoires, ed. Vèze, VII, 182. – [170] To be seen on a painting by F. Diofebi ("S. Giuseppe-festen") in the Thorvaldsen Museum. – [171] The latter arco is reproduced in Vasi, IV, Pl. 75. – [172] Cf Vald. Vedel: Liv og Kunst, I (Copenhagen 1949), 105 ff. – [173] L'Orange: Romersk Idyll, 23-26. – [174] "Arch. min.", I, Pl. 108-123. – [175] Axel Boëthius: Hur Rom byggdes under Antiken (Sth. 1938), 265-286; Figs. 108, 110-112, 114-115, 117. Christian Elling: Fra Sabinerbjergene (Copenhagen 1954), 37 (Fig.) – [176] In the Middle Ages there was no tax on trade from booth and workshop, the Roman had to pay a little duty for the "stone" on which he offered his goods for sale (P. Gregorovius: Papst Alexander VI und seine Zeit, Berlin 1942, 156). – [177] E. R. Trincanato: Venezia minore (Milan 1948), 93, 100 (Fig.). – [178] External galleries on façades are reproduced in Vasi, II, 28, 40; IV, 67; IX, 170. – [179] "Improvisatoren". Illustrated by the author (Copenhagen 1945), 29 (Fig.). – [180] Mme Du Boccage: Lettres contenant ses voyages (Dresden 1771), 188. – [181] F. Gregorovius: Die Stadt Rom zu Ende der Renaissance (Freiburg i. B. 1925), Fig. 50. – [182] Hugo Matthiessen: Gamle københavnske Skilte og Bomærker (Copenhagen 1919), 12-41. – [183] Publio Parsi: Edicole di fede e di pietà per le vie di Roma (Rome 1939); Trompeo: Piazza Margana, 100-104. – [184] Souvenirs de Madame Vigée-Lebrun (Paris 1869), I, 158. – [185] Norb. von Grund: Malerische Reise eines deutschen Künstlers nach Rom (Vienna 1789), II, 154. – [186] Ibid., 153. – [187] Mme Du Boccage: Lettres, 188. – [188] Silvagni, I, 528-529. – [189] Le Magnificenze, VIII, Pl. 144. – [190] Parsi, op.cit., 58-60; the play is late 18. century. – [191] De Blainville, II, 68. – [192] Glimpses of Italian Society in the 18th Century (London 1892), 211. – [193] Christian Elling: Den italienske Nat (Copenhagen 1947), 93-98. – [194] Where no authority is stated the following account is based on contemporary guides, and also on Silvagni, I, 45-66, and on Romano's topographical Lex. A useful survey by Louis Bobé in "Rom og Danmark", I, 314-342. On life on Piazza Navona see P. Romano and P. Partini: Piazza Navona nella storia e nell' arte (Rome n. d.), Chap. VI and VII, and Bengt von Törne: Från Domitianus till Gustav III (Uppsala 1933), 215 ff. – [195] Egger: Röm. Veduten, II, Figs. 21, 22. – [196] Pascoli, I, 311. – [197] Vasi, IV, 38. – [198] Lalande, IV, 96. – [199] G. Briganti: I Bamboccianti (Rome 1950), 50-51; Fig. 43. – [200] P. Romano: Il quartiere del Rinascimento, 101-102. – [201] Corresp. XII, 460; on bookselling in Rome see J. G. C. Adler: Reisebemerkungen auf einer Reise nach Rom (1783), 129; a visit at Pagliarini's is mentioned in Christopher Hervey: Letters, III, 185. – [202] Rome moderne, II, 388. – [203] Pierre Champion: Mon vieux quartier (Paris 1932), 43-49. – [204] De Blainville: Voyage histor., II, 104 ff. – [205] L. Holbergs Memoirer, ed. F. J. Billeskov Jansen (Copenhagen 1943), 68, 266-267; Th. A. Müller: Den unge Ludvig Holberg (Copenhagen 1943), 190. – [206] Deseine, II, 342. – [207] E. Portal: L'Arcadia (1922), 129; according to this authority the meeting is held on Piazza Cesarini; cf also Luigi Russo: Metastasio, 3. ed. (Bari 1945), 3 ff. It can be added that Metastasio is later said to to have lived in a small house near Pal. Testa-Piccolomini (A. Belli: Delle case abitate in Roma da parecchi uomini illustri, Rome 1850, 5); cf Pl. 116 in this book. – [208] Archivo del General Miranda,

II (Caracas 1929), 59. – [209] Trompeo: La Scala del Sole, 266-272. – [210] Pastor, XV, 739; moved to Montecitorio in 1762. – [211] E. Zilliacus: Romerska Vandringar, 95. – [212] Deseine, II, 361; Lalande, IV, 122. – [213] VII, Pl. 133. – [214] H. Focillon: Piranesi, 51, 53, 63; Corresp. XI No. 5163. – [215] Vasi, IV, Pl. 67. – [216] Silvagni, I, 49; H. Voelcker: Die Stadt Goethes. Frankfurt am Main im 18. Jahrh. (Frankf. 1932), 127. – [217] When Crown Prince Frederik (VI) was expected in Rome in 1692 some Jews were instrumental in furnishing Pal. Sciarra-Carbognano on the Corso, which he had rented (Fr. Weilbach: Frederik IV's Italiensrejser, Copenhagen 1933, 28). See also Russel: Letters from a young painter, II (1951), 197. – [218] On the ghetto in general see (apart from Gregorius' classic monograph in "Wanderjahre") especially A. von Reumont: Röm. Briefe, III, 205-208; Fernow, 179-184; Gorani, II, 381-387; Russel, II, 196-199. – [219] P. Romano: Il Rione Campo Marzio, I (Rome 1939), 84-117; G. J. Hoogewerff in "Studi Romani", I (Rome 1953), 138-139. – [220] Bandini: Galanterie, 346; on the Roman prostitutes see U. Gnoli: Cortigiane romane (Rome 1941). – [221] A. von Kotzebue: Erinnerungen von einer Reise aus Liefland nach Rom u. Neapel, III (Berlin 1805), 267. – [222] Sitten- u. Kulturgem., 185. – [223] De Blainville, II, 125. – [224] Mme Du Boccage: Lettres, 301. – [225] E. C. Werlauff: Hist. Ant. til L. Holbergs atten første Lystspil (Copenhagen 1858), 113; C. Elling: Fra Vestergade (Copenhagen 1947), 4. – [226] Silvagni, I, 51. – [227] U. Gnoli: Alberghi ed osterie di Roma nella Rinascenza (Spoleto 1935), 119-120. – [228] Pastor: Die Stadt Rom zu Ende der Renaiss., 51. – [229] Deseine, II, 411-412; as late as in 1846 H. C. Andersen engaged his Veturin to Naples in Albergo dell'Orso (Dagbøger, April 15. 1846). – [230] Ibid., I, 6. – [231] Journal d'un voyage en Italie, ed. Pilon (Paris 1932), 155. – [232] Pastor, op.cit., Fig. 25. – [233] P. Romano: Roma nelle sue strade, verbo "Campana". – [234] Clementi, II, 163. – [235] P. P. Trompeo: Sulle orme di Stendhal (Rome 1924), 223-235. – [236] Hoogewerff in "Studi Romani", I (1953), 144-150. – [237] L. Holbergs Memoirer, ed. Billeskov Jansen, 62. – [238] Pio Pecchiai: La Scalinata (Rome 1941), 34. – [239] On hos sojourn see F. Ahlefeldt Laurvig: Prins Carls Rejse (Copenhagen 1925), 66-68. – [240] Cf P. Romana & P. Partini: Piazza di Spagna (Rome n. d.) 83. – [241] Ibid., 84. – [242] Comte de Caylus: Voyage d'Italie 1714-1715, ed. A. Pons (Paris 1914), 173. – [243] Viaggio in Italia, I, 197. – [244] Vertraul. Briefe, I, 8. – [245] De Brosses has given the recipe for an excellent pudding which was served in Monte D'Oro. – [246] Deseine, I, 24. – [247] Cf Souvenirs de Charles-Henri Baron de Gleichen, ed. P. Grimblot (Paris 1869), pag. VI-IX, 202-203, 208-209 and elsewhere, and G. Maugras: Le Duc et la Duchesse de Choiseul, 12. ed. (Paris 1924), 60-62. – [248] Mémoires, ed. Vèze, VII, 169. – [249] Romano & Partini, op.cit. 79 (Fig.), 90. – [250] The Pembroke Papers, ed. Lord Herbert (London 1942), 261. – [251] Clementi, II, 204. – [252] Noack, II, 106; on this eccentric personality and grandiose traveller after whom all "Bristol" hotels are named see W. S. Childe-Pemberton: The Earl Bishop. The life of Frederik Hervey, I-II (London 1924). On his Roman Country house Ickworth Park (Suffolk) see Country Life, March 10. 1955. – [253] Röm. Leben, II, 315-316 and elsewhere. – [254] Mannlich, 172. – [255] Mémoires, XII, 4, 241; in 1773 she married an Englishman. – [256] On an etching from 1841 (reproduced on a plate facing p. 56 in Romano & Partini, op.cit.) a sign above the door of "Keats' House" is to be seen with a painting of the Spanish Steps. – [257] Vertraul. Briefe, II, 9-10. – [258] Silvagni, I, 386. – [259] Petraccone: Cagliostro, 103; W. R. H. Trowbridge: Casanova (London 1910), 34. – [260] Neville Rogers: Keats, Shelley and Rome (London 1949), 34-35, 65 ff.; Ernest Raymond: Two Gentlemen of Rome (London 1952), 186-196. – [261] In a letter Björnst. Björnson has given a malicious description of the interior of Munthe's home (Gustaf Munthe: Axel Munthe, Sth. 1949, 160-161). – [262]

Herders Reise nach Italien. Herders Briefwechsel mit seiner Gattin 1788-1789, edd. H. Düntzer & F. G. v. Herder (Giessen 1859), 178. – [263] C. Elling in "Artes", V, 146. – [264] Mrs. Millar, II, 189-190. – [265] Ibid., II, 379. – [266] Lalande, V, 134. – [267] Briefe, ed. Rehm, I, 262. – [268] Reisen eines Deutschen, III, 243. – [269] Roland de la Platière, V, 62. – [270] Noack, II, 255. – [271] Casanova: Mémoires, XI, 228. – [272] A. Valeri: Casanova a Roma (Rome 1899), 49. – [273] Mémoires, XI, 227. – [274] Noack, II, 125. – [275] Herders Reise nach Italien. Herders Briefwechsel mit seiner Gattin, edd. H. Düntzer & F. G. v. Herder (Giessen 1859), 94. – [276] Ibid., 128. – [277] L. Bobé ("Rom og Danmark", I, 318), who uses Pierre's statement without giving his authority, identifies it wrongly with Via Condotti. – [278] Corresp. XV No. 8718. – [279] Silvagni, I, 30-34. – [280] Voyage hist. et crit., II, 72. – [281] Lettere dell' Abate Pietro Metastasio, I (Trieste 1795), 25. – [282] Rome, Naples et Florence, ed. D. Muller (Paris 1919), II, 137-138; cf C. Molbech: Reise ... 1819-1820, III (Copenhagen 1822), 256. Frequently mentioned in Andersen's Roman Diaries. – [284] Mémoires, I, 210, 329. – [285] Diego Angeli: Le cronache del Caffè Greco, 3. ed. (Milan 1939), 1-4. – [286] Briefe, II, 142-143; cf Moritz, I, 152. – [287] F. Mendelssohn-Bartholdy: Briefe aus den Jahren 1830 bis 1847, 7. ed (Lpz. 1899), 63. – [288] Angeli, 45. – [289] Moritz, III, 13. – [290] Maler. Reise, II, 110. – [291] Concerning Sergel's studies see O. Antonsson: Sergels Ungdom och Romtid (Sth. 1942), 196. – [292] W. G. Constable: Richard Wilson (London 1953), 27. – [293] Wm. T. Whitley: Artists and their friends in England (London 1928), II, 307. – [294] Travels through France and Italy, 2. ed. (London 1766), II, 91-92. – [295] The Pembroke Papers 261, 271; Boswell on the Grand Tour. Italy, Corsica, and France 1765-1766, edd. F. Brady & Frederick A. Pottle (London 1955), 52 ("gloomy café"), 74. Also Reynolds visited the café (Whitley, I, 147). – [296] Gorani, II, 26-28. Goethe stayed in his house in Castelgandolfo (Ital. Reise, 1787, "Bericht Oktober"). – [297] Briefe über Rom, I (Dresden 1782), 18. – [298] Charles Burney: The present state of Music in France and Italy, 2. ed. (London 1773), 276. – [299] W. G. Constable: Rich. Wilson, 27. – [300] Mal. Reise (Vienna 1789), II, 34. – [301] "Rom og Danmark", II, Fig. 48; the address is stated to be Porto di Ripa Grande 26-27 (ibid. 23). See also Joseph von Führich: Briefe aus Italien an seine Eltern (Freiburg i. B. 1883), 91. – [302] Correspondance, edd. Paupe & Cheramy, II, 399. – [303] U. von Wilamowitz-Moellendorff: Erinnerungen 1848-1914 (Lpz. 1928), 139-140. – [304] Corresp. XV No. 8859. – [305] Mrs. Piozzi: Glimpses of Italian Society, 211. – [306] Labat, III, 46. – [307] Fernow: Kultur- und Sittengem., 101-102. – [308] II, 98. – [309] Travels, 2. ed., II, 95. – [310] Fernow, 101-102. – [311] Erinnerungen von einer Reise nach Rom, III, 249; cf Adlerbeth, 106 and Bonstetten: Reise in die klass. Gegenden Roms, II, 43-44. – [312] Holger Jacobæus' Rejsebog (1671-1692), ed. Vilh. Maar (Copenhagen 1910), 133-136. – [313] N. von Grund (II, 86) states "Aoo", i.e. the mewing of a cat, to be a call signal. – [314] A rather short survey over rococo houses is found in Rotili: Fil. Raguzzini (c. 1950), 103-104. The author of this work prepared a temporary catalogue in 1926. – [315] Silvagni, I, 115. – [316] Travels, 364. – [317] A splendid review of the present state of research in this field was given by Axel Boethius on the Congress of Antique Studies in Copenhagen 1954 (Urbanism in Italy, is available in a typewritten copy); also noteworthy is the same author's work: Kejsarnas Rom och Medeltidens Städer (Göteborg Högskolas Årsskr. LIX, 1953); cf C. Elling: Form and Function, § 4. – [318] Vasi, II, Pl. 28. – [319] Ital. Reise, Aug. 28. 1787; Münter held masonic lodge here sometimes (Tageb. I, 328, 345, 373, II, 134; III, 74). – [320] II, 150. – [321] Erik Palmstedt: Resedagbok 1778-1786, ed. Martin Olsson (Upps. 1927), 102-103. – [322] C. Elling: Rejse paa Amager (Copenhagen 1945), Pl. 4-7, 16. – [323] But it occurs frequently in Venice (cf for instance Calle delle Botteghe ved S. Barnaba). – [324] Reproduced in "Studi Romani", I, part 2 Pl. 17, also mentioned p. 142-143 (G. J. Hoogewerff). – [325] The district around the Rialto bridge, rebuilt after the fire in 1514, cf Rob. Cessi & Annibale Alberti: Rialto (Bologna 1934), 91-143. – [326] Wölfflin-Rose: Renaiss. u. Barock (4. ed.), Figs. 2, 4, 73-75. – [327] Egger, II, Pl. 97. – [328] Venuti, 208. – [329] G. Donati in "L'Urbe" 1940, 20-26. – [330] Noack, II, 223. – [331] A. Ravà: I teatri di Roma (Rome 1953), 62-63. – [332] Moritz, III, 153-154. – [333] Egger, II, Pl. 78. – [334] Vasi, X, Pl. 194. – [335] Silvagni, I, 47, 115. – [336] Vasi, VI, Pl. 105. – [337] Max Lamberg: Le Mémorial d'un Mondain (Frankf. 1775), 31. – [338] "Arch. min.", II, Pl. 44; Vasi, II, Pl. 30. – [339] Vasi, II, Pl. 70. – [340] Partini & Romano: Piazza di Spagna, 69-70. – [341] Noack, II, 165. – [342] Etching and text in J. Vogel: Aus Goethes röm. Tagen (Lpz. 1905), Pl. 2. – [343] Ibid., 143. – [344] F. Landberger: Wilh. Tischbein (Lpz. 1908), 68. – [345] Monti: Le case abitate in Roma da V. Monti (Rome 1868), 6 ff., 9, 11; Noack, II, 407. Later on Mendelssohn stayed in the house. – [346] Ravà, op.cit., 115. – [347] Clementi, II, 102. – [348] P. Tomei: L'arch. a Roma nel Quattrocento (Rome 1942), 62. – [349] Vasi (II, plate without no.) depicts the excavation; a similar print from a sketch made on the spot is reproduced in Russel: Letters from a young painter, II (London 1750), between p. 138 and 139. – [350] Trompeo: Sulle orme di Stendhal, 248. – [351] "Arch. min.", I, Pl. 59. – [352] Seen before the restauration on a plate in Vasi (II, 1762, Fol. XXIV). – [353] Le Chiese di Roma XXXIII. – [354] Silvagni, II, 404-405. – [355] Corresp. VIII No. 3658. – [356] The street was extended during Clement XII according to Romano, verbo "Zingari". – [357] Venuti: Descr. delle Antichità di Roma, 3. ed. (Rome 1824), II, 143. – [358] On Casa Raffaelli in Via del Babuino see Eugenio di Castro in "L'Urbe", Sept.-Okt. 1954, 30.

HOUSES IN THE COUNTRY

[1] Negro: Seconda Roma, 21 ff; Diego Angeli: Roma romantica (Milan 1935), Chap. II. – [2] "Cette ville d'un attrait mystérieux et d'un paix incomparable" (Charles Gounod: Mémoires d'un artiste, 3. ed., Paris 1896, 125); "trudged around in Rome! how peaceful and deserted in comparison to Naples ... it is as if I had come back to Odense ... (H. C. Andersen: Romerske Dagbøger, March 24. 1834). Cf A. P. Adler: Optegn. fra en Reise (Kbh. 1849), 148, Adlerbeth, 116, and Moritz, II, 104. – [3] Trompeo: Piazza Margana, 125. – [4] [Anon.:] Le vie di Roma (Rome 1915), 38; P. Romano: Roma, 90. – [5] H. Focillon: Piranesi, 90. – [6] The inscription says: "Clemens XII ... Viam Hanc Inter Thermas Olympiadis In Collo Viminali Publicae Commoditati Aperuerit ...". – [7] Egger: Röm. Veduten, I, Pl. 106-109. – [8] Valerio Mariani: Bart. Pinelli (Rome 1948), Pl. XXIII. – [9] Le Chiese di Roma, XXXVI. S. Salvatore della Corte. – [10] Trompeo: La Scala del Sole, 225 ff. – [11] H. C. Andersen's Roman Diary, April 26. 1846; also an extempore poem to Tasso's Oak, Nov. 23. 1833. – [12] C. Elling: Function and Form of the Roman Belvedere (Copenhagen 1950), pass. – [13] Abel Bonnard: Rome (Paris 1931), 38-39. – [14] Eberh. Hempel: Carlo Rainaldi (Bibl. d'arte illustr.), Pl. XXIV-XXV. – [15] Deseine, I, 64; Volkmann, II, 364-365. – [16] P. Romano: Roma, 38-39. – [17] Compton Mackenzie: Prince Charlie (London 1932), 20-21. – [18] C. Chledowski: Barocktidsmänniskorna i Rom (Sth. 1920), 20 f.; L. von Pastor: Die Stadt Rom zu Ende der Renaiss. (Freib. im Briesgau 1925), 24; Trompeo: La Scala del Sole, 266-268. – [19] G. Baglione: Le vite de' pittori ... (Rome 1642), 340. – [20] T. Valenti: Papa Lambertini umoristico (Rome 1938), 152. – [21] In the friezes over the door is carved: "Carolus Cardellus". – [22] The fountain is crowned with a cardinal's hat. Judging from the soft modelled style the fountain has most likely been put up under Andrea Santacroce, Cardinal 1699, died 1712

(Corresp. III, 21). – [23] K. von Schlözer: Röm. Briefe (Stuttg. & Berlin 1913), 173. – [24] "M. ordinò che si dovessi a quella [opera ɔ: Pal. Farnese] dirittura fare un ponte, chi attraversasso il fiume del Tevere". Cf the bridges seen from the backs of Pal. Barberini and Villa Ludovisi. – [25] Andrea Fulvio: L'Antichità di Roma (Venice 1588), 62. – [26] Nolli's plan from 1748 shows only two bridges, Vasi's etching three, the prospect is taken from the fourth; the etching is found (Pl. 193) in the 10th book of "La Magnificenze", published in 1761 with dedication from Jan. 12. 1760. A. Petrucci: Le Magnificenze di Roma di G. Vasi, 87). – [27] Reproduced in Maurice Fouche: Percier et Fontaine (Paris n. d.), 21. – [28] Wright: Travels, 307. – [29] N. Tessins Studieresor, 176. – [30] I, 210; Giardino Colonna is also mentioned by Roland de la Platière, V (1780), 334. – [31] Keyssler, II, 105. – [32] C. Elling in Festskr. til L. L. Hammerich (Copenhagen 1952), 114. – [33] C. Elling in "Architekten", Maanedshefte, 1930, 100-104. – [34] Lalande, IV, 356; Vasi, V, Fol. XXXV (Fig.). – [35] Deseine, II, 456; Volkmann, II, 405. – [36] Roma moderna (1727), 155; Deseine, IV, 901. – [37] II, 618. – [38] Lalande, V, 513. – [39] In Nolli is seen a fountain in the middle surrounded by trees. – [40] Lalande, IV, 524; Volkmann, II, 623. – [41] Roland de la Platière, V, 73-74. – [42] Mrs. Piozzi: Glimpses, 210. – [43] Roland, as mentioned above, 75. On the avertion to the scent of flowers see also De Brosses, II, 168; D'Orbessan, 570 ("indoors, smoke isn't feared, but the scent of flowers makes the delicate ladies of the country swoon"); Lalande, V, 163; Nugent: The Grand Tour, 2. ed., III (London 1756), 26; N. von Grund, II, 81; N. Brooke: Voyage à Naples et en Toscane, 57. – [44] "Benedicto XIV P. M. /Quod/ Liberalitate Optimi Principis /Sacrae Huic Domui/ Uberrimam Aquae Virginis Copiam / Suppeditaverit / Universus Eremitarum S. Augustini Ordo / M. P. Anno Iubilaei MDCCL." – [45] Lina Montalto: Il Clementino 1595-1875 (Rome 1939), 72-77; Volkmann, II, 567. – [46] In 1732 he published "La bolla d'oro de' fanciulli nobili romani e quella dei libertini" which were found in the Vigne. – [47] Francesco Basile: Studi sull' architettura di Sicilia (Rome 1942), 87. – [48] A. Boëthius: Hur Rom byggdes under Antiken (Sth. 1938), 257-286. – [49] Otto Haslund, among several Danish painters, has made use of the subject, also in a genre painting (F. Hendriksen: En dansk Kunstnerkreds, Copenhagen 1928, 141, 149). – [50] R. Villedieu: La Villa Médicis (Rome 1950), 10, 311. – [51] Deseine, I, 159. – [52] Noack, II, 272; the street was then called Via di S. Isidoro. – [53] Emma Amadei: Roma turrita (Rome 1943), 38-39. – [54] Thus Hubert Robert, cf Gabillot's and P. de Nolhac's monographs; the latter's work La Rome d'Hubert Robert hasn't been available to me. – [55] II, 223. – [56] Egger, I, Pl. 104. – [57] Remarks (London 1753), 194-195. – [58] The working Scavatori is mentioned by Wright (Travels, 336); a drawing, dated 1724, by G. Piccini shows the excavation (Egger, I, Pl. 103). – [59] Guidi: Lettres (Genève 1783), I, 234-235; Pierre Paul: Le Cardinal Melchior de Polignac (Paris 1922), 372-374. – [60] Del Palazzo de' Cesari (Verona 1738). – [61] Montesquieu: Voyages (1894), I, 246-247, cf 211-212. – [62] II, 221; cf Grosley (ed. 1764), II, 234-236. – [63] Deseine, III, 802: Lalande, IV, Reumont: Briefe von einem Florentiner, I, 89; Filippo Mercuri: Nouv. Descript. de Rome (Rome 1853), I, 205. – [64] Chr. Huelsen: Forum und Lalatin (Munich 1926), 90. – [65] Archivo del General Miranda, II, 72. – [66] Vald. Thisted: Romerske Mosaiker (Copenhagen 1951), 389 ff. – [67] M. Galschiøt: Skandinaver i Rom (Copenhagen 1923), 164. – [68] Venuti, 371; Volkmann, II, 778. – [69] After the editing of the present text, mainly based on observations made in 1949-1950, the country estate has been partly renewed; the work was in hand in 1953. – [70] Nolli's Plan 1748, No. 1078. – [71] An antiquarian survey in G. C. Adler: Beschr. der stadt Rom (Altona 1781), 115-116. – [72] Röm. Leben, I, 121-122. – [73] Now dated to 378 B.C. and after (Schück-Sjöqvist: Rom, Sth. 1949, 75). – [74] Rom under Pius IX (Copenhagen 1877), 393.

– [75] Lalande, IV, 497; Volkmann, II, 612; Vasi, X, Pl. 198. Also the garden behind Pal. Salviati, "in the French manner" (D'Orbessan, 546); on Duke Salviati's French symphaties see Corresp. II, No. 956. – [76] Labat, III, 42; IV, 119. – [77] G. Maugras: Le Duc et la Duchesse de Choiseul (Paris 1924), 35. – [78] Cf note 219 to the chapter: Squares and Streets. – [79] Röm. Eleg. XIII. – [80] Deseine, I, 8; Casino Sinibaldi is to be seen in Vasi, X, Pl. 186. – [81] Röm. Leben, I, 255. – [82] Voyage d'Italie 1773-1774, ed. Wilhelm (Paris 1948), 63. – [83] Deseine, III, 623. – [84] Lady Morgan, III, 211. – [85] Welcker: Zoëgas Leben (Halle 1912), 256; S. Maria in Navicella was most often closed "as it is situated in a quite secluded area" (Keyssler, I, 725). On Nov. 5. H. C. Andersen makes the following note in his diary: "Walked over Monte Cavallo and got lost among vineyards and ruins, so I had to climb a fence in order to find my bearings, but I didn't succeed". – [86] Quotation from Lady Morgan, III, 211. – [87] Keyssler, II, 118; J. C. Goethe, I, 270. – [88] Lalande, III, 553. – [89] Wright, 327. – [90] II, 52-53. – [91] Typical French reflections in Richard: Descript. hist. et critique de l'Italie (Paris 1766), VI, 134-139; a contemporary German view in Keyssler (II, 147). – [92] Wright, as mentioned above, 327. – [93] The Grand Tour, 2. ed. (London 1756), III, 245. – [94] Lady Morgan, III, 274. – [95] Corresp. IV No. 1800. – [96] The Works, ed. Fraser, IV (Oxford 1871), 522. On the fear of "aria cattiva" see among others Jacobæus, 121; Bonstetten: Reise in die klass. Gegenden Roms, II, 9-10; Russel, I, 183; F. Brun: Röm. Leben, II, 302. – [97] Clementi, I, 654. – [98] Corresp. of Thomas Gray, I (Oxford 1935), 146. – [99] Ibid., I, 158; Roland de la Platière, V, 60-61; Fernow: Sitten- u. Kulturgem., 91-92. – [100] Mrs. Millar, III, 140. – [101] Guidi: Lettres (1783), II, 97. – [102] C. Elling: Operahus og Casino (Copenhagen 1942), § 18; also: D'Orbessan, 567; Mrs Piozzi, 206; Moritz, III, 33. J. Russel (Letters from a young painter, I, 183) emphasizes: "the modern Romans ... return from Tivoli, Frescati, etc., to Rome before the Dogdays begin. The reason is, because it is reckoned dangerous for one who has resided constantly at Rome for a considerable time, to change his lodgings and lye in the Campania, during the months of July and August". – Mme Du Boccage (Lettres, 301) makes a similar remark, i.e. that in the warmest time of the year the nobility "demeure rarement en campagne". – [103] F. Cancellieri: Il Mercato, il Lago ed il Pal. Pamfiliano (Rome 1801); Blainville, II, 169-170; Labat, VI, 150; Lalande, IV, 111-112; Richard, V, 207; Reumont, II, 144; old photograph in Negro: Seconda Roma, at p. 352; P. Romano & P. Partini: Piazza Navona, 143-147. – [104] Archenholtz, II^2, 83. – [105] Corresp. VII No. 3012; Roland, V, 340; Kotzebue, III, 117; The Pembroke Papers, 197. – [106] Reumont, I, 434. – [107] Duclos, 113. – [108] Briefe, ed. Rehm, I, 213, 220, 237. – [109] Briefe, I, 247-248. – [110] Lalande, V, 172-173; Reumont, II, 135-136. – [111] Voyage ... 1685-1686 (2. ed. 1688), 383; Grosley (II, 437) however, stresses that herb gardens were always well kept. – [112] Roma moderna (1727), 698. – [113] Corresp. IV No. 1677. – [114] III, 656. – [115] Silvagni, II, 262. – [116] Roland, V, 342; Meyer: Darstell., 239; Moritz, III, 211. – [117] Rogissart: Les Délices de l'Italie, II (1707), 176; cf Blainville, II, 257. – [118] Rogissart, II, 326. – [119] II, 53. – [120] III, 117. – [121] Bergeret, 64; Pembroke Papers, 274. – [122] As late as in 1902 the place was considered unhealthy (R. Villedieu: La Villa Médicis, Rome 1950, 212-213). – [123] Lalande, V, 172-173; Volkmann, II, 340, 722. Around 1780 it was called "Villa de Passione" because lovers used to come here, a fact which indicates that the park was rather deserted. – [124] Montesquieu remarks (I, 31) that the promenade is a requirement for the French, but not for the people of the South as they are rather indolent; the promenade at Villa Medici is only "in vogue" with the common people (Lalande, V, 172-173); cf Volkmann, II, 722. See also Reumont, II, 136; Fernow, 91-92; Silvagni, I, 401. – [125] Blainville, II, 172; Kotzebue, III, 263; Moritz, II, 175; Vasi, II, Pl. 20. – [126]

Mémoires, ed. Vèze, I, 212. – [127] O. Antonsson: Sergels Ungdom och Romtid (Sth. 1942), 143; cf Mannlich, 105-107. On October excursions to Villa Borghese in 1705 see Corresp. III No. 1225, and to the area outside Porta del Popolo see N. von Grund, II, 172. – [128] Baretti: Les Italiens, 260; Richard, V, 208-209. – [129] Richard, as mentioned above; even Blainville mentions that nocturnal promenades in the city is in vogue and that the participants are dressed in "deshabillés galants" (II, 146-147); "ces peuples errans, vêtus de blanc ... me les fait comparer à des ombres heureuses", says Mme Du Boccage (Lettres, 188). – [130] C. Elling: Breve om Italien (Copenhagen 1945), 27-44. – [131] Corresp. VII No. 3014. – [132] Briefe, ed. Rehm, I, 313. – [133] Volkmann, II, 172-173. – [134] Bergeret, 63. – [135] Volkmann, loc.cit. – [136] Ramdohr: Ueber Mahlerei und Bildhauerarbeit in Rom (Lpz. 1787), II, 111-112. – [137] Volkmann, II, 254-255; cf Roland, V, 340 (its regularity is criticized). – [138] Bergeret, 61-63. – [139] A survey of this repertoire in Wilh. Waetzoldt: Das klassische Land (Lpz. 1927). – [140] H. F. Clark: The English Landscape Garden (London 1948), 13, 37-39. – [141] The Spectator, 1712, No. 414, June 25. – [142] The Pembroke Papers, 276. – [143] III, 143-144. – [144] Ibid., III, 138-139. – [145] Tagebuch I, 315. Rich. Wilson has made fine studies in the park of Villa Chigi. – [146] Tagebücher und Briefe Goethes aus Italien an Frau von Stein (Weimar 1886), 232; cf Ital. Reise, Dec. 2. 1786. – [147] Moritz, I, 149. – [148] According to an inscription on Specchi's etching; not listed in Pascoli among De Rossi's works. – [149] Not mentioned in M. L. Gotheins Gesh. der Gartenkunst (Jena 1914), and neither by Fokker; the short description in L. Càllari: Le ville di Roma (2. ed., Rome 1943) is so faulty that the author seems not even to have seen the building. – [150] C. Elling: Function and Form, 56-57, Pl. 45. – [151] Lalande, III, 402-403. – [152] Aug. Hare: Walks, II, 132. – [153] A. Schiavo: Villa Doria Pamphili (Milan 1942), Fig. 116. – [154] De Rossi: Descr. di Roma antica, I (1727), 288-289. – [155] Pastor, XV, 376, Note 8. – [156] Cf Schiavo, Fig. 113 (after Piranesi). – [157] Cf for instance Villa Corsini in Castello, Villa Corsi and others. – [158] Càllari, op.cit. 297-300. – [159] On Carpegna as an antiquarian see Keyssler, I, 733; Venuti, 498. He decorated S. Anastasia (Deseine, IV, 812). – [160] Clementi, I, 617. – [161] Pascoli, I 319. – [162] According to Pascoli (I, 192) Pierfrancesco Garoli (died 1716) had painted in Villa Carpegna's Casino; it may be noted that Garoli, who in 1679 became teacher of perspective and architecture at the San Luca Academy, also has worked as an architect. In 1713 he was commissioned to make designs for the university in Turin ("Filippo Juvara", I, 73), they were never executed. – [163] Coudenhove-Erthal, Fig. 46. – [164] Deseine, V, 1229. He died in 1720 (Corresp. V, 2228). – [165] Coudenhove-Erthal, 109. – [166] C. Elling in "Arch.", Maanedshefte 1930, 100-104. – [167] "Protegé de la France" (Blainville, II, 245). – [168] Not mentioned in Càllari: Le ville di Roma, 2. ed. 1943. – [169] A. Cametti: Il Teatro di Tordinona (Tivoli 1938), I, 19-20. – [170] A. Ravà: I teatri di Roma (Rome 1953), 131. – [171] Ibid., 68. – [172] Clementi, II, 34, 50. – [173] Corresp. VI No. 2408. – [174] See H. Tintelnot: Barocktheater und barocke Kunst (Berlin 1939), 75 ff. – [175] Ravà, 64. – [176] Lina Montalto: Il Clementino, 179. – [177] It was a rather regular practice that distinguished families of the gentry took their coats of arms – though somewhat changed – after the pope by whom they had risen; cf Labat, VI, 54. – [178] Wright: Travels, 340; Venuti, 5; Volkmann, II, 175-176; L. Bobè: F. Brun, 336 (full bibliography). On Mattei see Pascoli, II, 549. – [179] Deseine, III, 637; Venuti, 71; Vasi, X, Pl. 191. – [180] Pecchiai: La Scalinata, Pl. VI. – [181] Ital. Reise, July 24. 1787; on the view see also Heinse: Tagebucher, Sämmtl. Werke VII (Lpz. 1909), 77. Clement XIV rented the casino and recuperated by playing billiards (Guidi: Lettres, II, 97). A painting of the villa seen from the garden is reproduced in Mostra del Giardino italiano, 2. ed., Florence 1931, plate 49. – [182] Corresp. VI

No. 2579; E. Portal: L'Arcadia (1921), 37-44; Lalande, IV, 499. Volkmann, II, 613. – On the amphitheatre in the Oratorians' garden on Gianicolo see Torsten Steinby: Romerske Bilder (Sth. 1953), 40-41; on Evodio Assemani's garden there see Lalande, IV, 471-472. – [183] I am grateful to the Director of the American Academy in Rome for being allowed to reproduce this and other measurings of Roman gardens. – [184] Briefwechsel mit Frau von Stein, 252. – [185] Archenholtz, II[2], 105 ff. – [186] Lettres sur l'Italie, II, 8. Also Björnståhl: Briefe auf seinen ausländischen Reisen, II, 70; Adler: Reisebemerkungen, 191; Baretti: Les Italiens (Paris 1773), 128-132; Lettere dell' Abate Pietro Metastasio, II (Trieste 1795), 309. – [187] As a boy Goethe heard his mother sing this aria (by Rolli); and it made him yearn for Italy. – [188] A. Schiavo: Villa Doria Pamphili, 35-40. – [189] Ibid., Fig. 32. – [190] Ibid., 130. – [191] Pastor, XVI[1], 119; G. Matthiae: Ferd. Fuga, 39-40, 78. – [192] Grosley, 2. ed., II, 344. – [193] Gorani: Mémoires, II, 29-30. – [194] Lalande (III, 565) calls it "dans un gout anglois". – [195] Weinlig, II, 9; Volkmann, II, 279. – [196] According to Mattiae: Fuga, 40, the building is influenced by the Cinquecento-tradition, but it is hardly correct. – [197] Pastor, XVI, 32, 110 (on Maréchal), 123 (on the decoration); Venuti, 71; Càllari: Le ville di Roma, 2. ed. (1943), 320-321. – [198] Choix des plus célèbres maisons de plaisance de Rome et des environs (Paris 1812). Winckelmann writes in a letter from Sept. 25. 1756 that Cardinal B. had found a statue of Hermaphrodite when digging foundations for a building ("un palais") he was erecting (W.'s Briefe, ed. Rehm, I, 248); is this the villa? B. died that year. – [199] Schiavo, 125; a short description in Riesch: Observations faites pendant un voyage en Italie, II (Dresden 1781), 151. – [200] Remarks (London 1753), 195. – [201] Travels, 312-315. – [202] II, 180. – [203] Mémoires inédits de Mme la Comtesse de Genlis, III (Bruxelles 1825), 35 ff. – [204] Venuti (1766), 531; Vasi, X, Fol. XXV. – [205] Brinckmann (1919): 1764-60; Càllari: I palazzi di Roma (1943): 1737; Josephson: Barocken (1948), 1744; "Guida di Roma", (1950, C.I.T.): 1760, etc. – [206] Winckelmanns Briefe, ed. Rehm, I, 277. – [207] Letter of Feb. 4. 1758 (ibid., I, 326). – [208] Ibid., I, 248. – [209] Ibid., I, 326. – [210] Mémoires, ed. Vèze, VII, 172. – [211] W.'s Briefe, ed. Dassdorf. II, 188. – [212] They had hardly begun in 1762 (Richard, VI, 209). – [213] Grosley, II, 256-258. Mme Du Boccage, who saw the villa in Dec. 1757, was rather bewildered: "Cette habitation est d'un goût d'Architecture singulier. Je ne sais à quoi vous le comparer, mais il me plaît infiniment" (Lettres, Dresden 1771, 271). – [214] Briefe, ed. Dassdorf, I, 154. – [215] VI, 213. – [216] Briefe über Rom, I (Dresden 1782), 27-29. In 1765 Smollett called the casino "light, gay and airy" (Travels, 2. ed., London 1766, II, 104). Boswell visited the villa in May that year with Winckelmann acting as a cicerone; he didn't like the garden: "Garden like spread periwig" (Boswell on the Grand Tour. Italy, Corsica, and France 1765-1766, edd. Frank Brady & F. A. Pottle, London 1955, 81). – [217] Lettres (Genève 1783), II, 92. – [218] Voyage d'Italie 1773-1774, ed. Wilhelm, 64. – [210] V, 341. Roland seems to have visited the villa guided by Winckelmann. – [220] Tagebücher, Sämmtl. Werke VII (Lpz. 1909), 77. But the nightingales sang beautifully and the grashoppers warbled. – [221] Reise, III, 40. – [222] Reisebemerkungen, 190. The garden is "pure art" and has hardly any shadow. – [223] Ueber Mahlerei ... in Rom, II (Lpz. 1787), 8. – [224] Röm. Briefe, I, 126. Gierlew (II, 106) calls the garden "somewhat stiff, but laid out with grandeur"; here he succeeded in remembering Goethe's "Kennst du das Land ...". – [225] Pascoli, II, 549. – [226] K. Escher: Barock und Klassizismus in Rom (Lpz. 1910), 154. – [227] It was then (1950) summer residence for the Grand Master of the Order of Malta, Prince Ludovico Chigi Albani Della Rovere. – [228] De Brosses, II, 319. – [229] Justi: Winckelmann, II[1], 309. – [230] A reference to Pal. del Tè in Mantova is not to the point (Hautecœur: Rome et la renaiss. de l'antiquité, 63). – [231] A beautiful impression in

C. Justi: Briefe aus Italien (Bonn 1922), 78. – [232] Cf my small study in "Danske Herregaardshaver", (Copenhagen 1939) part 13, 357-368. – [233] Vagn Häger Poulsen in Kunstm. Aarsskr. XXVIII, 143 f. – [234] L. Càllari: Le ville di Roma, 2. ed. (1943), 330-336. – [235] The Pembroke Papers, 277. – [236] Focillon, 297; P. Romano & P. Partini: Piazza di Spagna, 96-97; W. G. Constable: Richard Wilson (London 1953), 27. – [237] Welcker: Zoëgas Leben (1912), I, 186. – [238] Wright, 341. – [239] Pembroke Papers, 276. – [240] Mrs. Millar, III, 155. – [241] Hautecœur, op.cit., 71. On More see also Wm. T. Whitley: Artists and their Friends in England 1700-1799 (London 1928), I, 201-204; Norb. von Grund: Mal. Reise eines deutschen Künstlers, II, 197; Münter, Tageb., II, 197-198; Herders Briefwechsel mit seiner Gattin (Giessen 1859), 105. – [242] Whitley, I, 200. Reynolds admired More and bought paintings by him. – [243] C. Elling: Den italienske Nat, 174-175. – [244] Pembroke Papers, 273. – [245] Whitley, I, 380. – [246] H. F. Clark: The English Landscape Garden (London 1948), 21, 23, 24. – [247] Smollett (op.cit. II, 113-114) by the way, has compared Villa Borghese to this English park and finds the former "a very contemptible garden" compared to Stowe. – [248] Archenholtz, II², 78. – [249] Silvagni, I, 119. – [250] Moritz, II, 222 ff.; Kotzebue, III, 208. – [251] Gierlew, I, 464. – [252] Darstell. aus Italien, 242. – [253] Kultur- und Sittengem., 71. – [254] Archenholtz, II², 77.

THE CALL OF THE RUINS

[1] Louis Bertrand: La fin du classicisme et le retour à l'antique (Paris 1897) and Louis Hautecœur: Rome et la renaissance de l'antiquité à la fin du XVIIIe siècle (Paris 1912) are the basic monographs. – [2] J. C. Goethe: Viaggio in Italia, I, 209. – [3] S. Negro: Seconda Roma, frontispiece. – [4] H. P. L'Orange: Romersk Idyll (Oslo 1952), 42-45. – [5] Silvagni, I, 48. – [6] When our romantic genre painters in Rome liked to depict street-barbers in front of monumental antique architecture (Ernst Meyer has for instance used Octavia's Porticus and Arco del Pantano as backgrounds) it need not, therefore, be arranged. – [7] See for instance K. F. Scholler: Ital. Reise, II (Lpz. 1832), 167-168. – [8] II, 569. – [9] Roland, V, 287; Moritz, II, 198-199. – [10] It was called S. Stefano alle Carrozze (Deseine, IV, 873); c. 1780 the temple was inhabited by a fisherman (N. von Grund, II, 45). – [11] Reisen eines Officiers durch die Schweiz und Italien (Hannover 1786), 211; Volkmann, II, 521; John Moore: Abriss des gesellsch. Lebens und der Sitten in Italien, I (Lpz. 1781), 239. – [12] Reisen eines Officiers, 214. – [13] Lettres contenant ses voyages (Dresden 1771). – [14] IV, 239-240. – [15] Dupaty: Lettres, I, 291-291. – [16] Richard, V, 211-212. – [17] Mrs. Piozzi: Glimpses, 207-208. – [18] Adlerbeth, 141. – [19] Reise durch verschiedene Städte Italiens, I, (Weimar 1792), 152-153. – [20] Wright, 343. – [21] Lettres d'un voyageur anglois, I (Neuchâtel 1781), 147. – [22] I, 221. – [23] Ein deutscher Maler und Hofmann. Lebenserinnerungen des Joh. Chr. von Mannlich (Berlin 1910), 165. – [24] Reise in die klass. Gegenden Roms, II, (Lpz. 1805), 25. – [25] 188. – [26] Cf The Autobiographies of Edward Gibbon, ed. John Murray (London 1897), 405. – [27] Promenades dans Rome, June 19. 1828. – [28] The painting is reproduced in Neville Rogers: Keats, Shelley and Rome (London 1949), plate facing p. 17; cf Henning Krabbe: Shelley's Poesi (Copenhagen 1959), 275. Maybe the proudest poetic picture of the ruins of Rome is given us by Shelley: "that high capital, where kingly Death/ keeps his pale court in beauty and decay". Ingemann walked through Rome in 1818 "with Livius in sight, and map in hand". – [29] Moritz, II, 253. – [30] Ibid. – [31] De Brosses used Deseine as a guide, Goethe used Volkmann, and his father J. C. Goethe, particularly Keyssler. – [32] Remarks, 177. – [33] L. Holbergs Erindringer, ed. F. J. Billeskov Jansen, 69. – [34]

F. J. L. Meyer: Darstell., 235. – [35] Dupaty, I, 292. – [36] Wright, 343. – [37] The Autobiographies of Edward Gibbon, 257. – [38] Boswell on the Grand Tour. Italy, Corsica and France (London 1955), 65. – [39] Justi, II¹, 13. – [40] Voyage d'Italie, 77. – [41] De Brosses, II, 221, 420; Grosley, II, 234-236. – [42] Barthélemy: Voyage en Italie (Paris 1801), 164. – [43] C. Gabillot: Hub. Robert (Paris 1895), 84-86. Percier was in great danger when measuring up Trajan's Column (Corresp. XXV No. 8920). – [44] Weinlig, II, 54. – [45] Cf M. Mackeprang in "Rom og Danmark", III, (1942), 1. – [46] Winckelmanns Briefe, ed. Dassdorf, I, 71. – [47] Focillon: Piranesi, 129. – [48] Justi, II¹, 12. – [49] De Brosses, II, 76-77. – [50] He was a member of the Académie des Inscriptions. His chief topographical work on Rome is Le vestigia e rarità di Roma (1744). – [51] On him see also Mannlich, 94. – [52] Welcker: Zoëgas Leben, I, 256. – [53] Sitten- u. Kulturgem., 255-256. – [54] Voyage en Italie, 222. – [55] Meyer: Darstell, 227-229. – [56] Voyage en Italie (Lausanne 1791), 61. – [57] Gorani: Mémoires, II, 49-53. – [58] John Moore: Abriss des gesellschaftl. Lebens und der Sitten in Italien, I (Lpz. 1781), 264. In 1765 Boswell attended a 6-day-course conducted by Colin Morrison, the antiquarian (Boswell on the Grand Tour. Italy, 62 ff). By the way, John Russel, the author of "Letters from a young painter" (1750), was also a cicerone. – [59] G. Maugras: Le Duc et la Duchesse de Choiseul (Paris 1924), 54. – [60] Winckelmann: Briefe, ed. Rehm, I (Berlin 1952), 216. – [61] Herders Reise nach Italien. Briefwechsel mit seiner Gattin. 1788-89 (Giessen 1859), 139-140, 158. – [62] The Travel-Diaries, I, 190. – [63] Lady Morgan: Italien, III, 209. – [64] "a Man who is in Rome can scarce see an Object that does not call to mind a Piece of a Latin Poet or Historian" (Addison: Remarks, 177). – [65] Dupaty: Lettres, II, 6-7. – [66] C. Elling: Den romantiske Have (Copenhagen 1942), pass. – [67] G. J. Hoogewerff: De Bentvueghels (1952); Léo van Puyvelde: La peinture flamande à Rome (1950); [Denys Sutton:] Artists in 17th Century Rome (London 1955). – [68] Corresp. VII No. 2818, 2820. – [69] Moritz, III, 152. – [70] Welcker: Zoëgas Leben, I, 186. – [71] F. Landsberger: Wilh. Tischbein (Lpz. 1908), 172; Waetzoldt: Das klass. Land. (Lpz. 1927), 134. – [72] Breve over Italien og Sicilien (Copenhagen 1807), II, 48. A similar view in H. N. Clausen: Rejsebreve 1818-1820, ed. Bjørn Kornerup (Copenhagen 1946), 32. – [73] Moritz, III, 203; Lalande, IV, 314. – [74] IV, 323-324; cf Moritz, I, 209. – [75] III, 142. – [76] Egger: Röm. Veduten, II, Fig. 25. – [77] The Tessin-collection, Nationalmuseum, Sth. – [78] Egger, II, Pl. 101. On the studies of a French artist at S. Constanza see Grosley, II, 252. – [79] Corresp. II No. 739. – [80] Ibid. III No. 1288. – [81] Cf C. Elling in "Kunstbladet" 1927, 217 ff. – [82] II, 188. – [83] III, 192; an engaged column is noticed (Grosley, II, 262). – [84] F. Brun: Röm. Leben I, 209. – [85] Voyage d'Italie, ed. Wilhelm, 93. – [86] Wright, 256. – [87] "Die runde antike Form ist alles", Heinse decreed in front of S. Bernado (Tagebücher 1780-1800, 81); cf Wright, 215. – [88] Dupaty, I, 213. – [89] Tanker om Smagen udi Konsterne i Almindelighed (Copenhagen 1762), 10. – [90] Welcker: Zoëgas Leben, I, 233. – [91] Heinse: Briefe, II (Sämmtl. Werke X, Lpz. 1910), 139-140. – [92] Ibid. – [93] The Travel-Diaries, I, 189. – [94] Rud. Bay: I Algier og Italien 1816-1821 (Memoirer og Breve, XXXIII, Copenhagen 1920), 118. On F. Hartmann's full length portrait of Fr. von Matthisson, painted in Rome 1796, the latter is depicted with folded arms and with the Colosseum as a background (L. Bobé: F. Brun, 139). See also C. Elling: Den ital. Nat. 170-174. – [95] Old photograph in Negro: Seconda Roma, facing p. 64. – [96] [C. Elling:] Documents inédits concern. les projets de J.-A. Gabriel et N.-H. Jardin pour l'église Frédéric à Copenhague (Copenhagen 1931), 36. – [97] Works, IV (1871), 526. – [98] See also Vasi-Nibby: Itinéraire (1818), I, 133-135. – [99] II, 262-263. – [100] Corresp. of Ths. Gray, ed. Paget Toynbee & L. Whibley (Oxford 1935), I 148. – [101] Roland, V, 261; Lalande, III, 403. – [102] Platner-Ashby: A

Topographical Dictionary of Ancient Rome (1929), 364; F. S. Robertson: A Handbook of Greek and Roman Architecture, 2. ed. (Cambridge 1945), 254, 345. – [103] Promenades dans Rome, Dec. 30. 1828. – [104] In 1765 when it was shown to Boswell "he spouted Horace's ode on the spot" (op.cit., 87). See also Vilh. Andersen: Horats I (Copenhagen 1939), 38-39, IV¹ (1948), 254-255, 298-299. – [105] C. Elling: Den romantiske Have, 146-147. – [106] Travels, 355. – [107] 573-574. – [108] IV, 402. – [109] II, 564. – [110] III, 46-47. – [111] III, 167. – [112] Tageb., II, 127. – [113] Lettres, I, 302-303. – [114] Archivo, II, 78. – [115] Reise, III, 368. Pauline Dorothea Frisch, née Tutein, who visited the grotto in 1804 picked off some of the maiden hair (Adiantum Veneris) in order to dry it (Reise durch Teutschland, Holland, Frankreich, die Schweitz u. Italien, Altona 1816, 365-366). – [116] Gustaf III's Resa i Italien. Anteckningar (Sth. 1902), 74. – [117] Carl Fehrman: Kyrkogårdsromantik (Lund 1954), pass. – [118] Cf Joseph Gregor: Kulturgesch. der Oper (Zürich 1941), 238-240; Ludwig Schiedermair: Die deutsche Oper (Lpz. 1930), Fig. 21; 164 ff., Alfred Einstein: Mozart (Sth. 1947), 606-607. – [119] Egger: Röm. Veduten, I, Pl. 79. – [120] Eugen Lennhoff: The Freemasons (London 1934), 67, 76. – [121] Voyage, IV, 374. – [122] C. Elling: Die Baugesch. der Schlosskirche von Christiansborg (Artes VI, 1938, Fig. p. 121). – [123] C. Elling: Jardin i Rom (Copenhagen 1943), 20, 28, 29. – [124] James Lees-Milne: The Age of Adam (London 1947), Fig. 33. – [125] Meyer: Darstell., 158-159. – [126] Welcker: Zoëgas Leben, I, 88. – [127] L. Bobé in "Rom og Danmark", I, 320. – [128] N. von Grund, II, 47. – [129] Breve over Italien, II (1807), 52-55. – [130] Sitten- u. Kulturgem., 177-179. – [131] John Lehmann: Shelley in Italy. An Anthology (London 1947), 13-14. – [132] Louis Guimbaud: Saint-Non et Fragonard (Paris 1928), 165. – [133] Duclos: Voyage en Italie (Lausanne 1791), 60-61. – [134] Kotzebue, III, 153. – [135] Meyer: Darstell., 169. – [136] Briefe, II, 141. – [137] The Travel-Diaries, I, 192. – [138] Lettres, I, 237-238. – [139] Reise durch verschiedene Städte Italiens in den Jahren 1785 u. 1786 (Weimar 1792), I, 159. – [140] Leone Vicchi: Villa Borghese nella storia e nella tradizione del popolo romano (Rome 1885), 212-213; Kotzebue, III, 208. – [141] Tageb. u. Briefe Goethes aus Italien an Frau von Stein (Weimar 1886), 403. – [142] Moritz (II, 226) states the place. – [143] J. Vogel: Aus Goethes röm. Tagen, 169. – [144] Ital. Reise, July 9. 1787. – [145] Goethes Briefwechsel mit den Gebrüdern von Humboldt (Lpz. 1876), 217. – [146] F. Brun: Röm. Leben, II, 123. – [147] Hautecœur, op.cit., 62-70; A. Michaelis: Die archäol. Entdeckungen des 19. Jahrh.'s (Lpz. 1906), 1-13. – [148] Chr. Huelsen in Abh. d. Heidelberger Akad. d. Wiss. 1917. – [149] Corresp. IV No. 1911; Wright: Travels, 321-322. – [150] Voyage en Italie (Paris 1801), 29. – [151] Travels, 2. ed. (London 1766), II, 104. – [152] A preliminary study for the ideal museum of antiques is Maffei's Lapidarium (founded in 1714) in the peristyle (1744-49) in front of the philharmonic Academy in Verona; has been described in Charles Burney: The present State of Music in France and Italy, 2. ed. (London 1773), 122-123. – [153] Voyages, I, 272. – [154] Travels, II, 125. – [155] Maler. Reise, II, 69. – [156] II, 208. – [157] Roland, V, 320. – [158] Fernow: Kultur- u. Sittengem., 246; the rotunda finished: Münter, Tageb. II, 117. A beautiful plan of Pius VI's Vatican Museum prefaces G. B. & Ennio Quirino Visconti: Il Museo Pio-Clementino, I (Rome 1782); on Gagnereaux's prospects of the gallery, executed on the occasion of Gustav III's visit in 1784, see Nationalmusei Årsbok, Ny Serie, VI (1936), 55-65; Adlerbeth (82-83) describes the visit. Cf also C. Bildt: Svenska Minnen och Märken i Rom (Sth. 1900), 235-236. – [159] Reise, I, 105-106. – [160] Moritz, III, 75; cf Münter: Tageb. II, 220. – [161] On this practice see C. Elling: Den ital. Nat, 182-185. Concerning the dating it may be added that Norb. von Grund, who was in Rome before 1779, has described the feast (Maler. Reise, II, 169). – [162] R. Venuti: Descr. top. delle Antichità di Roma,

3. ed., II (1824), 6 ff. – [163] On the light cultus see Elling, op.cit., 186-191. – [164] Tageb., I, 263. – [165] Ibid., 277. – [166] II, 155. – [167] Ital. Reise, Nov. 24. 1787. – [168] Corinne ou l'Italie (Paris 1807), I, 317. – [169] Miranda i Sverige och Norge 1787. General Francisco de Mirandas Dagbok, ed. Stig Rydén (Sth. 1950), 140, 145. – [170] Elling, op.cit., 302. See also Carl Justi: Briefe aus Italien (Bonn 1922), 56-57, on torchlight in Mus. Capit. (1867). – [171] Ital. Reise, the end.

INDEX

LIST OF PERSONS

Clement I (c. 97) 79
Liberius (4th Century) 46
Martin V Colonna (1417–31) 252
Paul II Barbo (1464–71) 19 27 274
Sixtus IV Della Rovere (1471–84) 15 241
Alexander VI Borgia (1492–1503) 16
Julius II Della Rovere (1503–13) 16 47 83 244
Leo X Medici (1513–21) 15 39
Clement VII Medici (1523–34) 16
Paul III Farnese (1534–49) 6 15f. 444
Pius IV Medici (1559–65) 14 16 451
Sixtus V Peretti (1585–90) 16f. 361
Clement VIII Aldobrandini (1592–1605) 221 442
Paul V Borghese (1605–21) 6 138
Gregory XV Ludovisi (1621–23) 304
Urban VIII Barberini (1623–44) 55 180 218 350 412 452
Innocent X Pamphili (1644–55) 121 214 245 304 437
Alexander VII Chigi (1655–67) 54 205 244 299 331 514
Clement IX Rospigliosi (1667–69) 54
Clement X Altieri (1670–76) 42 54f. 76 170 185 268 463 468
Innocent XI Odescalchi (1676–89) 55 62 219 228 237
Alexander VIII Ottoboni (1689–91) 55
Innocent XII Pignatelli (1691–1700) 55 99 196 209 230 299 319 433 455 468f.
Clement XI Albani (1700–21) 33 70 72 75 82–90 93 106 158 193 202 215 224 230 240 279 321–25 331 357 455 474 476 480 526
Innocent XIII Conti (1721–24) 72 82 90f. 96 121 168 207 252 297 318 332f. 335–38 341 352 434

Benedict XIII Orsini (1724–30) 96–102 104ff. 109 113ff. 117 134 207 212 237f. 244f. 252 347 352
Clement XII Corsini (1730–40) 116–130 135 169 204 287 297f. 352f. 358f. 419 423 464 477 526
Benedict XIV Lambertini (1740–58) 118 131–48 151 156ff. 162 171 207 211 232 241 285 359f. 385 431 439 450 475 482 526
Clement XIII Rezzonico (1758–69) 50 148–54 300 354 478
Clement XIV Ganganelli (1769–74) 154 208 245 310 455 527
Pius VI Braschi (1775–99) 154 158 233 312 362ff. 527
Pius VII Chiaramonti (1800–23) 9 245 249 363 380
Pius IX Mastai-Ferretti (1846–78) 208 249 300 486
Pius X Sarto (1903–14) 97
Pius XII Pacelli (1939–) 22 42

Abildgaard, Nicolai 124 398 502
Acquasparta family 169
Acquaviva, Francesco 112 137 346
    – , Troiano 137–8
Adam, Lambert-Sigismond 353
    – , Robert 515
Addison, Joseph 75 445 461 477 484 495 512
Adler, J. G. C. 479
Adlerbeth, G. G. 81 514
Afflisio (Affligio), Giuseppe d' 136
    – , Lisabetta (Passalacqua) 136
Albani family 84 322 325
    – , Alessandro 30 72 222 256 476–81

565

483 520 526
—, Annibale 79 82 87 90 481
Albany, Countess d', née Stolberg-Gedern 190
Alberoni, Giulio 287
Alberti, Leon Battista 27
Albertoni, Lodovica 42
Alfieri, Vittorio 274 356 394
Algardi, Alessandro 474
Algarotti, Francesco 153
Alibert, Antonio d' 469ff.
—, Giacomo 469f.
Althan, Michael Friederich 111
Altieri family 43 59 268 272 467
—, Emilio 310
—, Gaspare 463
—, Paluzzi 463
Amalie, Dowager Duchess of Weimar 395 500
Ameli, Paolo 309 474
Ammanati, Bartolomeo 14
Andersen, H. C. 4 164 193 210 237 356 375 427
Andres, Juan 494 520 528
Anglada, Raffaele 401
Antin d', Louis-Antoine 339
Antinori, Giuseppe 363
Antoine, Etienne d' 60
Archenholtz, Johan Wilhelm von 473 486
Archinto, Giovanni 202
Ariosto, Lodovico 390
Asprucci, Antonio 483 486 521

Baggesen, Jens 513
"Bajocco" (Francesco Ravai) 400
Balsamo, Giuseppe (Cagliostro) 172 212 312 372 390 394
Barbaruccia 324
Barberini, Francesco 173
Baretti, Giuseppe 27 54 167 473
Barigioni, Filippo 72 113 134 357
Barthélemy, Jean-Jacques 498 526
Bartoli, Francesco 464
Basseville, Hugon de 419
Batoni, Pompeo 148
Bay, Rudolph 177 510
Bayle, Pierre 384
Beccaria, Cesare 214

Beckford, William 157 500 510 519
Belli, Gioacchino 13 237 350 385 419
Bellicard, Jér.-Ch. 83
Benaglia, Paolo 352
Benedetti, Elpidio 329ff.
Bérain, Jean, the Elder 470 481
Bergeret, P.-J.-O. 155 364 451 479 496 508
Bergonzoni, Giambattista 92
Bergsøe, Vilhelm 211 366 444 449
Berkeley, George 47 455 510
Berlioz, Hector 399
Bernini, Domenico 56
—, Lorenzo 13 21–23 27 42 55–58 65 123 209f. 218 228 265 286 305f. 330 334 350f. 355
Bernis, Francois-Joachin de 255 285 311 431
Bessarion, Cardinal 441f.
Beyle, Henri, see Stendhal
Bianchi, Tommaso 483
Bianchini, Francesco 445f. 497
Bibiena, Giuseppe Galli 141
—, Francesco Galli 470
Bighazzini (Bigazzini) Giovanni Antonio 272
Bindesbøll, Gottlieb 29 313
Bizzaccheri, Carlo 21 86 89 188 282 357
Blainville, de 325f. 378 384 398
Blondel, Jacques-Francois 267
Blunck, Ditlev Conrad 425
Boccage, Marie-Anne du 147 356 375 490
Boccapaduli family 450
—, Marchese and Marchesa Margherita 282
Bolognetti family 42 274
—, Maria Costanza 169
—, Mario 476
Bonaparte, Josef 302
—, Napoleon 1 175 249 362
Boncompagni, Gregorio 304
—, Giulia 305
— Ludovisi, Eleonora 304
— —, Gaetano 305
— —, Maria Francesca 305
— —, Pietro 305
Bonnard, Abel 428
Bonstetten, Karl Viktor von 225 451 495
Borghese family 46 260 376 429 454
—, Marc' Antonio 185 483–87 521

Borgia family 390
Borioni, Antonio 72 101 186
Borromeo, Carlo 38
Borromini, Francesco 28 59f. 65 86f. 92 109
    120 145 171 178 179 198 205 218 267
    291 384
Boswell, James 400 496
Bottari, Giovanni 302
Bouchard & Gravier 387
Bouchardon, Edme 276 353
Bracci, Pietro 207 325 355
Bramante, Donato 21 25 27 37 125 411
Brandes, Georg 410
Braschi-Onesti, Luigi 312
    – , Romualdo 312
Breenbergh, Bartolomaeus 506
Breteuil, de 155
Brigante Colonna, Giulio 312
Bril, Paul 391 503
Bristol, see Hervey
Brosses, Charles de 109 114 137 149 198
    204 251 262f. 285 288–92 300 339 353
    393f. 403 445f. 453 458 477 508 511 527
Brun, Frederikke, née Münter 233 313 394
    449 451 498 522
    – , Ida (Bombelles) 508 522f.
Bufalo, Marchese Del 284
Bulgarini, Marianna Benti 398
Buratti, Carlo 128
Burlington, Lord 118
Burnet, Gilbert 219 457
Burney, Charles 401
Bødtcher, Ludvig 422

Caetani family 25 251
Caffarelli (Gaetano Majorano) 469
Cagliostro, see Balsamo
Campiglia, Giovanni Domenico 353
Camporese, Giuseppe 528
Canaletto (Canal), Antonio 503
Cancellieri, Francesco 362 366 482
Canevari family 421
    – , Antonio 82 91f. 120 135 193 473
Canillac, Abbé de 285
Canova, Antonio 274 362 365 531
Carapecchia, Romano 71 143
Carducci, Giosuè 350
Carl, Prince of Denmark 292

Carlos III (IV) King of Spain 146 475 492
Carnevale 36
Carolis, Marchese de 283
Carpegna family 252
    – , Gasparo 467
Carracci 400 503
Caruso, Lionardo 228
Casanate, Girolamo 186
Casanova, Giacomo 137 152 213 324 371
    394 396 459 478
Casimira, Queen of Poland 169 279 455
Casoni, Antonio 180
Castelli, Domenico 186
Catel, Franz 401
Caucig, Franz 506
Caylus, Anne-Claude Philippe de 393
Celsius, Olof, the Elder 328
Cenci, Beatrice 405
Cesarini family 169 454
Chateaubriand, François-René 4 159
Chausse, Michel-Ange de la 337
Chigi family 68 233 454 471
    – , Flavio, the Elder 305
    – , Flavio, the Younger 483
    – , Sigismondo 462
Choiseul, Etienne de 259
Christ, Joh. Fr. 362
Christian I, King of Denmark 234
Christian Friederich, Margrave of Ansbach
    396
Christina, Queen of Sweden 70 80 301 318
    357 467 469f. 471
Cimarra family 278 450
Cini family 450
    – , Joseph 266
Ciolli, Domenico 92
Cipriani, Sebastiano 71 206 332 340 471
Clérisseau, Ch.-L. 155
Cloche, Antonin 73 171f. 186 212 384
Colbert, Jean-Baptiste 56
Colonna family 42 72 120 136 251ff. 260
    287 294 377 398 432–34 454
    – , Fabrizio 296 451
    – , Filippo 433f. 451
    – , Girolamo 297
    – , Marc' Antonio 433
Conca, Sebast. 122
Consalvi, Ercole 249

Conti family 90f. 95 251f. 376
— , Guiseppe Lotario 333–36 352
— , Torquato II 333
Contini, Giambattista 21 58f. 92 120 185 224 380 413
Corazzini, Sergio 48
Corelli, Arcangelo 240 474
Corot, Camille 12
Corsini family 219 475
— , Bartolomeo 300
— , Neri Maria 118 204 259 300 353
Cortona, Pietro da 40 56 317 326
Coscia, Niccolò 98 100
Costaguti family 255
Courtois, Jacques 73
Crescenzi family 251
Crescimbeni, Giovanni Maria 88
Crovara (Corvara), Cesare 92
Cruyl, Lieven 269 351 413f.
Cuccovilla, Maria (Pizzelli) 274 282
Cuochetta, la 396

Dalberg, Joh. Fr. v. 397
Damon, hotelier 395
Daun, Wierich Philippe Lorenz 111
Davia, Giovanni Antonio 445
David, Marco 153
Delille, Jacques 501 514
Dérizet, Antoine 115 122 130
Deseine, François 269 278 321 384 390 393 434 457 495
Dickens, Charles 4 233
Domenichino 148
Dominicis, Carlo de 128–29 219
Donati, Alessandro 320
Dorbay, François 329
Doria family 293 456
Duca, Jacopo del 442
Duclos, Charles Pinot 3 199 277 458 499 518
Dupaty, Jean-Baptiste Mercy 473 491 501 514 519

Eckersberg, C. W. 23 97 240 482 523
Ehrensvärd, Carl Augustin 23 151
Eigtved, Niels 115 294 395
Elsheimer, Adam 503
Engelbreth, W. F. 498
Eugene, Prince of Savoia 112

Falda, Giambattista 68 192 194 234 277 316 353 385 411 414 422 425 432 441 443 448 463
Fansaga (Fonsaga), Cosimo 40
Farinelli (Carlo Broschi) 469
Farnese family 202
— , Francesca 173
— , Virginia 170
Fauno, Lucio 426
Feliciani, Serafina (Balsamo) 172
Fernow, K. L. 365 389 486 498 516
Ferrari, Francesco 112
Ferroni, Giuseppe Maria 309 476
Ficoroni, Francesco 442 494 500
Fiori, Giovanni Francesco 190
Fiorini, Luigi 363
Fischer von Erlach, Joh. Bernh. 60 111
Florenzi, Marianna 274
Foggini, P. L. 302
Fontana, Carlo 56 63 68 70 74–78 82ff. 93 96 129 142 147 176 186 197 207 209f. 215f. 219 228f. 269–72 280f. 284 293 315 317 319ff. 324–26 350 358f. 364 413 465 468
— , Carlo Stefano 71f. 79 82 85
— , Domenico 12 45 126 228
— , Francesco 12 71f. 82f. 197 324
— , Mauro 189
Ford, Richard 426
Fragonard, Honoré 276 461
France, Anatole 22 172
Franceschini, Marc' Antonio 202
Frangipani family 251
Francis of Assisi 240
Freddi, Padre 66
Frederick IV, King of Denmark 75 319
Fuga, Ferdinando 119 127f. 133 137–39 144 148 203f. 216 220 241f. 248 299–302 309 339 358 475

Gabrielli family 257 260 398
— , Caterina 257 396
Gaddi, G. B. 118 298
Galilei family 118
— , Alessandro 39 118 122–27 139
Galschiøt, M. 446
Gastaldi, Girolamo 63
Gaulli, Alessandro 332

Gellée, Claude, see Lorrain, Claude le
Gentili, Antonio 282
Gessner, Salomon 502
Ghezzi, Pier Leone 100f. 107ff. 122
   285
Giacinta, Madama 391
Giannini, Carlo 418
Gibbon, Edward 4 495f.
Gibbs, James 126
Gierlew, A. C. 363 504 515
Ginnasi family 447
Gioia 190
Giotto 240
Giudice, Antonio 119
  —, Nicola 119 322 336f.
Giulio Romano 412
Gleichen, C. H. v. 393
Goethe, Joh. Caspar 5 130 393 489
  —, Johann Wolfgang v. 4 23 47 157 224
   274 298 324 363 373 392 397 409f. 417
   425 440 450 462 471 473 489 495–98 500
   504ff. 510ff. 515 519 521f. 530f.
Goldoni, Carlo 136 152 418ff. 436
Gonzáles Velázquez, Antonio 143
Gorani, Guiseppe 162 244
Goya, Francisco 143
Grande Antonio del 29 215 289
Gravina, Gian Vincenzo 384
Gray, Thomas 51 194 455 511
Greca, Vincenzo della 432
Gregorini, Domenico 113f. 122 134 139–41
  305
  —, Lodovico 113
Grillo, Bernardino Del 278 436
  —, Cosimo Del 278
  —, Onofrio Del 436
Grimaldi, Girolamo 259
  —, Niccolò 282f.
Grimani, Vincenzo 260
Grosley, Pierre-Jean 27 174 256 302 479
Grund, Norbert von 130 400f. 527
Guardi, Francesco 435
Gueffier, Etienne 328f. 331 335
Guernieri (Guarnieri), Giovanni Francesco
  413
Guglielmi, Gregorio 143 241f.
Guidi, Jean-Baptiste 175 356 479
Gurlitt, Cornelius 306

Hårleman, Carl 115
Hackert, Philipp 317
Handel, Georg Friederich 280
Hansen, Constantin 89 482
Harrach, Alois Th. Raim. 111
Harsdorff, Caspar Frederik 156 527
Heinse, Wilhelm 195 357 399 479 497 510
  519
Hélyot, Hippolyte 170
Herbert, George, Lord 394 400 461 483–4
  —, Henry, 9th Earl of Pembroke 461
Herder, Johann Gottfried v. 274 395–97
  499f.
Hervey, Charles 210
  —, Frederick Augustus, 4th Earl of
  Bristol 394 485
Hildebrandt, Johann Lucas v. 60 111
Hirt, Alois 498ff.
Hohenlohe, Gustav 169
Holbech, Carl Frederik 444
Holberg, Ludvig 3 51 75 257 384 392 495
Houdon, Jean-Antoine 148
Howard, John 213f. 230 235
  —, Thomas Philip 219
Humboldt, Karl Wilhelm von 522

Imperiali, Renato 83

Jacobæus, Holger 404f.
Jagemann, Chr. Jos. 140
Jardin, Nicolas-Henri 9 276 451 482 510
  514
Jenkins, Thomas 400
John (João) V, King of Portugal 91 135
  470 472
Johnson, Samuel 512
Jones, Thomas 401
Joseph II, Holy Roman Emperor 358
Juel, Jens 400
Justi, Carl 125 136
Juvara, Filippo 74 82f. 95f. 114 116 119
  122 134 140 142 279f. 294 312 319 332ff.
  341f.

Keats, John 394
Keyssler, J. G. 207 283
Kotzebue, August v. 357 389 403 458 480
  513

Küchler, Albert 193 446

Labat, Père 27 79 167 212f. 231
Labre, Benoit-Joseph 173
Laer, Pieter van 391
Lafont, François 396
Lalande, J.-J. François de 27 124 139 159
   168 230 256 277 293 356 382 490 505 513f.
Lambardi, Carlo 124
Lancisi, Giovanni Maria 240f.
Langen, Ignazio 395
Lanzi, Luigi 494
Laugier, Père 508
Le Clerc, Louis-Auguste 439
Lenôtre, André 460
Leoni, Giacomo 119 126
Leseur, Père 155
Ligorio, Pirro 71
Liguori, Alfonso de' 189
Linnaeus, Carl v. 224
Lint, Hendr. Fr. van 444
Loret, Mathias 340
Lorrain, Claude le (Gellée) 31 391 443 461
   485f. 503
Louis XIV, King of France 468
Louis XV, King of France 26 312 336f.
   363 475
Ludovisi family, see Boncompagni
   – , Antonio 304
   – , Ippolita 304 359
   – , Niccolò 304
Ludwig I, King of Bavaria 274
Lund, J. P. 157
Lunghi, Onorio 357

MacCormack, James 194
Madelin, Louis 175
Maderno, Carlo 33 93 123 206
Maffei, Scipione 332f.
Maggi, Paolo 93 426 441
Magnani, Pietro 446
Maidalchini, Francesco 437
Maini, Giambattista 204
Mancini, Philippe-Julien 276
Manilio, Lorenzo 388
Mannlich, Chr. v. 495
Mansart, Jules Hardouin 308 507
Maratta (Maratti), Carlo 91 148

Marchionni, Carlo 98 477
Marchis, Tommaso de 136 146 224 310f.
Maréchal 476
"Margherita, Köchin" 394
Maria Clementina, Queen of Great Britain
   167
Marselis, Christof 60
Marstrand, Vilhelm 425
Martelli, Nicola 224
Massimo family 251
Mattei family 446
   – , Ciriaco 442
   – , Tommaso 72 101 471
Mau, August 402
Mazarin, Giulio 329ff.
Medici family 39
Mellini, Mario 310
Mendelssohn-Bartholdy, Felix 399
Mengs, Rafael 371 478
Merolli family 415
Metastasio (Pietro Trapassi) 382 384 398
   474
Meyer, Ernst 413
Meyer, F. J. L. 157 486 518 530
Michelangelo 22f. 33 125 127 146 148 165
   200 299 319 394 432 519 531
Micheli, Benedetto 356
Michetti, Niccolò 83 114 296f. 307
Milizia, Francesco 73 93 118 122 332 349
Millar, Mrs M. 155 395 462 505 513
Mills, Charles 446
Minassi, Padre 224
Miranda, Francisco 164 385 446 514 531
Misson, François-Maximilien 3 199 495
Mola, Giacomo 234
Molbech, Chr. 199 514
Monnoyer, Jean-Baptiste 212
Montaigne, M. de 3 390
Montelibretti, Duke of 455
Montesquieu, Charles de Secondat,
   Baron de 53 100 109 116 230 254 339
   446 526
Monti, Teresa, née Pichler 417
   – , Vincenzio 417 486
Moore, John 27 299
Moratti (Maratta), Francesco 357
More, Jacob 485 522
Moreau-Desproux, P.-L. 497

Morelli, Cosimo 312f.
Morgan, Lady Sidney 454 500
Moritz, Karl Philipp 157 193 395 400 410 414 462f. 495 508 514 521 529 530
Mornet, J. B. 157
Mozart, Wolfgang Amadeus 434 439 471 514
Munthe, Axel 395
Muti family 268
— , Maria Arcangela 84
Müller, Friedrich 498
Münter, Frederik 37 124 140 157 162 194 235 362f. 462 514 530

Napoléon, see Bonaparte
Natoire, Charles-Joseph 445
Negroni, Giovanni Francesco 457 460
Nemeitz, J. C. 495
Neri, Filippo 95 104 312 472
Nolli, Antonio 477
— , Giambattista 17 103 132 145 159 239 258 271 307 360 396 411 413 415 423 435 436
Northcote, James 400
Nugent, Thomas 263 453

Odescalchi family 42 62f. 280
— , Baldassarre 62 306
— , Livio 62 306 450
— , Tommaso 228
Omodei, Luigi 61
Oppenordt, Gilles-Marie 60 436 507
Orbessan, d'Agnan d' 170 254 513
Orlandi, Clemente 169
Orsini family 25 251ff. 429
— , Camilla 185 194
— , Domenico 430
Ottoboni, Marco 305
— , Pietro 75 113f. 122 140 279 297 305 318

Paciaudi, P. M. 302
Pagliarini, Nicola 383
Paisiello, Giovanni 240
Palazzi, Giuseppe 136
Palladio, Andrea 125 154 180 421
Palmstedt, Erik 158 410
Paluzzi-Altieri (degli Albertoni) 268

Pamphili family 43 120 251 287 376 454 474
— , Benedetto 288
— , Camillo 55 288ff. 293 308
— , Carlo Doria 437
— , Costanza 304
— , Giambattista 82
— , Girolamo 293
— , Olimpia 437
Panciatichi family 282
Pannini, Gian Paolo 122 204f. 223 287 475f. 503
— , Giuseppe 354
S. Paolo della Croce 195
Paolucci, Fabrizio 82 357
Paradis, Domenico 112
Parini, Giuseppe 222
Pascarella, Cesare 350 355
Pascoli, Lione 59 93 382 468
Passalacqua see Afflisio, Lisabetta d'
— , Pietro 135-36 139 142
Passionei, Domenico 203
Patriarca, Pietro 81
Patrizi family 255
— , Giovanni 471
Pecchaiai, Pio 327 329 332 335 339f.
Pembroke, see Herbert
Percier, Charles 434
Pereira, José 187 470
Peruzzi, Baldassarre 25 412
Peti, Madama 394
Petroni, Alessandro 310
Piacentini, Marcello 315
Piale, Stefano 417
Piccini, Nicola 240 398
Pichler, Giovanni 417
Piccolomini family 376
Pierleoni family 25
Pierre, J. B. 397 399
Pigalle, Jean-Baptiste 276
Pignata, Giuseppe 213f.
Pinelli, Bartolomeo 237 398 424
Pinto, Abbate 420
Piozzi, Esther Lynch, née Thale 378 403
Piranesi, Giambattista 11 148 151-54 276 307 342 361 372 387 391ff. 401 414 417 422f. 482 484 497 501 503 509 515 519 527

Poerson, Ch.-Fr. 297 335 339 352 507
Poli, Bartolomeo 294
Polinac, Melchior de 115 337 339 346 445f.
Pope, Alexander 485 512ff.
Porta, Giacomo della 27 144 218 265 273
Porto Maurizio, Leonardo da 192 312
Posi, Paolo 136 297 432
Poussin, Gaspard 485
– , Nicolas 503
Pozzobonelli family 392
Proust, Marcel 389
Pöllnitz, K. L. v. 288 346

Quadri, Carlo 130
Querini, Angelo Maria 145

Ragozzini, Orazio 99
Rainaldi, Carlo 43 56 58 62 64 127 275 277f. 292 382 413 429
Ramdohr, F. W. B. v. 357 480
Rancoureuil, Abbé 446
Randi, Lorenzo 211
Raphael 2 11 15 22 25 261 337 411 503
Rauzzini (Raguzzini), Filippo 99–112 115f. 129 134 223 238 339f. 347ff. 419f.
– , Giacomo 111
– , Venanzio 111
Ravai, Francesco, see "Bajocco"
Recalcati, Giacomo Onorato 73 87
Recke, Elisa v. d. 498
Reggi (Riggi), Maddalena 324
Reiffenstein, J. F. 498
Rembrandt 45
Reni, Guido 260 435
Reumont, Alfred v. 193 480
Reuterholm, Gustav Adolf 164
Rezzonico, Giambattista 153 360
Ricci, Lorenzo de' 219
Ricciolini, Niccolò 122
Riccoboni, Luigi 110
Richard, Abbé 124 140 255 479 491
Riegl, Alois 306f.
Robert, Hubert 157 276 354 461 467 497 503
Rodriguez dos Santos, Manoel 143
Rondinini family 79
– , Guiseppe 312 440

Rospigliosi family 42 260f. 435 454
Rossi, Domenico de 84
– , Giovanni Antonio de 58 67f. 84 129 238 267–72 284 463 467
– , Giuseppe de 95
– , Mariano 483
– , Mattia de 56 58 62ff. 176 197 228
– , de, publishers 71 385
Rossini, Gioacchino 75 383
Rousseau, Jean-Jacques 4 460
Rubens 391 502
Rubio, Diego 143
Ruffo, Tommaso 74 280
Ruggieri, Fernando 301
Rusconi, Giuseppe 122
Ruspoli family 59 169 280 318 472

Sacchetti family 255
Saint-Lambert, Jean-François 501
Salvi, Nicola 91 120 134 206 306ff. 318 353ff. 415 476
– , Simone 475
Saly, Jacques-François-Joseph 276
Sanctis, Francesco de 94 335 337 339ff. 345
Sangallo, Antonio da, the Younger 6 144 206 242
Santacroce family 42 251 311 431
– , Antonio 311
– , Giuliana, née Falconieri 311 431
– , Prospero 311
Sardi, Giuseppe, the Elder 74 88f. 92f. 130 134 142f. 190 420
– , Giuseppe, the Younger 142
Sassi, Ludovico Rusconi 71 122 129
– , Matteo 71 84 414
Savelli family 7 25 251f. 449
Scarlatti, Alessandro 474
Schlegel, A. W. 365
Schlözer, Kurt v. 169
Scorza, Sinibaldo 383 410
Seckendorf, Frau v. 397
Sergel, Johan Tobias 400 459 531
Severn, Joseph 495
Sforza-Cesarini family 135
Shakespeare 502
Sharp, Samuel 50
Shelley, Percy Bysshe 6 405 495 516
Sherlock, Martin 494

Silvagni, David 406
Simonetti, Michelangelo 528
Smollett, Tobias 400 403 526f.
Spada, Orazio 205
— , Ridolfo 446
— , Virgilio 205
Specchi, Alessandro 71 96 197 229 283–87 290 292 296 298 321f. 335f. 340f. 382 465 480
— , Michelangelo 298
Spinola, Cardinal 216
— , Marchese 429
Staël-Holstein, Anne-Louise, née Necker 4 193 365 531
Stendhal 22 26 29 33 96 164 249 263 266 274 288 391 399 402 419 495 511 522
Stosch, Philip v. 429
Stuart, Charles Edward 190 195 280 455 484
— , Henry, Cardinal 195 455 484
— , James III 167 280 429
Subleyras, Pierre 148
Swanevelt, Herman van 391

Taine, Hippolyte 125 165
Tamburini, Michelangelo 172
Tasso, Torquato 240 426f. 472
Tempesta, Antonio 235 441
Temple, Lancelot 27
Tencin, Pierre-Guérin de 336–39 343 363
Teodoli, see Theodoli
Terribilini 142
Tessin, Nicodemus, the Younger 58 61 66 270 278 330 355 430 434 506
Tettoni, Filippo 319
Theodoli family 255
— , Girolamo 90 121 135f. 146 169 189 231 282 337
Thomson, James 501
Thorvaldsen, Bertel 261 274 313 364 387 421 513 522f. 531
Thurah, Lauritz de 78
Tiepolo, Giambattista 342
Tischbein, Wilhelm 417 504
Torlonia family 42 274 513
— , Giovanni 259 274
— , Marino 387
Torriani, Orazio 328 331

Trippel, Alexander 409f.
Tuscher, Marcus 429

Ulfeldt, Counts 221

Vahl, Martin 224
Vaini, Guido 318 468
Valadier, Giuseppe 84 178 249 365f. 380 411 414 420
Valenti, Silvio 136 297
Valeri, Antonio 72 82 122 134 299
— , Ugo 386
Valesio, Francesco 97 101 105 108 127 189 296 346f. 349 392 433 472
Valvassori, Gabriele 109 115f. 134 188 282 289–93 309 339 420 424 474
Vanbrugh, John 60 486
Vanvitelli (van Wittel), Gasparo 353ff. 439
— , Luigi 122 134 148 190f. 312
Vasanzio, Giovanni 483
Vasari, Giorgio 126 432
Vasconi, Filippo 119
Vasi, Giuseppe 92 130 132 166 173 185 202 208 232 238f. 261 282 309 372 378 380 382 387 396ff. 408 415ff. 437 470 473 495 501 516
Vasquez, General 190
Velásques 37
Venuti, Ridolfino 159 188 307 311 417 477 499
Vernet, Joseph 11 323
Verri, Alessandro 282
— , Pietro 222 366
Veuillot, Louis 439
Vigée-Lebrun, Elisabeth 377
Vignola, Giacomo 444ff. 481
Vleugels (Vleughels), Nicolas 116 122 134 503
Volkmann, Joh. Jak. 124 437 490 495 513
Voltaire 33 98 146 489

Wailly, Charles de 497
Walpole, Horace 133 246
— , Robert 257
Watteau, Antoine 111
Weinlig, Chr. Traug. 234f. 401 417 479
Wiedewelt, Johs. 151 482f. 510 512 517
Wilson, Richard 400 461f. 485

Winckelmann, Joh. Joach. 4 111 148f. 151 202 225 279 302 366 371 395 457 459 473 477–82 496–99 525
Wright, Thomas 332 406 434 453 471 477 513

Young, Edward 505

Zabaglia, Nicola 49 172 364
Zagarolo, Dukes of, see Rospigliosi
Zenobia, Queen 492f.
Zoëga, Georg 194 313 364 449 451 484 498 504 510 515 530
Zoppoli, Carmine 100
– , Vito 100 106f.

Oehlenschläger, Adam 523

LIST OF PLACES AND SUBJECT INDEX

Accademia degli Arcadi 88 91 450 467 471–74
- di Francia 276 288 292 387 397 402 507
- degli Infecondi 447
- di S. Luca 120 129 135 296
- dei Virtuosi 36

Acqua, see also Fountains
- Acetosa 451
- Felice 13 71
- Lancisiana 240
- Paola 6 13
- Vergine 14 326 349ff. 439

Albergo Aquila d'Oro 312
- Campana 390
- Monte d'Oro 392f.
- dell' Orso 390
- Il Paradiso 389f.
- Pio 395
- Roland 396–97
- Lo Scudo di Francia (La Villa di Londra) 393 396
- Vacca 390

Amphitheatrum Castrense 19 360
Aqueducts 4 6 13
Arcades (Teatro di Marcello) 26
Arches (Archi, Cavalcavie) 63 431–34
Arco dei Capellari 373
- di Carbognano 398
- dei Cenci 373
- di Costantino 355
- di Dorabella 442
- di Giano 465
- di Grottapinta 373
- del Monte 227
- della Pace 373
- di Parma 373

Arco di S. Marco 373
- delle Sette Vespe 447
- di Settimo Severo 490
- di Tito 388
- dei Tolomei 373

Banco di S. Spirito (Pal. Spada) 205
Basilica di Costantino 233 505
Belrespiro (Villa Doria-Pamphili) 475f.
Belvederes 9 124 159 169 177 181 183 194 328f. 447 463f. 467 471 480
Biblioteca Casanatense (Minerva) 171 186 383f.
- Corsini 302
Bocca della Verità 47
Boschetto, Il 422
Bosco Parrhasio 472–74

Caffè 397–407 475f. 482
- sotto l'Arco di Carbognano 398
- Greco 399–400
- Inglese 400–01
- Nuovo 399
- del Veneziano 398

Calcografia Pontificia 385
Campagna 2–6 123f. 369 381 415 441 449 471 477 483 513
Campo dei Fiori 248
- Marzio 15
- Vaccino (Forum Romanum) 14 124f. 363 379 422f. 490 497 505 507f. 518f.

Canopus 481
Cappella Albani 72
- Borghese 46
- Corsini 126
- di S. Domenico 102 108
- di S. Maria della Pietà 147
- Sistina 126 153 394

50*   575

Carcere Capitolino 211
— Mamertino (S. Pietro in Carcere) 45
Carceri Nuove 29 214f.
Casa Giannini 418
— Guarnieri 413 443
— Mengarini 397
— Raffaelli 420
— Sterbini 205
— Tomati 387
— Turci 469
Casino Altieri 463f.
— Bolognetti 476
— Borghese 483–84
— Colonna 432f.
— Ferroni 476
— Pius IV (Villa Pia) 32 71 451 476
— dei Quattro Venti 464f.
— Rospigliosi 260
— Vaini 468–69
— Valadier 366
— Valenti 476
Castel Sant' Angelo, see Graves
Cestius Pyramid 6; see also Churchyards
Chinea, La 294f.
Churches 33–54
  S. Agata dei Goti 87 112
  S. Agnese (Piazza Navona) 43 61 75 77
  S. Agnese fuori le Mura 43 46
  S. Agostino 372
  S. Alessio 136 145–46 447
  SS. Ambrogio e Carlo 38
  S. Anastasia 44–45 423
  S. Anastasio 37 220
  S. Andrea delle Fratte 426
  S. Andrea al Quirinale 18 56 129
  S. Andrea della Valle 7 18 28 274 369 372
  SS. Angeli Custodi al Tritone 417
  S. Angelo in Pescheria 52
  S. Anna dei Palafrenieri 96
  S. Antonio 37
  S. Antonio Abbate 46
  S. Antonio dei Portoghesi 37 63
  S. Apollinare 144–45 177
  S. Apollonia 64
  SS. Apostoli 42 83 120
  S. Balbina 43 448
  Bambin Gesù, Chiesa del 128 233
  S. Bartolomeo 39
  S. Bartolomeo all' Isola 36
  S. Bartolomeo degli Bergamaschi 128
  S. Basilio 37
  S. Benedetto 369
  S. Biagio in Campitelli (S. Rita da Cascia) 67–69
  S. Biagio della Pagnotta 47
  SS. Biagio e Cecilia 105
  S. Brigida 37 80–81
  S. Carlino 28 67
  S. Carlo alla Corso 42 61 380
  S. Caterina della Ruota 114
  S. Caterina da Siena 136
  S. Cecilia in Trastevere 112 136–37
  SS. Celso e Giuliano 128
  S. Cesareo 43 442
  S. Claudio 37 115f.
  S. Clemente 79
  SS. Concezione, Chiesa della 173
  SS. Cosma e Damiano 36 438
  S. Costanza 506
  S. Crisogono 80
  S. Croce in Gerusalemme 17 19 39 44 132 134 139–41 360
  S. Croce dei Lucchesi 64–65
  SS. Domenico e Sisto 341
  Domine quo vadis? 45
  S. Dorotea 145 147
  S. Egidio 128
  S. Eligio 129
  S. Eusebio 43 85
  S. Eustachio 46 91–92 380 413
  S. Filippo Neri (S. Filippino) 95 104
  S. Francesco al Monte Mario 106
  S. Galla 62
  Gesù, Il 28
  Gesù e Maria 42 60 62 64
  S. Giacomo degli Spagnuoli (S. Jago) 37
  S. Giorgio in Velabro 83
  S. Giovanni Battista 39
  S. Giovanni Calibita 143 236
  S. Giovanni Decollato 52
  S. Giovanni dei Fiorentini 38–39 126–27
  S. Giovanni in Laterano 17 90 121–26 307 359f. 422 459
  S. Giovanni e Paolo 82f. 442f.
  S. Girolamo 37
  S. Girolamo della Carità 312

S. Girolamo degli Schiavoni 321
S. Giuseppe 36
S. Giuseppe alla Lungara 129
S. Gregorio Magno 112 442
S. Gregorio a Quattro Capi
  (S. Gregorietto) 53 112 248
S. Ignazio 28 317 507
S. Isidoro 9 86
S. Ivo 37
SS. Leonardo e Romualdo 114
S. Lorenzo in Damaso 114 316
S. Lorenzo in Lucina 364
S. Lorenzo in Miranda 36
S. Lorenzo in Panisperna 44
S. Lucia del Gonfalone 153
S. Luigi dei Francesi 37 328
S. Macuto 346 357
S. Maddalena in Campo Marzio 413
Madonna alle Fornaci, see S. Maria alle
  Fornaci
Madonna dei Monti, see S. Maria dei Monti
Madonna del Rosario 97 107
SS. Marcellino e Pietro 146–47
S. Marcello al Corso (de' Serviti) 42
  64–66 93–94 181 283 286 387
S. Marco 145
S. Margherita 63 68 145
S. Maria degli Angeli 147 312
S. Maria dell' Anima 37
S. Maria in Aquiro 418
S. Maria in Aracoeli 9 40 47 319
S. Maria Aventina (S. Maria del Priorato)
  41 153–54
S. Maria in Campitelli 42 61 274
S. Maria in Campo Marzio 68–69
S. Maria della Concezione
  (dei Cappuccini) 40 121 444
S. Maria in Coppella 36
S. Maria in Cosmedin 47 87f.
S. Maria in Domnica 47
S. Maria Egiziaca 80 88
S. Maria alle Fornaci 105 450
S. Maria Liberatrice 379
S. Maria Maggiore 8 17 44ff. 132 138–39
  182 185 194
S. Maria sopra Minerva 41 101 108
S. Maria de' Miracoli 178
S. Maria di Monserrato 37

S. Maria dei Monti 144 173 381
S. Maria in Monterone 63
S. Maria in Montesanto 17 20 178 189
S. Maria in Monticelli 84
S. Maria ad Nives 142
S. Maria Nova (S. Francesca Romano)
  124–25
S. Maria dell' Orazione e Morte 127
S. Maria dell' Orto 36 438
S. Maria della Pace 40 77 280 317
S. Maria del Popolo 13 16 305
S. Maria del Priorato, see S. Maria
  Aventina
S. Maria in Publicolis 42
S. Maria del Riposo 465ff.
S. Maria della Scala 45 63
S. Maria del Sole 88 511
S. Maria in Trastevere 73–74 80
S. Maria dell' Umiltà 128
S. Maria in Vallicella (Chiesa Nuova)
  7 114 316 413
S. Maria in Via Lata 288
S. Maria Maddalena in Campo Marzio
  129f. 188–89
S. Marta 82
S. Martino 247
SS. Michele e Magno 9 182
SS. Nereo e Achilleo 43
S. Nicola in Arcione 281
S. Nicola dei Prefetti 112
S. Niccolò da Tolentino 37
SS. Nome di Maria 130
S. Onofrio (al Gianicolo) 426 472
S. Paolino alla Regola 92
S. Paolo alle Tre Fontane 46
S. Pietro in Carcere (Carcer Mamertinus)
  45
S. Pietro in Montorio 472
S. Pietro in Vaticano 2 7 8 21 33 38 47
  55f. 77 82 91 116 123 133 148 154 158
  298 360 479
S. Pietro in Vincoli 9 45 82 427 444
S. Prassede 43
S. Prisca 43 448
SS. Quaranta Martiri e S. Pasquale
  Baylon 141
SS. Quirico e Giulitta 188
S. Rocco 36ff. 362

S. Saba 448
S. Sabina 44 447
S. Salvatore della Corte (S. Maria della Luce) 424
S. Salvatore in Lauro 40
S. Sebastiano 72
S. Sebastiano al Palatino 447
S. Silvestro in Capite 42 84
S. Sisto Vecchio 43 102 441
S. Spirito 39 144
S. Stanislao (dei Polacchi) 129
S. Stefano delle Carrozze, see S. Maria del Sole
S. Stefano degli Indiani (de' Mori) 38 82
SS. Stimmate di S. Francesco 93
SS. Sudario 39
S. Teodoro 78
S. Tommaso di Canterbury 37
S. Tommaso in Parione 372
SS. Trinità dei Monti 8 16 37 327 343 363 391f. 420 426
SS. Trinità dei Pellegrini 52 93f. 341
SS. Trinità degli Spagnuoli 143 419
S. Venanzio 40 268
SS. Vincenzo e Anastasio (a Trevi) 29 326 368
SS. Vincenzo e Anastasio alla Regola (de' Cuochi) 36 129
Churchyards
  Campo Santo (al Gianicolo) 243
  Campo Santo Teutonico 37
  Cestius Pyramid (the Protestant Churchyard) 514–16
  the Jews' Churchyard (on the Aventine) 448
Circus Maximus 365
Clivus Scauri 443
Cloaca Maxima 88 437
Collegium Angelicum 168
Collegio Bandinelli 39 218
  – Calasanzio 223–24
  – Cerasoli 219
  – Clementino 10 107 221 282 442 470
Collegium Germanicum 41 220
Collegio Greco 220
  – dei Cento preti poveri (the hundred poor priests) 182
  – degli Ibernesi 219

Collegio Inglese 219
  – dei Maroniti 220
  – Nazareno 221 526
  – dei Neofiti 172 220
  – di Propaganda Fide 182 218 243 291 529
  – Romano 28 217 347
Colonnacce, Le 372 489 507f.
Colonne 20 381
  colonna di Foca 380 507
  columna Antonini Pii 71 324 326 351 359
Colosseum 17 21 76 147 156f. 192 249 321 324 360 422 497 507 531
Conservatories 173–176
Conservatorio dell' Assunta 208 232f.
  – della Divina Providenza 231
  – S. Croce della Penitenza (delle Scalette) 231
  – di S. Pasquale Baylon 232
  – delle Zoccolette 231
Convents and monasteries 159–195
  S. Agostino 172 177 190–91 439
  S. Andrea (Jesuit Noviciate) 178
  S. Andrea della Valle (Theatines) 28 161
  S. Apollonia 172
  S. Balbina 191
  S. Bonaventura (Franciscans) 183–93 446
  S. Carlino 28
  Casa professa dei Gesuiti 28 383 437 448
  S. Caterina da Siena (Dominican nuns) 168–69
  S. Cecilia in Trastevere 167
  S. Cosimato 438–39
  SS. Domenico e Sisto (Dominican nuns) 168
  S. Eusebio 195
  S. Francesca Romana, see convent of Tor' de' Specchi
  S. Giacomo delle Convertite (Conservatorio) 175
  SS. Giovanni e Paolo (Padri della Missione) 193
  S. Giuseppe alla Lungara (Pii Operai) 190
  S. Isidoro (Irish Monks) 193f. 443
  S. Lorenzo in Lucina (Clerici minori) 188

S. Lorenzo in Panisperna 167 277–78
S. Lucia in Selci (Benedictine nuns) 166
S. Marcello de' Serviti (al Corso) 65 177 180–82
S. Margherita 64 177 186
S. Maria degli Angeli (Carthusians) 164f. 312
S. Maria in Campo Marzio (Benedictine nuns) 68 84 168 178 270
S. Maria della Concezione (Capuchins) 40 161 180
S. Maria sopra Minerva (Dominicans) 41 171 176–77 180f. 183 186 438
S. Maria in Monterone (Redemptorists) 189
S. Maria di Montesanto (Carmelites) 189
S. Maria della Pace (Canonici Lateranensi) 40–41
S. Maria dei Sette Dolori (Oblates) 170–71 208
S. Maria delle Vergini (Augustine nuns) 176 438
S. Maria Maddalena in Campo Marzio 188–89
S. Maria Maddalena delle Convertite 187 316
S. Marta (Augustine nuns) 170 186
S. Pietro in Vincoli 191
SS. Pietro e Marcellino (Teresians) 194
SS. Quattro Coronati 191
S. Rufina 177
S. Silvestro in Capite (Franciscan nuns) 187
Tor' de' Specchi, convent of, (Oblates) 166 191 372
SS. Trinità dei Monti (Minims) 155 180
SS. Trinità degli Spagnuoli (Trinitarians) 190
SS. Vincenzo e Anastasio (Clerici minori) 187
Umiltà cloister 176
Clares, convent of the 173
Philippines, convent of the, (Villa Sforza) 194
Jesuit Headquarters 181
Jesuit Noviciate (al Monte Cavallo) 172
Passionists, monastery of the, on Monte Cavo 195
Turchines, convent of the 185
Ursuline convent 189–90
Cortili 69

Dataria Apostolica 205
Dioscuri (Monte Cavallo) 363 365
Dogana 196f.
– di Ripa Grande 197
– di Terra 197f.
Domus Augustana 446
– Mendicantium Pupillarum 233
– aurea Neronis 444 505

Fora Caesarum 8 320f.
Forum Boarium 423
Forum Romanum, see Campo Vaccino
Fountains (wells, springs):
  Fontana delle Api 14
  La Barcaccia 13 331
  Fonte della Barchetta (Acqua Lancisiana) 240
  Il Facchino 14 284
  Fontana del Mascherone 13
  Quattro Fontane 13
  Fontanone di S. Sisto 13
  Fontana Secca 142
  – delle Tartarughe 13
  – di Trevi (Acqua Vergine) 12 20 120 325–26 336 349–57 414
  – del Tritone 12f.

Galleria Albani 480
– Colonna 290 295–96 433
– Doria-Pamphili 290 444
– del Quirinale 122
Galluzze, Le, see Minerva Medica
Gardens 428–40
  Orti Alibert 469
  Vigna Barberini 447
  Giardino segreto del Pal. Borghese 429
  Otto botanico 224
  Vigna Caffarelli 513
  Pal. Cardelli 431
  Casa professa del Gesù 438
  Vigna Cavalieri 449
  Vigna Cenci 437
  Giardino Colonna 297 426 432 436
  – Corsini (Riario) 449 472
  Pal. Farnese 432

Orti Farnesiani 379 445–46
Pal. Del Grillo 435–36
Horti Liciniani 511
Vigna Maccarani 449
Giardino Maidalchini 437–38
Pal. Orsini-Taverna 429
Pal. Rospigliosi 435
Orti Sallustiani 359
S. Francesco a Ripa 438
S. Isidoro 9 443
S. Maria delle Vergini convent 438
Pal. Santacroce 431
Vigna Sassi 530
Vigna Sinibaldi 450
Pal. Spada a Capo di Ferro 437
Vaticano 71
Ghetto 7 53 113 235 373 387–89
— degli Artisti (Via della Purificazione) 409
Grave(s):
Augustus' 362 394 490
Cecilia Metella's 350
Hadrian's (Castel Sant' Angelo) 34 197f. 211 243f. 245
Scipios' 530
Grotta di Egeria 495 505 511–14

Hills (colli) 6–9
Aventine 41 145 153 191 251 360f. 440 447–49 482
Campidoglio (Capitol) 7 17 19 67 124f. 200 314 319 480f. 491 519 525–26 531
Monte Celio (Caelius) 16 47 440 442
— Cenci 7
Citorio 7 311
Esquiline 8 16 43 46 185 194 425 440 444 457 472
Gianicolo 6 8 13 208 224 233 242 300 424 440 449 468ff. 472
Monte Giordano 6 383 384 430
Monte Mario 97 106
Palatine 7 45 192 423 440 444–47 472 502 504 516
Monti Parioli 450f.
Monte Pincio (Collis hortorum) 7f. 17 31 366 440 443 455
Quirinal 7f. 16 32 202 247 287 297–300 326 353 362 365 432 435 452 475

Monte Savello 7 26
— del Serpente 447
— Testaccio 7 458 514
— della Trinità 330
Viminal 16 278 422 440
Hospices:
Ospizio dei Mendicanti 227
— Apostolico di S. Michele 197 215 228f. 468
Ospizio degli Orfanelli (foundling hospital) 241–42
Passionists, the hospice of the, (Monte Cavo) 195
Ospizio della SS. Trinita dei Pellegrini 226 396
Trinitarians, the hospice of the Spanish 190 396
Hospitals 233–43
Ospedale della Consolazione 233–35
— dei Genovesi 427
— de' Pazzarelli 239
— di S. Galla 62
— di S. Gallicano 237f.
— di S. Giovanni di Dio 236–37
Arcispedale del SS. Salvatore 233
Arcispedale di S. Spirito in Sassia 205 233 241

Inscriptions 192 403 421 423

Largo Goldoni 318
— dell' Impresa 418
— Magnanapoli 168 307
Locanda Cesàri 390
— Margherita 394
— Sarmiento 395
— La Scalinata 394

Madonnelle, le 48
Markets 379–81
Marmorata, La 447
Minerva Medica 422 510–11
Misericordia Society 52
Mura 5 6
Museums 149 524–31
Museo Capitolino 126
— Vaticano 149

Obelisks 19 359 361–66
    Altieri obelisk 464
    Heliopolis obelisk 418
    Ludovisi obelisk 362–64
Oratorio della SS. Annunziata
    (la Nunziatella) 142 241
– in Borgo Nuovo (for the Cardinal's
    train-bearers) 36
– del Cuore di Gesù 52
– dei Filippini 87 179
– di S. Filippo Neri 472
– della S. Maria della Pietà del
    P. Caravita 51
– del SS. Sacramento di S. Maria in
    Via Lata 113
– del S. Simone Profeta 129
– dei Serviti 134 140
– della SS. Trinità dei Pellegrini, see
    Churches
Orphanages 228 233 316
L'Ortaccio 450
Osterie:
    La Barchetta 236
    del Gatto Nero 376
    La Gensola 425
    Spanish Wineshop 401–02
    La Villetta 425f.

Palazzi:
    Albani 283 477
    Alessandrino-Bonelli 313
    Altemps 149
    Altieri 21 262 268–72 309 372
    Altoviti 11
    Antonelli 9
    Dell' Aquila 25 411
    D'Aste (Bonaparte) 267 284
    Barberini 12 32 366
    Bernini 265
    Bighazzini 272–74 284
    Boncompagni-Cerasi 418
    Boncompagni-Ludovisi 303–05 359
    Bonelli (Ruspoli) 280 307
    Borghese 313 429
    Borgia 9
    Borgnana 403
    Braschi 383
    Del Bufalo 273

    Caetani 267
    della Cancelleria 21 114 201 276 316
        369 382
    Capizucchi-Gavotti 399
    Caprini 25 411
    Cardelli 431
    De Carolis 283–86 289 403
    Castellani 378
    Di Cellere (Macchi di C.) 358f. 418
    Cenci 224
    Chigi-Odescalchi 83 197 273 280 286
        305–08
    Cicciaporci 412
    Cimarra 276f. 411
    Cini 266
    Del Cinque 311–12
    Clementi 267
    Colonna 120 280 290 294–97 306–07
        432–34
    dei Conservatori 480f. 525
    della Consulta 32 202f. 247–48 300 359
        365
    Conti 364
    Corsini 300–02
    Costa 145 412
    Crescenzi 403
    Doria-Pamphili (al Corso) 29–30 109
        188 287–94 308–09
    Falconieri 39 437
    Farnese 7 13 74 202 432
    Fiano 387
    Gambirasi 280
    Gentili 281–82
    Del Grillo 278–79 435–36
    Grimaldi (Lazzaroni) 282
    Lancellotti 24
    Ludovisi 209
    Madama 211
    Mancini (Salviati) 274–77 284 288f. 292f.
    Massimo alle Colonne 25 369 381
    Massimo di Rignano 284
    Mastrozzi (Graziosi) 311
    Mattei di Giove 524
    Mellini 309 387
    Mignanelli 318 383
    di Montecitorio (Palace of Justice)
        209f. 305 311 319f. 324
    Muti (Bussi) 268 280

Nardini 211
Negroni 282
Odescalchi, see Chigi-Odescalchi
Orsini (Teatro di Marcello) 113
Orsini (now Braschi) 383
Orsini-Santobono 312–13
Orsini-Taverna 430
Pamphili (alla Piazza Navona) 61 116
Pediconi 312 385
dei Penitenzieri 209
Petroni (Cenci-Bolognetti) 309–10
Pichini 149 286–87 292
di Pio IV 22
Poli 92 326 336 351 354
del Quirinale 9 32
Riario (later Corsini) 81 301
Rondinini (Sanseverino) 312 440
Rospigliosi 23–24 434
Rossini 385
Ruffo 280
Ruspoli 399
Sacchetti 39
del Sacro Uffizio 212f.
Salviati 39 472
di S. Biagio 22
Santacroce 42 311 431
Savelli (Teatro di Marcello) 25
Sciarra 359
Sciarra-Carbognano 387
Sciarra-Colonna 284
Senatorio 211 490
Sforza-Cesarini 135
Spada (Banco di S. Spirito) 205
Testa-Peccolomini 303
Torres (Lancellotti) 223
della Trinità dei Pellegrini 396
Venezia 16 19 21 273
Verospi 283 405
Zuccari (Torres) 279 392
Palazzi di famiglia:
    Barberini 258
    Borghese 258 273
    Chigi 258
    Colonna 258 296
    Farnese 261
    Lancellotti 258
    della Famiglia Pontificia 298–99
    Santacroce 258
Pantheon (La Rotonda) 20 22f. 36 82 114 126 140 145 380 451 501 507 509–10 526ff.
Pasquino 269 318 383f. 526
Pescheria, La 207 380 490
Piazze:
    Argentina 507
    Barberini 12ff. 40 261 422 531
    del Biscione 369
    di Bocca della Verità 88–89 357 423
    Borghese 261 273 368
    del Campidoglio 519
    di Campitelli 62 67
    della Cancelleria 316
    Capranica 418
    Clementina (project) 325f. 358
    del Collegio Romano 29
    Colonna 39 239 273 317 320 326 359
    delle Coppelle 369 416
    Crescenzi 380
    della Crocetta (del Drago) 369
    Farnese 37 380
    del Febo 372
    di Firenze 115 416
    di Grottapinta 369
    Giudea 248
    Lancellotti 368
    del Laterano, see di S. Giovanni in Laterano
    in Lucina 188
    Madama 380
    Margana 388
    Mattei 13
    Mignanelli 395
    delle Monache di S. Silvestro 316
    Molara 236
    Montanara 25 381 416 490
    di Montecitorio 319f. 324 358–59 364
    Montedoro 389
    Montegiordano 312
    del Monte di Pietà 359
    alli Monti 381
    Navona 13 37 46 51 61 314 351 368 372 380 385f. 403 456
    degli Olmi 426
    dell' Orologio 205 384
    Padella 381
    Paganica (dell' Olmo) 426

del Paradiso 369 372 389
del Parlamento 418
di Pasquino 368 383ff. 419
del Pianto 387
di Pietra 197f. 248 359 409
della Pigna 369
della Pilotta (Olmo di Trejo) 426
in Piscinula 368 425
Pollarola 202 359 369 380 390
del Popolo 16 178 249 365 410
della Posta Vecchia 381
del Quirinale 12
della Rotonda 357 380 390 417 420
della Ruota 312
di SS. Apostoli 9 177 294 296 306–07
di S. Egidio 232 368
di S. Giovanni in Laterano 359–60 363
di S. Ignazio 177 180 346ff. 417
di S. Lorenzo in Lucina 416 419
di S. Maria Maggiore 47
di S. Maria in Trivio 350
di S. Pietro 13 21 315
di S. Silvestro 178
di S. Stefano del Cacco 372
dei Satiri 369
di Scanderbeg 368
Sforza Cesarini 359
di Spagna 7 9 16 72f. 326f. 331 342f.
 363 389 391f. 394 417
della Suburra 416
dei Termini 13 247
della Torretta 409
Venezia 318
Vittorio Emanuele 85
degli Zingari 9 416
Piazzette:
 del Biscione 373
 di Macel de' Corvi 380
 dell' Olmo Secco 426
Ponte Molle 12f. 250 450 455 486
 – Quattro Capi (Pons Fabricius) 11 144
 236f. 248
 – Rotto 10
 – S. Angelo 15f.
Porta Cavalleggeri 14 247
 – Pia 16
 – del Popolo 14f. 249
 – Portese 196f. 216 279

Porta di S. Pancrazio 6 441 464f.
 – di S. Paolo 6
 – di S. Spirito 241–42
 – Settimiana 8
Porticus Octaviae 207 380 490
Porto di Legno 359
 – di Ripa Grande 401
 – di Ripetta 36 321–24 335 341
Possesso, Il 307
Presepio, Il 47
Priorato di Malta 447 482

Quattro Fontane 13

Rioni 132
 Borgo 7 247 315 360
 Campitelli 7
 Campo Marzio 427–30
 Monti 7 16 377
 Ponte 7 11 241
 Regola 103 283
 Trastevere 7 36 43 87 141 145 248 368f.
  377 424ff. 437f.
Ripa Grande 15 196f. 231 321
Rupe Tarpeia 490

Salita della Dataria 204
 – del Gianicolo 472
 – Del Grillo 8
 – di S. Onofrio 9 232 242
Scala Mignanelli 9
 – Santa 45
 – del Sole (La Cordonata di Aracoeli)
  9 47 319
 – di Spagna, see Spanish Steps
Seminario Romano 222 347 490
 – di S. Pietro 223
Shops 374–75 407–08
Spanish Steps 9 91 317f. 326–46 363 392
Stalle Altieri 260
 – Barberini 261
 – Borghese 261
 – Colonna 261
 – Farnese 261
 – Rospigliosi 261
 – Santacroce 431
 – del Quirinale 14 32 261 298–99
Strada del Gesù (Via del Plebiscito) 308

Strada de' Librari 383f.
 – Pia (Via Venti Settembre) 13 16
 – di S. Francesco a Ripa 142
Street signs 375–76
Suburra quarter 172
Synagogue 388
Teatro d'Alibert (Alle Dame) 413 469f.
 – Argentina 36 135 369
 – Capranica 418
 – di Marcello 10 25 113 490
 – della Pace 418
 – di Pompeo 369
 – Tordinona 135 317 469f.
 – Valle 111 385
Temples:
 Castor and Pollux 507
 Concordia (Saturn) 491 507
 Faustina 36
 Fortuna Virilis 518
 Hadrianeum 71
 Jupitor Stator (Vespasian's Temple)
  490 507 509 519
 Nerva 507
 "Temple of Peace" (Templum Pacis),
  see Basilica (Constantine's)
 Vesta 490 499
Thermae 320
 "Agrippina"'s 320
 Caracalla's 43 441 490 495
 Diocletian's 147 207 490 497
Tiber 9–12 425 436f. 458
Tiber Island (Isola di S. Bartolomeo)
 10 143 184 235
Torre dei Borgia 444
 – Caetani 11 143 236
 – del Grillo 278f.
 – delle Milizie 21 169
 – di Nona 10 214
 – d'Orologio (Oratorio dei Filippini)
  179
 – della Scimia 37
 – del Palazzo Venezia 21
Traforo, Il 281

Universitas Gregoriana 433
 – La Sapienza 217 386

Valle dell' Inferno 31 106 449

Vicoli:
 Alibert 470
 dell' Arancio 426 429
 del Bollo 383
 del Buco 424
 della Campana 390 413
 della Campanella 385
 del Cardello 376
 dei Catinari 431
 dei Ciancaleoni 411
 del Cipresso 426
 del Corallo 385
 della Cuccagna 386
 del Fico 383
 del Gallinaccio 376
 delle Grotte 312 371
 Leonetto 413
 dei Leutari 75
 della Madonnella 371
 Mancini 377
 di Mazzamurelli 238
 Mazzarino 434
 del Melone 385
 del Melangolo (Merangolo) 429
 del Micio 385
 della Moletta 236
 del Monticello 176
 delle Orsoline 408
 degli Orti d'Alibert 471
 degli Osti 408
 delle Palle 39
 del Sambuco 423
 dello Scalone 9
 Scavolino 188
 della Scimia 375
 dello Sdrucciolo 405
 della Spada d'Orlando 376
 dello Struzzo 375
 delle Tre Cannelle 9
 delle Vacche 372
 della Volpe 372
Vie:
 Alessandrina (Borgo Nuovo) 16 36 360
 Alibert 413 469
 Appia 43 441
 in Arcione 281 371
 degli Artisti 444
 Aurelia Antica 6 441 449 464 474

delle Azzimelle 388
del Babuino 16 17f. 303 305 327 391 413 420
dei Balestrari 382
dei Banchi Nuovi 382
dei Banchi Vecchi 128
del Banco di S. Spirito 15 420
dei Baullari 382
Beato Angelico 177
Borgo Nuovo, see Alessandrina
Borgo Pio 373 386
Borgo S. Spirito 241–42
Borgo Vecchio 360
Borgognona 389 410
del Boschetto 422f.
delle Botteghe Oscure 37 194 382 490
dei Burrò 349
dei Calderai 382
di Campo Marzio 68 419
dei Canestrari 385
Capo di Ferro 371
di Capo le Case 316 409 426
dei Cappellari 382
dei Cappuccini 86
delle Carrette 423
delle Carrozze 374
Cassia 3 33
dei Cestari 93 382
dei Chiavari 382
di Chiesa Nuova 316
delle Cinque Lune 376
Clementina 423
del Colosseo 142
dei Condotti 16 143 327 343 399 403 419
del Consolato 39
dei Coronari 16 24 40 372 430
Corsini 302
del Corso 15–18 39 41 61 65 180 189 259 273f. 283 288 294 312 316 318 340 359 373 387 391 397f. 417 419 440 450 455 469 495 501 530f.
della Croce 339 395
Crucis 192
della Dataria 247 249 326
De Pretis 8
dei Falegnami 371 382
dei Farnesi 409 416
Felice, see Sistina

dei Fienili 423
della Fiumara 388
Flaminia 6 450f.
della Fontanella di Borghese 16
delle Fornaci 449
Francesco Crispi 409
delle Fratte (Frasche) 426
Frattina 389
Garibaldi 6 208 232
della Gensola 425
dei Giardini 452
dei Giubbonari 227 371 382
Giulia 13 16 22 29 40 47 52 104 127 227 240 261 432 437
Giulio Romano 67
del Governo Vecchio 211 314 368 383ff. 409
Gregoriana 371 451
delle Grotte 382
Labicana 194
Lata 14f. 17f.
del Lavatore 14 187f.
del Leoncino 375
dei Leutari 382f.
della Lungara 14 232 240f. 261 300
della Lungaretta 177 368
Lungotevere 242
dei Maddalena 68f.
Madonna dei Monti 173
Margutta 391 469
di Mario de' Fiori 389 403
della Maschera d'Oro 24 376
della Mercede 316
Merulana 17
della Missione 324
di Monserrato 37 217 311 371 428
di Monte Brianzo 371
del Montonaccio 430
Nomentana 476
dell' Olmata 8 425
degli Ombrellari 386
dell' Orso 371 375 390 413
della Pace 385
della Paglia 87 424
di Pallacorda 431
di Panico 15 385
Panisperna 17f. 409
Paola 15

di Parione 383
del Pavone 375
del Pellegrino (degli Orefici) 371 382f.
della Pescheria 371
dei Pettinari 7
dei Pianellari 372 386 421
di Piè di Marmo 376 385
della Pilotta 297 432–34
dei Polacchi 372
di Porta Pinciana 8 194 413 443
di Porta S. Sebastiano 441
dei Portoghesi 190 439
della Purificazione 409
dei Quattro Cantoni 185
delle Quattro Fontane 8 16
Quattro Novembre 308
del Quirinale 178
dei Riari 302
di Ripetta 15 391
Sacra 490
Salaria 451
di S. Agata de' Goti 420
di S. Basilio 180
di S. Giovanni in Laterano 17 415 451
di S. Nicola da Tolentino 41
di S. Pancrazio 473
di S. Spirito 142
della Scrofa 177 191
delle Scuderie 371
dei Sediari (Corso del Rinascimento) 37
del Seminario 178 417
dei Serpenti 173 423
delle Sette Sale 444
Sistina 8 17 19 279 363 371 387
di S. Sebastianello 339 393 426
di S. Stefano del Cacco 7
della Testa Spaccata 376
delle Tre Cannelle 309
dei Tre Ladroni 376
delle Tre Pile 319
dell' Umiltà 176
Urbana 128
delle Vergini 176
della Vetrina 372 385

della Vite 389 409
Vittorio Veneto 12
degli Zingari 420 423
Vignaccia, La 419
Vigna, see Gardens
Ville:
  Albani 451 477–82 485 520 526
  Aldobrandini 168 452
  Altieri 463–64
  Barberini 455 462
  Benedetti (Il Fascello) 6 330
  di Bessarione 441
  Boncompagni 359
  Borghese (Pinciana) 32 443 452 455 457 462 480 483–89 521–23
  Carpegna 465–68
  Casali 471 480
  Catena 333ff. 341f.
  Chigi (fuori Porta Salaria) 483
  Chigi (in Arriccia) 462
  Corsini 464 475
  Doria-Pamphili (Belrespiro) 6 456f. 461 465 474f. 481
  Farnesina 261 432
  Giustiniani 457 472
  Ludovisi 304f. 443f. 452 456 458 460 497
  Madama 459
  Malta 155
  Massimo 452
  Mattei 104 442 458 460 462 505
  Medici 32 344 391 443 452 458 480
  Mills 192 446
  Montalto-Peretti (Negroni) 415 457 460 464 465
  di Papa Giulio 22 32 146 450
  Patrizi 471
  Pia (in Vaticano), see Casino
  del Priorato di Malta 9 361
  Sacchetti 455
  Sforza (on the Esquiline), see Convents and Monasteries
  Vaini 297
  Valenti 126

MAPS OF ROME
by Giambattista Nolli
1748

I. *The southern part of Trastevere and Monte Aventino, Monte Palatino, and Monte Celio.*

II. *The northern parts of the town.*

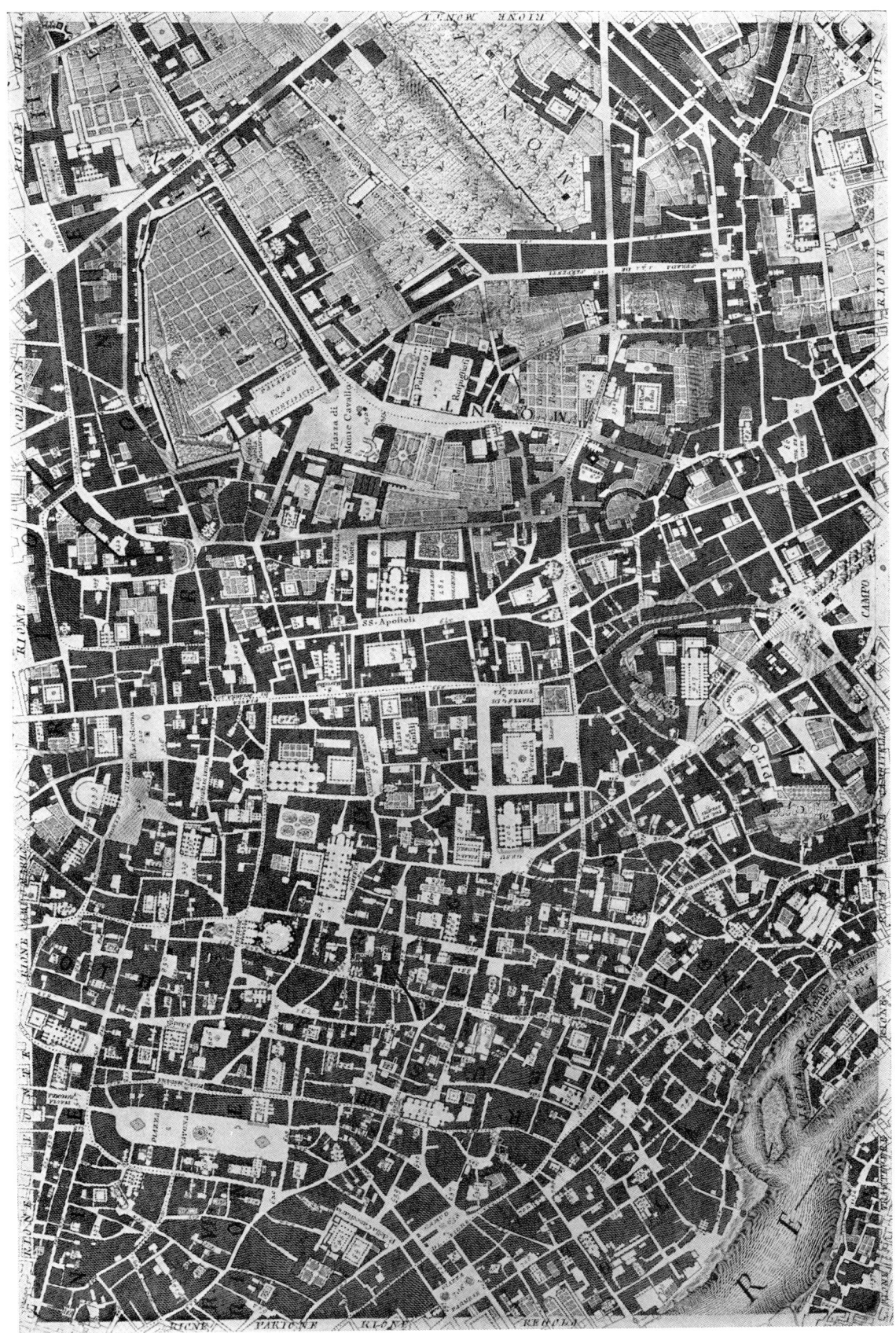

III. *The city centre.*

IV. *The neighbourhood around the Borgo, Castel S. Angelo, and part of the Rione Ponte.*

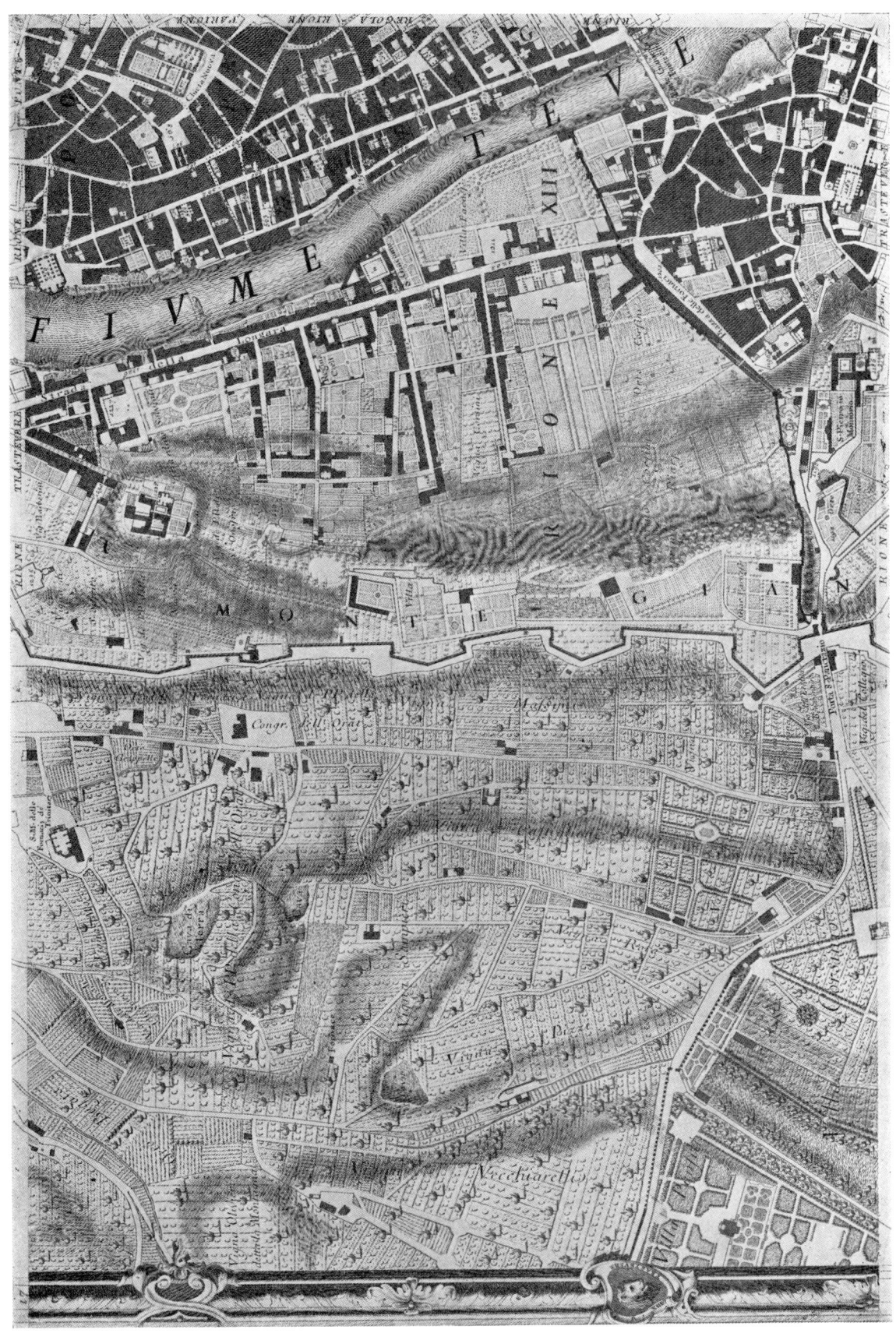

V. *Rione Regola, Trastevere, Lungara, and Monte Gianicolo.*

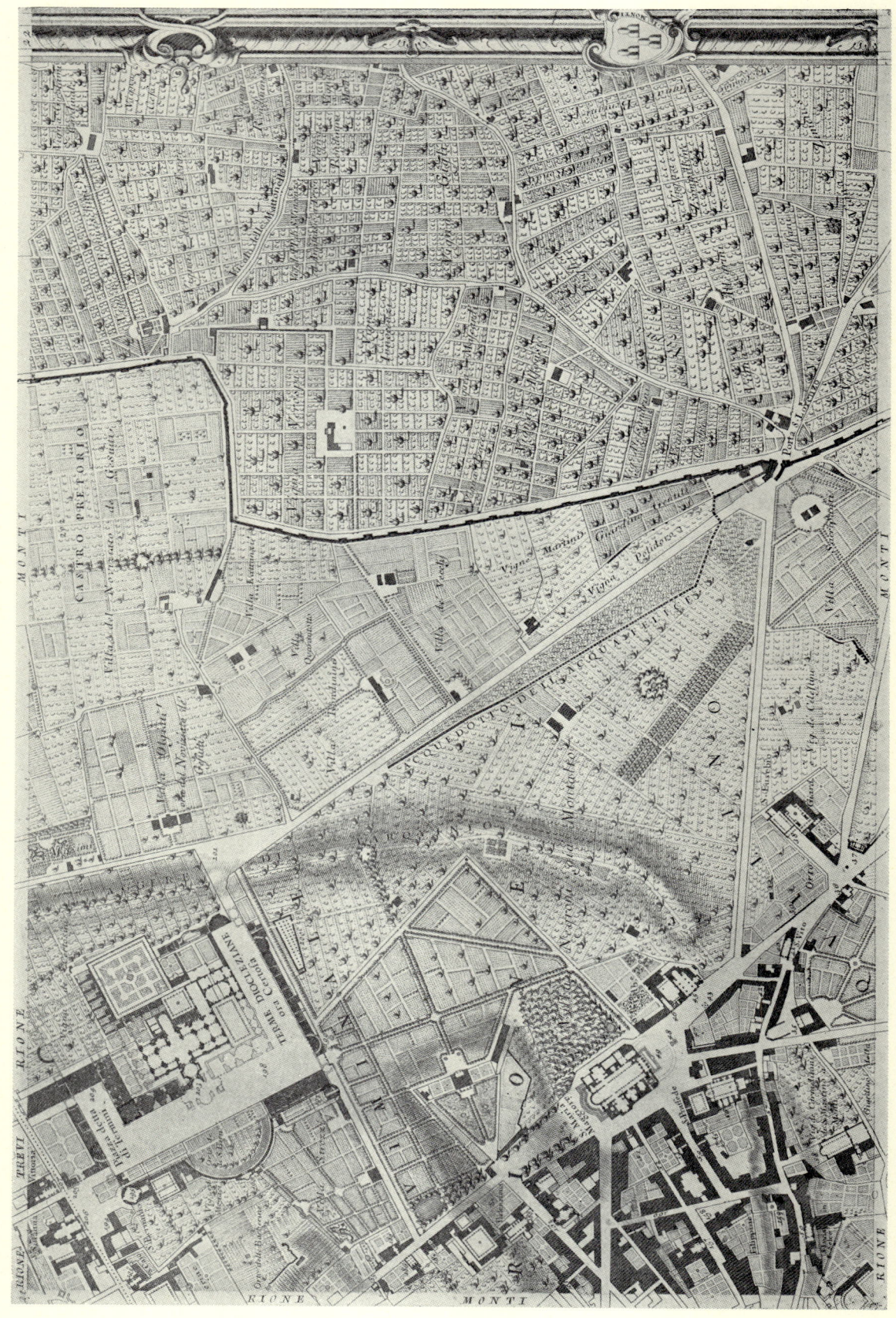

VI. *Monte Viminale, part of Monte Esquilino, and the outskirts of Rione Monti.*

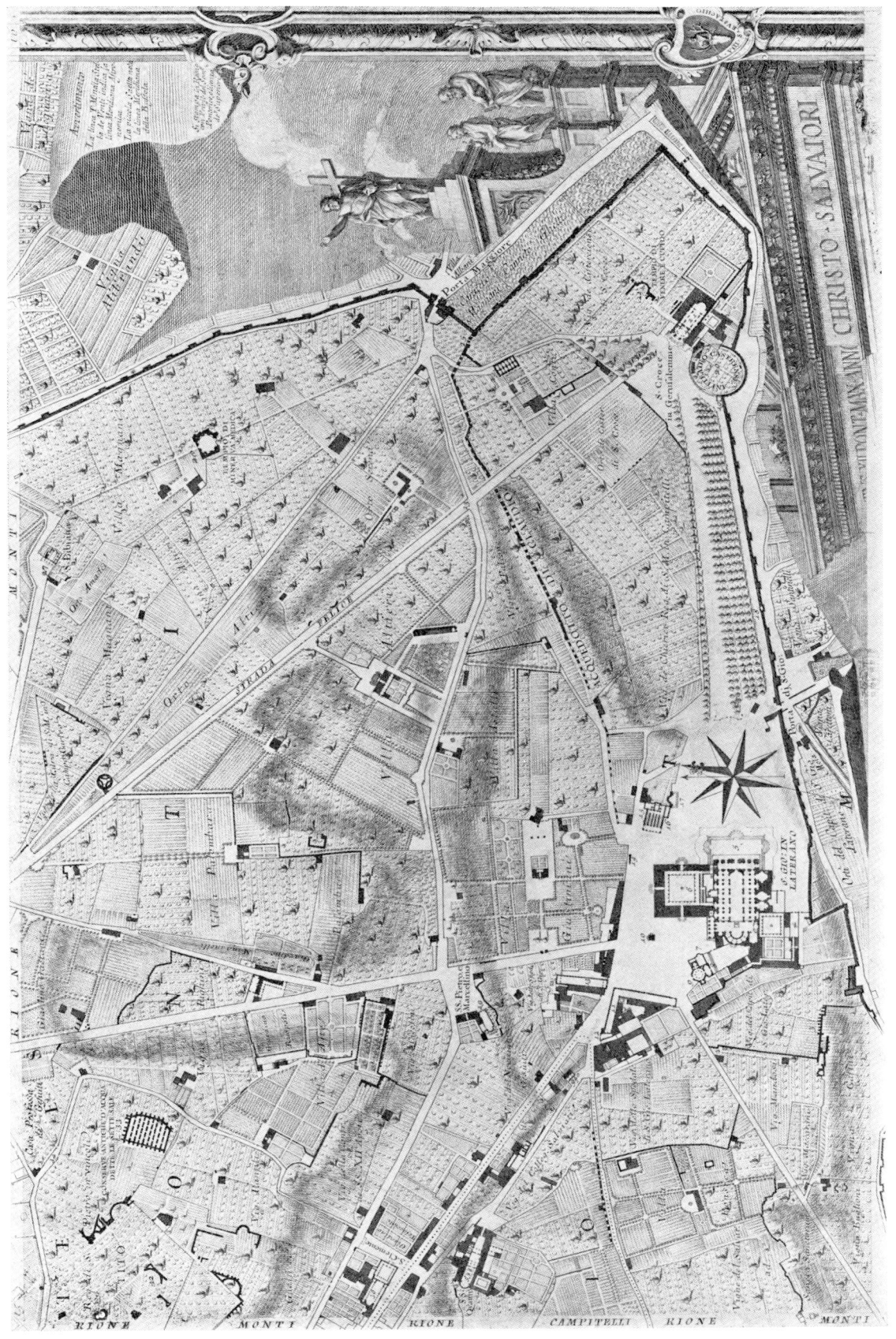

VII. *The Lateran and the outskirts of Rione Monti.*

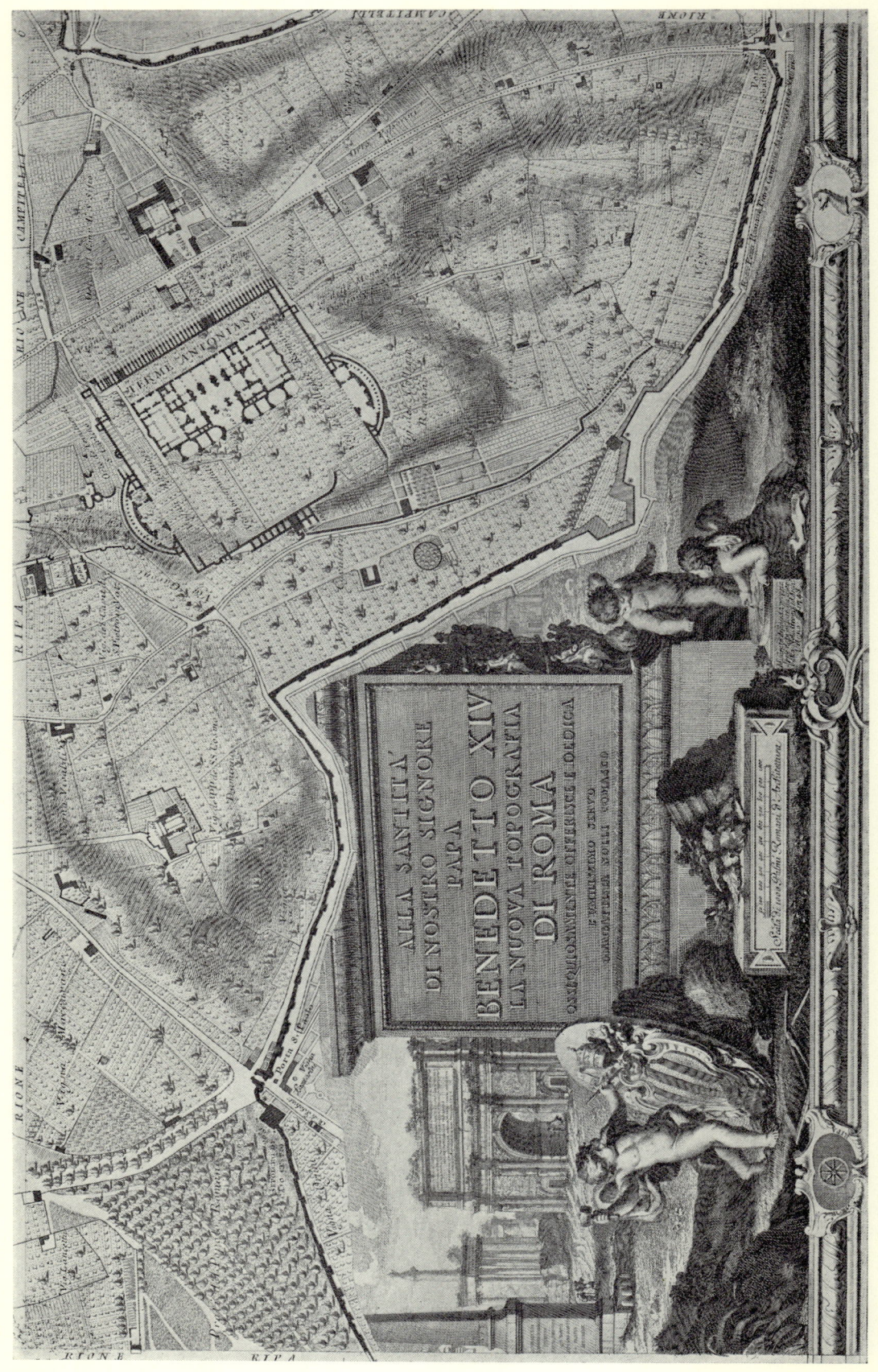

VIII. *The city wall between Porta S. Paolo and Porta S. Sebastiano, and the inner part of the Via Appia.*